NAVIGATIONS

Collected Irish Essays 1976–2006

Richard Kearney

Doras feasa fiafraighe
('The door of knowledge is questioning' – Irish proverb)

We do not want uniformity in our culture,
but the balancing of our diversities in a wide tolerance.
The moment we had complete uniformity our national life
would be stagnant. (George Russell)

THE LILLIPUT PRESS
DUBLIN

First published 2006 by
THE LILLIPUT PRESS LTD
62-63 Sitric Rd, Arbour Hill
Dublin 7, Ireland
www.lilliputpress.ie

A CIP record for this title is available from
The British Library.

ISBN 1 84351 032 4 (pbk)
1 84351 031 6 (hbk)

1 3 5 7 9 10 8 6 4 2

Set by Siobhán McAuley in 10.5 on 13 Bembo
Printed in England by MPG Books, Bodmin, Cornwall

Acknowledgments
I wish to acknowledge the following journals and collections where
earlier versions of various studies in this book were first published:
*The Crane Bag, Studies, Esprit, Third Degree, Screen, The Irish Literary Supplement,
The Honest Ulsterman, The Irish Philosophical Journal, The Irish Theological Quarterly,
Mythes et Histoire, Cahier de l'Herne, Keltisches Bewusstsein,
Reconciling Memories, Irishness in a Changing Society,
The Edinburgh Review, Theoria, Index, Céide, Ireland Today.*
Quotations from various writers cited are credited in the notes or text and are
gratefully acknowledged. I have added my own italic emphasis to some quotes.
The kind assistance of the Academic Publications Committee of the
National University of Ireland (UCD) is also gratefully acknowledged.

For Anne, Simone and Sarah

By the same author

La Poétique du Possible
Dialogues with Contemporary Continental Thinkers
Myth and Motherland
Modern Movements in European Philosophy
The Wake of Imagination: Ideas of Creativity in Western Culture
Transitions: Narratives in Modern Irish Culture
Angel of Patrick's Hill
Poetics of Imagining: From Husserl to Lyotard
Heidegger's Three Gods
Visions of Europe: Conversations on the Legacy and Future of Europe
Poetics of Modernity: Towards a Hermeneutic Imagination
Sam's Fall
States of Mind: Dialogues with Contemporary Thinkers on the European Mind
Postnationalist Ireland
Il Desiderio e Dio (co-authored with Ghislain Lafont)
Walking at Sea Level
The God who May Be: A Hermeneutics of Religion
On Stories
Strangers, Gods and Monsters
Debates in Continental Philosophy
On Paul Ricoeur: The Owl of Minerva

Edited and co-edited by the same author

The Black Book: On Third Level Education
Heidegger et la Question de Dieu
The Crane Bag Book of Irish Studies, Volume 1
The Irish Mind: Exploring Intellectual Traditions
The Crane Bag Book of Irish Studies, Volume 2
The No Word Image
Across the Frontiers: Ireland in the 1990s
Migrations: The Irish at Home and Abroad
Paul Ricoeur et les Métamorphoses de la Raison Herméneutique
Continental Philosophy in the Twentieth Century
Paul Ricoeur: The Hermeneutics of Action
The Continental Philosophy Reader
John Toland's Christianity not Mysterious: Texts, Assorted Works and Critical Essays
Questioning Ethics: Contemporary Debates in Philosophy
The Continental Aesthetics Reader

Contents

Preface

The studies collected here are part of a continuing endeavour to rethink Irish culture in terms of its operative narratives. I treat these under four main headings: Political, Literary, Dramatic and Visual. In a fifth section, I attempt to tease out some of the issues arising in the preceding sections with a number of contemporary artists and thinkers, Irish and non-Irish. These include writers like Durcan, Heaney, Borges and Jordan; artists like Ballagh, Coleman, Bono and Madden; thinkers and academics like Dumézil, Witoszek and Sheeran. But while 'dialogue' is the explicit medium of the concluding section, I would like to think it gives the signature tune to the more formal and scholarly studies of the work as a whole.

This volume includes a selection of my Irish essays drawn from a variety of publications between the years 1976 and 2006. These include *The Crane Bag*, *Across the Frontier*, *The Irish Mind*, *Debates in Continental Philosophy* and *The Edinburgh Review*, in addition to thirteen studies from *Transitions*, first published in 1988 and here revised and updated. The volume also includes a number of previously unpublished pieces such as 'Joyce II: A Tale of Two Cities – Rome and Trieste', 'Joyce III: Epiphanies and Triangles', 'Exchanging Memories: New York Famine Memorial' and 'Philosophy at the Limits of Reason Alone'. What all of these texts, written over the last thirty years, have in common, is a resolve to grapple with one of the most abiding dilemmas of Irish society – how to reconcile tradition (myth, memory, heritage, identity) with the overtures and exigencies of modernity. Each study seeks to interrogate specific texts, images and symbols that tell the story of modern Ireland as it makes and remakes history. While the twenty-seven pieces often interanimate and intersect, I would recommend the reader approach each separately according to one's particular interests.

The strength of Irish culture lies, I believe, in plurality rather than uniformity. The view that 'national culture' is a guarantor of homogeneous identity is no longer tenable. A living culture fosters a multiplicity of voices. It keeps history ticking over, encouraging us always to think and imagine otherwise. Authentic culture is not a matter of ourselves alone. It is most true to itself when most alert to others, engaging in robust dialectic, welcoming differences (*dialegein*), transmuting responses back into questions. And it is with this in mind that I wish to thank both allies and adversaries in the Irish-British cultural debate who, with their challenging comments and critiques, have helped me rethink my own ideas, keeping me always open to question.

A word about the title. In antiquity Irish scholars were known, amongst other things, for their practice of *navigatio*. This generally consisted of a journey undertaken by boat around the island or islands one inhabited. It followed a circular itinerary of exodus and return, the idea being that it was only when one was prepared to navigate foreign and uncharted waters – negotiating shallows and deeps, shores and reefs, storms and doldrums, south-westerlies and north-easterlies – that one would be finally ready to pursue questions of wisdom and justice. The odyssey could be literal or figural, or both. But whichever form it took, the aim was to undergo an apprenticeship to signs of strangeness with a view to becoming more attentive to the meanings of one's own time and place – geographical, spiritual, intellectual. It was a circumnavigation of body and soul, a journey of dispossession and repossession, a way back home through homelessness. The authors and artists I have chosen to engage with in this volume have almost all, I believe, undertaken some such navigation. And it is my wager that they have not returned empty-handed.

I wish to thank all those who came on board the ship as it travelled from port to port over the three decades – willing to perpetuate discussions in agreement or disagreement. And, finally, a word of deep appreciation to Antony Farrell and to his energetic Lilliput crew for believing in this return voyage. Without the keen editorial eyes and rigorous research skills of Marsha Swan, Maria Pizutti and Declan Sheerin I would not have touched shore this time. I am grateful beyond words to these young scholars. And to my vigilant proof-readers, Noah Chafet and Kascha Semon.

Introduction:
The Transitional Paradigm

The appeal to thought arose in the odd in-between period which sometimes inserts itself into historical time when not only the later historians but the actors and witnesses, the living themselves, become aware of an interval in time which is altogether determined by things which are no longer and by things which are not yet. In history, these intervals have shown more than once that they may contain the moment of truth.

Hannah Arendt, *Between Past and Future*

Ireland is witnessing a crisis of culture. This is often experienced as a conflict between the claims of tradition and modernity. Such an experience of residing between two worlds – one dying, the other struggling to be born – has given rise in turn to a crisis of consciousness. How is one to confront the prevailing sense of discontinuity, the absence of a coherent identity, the breakdown of inherited ideologies and beliefs, the insecurities of fragmentation? Is it possible to make the *transition* between past and future, between that which is familiar to us and that which is foreign?

Irish people have, over the last hundred years, experienced fundamental changes in their political and economic status. The South has become a post-colonial independent republic with a hugely urbanized population and an expanding industrial and technological sector. Traditional mores have been chided. And the 'filthy modern tide' that Yeats deplored as a threat to indigenous Irish culture has turned into the 'rising tide' of multinational prosperity. More-over, the traditional ideology of cultural nationalism that claimed Gaelic to be Ireland's first language, Catholicism its first religion and the reunification of North and South its first political priority, has been increasingly eroded by the pressures of contemporary events. The Irish Republic has become a secular state of the European Community. And needless to add, the dominant ideology of the old Northern Irish state (political and cultural unionism) has been subjected by the tumultuous events of recent decades to an even more unsettling crisis of identity. In short, both the 'unitarist' ideology of the South and the 'unionist' ideology of the North have proved untenable in the face of the growing exigencies of current history. The tensions between traditional aspirations and present actualities have combined to make various modes of transition inevitable.

This work offers a number of studies of this transitional crisis in Irish culture. It analyses different attempts – in our politics, literature, drama, art and ideologies – to narrate the problematic relationship between tradition and modernity. Such a narrative impulse has been described by Seamus Heaney as a 'search for symbols and images adequate to our predicament'. In this respect, one might say that the narratives examined in this volume represent a dialogue of sorts, however conflictual, between various Irish minds and the traditions from which they derive, and which they often seek to transcend or transform. Every cultural narrative – be it a poem, play, painting, film, novel or political discourse – is in some sense a reinterpretation of its own history; an attempt to retell the story of the past as it relates to the present; an act of understanding otherwise the subworld of symbols that informs our consciousness of society. Narrative, in short, is where the text of imagination interweaves with the context of history.[1] It is a point of transit between past and future.

Some narrative reinterpretations seek to revive the past; others choose to rewrite or repudiate it altogether. Apropos of Irish culture, we call the former option *revivalism* and the latter *modernism*. Since most of the narratives featured in this book mark, to a greater or lesser degree, a transitional tension between revivalist and modernist perspectives, it may be useful to begin with an introductory sketch of these two cultural paradigms.

Revivalism is a well-established phenomenon. It became something of a cultural orthodoxy in the early decades of the twentieth century, playing a powerful role in the debate about identity inaugurated by Hyde, Pearse, Yeats and other exponents of the Irish cultural revival (in both languages). Revivalism often took the form of 'cultural nationalism'. Hyde epitomized this attitude when he called for the de-anglicization of Irish culture. The basic argument of the Gaelic League, founded by Hyde, was that Ireland must cease to be a mere 'province' of England and become instead an independent nation through the restoration of its ancient Gaelic traditions and, of course, its language. 'The bulk of Irish minds,' wrote Hyde, 'as the Gaelic League has proved, can only be emotionalised through our own ancestral culture.' Hyde saw the Irish Literary Revival as an 'intellectual movement' that would make 'Ireland interesting for the Irish' by making the 'present a rational continuation of the past'. Once the educational system was 'intellectually nationalized', then Ireland's economic and political systems would follow suit and Irish people once again 'desire to live in Ireland and to develop it'. Pearse added more grist to the revivalist mill when he denounced the 'alien' system of education practised in Ireland: he called it a 'murder machine' that quenched every spark of national pride, prohibited the teaching of the 'true history' of the people, discouraged the playing of Gaelic games and made the speaking of the 'native language' an offence punishable by law. Pearse's remedy was to promote a general rehabilitation of Ireland's repressed national heritage, one that would lead in turn, he believed, to the political restoration of a nation 'Gaelic and free'.

Yeats, George Russell and Lady Gregory prescribed a similar campaign within the distinct terms of the Irish Literary Revival. Russell affirmed that to 'create the Ireland in the heart, is the province of a national literature. Other arts would add to this ideal hereafter, and social life and politics must in the end be in harmony.' Such exponents of the Celtic Twilight movement held that Ireland could only be redeemed from the spiritlessness of modernity, and reborn into its proper destiny, by retrieving the myths of the Celtic past. A mythological renaissance of the national spirit was what was needed. 'We are yet before our dawn', wrote Russell, but 'we can see as the ideal of Ireland grows from mind to mind, it tends to assume the character of a sacred land. The Dark Rosaleen … expresses an almost religious adoration'. It was Yeats and Lady Gregory, however, who brought this revivalist tendency in Irish literature into sharpest relief by founding an indigenous theatre, the Abbey, where the ideals of both the Anglo-Irish Ascendancy and the Gaelic peasantry could find common cause in a shared reliving of their ancient Celtic heritage. A primary purpose of this Literary Revival was to offset the influence of bourgeois Enlightenment materialism by restoring a sense of spiritual continuity with the past. Only by returning to what Yeats called the 'proper dark' of pre-Enlightenment Celtic mythology could Irish culture begin to repossess its true identity. It was, no doubt, with such sentiments in mind that Yeats wrote in 'The Statues':

> We Irish, born into that ancient sect
> But thrown upon this filthy modern tide
> And by its formless spawning fury wrecked,
> Climb to our proper dark, that we may trace
> The lineaments of a plummet-measured face.

The revivalist project to renew the link with tradition in order to rescue Ireland from spiritual homelessness and colonial dependency was also endorsed in large part by the nationalist tendency within the Irish Catholic Church and by the Irish republican movement of 1916 and Sinn Féin. Thus we witness a number of revivalist currents – literary, linguistic, religious and political – converging in the early decades of the twentieth century in response to a common cultural crisis. Desmond Fennell records the basic motivations of this revivalist tendency as follows:

'Modern' has always meant what is in vogue, in the way of life-styles, tech-nology and opinions, in the power-centres of the capitalist world – in London, Paris, New York, etc. Secondary nations have had the choice either of aping that, provincially, and finding themselves always lagging, or of striking out on their own for a better-than-modern life. Ireland ... at the beginning of this century [was a] secondary nation which opted to attempt the latter course ... Pearse in the educational field ... Russell and Yeats by working for the restoration of myth and sacredness, the Catholic clergy by building a Holy Ireland to convert the world, almost all the leading revolu-tionaries by exalting rural civilisation, set their faces against the 'filthy modern tide' and aimed to create a new ... truly human life which would radiate from Ireland and transform the age.[2]

Revivalism may be characterized, accordingly, as a movement from cultural provincialism (the experience of being a secondary or dispossessed culture) to cultural nationalism (the experience of being a primary or self-possessed culture).

Modernism rejects both the aims and idioms of revivalism. It affirms a break with tradition and endorses a practice of radical self-reflection. Modernism is essen-tially a 'critical' movement in the philosophical sense of questioning the very notion of *origins*. And as such it challenges the *ideology of identity* that revivalism presupposes. The modernist mind prefers discontinuity to continuity, diversity to unity, conflict to harmony, novelty to heritage. Rimbaud offers one of the earliest manifestos of this modernist attitude in his *Lettre du voyant*: 'Newcomers are free to condemn their ancestors ... The poet makes himself a seer by a long, gigantic and rational derangement of all the senses ... he leaps through unheard of and unnameable things ... Let us ask the poet for the *new*.'

Modernism is, consequently, suspicious of attempts to re-establish national literatures or resurrect cultural traditions. And most of those we might call Irish modernists deny the possibility of sustaining a continuous link between past and present. The contemporary crisis of culture is, as it were, their point of departure, their *raison d'être*. It is something to be exploited, not resolved.

The modernist tendency in Irish culture is characterized by a determination to *demythologize* the orthodox heritage of tradition in so far as it lays constraints upon the openness and plurality of experience. Joyce's Stephen Dedalus exemplifies this impulse when he speaks of trying to awaken from the 'nightmare of history'. He refuses to serve that in which he no longer believes, whether it call itself 'home, fatherland or church'. The revivalist credos of 'nationality, language and religion' are derided as nets that hold the creative spirit back from flight. For Stephen the 'conscience of his race' is not something inherited from the past but something still 'uncreated' and therefore, by definition, still to be invented. Repudiating revivalist nationalism as a 'pale afterthought of Europe', Joyce went into exile and chose an experimental aesthetic. Beckett too rejected the myths of the Irish Literary Revival, concentrating instead on the modernist problematic of language itself – what he termed 'the breakdown of the lines of communication'. The privileged province of his exploration was to be the no-man's-land of the author's own interior existence: an existence condemned to perpetual disorientation.

For Joyce and Beckett – and the Irish modernists who succeeded them – it is not what one writes about that is of primary importance but the process of writing itself. Or as Beckett said of Joyce, 'his writing is not *about* something, it *is* that something'. What matters, in other words, is less the content than the form of language. The modes of communication are more significant than the message communicated, since there no longer exists any inherited reservoir of meaning that can be taken for granted. Not surprisingly then, the very notion of culture as a transmission of collective experience is itself at issue. Language becomes self-conscious, reflexive; it begins to scrutinize its own conditions of possibility. It is in this context that we may best understand John Banville's claim that there is no such thing as an Irish national literature, only Irish writers engaged in the practice of writing. We might say that the modernist tendency of certain Irish writers, artists and intellectuals generally represents a shift away from the cultural nationalism of the Revival to a cultural internationalism committed to formal and critical experimentation. Turning its back on the political agenda of national revival, modernism espouses an aesthetic 'revolution of the word'. Seamus Deane puts this well: 'In the place of political ideology we discover a whole series of ideologies of writing – those of Joyce, Beckett, Francis Stuart … and others – in which politics is regarded as a threat to artistic integrity; the heroics of the spirit which formerly were indulged for the sake of the Yeatsian "Unity of Being" become a doctrinaire aesthetic of privacy, insulation, isolation and exile.'[3]

Instead of attempting to rekindle tradition, the modernist movement in Irish culture disassembles it by critically exploring language itself as the privileged site of innovation and difference. The contemporary sense of 'homelessness', which revivalism sought to remedy by the reinstatement of a lost homeland, becomes for modernism the irrevocable condition not only of Irish culture but of world culture. The 'filthy modern tide' is here to stay. At worst, one must attest to its divisive ravages, without alibi or illusion. At best, one might discover in the flotsam and jetsam of its wake, the still-floating possibilities of other, postmodern, modes of consciousness. Either way, the modernist prefers, as Brecht put it, to begin with 'the bad new things' rather than the 'good old ones'.

Most of the narratives analysed in this book bear witness to a tension between revivalism and modernism. There are, of course, different degrees of attraction towards either pole. Some narratives gravitate towards tradition and the past: an attitude that might be described, paradoxically, as 'revivalist modernism'. Others veer in the opposite direction, resisting the pull of tradition and its attendant idioms of national renewal: this attitude may be described as 'radicalist modernism'. Others again comprise a third set of narratives occupying a middle position in the transitional compass: a position that we might call 'mediational modernism' or 'postmodernism'.* But whatever their individual leanings, all of the narratives examined in this work reflect, to one degree or another, a crisis of mutation.[4]

The transitional paradigm exemplifies the essentially conflictual nature of contemporary Irish experience; it expresses the multiple complexities and aporias that inform our sense of history. It is striking how many modern Irish authors have spoken of being in transit between two worlds, divided between opposing allegiances. They often write as *émigrés* of the imagination, conveying the feeling of being both part and not part of their culture, of being estranged from the very traditions to which they belong, of being in exile even while at home. Joyce described his own work as a dual fidelity to the 'familiar' and the 'foreign', inhabiting a sort of liminal space between 'twosome twiminds'. And Heaney defines his poetry as 'journeywork' – a migrant preoccupation with threshold and transit, passage and pilgrimage, with the traversing of frontiers and divisions. The chosen emblems of his work are, accordingly, Terminus (the god of boundaries), Sweeney Astray (the displaced, wandering king) and Janus (the double-faced god who looks simultaneously backward to the myths of indigenous culture and forward to the horizons of hope). But Heaney's journeywork is nowhere more evident than in his relentless probings of the hidden ambiguities and duplicities that enseam the very language he inscribes. While this preoccupation with language is a common feature of international modernism in general, it carries a singular resonance for those Irish writers who remain aware of their dual linguistic heritage. Modern Irish literature often dwells on the medium in which it is written because 'it is difficult not to be self-conscious about a language which has become simultaneously native and foreign'.[5]

Brian Friel marks yet another inflection in the transitional paradigm when he affirms that his plays are concerned with 'man in society, in conflict with community, government, academy, church, family – and essentially in conflict with himself'. A consequence of this recognition of conflict is the impulse to negotiate between the terms of the opposition, to mediate between the split selves – in short, the need for translation. The problem of transition thus becomes a problem of *translation* (*transferere-translatum*, meaning to carry over or across). The schoolmaster of Friel's play *Translations* recognizes the necessity of transition, poised as he is between the vanishing ancestral order and the emerging new one.

---

* Precisely as a collage of modern and traditional motifs, this third narrative tendency cannot strictly be confined to either modernist or revivalist categories. It may be termed post-modern to the extent that it borrows freely from the idioms of both modernity and tradition, one moment endorsing a demantling of tradition, another reinventing and rewriting the stories of the past transmitted by cultural memory.

'It is not the literal past, the "facts" of history, that shape us,' he acknowledges, 'but the images of the past embodied in language. We must never cease renewing those images because once we do we fossilise.' But Friel is aware that one does not cross the frontiers dividing cultures with ease or impunity. The translation from the old set of images to the new is frequently seen as a *transgression* – even as betrayal. Another of Friel's characters observes: 'You don't cross those borders casually – both sides get very angry.' Our transitional culture has its share of victims as well as its survivors. While some manage a successful navigation from the traditional to the modern order of images, there are many who fail to do so. In one 'Diary Entry' on *Translations* (18 June 1979), Friel describes the casualties as follows: 'The cultural climate is a dying climate – no longer quickened by its past, about to be plunged almost overnight into an alien future. The victims in this situation are the transitional generation. The old can retreat into and find immunity in the past. The young acquire some facility with the new cultural implements. The in-between ages become lost, wandering around in a strange land. Strays.' The winners and the losers of the transitional crisis are, as it were, two sides of the same dialectic, Siamese twins of the migratory imagination.

A central problem facing contemporary Irish culture is how to navigate between the images of past and future; how to avoid the petrifaction of tradition and the alienation of the hyper-new; how, in short, to obviate the extremes of either a reactionary Re-Evangelization or a multi-national Los-Angelization of society. In a study entitled 'Universal civilisation and national cultures', the French philosopher Paul Ricoeur provides this account of the dilemma facing many post-colonial societies. Acknowledging that the contemporary phenomenon of universalization generally represents an advancement for mankind, he notes how it sometimes constitutes a subtle attrition not only of traditional cultures – which he admits might not be an irreparable loss – but also of what he calls 'the creative, mythical and ethical nucleus of all great cultures': the nucleus on the basis of which we interpret our history and make sense of our lives. Ricoeur describes the resulting conflict of conscience:

> In order to get onto the road towards modernisation, is it necessary to jettison the old cultural past which has been the raison d'être of a nation? ...Whence the paradox: on the one hand, it has to root itself in the soil of its past, forge a national spirit and unfurl this spiritual and cultural revindication before the colonialist's personality. But in order to take part in modern civilisation, it is necessary to take part in scientific, technical and political rationality, something which very often requires the pure and simple abandonment of a whole cultural past ... There is the paradox: how to become modern and return to sources; how to respect an old dormant civilisation and take part in universal civilisation.[6]

The studies featured in this volume offer a variety of responses to the above paradox. One of our main objectives is to analyse certain representative texts –

ranging from poetry, fiction, drama, painting and film to ideological debates on the 'national question' – that have reflected the transitional crisis in diverse ways. Considered as a whole, I think there is much evidence here to counter the received wisdom that Irish culture constitutes a single entity. These texts suggest, on the contrary, that our culture may be more properly understood as a manifold of narratives that resist the uniformity of a closed system. There is no single Master Narrative of Irish culture, but a plurality of transitions between different perspectives. Moreover, this very plurality is perhaps our greatest asset; something to be celebrated rather than censored.

As I have suggested elsewhere, the notion of an 'Irish mind' should be comprehended in terms of a multiplicity of Irish minds.[7] This tension between unity and difference is crucial. It must be preserved in the face of ideological reductionism. Modern Irish culture is larger than the distinct traditions – nationalist, unionist or otherwise – from which it derives and which it critically reinterprets.[*] And it is this *surplus* of cultural meaning that makes it possible for contemporary Irish minds to engage in a dialogue that resists both the tyranny of a unitary identity and the sectarianism of embattled tribes. Such dialogue has the beneficial effect of encouraging us to reinvent the past as a living transmission of meaning rather than revere it as a deposit of unchangeable truth. It is only when we abandon what Russell called the 'infantile simplicity of a single idea' that we can properly embrace cultural diversity.

The commitment to a transitional model of open-endedness has meant, furthermore, that the narratives analysed in this collection not only attest to an interplay between habitual (national) and alien (international) ideas, but also lend themselves to the kinds of reading I have attempted here. I see no good reason why the critical methods of contemporary European thought – hermeneutics, existentialism, structuralism, psychoanalysis, dialectics or deconstruction – cannot

---

*Our particular selection of narratives does not claim to be comprehensive. Apart from chapter 17, 'Modern Irish Cinema', there is little mention, for example, of the decisive influence of the technological media and popular culture generally on contemporary Irish life. Nor is there analysis of those cultural narratives that address the problem of the 'unionist' culture or tradition. Most of our discussion of the transitional paradigm concentrates on texts engaged, directly or indirectly, in the debate concerning Irish 'nationalist' culture – in the broadest sense of the phrase. However critical Joyce, Flann O'Brien, Heaney, Friel, Jordan or Murphy may be apropos of tradition, it is largely the nationalist tradition that is in question. I have no doubt that similar tensions between tradition and modernity exist for those contemporary Irish writers who seek to revoke or revise what we might term, by way of distinction, Irish unionist culture. Some obvious examples would be the work of Hewitt, Mahon, Longley, Paulin, Simmons, Parker and Devlin. Transitional paradigms are also at work here; though admittedly the opposition between revivalist and modernist tendencies has not been as explicit. And this for the reason, perhaps, that the mythological past of the 'Planter' (to borrow Hewitt's term) has rarely been invoked by Ulster poets to compensate at a *cultural* level for the historical experience of *political* failure or dispossession. Nevertheless, both traditions of Irish culture, nationalist and unionist (in the sense of traditions that the modernist impulse interrogates, demythologizes or rewrites), have produced literary works preoccupied with the transition

be usefully employed in the interpretation of the texts of Irish culture. And so I have not hesitated to read Joyce and Beckett, for example, in the light of Derrida or the structuralists; Heaney in the light of Heidegger and Freud; Friel and Jordan in the light of Lévi-Strauss or Saussure; le Brocquy and Ballagh in the light of Marcuse; or the ideology of Irish republicanism in the light of Ricoeur or Sartre. These readings stem from the conviction that it is neither necessary nor always illuminating to interpret Irish culture exclusively in terms of Ireland, literary works exclusively in terms of literature, political ideologies exclusively in terms of politics. The interdisciplinary character of this work is intended to resist the academic habit of consigning the multiple and cross-referential discourses of intellectual life to ghettos of specialization. Against such academic apartheid, I have sought to chart a series of navigations between Irish and European culture, between thinking and writing, between politics and art. Such boundaries, I submit, cannot be sustained in any absolute fashion without leading to cultural indifference, or worse, dogmatism. And if the crossing of boundaries causes some degree of interference, I reckon it is an interference worth experiencing.[8] The ability to traverse and transit, free and fearless, is surely the sign of a salutary mind.

from past to future. And at times, of course, these two traditions have overlapped and complemented each other.

One must be wary, too, of hasty oppositions. For just as it is a mistake to conceive of Irish culture as a seamless continuum, it would be equally erroneous to posit two or more Irish cultures that are absolutely polarized or mutually exclusive by virtue of their differences. Here again, Irish culture is best conceived as a complex web of interweaving narratives that refuse the facility of a homogeneous totality.

Navigations

Collected Irish Essays 1976–2006

Part One:

POLITICAL NARRATIVES

CHAPTER ONE

Towards a Postnationalist Archipelago

Nation-states are rather like teenagers: fine when full of questions but impossible when they get too sure of themselves. What we are witnessing on the Irish-British archipelago as we pass into a new millennium is little short of a revolution in our political understanding. With the ratification of the 1998 Belfast Agreement, both sovereign governments effectively signed away their exclusivist sovereignty claims over Northern Ireland – and came of age. This signalled, I believe, the last chapter in the long constitutional battle over the territory of Ulster: that contentious piece of land conjoining and separating the islands of Britain and Ireland. The Siamese twins can now, one hopes, learn to live in real peace, accepting that their adversarial offspring in Northern Ireland may at last be 'British or Irish or both'.

Unitary sovereignty could not be exercised by two separate nation-states over the same place at the same time. Especially if we were talking 'absolutist' sovereignty – which we were – and understood this to mean something like 'one and indivisible' (as defined by Hobbes, Bodin and Rousseau) – which we did. The Agreement marked the attenuation of the age-old conflict between the rival ideologies of a United Kingdom and a United Ireland: a conflict made inevitable by the fact that two into one wouldn't go.

The British and Irish nation-states are now compelled to redefine themselves. The 'hyphen' has been reinserted into their relations, epitomized in the new British-Irish Council of Isles, which held its first meeting on 18 December 1999, and whose aim is 'to promote the harmonious and mutually beneficial development of the totality of relationships among the peoples of the British and Irish islands'. The Irish government endorsed the removal of articles 2 and 3 from the Constitution of the Republic (a move ratified by the vast majority of the electorate), while the British government revised the 1922 Government of Ireland

Act, instituting the partition of Ireland, and has held referenda to establish regional assemblies in Scotland, Wales and Northern Ireland. The zero-sum game of exclusive 'national identities' seems to be approaching its final end.

The emerging postnationalist scenario allows, for the first time in history, that citizens of Northern Ireland can owe differing degrees of allegiance to an expanding range of identifications: from regional townland, parish or province to national constitution ('British or Irish or both') and, larger still, to the trans-national union of Europe. As John Hewitt wrote foresightedly to his fellow Ulster poet John Montague: 'I always maintained that our loyalties had an order: to Ulster, to Ireland, to the British archipelago, to Europe, and that anyone who skipped a step or missed a link falsified the total'. How right he was.

I

But how did the game of exclusive nationalities first originate? Like most stories of national genesis, the Irish and British one began with a mirror-stage. The peoples of the two islands first identified themselves as separate and unique by differentiating themselves from one another. One of the earliest chapters in this process, noted by the Welsh historian, R.R. Davies, was the attempt to forge the notion of an English (proto-British) nation – *nacio or gens* – over and against that of a colonized Irish nation in the fourteenth century. The English settlers of the time felt so fearful of mingling with the natives, thereby becoming 'more Irish than the Irish themselves', that they invented the infamous Statutes of Kilkenny. These Statutes, passed into law in 1366, instigated segregation between colonizer and colonized, fomenting political divisions between two supposedly incompat-ible 'peoples'. Non-observance of the Statutes was called 'degeneracy' – that is, the falling outside the Pale of the *gens*. To marry outside the *nacio* or *gens* was to cease to be a proper English 'gentleman', thereby forfeiting the attendant virtues of gentility and gentrification. Commingling with the so-called natives was, as the old phrase went, 'going beyond the Pale' (literally, exiting from the frontier-walls of the city of settlers, Dublin). To transgress this limit was to betray the tribe. The colonizing *gens* thus came to define itself over and against its *de-gens*, its alter-ego: namely the indigenous Irish. Thus, even though it was the venerable Bede who initially invoked the idea of an English *gens*, and while it was Alfred's expansion of Wessex (871–99) that opened the way, it was actually in the laboratory of Ireland that the English nation first saw itself in the glass and believed its image. If the Irish hadn't existed, the English would have had to invent them.

By virtue of this mimetic logic, the Irish in turn began redefining themselves as an equally pure and distinct *nacio*. In response to the colonial campaign of segregation, King Donald O'Neill of Ulster wrote to the Pope in 1317 declaring himself heir of the 'whole of Ireland' and affirming an unbroken historical continuity of the Irish people (*gens*) through their laws, speech and long memory of tribulations suffered at the hands of the colonial invaders. (This move conveniently masked the fact that the 'natives', no less than the colonial 'settlers', were a mongrelized ethnic mix of successive migrations.) Ever since this act of reciprocal invention and definition in the fourteenth century, the Irish and English/British nations have evolved like twins, inseparable in their loves and hates, joined at the hip of Ulster and forever bound to a dialectic of conflict and reconciliation.

It is, of course, true that the Irish nation had some primitive sense of itself before this reaction to the fourteenth-century plantation. It has been argued, by Proinsias McCana for example, that some form of unitary government began to emerge as early as the ninth century in response to Viking incursions, and again in the twelfth century in response to the Anglo-Norman invasion. But these intermittent efforts at all-island structures of self-rule were largely a matter of defence rather than any self-conscious assertion of enduring national identity. After all, the term 'scotus' could as easily refer to an inhabitant of Ireland as of Britain up to the eleventh century (e.g. John Scotus Eriugena from the former, Duns Scotus from the latter). In short, the first successful attempt to identify the Irish and British as two radically separate peoples really only took hold after the fourteenth-century invasionary settlement made it in the interests of the colonizers, and the colonized, to differentiate themselves as two distinct nations.

The criteria of discrimination were conventional rather than natural. They were, in other words, largely of a cultural and legal character – e.g. apparel, name-forms, language, decorum, property rights – than of ethnic foundation. (Indeed it is well accepted that the inhabitants of our respective islands share a virtually homogeneous gene pool due to their common experience of successive invasions and migrations: pre-Celtic, Celtic, Viking, Anglo-Norman, etc. The first book of Irish letters is, after all, called the Book of Invasions!) The *gens* actually 'looked' almost identical to the *de-gens*. But this absence of racial distinguishing marks made it all the more necessary to compensate at the level of contrived legislation and statute. Where nature could not segregate, law would.

But law in itself was not enough. The border of the Pale separating *gens* from *de-gens* remained constantly porous and indeterminable, requiring repeated recourse to propaganda. The stereotyping usually took the form of prejudice and snobbery ('the natives are not gentlemen' ...), drawing great ammunition from Giraldus Cambrensis' twelfth-century *History and Topography of Ireland*. Cambrensis himself was, tellingly, a secretary to Prince John on one of his invasionary expeditions to Ireland and his depiction of the natives as 'a wild and inhospitable people who live like beasts' well served its colonial purposes. As the Irish historian Art Cosgrove would later observe: 'The picture drawn by Gerald was unflattering; the Irish were economically backward, politically fragmented, wild, untrustworthy and semi-pagan, and guilty of sexual immorality. Doubtless the picture was much influenced by the need to justify conquest and dispossession.' But the prize for colonial stereotypes must surely go to the British historian Charles Kingsley who remarked on a visit to Ireland in the nineteenth century: 'to see white chimpanzees is dreadful; if they were black, one would not feel it so much, but their skins … are as white as ours'!

The Irish, of course, responded with their own version of self-conscious national pride, their spalpeen poets and bards spinning tales of the virginal motherland being raped and plundered by the invading Sassenach. And this widening gender opposition between Ireland as female virgin (Róisín Dubh, Cathleen Ni Houlihan, Spéirbhean, etc.) and England as male master (fatherland, King and Country, etc.) served to aggravate the divide between the two peoples.

But while literary propaganda worked, it was nothing compared to the divisive power of religion. Arguably, it wasn't really until the seventeenth-century plantation of Ulster, after the reformation, that the colonization of Ireland ultimately succeeded – and with a vengeance. The disenfranchizing of Irish Catholics *en masse* in favour of Planter Protestants, subsequently backed up by the infamous Penal Laws, was evidence of how fatally religion could be deployed as a galvanizing force of apartheid. Where neither nature, nor ultimately even law or propaganda, could succeed in separating the peoples of these islands, faith in the one true church would! After Cromwellian zeal and Elizabethan ruthlessness had taken their toll, there were many Protestants and Catholics in the island of Ireland who preferred to die rather than to commingle. And not even Wolfe Tone and the United Irishmen, with their valiant appeal to a single nation of 'Catholic, Protestant and Dissenter' in the 1790s, could put the Hibernian Humpty Dumpty back together again. Sectarianism was here to stay.

It would take another two hundred years after the failed Rebellion of 1798 for Britain and Ireland to mutually renounce their separatist claims to Northern Ireland, thereby permitting Irish Catholics, Protestants and Dissenters to peaceably cohabit for the first time since the Reformation. It was only when the two communities inhabiting Ulster acknowledged that they could be 'British or Irish or both' that they could be united once again. Not, to be sure, as a unitary national identity as Tone hoped, but as a multiple postnational one.

II

The story of the genesis and evolution of the Irish and British nations might thus be said to run broadly in parallel. As R.R. Davies again points out in his landmark study 'The peoples of Britain and Ireland 1100–1400', what the English, and later the British, had great difficulty accepting was that after the Viking and Norman invasions, the various parts of these islands were already countries of 'multiple' peoples, which included, in part at least, the culture of the

colonizer who was so desperately struggling to retain (even if it meant reinventing) its own sense of pure, uncontaminated identity. The settlers in Ireland
were so insecure and unsure of their own ambiguous status as a 'middle nation'
– neither fully English nor fully Irish – that they portrayed the native Irish as
their Other in order to more emphatically insist on their belonging to the former.
This scapegoating campaign led to the exacerbation of existing conflicts. Thus
the match between people and polity that was achieved in England (and to a
lesser extent Scotland) was not replicated in Ireland. But while the peoples of
England (including the Normans) were by the fifteenth century welded into an
integrative unit by virtue of such strategies of alien-nation – namely, establishing
oneself as a single nation over against an alternative one – the island of Ireland
remained a victim of such divisions. What would continue, however, to haunt
the contrived national unity of Englishness – and of Britishness after the union with
Wales and Scotland – was the ghost of their alien and alienated double: Ireland.
The very difference from Irishness became part and parcel of English/British identity. Their Hibernian Other was uncannily mirrored in themselves, the familiar
spectre hidden in strangeness, the original double they had forgotten to
remember, the threatened revenant of their own repressed political unconscious.

Linda Colley provides further evidence for this mirror-imaging of Irish and
British nationalism in the last two centuries. In *Britons: Forging the Nation,
1707–1837*, she reinforces the point that the peoples who made up the British
nation were brought together as a national unit by confrontation with the Other.
In keeping with the theses of the new British history advocated by Hugh Kearney,
Benedict Anderson, J.G.A. Pocock and Tom Nairn, Colley suggests that British
national identity is contingent and relational (like most others) and is best understood as an interaction between several different histories and peoples. Without
necessarily endorsing the Four Nations model of Britain, Colley contends that
most inhabitants of the 'British Isles' laid claim to a double, triple or multiple identity – even with the consolidation of British national identity after 1700. So it
would not be unusual, for example, to find someone identifying him/herself as a
citizen of Edinburgh, a Lowlander, a Scot and a Briton. It was over and against this
pluralist practice of identification, on the ground, that the artificial nation of Great
Britain managed to forge itself, not only by its Tudor conquests and successive
annexations of Wales in 1536, Scotland in 1707 and Ireland in 1800, but also by its
homogenizing Industrial Revolution and a series of massive external wars
between 1689 and 1815. Due to the latter especially, Britain managed to expand its
empire overseas and unify its citizens back home, repeating on a world stage what
England had first tried out in Ireland in the fourteenth century. It galvanized itself
into national unity by pitting itself against external enemies.

The strategic benefits of British imperialism were not just commercial and
political, therefore, but psychic as well. And the biggest advantage of the overseas African and Asian colonies was that, unlike Britain's traditional enemies

closer to home (the Irish and the French), these Others actually looked entirely different. But as the empire began to fracture and fragment in the first part of the twentieth century, the British resorted to religion once again to cement the sense of real national identity. What united the British above all else in their times of trouble and decline, was their 'common Protestantism'. Hence the emblematic importance of the famous photo of St Paul's in London during the Blitz – the parish church of the besieged empire par excellence – 'emerging defiantly and unscathed from the fire and devastation surrounding it ... a Protestant citadel, encircled by enemies, but safe under the watchful eye of a strictly English-speaking deity'.[1] The British nation thus emerged, like many another nation, as an 'imagined community' that invented itself in dialectical opposition to its 'Others' – and none more fundamentally than Ireland, its first, last and most intimate 'Other'. For Ireland was unique in combining the three most salient characteristics of alien-nation: 1) Ireland was majority Catholic (non-Protestant); 2) it was a colony (overseas, if only a little over – but sufficiently so to be treated like a subordinate neighbour, *pace* Wales or Scotland); and 3) Ireland was a traditional ally of France, the main military rival to British imperial designs, and inspirational insurrectionary model, along with Ireland, for rebellious movements in India, Israel and elsewhere. Thus Ireland came to serve as the untrustworthy 'poor relation' of the United Kingdom:

> [Ireland's] population was more Catholic than Protestant. It was the ideal jumping-off point for a French invasion, and both its Protestant and its Catholic dissidents traditionally looked to France for aid. And although Irishmen were always an important component of the British armed forces, and individual Scots-Irishmen like Macartney and Anglo-Irishmen like the Wellesley clan played leading imperial roles as diplomats, generals and proconsuls, Ireland's relationship with the empire was always a deeply ambiguous one. How could it not be, when London so persistently treated the country in a way that it never treated Scotland and Wales, as a colony rather than as an integral part of a truly united Kingdom?

In many respects, Ireland was the laboratory of the British empire. 'Much of the legal and land reform which the British sought to implement in India, for example, was based on experiments first implemented in Ireland.'[2]

It is of course the very ambiguity of Ireland's insider-outsider relation with Britain that made it at once so fascinating for the British (witnessed in their passion for Irish literature from Swift and Sheridan to Wilde, Yeats and Shaw) and so repellent (evidenced in the portrayals of the Irish as brainless simians in London's Fleet Street media).

This paradox of attraction and recoil is typical of what Edward Said calls 'orientalism': Ireland serving as Britain's Orient in its own occidental backyard! It also approximates to what Freud describes as the 'uncanny' (*das Unheimliche*)

– the return of the familiar as unfamiliar, of friend as stranger. Ireland served, one might say, as Britain's unconscious reminding it that it was ultimately and irrevocably a stranger to itself: that its self-identity was in fact constructed upon the screening of its forgotten other – in both senses of 'screen': to conceal and to project.

The nature of this unsettling rapport was evident not only in the mirror-plays of Irish dramatists like Shaw and Wilde, but also in the works of English drama-tists who reflected on the neighbouring island. Already in Shakespeare we find echoes of this. In *Henry V*, for example, we find Captain MacMorris, the first true-blue Irishman to appear in English letters, posing the conundrum: 'What ish my nation?' – thereby recalling not only that Ireland is a nation still in ques-tion, but that England is too. And we find an even more explicit example in *Richard II*, when the King visits Ireland only to regain the British mainland disoriented and dismayed. Having set out secure in his sovereignty, he returns wondering what exactly is his identity, and by implication, his legitimacy as monarch: 'I had forgot myself, am I not king?' he puzzles. 'Is not the king's name twenty thousand names?' (III, ii). In short, Ireland takes its revenge on the king by deconstructing and multiplying the one and indivisible character of his sover-eignty. Richard is shaken from his slumber by his sojourn in the Irish colony, discovering that the very notion of a united national kingdom is nominal rather than real, imaginary rather than actual.

Paradoxically, where Ireland had some advantage over England/Britain was that it never achieved indivisible sovereignty as a unitary nation – and so was less liable to mistake the symbol for a literal reality. For the Irish, from ancient legend to the present day, the idea of sovereignty was linked to the notion of a 'fifth province': a place of mind rather than of territory, a symbol rather than a *fait accompli*. The Irish for province is *coicead*, meaning a fifth, but there are only four provinces in Ireland. Or to put it another way, when it came to sovereignty, Ireland had less to lose than Britain because it never enjoyed all-island territo-rial sovereignty as a legally instituted nation-state in the first place. The Irish knew in their hearts and souls that *the nation* as such does not literally exist. They knew it was an imagined and imaginary entity. Which did not, of course, prevent it being often elevated to the status of poetic myth and theological mystique.

The British crisis of sovereignty reached its own peak in recent times. This was brought on by a variety of factors: 1) the final fracturing of the empire (with the Falklands, Gibraltar and Hong Kong controversies); 2) the end of the Protestant hegemony (with the mass immigration of non-Protestants from the ex-colonies in Asia, Africa, the Caribbean and Ireland); 3) the entry of the UK, however hesitantly, into the European Union, which ended Britain's isolationist stance *vis-à-vis* its traditional alien-nations, Ireland and France; 4) the ineluctable impact of global technology and communications, proving the point made by Jürgen Habermas that the growing interdependencies of a world society 'challenge the basic premise that national politics, circumscribed within a determinate national territory, is still adequate to address the actual fates of individual nation-states';[3] 5) the devolution of power from over-centralized government in Westminster to regional assemblies in Edinburgh, Cardiff and Belfast – and probably, in time, to different English regions as well; and finally, 6) the ultimate acknowledgment, with the mourning of Princess Diana and the birth of New Labour in the late 1990s, that Britain is now a multi-ethnic, multi-cultural, multi-confessional community that can no longer sustain the illusion of an eternally perduring sovereignty.

To be sure, Thatcherism represented one last desperate exercise in 'denial' fantasy, finding its perfect foil in the IRA. Terrorist bombings of London and Birmingham momentarily served to rally the British people against the alien Irish in their midst: people who looked and spoke like them but were secretly dedicated to their destruction. But even the IRA at their most menacing – and however associated with similar anti-British 'monsters' like Galtieri, Ghaddafi and Saddam Hussein – could not save Britain from itself. Thatcher's last stand to revive one-nation Toryism was just that, a last stand. It could not prevent the dissolution of absolute unitary power, ultimately giving way to the formation of regional parliaments in Edinburgh, Cardiff and Belfast. The break-up of Britain was as inevitable as it was overdue. So much so that the enormous outpouring of grief at Princess Diana's demise was not, I submit, just mourning for a partic-ular person but for the passing of an imperial nation.

If Ireland was present at the origin of the British *natio*, as I have suggested, then it is equally present today – in the guise of the Ulster crisis and resolution precipitating its end. Ireland is the deconstructive seed at the heart of the British body politic. The cracked mirror reflecting Royal Britannia's primal image of its split-self. John Bull's other island sending shock waves back to the mainland. The island behind the island returning to haunt its inventor.

III

A new postnational constellation is emerging in the British-Irish context. The seminal idea of a British-Irish Council (BIC), alongside the internal NI Assembly and the North–South cross-border bodies, harbours great promise. What this transnational model effectively recognizes is that citizens of Britain and Ireland are inextricably bound up with each other – mongrel islanders from East to West sharing an increasingly common civic and economic space. In addition to the obvious contemporary overlapping of sports and popular cultures, the citizens of Britain and Ireland are becoming ever more mindful of how much of their respective histories were shared during centuries when the Irish Sea served as a waterway connecting the two islands rather than a *cordon sanitaire* keeping them apart. And this is becoming true again in our own time with over 25,000 trips being made daily across the Irish Sea, in both directions. It is not entirely surprising then that over eight million subjects of the United Kingdom today claim Irish origin, with over four million of these having an Irish parent. Indeed a recent survey shows that only 6 per cent of British people consider Irish people living in Britain to be 'foreigners'. And we don't need reminding that almost a quarter of the inhabitants of the island of Ireland claim to be at least part British. Finally, at a symbolic level, few can fail to have been moved by the image of the President of the Irish Republic, Mary McAleese, standing beside the Queen of England on the battlefield of Flanders commemorating the dead of their respective peoples – poppies and shamrocks no longer considered symbols of irreconcilable identity.

In light of this reawakening to our common memories and experiences, it was not surprising to find Prime Minister Blair receiving a standing ovation from Dáil Éireann, the parliament of the Irish Republic, following the 1998 Agreement. Such a visitation had not occurred for over a century, and the ghost of Gladstone was not entirely absent from the proceedings. Blair acknowledged openly on that occasion that Britain was at last leaving its 'post-colonial malaise' behind it and promised that a newly confident Republic and a more decentralized UK would have more common tasks in the scenario of European convergence than any other two member states. East-West reciprocity was back on track for the first time since the divisive Statutes of Kilkenny. We had come a long way from 1366 to 1998.

Though no one was shouting about it, a practical form of joint-sovereignty had now been endorsed by the Irish and British peoples. The pluralization of national identity epitomized by the British-Irish Council entailed, I believe, a radical rethinking of our hallowed notions of sovereignty. In essence, it meant the deterritorialization of national sovereignty – namely, the attribution of sovereignty to peoples rather than land. A fact that found symbolic correlation in the Agreement's extension of national 'belonging' to embrace the Irish diaspora, which now numbers over seventy million world wide.

The term sovereignty (from the Latin *superanus*) originally referred to the supreme power of a divine ruler, before being delegated to divinely elected 'representatives' in this world – kings, pontiffs, emperors, czars, monarchs – and, finally, to the 'people' in most modern states. A problem arose, however, in that many modern democracies recognize the existence of several different peoples within a single state. And many peoples means many centres of sovereignty. Yet the traditional concept of sovereignty, as already noted, was always unitary, that is, 'one and indivisible'. Whence the dilemma: how to divide the indivisible? This is why, today, sovereignty has become one of the most controversial concepts in political theory and international law, intimately related to issues of state government, national independence and minority rights.

Inherited notions of absolutist sovereignty are being challenged from both within nation-states and by developments in international legislation. With the Hague Conferences of 1899 and 1907, followed by the Covenant of the League of Nations and the Charter of the UN, significant restrictions on the actions of nation-states were already laid down. A system of international checks and balances was introduced limiting the right of sovereign states to act as they pleased in all matters. Moreover, the increasing interdependence of states – in the interests of greater *entente*, social justice, economic exchange and information technology – qualified the very principle of absolute sovereignty. 'The people of the world have recognised that there can be no peace without law, and that there can be no law without some limitations on sovereignty. They have started, therefore, to pool sovereignties to the extent needed to maintain peace; and sovereignty is being increasingly exercised on behalf of the peoples of the world not only by national governments but also by organisations of the world community.'[4]

If this pertains to the 'peoples of the world' generally, how much more does it pertain to the peoples of the islands of Britain and Ireland? This is why I argued in *Postnationalist Ireland* (1997) for a surpassing of the existing nation-states in the direction of both an Irish-British Council and a federal Europe of regions. The nation-state has become too large and too small as a model of government. Too large for the growing needs of regional participatory democracy; too small for the increasing drift towards transnational exchange and power-sharing. Hence the relevance of the Nordic Council as a model for resolving our sovereignty disputes – in particular the way in which these five nation-states and three autonomous regions succeeded in sorting out territorial conflicts, declaring the Åland and Spitsbergen islands as Europe's two first demilitarized zones. Could we not do likewise under the aegis of a new transnational British-Irish Council, declaring Northern Ireland a third demilitarized zone?

Up until recently, such sovereignty sharing had been largely opposed by British nationalism that went by the name of unionism. It was, ironically, the Irish republican tradition (comprising all democratic parties in the Irish Republic as well as the SDLP and Sinn Féin in the North) that was usually labelled 'nationalist', even though the most uncompromising nationalists in the vexed history of Northern Ireland have been the unionists. It was the latter, after all, who clung to an anachronistic notion of undiluted British sovereignty, refusing any compromise with their Irish neighbours; until Tony Blair blew the whistle and moderate unionism realized the tribal march was over. The final showdown probably came when the unionists faced off against Her Majesty's Army in Drumcree, prepared to do combat with the very Crown to which they swore unconditional loyalty. At that fateful moment it must have dawned on even the most fervid loyalists that the United Kingdom was no longer united. By contrast, John Hume's 'new republicanism' – a vision of shared sovereignty between the different peoples of this island – had little difficulty with the new 'postnationalist' scenario. Indeed Hume had declared himself a postnationalist for many years without many taking heed. And, curiously, one might even argue that Michael Collins, one of the leading figures in the Irish war for Independence, was himself something of a postnationalist when he wrote in 1921 that as a 'free and equal country' Ireland would be willing to 'co-operate in a free association on all matters which would be naturally the common concern of two nations, living so closely together' as part of a 'real league of nations of the World'.[5]

That recent British governments seem prepared to grasp the sovereignty nettle and acknowledge the inevitable long-term dissemination of Britain, qua absolute centralized state, is to their credit. But it is not a decision taken in a vacuum. There are precedents for sovereignty-sharing in Britain's recent experience, including Westminster's consent to a limitation and dilution of sovereign power in its subscription to the European Convention on Human Rights, the Single European Act, the European Common Defence and Security Policy and the European Court of Justice. If Britain has been able to pool sovereignty in these ways with the other nation-states of the EU, surely it is only logical to do so with its closest neighbour, the Irish Republic! Moreover, the EU principles of subsidiarity and local democracy, promoted in the European Charter of Self-Government, offer a real alternative to the clash of British-Irish nationalisms that paralysed Ulster for decades.

In this respect, one should not forget either that the forging of Britain into a multinational state constitution was predicated, at its best, on a civic rather than ethnic notion of citizenship. We need only recall how radically the borders of the British nation have shifted and altered in history (e.g. in 1536, 1707, 1800 and 1921) to envisage how they may shift and alter yet again – perhaps this time so radically as to remove all borders from these islands. The fact that British nationalism was often little more than English nationalism in drag does not take from its salutary constitutional principle of civic – that is, supra-ethnic – belonging.

IV

The conflict of sovereignty claims exercised over the same territory by two independent governments – issuing in decades of violence – is now being superseded by a postnationalist paradigm of intergovernmental power. The dual identities of Northern Ireland, which long belied the feasibility of 'unitary' government, show the necessity of ultimately separating the notion of nation (identity) from that of state (sovereignty) and even, to some extent, from that of land (territory). Such a separation is, I submit, a precondition for allowing the coexistence of different communities in the same society; and, by extension, amplifying the models of identity to include more pluralist forms of association – a British-Irish Council, a European Network of Regions, and the Irish and British diasporas. In sum, it is becoming abundantly clear that Bossuet's famous seventeenth-century definition of the nation as a perfect match of people and place – where citizens 'lived and died in the land of their birth' – is no longer wholly tenable.

The fact is there are no pristine nations around which definitive state boundaries – demarcating exclusivist sovereignty status – can be fixed. (Germany's attempts to do this from Bismarck to Hitler led to successive and disastrous wars). The post-1998 paradigm acknowledges the historic futility of both British and Irish constitutional claims on Northern Ireland as natural 'national territories'. Instead, such seminal models as the Intergovernmental Council or the BIC hopefully foreshadow a network of interconnecting assemblies guaranteeing parity of esteem for cultural and political diversity and an effective co-management of practical common concerns such as transport, environment, social equity and e-commerce. British and Irish citizens are, in effect, being challenged 1) to abandon their mutually reinforcing myths of mastery (largely British) and martyrdom (largely Irish), going back to the fourteenth century, and 2) to face their more mundane post-imperial, postnational reality. Might the project of a transnational council not, as Simon Partridge suggests, even serve as an inspiration to other parts of Europe and the globe still enmired in the devastations of ethnic nationalism?

What the postnationalist paradigm allows, in short, is that our ineradicable need for identity and allegiance be gradually channelled away from the exclusive focus of the nation-state, where history has shown its tenure to be insecure and belligerent, to supplementary levels of regional and federal expression. In the Irish-British context, this means that citizens of these islands may come to express their identity less in terms of rival nation-states and more in terms of both locally empowered provinces (Ulster, Scotland, Wales, North and South England, the Republic, etc.) and larger international associations (e.g. the BIC and EU). The new dispensation, I repeat, fosters variable layers of compatible identification – regional, national and transnational – allowing anyone in Northern Ireland to declare allegiance to the Ulster region, the Irish and/or British nation, the European community, and in the widest sense, the cosmopolitan order of world citizenry.

Citizens of the British-Irish archipelago might, I suggest, do better to think of themselves as mobile mongrel islanders than as eternal dwellers of two pure, God-given nation-states. There is no such thing as primordial nationality. If the nation is indeed a hybrid construct, an 'imagined community', then it can be reimagined again in alternative versions. The task is to embrace this process of hybridization from which we derive and to which we are committed willy nilly. In the face of resurgent nationalisms in these islands and elsewhere, fired by rhetorics of purity and purification, we do well to remember that we are all mongrelized, interdependent, marvellously mixed up.

CHAPTER TWO

The Irish Mind Debate

The slamming of the door on the long galleries of historical consciousness is understandable. It has a fierce innocence ... But it is an innocence destructive of civilisation ... without the true fiction of history, without the unbroken animation of a chosen past, we become flat shadows.

George Steiner, *After Babel*

The Irish Mind was specifically devoted to Ireland's contribution to the world of thought.[1] Content with the cliché that this island was inhabited by irrational dreamers, people had tended to ignore the intellectual adventures of the Irish mind over the centuries, at the level of mytho-poetic, metaphysical, political, aesthetic and scientific thought. We heard much of the *images* in Irish cultural history (and rightly so), but little or nothing of its *concepts*. The publication of *The Irish Mind* in 1985 hoped to redress the balance and to challenge the colonial and racial stereotype of the 'thoughtless Celt'.[2]

The existence of an Irish mind had frequently been contested; but the main lines of the argument reached their most explicit form in the nineteenth century.[3] This was expressed as both a negative and a positive discrimination. The former was vividly epitomized by the colonialist portrayals of the Irish as brainless savages. In 1836, Disraeli, the future Prime Minister of England, stated: 'The Irish hate our order, our civilization, our enterprising industry, our pure religion. This wild, reckless, indolent, uncertain and superstitious race have no sympathy with the English character. Their ideal of human felicity is an alternation of clannish broils and coarse idolatry. Their history describes an unbroken cycle of bigotry and blood.' The British historian Charles Kingsley provided further justification for the cultural and military suppression of his Irish neighbours when he composed this racist portrait in 1860:

> I am daunted by the human chimpanzees I saw along that hundred miles of horrible country. I don't believe they are our fault. I believe that there are not only many more of them than of old, but that they are happier, better and more comfortably fed and lodged under our rule than they ever were. But to see white chimpanzees is dreadful; if they were black, one would not feel it so much, but their skins, except where tanned by exposure, are as white as ours.[4]

So much for the colonial scapegoating of the Irish.

The positive discrimination against the Irish mind was more subtle, more benevolent, and for this very reason, more effective. This discrimination derived from the conviction, perhaps best summed up by Matthew Arnold and his Victorian peers, that the Irish were great fantasizers, great pedlars of ballads, mysteries and dreams, but ultimately incompetent when it came to translating dream into decision, when it came to responsibly ordering and organizing their boundless fancies. Accordingly, Arnold could enthusiastically commend the 'Celtic soul' for its readiness to revolt against the despotism of fact; but he never recognized the existence of a *Celtic mind*. Thinking minds were the prerogative of Angles and Saxons. This racial discrimination was manifested in Arnold's unambiguous opposition to the Home Rule for Ireland Bill of 1886. Commenting on this cultural prejudice, one critic caustically remarked: 'By means of it, Celts could stay quaint and stay put'.[5]

Both these positive and negative strategies of discrimination had as their attendant aim the provision of an ideological vindication of colonial domination in Ireland. The Irish Revival, when it finally flowered in the early decades of the twentieth century, operated on a number of fronts – linguistic, literary and political – to counteract the colonial prejudice against, among other things, the Irish mind. The Revival's campaign to liberate the Irish from their incarcerating colonial self-image was pursued with the idea of reconquest, but reconquest not only of territory but more fundamentally of mind.[6]

This is clearly one of the reasons why Douglas Hyde insisted that the Gaelic League was primarily 'an *intellectual* movement' to repossess Ireland's dispossessed culture. The Irish – Catholic, Protestant and Dissenter – have over time come to espouse some of the intellectual, or rather anti-intellectual, prejudices of their historical opponents. An Irish philosopher, Garrett Barden, has remarked that:

> in the dialectic of master and slave, the slave's image of himself is precisely that – an image. His speech is taken from him not only by the master but by himself ... he is a slave because he identifies with his servile discourse ... Speech or will is the fundamental possibility of thinking through and overcoming servile discourse.[7]

The task of cultivating such an intellectually liberating speech is not an easy one: for the colonial image of the master has been adopted by a considerable section of our population, including some of our most influential authors and critics. The early Yeats, for example, while still under the influence of Arnold's cultural apartheid, enthused about an Ireland whose socio-political inferiority to the English was compensated for by its 'poetic … idyllic and fanciful' life of the Spirit![8] 'Poetry', he declared in 'Hopes and Fears for Irish Literature' (1892), 'has nothing to do with thought, nothing to do with philosophy'. (A sentiment he had the good sense to revoke later – to the benefit of both his thought and his poetry.) But Yeats is not an isolated example. Frank O'Connor spoke of the Irish 'choosing the imagination over the intellect';[9] Sean O'Faolain endorsed the thesis that early Irish texts 'revealed a total inability of the Irish mind to form a concept';[10] and Seán Ó Tuama declared: 'One doubts if we have added anything of real importance to sociological or theological or philosophical or aesthetic thought.'[11] (Though to be fair, Ó Tuama is regretting rather than sponsoring this doubt.) It is perhaps time to question the validity of such self-wounding affirmations. We must reclaim the idea of ourselves.[12]

But if an Irish mind does exist, what *is* this mind? What are the distinguishing characteristics, if any, of its historical expression? These questions may best be broached by situating the debate within philosophical and cultural contexts.

The Philosophical Context

I begin with a hypothesis. The Irish mind does not reveal itself as a fixed homogeneous identity. From the earliest times, the Irish mind remained free, in significant measure, of the linear, centralizing logic of the Graeco-Roman culture that dominated most of western Europe. This prevailing culture was based on the Platonic-Aristotelian logic of non-contradiction that operated on the assumption that order and organization result from the dualistic separation of opposite or contradictory terms.[13] Hence the mainstream of Western thought rested upon a series of fundamental oppositions – between being and non-being, reason and imagination, the soul and the body, the transcendentally divine and the immanently temporal and so on.

Could it be that Irish intellectual traditions represent something of a countermovement to the mainstream of hegemonic rationalism? Could it be that the Irish mind, in its various expressions, often flew in the face of such logocentrism by showing that meaning is not only determined by a logic that centralizes and censors but also by a logic that disseminates: a structured dispersal exploring what is *other*, what is irreducibly diverse.

In contradistinction to the orthodox dualist logic of *either/or*, the Irish mind may be seen to favour a more dialectical logic of *both/and*: an intellectual ability to hold the traditional oppositions of classical reason together in creative confluence. This would not mean, as the colonial slur presumed, that the Irish abandoned order for disorder or reneged on conceptual rigour to embrace formless chaos. The highly complex *mythos* of life and death articulated by the symbolic systems of neolithic Newgrange or Celtic mythology, to take some of the most ancient instances, do not bespeak primitivistic unrule. As the modern scholarship of such anthropologists as Lévi-Strauss, Dumézil and Eliade enables us to recognize, these symbolic structures testify to an alternative order and organization.[14] We have here not meaninglessness but another kind of meaning, not confusion but another kind of coherence. Lévi-Strauss makes this point succinctly in *Structural Anthropology*, when he states that 'the kind of logic in mythical thought is quite as rigorous as that of modern science'. But is there any evidence to suggest that this more open-ended and paradoxical logic has been reformulated in post-mythic Irish intellectual traditions?

The Cultural Context

Which modern Irish intellectuals have acknowledged the cultural possibility of this *other* quality of mind? To begin with some modern writers: Joyce, for one, repeatedly insisted that his own work was not a surrender to a capricious anarchy of word play, but a challenge to the reader to discover different and deeper models of understanding. In this regard, Joyce might well have sympathized with the psychoanalytic belief in the existence of a 'non-casual and synchronistic order' in those regions of the mind suppressed by logocentrism. Joyce subverted the established modes of linear or sequential thinking in order to recreate a mode of expression that would foster rather than annul heterogeneous meanings, which would, in his own words, permit us to have 'two thinks at a time'. To cite some common examples, Joyce could refer to Dublin as 'lugly' (conveying his native city as both lovely and ugly); Dublin is, as he reminds us in *Finnegans Wake*, 'doublin'. Yeats wrote of a 'beauty born out of its own despair' and referred to the 1916 Rising as a 'terrible beauty'. Wilde boasted that in his art 'a truth was that whose contradictory was also true'. And this fecund double-mindedness is also a decisive factor in Beckett's own aesthetic maxim: 'Where we have *both* darkness *and* light, there we also have the inexplicable. The key word of my work is *perhaps.*'

Thomas Kinsella has adverted to the decisive role played by psychic ambivalence in Irish culture in his essay 'The Divided Mind'. Whereas the English writer, says Kinsella, can easily identify with the continuous tradition of English literature, 'an Irish poet has access to the English poetic heritage through his use of the English language, but he is unlikely to feel at home in it.' Kinsella observes that the real condition of Irish culture in the nineteenth century preceding Yeats was silence – the silence surrounding the demise of the Irish language and of half of the famine-stricken population. Moving back into the eighteenth

century Kinsella discovers, in contrast, the voices of those Gaelic poets resurrected for posterity in Corkery's *Hidden Ireland* and *An Duanaire: Poems of the
Dispossessed* (translated by Kinsella and Ó Tuama). Before them again, Kinsella
points to a literary tradition stretching back some thousand years.

> In all this, I recognise a great inheritance and simultaneously a great loss. The
> inheritance is certainly mine but only at two enormous removes − across a
> century's silence and through an exchange of worlds ... I recognise that I
> stand on one side of a great rift and can feel the discontinuity in myself. It
> is a matter of peoples and places as well as writing − of coming from a
> broken and uprooted family, of being drawn to those who share my origins
> and finding that we cannot share our lives.

Hence a *double* vision that characterizes the Irish mind as discontinuous, divided
and, at times, *comic*. For perhaps there also exists an Irish comic vision, as Vivian
Mercier has argued, extending from the medieval bards to Swift, Shaw, Wilde,
Joyce and Beckett − a comic intellectual heritage typified by an ability to
respond creatively to dislocation and incongruity.[15]

The question arises, however, as to whether this double vision is a quality
inherited by the Irish mind or a quality *imposed* on it by divisive historical circumstances − e.g. the various invasions, the break between the Gaelic and Anglo-
Irish traditions, and so on. In other words, is the ambivalence of the Irish mind
something that produces or something that is produced by history? In all prob-
ability it is a dialectical combination of both. But in thus suggesting the possibility of some intellectual disposition towards history, I would insist that this be
understood as a *cultural* phenomenon that develops and alters as history
progresses, and *not* as some innate ethnic characteristic.

In the case of many Irish writers the double vision assumed the focus of exile
or estrangement, the unmistakable sentiment of residing on the outside or
periphery, of being *other* − for better or for worse. Joyce's experience of exile, for
example, was not only geographical but also cultural and linguistic. Even though
he wrote in English, Joyce was mindful of the fact that he was never quite at ease
with its vocabulary; and this uneasiness perhaps also accounts for his exceptional
capacity to deconstruct and reconstruct it. Joyce exulted in the knowledge that
his writing was a Trojan horse in the city of the Anglo-Saxon tongue. As Stephen
Dedalus ruminated after his exchange with the English Dean of Studies in *A
Portrait of the Artist*:

> The language in which we are speaking is his before it is mine ... I cannot
> speak or write these words without unrest of spirit. His language *so familiar
> and so foreign*, will always be for me an acquired speech. I have not made or
> accepted its words. My voice holds them at bay. My soul frets in the shadow
> of his language.

Joyce could only inhabit the English language as an outsider. But if he was not at home in English, he was not at home in his native culture either. Joyce derided familiarity whenever it took the form of narrow chauvinism – those 'nets of nationality, language and religion' that Stephen deplores – and chided the ideology of insular nationalism as a pale 'afterthought of Europe'. But while he felt himself a foreigner in Ireland, he prided himself on being an Irishman in foreign lands. After only three years in Europe, Joyce wrote to his brother Stanislaus: 'The Irish are the most intelligent, most spiritual and most civilised people in Europe ... If once it could assert itself, [the Irish mind] would contribute a new force to civilisation.' Throughout his life and work Joyce retained a dual fidelity to both the foreign and the familiar. He wanted to Europeanize Ireland and to Hibernicize Europe – no less.[16] John Montague provides this portrait of Joyce's bifocal vision:

> He is the first great artist of his race in the English language, the master forger of his conscience ... His texts grow and grow like an interlaced Celtic manuscript, corrections and additions serpenting along the margins ... His whole being is a blackness, a battlefield of contradictions. An Irishman who retains his British passport, he loathes British officialdom, and is obsessed with the land he left behind ... Sadness and gaiety, seriousness and anarchic humour, he makes his contradictions dance.[17]

This Joycean counterpointing of the foreign and the familiar is arguably one of the most recognizable watermarks of the Irish intellect. Seamus Heaney, a Northern Irish poet who migrated south, at once exiled and at home, haunted by borders and partitions, exposed to the cultures of colonizer and colonized, Catholic and Protestant, Gael and Saxon, has also practised the art of making contradictions dance. The following statement of his intellectual position is instructive in this regard:

> I am convinced that one can be faithful to the nature of the English language and at the same time to one's own non-English origins. This is a proper aspiration for our poetry. In the Sweeney story we have a northern sacral king, Sweeney, who is driven out of Rasharkin in County Antrim. There is a sort of schizophrenia in him. On the one hand he is always whinging for Rasharkin, but on the other he is celebrating his free creative imagination. Maybe here there was a presence, a fable which could lead to the discovery of feelings in myself which I could not otherwise find words for, and which could cast a dream or possibility or myth across the swirl of private feelings: an objective correlative. But one must not forget the other side of the poetic enterprise, which is precisely the arbitrariness and the innocence of the day to day poetic impulse ... This inner impulse has to be preserved, however essential the outward (mythic) structures may be for communication, commu-
> ████████████████ universal significance ... Yeats and Kavanagh point up these contra-

dictions: Yeats with his search for myths and sagas, the need for a structure and a sustaining landscape; Kavanagh with his need to be liberated and distanced from it, the need to be open, unpredictably susceptible, lyrically opportunistic ... You need both.[18]

Derek Mahon, speaking for and from the Northern Protestant tradition, makes a similar plea for the validity of a double cultural residence:

I still consider myself in the tradition of Louis MacNeice, that is an Irish poet who is no more at home in the specific culture of Ireland than in the English culture imparted by a Protestant education and a London residence. The tensions are, I hope, fruitful.[19]

And extending the analysis of intellectual dialectics to the Irish visual arts, Louis le Brocquy describes how his own painting attempts to articulate a secret logic of ambivalence. He explains:

It would appear that this ambivalent attitude ... was especially linked to the prehistoric Celtic world, and there is further evidence that it persists to some extent today ... I myself have learned from the canvas that emergence and immergence – twin phenomena of time – are ambivalent; that one implies the other and that the matrix in which they exist dissolves the normal sense of time, producing a characteristic stillness.[20]

One recalls here the spiral mandala and interlacement motifs that recur in Newgrange, the Celtic crosses and the *Book of Kells*.[21] Le Brocquy leaves us with the following thought-provoking question:

Is this the underlying ambivalence which we in Ireland tend to stress; the continued presence of the historic past, the indivisibility of birth and funeral, spanning the apparent chasm between past and present, between conscious-ness and fact ... day-consciousness/night-consciousness, like [Joyce's] Ulysses and Finnegan?

It is certain that Joyce's own choice of the word 'wake', where the antithetical worlds of life and death overlap and embrace, is no accident.

Finally, several Irish philosophers and scholars appear to bear witness to parallel preoccupations of mind. It is a curious if much neglected fact that two of Ireland's most reputed thinkers, John Scotus Eriugena in the ninth century and Bishop George Berkeley in the eighteenth, reacted against the mainstream logocentric philosophies of their time in an effort to espouse heterodox currents of thought. In Eriugena this decentralizing scruple was marked by a resistance to the Latin orthodoxy of his time (in particular the primacy of substantial being). Eriugena turned instead to the marginal Eastern spirituality of thinkers like Maximus the Confessor and the Pseudo-Dionysius. For his pains he was branded a heretic by Pope Honorius III in 1225. Berkeley was no less icono-clastic in his response to the established mechanist-materialist philosophy of British empiricism (inaugurated by Hobbes and Locke). 'We Irish think other-wise', as he quipped in the margins of Locke's famous *Essay*. Looking beyond the colonial curtain to the anathematized thought of the Continent, Berkeley fashioned an Irish version of Cartesian idealism. For Berkeley, as for Eriugena, this radical movement towards the intellectual *other* – French metaphysics for Berkeley, Oriental theology for Eriugena – also involved a surmounting of confessional divides between Catholic and Protestant for the former, between Oriental and Roman for the latter. In short, both Irish thinkers considered themselves alien to the prevailing philosophical orthodoxies and responded by embracing what were for them *alternative* modes of thought.

The pattern of intellectual exodus towards 'otherness' recurs in the experi-ence of certain Irish scholars as a *peregrinatio* to foreign lands. One could mention here Eriugena's emigration to Laon in France to translate, write and teach philosophy; St Columbanus's holy quest for the 'solitude of contemplation' at Lake Constance in Switzerland; the European wanderings of Gallus, Sedulius Scottus, Cilian and Clement Maelcomer (whose teachings were also condemned by Rome). So profound indeed was the impact of these émigré scholars between the sixth and ninth centuries that one German abbot was prompted to proclaim: 'How can we ever forget Ireland, she fills the church with her science and her teaching.'[22] The *peregrinatio* cult may, in reality, have been necessitated by the Viking invasions of Ireland, but in cultural memory it was recorded as a spiri-tual movement outwards to alien lands.[23] Moreover, this link between Irish and continental spiritualities re-emerged between the seventeenth and nineteenth centuries, when many Irish priests and scholars, unable to study in Ireland due to penal colonial regulations, travelled abroad to receive their education in the Irish colleges established in Paris, Salamanca, Rome, Crakow and other conti-nental cities. And then we have the wanderings through Europe of exiled Irish intellectuals such as John Toland or Oscar Wilde, paving the expatriate path to Paris and beyond, travelled by not only Joyce, Beckett and Stephens, but also by Devlin, Coffey, MacGreevy and many other Irish writers of the twentieth century.

No formal distinction has been made in the preceding account between poets and philosophers; both testify to what would seem to be common, if fluc-tuating, characteristics of the Irish mind – *decentredness, double-vision* and *exile*. The conventional practice of rigidly separating the artist and the thinker, imag-ination and reason, must be questioned if we are to appreciate fully the complexity of the Irish mind.

Poets, philosophers, and other creative thinkers are not, however, the only repre-sentatives of an Irish mind. The characteristics of such a mind have also found *negative* intellectual expression. For example, the logic of ambivalence, the ability to have 'two thinks at a time', can equally manifest itself in a particular brand of 'double-think', a peculiar relish for moral equivocation and evasiveness, for having it both ways: *Tadhg an dá thaobh*. No culture, Irish or otherwise, is above critical reproach. In the light of the above reflections, we are perhaps more justified to speak not of *the* Irish mind, but of *an* Irish mind; or better still, of Irish *minds*.

Interpreting the Past

There are only facts – I would say: No, facts are precisely what there are not, only interpretations.

(Frederick Nietzsche, *The Will to Power*)

The traditional devices for constructing a comprehensive view of history and for retracing the past as a patient and continuous development must be systematically dismantled ... History becomes 'effective' to the degree that it introduces discontinuity into our very being.

(Michel Foucault, *Language, Counter-Memory, Practice*)

How are we to distinguish between the Irish mind the poets and philosophers have invented and the Irish mind as it really existed in history? In a way, this kind of question presupposes an artificial opposition. But it may be usefully employed to clarify the fundamental problem of trying to interpret the meaning of our intellectual history, of trying to make sense of our past by creating or recreating a tradition. Seamus Deane has argued that we should divest ourselves of the cultural myths of the Irish Revival, and particularly the myth, endorsed by Yeats, of a native Anglo-Irish tradition comprising Berkeley, Goldsmith, Sheridan and other Ascendancy intellectuals.[24] Yeats regrouped these disparate minds under the common banner of anti-modernism. He attributed this anti-modernist quality to the Irishness of their intellectual endeavours, which for him amounted to a concerted hostility to the mechanistic spirit unleashed by English philosophy. Yeats commented:

Born in such a community, Berkeley with his belief in perception, that abstract ideas are mere words, Swift with his love of perfect nature, of the Houyhnhnms, his disbelief in Newton's system and every sort of machine, Goldsmith and his delight in the particulars of common life that shocked his contemporaries, Burke with his conviction that all states not grown slowly like a forest tree are tyrannies, found in England the opposite that stung their own thought into expression and made it lucid.[25]

Deane ascribes Yeats's 'mythologizing' of the past to his intellectual and aesthetic need for coherent 'arrangements of history' (for a *continuous* tradition), identifying this with a Hegelian rage for retrospective order. But while Deane credits the aesthetic force of such 'historical fictions', he deems it a betrayal of what he calls 'the brute facts of history' – the signal feature of our *discontinuous* tradition as 'an inheritance of colonial history'. Hence his plea for the abandonment of the fiction of continuity.

I would not dispute the content of Deane's analysis, only some of his methodological presuppositions. Is not history always translated into a quasi-story (the French use the same term for both: *histoire*) as soon as it is interpreted by the human mind? How is the past remembered if it is not written or recounted? Deane seems to oppose the fictive claims of myth to the truth claims of sociological analysis. He does not wish to privilege either. He simply exhorts us to acknowledge them as two mutually exclusive orders: one pertaining to imagination, the other to reality. But is not the 'realist' methodology of sociological history itself a fictional construct of the mind? Does the scientific reliance upon empirical verification not itself presuppose the positivistic myth of *truth as an objectively observable fact*? In short, is not the abandonment of all myths itself a kind of myth?

I would suggest that what we are dealing with in the Yeatsian view of an Irish intellectual tradition is not so much an *unreal* historical fiction to be pitted against the social literalism of *real* historical truth, as a myth of one order (Yeats's Romantic interpretation) opposing a myth of another order (the enlightenment positivist interpretation). *Both* are hermeneutic constructs. History is never literal; it is a *figurative* reading of events by means of human thought and language. And it is precisely because history is figurative that it is subject to the ethical laws of hermeneutic transfiguration or disfiguration, of liberation or distortion.[26] Every reading of history involves a choice between different interpretative models.

Irish intellectual history, like any other, can be interpreted in a variety of ways. Four of the most obvious hermeneutic models are 1) an Anglo-Irish Ascendancy reading; 2) a nationalist/republican reading; 3) a positivist/enlightenment reading; 4) a socio-economic or materialist reading. The existence of these rival hermeneutics simply testifies that history is a carrier of multiple, and often conflicting, readings of the same historical phenomena. And one cannot appeal to the putatively *neutral* court of fact – the way it *really* was – without in turn resorting to a particular mode of *interpretation* (i.e. the hermeneutic of positivism). Facts are devoid of meaning until they are configured by human thinking and praxis. 'Tradition', as Terry Eagleton reminds us, 'is the practice of ceaselessly excavating, safe-guarding, violating, discarding and reinscribing the past ... history is not a fair copy but a palimpsest, whose deleted layers must be thrust to light.'[27]

This is not to deny that it is the ethical duty of the critical, discerning mind to discriminate between hermeneutic rivals. (What, after all, is my present reading if not an attempt, amongst other things, to debunk the myth of the mindless Irish?) But one cannot discriminate and debunk by presuming privileged access to some pre-interpretative experience. History cannot pre-exist hermeneutic invention.[28] And here we must restore to this word, invention, the double etymological connotation originally carried (before its Romantic idealist distortion) by the Latin *inventio*, meaning both *creation* and *discovery*: the hermeneutic projection of that reading that resides in latent or potential form in the events of history. Historical meaning is neither exclusively subjective (as the Romantic idealist claims) nor exclusively objective (as the positive empiricist holds). It precedes the division into such extremes of subjectivism and objectivism. The meanings of our past emerge from a reciprocal act in which interpreter and what is interpreted each contribute to the identification of a pattern. This is perhaps the single most revolutionary discovery of contemporary philosophical hermeneutics as formulated by Heidegger, Ricoeur and the Frankfurt school.

Deane asserts that Yeats's readings of an Anglo-Irish intellectual tradition 'can only be understood as myths, as versions of history converted into a metaphor'. I agree. But I would reread the 'only' in this sentence as denoting a condition of possibility rather than of disqualification. This is not to suggest that we dispense with the critical duty to demythologize cultural myths and metaphors whenever they assume a reactionary or perverse guise. But in discharging our hermeneutic duties we should not delude ourselves into thinking that such a critique can ever lead us back to some pristine, pre-interpreted world of fact. An authentic hermeneutic demythologizes the dehumanizing myths of history in order to recreate new and more liberating ones.[29]

Deane does, however, appear to recognize implicitly the unavoidable existence of the hermeneutic circle when he concedes that the Yeatsian Revival myths 'survive because they have no serious competitors' (presumably no serious alternative myths); or when he regrets that the influence of the Joycean hermeneutic 'on Irish modes of thought has been negligible compared with that of Yeats and even Synge.'[30]

What hermeneutic competitors to the Yeatsian reading might we consider? First there is, as Deane observes, Joyce's critical rereading of the Irish Revival tradition of the heroic imagination. The main target here is Stephen Dedalus who prides himself, like Yeats and Wilde, on being a 'priest of the eternal imagination', a *salvator mundi* transmuting the daily bread of history into the hieratic word of art. Through his deflation of Stephen's aesthetic pretensions (ironically played off against the more humane and life-embracing aesthetic of Bloom and Molly), Joyce repudiates the imperial wilfulness of the romantic hero at war with history. But by presuming that history, in this context, comprises a 'literal' world of 'class problems, economics, bureaucratic systems and the like', Deane finds himself, paradoxically, invoking the old dualism between subjective imaginings and objective 'brute facts', which he lauds Joyce for trying to surpass. What this dualistic presupposition fails to adequately appreciate is that the 'brute facts' of class exploitation and economic bureaucracy are themselves products of dehumanizing political ideologies. As Habermas and the Frankfurt school have taught us, capitalism and communism are themselves derived from hermeneutic rereadings of history.[31]

While Deane and Kinsella interpret Irish intellectual history in terms of a hermeneutic of discontinuity, other critics such as Frank O'Connor and Vivian Mercier have chosen to reaffirm a hermeneutic of continuity – albeit from a perspective different to that of Yeats. In *The Irish Comic Tradition* (1962), Mercier advances a retrospective overview of Irish culture ranging from early Gaelic to late Anglo-Irish literature. He isolates the comic character of the Irish mind as a recurring feature of our tradition. But Mercier's unfamiliarity with the Gaelic tradition left him vulnerable to the charge of underestimating the basic disruption in Irish culture occasioned by the break-up of the Gaelic tradition. The hermeneutic of continuity may not, however, be so easily dismissed. Frank O'Connor, one of Ireland's most eminent translators from Gaelic,[32] also promoted the idea of a single Irish tradition. In *The Backward Look* (1967), O'Connor composed a critical survey spanning the entire course of Gaelic and Anglo-Irish literature. His argument for continuity stems from the conviction that both literatures share a common retrospective vision, whence the title. 'I am not sure,' he writes, 'that any country can afford to discard what I have called the backward look, but we in Ireland can afford it less than any other because without it we have nothing and are nothing.' His study is divided into two parts: the first dealing with Gaelic literature down to the seventeenth century, the second with Irish literature in English from the seventeenth century to the present with special emphasis on Yeats, O'Casey, Synge, Stephens and Joyce. O'Connor's reading is facilitated by his omission of any serious reference to the literature written in Irish since the Revival.[33] Notwithstanding this, he does make a strong case for a certain connection across disconnection. Speaking of the structural composition of the *Táin*, for example, O'Connor sees it as a multi-layered excavation site with a transversal vein of reinterpretations:

> Some I cannot identify at all, but I think I can isolate a seventh century substratum in archaic verse; an eighth century rendering of this in good narrative prose, which more or less corresponds with what the lawyers were trying to do at the same time with the charted laws; definitely there is a ninth century layer, very elegant, but less vigorous than the earlier strata; and finally as the influence of the Norse invasions becomes felt, there is a recrudescence of the oral element ...

and so on. O'Connor's account illustrates the hermeneutic lesson that meaning can only be historically constituted and transmitted as a palimpsest of ever-receding, ever-recurring readings. There is no original *arche* that could be recovered as some sort of pure pre-linguistic presence. History is an endless text incorporating a horizonal context of possible readings that can only be actualized by each interpretation. History is, in sum, an interplay of multiple pre-inscriptions: a play of recreation. As the old Irish epigram on pilgrimages to Rome reminds us:

> The King you seek there,
> unless you bring Him with you, You will not find him.

O'Connor finds interconnections everywhere in the 'immense mass' of a thousand years and more of Irish literature, in both English and Gaelic. He divines links between the literary revivals inaugurated by Ferguson, Mangan, Hyde, Pearse and Yeats and the 1916 Rising; and between both of these and the ancient Celtic saga tradition. Emphasizing Ireland's Indo-European roots, O'Connor concludes that we are 'a people of The Book', and as such can 'no more escape from the burden of tradition than the Jews have been able to escape from the Pentateuch'.[34]

Is it a mere coincidence that O'Connor, like Deane and Kinsella, is both a critical and creative writer? Probably not. These three interpreters of our cultural tradition have successfully combined intellectual and poetic sensibilities. This bifocal fidelity exemplifies one of the central hypotheses of our analysis: that Irish minds have succeeded, in several important respects, in eschewing the orthodox dualism between intellect and imagination, between conceptual and aesthetic creativity – a dualism that has hamstrung the Western logocentric tradition.[35]

I am not, of course, suggesting that Irish culture is the only European instance of non-logocentric expression. One could, no doubt, cite examples of other European – not to mention non-European – cultures that resisted, debunked or simply remained on the periphery of Graeco-Roman logocentrism.[36] It is undeniable, however, that the Irish mind is one of the most sustained examples of such intellectual difference and dissent.

Some might object that the debate concerning the conflicting readings of Irish intellectual history, and in particular the rival interpretations of continuity and discontinuity, is simply not worth such expense of time, space and energy. Sean O'Faolain, for one, has expressed the view that the main trouble with modern Ireland stems from 'that old curse and bore', our 'revered, unforgettable, indestructible, irretrievable past ... the underground stream that keeps on vanishing and reappearing'.[37] O'Faolain attributes such preoccupations to the mesmerizing atavisms of 'myth and mystique', epitomized in what he calls the 'atrocity' of nationalism. The curse and bore of the past is also evinced, he insists, in our political ineptitude and inability to govern ourselves: 'All our life-ways remained for far too long based on social structures dependent on the primitive idea of the local ruler, while Europe was developing the more powerful concept of the centralised state.' Against this intellectual self-excoriation, so typical of that post-colonial servility that repudiates its own past, I would invoke the pronouncement of Sir Samuel Ferguson that we should attend to the records of our past in order that we may liberate our minds by 'living back in the land we live in'.[38]

But can we *look back* without anger or nostalgia? Can we *live back* without resorting to the opiates of ethnic nationalism or reactionary conservatism? Or to put it in more pertinent terms for our present purposes, how may we *think back* in order to think forward in an intellectually emancipating manner?

The first assumption to be dispelled is that the past constitutes some abstract evolutionary chain leading from the bad, to the better, to the best (the progressivist illusion); or from the best to the worst (the regressivist illusion). We might take our cue here from the philosopher Walter Benjamin who wrote that 'in every era the attempt must be made anew to wrest tradition away from the conformism that is about to overpower it.'[39] Benjamin recognized that the only way to confront such conformism is to think through the tradition in a critical and creative fashion. The deletion of the past from our minds is the best recipe for enslavement to it. Or as Arland Ussher, the Irish thinker, remarked: 'The sentimentalist would like to look at the past as a mere picture hung upon the wall. But the past is throbbing with a secret life, like a dragon's egg.'[40] One of the most insidious kinds of conformism to overpower the sense of Irish tradition is, I have argued, the ethnic stereotype of the heroic, thoughtless Celt (a stereotype that has been variously deployed for colonial and also chauvinistic nationalist reasons). Accordingly, history must be constantly reinvestigated and revised not just so that we may expose its prejudices, but so that we may restore its forfeited or discarded fragments. Corkery's 'hidden Ireland', Kinsella's and Ó Tuama's 'poems of the dispossessed' or Montague's 'lost tradition' are retrieved from oblivion only after an initial acknowledgment of loss. In similar fashion, the neglected heritage of Irish minds can only be reclaimed by challenging the blindnesses that occasioned such neglect.

Tradition is not just a homogeneous totality; it is a multilayered manuscript with each layer recording some new crisis, rupture or spasm that has altered the course of history. Consequently, while historicism – as advanced by the liberal humanists or the Second Marxist International – tended to read history teleologically as a causally determined sequence of events, a more authentic hermeneutic will, in Benjamin's words, 'brush history against the grain', thereby salvaging its repressed lineages, unmasking reactionary ideologies and reminding us that 'there is no cultural document that is not at the same time a record of barbarism'.[41] To ignore or disregard our past is, ironically, to remain in corrosive collusion with it. The past is thus taken for granted and robbed of its critical potentiality to challenge the imposing ideologies of the present. The question of tradition is too often consigned to quarantined remoteness, or misconstrued as an exclusive dialect of the tribe to be purified by the elect. In this regard one must be equally wary of the Eliotic view of tradition as a pantheon of eternal monuments that 'form an ideal order among themselves', an order that is 'complete before (any) new work arrives'.[42] More authentic is the view that tradition is a seedbed of multiple readings that subvert any pretension to univocal self-identity or self-completion.

In the field of Irish intellectual history that concerns us, this means accepting our tradition as a medley of rupturing, irregular and often suppressed perspectives, a tradition that comprises such diverse claimants as the pre-Celtic ideology of Newgrange; the Celtic ideologies of old and middle Irish myth; the medieval, Christian vision of Eriugena and the wandering monk-scholars; the dispossessed mind of the Gaelic 'hidden' Ireland; the Anglo-Irish Ascendancy tradition of Berkeley, Swift, Burke, Shaw, Wilde, Yeats and many of our scientific thinkers; the political ideologies of Irish socialism, republicanism and liberalism; the nationalist aesthetic of the Fenian poets Mangan, Davis and Pearse; and the self-scrutinizing critical modernism of Joyce, Beckett and many of our contemporary writers.

To interrogate this plurality of conflicting interpretations is to open ourselves to those other, often occluded possibilities of being ourselves from which our constricting present may alienate us. Hence the necessity for an open-ended 'science of history whose subject matter is not a tangle of purely factual details, but consists rather of the numbered group of threads that represent the weft of the past as it feeds into the warp of the present'.[43] Such a view disengages us from the predeterminism of history. It sidesteps both the historicist cult of a pre-ordained continuum and the postmodernist cult of arbitrary fragmentation, in order to engage us with robust questioning. There is, I suggest, no better hermeneutic guide to the present work than Benjamin's own blueprint:

> For successful excavation a plan is needed. Yet no less indispensable is the cautious probing of the spade in the loam; it is to cheat oneself of the richest prize to preserve as a record merely the inventory of one's discoveries, and not this dark joy of the place of the finding itself. Fruitless searching is as much a part of this as succeeding, and consequently remembrance must not proceed in the manner of a narrative or still less of a report, but must, in the strictest epic or rhapsodic fashion, assay its spade in ever-new places, and in the old ones delve to ever-deeper layers.[44]

Such careful, critical excavation may well result in the discovery of the Irish mind as a creative historical interplay of Irish *minds*.

CHAPTER THREE

Myth and Martyrdom: Foundational Symbols in Irish Republicanism

In an essay entitled 'Universal civilisation and national cultures', the French philosopher Paul Ricoeur suggests that nationalist movements are almost invariably motivated, at some deep and often preconceptual level, by a 'mythical-nucleus'. If one wishes to analyse this ideological deep-structure, Ricoeur argues, one has to cut through to that 'layer of images and symbols which make up the basic ideals of a nation or national group'.[1] Was such a 'mythical-nucleus' detectable in the extreme nationalist ideology of the Provisional IRA? To what extent could this ideology be said to represent, however indirectly, the 'basic ideals of a national group'? And where might one locate the mythical paradigms and symbols to serve as guidelines for such an analysis? The following study is an attempt to provide a partial answer to these questions.

I. The Militant Nationalist Tradition

With the emergence of leaders like Gerry Adams and Danny Morrison in the seventies and eighties, the Provisional IRA was said to have taken a turn to the left. This appeared to signify a movement beyond the 'traditional republicanism' of Daithí Ó Conaill, Ruardhí Ó Brádaigh and Seamus Twomey toward a more 'radical republicanism' that combined nationalism with revolutionary socialism. It could be argued that these two ideologies had always coexisted to some degree in the militant republican tradition; but it was clearly the rhetoric of extreme political nationalism that dominated the Provisional movement when it first emerged in the late sixties.

In January 1970, the Kevin St headquarters of the Provisional IRA issued a statement entitled *Where Sinn Féin Stands*. Here they outlined their aims, policies and major points of difference from other 'parliamentary' radical groups (in particular Official Sinn Féin and the Irish Communist Party). In this publication the Provisionals declared: 'Ours is a socialism based on *the native Irish tradition* of Comhar na gComharsan, which is founded on ... our Irish and Christian values.' To this they added the all-important qualification – '*we take our inspiration and experience from the past*'. But what precisely did the Provisionals mean when they claimed to take their inspiration from the 'past'? Although the Provisionals called themselves socialists, at their annual conference in Dublin, October 1971, they explicitly proscribed all 'members of the communist party or *any other radical group*'. They also took this opportunity to denounce the efforts of the left-wing Officials (later to become The Workers Party) to seek a parliamentary socialist solution to the Northern problem by concentrating on 1) the democratic election of a working-class party, and 2) the Two-Nations theory (i.e. the renunciation of the nationalist ideal of a United Ireland). The Provisionals' dissociation from the anti-nationalist Marxism of the Officials is unequivocal: 'We call on them to cease describing themselves as Sinn Féin. That honoured name has never belonged in Westminster, Stormont or Leinster House. Let them join with their new-found friends in their "Liberation Front" or whatever they wish to call it and leave the Republican Movement alone.'[2] A commander-in-chief of the Provisional IRA in the seventies, Seamus Twomey, confirmed this preoccupation with traditional nationalist aims when he stated: 'At heart I am a socialist ... but at the same time a right-winger ... our prime and main objective is the unification of our country ... and our definition of nationalism is implied in the *militant Republican tradition*.'[3]

What exactly was this native republican 'tradition' that the Provisionals invoked to sanction their military campaign? What was this 'past' from which they claimed to take their 'inspiration and experience'? In short, where might we seek out the ideological origins of the Provisionals' rhetoric, and by extension, action? The most obvious pointer would seem to lie in the very appellation of the movement itself – 'Provisional'. This title was borrowed from the 1916 Proclamation of the 'Provisional Government of the Irish Republic'. What is more, the most cursory perusal of any page of the Provisional IRA's publication *An Phoblacht* (itself derived from the titular address of the same 1916 Proclamation – 'Poblacht na hÉireann') confirms the Provisionals' deep identification with the heroes of Easter Week.

Taking this as a clue to the locus of the 'past' that the Provisionals invoked, we may decipher the 'mythical-nucleus' latent in the symbols of the 1916 Proclamation itself. The opening phrases of this foundational document of traditional Irish nationalism are highly instructive: 'Irishmen and Irishwomen: In the name of God and of the dead generations from which she receives her old tradition of nationhood, Ireland, through us, summons her children to her flag and strikes for her freedom.' The appeal to Irishmen and women is not made by the signatories themselves, but only 'through' them by Ireland. Ireland is addressed here as a maternal and mythical personification of the nation who addresses her children in the name of God and those 'dead generations' who have sacrificed themselves for her nationhood.

It would seem, therefore, that just as the Provisionals conceived of themselves as the legatees of the 'past' generation of 1916 (a conception that most Irish nationalists would, of course, dispute), that original generation in turn had acted on behalf of an even older heritage of 'dead generations'. This extended genealogical invocation would have linked the 1916 heroes not only with their founding Fenian forebears of the preceding century, but also with former Irish patriots such as O'Donnell and O'Neill, and ultimately with the legendary heroes of mythological Erin, i.e. Oisín, Cuchulain, Mananán, Cathleen Ni Houlihan and most importantly Fionn MacCumhaill and his warrior band, the Fianna. It is essential to recall that it was from this mythological Fianna that the whole Fenian movement leading up to 1916 took its name and 'inspiration'. And as we shall remark below, the *symbols* of the Rising stemmed largely from the Fenian revival of ancient mythological lore.

The suggestion here is that the *rationale* of the 1916 republican movement – and by implication the Provisional republican movement that laid claim to its heritage – may have had as much to do with the mythic resuscitation of some sacred national 'tradition' as with revolutionary socialist scruples (although James Connolly would seem to be an exception here). Is it possible that one guiding motivation of militant republicanism had less to do with the appropriation of the socio-economic means of production, than with an exigency of sacrifice to a mythological Ireland: an ancestral deity who would respond to the martyrdom of her sons by rising from her ancient slumber to avenge them? Is this possibility not strongly suggested by the fact that the operative terms of 1916 were 'sacrifice' and 'rising' – originally scheduled, let us not forget for Easter Sunday! – rather than 'proletarian revolt' or 'class war'?[4] The concluding sentences of the Proclamation would seem to furnish additional evidence for such a hypothesis: 'In this supreme hour the Irish nation must, by its valour and discipline and by the readiness of its children to sacrifice themselves for the common good, prove itself worthy of the august destiny to which it is called.' On Easter Monday, 1916, amidst much confusion and alarm the General Post Office in Dublin was occupied by Pearse's troops and the Rising began.

But the ultimate triumph of the Rising was really secured when Pearse and his fellow signatories were executed by the British in Kilmainham Jail. The very rebels who had been spat upon by the Dublin people as they were led as prisoners from the General Post Office became national heroes overnight as soon as their lives had been sacrificed. As Bernard Shaw observed: 'Those who were executed became ... martyrs whose blood was the seed of the Irish Free State.'

The mythological interpretation of militant republicanism is not entirely unprecedented. Augustine Martin in 'Reflections on the Poetry of 1916' and Ruth Dudley Edwards in her biography of Pearse have each alluded to the link between Irish nationalism and the mythic ideology of sacrificial blood-letting, martyrdom and the ancestor cult. And the seasoned civil rights campaigner, Eamonn MacCann, writes as follows of the redemptorist martyr cult of Irish nationalism in his *War and an Irish Town*: 'One learned, quite literally at one's mother's knee, that Christ died for the human race, and Patrick Pearse for the Irish section of it ... Nationalist candidates were not selected, they were anointed. Religion and politics were bound up together, were regarded, indeed, as being in many ways the same thing.'[5] But while these and other commentators have succeeded in identifying this mythic dimension they have not proceeded to interrogate its origins or presuppositions *qua* myth. The analysis undertaken here attempts such an interrogation. By isolating the mythological essence of the foundational symbols of the 'militant republican tradition' we hope to shed some light on the Provisionals' claim to have taken therefrom both their 'inspiration and experience'.

II. The Myth of a Recurring Past

We have come to the holiest place in Ireland; holier to us even than the place where Patrick sleeps in Down. Patrick brought us life, but this man died for us ...

(Patrick Pearse at the graveside of Wolfe Tone)

Our reading of the textual symbols of the Easter Proclamation has identified the primary motif of sacrifice in the name of the deities and dead generations of the 'past'. This motif is fundamentally mythological as Mircea Eliade points out in his *Myths, Dreams and Mysteries*:

Myth is thought to express the *absolute truth* because it narrates a *sacred history*; that is, a trans-human revelation which took place at the dawn of the Great Time, in the holy time of the beginning ... The myth becomes exemplary and consequently *repeatable*, and thus serves as a model and justification for all human actions ... [By] *imitating* the exemplary acts of a god or of a mythic hero and heroes ... [man] detaches himself from profane time and magically re-enters the Great Time, the sacred time.[6]

By means of a mythological repetition of the 'past', the nationalist leaders, it might be argued, sought to redeem Ireland. Incarcerated in a history of colonial oppression, the evangelists of the Provisional Republic appealed to a prehistorical mythic power whereby their present paralysis might be miraculously transcended.

By *repeating* the names and deeds of the ancient heroes and martyrs of Erin they sought to revive her sacred destiny. The only way to redeem the nation seemed to be the negation of present history in favour of some Holy Beginning, some eternally recurring Past. And this recurrence of the primordial Spirit of Erin would be brought about, following the laws of myth, by blood-sacrifice. This is certainly the *mythos* to which Pearse subscribed when he claimed that 'blood-shed is a cleansing and sanctifying thing'. In brief, sacrifice obeys the laws of myth, not politics: it operates on the assumption that victory can only spring from defeat, and total rejuvenation of the community from the oblation of a chosen hero or heroic elite. But while myth seeks to transcend the logic of prag-matic political action, it can nonetheless influence the political consciousness of a people in a significant manner. In *States of Mind: A Study of Anglo-Irish Conflict, 1780–1980*, Oliver MacDonagh argues that the pervasive optimism of Ireland's political *myths* is the logical counterpart of the pessimism of its political *history*:

> ... a past seen in terms of subjection and struggle, seen as a pageant or tour-nament of heroic defeat, is one of the roads towards fundamental distrust of or even disbelief in achievement ... it is true that the characteristic Irish time-frame inclines Irishmen to a repetitive view of history and that such a view inclines them – perhaps in defensive wariness and from fear of failure – to prize the moral as against the actual, and the bearing of witness as against success.[7]

The predominant symbols of the 1916 leaders' own rhetoric would appear to corroborate this seemingly extravagant reading. Pearse was perhaps the most artic-ulate spokesman of this mythic consciousness. In a farewell letter to his mother written from his cell in Kilmainham Jail shortly before his execution, he bade her 'not to grieve for all this but to think of it as a sacrifice'. He included a poem enti-tled 'A Mother Speaks' in which he identifies himself with the sacrificed Christ 'who had gone forth to die for men' and compares his mother's faith in his powers of renewal with Mary's faith in the resurrection: 'Dear Mary, I have shared thy sorrow and soon shall share thy joy'. This motif of blood sacrifice is even more explicitly evinced in the final lines of Pearse's play *The Singer* when the hero MacDara exclaims: 'I will stand up before the Gall as Christ hung naked before men on the tree!' But the *mythos* of sacrifice was not merely a private fantasy. In the months following the Rising numerous posters with the caption 'All is Changed' were to be seen in Dublin depicting the martyred Pearse in a *pietà* posi-tion supported by the mythic figure of Mother Erin (brandishing a tricolour).[8]

It was this same Pearse who had, just twelve months previously, reverently solicited the authority of the 'dead generations' in his panegyric over O'Donovan Rossa's grave. In this address, steeped throughout in mythological idioms of seasonal and generational renewal by blood, Pearse claimed that the 'new generations' that had been 'rebaptised in the Fenian faith' would shortly come of age as a 'miraculous ripening seed'. He concluded with the now immortal lines: 'Life springs from death, and from the graves of patriotic men and women spring living nations ... The fools, the fools, the fools, they have left us our Fenian dead and while Ireland holds these graves Ireland unfree shall never be at peace.' But Pearse's most unequivocal rendering of the sacrifice myth is perhaps to be found in 'The Coming Revolution' where he writes: 'We may make mistakes in the beginning and shoot the wrong people; but bloodshed is a cleansing and sanctifying thing, and the nation which regards it as the final horror has lost its manhood.'

Thomas MacDonagh was another of the signatories instrumental in the propagation of the myth of sacrificial renewal. In his *Literature in Ireland* he described the revival of the national spirit as the 'supreme song of victory on the dying lips of martyrs' and elsewhere declared his own death to be but a 'little phase of an Eternal Song'. The allusion here to Pearse's symbol of the 'singer' is not accidental. Both of these leaders were poets who conceived of the Rising in fundamentally mytho-poetic terms. Both envisaged their imminent martyrdom as a sort of leitmotif recapitulating the Eternal Song of sacrifice-and-rebirth that harmonized all those 'dead generations' of Irish heroes. While a purely political revolution could provide only a temporary – because 'temporal' – solution, a *mythic* Rising reaching back to the roots of the national spirit could ensure an 'eternal' victory. These leaders realized from the outset that their heroic stand would constitute no more than a *symbolic* Rising with little or no hope of prac-tical political success. But their conviction seems to have been that by their temporal defeat an Eternal Nation might be induced to *recur* and reinstate itself. This attitude is epitomized by Pearse's surrender-statement that though the Irish had lost their victory in life 'they would win it in death'. It was on similar grounds that MacDonagh defended the Proclamation at his trial: 'You think it a dead and buried letter, but it lives, it lives; from minds alight with Ireland's vivid intellect it sprang; in hearts aflame with Ireland's mighty love it was conceived. Such documents do not die.'

Mary Ryan, one of the last acquaintances to visit MacDonagh before his death, reported that his last words aside from prayers were 'God save Ireland'; and added, betraying a nuance she herself could scarcely have suspected: 'At four o'clock when the shooting was done a gentle rain began to fall – the tears of Dark Rosaleen.' Dark Rosaleen was, of course, one of the several mythic person-ifications of Ireland. She had been immortalized in a James Clarence Mangan poem and had served as a common motif in the Fenian rhetoric of the preceding century. Indeed, the mythological symbol of the red rose – emblem of Ireland's eternally self-renewing spirit – played a central role in both the Fenian and 1916 poetics. In the nineteenth century such poets as Mangan, Davis, Ferguson and de Vere had richly exploited the sacrificial resonances of the rose symbol (renewal through blood, dawn, spring, crucifixion) in their evocation of a 'hidden mythological Ireland'.[9] The primary images of this mythologized Erin had, in turn, been handed down from the previous generations of Spalpín poets: Ó Rathaille, Ó Súilleabháin and Ó Longáin. These Gaelic bards had personified the sufferings of the native community in the form of visionary evocations (*aisling* or *spéir-bhruinneal*) of ancient Celtic heroes and deities. Thus, for example, MacDonagh's appeal to the 'passionate proud woes of *Róisín Dubh*' is an adaptation of Mangan's poem 'Róisín Dubh', which is itself a borrowing from the earlier Gaelic poetics of devotion to this mythic goddess. Similarly, Joseph Plunkett − another of the 1916 leaders − wrote a poem entitled 'The Little Black Rose Shall Be Red at Last' in which he rewords de Vere's lyric of the same title. Plunkett dedicates this poem to the mythic figure, Caitlín Ní hÚllacháin, and prays in the final lines that by sacrificing himself to inevitable 'doom', the 'dark rose shall redden into bloom'. The reference to 'doom' at this key point in the poem is significant for it confirms our suggestion that the *mythic* recourse to miraculous powers of transmutation is primarily motivated by the closing off of all normal channels for effecting political change *in* history. A certain *fatalism* is inherent in most invocations of the mythic past.

The translation at the turn of the century of the Celtic mythological sagas (the Táin and Ossianic cycles, etc.) by O'Grady and O'Shaughnessy was, no doubt, a further source of inspiration for the ancestral myths of 1916. These translations helped in particular to focus the minds of the Anglo-Irish members of the Irish Revival on the mythological heritage of what Daniel Corkery called the 'hidden Ireland of the Gaels' that had survived in the poetic symbols of the native Gaelic tradition. This hidden Ireland was perhaps most powerfully represented by the eighteenth-century Gaelic poetry of 'dispossession' known as *an duanaire*. In these poems the recognition of tragic failure and defeat in the political *present* was compensated for by the recollection of a mythic *past* (or the anticipation of a mythic *future*) where the fatalities of history could be redeemed. The Gaelic poets of *an duanaire* frequently invoked such ancestral myths in order to resuscitate the morale of a people bent low by famine, colonization and religious apartheid. As Corkery points out in his study of this period, the poetry was more racial and national than personal in character.[10]

This subordination of individual utterance to the archetypes of national experience is typical of mythic forms of expression. In this spirit, Ó Rathaille described Ireland as 'some fair daughter of celestial powers' (*do geineadh ar gheineamhain / di-se an tír uachtaraigh*), and declares that he will suffer 'amid a ruffian hoarde' until the ancient heroes return from over the sea of death (*go bhfuillid na leoghain tar tuinn*). In another poem one finds an even more explicit appeal to the ancestral genealogy that unites the poet with his deceased forebears:

> I will stop now—my death is hurrying near
> now the dragons of the Leamhan, Loch Léin and the Laoi are destroyed.

> In the grave with this cherished chief I'll join those kings
> my people served before the death of Christ.

In the nineteenth century these same preoccupations with some Holy Time of the Great Beginning were evidenced in the Fenian poets. The following opening lines from Darcy Magee's poem 'The Celts' are exemplary:

> Long, long ago, beyond the misty space
> of twice a thousand years
> in Erin old there dwelt a mighty race.

Contemporary commentators of the 1916 Rising seemed to grasp the significant role of sacrifice more readily than the more empirically minded critics of our own day. Chesterton immediately recognized this mythic dimension: 'Pearse and his colleagues died to be in the Greek and literal sense martyrs: they wished not so much to win as to witness. They thought that nothing but their own dead bodies could prove that Ireland was not dead.'[11] Indeed we need only recall the incredible transformation that their martyrdom effected to realize just how deeply rooted in the Irish national psyche is this mythological cult of sacrifice. As Lennox Robinson remarked as early as 1918: 'Everything in Ireland has either taken place *before Easter Week* or *after Easter Week*. Right down to the heart of Irish nationality it cut, and the generations to come will continue to feel the piercing terror of the sword thrust.'[12] James Stephens adverts to this same sacrificial motif in his *Insurrection in Dublin* written several months after the Rising: 'The day before the rising was Easter Sunday and they were crying joyfully in the churches "Christ has Risen". On the following day they were saying in the streets "Ireland has risen".' In a poem entitled 'Spring 1916' Stephens elaborates on this theme, substituting the Celtic hero, Mananán, for Christ.

> Be green upon their graves, O happy Spring! …
> Now are we born again, and now are we,
> —Wintered so long beneath an icy hand!—
> New-risen into life and liberty,
> Because the Spring is come into our land! …
> … Be with us Mananán![13]

III. Yeats and the Symbolism of Sacrifice

It is in Yeats's poetic testimony of the Irish nationalist uprising, however, that the whole *mythos* of sacrifice finds its most eloquent formulation. In his much quoted poem, 'Easter, 1916', Yeats confesses astonishment at how such ordinary men as MacDonagh, Connolly and Pearse had been totally transformed by sacrifice

> Now and in time to be,
> Wherever green is worn,
> [They] Are changed, changed utterly:
> A terrible beauty is born.

Two themes of major importance emerge here. Firstly the theme – central to mythic logic – that 'beauty' is the offspring of 'terror'. In other words (though we are reading freely here between Yeats's lines), the terror inspired by the Easter sacrifice served as some sort of magic passport ferrying the martyrs from their local time to a sacred time where they might secure the beatific power of renewal. Yeats, of course, made no secret of his admiration for ancient mystery-rites and even fostered a project of establishing a mystical Celtic order of such practices in the Castle on the Rock at Lough Key. His perpetual yearning for a Unity of Culture capable of transmuting the Irish people into an 'enduring nation' and his belief in the existence of a 'supernatural racial Memory' also testify to his mystic temperament. 'Was not a nation,' Yeats ponders in *The Trembling of the Veil*, 'as distinguished from a crowd of chance comers, bound together by that Unity of Image which I sought in national literature!' And would not such a Unity of Culture and Image be impossible without some apocalyptic terror? Talking of the great cultural martyrs, who sought in the past to forge such a unity, he writes: 'We gaze at such men in awe, because we gaze not at a work of art but at the re-creation of the man through that art, the birth of a new species of man, and it may even seem that the hairs of our heads stand up, because that birth, that recreation, is from *terror*.'[14] Yeats adds, appropriately, that 'these things are true also of nations', and 'though the gate-keepers who drive the nation to war or anarchy, that it may find its image, are different from those who drive individual men … they work together'. It requires no great feat of imagination to identify these gate-keepers as those 'dead generations' invoked by the 1916 martyrs.

The second theme of key importance in Yeats's 'Easter, 1916' is the cultic immortalization of an act. The mediocre men who are so utterly changed by their 'terrible' deed are not only changed 'now' but also 'in time to be'. The significance of their action is not buried with their bones but flows eternally from their graves and nourishes all those subsequent generations of martyrs who sacrifice themselves for an 'enduring nation'. The 'terrible beauty' is not, strictly speaking, something 'born' but something perpetually re-born in periodic rites of terror. Yeats leaves us in no doubt as to his intended meaning when, in another poem 'Three Songs to the One Burden', he reminds us that,

> For Patrick Pearse had said
> That in every generation
> Must Ireland's blood be shed.

Only by means of such sacrificial commemoration can the Sacred Time of the nation return. 'When supernatural events begin,' writes Yeats, 'a man first doubts his own testimony, but when they repeat themselves again and again, he doubts all *human* testimony.'[15] To illustrate this point, Yeats cites the example of the ancient priests who received their supernatural power through repeated contemplation of the image of Apollo, and closer to home, the case of Gemma Galgaris who, in 1889, was said to have caused deep wounds to appear in her body by contemplating her crucifix. Similarly, by reiterating the sacrificial deeds of 'dead generations', the national martyr reactivates the primordial spirit of his sacred ancestors. This is what Yeats had in mind when he concluded his poem 'The Statues' with the rhetorical question:

> When Pearse summoned Cuchulain to his side,
> What stalked through the Post Office? ...[16]

In several other poems, Yeats develops the central Fenian symbol of Ireland as a rose. Thus in 'To the rose upon the Rood of Time' he celebrates the mythic spirit of Éire as the mystical rose of sacrifice and rebirth:

> I would ... Sing of old Éire and the ancient ways:
> Red Rose, proud Rose, sad Rose of all my days.

And in 'The Rose Tree', Yeats features an imaginary dialogue where Pearse laments to Connolly that the rose tree of Ireland is withered. The latter replies that it needs to be watered if the 'green' is to re-emerge and the garden to blossom again. The last verse provides us with one of the most succinct expressions of the whole mythic cult of sacrifice:

> 'But where can we draw water,'
> Said Pearse to Connolly,
> 'When all the walls are parched away?
> O plain as plain can be
> There's nothing but our own red blood
> Can make a right Rose Tree.'

Another mythic symbol of nationalist sentiment that Yeats rehearsed and refined was that of Cathleen Ni Houlihan. In a note dated 1903 and addressed to Lady Gregory, Yeats describes this figure as 'Ireland herself ... for whom so many songs had been sung and for whom so many had gone to their death'. His famous play, called after this mythological goddess, was set during the 1798 Rebellion and enacts the myth of Erin being revived by the blood of her heroes. Cathleen summons Michael Darcy, a young peasant about to be married, to revolt, counselling blood-sacrifice as the only means to redeem the nation. In return for such sacrifice, she promises that the heroes 'shall be remembered for ever'. The play aroused deep reverberations in the Irish nationalist consciousness when it first appeared in 1902. Stephen Gwynn declared that the effect was such 'that I went home asking myself if such plays should be produced unless one was prepared for people to go out and to shoot and be shot'. P.S. Hegarty, a republican rebel, referred to it as a 'sort of sacrament'; and Constance Markievicz hailed it from her execution cell in 1916 as a 'gospel'. What is more, Pearse himself enthusiastically acclaimed the play; and Plunkett was inspired to dedicate his nationalist poem, 'The Little Black Rose Shall Be Red at Last', to this same Celtic goddess. Yeats was by no means unmindful of this extensive influence and asked himself remorsefully, in later years, whether his play did in fact 'send out / Certain men the English shot?'[17]

But it is perhaps in Sean O'Faolain's autobiography *Vive Moi!* that we find the most lucid and critical acknowledgment of the mythico-cultic preoccupations – sacrificial and ancestral – that enlivened the republican ideology. O'Faolain himself had fought in the Irish Republican Army before becoming a writer and reveals here an intimate understanding of the mythic spirit that informed the whole nationalist movement:

> And so blinded and dazzled as we were by our Icons, caught in the labyrinth of our dearest symbols – our Ancient Past, our Broken Chains, our Seven Centuries of Slavery, the Silenced Harp, the Glorious Dead, the tears of Dark Rosaleen, the Miseries of the Poor Old Woman, the Sunburst of Freedom that we had almost always believed would end our night and solve all our problems with the descent of a heavenly human order which we would immediately recognise as the reality of our never articulated dream … I had nothing to guide me but those flickering lights before the golden Icons of the past … the simplest pieties of Old Ireland.

Thus exposing the underlying *mythos* of the post-1916 republican movement, O'Faolain goes on to explain the split of the Irregular IRA from the Regular IRA (i.e. Free State Army) in 1922 in terms of a profound conviction that they alone – the Irregulars – 'represented the Symbolical Living Republic first declared during the 1916 Rebellion and set up as a *de jure* … underground government during the troubles'.[18]

This statement of O'Faolain demonstrates that the mythic pietism of the 1916 Rising continued as a motivating ideology in the subsequent republican struggle against the British (War of Independence) and Free State government (Civil War). It is not difficult to trace the line of continuity from this 'old' republicanism to the later republicanism of the Provisional IRA. The Provisionals' campaign from the sixties to the nineties may be said to have constituted, to some extent at least, a repetition of Pearse's attempt to 'rebaptise' the nation in the 'Fenian Faith'. Now, as before with Pearse, and before him again with the Fenian fathers and their ancestors, it is a baptism by blood. In this mythological perspective there seems but a thin line between Pearse's statement that blood-shed is a sanctifying thing and Seamus Twomey's suggestion in his *Crane Bag* interview (1978) that a lasting peace in Ulster can only come from the terror of apocalyptic violence: 'From all wars peace has sprung. Peace has never been built out of anything else but violence.'[19]

The point here, however, is not that the old IRA would have acknowledged a link between their faith in a Symbolical Underground Republic and the faith of the Provisionals in an identical ideal. (Indeed, it is almost certain that most of them would not.) The point is that the Provisionals *did* insist on such a link — the all-important difference being, of course, that they believed this Symbolical Living Republic to be *still* 'underground' in the second half of the twentieth century. This faith constituted the Provisionals' loyalty to a 'native tradition of Irish Christian values' extending beyond the established Republic of the twenty-six counties. It was moreover to this eternal Symbolical Republic — with its *mythos* of renewal through sacrifice — that the Provisionals referred when they spoke of 'taking their inspiration and experience from the past'.

IV. On the Sacrifice Myth

The sacrifice myth that animated the 1916 ideology sprang as much from the pagan *mythos* of seasonal rejuvenation and blood-letting rites as from the Christian message of salvation. This is an essential point ignored by many critics who explain the 1916 ideology of sacrifice in terms of a standard Christian devotionalism, thereby disregarding its fundamentally *mythological* nature. As several modern theologians, among them Bultmann and Moltmann, have claimed, the common interpretation of Christ as a propitiatory sacrifice in which humans could subsequently share by means of ritual repetition arises from the superimposition of a pagan *mythos* of cult-sacrifice (based largely on Hellenic mystery rites) onto the original biblical and *anti-cultic* understanding of Christ as Messiah. Whereas the Gospels saw Christ's death and resurrection in the eschatological light of a future Second Coming, the derived Hellenized notion conceived the Christian event in terms of a mythological remembrance of a past cosmic sacrifice along the model of the mystery-cults of Attis, Osiris and Dionysius. The basic conviction of these pagan mystery-cults was that by ritually rehearsing the violent sacrifice of the cult-hero or *Kyrios*, one could likewise participate in his renewal. As Jürgen Moltmann observes in *Theology of Hope*:

> The influence of cultic piety shows itself not only as a formal event in the self-presentation of Christianity on Hellenistic soil, but quite certainly

> extends also to the understanding of the event of Christ. The Christ event is
> here understood as an epiphany of the eternal [past] in the form of a dying
> and rising Kyrios of the *cultus* ... Initiation into the death and resurrection
> of Christ then means that the goal of redemption is already determined for
> in this baptism eternity is sacramentally present ... the Cross becomes a
> timeless sacrament of martyrdom which perfects the martyr and unites him
> with the heavenly Christ.[20]

Whether one accepts that the mythic strain in Christianity stems from a derivative Hellenic (rather than original Hebraic) influence, the fact remains that the
sacrificial component of much traditional Christianity *is* mythic and must be
recognized as such. We are thus reminded that the basic religious notions of
martyrdom, apocalypse and ritualistic commemoration, which exerted such a
profound influence on Pearse and his colleagues, stand – at least in part – in the
lineage of sacrificial cultism that dates back to the ancient mythological cycles
of renewal and rebirth.

But what are the philosophical and anthropological explanations for the
extraordinary perdurance of sacrificial myths? Myth has frequently been used to
translate the impotence of man's historical existence into the omnipotence of a
prehistory. As Eliade has shown in his analysis of the structures of primitive myth,
the power (*Mana*) of ancestral deities was considered capable of magically intervening in this world to vanquish an oppressive enemy, produce a double-harvest
or overcome pestilence. When all the practical possibilities of dealing with
suffering seemed exhausted, this Sacred Power of the Beginning could be
prevailed upon. But in order to reactivate this primordial power mortals first had
to sacrifice themselves to the mythological deities and heroes of the tribe.[21]

From its origins, myth frequently assumed the form of a *cult* based on the
violent practices of mutilation and blood-letting (as its Latin etymology indicates – *cultivare*: to cut, till or worship by cutting). In many instances, blood was
an indispensable ingredient, the coveted ambrosia of the gods. Eugen Fink, the
German philosopher, has defined the mythic cult accordingly:

> The cult is integrally related to the consecration of a victim or scapegoat; it
> is a great ritual gesture which reaches out towards a Totum or Whole. The
> cult participant allows himself to be magically 'possessed' by this power
> which the cult symbolises ... The Totum thus reinvests one of its parts [the
> sacrificial victim] and transports this worldly fragment beyond this world,
> absorbing it back into its Total Self ... The cult may therefore be defined as
> that point of confluence between the human and the divine run through
> with terror.[22]

This identification of myth as the nexus of exchange between supernatural
power and sacrificial terror is all important. Blood sacrifice is the ransom exacted

44

by the mythic deities in return for the privilege of miraculous intervention. But the cult sacrifice never constitutes more than a *provisional* purchase of power. Humans never succeed in securing this power once and for all; for they are, at all times, creatures bound to historical time. They must return, therefore, to the sacrificial cult at certain regular intervals. They must periodically open their veins to the flow of divine power in order to renew the community. By means of such periodic blood-letting, the cult enables mortals to pre-empt history. It empowers them to give the lie to the intractable world of fact, sanctioning their accession to another world of consciousness where different laws apply and where they may be relieved of all the onerous inconveniences that bear them down. If only one is prepared to submit one's world to the terror of a purging apocalypse, the mythological deities will permit one to feel free, unfettered and divine – that is, of course, *for a time*. One of the main purposes of initiatory and sacrificial rites is to bring historical time to a standstill and revivify those mythic paradigms that have survived as the *depositium* of ancestral experience. To re-enact these paradigms is to participate once again in the Golden Age of the ancestral *Majores*. In other words, by participating in an original sacred time that represents all times, men cease to be men and become *Man*. Under the penumbra of myth, experience escapes its contingent singularity and is transformed into a recurring Archetype. Through cultic identification with the archetypal figure of the hero, the individual seeks to recapitulate the Archetype in its own self and to subsume this self into the Archetype.[23]

The sacrificial cult thus promises to grant the community a victory over history by permitting it to return to its prehistoric origin, where it might be contemporaneous with its heroic founders. We may say then that myth is fundamentally 'ecstatic' in so far as it endorses our magical participation in an immemorial past. That is to say, through myth we stand outside (*ex-stasis*) the futile flow of profane history that no longer seems to offer any prospect of rational reform or progress. We have recourse to the mythic law of the 'eternal recurrence of the same' (i.e. the recurrence of the same ancestral heroes, of the same paradigms of destruction and renewal, of the same time of the Holy Beginning). Since no solution to our alienation is to be found in the present, we submit ourselves to a transforming myth, thereby reactivating the original sacred power that exists before and beyond history.

The experience of renewal through bloodshed central to sacrificial myths is perhaps most plausibly explained in terms of a community's experience of despair before a cruel history. This experience gives rise to feelings of revenge and resentment that ultimately express themselves in acts of violence. Just as this 'cruel history' was the cosmic evil of famine and disease for primitive humanity, and the political evil of the Roman Empire for the early Christians, it was British Rule for many Irish republicans. Max Scheler's analysis of the violence arising from such an experience of impotence is most suggestive:

Revenge tends to be transformed into resentment the more it is directed against lasting situations which are felt to be injurious but beyond one's 'control' – in other words, the more the injury is experienced as a destiny. This will be most pronounced when a person or group feels that the very fact and quality of its existence is a matter which calls for revenge … When the repression is complete, the result is a general negativism – a sudden, violent, seemingly indiscriminate and unfounded reprisal on things, situations or persons whose loose connections with the original cause of the hatred can only be discovered by a complicated analysis.[24]

Jean-Paul Sartre offers another interesting perspective on the human recourse to mythic modes of behaviour in his *Sketch for a Theory of the Emotions*.[25] The mythical consciousness, Sartre argues, is not some lawless disorder but 'an ordered pattern of means directed towards an end'. Myth, in other words, is a strategic mode of consciousness whereby we seek to negate a real world that has grown intolerable in order to transform it into an imaginary one that we can tolerate. This may occur whenever our normal avenues of behaviour – what Sartre calls our 'hodological maps' (Greek, *hodos*, path or way) – no longer seem functional or practicable. Thus confronted with what appear to be 'impossible situations', we depart from the pragmatic patterns of so-called *rational* behaviour and have recourse instead to *magical* behaviour. But this magical behaviour is just as intentionally structured as the rational behaviour it replaces. Put in another way, once the real world proves 'non-utilizable' or 'unmanageable', we deploy emotion to transpose this world into an unreal one where the normal laws of experience no longer operate. In short, we negate the world in order to better cope with what appears to be an intractable problem. Far from being a 'passing disorder of the organism', therefore, myth is revealed as a highly ordered strategy that 'transforms the determinist world in which we live into a magical world'. Of course, strictly speaking, what myth transforms is not the world itself – which remains as unmanageable as before – but the *manner in which we intend the world*. By altering our *attitude* to the world, myth provides imaginary solutions to real conflicts. Hence the enormous appeal of mythological paradigms of belief for the consciousness of an oppressed or colonized people.

All of these philosophical commentators of mythic consciousness agree that myth is not some innocuous museum piece of the antique past. Because the very structure of myth lays claim to a certain timeless and repeatable experience that promises to redeem human history, it can be said to have as much stake in the present as in the past. In this sense, myth is not without relevance to the ideologies and actions of contemporary societies. 'While myth relates to events that happened at the beginning of time,' as Paul Ricoeur remarks, 'it also has the purpose of providing grounds for the ritual actions of men today.'[26] It is our conviction that it was with just such a purpose in mind that Provisional Sinn

Féin claimed in their inaugural manifesto to take their 'inspiration' from the tradition of the 'past'.

This is not, of course, to deny that other factors of a more pragmatic social, economic and military nature have fundamentally motivated the actions and strategies of extreme republicanism. Indeed, these factors constituted the official rhetoric of the movement. Our analysis of some of the foundational symbols of Irish republicanism simply intends to recall that there also existed a hidden *mythic* dimension, ignored by most commentators, which played a formative role in what might be described as the 'ideological unconscious' of the militant nationalist tradition in Ireland.

CHAPTER FOUR

The Triumph of Failure:
The Irish Prison Tradition

On 9 April 1981, Bobby Sands, a republican hunger-striker in the H-Block of Long Kesh prison in Belfast, was elected with a massive 30,000 vote to the Westminster parliament. On 5 May of the same year, Sands died and was buried with full military regalia in Milltown Cemetery in Belfast. He had become a national martyr.

In the months that followed, nine other republican hunger-strikers in Long Kesh followed Sands to the grave in pursuit of a 'political status' that the British government refused to grant. The death of Sands and his fellow hunger-strikers bore the unmistakable stamp of sacrificial martyrdom and captured the sympathy not only of a vast number of Irish nationalists but also of a considerable body of international opinion. During his fast Sands wrote a diary in his cell using pen refills and sheets of toilet paper. His final entry testifies to the sacrificial character of his 'endurance campaign' – his firm belief that victory could only be attained through death:

> It had been a hard day but wasn't every day the same and God only knew what tomorrow would bring. Who would be the unlucky unfortunates tomorrow, supplying the battered bloody bodies for the punishment block? Who would be hosed down, beaten up or torn apart during a wing shift? Tomorrow would only bring more pain and torture and suffering, boredom and fear and God knows how many humiliations, inhumanities and horrors. Darkness and intense cold, an empty stomach and the four screaming walls of a filthy nightmare-filled tomb to remind me of my plight, that's what lay ahead tomorrow for hundreds of naked Republican Political Prisoners-of-War, but just as sure as the morrow would be filled with torture so would we carry on and remain unbroken. It was hard, it was very, very hard, I thought, lying down upon my damp mattress and pulling the blankets

around me. But some day victory would be ours and never again would another Irish man or woman rot in an English hell-hole ... That's anoher day nearer to victory, I thought, feeling very hungry. I was a skeleton compared to what I used to be but I didn't matter ... They have nothing in their entire imperial arsenal to break the spirirt of one single Republican Political Prisoner-of-War who refuses to be broken, I thought, and that was very true. They can not or never will break our spirit. *Tiocfaidh ár lá,* I said to myself. *Tiocfaidh ár lá.* [Our day will come.][1]

The election of Bobby Sands as a Westminster MP marked a watershed in the republican movement in the North. On 20 August 1981, several months after Sands' death, Owen Carron, his election agent, won the vacated seat as Provisional Sinn Féin candidate for Fermanagh-South Tyrone. And on 9 June 1983, Gerry Adams, the leader of Provisional Sinn Féin, was elected as Westminster MP for West Belfast, thereby confirming the significant rise of electoral support for non-constitutional nationalism in Northern Ireland in the immediate wake of the H-Block campaign.

In this study I want to examine the 'sacrificial' dimension of this campaign in the light of the republican prison tradition and its relation to the nationalist ideology of martyrdom analysed in the preceding study.

I

Seán MacBride, a leading Dublin jurist, recipient of the Nobel Peace Prize and a founder member of Amnesty International, wrote a lengthy introduction to Bobby Sands' prison diary when it was published after his death.[2] MacBride begins with a quotation from a poem by the 1916 martyr, Patrick Pearse, evoking the sacrificial status of the hunger-strike campaign:

> What if the dream come true? ...
> And if the millions unborn shall dwell
> In the house that I shaped in my heart,
> The noble house of my thought? ...
> Was it folly or grace?
> No man shall judge me, but God.

The implication here was that Bobby Sands and his fellow hunger-strikers had, through their sacrifice, earned a sacred place in the 'noble house' of Pearse's nationalist dream, defying the official laws of human judgement (which dismisses their death as 'folly') in an appeal to a divine judgement (which bestows upon them the 'grace' of martyrdom). Pearse, as we noted in the previous study, conceived of his own death as a sacrifice for the motherland, explicitly identifying with the crucified Christ 'who had gone forth to die for men' in his eve-of-execution poem, 'A Mother Speaks'. The Catholic concept of the Mass as a 'real sacrifice' has been a central symbol for the republican tradition of martyrdom; and the H-Block hunger-strikers, going to their death over sixty years after Pearse, acknowledged that daily Mass in the prison was one of the main sources of their strength.[3] Nor was this sacrificial identification with Christ lost on the H-Block sympathizers. Many of the placards carried in the hunger-strike support marches portrayed Sands and his colleagues in crucified postures (recalling the 1916 posters of the pietà-like Pearse), the barbed wire of Long Kesh transformed into a crown of thorns, the H-Block blanket into a burial shroud. Indeed, during several such marches, the prisoners' families themselves wore blankets and wire crowns to symbolically express their conviction that the hunger-strikers who were sharing in Christ's martyrdom would one day rise up victorious from their ashes. One H-Block document even showed a drawing of the Pope blessing the kneeling prisoners under the title, 'Pope John Paul II and Human Rights', and quoted the Pope's pointed statement during his Drogheda address in September 1979, that 'the law of God stands in judgement over all reasons of state'. (This same document associated the prisoners' fasting protest with the historic suffering of the Irish Catholic people during the Famine.)[4]

It was Pearse's dream above all that informed the traditional ideals of Gaelic Catholic nationalism. And while it is probably true that Sands and his fellow inmates would have given only passing allegiance to these ideals before their imprisonment, once confined to Long Kesh, deprived of 'political status' and subjected to degrading treatment, the Catholic religion and the Gaelic language became (as Sands' diary testified) symbols of primary significance. In prison, to be Gaelic and Catholic was almost synonymous with being nationalist; for all three categories of identification served to remind the republican inmates of their forefathers' long history of persecution. The Pearsean dream, in short, was more relevant to the *sacrificial* ideology of the republicans' prison campaign than to the *revolutionary* ideology of their military campaign.

MacBride described Sands' prison testimony as a 'tale of faith' and 'triumph of endurance' that became a 'morale booster' for a cause that depended 'more on integrity and courage than on what politicians and lawyers term reason and common sense'. He went on to observe that the death of Sands and his fellow hunger-strikers was 'to the bulk of the Irish people … a tragedy that tore asunder the strings of their hearts and their consciences'. Only a small minority of the nation still suffering from a 'slave mentality' that hankers after the 'trappings of British influence in Ireland' were, he argued, hostile to the hunger-strikers' aim of a United Ireland (however much they might, like MacBride himself, abhor the IRA's use of violence). MacBride was probably representative of majority nationalist opinion when he claimed that the hunger-strike phenomenon must be understood in terms of the Irish people's *historical memory* of British colonial misrule. In reply to those, particularly in Britain, who complained that 'our memories are too long and that we should forget the past', MacBride declared that it is only by *remembering* the colonial heritage of partition, imprisonment and 'every conceivable form of coercive and repressive legislation', that we may begin to comprehend the real implications of the H-Block campaign. The hunger strike, MacBride concluded, was not some isolated political happening of our time but a deep symptom of a historically recurring persecution: 'a fall-out resulting from the cruel interference by Britain in the affairs of the Irish nation'. MacBride's introduction to the Bobby Sands diary thus identified the basic *rationale* of the republican prison campaign in terms of the memory of the nationalist people's historical suffering, a memory of heroic martyrdom invoked not only in MacBride's opening quotation from Pearse but also in his final quotation from W.B. Yeats:

> Some had no thought of victory
> But had gone out to die
> That Ireland's mind be greater,
> Her heart mount up on high;
> And no one who knows what's yet to come

MacBride's quotation does not include the remaining lines of Yeats's stanza, but the sentiment is already clear, and the reader can supply it for himself:

> For Patrick Pearse had said
> That in every generation
> Must Ireland's blood be shed.

II

It might be useful at this point to examine in more detail the republican prison tradition that so powerfully informed the response of the nationalist population to the H-Block hunger strike. This tradition corresponds to what Tim Pat Coogan, editor of *The Irish Press* and author of a best-selling book on the H-Block campaign, called the 'endurance' strategy of the republican movement.[5] The national heroes of this endurance tradition are legion, but it was perhaps Terence MacSwiney, the Sinn Féin Lord Mayor of Cork who died on hunger strike in an English prison in 1920, who most concisely articulated this ideology of suffering. In his inaugural speech as Lord Mayor he stated:

The contest on our side is not one of rivalry or vengeance but of endurance. It is not those who can inflict the most but those who can suffer the most who will conquer ... It is conceivable that the army of occupation could stop us functioning for a time. Then it becomes simply a question of endurance. Those whose faith is strong will endure to the end in triumph.[6]

Coogan has argued that MacSwiney's was a 'particularly Irish form of self-sacrifice' that caught 'the imagination of the world at the time, and of the IRA ever since'.[7] He also makes the interesting observation that during the time of the native Brehon laws that governed Ireland prior to the Anglo-Norman invasion, one of the most effective ways of retaliating against a wrongdoer was for the offended party to starve himself outside the guilty person's house!

The republican tradition of prison endurance is certainly longstanding. It has found many adherents throughout this century. Tom Clarke's prison experience earned him the honour of heading the 1916 Proclamation of the Irish Republic. Joseph McGuinness, while still in Lewes Jail, won the first seat for Sinn Féin, largely due to his popular appeal as an 'endurance' candidate. Other instructive examples include the release of IRA leader Patrick McGrath from prison in 1939 as a result of the massive public outcry caused by his 43-day hunger strike, and the similar release of another republican hunger-striker, Davy Fleming, from an Ulster prison in 1946. Furthermore, the significant lobbying power of Seán MacBride's Clann na Poblachta party in 1948 was in large part due to its spectacular 'release the prisoners' campaign. And the popular prestige of such provisional leaders as Daithí Ó Conaill, Ruardhí Ó Brádaigh and Gerry Adams would appear to be related to the fact that each served his time as a prison 'martyr'. (Indeed, the relegation of a leader such as MacStíofáin was surely not unrelated to his last-minute decision to call off his much-publicized hunger strike in Portlaoise prison). Indeed, up to recent times, it was often the case that even elected political leaders in the Republic owed part of their status in the community to the fact that they themselves, or their fathers before them, had suffered imprisonment or death at the hands of the 'colonial oppressor'. Obvious names here included de Valera, MacBride, Fitzgerald, Cosgrave, Boland etc. (And it is arguable, ironically, that the humiliating public trial of Charles Haughey, on charges of gun-running while a government minister in 1970 did more, in retrospect, to help than to hinder his popular standing in the South, and even his eventual election as Taoiseach of the Irish Republic).[8]

It is against the background of this long republican tradition of prison endurance that we may best understand the extraordinary impact of the H-Block campaign. This campaign began as far back as 1976 when the British government removed the 'special category' status for political prisoners in Long Kesh. Ciaran Nugent was the first to go 'on the blanket' on 15 September of that year and was soon followed by some 370 Long Kesh internees who immediately grasped the national and international impact of his protest. By declining to grant the prisoners' demands the British hastened the deterioration of events. The republican prisoners reacted by disobeying prison regulations and were soon living in excrement-covered cells that Cardinal Tomás Ó Fiaich, Primate of the Irish Catholic Church, described as 'unfit for animals'. After his visit to

Long Kesh on 19 July 1978, the Cardinal issued this controversial statement:

> In the circumstances I was surprised that the morale of the prisoners was
> high. From talking to them it is evident that they intend to continue their
> protest indefinitely and it seems they prefer to face death rather than submit
> to being classed as criminals. Anyone with the least knowledge of Irish
> history knows how deeply rooted this attitude is in our country's past. In
> isolation and perpetual boredom they maintain their sanity by studying Irish.
> It was an indication of the triumph of the human spirit over adverse mate-
> rial surroundings to notice Irish words, phrases and songs being shouted
> from cell to cell and then written on each cell wall with the remnants of
> toothpaste tubes.[9]

The Cardinal went even further to explicitly defend the prisoners' demand to
be recognised as special prisoners, pointing out that the rapid jump in the prison
population of Ulster from 500 to 3000 was inexplicable unless a new type of
political prisoner had emerged.[10]

Other prominent Catholic churchmen expressed similar sympathy with the
prisoners' plight, thereby considerably increasing public awareness of the situation. Bishop Cahal B. Daly of Ardagh and Clonmacnoise was quick to take up
the cause while adverting to the implications of IRA propaganda in this regard.
In his address for World Peace Day on 1 January 1979, Bishop Daly was the first
to acknowledge that the IRA 'are exploiting the H-Block situation with disqui-
eting success'; to such an extent indeed that in the United States where the
funds campaign had been virtually neutralized there had been 'a new upsurge of
financial support on behalf of this organisation'. But while denouncing the IRA's
'unscrupulous manipulation of the human rights aspect' of H-Block, Bishop
Daly felt obliged to point out the British government's share in the blame:

> These conditions are objectively in conflict with all recognised codes governing
> the environment in which prisoners are allowed to live. The Provisional IRA
> have, however, by a strange paradox, received great help from an unexpected
> source – the mistakes of the British administration and security chiefs,
> mistakes in which they have persisted with remarkable obstinacy in the face
> of the lesson of all Anglo-Irish history and all experience. The IRA was prac-
> tically a spent and discredited force until they were handed the H-Block
> situation as a propaganda gift. This, and the unnecessary army harassment of
> innocent people, especially young people, among the 'men of no property',
> are now virtually the only source of vestigial sympathy or of recruitment for
> the IRA.[11]

While the sacrificial propaganda of the H-Block campaign was most immediately recognized by the alarmed leaders of the Catholic community in the
North, they were not the only ones to raise a voice of warning. Several Protestant churchmen – most notably Dr Coggan, the Archbishop of Canterbury, and

Dr John Austin Baker, chaplain to the speaker of the House of Commons – clearly acknowledged the historical connotations of the H-Block campaign and appealed (in vain) to the British government for concessions.[12] Many constitutional nationalist leaders, both North and South, together with prominent Irish-American senators in Washington (like Kennedy, Cary, Moynihan and O'Neill) also made repeated efforts to convince Mrs Thatcher to compromise on the issue. The Irish media were highly conscious of the explosive nature of the H-Block protest, with an *Irish Press* editorial describing it as a 'major obstacle along the road to eventual peace'[13] and a distinguished columnist in *The Cork Examiner* speaking indignantly of the British government's 'Nazi-like behaviour in Long Kesh'.[14]

Witnessing the massive impact that their campaign was having on public opinion at home and abroad, the Long Kesh inmates must surely have been tempted to believe that William McKee, a former IRA leader in Belfast, was right when he claimed that 'this war will be won in prisons'. Standing in their 'filthy cold tombs', their blankets cloaked about them as they chanted Gaelic phrases and prayers from cell to cell, like some chorus in an ancient tragedy, the H-Block prisoners might have seen themselves – at moments at least – as sacrificial victims of a fallen and divided nation that could only be redeemed by their deaths, rising up miraculously from their excrement and ashes. The prisoners' ultimate decision to perish of hunger was, no doubt, for them and for many of their sympathizers, the final seal on the coffin of martyrdom.

III

Whereas constitutional politicians objected that violence can only beget violence, the IRA replied that theirs was a violence to end all violence. This latter attitude to violence was sacrificial in that it saw suffering and bloodshed as prerequisite to the ultimate attainment of justice, freedom and peace.[15] But the violence of the IRA was also sacrificial, as we have seen, to the extent that it was as much a violence suffered as a violence inflicted. From the point of view of the age-old nationalist tradition of martyrdom, violence 'endured' often proved the most effective way to gain widespread community support. The republican militants in Northern Ireland in the 1970s and 1980s continued to invoke the authority of the executed founders of the Republic. In 1978 a spokesman for Provisional Sinn Féin proudly stated that the IRA was 'not ten years old but over sixty years old';[16] and for many republicans the frequent invocation of the 1916 and Fenian martyrs at IRA funeral orations or in the daily columns of the Provisionals' newspaper, *An Phoblacht,* invested their campaign of 'resistance and suffering' with the sanctity of an ancestral rite. The following extract from the popular republican ballad 'Who is Ireland's Enemy?' provides a typical example of the traditional ideology of sacrifice that conceived the history of Fenian martyrdom as a 'sacred debt' that remained to be paid in the present:

> Who shattered many a Fenian mind in dungeons o'er the foam
> And broke the loyal Fenian hearts that pined for them at home?
> Who shot down Clark and Connolly and Pearse at dawn of day,
> And Plunkett and McDermott and all who died as they ...
> Who robbed us of MacSwiney brave, who murdered Mellows too,
> Sent Barry to a felon's grave and slaughtered Cathal Brugha?
> 'Twas England robbed our Motherland,
> 'Twas England laid her low,
> Rise up, oh dead of Ireland, and rouse our living men,
> The chance has come to us at last to win our own again ...
> And in your name, oh holy dead,
> Our Sacred Debt to pay.

The sacrificial victim must undergo passion and demise before arising to liberate the community from its historical bondage. By commemorating the sufferings of their Fenian forebears, the IRA were operating on the conviction that they could fulfil the redemptive promise of their martyrdom.[17]

That the military odds were stacked high against an IRA military victory was indubitable. By the early eighties they counted no more than 200 active members against 20,000 British troops, 7000 armed police and twice that number of loyalist paramilitary, not to mention the Irish army and police force south of the border. But for the IRA, strength was not in numbers. The power they wielded in the republican community, both north and south of the border, derived largely from their outnumbered status. It was only when they stepped back into the shadow of their persecuted ancestors, as the H-Block protests and hunger strikes showed, that they succeeded in reanimating the hidden and often unconscious sympathies of the Irish people. Their suffering (*pathos*) was the surest way of soliciting sympathy (*sym-pathein:* to suffer with). Without it, Sands, Carron or Adams might never have been elected Westminster MPs.

It was because the IRA campaign *could not* achieve military victory (and was at times even suicidal) that it *could* assume a sacrificial mystique. The Provisionals might well have replied to the threats and entreaties of the politicians from Westminster and Dublin what the 1916 insurgents in Bolands Mills replied to the offer of surrender: 'We came here to die, not to win.' This was, moreover, why the boasts of successive British Secretaries in Northern Ireland that the IRA was finally defeated merely served to augment the stigmata prestige of this tiny sect. Political impotence at the constitutional or parliamentary level (and it must be recalled that no Provisional Sinn Féin MP ever took his seat at Westminster), was the *sine qua non* of their sacrificial potency.

As observed in our preceding study, it was whenever the official channels of constitutional change appeared inoperative that the Irish republican movement had most effective recourse to the strategy of seeking a national renewal through martyrdom. The IRA knew only too well that the most important step towards the founding of the Irish Republic was not the half-baked revolt of a few badly armed patriots in 1916, but the subsequent execution of these patriots by the British. Connolly on a wheelchair before a British firing squad gained far more than Connolly with a gun. The IRA knew that the most useful republican for the propaganda cause was a dead one. Deep in their memory was inscribed Pearse's motto that 'from the graves of patriot men and women spring living nations'.

By playing the role of sacrificial executioner, the British Empire contributed greatly to its loss of the south of Ireland in the first part of the nineteenth century. By ensuring that the British continued to play that role in Ulster in the latter part of the same century, the IRA believed they held the key to a United Ireland. In their exclusive concentration on the security and economic dimensions of the Ulster crisis and their general ignorance of the persuasive sacrificial factor, the British unwittingly perpetuated violence in Northern Ireland. They repeatedly assumed the role of the magistrate Creon before the republican Antigone. The self-righteous intransigence of the British Northern Secretary, Roy Jenkins, for example, before the requests of the imprisoned and hunger-striking Price sisters in 1974, reset the scene for the timeless defence of the tragic heroine: 'I do not heed your mortal edicts which cannot invalidate the unwritten laws of the gods … laws which are not of today or yesterday, but of all times.' And Margaret Thatcher's adamant refusal to grant 'political status' or alter concessions regarding visits and clothing to the Long Kesh hunger-strikers in October 1980, and again in March 1981, further confirmed the British government's misjudgment of nationalist reaction. Thus 'Ireland's enemy' became an indispensable accomplice to the rites of sacrifice.

By committing acts of violence, the IRA drew upon themselves the retaliatory wrath of the ruling authorities. Indeed, it almost seemed at times that one of the reasons for the IRA's offensive was to invite reaction. Though it is important to recall here that this sacrificial motivation was merely one side of the coin, i.e. the largely unconscious ideological identification with the Fenian tradition of martyrdom. The IRA's *explicit* aim remained that of military attack and victory as illustrated in this typical statement by an IRA army council spokesman in the 1980s: 'The British know we are not a spent force and that we will continue.'[18]

The IRA could be sacrifically effective only when the oppressor conspired to oppress, when the executor agreed to execute, in short when they stirred up national and international sympathies by being interned without trial, tortured, and denied other basic human rights. In fact, it is probably accurate to say that, apart from the death of the ten H-Block hunger-strikers in the spring of 1981, the IRA rarely received more support throughout the entire Irish nation (or elsewhere) than the day thirteen innocent civilians were shot dead by the British army in Derry in 1972. The IRA subsequently christened the event Bloody Sunday, exploiting the full sacrificial connotations of Bloody Sunday in 1920 (when British agents indiscriminately murdered members of the crowd at a Gaelic football match in Croke Park in Dublin). This symbolic appelation soon gained currency throughout the four provinces. Three days after the Derry massacre, 30,000 people marched on the British Embassy in Dublin and watched it burn to the ground. 20,000 attended the funerals in Derry and a national day of mourning was declared. Years later, thousands still commemorate Bloody Sunday on 30 January. Seán MacBride accurately identified the consequence of the Bloody Sunday massacre for the IRA's cause: 'This act of oppression by the British forces ... influenced the young people to turn more and more towards the IRA and physical force. The IRA availed of this situation to become the defenders of the Catholic population against the attacks of the police and the British military forces.'[19]

The British mishandling of the republican endurance campaign led to other sacrificial victories for the IRA. One might cite, for example, the British government's introduction of internment without trial on 9 August 1971. Three hundred suspected 'terrorists' were arrested in their beds during a series of dawn raids by the British army: 6000 refugees fled southwards to the Republic, generating widespread public concern. On 16 August a strike was staged to denounce internment and on 12 September 10,000 people held a follow-up protest meeting in Casement Park in Belfast, the first of a long series. The IRA had once again succeeded in recharging their dwindling support.

More grist to the sacrificial mill came with the moves to censure media broadcasts or publications supportive of the republican campaign or even featuring members of Provisional Sinn Féin. On 18 October 1976, Conor Cruise O'Brien, then Minister for Posts and Telegraphs in the Republic, introduced measures to this effect, causing an immediate public outcry. The British government's decision on 4 June 1980 to censor an ITV programme dealing with the Amnesty International report on British Army torture in Northern Ireland met with similar disapproval and once again highlighted the IRA as a 'victimized' body. But the most blatant act of media censorship, which provided the IRA with a massive propaganda victory, was the decision taken in August 1985 by the BBC Board of Governors (in response to British government pressure), to ban an interview with the Provisional Sinn Féin spokesman, Martin McGuinness. This decision resulted in mounting support for the censored party not only in Ireland but also in the British Broadcasting Service, which called a nationwide one-day strike, sparking off what one member of the BBC Board of Governors described as the 'worst crisis in the station's history'. In her attempt to 'starve the terrorists of the oxygen of publicity', Mrs Thatcher succeeded, ironically, where McGuinness himself would have surely failed (had the interview *not* been censored) – that is, in providing Provisional Sinn Féin with a most significant propaganda triumph.

This image of *victimization* was reinforced down through the years by the

British Army's infliction of 'cruel, inhuman and degrading treatment' on IRA prisoners (as condemned by the European Commission of Human Rights in Strasbourg, August 1976). The employment of sensory-deprivation torture methods on twelve republican detainees in 1971, both in Castlereagh barracks in Belfast and in certain army bases in England, gave rise to a series of influential protest publications (in particular *The Guinea Pigs* by John McGuffin, *Le Laboratoire Irlandais* by Roger Faligot, and the information bulletins of Denis Faul and Raymond Murray sent to all major international associations for the defence of human rights). The controversial use in Ulster of Diplock Courts (trial without jury), of rubber bullets, which killed several women and children, in addition to a shoot-to-kill policy and the controversial conviction of suspects of IRA bombing in Britain (subsequently turned into a hugely popular feature film, *In the Name of the Father,* by Jim Sheridan) might also be mentioned here.[20] Furthermore, the extensively publicized hunger strikes staged by the Price sisters and Francis Stagg, and the beatings meted out to thirty-two republican women prisoners in Armagh prison in February 1980, furnished additional evidence of the 'oppressive' role of the British authorities – a role that arguably achieved its most conspicuous manifestation in the mishandling of the H-Block Campaigns.

In each of these cases, the IRA won public sympathy not when they perpetrated violence but when they drew it upon themselves. At the level of tacit popular support, their 'patriot game' (to cite another republican ballad) was more likely to win when it was conducted according to the rules of sacrifice than of military aggression. They played to capacity audiences as vanquished rather than as vanquishers. This may account, indeed, for the curious fact that IRA activists could be denounced for their campaigns of bombing and killing by the majority of the nationalist community and yet acclaimed as martyrs by many in this same community once they were harassed by the British security forces, censored, tortured, imprisoned or assassinated. It was certainly this sacrificial logic of martyrdom that operated in the minds of the nationalist community when Bobby Sands and his nine fellow hunger-strikers were transformed, in the popular perception, from 'delinquent criminals' into 'national heroes'.

Conclusion

Our analysis of the strategy of sacrifice has confined itself to the Catholic and nationalist community in Northern Ireland. That members of the Protestant community also endured hardship and injustice is undeniable (particularly in the border areas); and it must not be forgotten that loyalist paramilitaries were also interned, tortured and deprived of Special Category status. Loyalists too were victims of the Ulster troubles. But while the unionist/loyalist community certainly had its share of suffering, it did not identify with this suffering as a fundamental symbol of its own specific tradition or ideology.[21] Suffering for them was seldom transformed into sacrifice and martyrdom; it was not commemorated but feared rather as a threat to their very existence as a distinct community. Hence while the republicans revered the graves of their martyred heroes (be it the 1916 leaders in Dublin, Wolfe Tone in Bodenstown, the Bloody Sunday victims in Derry or the hunger-strikers in H-Block), the loyalists tended to identify more with the triumphalist emblems of their historical victories: King Billy and Carson. The Apprentice Boys parade and the Orange Day marches celebrated political and military success, not failure. And when the loyalists staged an annual ritualistic burning of the Lundy simulacrum (Lundy was the 'traitor' who attempted to open the gates of Derry to the besieging army of King James), it was not to sanctify the sacrificial victim but to pour scorn upon him.[22] The loyalist ideology was perhaps best summed up in the catchcry of Randolph Churchill, who first played the Orange card in 1886 against Gladstone's Home Rule Bill: 'Ulster will fight and Ulster will be right'. This was in stark contrast to the sacrificial ideology of republicanism that found typical expression, as we saw, in MacSwiney's credo that 'it is not those who inflict the most but those who suffer the most who will conquer'. This credo, invoking the deep-rooted Catholic Fenian tradition of martyrdom, was reinvoked throughout the entire republican 'endurance' campaign. A typical example was to be found on the wall of an Ulster prison cell where a republican inmate had written the following confiteor: 'I am one of many who die for my country ... If death is the only way I am prepared to die. To be free is all I want and many like me think the same.' Our study has tried to adduce some evidence to suggest that many people inside and outside the prison walls of Ulster, consciously or unconsciously, thought the same.

The republican myths of martyrdom were, of course, no less susceptible to moral judgement than the loyalist myths of triumph. A French commentator of the hunger-strike campaign, Manuel de Diéguez, observed that it was

> frightening to think that the call to sacrifice and salvation through martyrdom is a source of motivation for a devoted population to obediently die in order to receive the rewards of their sacrifice. This mechanism appears indiscriminate: one can die in this fashion as easily for Hitler, Napoleon, Caesar or Alexander as by the side of Demosthenes for the liberty of Greece.[23]

Whatever about the justice of de Diéguez's remarks in relation to the H-Block campaign, they do raise an important philosophical issue – that of the ethical discrimination between different ideological interpretations of national myths (sacrificial or otherwise). This question will be considered in chapter 27, 'Myth and the Critique of Ideology'.

CHAPTER FIVE

Faith and Fatherland

Many people in Ireland still consider their identity to be linked in some vague but deep sense with their religion. In the North, for example, it has become commonplace to use the label 'Catholic' to identify the nationalist community and the label 'Protestant' to identify the loyalist community. While this mix of national and religious identities is not as obvious or sectarian in the South, it remains implicit; and in times of internal conflict – as debates on constitutional changes with regard to public and private morality have shown – many of the citizens of the Republic still consider a challenge to their confessional convictions as a threat to their unique sense of 'Irishness'.

I

Outsiders often tend to view this continuing equation of political and religious identities as a symptom of eccentric backwardness or heroic conservatism. I suspect, however, that in the face of such 'outside' opinion, many Irish citizens would respond: 'But you foreigners don't really understand us; you don't appreciate that the conflict in Northern Ireland, for instance, was not in fact a religious war at all – the IRA or the UDA didn't care about the theological doctrines of their religious traditions – the violence was *really* about opposed tribal fidelities or economic class interests,' and so on.

Similarly, in response to the suggestion that the South displayed a conservative religious outlook in its laws on divorce, contraception or homosexuality, many might wish to distinguish between the conservative *ought* of the official legislation and the more liberal *is* of people's everyday lives. After all, were there not thousands attending family-planning clinics and flouting the anti-contraception laws of the Republic up to 1985 (laws that one leading politician referred to as an 'Irish solution to an Irish problem')? Some might claim accordingly that we are not really as backward as we appear to be, and that when the time is ripe we will be prepared to make all kinds of generous concessions to a more pluralist society. Or to juggle with Saint Augustine: 'Lord, make us pluralist, but not yet!' Some might well go on to cite the fact that a large proportion of our people can tune into the 'permissive' BBC, and that even our own RTÉ has itself done much in recent times to open the windows to the outside world and ventilate controversial matters hitherto confined to the confessional.

But what is at issue here? Are we in the Republic not in fact saying that we want to have our cake and eat it? That we want our *ideals* to reflect one set of values (often synonymous in the South with the anti-materialist teachings of the Church) and in *real* life to enjoy quite another set of values, i.e. the benefits of advanced technological affluence, Anglo-American liberalism and EU consumerism? In short, are we not saying that we are prepared to give the nod to the old isolationist rhetoric of a rural holy Ireland with comely maidens dancing at the crossroads, while practising a cosmopolitan code of modern materialism?

This double-think has been reflected in a variety of contradictory practices. We believed it our national duty to buy Irish but bought British whenever the opportunity arose (as the Newry bus route amply testified). We ritually deplored the spread of alien permissiveness but switched from home-produced programmes like *Folio* or *Féach* to the Hollywood soap operas *Dallas* or *Dynasty* without hesitation. In other words, political corruption and narcotic-erotic high-jinks could be vicariously consumed in Californian other-worlds, yet we preferred to deny that they might exist on our own Holy Ground here in Ireland. Further instances of our double-think were, arguably, evidenced in the debate on the constitutional amendment on abortion in 1984. Here many appeared willing to run with the secular hare and hunt with the sacred hounds; that is, do everything to amend our constitution to reinforce the existing legal prohibition on abortion, while continuing to do little to amend our punitive attitudes to those unmarried mothers who had chosen *not* to abort that life that, once born, our society would stigmatize as 'illegitimate' for the rest of its days. I mention this to illustrate a contradiction in our moral attitude; a contradiction which, from the point of view of some unmarried pregnant women of our society, amounts to this: the constitutional *law* of our land proclaims 'do not abort', while the social *practice* of our land often whispers the very opposite – 'if you do not abort then do not expect to keep your job, or your good name or the potential status of legitimacy for your child'. Translated into plain language this means: in Ireland it is constitutionally illegitimate to abort and socially illegitimate not to.

Southern Catholics might well ask themselves why they have such little confidence in the teachings of their majority Church that they need the constitution of the State to copperfasten these teachings in law? Or why they have so little confidence in their national identity that they somehow feel that any further attempt to separate the laws of the majority Church from those of the State would result in a diminution of their sense of 'Irishness', opening the gates to an irresistible immoralism that would swamp us all?

I am not implying that a nation should dispense with its religious traditions or cultural ideals. Each nation needs to preserve a set of values by means of which it can provide itself with a sense of rootedness and self-identity, thereby differentiating itself from other national identities. Nobody wants an anonymous world-state in which all the customs and characteristics of the various peoples would be annihilated. But while every self-respecting society requires a set of *oughts* to motivate the *is* of its everyday life, is there not a danger of allowing those *oughts* to become so abstract or removed from our real experience that they cease to positively inform it? If this happens our ideal of ourselves will congeal into a lifeless cliché. What is required therefore is not a total renunciation of our most cherished ideals, but a critical discrimination between those ideals that keep us imprisoned in a dead past and those that liberate us into a living future.

It is arguable that just as we in Ireland have allowed a purely rhetorical aspiration for a United Ireland to replace any policy for achieving it in reality, so too we may have so elevated certain of our religious aspirations that we now risk depriving much in our everyday experience of its genuinely religious dimensions. If what we believe we *ought* to be becomes totally disconnected from what we know in our hearts we *are*, then the relationship between the ideal and the real ceases to be a creative dialogue: it becomes instead a schizophrenic split between an authoritarian master-mentality and a resentful slave-mentality.

To prevent such a schizophrenia from taking hold we might well compare some of our idealized religious self-portraits with the harsh facts of contemporary reality: we might ask why religious vocations and church observances have been falling so drastically in recent years; why anti-clericalism has become so rampant in the younger generation; why many of those struggling for women's or minority rights feel hard done by by the Irish Church; why violence and heroin addiction have become endemic in our urban communities North and South; or why the Irish Church, once famed throughout Europe for its learning and missionary enlightenment, and capable of producing an innovative philosopher of the calibre of John Scotus Eriugena, should now be more renowned – at least at home – for its anti-intellectualism.[1]

And why is it, lastly, that the same Catholic Church that, throughout the centuries, was such a powerful agency of liberation and education for the dispossessed Irish – providing them with a basic sense of human dignity and self-respect – has become in more recent times the very opposite: that is, an agency so preoccupied with a conservative defence of 'faith and morals' (which all too frequently means blind faith and sexual morals), that a considerable number of young Irish citizens today regard it as a reactionary apologist, rather than a radical challenger of the status quo? Such questions are not intended to condemn Irish religion *per se* but, on the contrary, to identify some of the difficulties that have to be faced if religion is to be taken seriously by the generations growing up in Ireland today.

II

The problems outlined above have a complex history that in some respects is particular to the Irish problem of identity. We cannot properly understand our present crisis of value without paying some attention to the cultural and ideological background that has shaped many of our religious assumptions. In attempting here to analyse the origin of some of these assumptions our method will be less that of the historian concerned with 'hard facts' than that of a philosopher concerned with a specific interpretation of these facts: that is, with the emergence of a national consciousness governed by a chosen set of ideals and ideologies. In short, we will focus on the ways in which we as a nation have chosen to represent ourselves, and examine the central role played by religion, and particularly Catholicism, in the creation of this national self-image.

One of the first clear instances of an overlap between religious and national identities in Ireland was witnessed when the colonial fanaticism of the Cromwellian plantation forged the self-protective alliance of 'faith and fatherland' in the minds of the colonized natives. As one Protestant Planter put it as early as 1625: 'The very ground the Irish tread, the air they breathe, the climate they share, the very sky above them, all seem to draw them to the religion of Rome.' The Cromwellian Act of Settlement of 1652 in effect divided the inhabitants of Ireland into 'English Protestants' and 'Irish Papists'.[2]

This division was to re-emerge with the campaign for the emancipation of Catholics in the nineteenth century: a campaign that challenged the fusion of Protestant and imperial interests exemplified in the rise of the Orange Order after the 1830s. The ranks were now drawn up along confessional lines with the largely Catholic nationalists promoting a Home Rule for Ireland Bill and the Protestant unionist party opposing and ultimately defeating it. It was out of such protracted antagonism between the ideological interests of nationalism and unionism that there arose the Orange protest that Home Rule is Rome Rule, and the answering reply that Protestant Rule is British Imperial Rule.

The resulting equation of Catholic with nationalist and Protestant with antinationalist was thus less a question of theology than of ideology: a political rhetoric whereby the two communities reinforced their opposing identities. This equation, in other words, served as an ideological strategy deployed by both the unionist and nationalist parties to simplify reality by 'fastening the loyalty of their members on central symbols'.[3] Catholic and Gaelic became symbols used by many nationalists as a way of achieving separation from Britain. And the reverse was equally true: Protestant and British became symbols used by unionists to preserve the union with the United Kingdom.

So what role did the ideal of 'Holy Ireland' play in all this? And how did this ideal relate to the confessional difference between Irish Catholicism and Irish Protestantism? In 1906, Douglas Hyde, founder of the Gaelic League and future first President of Ireland, offered the following quaint description of Irish religion in *Religious Songs of Connaught*:

> A pious race is the Gaelic race. The Irish Gael is pious by nature. He sees the hand of god in every place, in every time and in every thing ... The things of the Spirit ... affect him more powerfully than the things of the body ... What is invisible for other people is visible for him.

Hyde was speaking as a Protestant cultural nationalist about a national Catholic culture. He knew that it was considered far more 'natural' for a Catholic to subscribe to the terms *Gaelic* and *nationalist* than for a Protestant to do so. Thus his rather uncritical appraisal of the piety of the Gael may have been motivated by his eagerness to accommodate himself, as a Protestant, to the desired definition of a Gaelic nationalist. Hyde's eulogy of the pious Gael might be described as a Protestant's ideal of Gaelic Catholicism dressed up in romanticized peasant garb.

Hyde was by no means an isolated example of this attitude. Yeats, Lady Gregory, Russell and other Protestants of the Literary Revival, subscribed to a similarly sacralized view of the Irish Catholic peasant – particularly up to Independence when the Catholic culture was seen (rightly) as the victim of colonial persecution. Yeats, for example, would conclude his poem, 'Under Ben Bulben', by championing the Gaelic-Catholic peasantry over and above the Anglo-Irish Ascendancy:

> Sing the peasantry, and then
> Hard-riding country gentlemen.

In other words, even Yeats would have horse-trotting 'Prods' play second fiddle to bog-trotting 'Papists' ... in literature at any rate.

But what prompted Irish Protestant nationalists such as Hyde and Yeats to sponsor an idealized portrait of the Catholic peasantry? There may well have been a touch of residual colonial guilt in such idealization: a secret regret almost that they, as Protestants, were born into the winning side and so bore a special responsibility to undo not only the *political*, but also the *cultural* wrongs of colonial history.

But this Protestant nationalist view of Catholicism was to change somewhat *after* Independence when the Catholic nationalist culture was restored to power. While the constitution of 1937, for example, pledged to honour all religious denominations on the island, it was clear that it privileged a Catholic ethos in certain aspects of legislation. So that instead of the sectarian wrongs of colonial history being righted (by establishing laws equally acceptable to both traditions), there was a feeling among many Irish Protestants that they were simply being reversed, i.e. that a new form of discrimination was creeping in.

Such accusations of complicity between Catholic Church and Southern State were not, however, confined to Protestants. In fact they assumed far more aggressive expression in the writings of such Catholic authors as Joyce, O'Faolain and O'Flaherty: writers who felt that Catholicism, having ceased to be the colonial victim of oppression, had now become a post-colonial oppressor in its own right. As Sean O'Faolain remarked: 'Here in the Republic ... we have two parliaments: A parliament at Maynooth and a Parliament at Dublin ... The Dáil proposes; Maynooth disposes.'[4] Such writers implied that Irish Catholicism had somehow *internalized* its colonial master in its historical memory; so that liberated at last, it sought subtly to emulate this master. Perhaps Hyde had something similar in mind when he claimed that the English are the old masters whom 'we love to hate yet never cease to imitate'.

III

But the stereotype of the 'pious Gael' was also cultivated by the Catholic community, and particularly by the Church. It was quite logical in a sense for the Catholic Church to lay claim to an idealized view of its own religion; for the Gaelic Catholic peasantry had been deprived of legitimate power for centuries (particularly during the period of the Penal Laws). And over these same centuries the Church had survived as not only the protector of its persecuted flock but also as a *sanctuary of its dreams*.

The notion of 'Holy Ireland' was a popular example of such a dream, in so far as it referred *back* to an idealized past of saints and scholars before the arrival of the Protestant Planters; or else *forward* to an idealized future after Ireland became an independent Catholic nation once again. In short, as long as colonial oppression reigned, the name of holy Catholic Ireland could remain unblemished for the simple reason that a *religion of aspiration* remained precisely a utopian ideal and not a concrete reality. And perhaps this tendency to idealize had something to do with the *symbolizing process of sublimation* – a process whereby what we lack in history we compensate for in our dreams. The more colonially suppressed the Catholic identity, the more sublime the myth of a 'Holy Ireland'. Lévi-Strauss has described this aspect of religious mythologizing as 'the fantasy production of a society seeking passionately to give symbolic expression to the institutions it *might* have had in reality' (had the historical circumstances of that society been more conducive to the actualization of its projects). But since the 'remedies were lacking', the society finds itself unable to fulfil its desired goals and so begins 'to dream them, to project them into the imaginary'.[5] In short, for a colonially oppressed people, religion can readily serve the ideological purpose of inventing *mythic solutions* to problems that remain unsolvable at the socio-political level.

But what would happen once Ireland achieved independence? What would happen once we were provided with the possibility of translating our sublimated ideals into reality? For centuries the Catholic religion identified with its colonized flock against the colonial foreigner – to such an extent indeed that Cardinal Cullen was able to affirm in the nineteenth century that Irish 'nationality simply meant the Catholic Church'. After Independence, however, and particularly during the Civil War, the Church found itself divided against a significant portion of what it considered to be its own people. With the alien oppressor gone from the scene, the violence that exploded in the Civil War between Irishman and Irishman could no longer be attributed to an *external* cause (i.e. the colonial British occupation). It had to be acknowledged as 'our own', that is, as a rupture *within* the Catholic nationalist community itself. So that with the setting up of the Irish Free State after the treaty of 1921, the Church found itself in the ambiguous position of being at once the representative of the ideals of the Catholic nationalist population and at the same time of siding with one 'legitimate' portion of that population (the Free State) against another 'illegitimate' portion (those republicans who rejected the treaty in the name of the still unrealized ideal of a United Ireland).

In 1922, the Irish hierarchy declared that they thought the wisest course for Ireland was to accept the Treaty and make the most of the freedom it brought – 'freedom for the first time in seven hundred years'. The republicans who violently opposed the Free State were held to be guilty of a far greater crime than their Fenian predecessors, for these republicans were threatening to undermine the good name of holy independent Ireland itself. Accordingly, we find the hierarchy throwing their lot in with the Provisional Government, denouncing the republicans as 'parricides, not patriots'. As one veteran IRA campaigner, Connie Neenan, acerbically commented: '[Before] we were Saints and heroes – now we were burglars and bank robbers ... The ecclesiastical powers were against us, and they were very vocal ... They just wanted the status quo back in any shape or form.'[6]

Of course the hierarchy saw their condemnation of the republicans – which in some instances included excommunication and the denial of the sacraments – as a genuinely *nationalist* stance. They saw themselves as protecting the moral integrity of Ireland against those who had chosen 'to attack their own motherland ... as if she were a foreign power'. They even went so far as to declare that the IRA's campaign of violence against the Free State had done 'more damage in three months than could be laid to the charge of British rule in thirty decades!' Because the republican dissenters were tearing at the sacred vestment of Catholic nationalist unity, the Church endeavoured to win them from their 'evil ways'. What was at stake, insisted the hierarchy, was nothing less than 'our *Christian heritage* and our *name as a nation*'.[7]

But this civil war opposition between the hierarchy and the republicans was not to last long. In time, de Valera's men returned to the fold of Dáil Éireann under the name of Fianna Fáil. And by the same stroke, the prodigal sons were embraced by Mother Church.

The spirit of family reunion was evidenced in de Valera's constitution of 1937, which inserted articles acknowledging the special position of the Catholic Church and banning divorce. In the minds of some – not least members of the Protestant minority – de Valera had produced a Catholic constitution for a Catholic people. But whatever interpretation one chose, it was clear that the Church, having recovered from its insecure and embattled role during the Civil War, now found its teachings reflected in the constitutional law of the land for the first time in Irish history. Archbishop McQuaid was happy; so was de Valera, who had no hesitation in declaring, during a broadcast to the United States, that 'We are a Catholic nation'. A curious echo this, some might note, of the claim by Lord Craigavon, Northern Ireland's first prime minister, that he wanted a 'Protestant parliament for a Protestant people'. The confessional lines of partition thus seemed reinforced.

IV

But the relationship between Church and State did not end there. Once the quarrels between de Valera and the hierarchy had been patched up, it was still obvious that the dream of Holy Ireland was not yet a reality. There was a lingering suspicion that something remained a little malodorous, not to say rotten, in the state of Erin. The independent southern state was still a far cry from the promised land. But how was this continuing discrepancy between the ideal *ought* and the actual *is* of Irish national life to be accounted for? With the English gone, the majority of the IRA turned respectable, and the Protestant minority in the South as good as gold (since they had been relieved of their colonial status), what would now explain why the ideal of Holy Ireland had not yet been convincingly realized?

Several commentators have argued – among them the historian Margaret O'Callaghan – that between the twenties and the fifties, 'sexual immorality' became something of an ideological scapegoat in this regard.[8] In other words, the former *political* threat to our national integrity was now replaced by a *moral* threat. And since it was continually asserted in these rather insular years that this threat to our 'Faith and Morals' came principally from 'abroad' (that is from the liberal licentiousness of 'foreign' countries), the presumption could be sustained that the root cause of our evils came once again from *without*.

Let me take some examples. In a statement in 1924, Cardinal Logue set the tone for subsequent clerical attacks on the immoral nature of foreign dress, dance, cinema and evil literature that threatened to corrupt our chaste youth. Despite the fact that 'men are now engaged in a laudable effort to repair the rack and ruin of the past', wrote Logue, 'there are moral abuses which require to be condemned. The dress, or rather the want of dress, of women at the present day is a crying scandal.' He affirmed the hierarchy's commitment to 'make Ireland what she *ought* to be, a good, solid, Catholic nation', by denouncing the 'regular mania' for dancing, which is the 'outcrop of the corruption of the age'.

'It is no small commendation of Irish dances,' wrote the Maynooth Bishops in 1925, 'that they cannot be danced for long hours ... They may not be the fashion in London or Paris. They should be the fashion in Ireland. Irish dances', they concluded, 'do not make for degenerates.' (Ironically, it was this same Irish dancing, particularly at crossroads, which had been condemned by the clergy in the preceding century.)

But dance and dress were not considered the most pernicious of alien influences. 'Evil literature' emanating from foreign lands was decried by Archbishop O'Donnell as an even more corruptive carrier of immorality. And to immunize the national body against such disease, the archbishop appealed to the Church's educational system to interest the young 'in the beauties of the native tongue'. 'The spirit of Irish classes', they argued, 'is dead against this trash.'

Nor did other media such as cinema (or later television) escape the censorious scrutiny of the hierarchy. Bishop McNamee of Ardagh berated the 'powerful *anti-nationalism*' of films, which, he asserted, served to bring 'vivid representations of foreign ideals' before the vulnerable minds of the people; and he added his conviction that only the 'Gaelic movement provided a powerful antidote to the pleasure-seeking spirit of the times'.

Thus we find the revival of Gaelic culture being used – some would say abused – for the ideological purpose of innoculating the Irish people against the traffic of alien, immoral culture. And one can only assume that Merriman's 'Midnight Court' or *The Love Songs of Connaught* were not the staple diet in those 'Irish classes' prescribed by the bishops. One may also assume that many nationalists had forgotten that the Church that now so fervently espoused the Gaelic cause was the same institution that, in its support for the Act of Union in 1800 and in its rulings from Maynooth in the nineteenth century, had done much to aid and abet the anglicization of Ireland.

The Church's defense of national faith and morals against alien practices did not fall on deaf ears. The State responded with filial obedience, introducing a series of laws that embodied the Catholic moral code. To mention the most obvious examples, there was the Censorship of Publications Act of 1929; the Censorship of Films Act of 1923; the legislation prohibiting divorce in 1925; the legislation requiring the licensing of dance halls and banning contraceptives in the 1930s; Article 42 of the constitution, safeguarding the privileged role of the Church in education; the constitutional underwriting of the special position of the Catholic Church enshrined in Article 44 (repealed in 1972); the Church's controversial role in the mother-and-child-scheme crisis in 1951; and more recently the passing of a constitutional amendment in 1983, the wording of which was unacceptable to the minority churches and to a considerable number of the majority Church, and the defeat of the divorce referendum in 1986.

I rehearse this litany of Church-influenced legislation not to engage in unionist apologetics (for quite clearly the Stormont regime was far more confessionally biased in almost every respect), but to demonstrate that the ideological equation of Catholic Church and Irish nation was in fact reinforced after Independence rather than the reverse.

Margaret O'Callaghan is correct in interpreting the Church's desire, after Independence, to influence the laws of the State as a symptom of growing insecurity before the influx of a cosmopolitan liberalism; a liberalism which, it was felt, might further endanger the Church's historic role as the protector of the ideals of a threatened people. O'Callaghan concludes that the clergy's puritanical zeal during this period should be viewed 'not merely as an intensification of a Jansenist streak in Irish Catholicism, but as a reaction to the demands that they believed Independence made upon the people's moral calibre'.[9] In short, their almost obsessive concern to preserve the holy name of Ireland within a narrow sphere of faith and morals may perhaps best be understood in the historical context of a Church that had formerly served as the 'only institutional voice of a wronged Ireland and now found itself, in the absence of an external colonial enemy, with the same crusading spirit that history of the former centuries had made a part of its being'.[10] Moreover, since the very ideal of national self-identity had developed historically in *reaction* to the colonial outsider, it was not entirely surprising that once Independence was achieved, the Church's protectionist reaction against alien materialism could now be seen as a means of preserving this ideal of national identity. In other words, a new post-colonial outsider had been identified – the permissive pagan foreigner – whom we would love to hate yet never cease to imitate. Once again, we witness an *interiorization* of the colonial model, so well observed by post-colonial commentators like Franz Fanon and Edward Said.

V

Let me try to sum up the argument. It would seem that the Church's repeated attempts after Independence to promote an idealized version of Gaelic Catholic nationalism was motivated, in part at least, by a desire to preserve its traditional role as protector of the Irish people; and that it sought to fulfil this vocation by purging the nation of extraneous immoral influences: that is, by keeping it *pure*. Thus *sexual purity* became synonymous in an almost symbolic way with the ideal of *national purity*. In the process, the root cause of our national impurities could once again be attributed to the old master – pagan Britain. The central difference was, of course, that this alien culture was now exerting its nefarious influence on our moral as opposed to our political being.

To be fair, the hierarchy generally refrained from explicitly identifying the terms 'foreign' and 'pagan' with 'English' and 'Protestant', but it must have been obvious to most that the evil literature and cinema that so threatened the purity of Irish youth was unlikely to be scripted in Italian or Russian. Certainly, D.P. Moran's racist pleas for the protection of 'Irish Ireland' from all non-Catholic and non-Gaelic cultures, in *The Rosary* and *The Catholic Bulletin*, left his readers in little doubt as to his intentions. This influential author even went so far as to denounce Yeats's winning of the Nobel prize in 1923, declaring that 'the line of recipients of the Nobel prize shows that a reputation for paganism in thought and deed is of very considerable advantage ...' Indeed, so incensed was Russell by Moran's xenophobic stance and in particular by his assertion that 'the Gael must be the element that absorbs' lest 'pagan, alien and un-Irish philosophies' corrupt our national being, that he riposted as follows: 'We do not want uniformity in our culture, but the balancing of our diversities in a wide tolerance. The moment we had complete uniformity our national life would be stagnant.'[11]

Russell was simply confirming here Parnell's generous hope that all the children of the nation be cherished equally, regardless of the purity or impurity of their racial genes or their religion. And by the same token, he was, of course, reiterating the interdenominational project not only of the United Irishmen movement (which invoked a common heritage of Protestant, Catholic and Dissenter) but also, let it not be forgotten, of many of the 1916 leaders who stressed the need for non-sectarian institutions in a new independent Ireland. (Connolly was quite clear on this point and Pearse also in his pleas for interdenominational third-level education in *An Claidheamh Soluis*).[12]

Those rightly proud of the nationalist, Gaelic and Catholic traditions that have contributed to Irish culture over the centuries would, I suggest, best serve those traditions by dismantling the tribal ideology that has divided the different communities on this island and betrayed the 'common name of Irishman'. This does not require a jettisoning of all inherited ideals, only a critical discrimination between those ideals that discourage and those that encourage a more open understanding of our national identity. The ideological tendency, particularly since Independence, to identify Irish nationalism with stereotyped versions of Catholicism and Gaelicism has resulted in an exclusivist cliché: one, indeed, that has done a fundamental disservice to the unique qualities of each of these cultural heritages (that is, the nationalist, the Catholic and the Gaelic). In the process, religion has suffered, our sense of national identity has suffered and the Irish language has suffered. This ideological tendency has only exacerbated the partitionist mentality both north and south of the border, and done little to advance the cause of either Irish or Christian reconciliation. It has ensured, rather, that the border has been drawn not just on the outer geographical map but on the inner soul of our nation. Is it not time to disentangle the convoluted web of ideological hegemony and restore to each ideal – Gaelic, Catholic, nationalist – its distinctive promise?[13]

Let me conclude by putting some questions to our two major religious denominations, Protestant and Catholic: questions that require radical responses if future generations on this island are to acquire a genuine sense of the sacred and thus belie the Swiftean foreboding that we Irish 'have just enough religion to make us hate but not enough to make us love'.

Of Ireland's Protestant churches it might be asked: Are you prepared to repudiate the colonial stereotype of Irish Protestantism as inherently superior to Irish Catholicism? Are you prepared to live instead by the liberating heritage bequeathed by such Irish Protestants as Berkeley, Tone, Davis, Mitchel, Ferguson, Parnell, Hyde, Yeats, MacNeice, Hewitt and others? Are you prepared to foster the enlightening role of Protestantism as guarantor of 'civil and religious liberties', by *protesting* against all forms of discrimination, South *and* North? (I am thinking in particular of the collusion between certain Protestant leaders and paramilitary violence in the North.) In short, are you prepared to heed the words of a former Protestant dean of St Patrick's that here in Ireland 'we have had too much religion and not enough Christianity'?

Of Ireland's majority Catholic Church it might be asked: Are you prepared to disavow the stereotype of Irish Catholicism as sole protector of the 'Holy Name of Ireland'? Are you willing, accordingly, to accept that the doctrinal convictions of one Church should not be enshrined in the laws of the State to the exclusion of the aspirations of minority religions or, indeed, of those citizens who have chosen to have no religion? In other words, are you prepared to acknowledge that one cannot credibly denounce majority confessional rule in the North while defending it in the South? Did Vatican II really mean 'no change' as Archbishop McQuaid of Dublin once remarked? Or did not its rethinking of traditional Catholicism require, for example, a transformation of our institutions of education so that the generations now growing up learn a message of tolerance, critical questioning and social commitment to the outcast members of our society, rather than a message of authoritarian puritanism or blind obedience? As one Irish bishop put it, the Church must become less obsessed with the sexual morality of the bedroom and more concerned with the social morality of the boardroom.

The Irish churches might do well to abandon their holier-than-thou isolationism, admitting that while they have indeed produced their share of saints and scholars and withstood centuries of persecution, they are today no less nor no more holy than most other religious communities on this globe. Far from warranting the abandonment of our 'common religious heritage', such an admission would encourage the development of this heritage in the direction of a genuine pluralism. The provision or fortification of legal dykes are not viable methods of ensuring the preservation of religious values. The Irish Council of Churches was correct when it recommended: 'Churches will have to look to the faith of their members and the nurture of it.'[14] The laws of Church and State have been confused for too long in both parts of this island. This confusion is understandable, in the light of the protracted colonial (and post-colonial) conflict whereby Catholicism provided the symbols around which the sense of Irish nationalist identity was sustained, and Protestantism provided the symbols for the maintenance of the unionist identity as guaranteed by the link with Britain. But this confusion of ethnic and religious identities is no longer tenable. The historical overidentification of Protestantism with the unionist ideology of siege and of Catholicism with the nationalist ideology of grievance has nowhere to go but backwards. A pluralist Ireland is one in which the distinctive religious traditions can be respected without any one tradition being allowed to dominate the value system of the state – North or South – at the expense of minority religious communities. Any Christian Church that lays claim to hegemonic status ceases to be Christian. The religious triumphalism of 'majority rule', based on the crude calculation of sectarian headcounts has, one would hope, had its day.

CHAPTER SIX

Between Politics and Literature: The Irish Cultural Journal

Some argue that politics and literature should be kept separate. Any attempt to deviate from such a strategy of mutual exclusion can only lead, in Conor Cruise O'Brien's memorable formula, to an 'unhealthy intersection'. I wish to challenge this assumption, pointing out that some of this country's most inventive thinking and writing over the last one hundred and fifty years was produced in cultural journals such as *The Nation, The United Irishman, The Irish Statesman, An Claidheamh Soluis, The Bell* and others – journals that refused the polarization of literature and politics into opposed discourses and believed that the struggle for a new national identity was best served by combining imaginative creativity with a keen sense of social commitment.

I. The Historical Genesis of Journals in Ireland

a) The Propagandist Journal

The journal began to play an important role in Irish life in the early decades of the nineteenth century. Between the Act of Union in 1800 and the rising of 1848, over 150 periodicals were launched in Ireland.[1] Only a tiny portion of these managed to last more than five years; and those that did, did so, it appears, because they succeeded in aligning themselves with a specific ideological identity. One of the most conspicuous features of Irish society between 1800 and 1850 was that it was bitterly divided, so that the journals published during this period were for the most part of a polemical, and frequently sectarian, character. One finds an extensive list of journals dividing rather predictably along confessional and political lines. On the one hand, there were the periodicals that subscribed to the Catholic-Whig-Anti-Union grouping; on the other, those that represented the Protestant-Tory-Pro-Union grouping. On many occasions, indeed, a journal of one persuasion arose as a direct response to a journal of the opposite persuasion. For example, there was the *Protestant Penny Magazine* and the *Catholic Penny Magazine*, the *Union Magazine* and the *Anti-Union Magazine*, and so on.

One cannot fail to remark how the majority of journals published between 1800 and 1830 were propagandist responses to the colonial Act of Union.[2] The unionist journals aggressively defended the Union as the indispensable guarantee to their otherwise threatened identity as a non-Gaelic and Protestant community in Ireland, while the nationalist journals attacked the Union as the major threat to their native, Gaelic, Catholic identity as a community. The following passage from an editorial in the *Irish Magazine and Monthly National Advocate* (1822) is representative in this regard:

> We feel that the Union is not only the greatest evil with which the country is affected but that it is in reality the prolific source of many of the other evils under which we labour ... For this there is only one course to be taken, let every independent man in Ireland stand up for a Repeal of the Union ... If they wish the salvation of their country they will not delay ... The Orange idolaters of Ireland are too vicious to learn truth and too prejudicial to be convinced.

It is significant that both nationalist and unionist journals were written, published and read in the name of defending a specific communal identity against another that menaced it. The tribal conflicts that in preceding centuries had been fought out on the battle fields were now largely fought out in print. Ideas replaced arms as the weaponry of colonial confrontation. Thus, for example, the motto of the *Irish Catholic Magazine* (1829) reads 'Happy homes and altars free', while that of the *Irish Protestant* was 'Fear God, Honour the King'. This admixture of political and religious idioms to bolster up one community at the expense of another was a typical feature of early nineteenth-century journals. The anti-unionist *New Irish Magazine* carried pot-boiling pieces entitled 'The Hydra of Methodism' or 'Shameful Conduct of the Methodists: Addressed to Ladies who Circulated Bibles'; while the pro-unionist *Church of Ireland Magazine* was full of equally acrimonious rhetoric. Founded to combat 'Romish ignorance, superstition and idolatry', the *Church of Ireland Magazine* reminded its readers that 'popery, however painted, and however masked, remains always the same, the enemy of reform, the advocate of inquisitorial tyranny and the patroness of persecution'. This sectarian journal lasted an amazing twenty-four years from 1825 to 1849. Indeed, the more provocative the editorial policy, the longer the magazine was likely to be produced. These journals created a sense of communal solidarity by trading on the widespread feeling of tribal division. The sense of community in question was *intra-communal* rather than *cross-communal*, reactive rather than explorative: it resulted from the consolidation of the besieged Planters in one corner and the colonized natives in the other.[3]

b) The Literary Journal

It was not really until the 1820s and 1830s that another, less sectarian kind of journal began to emerge in Ireland – the literary journal. The literary journal focused on the world of *belles-lettres* and attempted to discover a common spiritual heritage that might surmount the sectarianism of the religious and political quarrels. Thus, for instance, *The Belfast Magazine and Literary Journal*, which appeared in 1825, declared its express determination to 'avoid controversial theology and party politics' in favour of the 'peaceful pursuit of literature'. In similar fashion, *The Dublin Magazine or General Repertory of Philosophy, Belles-Lettres and Miscellaneous Information* proclaimed its editorial policy to be above party politics, i.e. 'to arrest the decay of literature which has been generally considered the certain herald of declining greatness, in every age and nation'. The aristocratic journal, *Ancient Ireland* (1835), also promoted an ideal of aesthetic harmony and reconciliation, affirming itself to be 'solely and altogether a literary publication: Politics and polemics are totally excluded from these pages'.

While several of the sectarian magazines enjoyed life-spans of up to fifty years, none of the major literary magazines mentioned lasted for more than eleven months. *The Irish Monthly Magazine*, a sectarian periodical of the anti-unionist variety, explained the speedy demise of the literary *Dublin Magazine* as follows: 'In the first volume of this periodical we did not meet with a single political article. What a publication for a country suffering under political disabilities! The poor slave was either contented with servitude, or afraid to complain; and amused himself by playing with flowers of literature, which soon withered and died in his hands.' The implication here is that journals without a political commitment or *parti pris* are journals without guts – irrelevant, elitist, ephemeral. As a disenchanted editor of one of the many failed literary journals remarked in 1831: 'A thing impossible at the present moment, in the present state of affairs in this country, to establish a literary periodical, conducted in a fair, temperate, gentlemanly way ...'

This is not to suggest, of course, that the propaganda journals omitted all reference to literary or cultural matters. But when such non-political material was included, it served the purpose of either providing picturesque relief – e.g. travelogue articles such as 'Three weeks in Donegal', 'A Connaught ramble' – or of surreptitiously shoring up a sectarian viewpoint. When the Rev. Otway, for example, decided to publish some of William Carleton's early stories of Irish peasantry in his *Church of Ireland Magazine*, he did so under such slanted editorial headings as 'Popular Romish legends' or 'Irish superstitions'. In some

respects, this condescending nod to a native literature of peasant lore also corresponded to the fashionable anthropological interest of educated British opinion
typified in Arnold's vision of the quaint, dreamy, entertaining Celt. And it is no
accident that Arnold's benign portrait of the antiquated Celt went hand in glove
with his total opposition to the Home Rule for Ireland Bill. As Seamus Deane
has remarked, this Arnoldian attitude to the Irish expressed itself in the attitude:
'the Celts can stay quaint and stay put'.[4]

The anti-unionist journals also had their token literary articles; but here again
the literature was considered less in terms of its artistic merit than in terms of
its political implications for the 'cause'. A telling instance of this can be found in
the *Irish Catholic Magazine* (1829), which included comments on the 'gloomy
timidity of evangelical prudery' alongside essays on the upsurge of a new and
rebellious generation of Catholic readers. 'We who remember Ireland for the last
fifty years,' reads one contribution, 'view with astonishment the progress of
education in this country. There is at length, a popular mind in Ireland enlightened and organized. We are becoming a reading and thinking nation ...' But the
emergence of such a newly educated generation also spelt the possibility of a
new kind of journal, one that would combine genuine literary interests with
more broadly political ideas of interdenominational concern, ideals that sought
a broad cultural consensus for a new Ireland and could cut across the tribal
conflict between Planter and Gael. Thus we witness the gradual burgeoning of
non-sectarian cultural journals that transcend the format of the propaganda
pamphlet. These strove to rise above the narrow divisiveness of party politics
without being apolitical in the manner of the effete literary journals.

c) The Cultural Journal

The new cultural journal sought to provide a common forum for Catholic and
Protestant authors on both literary and socio-political matters. One of the
earliest examples of such a non-sectarian periodical was the *National Magazine*,
founded in 1830, which after the bitter polemics occasioned by the Act of
Union, looked forward to the possibility of a more inclusive national identity, a
new vision of united 'Irishness' that might give common cause to Protestant,
Catholic and Dissenter. The *National Magazine* featured many articles on Irish
literature, legends and cultural life, declaring at the same time an active interest
in political and social affairs. 'We propose to make politics a frequent subject of
discussion in our pages,' ran one editorial, 'though as the political world now
stands, we belong to no party.' In other words, if the old political framework
militated against a genuine sense of national partnership, a new framework
would have to be invented. Such journals ceased to be merely *reactive* (in the
sense of polemical responses to the latest sectarian squabble) and became *creative*
(in the sense of projecting novel visions of Irish culture and society).[5]

It should be mentioned, however, that the initial spate of non-sectarian cultural journals faced numerous obstacles and only a few survived for any considerable time. First, the established reading public were accustomed to partisan journals and found any departure from this format unsettling. Second, the hoped-for generation of new readers, rising up from the darkness of down-trodden peasantry, were still only semi-literate (particularly in English, which was the language used in the large circulation journals) and were often without sufficient money to purchase a quality magazine. Several penny magazines arose towards the middle of the nineteenth century to cater for this emerging mass readership, but these tended to slip back, once again, into the sure-bet saleability of sectarian cliché. The *Catholic Penny Magazine* equated Irish nationalism with Catholicism, while its *Protestant Penny* counterpart equated civilization with Protestantism (and included fanatical attacks on the doctrine of transubstantia-tion, the Virgin Mary, nuns and the Pope, with headings such as 'Jew horror-struck at the host assuming the form of a crucifix!'). The non-sectarian journals thus found themselves in something of a vicious circle: they invoked the support of the new generation of enlightened readers whom they set out to enlighten.

But there was yet another reason for the initial resistance to non-sectarian cultural journals in Ireland: namely, the deeply rooted prejudice, shared by both Protestant Ascendancy and Catholic middle class, that anything Irish was neces-sarily inferior to anything English and ultimately doomed to failure. As Barbara Hayley has observed: 'The ascendancy and would-be ascendancy, the trades-people and "comfortable" Irish ... were resistant to Irish periodicals for snob-bish reasons. Time and again one reads of their reluctance to take magazines of "local manufacture"; [periodicals of English provenance] had a more cosmopol-itan appeal, displayed on their literary tables.'[6] To add to the difficulties, the majority of Irish booksellers served as agents for the British periodicals and had no great desire to jeopardize this established market by supporting Irish rivals.

The various responses to this colonial mentality were instructive. Some Irish editors adopted a defensive or defeatist rhetoric, decrying their fellow countrymen for making Ireland a failed cultureless land by absconding to England or by subscribing to the latest cults of London fashion. Other Irish editors did a little double-think and continued to have their periodicals *published* in London so that Irish material could be seen to carry the seal of imperial approval. Moreover, this lamb-in-lion's-clothing solution was practised not only by Protestant journals but also by Catholic ones such as the *Dublin Review* (which lasted for a remark-able 133 years, from 1836 to 1969) and whose main contributors hailed from the Catholic seminary of Maynooth. A third response by Irish editors was to dig their heels in, refuse to pander to defeatist pessimism or colonial snobbery, insisting that non-sectarian journals *could* be written, published, sold and read in Ireland despite the odds. It was, arguably, this third defiant response to the colo-nial inferiority complex that ultimately provided the best kind of cultural journal, combining high-quality political and literary commentary.

First and foremost of such defiant cultural journals was *The Nation*. *The Nation*, whose first number appeared on 15 October 1842, was in many respects the great breakthrough. Published weekly, it promoted both literary excellence and socio-political reform. In other words, it refused the security of being exclusively polit-ical or exclusively literary. While committed to specific political objectives, such as the improvement of the land tenure system and the repeal of the Act of Union, it believed such reforms to be but half measures unless accompanied by a new vision of the Irish national community. This required a re-definition of our cultural identity beyond the conventional moulds of sect and party. Davis, himself a Protestant, resolved to break for good with the sectarian equation of religious confession and political purpose, declaring the creation of a common national identity to be the work of Catholic, Protestant and dissenter. Davis recognized the indispensable role of the cultural journal for this work and, as editor of *The Nation*, persuaded countless Irish writers to stay in Ireland and write for their people so that as many as possible might participate in open debate on the national question.

The Nation did not pander to the masses, as did the Penny magazines, nor did it scorn or snub them like the elitist, London-based, literary periodicals. And unlike the legion of sectarian journals that preceded it, *The Nation* refused to be content with preaching to the converted – be they Catholic or Protestant. It determined to interrogate ideas of cultural tradition and heritage not so as to sentimentalize the past or escape into its archaic irrelevancies, but so as to regain that sense of self-respect necessary to construct an alternative national literature and politics. This was the invaluable legacy of Mangan, Davis, Ferguson, Gavan Guffy and the other contributors to *The Nation*. Finally, *The Nation* recognized that the work of shaping a new cultural identity could be greatly assisted by reviewing the age-old, locked-in conflict between Ireland and England in the comparative light of other national struggles; and so we find numerous studies comparing Ireland's plight with that of America, France and the other European nations. In this respect, *The Nation* proved the point that a genuine national awareness presupposes an international awareness if it is not to stagnate into self-regarding insularity; that to understand ourselves we must also understand how other peoples in other countries think, feel, work, struggle and aspire.

II. In Search of a New Nation

The Nation was to serve as a positive blueprint for Irish cultural journals for the next century and more, championing as it did the twin virtues of literary adven-turousness and socio-political commitment. Amongst such journals we could mention *The United Irishman* edited by John Mitchell and Arthur Griffith, *An*

Claidheamh Soluis edited by Patrick Pearse, *The Workers' Republic* edited by James Connolly, *The Irish Statesman* and *The Irish Homestead* edited by George Russell and Horace Plunkett, and *The Bell* edited by Sean O'Faolain and Peader O'Donnell. Indeed it is interesting to note how this catalogue of editors reads like a list of honour of some of Ireland's finest literary and political minds. How strange to think that Griffith, Davis, Mitchell, Connolly and Pearse – minds that helped to shape the identity of the emerging Irish nation – all began as editors of journals (a sad reminder also of the present uninfluential role of journals in Ireland).

Let us take a closer look at the significance of some of these journals that emerged during what might be termed the Golden Age of Irish cultural debate.

Griffith's *United Irishman* flourished during the latter part of the nineteenth century. One of its major objectives was the ending of colonial landlordism and the attainment of land for the people in a new young Ireland. Much of Sinn Féin's ideological programme was thrashed out in these columns. As F.S.L. Lyons remarked in *Ireland since the Famine*: 'The United Irishman was to become for Griffith's contemporaries as potent a force as *The Nation* had become for the contemporaries of Thomas Davis.'[7] Griffith opened his columns to wide-ranging discussion on various types of new organization that might link together 'the scattered literary and political societies and produce a practical programme for the future'.[8] His principal hope for the journal was to develop what he called a 'disciplining of the mind', which he saw as a prerequisite to the practical political transformation of the nation. With *The United Irishman*, and later with its political offshoot, *Cumann na nGaedheal*, Griffith endeavoured to advance the struggle for Irish independence by 'cultivating a fraternal spirit among Irishmen' – in other words, by cultivating a new sense of community.

Another journal that contributed from a different angle to the promotion of a national community was Pearse's *An Claidheamh Soluis*. This journal drew from a variety of talented Gaelic scholars, both Catholic and Protestant, who saw it as essential to incorporate Ireland's Gaelic heritage in the shaping of a post-colonial Irish society. Responding to Douglas Hyde's plea for a de-anglicization of Ireland that might liberate the nation from colonial servility, *An Claidheamh Soluis* included a number of spirited contributions from Eoin MacNeill, The O'Rahilly and, of course, Pearse himself: all central figures in the founding of the Irish Republican Brotherhood. It was, moreover, MacNeill's essay 'The North Began', published in November 1913, which placed this journal at the hub of intellectual debate in the country and, as F.S.L. Lyons remarked, opened 'a whole new chapter of Irish history'. MacNeill appealed for an internal Irish settlement. 'It is evident', he wrote, 'that the only solution now possible is for the Empire to make terms with Ireland or let Ireland go her own way. In any case, it is manifest that all Irish people, unionist as well as nationalist, are determined to have their own way in Ireland.'

An Claidheamh Soluis was founded with a view to intellectually furthering this ideal of national self-determination. Though unashamedly nationalist in its convictions, this journal, like the best of its kind in the early years of this century, advocated a generous and inclusive nationalism. 'We never meant to be Gaelic leaguers and nothing more than Gaelic leaguers,' wrote Pearse. Indeed, it makes for chastening reading even today to see how Pearse used his journal as a platform to advance the idea of a non-sectarian national university system with Trinity as one of its central pivots (an idea that was strenuously opposed by both a Protestant 'Save Trinity' campaign and a Catholic 'Save the Catholic Universities' campaign). In this respect, Pearse parted company with an editor like D.P. Moran, whose journal *The Leader* (1900) advocated a xenophobic programme of sectarian nationalism and whose racialist motto ran as follows: 'The foundation of Ireland is the Gael and the Gael must be the element that absorbs'. It was Moran's editorials that furnished much of the ideological ammunition for that movement of cultural protectionism that joined forces with equally bigoted journals like the *Irish Rosary* and *The Catholic Bulletin* to champion the censorship laws of the twenties and thirties. One of the most notorious results of this was the establishment of the Commission on Evil Literature in 1926 that berated many of Ireland's finest writers for encouraging pagan, alien and un-Irish philosophies. One realizes just how grievous a loss to Ireland was Pearse and his journal when one considers the way in which his originally high-minded equation of a nation 'Gaelic and free' was travestied by D.P. Moran and his blinkered, racist colleagues.

A third important cultural-political journal to contribute to the formative debate on the Irish national question was James Connolly's *The Workers' Republic*. This journal argued, in an unprecedented manner, for a reconciliation of the aims of international socialism and national independence, a combination which Connolly believed to be an effective response to the particularity of the Irish situation. 'The struggle for Irish freedom has two aspects,' wrote Connolly,

> it is national and social. The national ideal can never be realised until Ireland stands forth before the world as a nation, free and independent. It is social and economic because no matter what the form of government may be, as long as one class owns as private property the land and instrument of labour from which mankind derive their subsistence, that class will always have it in their power to enslave the remainder of their fellow creatures.

Connolly's journal, like Pearse's and Griffith's, also had its attendant political expression: the Citizen Army and trade union movements. These were journals that managed to keep their heads above the clouds *and* their feet firmly planted on the ground.

A fourth influential journal that assisted greatly in the provision of innovative debate on the national question was George Russell's *Irish Statesman*.[9] Russell's journal – which he began editing in 1923 at the request of Horace Plunkett – has been described by Terence Brown in *Ireland: A Social and Cultural History 1922–79*, as 'one of the most remarkable cultural organs modern Ireland has known – humane, politically engaged and broadly literate'. This journal was nationalist in yet another sense, what might be termed Anglo-Irish nationalist. Russell waged a vigorous campaign against the Censorship bill and its ideological assumption that the only legitimate definition of Irishness was 'Catholic' and 'Gaelic'. While acknowledging the rich and indispensable resources of the Gaelic, Catholic heritage, *The Irish Statesman* persistently brought home to its readers that the Irish national community was a pluralist one that also contained a richly deserving Anglo-Irish component. 'The moment we had complete uniformity our national life would be stagnant,' Russell announced. 'We are glad to think that we shall never achieve that uniformity which is the dream of commonplace minds ...' In opposition to D.P. Moran's vision of a single, Gaelic hegemony, Russell sponsored a doctrine of national synthesis in which each cultural and ethnic group would have its legitimate place. 'We wish', he wrote, 'the Irish mind to develop to the utmost of which it is capable and we have always believed that the people now inhabiting Ireland, a new race, made up of Gael, Dane, Norman and Saxon, has infinitely greater intellectual possibilities in it than the old race which existed before the stranger came. The union of races has brought a more complex mentality. We can no more get rid of these new elements in our blood than we can get rid of the Gaelic blood.' Foregrounding the significant achievements of the Irish Literary Revival, Russell concluded that Ireland has not only 'the unique Gaelic tradition, but has given birth, if it accepts all its children, to many men who have influenced European culture and science, Berkeley, Swift, Goldsmith, Burke, Sheridan, Moore, Hamilton, Kelvin, Tyndall, Shaw, Yeats, Synge and many others. If we repudiate the Anglo-Irish tradition, if we say these are aliens, how poor does our life become.'[10]

The Irish Statesman – like its companion journal, *The Irish Homestead*, which Russell also edited for a time – was determined to keep Ireland free from self-righteous nationalism by keeping it open to cultural diversity at home and abroad. Hence one finds in these pages articles on Irish culture and politics juxtaposed with studies comparing these national concerns with those of other European nations confronting the challenge of modernity. Writing in 1923 on the question of national culture, Russell stated his own position accordingly:

> We say we cannot merely out of Irish traditions find solutions to all our modern problems ... We shall find much inspiration and beauty in our own past but we have to ransack world literature, world history, world science and study our national contemporaries and graft what we learn into our own national tradition, if we are not to fade out of the list of civilised nations.[11]

It is significant that Russell's resolve to conflate the Gaelic and Anglo-Irish traditions with international ideas from abroad led not only to a theory of pluralist culture, but also to a decentralized co-operative movement, which he set up with Horace Plunkett.

Thus we see how some of Ireland's most formative cultural journals served to inaugurate critical discussion on four of the central ideological standpoints that conjoined in the early decades of this century to found the national philosophy of modern Ireland: 1) progressive nationalism (*The United Irishman*); 2) Gaelic revivalism (*An Claidheamh Soluis*); 3) socialist republicanism (*Workers' Republic*); 4) Anglo-Irish liberalism (*The Irish Statesman*).

III. The Bell

Before concluding I would like to refer to one other publication that merits inclusion in the golden age of Irish cultural journals that lasted approximately from 1850 to 1950 – *The Bell*. This magazine was founded in 1940 by Sean O'Faolain and Peadar O'Donnell, two intellectuals actively engaged in the political struggle for Irish Independence as well as being amongst the most talented creative writers of their generation. *The Bell*, like the best of its predecessors, succeeded in combining an urgent commitment to social questions with a keen concern for literary excellence. It lasted for fourteen years, appearing monthly (with certain lapses) until 1954.

Unlike so many of its contemporaries in Britain, such as *Scrutiny* or *Penguin New Writing*, *The Bell* refused to be an exclusively literary review. It included many fascinating social and political studies on the transitional crises of Irish society in the forties and early fifties. Like *The Irish Statesman* before it, *The Bell* argued that Ireland was not some homogeneous cultural unit but a complex teeming synthesis of differing views and lifestyles. On the question of language, for example, O'Faolain spoke of the need to acknowledge that 'the sum of our local history is that long before 1900 we had become part and parcel of the general world-process with a distinct English pigmentation'; and this meant, for the editors of *The Bell*, that 'our object is not unilingualism, but that we should speak, according to our moods and needs, both Gaelic and English'. It also implied that *The Bell* should celebrate the fact that 'Irishmen writing in English have won distinctiveness for an Irish literature which stands apart from, and even challenges, the achievements of contemporary writers elsewhere.'

And so *The Bell* set about providing a reflective exploration of contemporary Irish life that would illustrate its national and cultural diversity. In 1941, for instance, the editors organized a symposium on Irish culture in which the Gaelic, classical, Norman and Anglo-Irish traditions were represented by a wide variety of contributors. Indeed this project of pluralistic, non-sectarian debate, inviting Irish readers of different traditions to participate in the creation of a new cultural community, is powerfully evidenced in O'Faolain's first editorial entitled 'This is your magazine'. It is worth quoting this editorial in some detail:

> *The Bell* has, in the usual sense of the word, no policy ... This magazine will grow into character and meaning. By the time you have read three issues you will be familiar with its character ... That would not happen with every magazine, but this is not so much a magazine as a bit of life itself, and we believe in life, and leave life to shape us after her own image and likeness.

It was no longer necessary for a journal to invoke the old shibboleths of ancient Gaeldom or Anglo-Irish Ascendancy, O'Faolain affirms, for such symbols belonged to the time when, as he put it, 'we growled in defeat and dreamt of the future'. All our symbols, he goes on,

> have to be created afresh and the only way to create a living symbol is to take a naked thing and clothe it with new life, new association, new meaning, with all the vigour in the life we live in the Here and Now. We wanted to refuse the word Irish, or Ireland, in the title. We said, 'It will plainly be that by being alive.' Our only job was to encourage life to speak. When she speaks, then *The Bell* will itself become a symbol, and its 'policy' will be self-evident.

Addressing the reader directly, O'Faolain then declares:

> You possess a precious store of (life). If you will share it with all of us you will make this bell peal out a living message. *The Bell* will ring a note this way and a note that way. The wind will move it and a faint sigh come from the top of the tower. Some traveller will finger the rope and send out his cry. Some man who knows how to ring a proper peal will make the clapper shout. People will hear these chance notes to the north and people will hear them to the south ... a linking, widening circle of notes, a very peal of bells, murmuring over the land.

This journal, concluded its editors, would aim to create a genuinely participatory community of minds, by making the collective order of practical facts answerable to the 'individual veracity' of imagination and vice versa:

> *The Bell* is quite clear about certain practical things and will, from time to time, deal with them – the language, partition, education and so forth ... we are living experimentally. Day after day we are all groping for reality, and many of our adventures must be a record of error and defeat ... In recording them all, the defeats and the victories, the squalors and the enchantment, how can we have any 'policy' other than to stir ourselves to a vivid awareness of what we are doing, what we are becoming, what we are? That is why this is your magazine.

I quote these passages from *The Bell's* first editorial at such length because they succinctly convey the preoccupations of this pioneering journal. Now that Ireland had reached its long-fought-for national Independence, the editors felt it possible to open Irish minds to life as it was lived in the present, that is, unencumbered by nostalgic abstractions from the past or millennial abstractions about the future. Ireland had come of age. The moment for critical stock-taking had arrived. Thus O'Faolain's Nietzchean appeal to life with a capital L and democratic plea to the reader, with a capital R, presupposes the possibility of a communal consensus that could reconcile the diverse elements, native and non-native, that make up contemporary life. Terence Brown supplies an apposite assessment of *The Bell's* contribution in this regard:

> O'Faolain and his contributors through attending in an empirical, investigative manner to Irish realities opened windows in *The Bell* to show how much Irish life was not some absolute state of national being but an expression of man's life in a particular place, bound up with European history, geography, economics and social forces of all kinds. *The Bell* was therefore a vital organ of empirical, humanistic self-consciousness at a moment when the new state was entering on a period of profound challenge. As such it probably helped to make more generally available ideals of rational reflection and social analysis without which the country could not have responded to the post-war crisis as capably as it did ... Perhaps *The Bell* helped to prepare the ground in the wider community for a period when social analysis was to become a crucial partner in a process of modernisation with economic development.[12]

Brown's verdict is undoubtedly just; but it only takes account of half of the evidence – the positive half. It is true that *The Bell* was one of Ireland's most successful and influential journals, being able to boast, in its heyday, of a print-run of 3000 copies. It is also true that it secured the collaboration of some of Ireland's finest literary and critical minds – amongst them John Hewitt, Patrick Kavanagh, Brendan Behan, Denis Johnston, Anthony Cronin, Louis MacNeice, Austin Clarke and many more. But it is equally true that *The Bell* was to be the last journal of its kind for a considerable time to come. This sense of an ending was recognized by O'Faolain himself in his ultimate 'signing-off' editorial. It is instructive to contrast the almost prophetic optimism of *The Bell's* first editorial with the pessimism of its final one. In this valedictory address, O'Faolain sounds a note of rueful disaffection in sharp contrast with his earlier messianism:

> I have, I confess, grown a little weary of abusing our bourgeoisie, Little Irelanders, chauvinists, puritans, stuffed-shirts, pietists, Tartuffes, Anglophobes, Celtophiles ... I am surprised to find myself suddenly grown detached and impersonal about them ... and when all is said and done, what I am left with is a certain amount of regret that we were born into this

thorny time when our task has been less that of cultivating our garden than of clearing away the brambles.

Thus we observe that the positive organic metaphor of Life, fructifying and expanding in all sorts of creative directions (which informed the first editorial), has been replaced here by the negative organic metaphor of a rank and overgrown garden. Cultivating exotic gardens was, it seems, the leisured luxury of the vanishing ascendancy class; the intellectuals of the New Ireland had been condemned to the more menial chore of distributing the weed-killer. The transition from the excited innocence of *The Bell*'s initial project to the sobering experience of reality is symptomatic of the editors' general disillusionment.

Similarly we find that the salvific connotations of the metaphor of the bell itself – annunciation, liberation, resurrection, revelation and so on – have ultimately fallen on unheeding ears. After eleven volumes O'Faolain looks back disenchantedly at his earlier boast that Life would create new symbols of consensus by creating in and through *The Bell* a new community. Far from congratulating himself on the establishment of a new community – as Davis, Griffith, or Pearse might have done – O'Faolain bemoans the fact that he, and by implication, the writers and readers of *The Bell*, are still as isolated as ever. He refers to himself with humorous self-mockery as an old campanologist, a lonely unheeded bell-ringer having more in common with Yeats's sixty-year-old smiling public man than the Nietzchean Yea-Sayer of a life-enchancing culture. Life with a capital L had, it appeared, become as vacuous an abstraction as those hackneyed symbols of ancient Ireland – Róisín Dubh and Cathleen Ni Houlihan, etc. – whose propensity to 'growl in defeat' and 'dream of a future' he had so sanguinely repudiated in his opening editorial. Now it is O'Faolain's turn to growl in defeat and dream of a future. We have seen, in the passage cited above, how he growled about thorns and brambles; his futuristic dreaming, however, is equally telling. O'Faolain conjures up some glimmer of hope by driving a wedge between politics and literature. If *The Bell* failed, it failed, notes O'Faolain, because 'politics and social problems had intruded' onto its pages; and so O'Faolain imagines a future time when it may be that 'poetic truth, which lives remote from the battle, is more to be sought for than political truth'. Forsaking the earlier claim of communal consensus, he now has recourse to the individualist model of the romantic solitary nursing his genius far from the madding crowd:

> It may be, and one hopes so, that somewhere, some young poet, scornful of us and our controversies, has been tending in his secret heart a lamp which will, in the end, light far more than we can ever do … It is one thing to have a noble vision of life to come and another to have to handle what does come.

In other words, O'Faolain is subordinating the quest for communal debate to the quest of each individual artist – 'the heart's search for the heart', as he puts it, 'that he may sooner or later come to himself.' He affirms the existence of an insurmountable gulf separating the public realm of political commitment and the private sanctuary of aesthetic purity. Denouncing present politicians and 'our censorious people' as tiresome 'haters of life', O'Faolain vows to hand over the intellectual reins to those apolitical artists who will 'purify the source of art, i.e. themselves'.

O'Faolain's acceptance of the impossibility of creating, or at least continuing, a non-sectarian cultural journal that might conscript the dual vehicles of political and literary debate into the service of a new communal identity was, doubtless, a response in large part to the Ireland of his time. Settled into a comfortable partitionist view of itself, the recently established Republic seemed disinclined to foster new debates about new identities. Things were fine as they were and anything threatening this sense of collective self-security should be ignored or allowed to suffer a slow death. 'The establishment of an efficient police force, an experienced civil service and an impartial judiciary,' as John A. Murphy remarked, 'though admirable in themselves, could hardly be hailed as the building of a new Jerusalem.' Even de Valera conceded after the election campaign of 1951: 'If I cannot say that there is a concrete plan for bringing in the six counties, then I am sure nobody else can either.'[13] The New Ireland seemed to want politicians to be politicians and artists to be artists; let politics do its pragmatic job without being led astray by fancy visions; and let poets and painters for their part look after their own reveries to their heart's content and paint harmless self-portraits to hang in the newly constructed national banks, civil service departments and life assurance companies.

This attitude was partitionist in at least two important respects. It was geographically partitionist in that it accepted the inevitability of partition as a solution to the problem of accommodating the troublesome half of the nation north of the border. But it was also partitionist in another and perhaps not unrelated sense: an intellectual sense based on the premise that the socio-political debate dealing with reality and the literary debate dealing with imaginative vision should be kept rigidly apart.

IV. Conclusion

The consequence of this partitionism for the future of cultural journals in Ireland was quite negative. Many journals of course survived the demise of The Bell, but their survival was almost invariably secured by assuming either an exclusively literary identity or an exclusively socio-political or religious one. This is not to minimize the excellence of these journals within their specific competency; it is simply a matter of acknowledging that they increasingly tended towards specialization. Even journals like Studies, Doctrine and Life or The

Furrow inclined after the 1950s almost entirely towards religious and social questions. And the sixties and seventies witnessed a new wave of high-powered, secular and socially committed magazines such as *Hibernia, Nusights, Magill, In Dublin* and so on. On the other hand, the realm of literary debate was also left to specialized journals. These divided into two distinct categories: 1) literary journals dealing primarily with poetry and 'creative' writing – *Poetry Ireland, Envoy, Irish Writing, The Honest Ulsterman, Innti, Quarterly of Ulster Poetry, Feasta, Kavanagh's Weekly, The Kilkenny Magazine, Era, Cyphers, Comhair*, etc.; 2) literary journals of a more critical, academic nature aimed mainly at universities and libraries – *The Irish University Review, Atlantis, Threshold, Aquarius, Irish Studies* and so on.

All these literary journals, and others besides, served the purpose of affording new generations of creative writers a forum for publication and discussion. They shared a desire to eschew socio-political debate in order to concentrate on their trade of well-made fictions: to purify, as O'Faolain recommended, 'the source of art'. This apolitical commitment to the private graph of artistic sensibility, echoing the policy of the literary journals of the preceding century, is aptly conveyed in a foreword to a 1950 issue of *Envoy*, which stated that 'the younger poets' no longer need to busy themselves with national questions because they can 'take their nationality for granted'. A similar view is advanced by Robert Greacen in *Irish Writing*, no. 3 (November 1947), apropos of the new generation of Irish intellectuals: 'If they set store on any one quality it is on personal integrity … The new Irish writers seek neither to deny nor accept Harp or Sickle or Hammer …'

The founding of *The Crane Bag* in 1977 was an *attempt* to counter this drift towards the polarization of intellectual journals into the exclusively literary and the exclusively political. In the following passage from the first editorial, our aims were clearly expressed:

> [In this journal we would hope that] the creativity of art and the commitment of politics might converge to challenge the assumption that the aesthetic and political are two mutually exclusive areas: the first a matter of the yearly visit to the gallery or concert; the second an item of daily news, but essentially other people's business. Our world is an imposition, pleasant or unpleasant as the case may be … We do have a choice, [however,] about the way we respond to this received world. Our way can be critical or uncritical. The latter says there is nothing I can do: there are politicians to run the country for me, as there are mechanics to look after my car; I am the *protégé* of a caretaker society; if there is meaning to it all, it was there before I arrived; if there is not, then I can do nothing about it. The critical way, by contrast, challenges this acquiescence. It recognises that even if history is irretrievably past, its meaning is still in the process of becoming. It holds things at a certain distance and suspends the paralysing immediacy of

facts by examining their roots and their reason for being there in the first place. Such critical freedom is what Socrates called irony: a blend of comic detachment and committed concern. Could a crane bag be for Ireland what the Socratic gad-fly was for Greece?[14]

The Crane Bag had its moments of frustration and of celebration; it produced eighteen issues between 1977 and 1986, some of which generated lively debate and others that sank like millstones into mute oblivion. I do not propose to rehearse the various fortunes of this journal, but simply to put on record this plea: we need more cultural journals in Ireland today, for without a renaissance of the kind of intellectual questioning that flourished in Ireland between 1850 and 1950, our culture will stagnate – either by uncritical reversion to tribal platitudes or by an equally uncritical immersion in the anonymous tide of modern consumerism. To juggle with the words of Pearse: cultural journals can be cleansing things and a nation that regards them as the final irrelevance has lost its sense of nationhood.

Appendix: A Note on the Journal Genre

The journal is neither a book nor a newspaper. This may seem all too obvious for us today. But it is interesting to recall the historical genesis of the modern journal and the way in which it came to distinguish itself as a unique genre of publication.

If we look at the etymology of the term journal (Old French, *diurnal*, meaning daily) – we are reminded that the journal was originally conceived as a daily record of events and impressions. In the post-Renaissance era, this conception of the daily record gave rise to two distinct kinds of journal: the *journal intime* dealing with the realm of subjective feelings and reflections, and the *journal populaire* (or *le journalisme*) dealing with the realm of objective facts.

The *journal intime* or private diary involved a highly individualized account of events and was generally registered in the first person singular. Its emergence as a common practice, particularly amongst the leisured classes, seems to have coincided with the birth of the modern era of subjectivity. This modern emphasis on subjective experience, epitomized by the *journal intime*, was a response to a combination of several different but related historical circumstances: 1) the Renaissance discovery of humanism with its central notions of personality, creativity and authorship; 2) the Cartesian and Enlightenment philosophy of the *cogito*, which taught that truth begins with the subjective act of the individual knower; 3) the Reformational and Romantic insistence upon a private spiritual relationship with the transcendent; 4) the emergence of a liberal 'soul-searching' bourgeoisie with the French Revolution on the Continent and the puritan and industrial revolutions in Great Britain. All of these historical and cultural movements conspired to provide conditions favourable to the conviction that the *individual* recording of events was a meaningful practice, indeed a necessary one, for the cultivation of value in a modern world of rapidly changing circumstances.

In time the *journal intime* took a public turn; it assumed the 'published' form of a book wherein the records of one's individual feelings and fantasies were offered the possibility of communicating with other individuals in printed volumes. Thus arose the modern notion of the autonomous author addressing his/her autonomous reader in the privacy of the boudoir or garden. The most direct literary offspring of the *journal intime* was the confessional novel where the author enjoined the reader to suspend the everyday world of facts and indulge in the fiction of a *tête-à-tête* communication. In this manner, the *journal intime* progressed from a spiritual monologue to a literary complicity of shared solitude. As Walter Benjamin observes in his celebrated essay on Leskov, the birth of the novel coincided with a cultural crisis resulting from the demise of traditional beliefs. Whereas the earlier epic genres of myth, legend and oral storytelling traded on such communally shared notions as universal wisdom, truth, counsel, remembrance, tradition and authority, the novel, by contrast, was a response to the crisis of culture engendered by the very loss of such notions. 'The novelist', writes Benjamin, 'has isolated himself. The birthplace of the novel is the solitary individual, who is no longer able to express himself by giving (universal) examples of his most important concerns, is himself uncounselled, and cannot counsel others ... the legitimacy it provides stands in direct opposition to reality (as a universally shared experience).'[15] Before the novel, literature believed in the 'moral of the story'. But the novel dispensed with such universal wisdom. It represented an individual search for the 'meaning of life' no longer deemed available in the resources of a communal tradition.

But the *journal intime*, with its attendant literary form, the novel, was not the only response to the cultural transitions of the post-Renaissance era. If the Enlightenment ushered in a cult of subjective sentiment, it also recognized a quite different order of experience worthy of published record: the realm of objective fact. This attention to the objective world of empirical observation gave rise to another kind of journal: the newspaper. The newspaper sponsored a different kind of writing known today as journalism. This kind of writing did not, originally at least, take its identity from individual authors. Indeed most of the articles or news reports were anonymously recorded, the idea of personalized authorship being suspect as an indication of bias or distortion. The journalistic reporting of facts required one to describe events 'objectively' and 'neutrally'. Newspapers were generally identified not by the signature of their editors or authors, but by their geographical origin – e.g. *The London Times, The Washington Post, The Skibbereen Eagle* and so on. Furthermore, the journalistic mode of communication was not that of intimate confession (as in the *journal intime*) but that of verifiable information. 'Information', writes Benjamin, 'lays claim to prompt verifiability. The prime requirement is that it appears "understandable in itself". Often it is no more exact than the intelligence of earlier centuries was. But while the latter was inclined to borrow from the *miraculous*, it is indispensable for information to sound *plausible*.'[16]

Now, alongside these two genres of the *journal intime* and the 'journalist' newspaper, emerged a third genre – the journal as review or magazine. When we speak of a journal today we usually intend it in this third sense. The journal-magazine was, as the root arabic word *makhazan* suggests, a storehouse that records both factual and fictional experience, and combines the resources of subjectivity (as cultivated by the *journal intime*) and objectivity (as invoked by newspaper journalism). The magazine-journal featured a miscellany of essays that carried their authors' names, but whose very diversity implied that no single personal vision was being privileged. In other words, the magazine-journal would try to respond to the objective world of facts while retaining something of the imaginative richness of subjective interpretation. The publication time span of the magazine-journal was also significant in this regard. While newspapers appeared daily and dealt with topical matters and while novels were almost 'timeless' by virtue of the unconditioned freedoms enjoyed by the artist, magazines appeared on a 'periodical' basis, that is, at regular intervals of a week, a month, every three months, every year, etc. Unlike the daily intervals of newspapers, these more prolonged intervals were intended to allow the authors and the readers of the magazine articles to reflect in a measured and critical fashion upon the events recorded. The purpose was not just to view but to re-view. In other words, the magazine-journal obeyed the laws of temporal regularity and periodicity while remaining sufficiently distanced from everyday events to foster considered debate. Its aim was to invite the reader to participate in the multiple interpretations of events represented by the different essays. Indeed the very term 'essay' is perhaps significant here, for it acknowledges that the various contributions printed in a single issue of a journal are no more than a variety of *attempts* (French, *essais*) to reach a consensus. The essays of a magazine are parts in search of a whole, diverse perspectives which require the reflective response of the reader if they are to achieve any sort of overall synthesis. There is no beginning, middle or end – as in a novel. The essays represent a series of beginnings whose end is the reader. The purpose of the magazine is, therefore, *dialogue*, and by extension, *community*. This is why it seems fair to say that the possibility of a journal always exceeds its actuality; it is of its nature to promise more than it can deliver.

In short, one might conclude by saying that if the artistic genre of the *journal intime* operated in terms of individuality, and if the journalistic form of the newspaper assumed the status of a collectivity, the magazine strove towards the provision of a sense of community; it served as a mediating link between the idioms of individualism and collectivism. This implied in turn the creation of a specific kind of writing and reading different from those solicited by artistic or journalistic literature. It is perhaps for this reason that certain social and cultural historians, desiring to take the pulse of a particular period of modern history, focus on the key debates and discussions featured in magazine-journals. A good case in point is Terence Brown's *Ireland: A Social and Cultural History 1922–79* (Fontana 1981), which draws its material more frequently from *The Bell, Envoy, Kavanagh's Weekly, Studies, Doctrine and Life* and others, than from novels or newspapers.

Part Two:

LITERARY NARRATIVES

CHAPTER SEVEN

Yeats and the Conflict of Imaginations

'No mind can engender till divided into two.'

The Trembling of the Veil

Yeats often canvassed the view that poets should seek inspiration in some great tradition of imaginary heroes. A question that appears to have obsessed Yeats throughout his lifetime, however, was whether it is tradition that shapes the poet's imagination or the poet's imagination that shapes tradition. In his *Autobiographical Writings*, Yeats informs us that already at the age of seventeen he had formulated the doctrine that because imaginary people are created to be man's measure, whatever we can imagine those mouths uttering may be the nearest we can go to truth. This statement can be read in two ways: either this imaginative norm refers to a power immanent in the individual poet, or it refers to an attitude of visionary obedience to a transcendent truth that comes from beyond the human mind. Otherwise put, either man is the measure of his imagination or he is not.

Yeats was well versed in the philosophical debates on images.[1] He was particularly impressed by the neo-Platonic notion of the *Anima Mundi* – a cosmic storehouse of symbols, based on Plato's world of Eternal Forms and reformulated in Carl Jung's psychology of a 'collective unconscious'. The main attraction of this notion for Yeats was that against the Enlightenment philosophies of individualism and empiricism, it set the theory of a Great Tradition still in contact with the accumulated memories of generations: 'Pre-natal memory, like Plato's assertion that all knowledge is recollection, also supports the doctrine of reincarnation. The *Anima Mundi* ... is the sum of human wisdom, to which the individual gains access through the symbols of dream and reverie, or through deliberate magical invocation. We are thus organically linked to each other, to the dead, and to our former and future selves: the history of the world is a stream of souls, and not a catalogue of facts.'[2]

The fascination that the old philosophical debate on imagination exerted on Yeats was not unrelated to the particular historical circumstances of modern Ireland. Yeats longed for a tradition that might transcend the bitter divisions that had bedevilled Irish life since the seventeenth century – most notably, the sectarian strife between Catholic and Protestant and the colonial strife between Gael and Planter. A Unity of Culture was needed, Yeats was convinced, to offset the 'filthy modern tide' of fragmentation and conflict.

Yet the matter is not so simple. For if Yeats is powerfully drawn to the unifying idioms of tradition, mythology and collective memory, he is also, in some measure, a proto-modernist who refuses to abandon the contrasting idioms of individual creativity, autonomy, desire, play and will. Yeats's complex attitude to the Irish Revival is an apt reminder of this collision of fidelities. While he championed a return to the pieties of a collective national culture, he also prided himself on being a perpetual dissident committed to the principles of intellectual freedom, cultural diversity and political pluralism. In short, if Yeats's desire to obviate the divisive ruptures of Ireland's colonial history found refuge in the mythic timelessness of the *Anima Mundi*, it was no more than provisional – a refuge repeatedly harassed by the intrusions of history. 'A colony', as Seamus Deane has remarked, 'always wants to escape from history. It longs for its own authenticity, the element it had before history came to disfigure it.'[3] Thus, if Yeats set out to invent an Ireland amenable to his imagination, he was to be confronted by an Ireland inhospitable to it.[4] Yeats's entire work may be viewed in this way as an endless vacillation between the rival claims of myth and history, that is, between the ideal of a timeless tradition and the reality of a fragmenting modernity.

I. The Imagination of Desire

In the essay 'Ireland After Parnell' (1922), Yeats makes a telling distinction between what he calls 'images of desire' and 'images of vision':[5]

> The *imagination of desire* is characteristic of the romantic artist who seeks to construct an anti-self or mask to complete the halfness of his natural self.

> The *imagination of vision*, by contrast, is described as the sacramental property of those 'who seek no image of desire, but await that which lies beyond their mind – unities not of the mind, but unities of nature, unities of God'.[6]

But where is Yeats himself to be situated in terms of this divide? Most critics tend to corroborate R.P. Blackmur's claim in *Anni Mirabiles* that Yeats is an 'erotic' rather than a 'sacramental' poet (a contrast corresponding to the distinction between images of desire and images of vision). In *The Romantic Image*, Frank

Kermode places Yeats in the 'central Romantic tradition', which held that the creative imagination must don a mask to ward off passive acceptance of any principle transcending, and thereby threatening, the sovereignty of its own dramatic energies. And Denis Donoghue enlarges the argument when he explains that 'the *romantic* imagination' that Yeats embodies is to be understood as 'exercising its freedom by playing widely ranging roles in a continuous drama: the poet is playwright and actor in his own play. The self is the object of its own attention ... creates and extends itself by a continuous act of imagination; thus it evades the penury of the given.'[7] According to this reading Yeats belongs to that Romantic movement, which runs from the German idealists, Coleridge and Nietzsche to several of the early modernists, where imagination is deemed a creative faculty and the self its final concern. A list of the operative terms of such a Romantic imagination would read as follows: desire, will, drama, conflict, energy, tension, style, personality, mimesis, mask, power, self and self-transformation.[8]

According to the Romantic canons of modern humanism, 'active virtue, as distinguished from the passive acceptance of a code, is ... theatrical, consciously dramatic, the wearing of a mask'.[9] The Romantic imagination always assumes postures of belligerence before the exteriority of the world. Its habitual attitude is warmongering and divisive. Indeed, Yeats tells in his *Autobiographies* of how he was accustomed to plan 'some great gesture, putting the whole world into one scale of the balance and my soul into the other, imagining that the whole world somehow kicked the beam'.[10] This is the Yeats who exchanged the traditional notion of *character* (epitomized by man's obedience to a naturally or divinely given vocation) for the modern notion of *personality* (e.g. wilful self-determination). Poetry thus becomes *mimesis*, the imitation of a mask or *persona*. The aim of the genuine poet, Yeats proclaimed, is the 'birth, the growth and the expansion of everlasting personalities'.[11] Art, or at least Romantic art, is the transmutation of character into the free play of personality. For, Yeats insists, 'we have all something within ourselves to batter down and we get our power from this fighting'. Moreover, 'without this conflict we have no passion', that is, no energy for artistic creation.[12] This accounts for the artist's fascination with what is difficult: the war of self on self waged by Yeats in *Deirdre*; the will to 'make the truth' out of one's struggle with oneself that his imaginary Cuchulain embodies. Yeats sums up the aesthetic of modern Romanticism in a letter to Russell in 1904 – the artist 'possesses nothing but the will ...'

Hence Yeats's enthusiasm for the medium of drama. Drama's end, he insists, 'is to turn the imagination in upon itself.'[13] Religion, being the opposite of drama, is denounced by Yeats accordingly as a denial of creative liberty: 'An enforced peace is set up among the warring feelings ... that is why the true poet is neither moral nor religious.'[14] Thus it comes as no surprise to find Yeats on one occasion advocating a move away from *vision* toward *self-portraiture*; a move that suspends anything that does not concern the self, anything that does not testify to the 'presence of man, thinking and feeling'.[15] In this mood, the French poets, Mallarmé, Ronsard and Villon, became his models, those who 'created marvellous drama out of their own lives'.[16] Mallarmé's typically modernist lines on Hérodiade especially intrigued Yeats:

> All about me lives but in mine own
> Image, the idolatrous mirror of my pride

In 'The Tragic Generation' he candidly admits that 'there was something in myself compelling me to attempt creation of an art as separate from everything heterogeneous … as some Hérodiade of our theatre, dancing seemingly alone in her narrow moving luminous circle.'[17]

It was this persuasion, abetted by a reading of Nietzsche, that prompted Yeats towards his celebrated formulation that poetry is created out of the quarrel with ourselves.[18] According to this reading even the transcendental images of the *Anima Mundi* are construed as dramatic antithetical inventions of man that can best rouse 'the will to full intensity': for Yeats firmly believed that 'no mind can engender till divided into two'.[19] This Romantic fascination with self-conflict is perhaps most vividly expressed in 'The Tower' where Yeats commends the 'Excited, passionate, fantastical Imagination' that stems from a 'troubled heart' and 'expected the impossible'. The Romantic imagination is imperious; it *calls* images from the ruin of the surrounding world so that the artist may 'Dream and so create / Translunar Paradise'. This is the Yeats that mocks the transcendental vision of Plato and Plotinus, concluding that 'Death and life were not / Till man made up the whole'.

The Romantic in Yeats cultivates genius in defiance of all constraints. The best art, he writes, occurs when 'Propinquity had brought / Imagination to that pitch where it casts out / All that is not itself'.[20] Thus while Yeats deplores 'the saint and sage' in the Irish philosopher Bishop Berkeley, he is 'attracted beyond expression' to him as sponsor of the 'intellectual fire' of creative imagination: that which he saw as the only genuine 'substitute for the old symbol God'.[21] Yeats hails here the Promethean Berkeley who shocked the elders of traditional belief by opening 'once more the great box of toys'. It is insofar as Berkeley's philosophy of imagination resists our servility to reality and usurps the creative function of the traditional god, that Yeats invokes it as the epistemological equivalent of Mallarmé's modernist doctrine of the artist as Priest of the Eternal Imagination. Yeats expresses here his preference for an aesthetic of play over one of prayer. He endorses the Symbolists' maxim, *le style c'est l'homme*. The best art is one of 'style and personality, deliberately adopted'.[22]

One final aspect of Yeats's commitment to the Romantic imagination is its relevance to Irish politics. Here we might cite his model of an 'Irish Imagination' fuelled by the 'romantic dreaming' of a group of isolated poets, including

Russell, Synge and himself: poets who had fled the sordid reality of post-Parnel-lite Ireland and created an imaginary Ireland to correspond with their affronted desires.[23] In brief, when Yeats interprets the notion of an Irish tradition as the expression of a visionary imagination, he sees it as a specific set of archetypal images that reveal themselves to the poetic seers of the nation. But when he interprets it as the expression of the Romantic imagination he sees it as a delib-erate invention of the defiant dreamer who insists on creating himself what history refuses to grant. This latter version is evidenced in Yeats's contention in *First Principles* (1904) that poets must *create the illusion* of a national tradition; and that in so doing they will do the people of history the honour of naming after them the inventions of their own imaginings. Yeats gives as example Shake-speare's creation of Richard II: 'He is typical not because he ever existed, but because he has made us know of something in our minds we had never known of had he never been imagined.'[24] It is no great leap of fancy from Shakespeare's Richard II to the inventions of Yeats's own mythic-historical drama: Deirdre, Cuchulain, Maud Gonne or Parnell. Indeed, it is in just such a mood that Yeats espouses the Romantic cult of shaping individual imagination in the conclusion to *First Principles*: 'In Ireland, where the tide of life is rising, we turn … to the imagination of personality – to drama, gesture.'

II. The Imagination of Vision

But while the imagination of personality and desire accounts for a good part of Yeats's aesthetic, it by no means tells the whole story. At times, we witness Yeats's poetic notion of the *self*, for example, moving from the Romantic idiom of self-transformation back to the sacramental idiom of self-abnegation, preferring a peace treaty between self and transcendence to a proclamation of the self's omnipotence. In this mood, Yeats pleads for an imagination of mystical vision that seeks unity with a life beyond the individual being.[25] Citing the religious examples of Saint Simon on his pillar and Saint Anthony in his cavern, Yeats praises such receptive and obedient imaginations 'whose preoccupation is to seem nothing; to hollow their hearts till they are void and without form, to summon a creator by revealing chaos, to become the lamp for another's wick and oil'. So that imagining becomes a matter of passive vigil rather than of active formation. For such men, explains Yeats, 'must cast all Masks away and fly the Image, till that Image, transfigured because of their cruelties of self-abasement, becomes itself some Image or epitome of the whole natural or supernatural world, and itself pursues'.[26] The guiding image of the shaping imagination – that of the 'perfectly proportioned human body' – suffers crucifixion in the saintly imagination; it becomes instead the contrary image of the crucified God, the sacrificed and emptied heart, *Kenosis*.

But Yeats does not deny that this visionary or saintly imagination is capable of poetry as well as prayer. He explicitly acknowledges that 'images of vision' inspired the religious poetry of George Herbert, Francis Thompson and George Russell: 'those whose imaginations grow more vivid in the expression of some-thing *they have not themselves created*, some historical religion or cause'.[27] But as soon as this visionary imagination abandons its passive vocation and aspires instead to become pursuer and hunter (as in the case of poets like Morris and Henley) then Yeats maintains that their art degenerates into a mere 'repetition of thoughts and images that have no relation to experience'. Yeats expresses disap-pointment with visionaries who permitted their sacramental imagination to be misled by modern subjective Romanticism away from the bedrock of 'traditional belief'. For such a fidelity to tradition, Yeats now argues, would have eliminated all those 'images of desire' that Romanticism admires, and redirected attention back to 'the images of his vision'.

In pronouncing thus Yeats was, of course, also pronouncing on himself. In a telling passage in *The Trembling of the Veil*, Yeats concedes that visionary art can only occur when the inclinations of Romantic will have been laid aside. And this requires that the poet 'exhausts personal emotion in action and desire so completely that something *impersonal*, something that has nothing to do with action and desire, suddenly starts into its place, something which is as unforeseen … as the images that pass before the mind between sleeping and waking'.[28] The sacramental imagination thus emerges as an *involuntary* agency. At extreme moments, this notion even prompted Yeats to plan a mystical order of contem-plation on the Castle Rock in Roscommon where he intended to re-establish Celtic mysteries like those of Eleusis and Samothrace. This project, both religious and aesthetic in inspiration, was a clear expression of the revivalist tendency in Yeats: 'I had an unshakeable conviction … that invisible gates would open as they opened for Blake … Swedenborg … and for Boehme, and that this philosophy would find its manual of devotion in all imaginative literature which, though made by many minds, would seem the work of a single mind, and turn our places of beauty or legendary association into holy symbols.'[29]

The single mind spoken of here is that *Anima Mundi* or Great Memory from which individual poets would receive a set of collective images. These images would be archetypal and mythological in contrast to the personal and psycho-logical images fashioned by the Romantic imagination. Yeats identifies them in mystical fashion with the 'strange things said / By God to the bright hearts of those long dead'.[30] Other times, he suggests that these archetypal images can be embodied in the mythic transmutation, often through terror or violent crisis, of certain national heroes such as the 1916 leaders or Maud Gonne MacBride. 'Are not such as she,' Yeats comments of the latter, 'aware at moments of great crisis, of some power beyond their own minds … there was an element in her beauty that moved minds full of old Gaelic stories and poems, for she looked as though she lived in an ancient civilisation where all superiorities whether of the body or the mind were a part of public ceremonial.'[31]

For the most part, Yeats's concern with the images of the *Anima Mundi* was less religious than literary. Due to the fact that these collective images are engendered by a 'memory independent of individual memories', Yeats saw them as constituting a Unity of Image that could ultimately serve as the originating symbol of a national literature.[32] It was thus the sacramental imagination that revealed to Yeats the possibility of a Unity of Culture.[33] This encouraged him in turn to privilege the primordial images of ancient Celtic mythology that predated all subsequent historical divisions into different religious (Catholic/ Protestant) or political (nationalist/unionist) beliefs. Yeats maintained that certain folk-images of ancient Ireland came to him in the waking visions that inspired much of his writing.[34] It was with such experiences in mind that Yeats confessed in a letter to the Fenian leader, John O'Leary, in 1892: 'The mystical life is the centre of all that I do and all that I think and all that I write.' On such occasions, Yeats tends to favour the involuntary and trans-personal characteristics of the sacramental imagination over the wilful energies of the Romantic imagination.[35] He renounces the modern aesthetic of mastery in deference to a mystical vision wherein images are *given* rather than *chosen*.[36] Consequently, while the Romantic poet in Yeats celebrated self-possession in life and style in art as products of a 'deliberate shaping of all things', the visionary in him recognized that in sacred or mystic experiences, the poet's 'imagination began to move of itself and to bring before [him] vivid images that ... though never too vivid to be imagination ... had yet a motion of their own, a life I could not change or shape'.[37]

Yeats's commentaries on other 'visionary' artists of the Irish Literary Revival (in particular George Russell and John Millington Synge) convey a similar scruple concerning the origin of images. In 'Ireland After Parnell'[38] he recalls how he had quarrelled with Russell because the latter refused to rationally examine his visions and record them as they occurred. Yeats had at first insisted that they were symbols of the subconscious whereas Russell claimed for them an objective exterior reality. So keenly attuned was Russell to the primordial images of the *Anima Mundi* that he saw 'all life as a mythological system'.[39] Russell's influence on Yeats was strong, so strong, in fact, that in *A Symbolic Artist and the Coming of Symbolist Art* (1898), Yeats asserts that to write of literature in Ireland is to write 'about a company of Irish mystics' whose 'religious philosophy' has changed both poet and non-poet alike into 'ecstatics and visionaries'. Under this influence, Yeats even subscribed to the doctrine that the source of literary inspiration was a 'divine flame' that revealed itself as a motion in the 'imagination of the world', thus affecting change in any specific culture through its impact on 'one or two' visionary individuals.[40] The imagination in question is transcendent of the individual artist and speaks to, or through, him.

The commentaries on Synge reinforce the sacramental interpretation. Yeats confesses in *Autobiographies* that Synge's writing has persuaded him to renounce 'the deliberate creation' of imagination. But this did not mean that Yeats felt compelled to abandon imagination altogether. On the contrary, he saw in Synge a further testimony to that visionary imagining that repudiates the controlling will or personality in favour of a more vigilant attitude to the images of language and community other and older than the author's own. In 'The Tragic Generation', Yeats commends Synge's renunciation of 'power and joy', which are generated by 'subjective dreaming'. He praises him as one who 'judged the images of his mind as if they had been created by some other mind'.[41] Thus Synge is enlisted in Yeats's inventory of visionary revivalists who remained faithful to the sacramental source of their inspiration. For such men, Yeats affirmed, this inspiration stemmed from the mystical 'earth' that had become 'not in rhetorical metaphor, but in reality, *sacred*'.[42]

But one could also give a political reading to Yeats's revivalist hankering after a transcendental Unity of Culture. It has been argued that Yeats mythologized the revolutionary dynamic of the Irish nationalist Rebellion – directed in part against the Anglo-Irish ascendancy to which Yeats and many other advocates of the Celtic Revival belonged – in order to take the subversive harm out of it. By gathering the anarchic energies of history into the 'artifice of eternity', he contrived to defuse the disruptive potential of the Rebellion in the very act of mythologizing.[43] According to this reading, Yeats's urge to reinstate sacred myths is informed by a political motivation to reconcile the historical antinomies of class and creed – which the revolutionary drive of Irish nationalism threatened to expose – within a timeless and seamless continuum. But the more spiritually idealized the collective memory of the nation becomes the more it assumes the form of a death cult erected upon the dual fetishizing of Past (the golden age of Celtic myth) and Motherland (Cathleen Ni Houlihan and the sacrificial Rosaleen). Yeats's revivalist nostalgia for a tradition guaranteeing a pre-historical Unity of Culture may be construed accordingly as a regressive death drive towards an imaginary reunification with the mythological mother. In short, the *Anima Mundi* of the collective unconscious becomes identical with the *Magna Mater* of the nation. Terry Eagleton summarizes the main aspects of this ideological reading of Yeats's revivalism as follows:

> Adherents of aristocratic ideology like Yeats are committed ... to the values of order, ceremony, peace, stability and tradition – that is to say, to an impersonal organic hierarchy to which the individual subject is – precisely – subjected ... The desire to merge gracefully into the impersonal matrix of an aristocratic matriarch is woman as desexualised, defused, rendered safe, and so an appropriate symbol of a non-violent, courteous social order. But this

process of sublimation is inescapably a kind of castration: by depleting your libidinal virility it renders you vulnerable to the forces of death which are equally associated with the woman … When your aristocratic order is threatened with violence from the people … you can turn to the ideal of womanhood, defending yourself against the grubby-handed plebs by unity, ceremony, innocence, Nature, rootedness and associated ideological illusions.[44]

We have already explored the ideological connotations of Yeats's 1916 poems – and particularly his symbolism of blood sacrifice – in chapter 3, 'Myth and Martyrdom'.

Conclusion

Yeats's endless vacillation between the rival claims of 'vision' and 'desire' would seem to indicate a fundamental incompatibility between the sacramental and Romantic impulses of imagination.[45] In several passages, however, Yeats expresses the conviction that these imaginative impulses may function as a kind of dialectic where vision is *revealed* to the poet and *invented* by him at one and the same time.[46]

In *Discoveries* Yeats suggests that the great artist will have his share of *both* 'the sadness that the Saints have known' *and* the 'Promethean fire' that engenders active desire. In *Poetry and Tradition* he contends that the finest poetry is one-half the 'self-surrender of sorrow', which characterizes tragedy, and one-half 'the freedom of self-delight', which is the expression of comedy. Tragedy is for Yeats closely identified here with the ecstasy of the saint in that it leads beyond the wilful personality to that 'sorrowful calm' that epitomizes the sacramental imagination.[47] Comedy, by contrast, is the genuine articulation of the Romantic spirit in that it fosters the personality and will of deliberate creation; the comic attitude celebrates, as Nietzsche taught Yeats, a gaiety that transfigures dread and transforms nay-saying into yea-saying.[48] On the final count, Yeats is prepared to compromise, dividing the spoils judiciously between the rival imaginative tendencies. And so he writes that while comic desire, 'because it must be always making and mastering, remains in the hands and in the tongue of the artist … with his eyes [the faculties of tragic vision] he enters upon a submissive, sorrowful contemplation of the great irremediable things'.[49] In such passages, Yeats seems to acknowledge that the two imaginations can function together in creative dialectic and indeed *must* do so, if the art is to be excellent. Yeats's ultimate position would appear to be that the best literature arises from a dialectical tension between the imaginations of saint and artist: 'That shaping joy has kept the sorrow pure … for *the nobleness of the arts is in the mingling of contraries*, the extremity of sorrow, the extremity of joy, perfection of personality, the perfection of its surrender, overflowing turbulent energy, and marmorean stillness; and its red rose opens at the meeting of the beams of the cross, and at the trysting-place of mortal and immortal, time and eternity.'[50]

It was a despondent Yeats who finally confessed that 'outside of myth ... the union cannot be'.[51] In the Irish context, this meant that Yeats came to realize that the myths of the Literary Revival that promised to reconcile the rival impulses of vision and desire – and by implication the opposing claims of tradition and modernity – were themselves imaginative constructs. In short, the revivalist myth of a Unity of Culture could not be translated into reality. Faced with the 'filthy modern tide', Yeats acknowledged that the sacramental need for harmony and the Romantic need for adversity could not be reconciled *within history*. Perhaps this was the greatness of Yeats's achievement – to have carried this impossibility of synthesis to its ultimate crisis, registering its full consequences in that dialectical conflict of imaginations that his work as a totality embodies. Indeed this very conflict is Yeats's own eloquent testimony to the transitional tension between revivalism and modernism.

Appendix: The Byzantine Imagination

Yeats's advocation of a dialectical mingling of contraries may *itself* be interpreted according to either the sacramental or Romantic perspective. If the sacramental reading prevails the dialectic is seen as a reconciliation of contraries, as a process of pacification. By contrast, the Romantic reading construes this dialectic of the two imaginations as itself merely another expression of the human need for dramatic conflict and tension. But it would be a mistake to favour this reading, as most critics have done, at the total expense of the sacramental. To do so is to reduce the rich bi-polarity of Yeats's art to just one of its terms; it is to ignore the independent validity of the sacramental imagination, to deny it the power, in itself, to engender its own specific form of art, its own 'pacifying' dialectic of contraries. Such a view caricatures the sacramental imagination as but a pale self-alienation of the Romantic imagination, as little more than a prop in its own comic drama.

Yeats does recognise a specific and autonomous form of sacramental art that dates from the artisans of Byzantine Christendom, Dante and the metaphysical poets to such visionary modern poets as Shelly, Synge, Russell and, at times, himself. By overestimating the significance of the Romantic imagination in Yeats, critical opinion has tended to completely ignore its visionary counterpart; or, at best, to dismiss it as the infrequent outburst of the occultist dabbler in him. The mistakenness of this assessment becomes evident as soon as we turn from the poetry of imperious desire – arguably much of his best – and try to account for the self-abnegation of *Supernatural Songs*, the sorrowful calm of *Wisdom with Time*, the humility of *A Coat, Hightalk* or *Among School Children*, the tragic acquiescence of *The Circus Animals' Desertion*. It is the sacramental and religious imagination in Yeats that regrets that it was but a 'dream', 'players and painted state' that took his love, and 'not the things that they were emblems of'. It is the same Yeats who acknowledges that 'masterful images' shaped by the mind amounted to little more than 'refuse or the sweepings of a street'; that 'the soul cannot take until her master gives'; or that as a solitary man of fifty, he could sit in a London café and contemplate a street until in ecstasy he 'was blessed and could bless'. How but in terms of the sacramental perspective can we explain the motive of an imagination, as featured in *Among School Children*, capable of repudiating the 'self-born' *images of desire*, that is, images revered by the same desire that created them in the first place: a nun's piety, a mother's affection or a lover's passion? Or an imagination able to embrace such archetypal and impersonal *images of vision* as the harmonious chestnut tree or the dancer that is inseparable from the dance? In short, the sacramental imagination habitually expresses itself as at once iconoclastic (concerning all images of desire) and utopian (concerning images of vision).

Perhaps the most representative example is to be found in the Byzantium poems. Byzantine art epitomized for Yeats a sacramental imagination based on the obedient imitation of a single Image – that of Christ and his Kingdom – before which the will and personality of the artist sacrificed itself: 'the work of many that seemed the work of one, that made building, picture, pattern, metal work of rail or lamp, seem but a single image' (*Selected Prose*, edited by A. Norman Jeffares [Macmillan 1964], p. 244). He described such art as a vision that proclaimed 'its invisible master', testifying to the conviction of an early, and still genuine, platonic Christianity that 'god's messengers ... who show His will in dreams or announce it in visionary speech, were *never* men' (*ibid.* p. 239). Yeats even insists that anyone today still capable of vision can recognise in the mosaics of Ravenna or Sicily the work of a sacramental imagination: an imagination dying unto itself in imitation of the Galilean whose 'assent to a full Divinity made possible this sinking in upon a supernatural splendour' (*ibid.* p. 245).

In the Holy City of Byzantium the artist *was* saint. There the sages 'standing in holy fire' could effectively serve as 'singing-masters' and thus transform 'the heart of desire' into the 'artifice of eternity'. The Song of Parnassus and Prayer of Galilee were reconciled here, for it was a privileged time and place – timeless and u-topic – combining Judaeo-Christian *holiness* with Greek *culture*. It was the place 'where religious and aesthetic life were one, as never before or since in recorded history' (*ibid.* p. 244). This qualifying admission is significant. It clearly foreshadows Yeats's final realization in *Byzantium* (1930) that the miraculous images of vision, which 'scorn ... all complexities of mire and blood', cannot in our time be reconciled with images of desire: 'those images that yet/Fresh images beget,/That dolphin-torn, that gong-tormented sea'. It was with a similar sense of reluctance that Yeats renounced, in his 1925 preface to *A Vision*, the sacramental ideal of a new age when 'men will no longer separate the ideal of God from that of human genius, human productivity in all its forms'. Such a beatific vision would have to remain merely a *vision*, a myth, a sacramental image for the sacramental poet. The time was not yet ripe for it to become a *reality*. Only in the refuge of a few visionary images could such a sacramental aspiration to reconcile our contrary instincts find asylum.

But we may ask – after Yeats, is it *there* that such a visionary aspiration must remain?

CHAPTER EIGHT

Joyce I: Questioning Narratives

Joyce responded to the crisis of modernity in a manner very different to Yeats and the Irish revivalists. Instead of seeking to transcend the fragmentation of modern consciousness by invoking a timeless mythic past, Joyce embraced the 'filthy modern tide' and resolved to create in its wake altogether different possibilities of experience. Whereas Yeats moved back towards a pre-modern culture, Joyce moved forward to a postmodern one. He opted for a radical rather than revivalist version of modernism; a version that revolted against traditional notions of both cultural identity and literary narrative.

Joyce had little patience with the revivalist dream of a unitary identity. He scorned the very idea of an Irish literary tradition (Anglo-Irish or Gaelic) and was particularly dismissive of the Celtic Twilight. As Yeats records in his account of their meeting in Dublin in 1902: 'He began to explain all his objections to everything I had ever done. Why had I concerned myself with politics, with folklore ... and so on? These were (for Joyce) all signs of the cooling of the iron, of the fading out of inspiration.' Joyce was even less charitable when he characterized Yeats and Gogarty elsewhere as the 'blacklegs of literature'. The revivalism of Douglas Hyde and the Gaelic league he found equally unattractive. He probably agreed with the young artist in *Stephen Hero* who remarked indignantly to his nationalist classmate, Madden: 'It seems to me you do not care what banality a man expresses so long as he expresses it in Irish.'

Unlike most of his Irish literary contemporaries Joyce did not champion the cause of an indigenous Revival. Stephen Dedalus seems to have been rehearsing Joyce's own sentiments when he declared in *A Portrait* that he would no longer 'serve' that in which he no longer 'believed', whether it call itself home, fatherland or church: 'You talk to me of nationality, language and religion. I shall try to fly by these nets.' These terms are, curiously, almost an exact paraphrase of those advanced by Patrick Pearse when he wrote: 'Patriotism is at once a faith and a service … and it is not sufficient to say "I believe" unless one can say also "I serve".'[1] Joyce's refusal of this kind of revivalist patriotism is also evident in his devastating parodies of the Fenian shibboleths of Owen Roe, Proud Spain, Dark Rosaleen and Earl Gerard's Steed etc. in the 'Citizen' episode of *Ulysses*. He would no doubt have sympathized with Stephen who, when asked if he would be remembered by Ireland, replied that Ireland would be remembered because of him! The Irish nationalist ideology, he maintained, was but a 'pale afterthought of Europe'. Even the 1916 uprising and subsequent establishment of the Irish Free State failed to impress Joyce as he made plain in refusing to carry a passport from what he called an 'Upstart Republic'. In short, Joyce resisted the various efforts of the Irish Revival, both literary and political, to reread history in terms of a *continuous* tradition. As Seamus Deane has observed: 'Yeats created an Anglo-Irish tradition out of Swift, Burke, Berkeley, Goldsmith. Pearse created a heroic revolutionary tradition out of Tone, Emmet, Mitchel, Lalor. Joyce created a tradition of repudiation. What was a principle of continuity to others was a principle of betrayal to Stephen Dedalus.'[2]

Instead of cultural revival, Joyce chose cultural revolt. He preferred to deconstruct rather than reconstruct the myth of a Unity of Culture. But if Joyce held no brief for 'Irishness' in the revivalist sense, he by no means turned his back on Ireland. While he felt oppressed by his nation as a resident, he was obsessed by it as an *émigré*. Like Wilde and Shaw before him, Joyce was no less sceptical of the allurements of imperial British culture than he was of national Irish culture. This resistance to all forms of cultural hegemony was best expressed at the level of *language*. While Joyce chose to use the English language, he did so as an alien, an iconoclast, a subversive. He worked inside the language as an outsider, forever mindful of the confusions, ambiguities and discontinuities that this language of empire – like most hegemonic languages of the European nation-states – sought to conceal in order to preserve the veneer of a pure homogeneous identity. English could never be his own as Stephen pointed out in his famous exchange with the English Dean of Studies in *A Portrait*: 'The language in which we are speaking is his before it is mine. How different are the words home, Christ, ale, master on his lips and mine! I cannot speak or write these words without unrest of spirit. His language, so familiar and so foreign, will always be for me an acquired speech. I have not made nor accepted its words. My voice holds them at bay. My soul frets in the shadow of his language.' It is primarily in this sense of linguistic dissidence that Joyce may be called an 'Irish' writer.

Joyce's writing rendered the English language self-reflexive and challenged its historic claim to a continuous literary tradition running from Chaucer and Milton to Fielding and Hardy. His linguistic restiveness was in itself a formal revolt against the presumed continuity of this august tradition (as evidenced in the 'Oxen of the Sun' episode in *Ulysses* when he parodies the 'artificial' nine-stage evolution of the English tradition of prose writing by contrasting it with the 'organic' nine-month evolution of Mrs Beaufoy-Purefoy's embryo).

Joyce's deconstructive approach to literary traditions was, however, motivated by other scruples besides that of the post-colonial rebel. He fully subscribed to the modernist motto of Eugene Jolas, his Paris friend and editor of the avant-garde literary journal *transition*, that 'the real metaphysical problem today is the word". He resolved accordingly to commit himself to what Jolas called the *revolution of the word*.[3] The very process and problem of writing would become Joyce's overriding concern.

For Joyce, language was that enigmatic medium which, as *Finnegans Wake* 'retales', first entered the world in the form of the biblical *Logos* and subsequently fell into non-meaning with the fall of Adam and Eve and the construction of the Tower of Babel. Indeed, Joyce declared to Frank Budgen, to write or read the *Wake* was to come to understand the story of Babel – that is, the genesis and evolution of the 'polygutteral' nature of language.

Finnegans Wake takes the form of a chronicle of human babbling. It is, in the author's own words, a 'collideorscape' of 'comparative accoustomology' which attests, by a play on language as *lapsus*, to the 'fallen' character of words. Joyce's language might be described accordingly as *lapsarian*, built as it is on lapses of pen and tongue, embodied in the legendary figures of falling – Humpty Dumpty who fell off the wall, Old Tim Finnegan who fell off the ladder, and of course Adam and Eve who fell out of paradise.[4] The transgression of the First Parents was a *felix culpa* not only because it ultimately enabled the Word to become flesh in the incarnation but also because it enabled the Word to become multiple, that is, to enter into *histoire* (in the dual sense of both history and story). The *Wake* reminds us that Adam was the one who invented naming by first saying 'goo to a goose', and that Eve, the instigator of the fall of language, is the 'grandmère of grammaires'. But modern European man, puffed up by his own sense of cultural purity or racial superiority, prefers to ignore the multilinguistic genesis of Western civilization; he does not want to think that 'his grandson's grandson will stammer up in Peruvian' or that 'his grandmother's grandmother coughed Russky in suchky husky accent (which) means I once was *otherwise*'. As the *Wake* makes plain, Joyce gave no quarter to ethnocentric imperialism with its smug refusal to accept that each society is composed of 'diversed tonguesed … antagonisms'. Behind the postures of imperial *consensus* Joyce's writings expose a cultural *conflict* expressive of the underlying polyvalence of language itself.

Writing thus became for Joyce a sort of semiotic psychoanalysis of the repressed genesis of Western culture. In the *Wake* he proposes to 'psoakoonaloose' the multi-voiced unconscious of language, to trace the original sin of the Word back to its fall from univocal meaning into a medley of different equivocal languages. This linguistic fall gave rise to what Joyce calls the 'law of the Jungerl' – a verbal play on the triple connotation of *jungle* (the aboriginal chaos from which modernity has sprung), *Jung* (a founder of the psychoanalytic method of exploring the unconscious through wordplay, symbol and myth) and *young girl* (Anna Livia's young daughter, Issy, who promises to reveal the secret formula of creation in the 'nightlessons' of the *Wake*). By composing a language that discloses this unconscious 'law of the jungerl', Joyce dismantles the conventional notion of narrative as a transparent representation of some univocal mental message. Against this representational model of language as mere instrument of the author's conscious intentions, the Joycean text shows – some fifty years before Lacan and the post-structuralists – how language is 1) structured like the unconscious, and 2) operates according to a deeper and more complex logic that allows for at least 'two thinks at a time'. Joyce called this the logic of 'nighttime consciousness' in contrast to the 'daytime consciousness' of formal logic based on the laws of identity and non-contradiction (see epilogue 'Joyce and Derrida: Jewgreek is Greekjew'). By exposing the unconscious structure of language as an interplay of 'intermisunderstanding' minds – where *I* becomes *other* – Joyce defied the classic myth of narrative as a one-dimensional communication of some fixed predetermined meaning. Consequently, his mischievous definition of the *Wake* as 'crums of trektalk' and 'messes of mottage and quashed quotatoes' should not be read as a biographical allusion to Nora Joyce's cuisine but as a comment on the pluralizing codes of language itself. Indeed Joyce's text provides an excellent illustration of Mikhail Bakhtin's notion of the 'dialogical imagination' as a carnivalesque rupturing and dispersal of the official norms of narration.[5]

Finnegans Wake is a self-deconstructing narrative that reveals language to be an infinite interplay of meanings, a 'bringer of plurabilities' that serves as matrix of all human culture. 'In writing of the night,' as Joyce explained, 'I felt I could not use words in their ordinary relations and connections. Used that way, they do not express how things are in the night, in the different stages – conscious, then semi-conscious, then unconscious.' And this is why the *Wake* is a book where 'the forms prolong and multiply themselves, where the visions pass from the trivial to the apocalyptic, where the brain uses the roots of vocables to make others from them which will be capable of naming its phantasms, its allegories, its allusions.'[6] Suspending the established relation between author and text and, by extension, author and reader, Joyce refuses the accredited autonomy of narrative and demonstrates its inextricable dependence on *language*. The reader of *Finnegans Wake* is compelled to acknowledge this work as 'writing which is calling attention to its written nature'.[7]

Joyce's debunking of the classical conventions of narrative did not confine itself, however, to *Finnegans Wake*. It was already under way in *A Portrait* and *Ulysses*.

When *Ulysses* was published in 1922 it seemed to many writers of the time that the resources of the traditional novel had been exhausted. D.H. Lawrence and Virginia Woolf declared it a literary scandal; F. Scott Fitzgerald offered to jump out of his hotel window to prove his admiration; and Hemingway hailed it as a 'goddam wonderful book'. No serious novelist could afford to ignore Joyce's revolt against the narrative form of the 'classical realist' novel.

From its emergence in the eighteenth century, the novel genre exhibited a specific structure of *quest*. This quest-structure was related to several dominant paradigms of modern European culture, in particular Cartesian idealism, bourgeois individualism and Reformational subjectivism. The quest-structure generally took the form of an individual subject's search for value in an alienated world. Its conventional theme was that of a journey from meaninglessness to meaning, from the insufficiency of the surrounding social environment to some new vision of things. The quest-structure thus presupposed the experience of a rupture between the internal imagination of the hero and the external reality that he is trying to explore or transcend. The novel of quest was characterized by a psychological preoccupation with the hero's solitary ego as it struggled with an alien world.

This quest-structure of the novel has been comprehensively analysed by such diverse critics as Lucien Goldmann, René Girard and George Lukács.[8] The bourgeois genre of the novel differs from the old genre of the epic, as Lukács explains in *Theory of the Novel*, in that it narrates a quest without the guaranteed resolution of a providential deity. The hero of the novel must invest meaning *ex nihilo*, drawing exclusively from the resources of his own subjective desire, for meaning has fled from the modern world and can no longer be expected as a miraculous gift from the gods. Hence the recurring theme of the great 'classical realist' novels: the attempt by an isolated human consciousness to provide a narrative coherence for its fragmented existence in a society devoid of value. The quest-structure operates on the basis of a radical discrepancy between the subjective desire of the hero and the objective reality of the historical world: a discrepancy between 'essence' and 'life' (to borrow Lukács' terms) that the narrative fails to overcome except as a *subjective project*. The contemporary Czech novelist, Milan Kundera, provides the following useful account of the development of the modern novel from Richardson's discovery of confessional narrative in the eighteenth century to Joyce's dissolution of such narrative in our own century:

> Richardson launched the novel on the path of the exploration of the interior life of man ... What is the self? How can the self be grasped? This is the fundamental question on which the novel as such is based. By the different responses to this question one can distinguish different tendencies and periods in the history of the novel ... But (with Joyce) the quest for the self finishes in a paradox: under the great Joycean lens which decomposes the soul into atoms, each one of us resembles everyone else.[9]

We may say, accordingly, that Joyce deconstructs the quest-structure of the novel by dissolving its *egological* constituents (i.e. the subjective ego of the author and his fictional characters) into an *ecological* system (i.e. the unconscious structures of the text as a language process). In other words, the Joycean transition from 'classical' to 'critical' forms of narrative is characterized by a surpassing of the ecology of the bourgeois novel, typified by the narrator's psychological exploration of himself and his world, towards an ecology where the language system assimilates the narrator's subjective consciousness to itself. Consequently, 'plot and theme, those elements which produce the story, are to be subdued, even abolished and replaced by language. Even though language will inevitably carry the traces of these story patterns, it will not allow them to dominate.'[10]

Joyce's first novel, *A Portrait of the Artist as a Young Man* is, as the self-reflexive title suggests, a parody of the quest-structure of the traditional bourgeois novel. Stephen is the alienated artist in search of beauty in a hostile world. He defines beauty in terms of the meta-physical triad of *integritas/consonantia/claritas* and pretentiously affirms the transcendental and quasi-divine status of art. Stephen aspires towards the condition of a Platonic demiurge who might transmute the dross of his surrounding reality in the 'silver womb of the imagination'. Like the 'fabulous artificer' he is named after, Dedalus seeks to forge the conscience of his race in the smithy of his own soul (in Greek mythology Dedalus was said to have invented the instruments of sculpture and forgery, which enabled him to imitate the gods by creating human-like figures from amorphous matter).

In order to recreate each other as 'artistic' father and son, Bloom and Stephen believe it necessary to abandon *memory* – that 'agenbite of inwit' that binds them to the procreative principles of history. It is Stephen's guilt-ridden memory that keeps him chained to Church, nation and family, just as it is Bloom's paranoid memory that feeds his obsession with an unfaithful wife and deceased son. Stephen and Bloom seek to bypass the oppressive 'mothers of memory' towards the liberating power of creative imagination. Through an art that transcends history, through an imagination that creates *ex nihilo*, they aspire to a transcendental condition of consubstantiality.

In similar fashion, Stephen is trying to move beyond the constraints of historical filiality towards an aesthetic principle of creation. Stephen has abandoned his allegiance both to his natural father and to his natural mother, whose death-bed request for prayers he rejected. But this refusal of his inherited filial condition is most vividly manifest in his repeated efforts to evade the threatening 'mothers of memory'. Thus in the opening chapters of *Ulysses*, Joyce portrays Stephen attempting to escape his oppressive matriarchal origins, as he seeks to awaken from the 'nightmare of history', which he identifies with the three mother-figures of the determining past: mother-nature (his biological mother); mother-church (the Virgin mother); and mother-Ireland (the Sean-Bhean-Bhocht Milk-woman or Cathleen Ni Houlihan, variously derided as an 'Old Gummy Granny' or a 'sow that eats her own farrow'). Joyce reinforces this son-versus-mother structure by means of a clever introductory *leitmotif* of omphalic signifiers: the shaving-bowl, sacrificial bowl, vomiting bowl, the bowl of Dublin bay, the hollow tower, etc. The suggestion seems to be that before Stephen can embark upon his journey toward a metaphysical father he must first transcend his bonds to the historical mothers of memory (a suggestion reinforced by Buck Mulligan's description of Stephen as 'Japhet in search of a father').

Both Bloom and Stephen, then, construe art as an 'eternal spirit' that promises to unite father and son in a new communion, one that transcends the oppressive transience of history and the sexual-maternal cycles of nature. Louis Gillet, Joyce's Parisian friend, confirmed the centrality of this theme in the Joycean aesthetic when he declared in 1949 that 'the problem of paternity ... is the essential basis of the Joyce problem'.[11] But it is Haines, in the very first chapter of *Ulysses*, who already provides us with the key to this narrative paradigm: 'the father and the son ideal. The son striving to be atoned with the father.' Stephen and Bloom. Telemachus and Ulysses. Prince Hamlet and King Hamlet. Christ the Son and God the Father.

This quest to discover in art a supra-historical rapport between father and son finds most explicit expression in the celebrated scene in the National Library (chapter 9). Here the trajectories of Stephen and Bloom briefly converge. Stephen poses the problem of how Shakespeare sought to recreate himself by 'writing and reading the book of himself'. Just as God was the original artist who 'wrote the folio of this world', so too Shakespeare/Hamlet sought to become a divine artist by creating an artistic world in which he could find 'as actual what was within his world as possible'. Thus Stephen demonstrates that the Godlike artist compounded of father and son and ghost is 'all in all, the father of his own grandfather' – and of everyone else, but most importantly, 'himself his own father' (i.e. a self-creation from nothing). But Stephen's seeking becomes self-conscious and ultimately self-parodying. Thus while Joyce ostensibly conforms to the quest-structure of the traditional novel to the extent that it recounts the efforts of a heroic imagination to redeem the degraded world from which it is severed, he is in fact subtly mocking this very project. Stephen's romantic desire to become an 'eternal priest of the imagination' who will transform the squalor of history into art, is treated ironically by Joyce. The 'sluggish matter of the earth' proves refractory to Dedalus' alchemical designs. As his friend Lynch exclaims: 'What do you mean by prating about beauty in this miserable god-forsaken land?'

Already in *A Portrait* we witness Joyce's modernist strategy of making writing reflect upon its own condition of possibility. Fiction becomes meta-fiction. Joyce the artist-author writes about himself as the artist-hero, Stephen, who in turn writes about himself as the artist-*manqué* (e.g. Stephen's confessional portrayal of himself in his introspective journal and 'dewy-wet' doggerel). Moreover, the artist's self-portrait as a Byronic pedant citing Aquinas and Newman in support of his own Romantic aesthetic further accentuates this sense of the narrative as critical self-reflexivity. In *A Portrait* the text as a closed product to be passively consumed by the reader is already being replaced by a text that represents itself as an open-ended process in which the reader may actively participate. And in this modernist impulse towards critical self-representation we find the *novel of quest* being subverted by the *novel of question* – or to be more precise, of *self-questioning*.[12]

If the *Portrait* ends with Stephen invoking the assistance of his mythic name-sake Dedalus – 'old father, old artificer' – in *Ulysses* the narrative quest of the 'artist' son (Stephen) for his 'artificer' father (Bloom) is brought to its absurd conclusion. It is significant that Stephen and Bloom journey towards each other in search of an *aesthetic* father-son relationship, rather than a *real* one. History has let them down, so they look towards art for their salvation.

Bloom's 'real' son, Rudy, died as soon as he entered life and his wife, Molly, is unfaithful. His alimentary condition (Joyce makes much of his corporeal infe-licities, in chapters 5, 6 and 7) is as poor as his sexual condition (he is a cuckold 'adorer of the adultress rump') and his social condition (a Jew in anti-Semitic Dublin). In brief, Bloom feels himself a failure in reality and so seeks to recreate himself in the artifice of eternity. Time and again Bloom fantasises about himself as a great prophet-artist. He inscribes the words 'I am A' on the Dollymount sand – a cryptic cabalist formula that may signify Artist, Alpha, Adonai, Abba (*Heb.* Father) or I Am who Am (Yahweh). Bloom uses fantasy to free himself from the 'accumulation of the past'. As Lenihan says of him: 'There's a touch of the artist about old Bloom.' In short, Bloom strives to relinquish his temporal familial bonds – both to his wife, Molly, and to his dead but remembered son, Rudy – in order to achieve an aesthetic 'atonement' with an 'eternal son'.

But the hope for such an aesthetic communion is exposed as illusory in the final 'Ithaca' chapter. Here Stephen-Telemachus and Bloom-Ulysses reach their journey's end (Eccles St/Itacha), only to find it is a *cul de sac*. This episode is presumably intended to demonstrate the impossibility of communication between Stephen and Bloom. The sheer encyclopaedic abstruseness of their dialogue – what Joyce referred to as the 'dry rocks' of 'mathematical catechism' – belies the dream of an exclusively aesthetic alliance. The auto-creative imagi-nation proves to be sterile, devoid of all genuine creativity, all intimacy and life. And so memory reasserts itself at last when the early morning chimes of St George's bell make Stephen remember the mother he thought himself rid of and make Bloom recall the dead. The 'Ithaca' chapter concludes with an acknowledgment of the futility of any artistic creation that seeks to censure the nightmare of history. The point seems to be that imagination must incorporate memory, opening itself to the fluxile temporality of history as it does in Molly's final soliloquy. Bloom reaches towards such an intuition, accepting his past in a spirit of equanimity: 'If it was it was. He bore no hate.' He curls up at Molly's feet, a 'childman weary, the man-child in the womb'. Stephen too ultimately assents to the reality of history he had previously scorned; he agrees to meet Molly, to trust in what 'he must come to ineluctably'. Stephen and Bloom cannot commune without Molly. She is the life-giving flesh to the skeleton of Ithaca. As Joyce himself put it in a letter to Valéry Larbaud: 'Ithaca is alien, Penelope the last word'. The world of creation cannot ignore the world of procreation. Art that excludes history cuts its own throat.[13]

In Molly's soliloquy the fertile chaos of everyday historical time coincides with the structuring principle of art. Joyce resists the temptation to reduce Molly to some *Magna Mater* archetype who is all matter and no mind. Molly is both a procreator and a creator (she is a mother, a lover and an opera singer). Her stream-of-consciousness epilogue is a welling up of suppressed images from memory *and* an aesthetic shaping of a new vision of things. It exemplifies how language may be liberated from a closed 'egological' narrative into an open 'ecological' system of textual play – one where conscious *imagination*, which leads beyond history, and unconscious *memory*, which leads back to history, become one and the same.

By thus conjoining the aesthetic principle of imagination and the reality principle of history, Joyce dismantles the linearity of the search-structure so indispensable to the traditional novel. Molly's mind moves in circles; it allows for no journey from one point to another. Her epilogue is therefore a sort of anti-novel. For once the two poles of the journey – the subjective pole of the ordering imagination and the objective pole of disordering reality – are superimposed, the novel would appear to forfeit its very *raison d'être*. It is exposed as *writing*: the textual play of language as an open-ended process of signification.

Joyce differs principally from Yeats in his belief that the dualistic opposition between creative desire and recreative memory can be overcome. This entails for Joyce a dismantling of both the traditional quest structure of narrative desire and the traditional constraints of oppressive memory – including the monolith of tradition itself. Thus while Yeats conceived of memory as a sacramental refuge from history, a Great Tradition of timeless myths restoring the dream of a lost Unity of Culture, Joyce redefines memory as a 'nightmare of history' – something to be interrogated and creatively explored so as to open up new possibilities of historical meaning. For Yeats memory offers the promise of cultural *identity* based on the retrieval of tradition; for Joyce it opens the possibility of cultural *difference*, of being always *otherwise*. Cathleen Ni Houlihan, the matriarch of national unity, is supplanted by Molly and Anna Livia, 'bringers of plurabilities'.

Appendix: Joyce and Derrida: Jewgreek is Greekjew

In *Writing and Difference*, Jacques Derrida offers the following comment on *Ulysses*: 'Are we Jews? Are we Greeks? We reside in the difference between Jew and Greek, which is perhaps the unity of what we call history ... What is the legitimacy or the meaning of (Joyce's) proposition – "*Jewgreek is Greekjew. Extremes meet*"?' In a footnote, Derrida elaborates: 'In constructing Bloom and Stephen (Jew-Greek), Joyce showed great interest in the thesis of Victor Bérard who saw Ulysses as a semite ... Furthermore, this proposition is attributed to feminine logic: "Woman's reason. Jewgreek is greekjew".'[14]

Derrida is suggesting here that Joyce's *Ulysses* is a narrative replay of the historical relationship between the two primary cultural movements that make up modern Western civilisation: *Greek metaphysics* (represented by the Aristotelian Stephen), and *Biblical messianism* (represented by the semitic-prophetic Bloom). Both cultures have remained dualistically opposed in Western history to the extent that they propounded rival 'logocentric' systems which excluded the mediating principle of 'woman's reason' (represented by Molly).

In the light of Derrida's hypothesis, let us briefly isolate and re-examine some of the philosophical implications of our preceding analysis. Bloom, the surrogate Hebraic father, sought 'atonement' with Stephen, the surrogate Hellenic son, through the holy ghost of an aesthetic discourse totally devoid of feminine creativity or procreativity. Quite appropriately, Stephen formulates his version of atonement with the eternal father, transcending the sexual-maternal chains of nature, in the idiom of Greek metaphysics. Already in *A Portrait* Stephen had coveted art's 'silver womb of the imagination' capable of dispensing with the corporeal womb of maternity, by creating quasi-mystical images of *consonantia, integritas* and *claritas*. It is not insignificant that Stephen's theory of aesthetic epiphany is derived here from Thomistic metaphysics. Thomas Aquinas originally advanced this triadic definition of beauty to account for the spiritual rapport of *similitudo* or consubstantiality between God the Son and God the Father.[15] In *Ulysses* Stephen frequently invokes the teaching of 'the bulldog of Aquin' and prides himself on reading his 'gorbellied works ... in the original'. Stephen's meditations on the Aristotelian-Thomistic model of a self-creating, self-thinking *Logos* beyond time, history and matter (the mothers of memory) reach their most conspicuous expression in the National Library scene. Here Stephen employs the model of metaphysical paternity to explain how Shakespeare essayed to recreate himself out of himself, in emulation of the divine *creatio ex nihilo*, by 'writing and reading the book of himself' – *Hamlet*. Thus, as we noted, the god-like artist assumes the metaphysical status of a self-identical trinity (*Ens Causi Sui*), becoming 'all in all the father of his own grandfather ... himself his own father ... It is a mystical estate, an apostolic succession, from only begetter to only begotten.' This idea of a patriarchal *Logos* in silent dialogue with itself through its exclusive self-creation as divine son, recurs in the 'Circe' episode when Stephen muses: 'What went forth to the ends of the world to traverse not itself. God, the Sun, Shakespeare, a commercial traveller, having itself traversed in reality itself, becomes that self.' It is in this context that we must interpret Stephen's search in the 'Proteus' chapter for the secret 'signature of things' (Boehme) and the 'form of forms' (Aristotle/Aquinas) which will serve as the divine-artistic Word of creation. (See the Dalkey meditation in chapter 3 of *Ulysses*).

This self-deconstructive language of substitution is epitomized by Molly's 'woman's reason'. In contrast to the logocentric principles of identity and non-contradiction (the traditional logic of *either/or*), Molly advances a deconstructive logic which allows for 'two thinks at a time'. Opposites are no longer dualistically opposed, as in the paternal code, but are subversively played off against one another until the opposition is undone. 'Jewgreek is greekjew': this ambivalence is accessible to the traditionally repressed 'woman's reason' (as we see in Molly's final soliloquy); but, it is incompatible with the phallogocentric fiction of self-presence coveted by Bloom and Stephen.

The projected atonement between the Hebraic father and the Hellenic son is, as we noted, humorously dismantled in the incomprehensible dialogue of 'Ithaca'. And it is certainly a clear reminder that the silver womb of the exclusively male imagination begets not a divine *creatio ex nihilo* but a *nihil ex creatione*: a slow slump into intellectual nothingness. By contrast, Molly's concluding 'anamnetic' soliloquy recollects the fragmented events of the day; her stream of consciousness serves as a 'chapter of accidents' which synchronizes the contrary and irreconcilable claims of Greek and Jew, of father and son. Stephen implicitly subscribes to Molly's 'woman's reason' by accepting 'what he must come to ineluctably' (i.e. history is transformed from a curse to the condition of existence); while Bloom explicitly acknowledges it when he faces up to his past history of betrayal and persecution, in a spirit 'less of envy than equanimity'. In short, Bloom the 'jewgreek' can only hope to be atoned with Stephen, 'the greekjew', through the historically mediating consciousness of Molly who is *both* a creator faithful to her imaginative vocation as chanteuse *and* a procreator (mother, wife and lover) devoted to the everyday claims of history. Her affirmative 'yes' transcends the nihilistic theology of father and son.

In *Finnegans Wake* the *both/and* logic of 'woman's reason' re-emerges in the equally equivocating language of Anna Livia Plurabelle. In this 'mistresspiece' Joyce leaves us in little doubt as to where his intellectual and linguistic sympathies lie: 'In the name of Annah the Allmaziful, the Everliving, the Bringer of Pluralities, haloed be her eve, her singtime sung, her rill be run, unhemmed as it is in heaven'. Anna's language ruptures the logocentric principles of *identity* (a is a), *non-contradiction* (a is not non a), *excluded middle* (truth is either a or b, but not both at once) and *linear causality* (a causes b). ALP reverses the traditional censure of the polyvalence of language. His word-play debunks the fallacy that language could ever be a 'pure dialect of the tribe', a vehicle for transmitting some unalloyed cultural or racial identity. It disinherits the patrimony of the word. This 'woman's reason' is what Derrida calls 'undecidability', adding that if a meaning is *both/and* it is also *neither/nor*. Once the accredited world of *either/or* is disrupted, new possibilities of meaning emerge from the irresolvable indeterminacies and unforeseen diversities of language. Beyond, or behind, the secure veneer of binary opposition, there resides a world of 'excluded middles' revealing 'another mode of meaning beyond the obvious one' (as Tom Pynchon remarks in *The Crying of Lot 49*). And this undecidable play of meaning is what *Finnegans Wake* aptly nominates as the interface 'between twosome twiminds'.

Finnegans Wake thus testifies to the fall of the metaphysical and biblical *Logos* into the babel of history. It is a 'mamafesta' which retells how Anna (the Celtic mother-goddess who reconciles the father-god, Mananaan, and the son-god Aengus Og) and Eve (the temptress who first challenged patriarchal self-sufficiency and self-presence) inaugurated the history of human creation and procreation. As such, Anna and Eve have become identified in Western consciousness with the subconscious and suppressed depths of language. Joyce seems to be saying that it is only by attending to this *other* language which subtends our logocentric culture – the 'nighttime' language of the *Wake* which sabotages 'the wideawake language of cut and dry grammar and go-ahead plot' – that we can become aware of the polyphonic legacy of 'woman's reason'.

This metaphysical relationship of *identity* between father and son is what Derrida calls *logocentrism*. Western metaphysics is fundamentally logocentric, Derrida explains, because it is founded on the ideal of a perfect self-immediacy which the Greeks called the *Logos* or the

Arche. From these founding notions the cardinal metaphysical terms of reason, logic and transcendent intellect were derived. Because the *Logos* was thought to reside beyond historical time and matter, and by extension beyond the so-called 'feminine' principles of desire and procreation, the logocentric era of the West, dating from Plato and Aristotle to the present, is also characterised by Derrida as '*phallogocentric*'. Consequently, the Platonic *Logos* became synonymous with an all-male self-referential relationship between father and son. As Derrida observes in *Dissemination*: 'The absolute invisibility of the origin of the visible, of the God-Sun-Father, Platonism, is the general rehearsal of this family scene and the most powerful effort ... to conceal it by drawing the curtains over the dawning of the West.'[16] Thus, for example, when the Stranger in Plato's *Theaetetus* (241–2) 'dares to lay unfilial hands on the paternal pronouncement' of the *Logos* (*toi patrikoi logoi*), he is accused of parricide.

Platonic metaphysics defined the paternal *Logos* as a 'silent dialogue of the soul with itself'; and it deemed language and writing to be an adulteration of this original self-presence. Accordingly, in the *Phaedrus*, Plato condemned writing because it acted as an intermediary detour of inscription which interrupted the dialogue of Father with Son, i.e. because it 'claimed to do without the Father of *Logos*'.[17] In short, once language is written and thus recollected and recorded, it no longer requires the unmediated speaking presence of the paternal *Logos*. Writing disrupts the *Logos* because it breaks from the original self-identity of the father and assumes a life of its own, an existence *other than the father*. The language of writing, as Derrida concludes, is the 'father's other', it 'cannot be assigned a fixed spot ... sly, slippery and masked ... a joker, a floating signifier, a wild card (which) puts play into play'.[18] This 'floating indetermination' and 'unstable ambivalence' which characterises the written form of language, deconstructs the paternal *Logos* of identity by permitting the play of *substitution*, i.e. the play of a re-presentation standing in for self-presence, of the derived replacing the original, the mediated replacing the immediate, the temporal replacing the eternal, the different replacing the same.

By dispensing with all quotation marks or 'perverted commas' in the *Wake*, Joyce shattered the illusion of the author as some extra-linguistic identity. In similar fashion, he demonstrated that language is not derived from some original, prelapsarian Word, but from compound multivocal 'thunderwords' made up from a wide variety of tongues. *Finnegans Wake*, as noted, proposes to reveal the secret 'law of the Jungerl' (*Jung's* law of the synchronistic and non-causal order of the unconscious) enunciated in Issy's 'nighlessons' (Anna's *young-girl*).[19] The nighttime logic of Anna and Issy discloses language as a fecund interplay between different meanings. The discourse of 'woman's reason' invites us to experience language itself *as language* through the destruction of the conventional model of the word as a servile mirroring of some univocal, pre-existing presence (residing *a priori* in the mind, in reality or in some transcendental world of Ideas). As Colin McCabe points out in his deconstructionist reading of Joyce: 'Through its constant demonstration of the differences and absences with which language is constituted, writing allows a constant openness to the feminine. *Finnegans Wake* lets the unconscious speak by investigating the very act of writing, it tells us the mother's secrets ... it suggests that there is a totally different attitude to language which can be characterised as female.'[20]

Anna and Issy destroy the myth of the father's phallic omnipotence (Persse O'Reilly/HCE/Tim Finnegan). They do so by frustrating the father's efforts to narrate a centralising, linear story of identity ('to identifine the individuone'). ALP dismantles HCE's claim to be 'constantly the same and equal to himself'; she shows him to be a 'multiplicity of personalities'. Anna is a 'site of salvoceon' for she permits the voices of feminine desire to speak and thus liberates language into its differing discourses. She thereby redeems not only herself and Issy from patriarchal dominance, but also her guilt-ridden husband (we are told 'she made him able') and her schizophrenic sons, Shem and Shaun.

The quasi-divine father of *Ulysses* inscribing 'I am A' in the sand has become in the *Wake* 'mushame' (myself, mise-same, my shame).[21] Shaun is portrayed as a Christ-like son who 'usupps' the paternal word by falling into the Liffey in a barrel, thus reducing his eschatological father to a scatological 'popodownapapa'. This passage ends significantly with the verbal deconstruction of the son's prayer to the omnipotent father; 'ah, mean' (Amen, Ah men, I mean). Shem and Shaun, the wielders of the authorial literary pen and of authoritative legal power respectively, attempt to take over the patriarchal *Logos* – by becoming 'two in one': an interchangeable, self-identical *Ens Causa Sui*. Because he admits to 'talking to myself' and to being 'me atar's ego in miniature', the judge accuses Shaun of homosexual narcissism: 'You have homosexual cathesis of empathy between narcissism of the expert and stetopygic invertedness. Get yourself psychoanalysed!' Moreover, the fact that Shem and Shaun metamorphose into Cain and Abel, Adam's sons, further highlights the Joycean critique of the established models of patriarchy.[22] In this way, the *Wake* rehearses the age-old 'family scene' of parricide which Derrida traced back to the Platonic metaphysics of language.

But if Shem and Shaun are to accede to the logocentric throne, they must first steal the secret letters of ALP; they must incestuously violate the mother's word, for she is that 'New Tree Woman with novel inside'. The salvation she offers is not that of a return to some prelinguistic presence but of an endless cycle of resurrection through language, through words 'returnally reproductive of themselves'. In the concluding pages of the *Wake*, Anna recovers her own voice; she celebrates her 'golden wending' with HCE, not by dying into his fiction of paternal identity, but by rejuvenating herself as the river of Life – the Liffey – flowing back to the sea only to recur again in her 'rain/reign'. This cyclical return of the prodigal mother disrupts the conventions of literary architectonics, founded on the illusion of a centering, authorial *arche*, and replaces it with an-archic, ex-centric discourse. Anna's repetitive word-flux reminds us that life, like language, can never end, can never even 'start to finish'. The logocentric promise to possess an original arche or final *telos*, outside of the fallen language of time, history and female desire, is indefinitely deferred. And as a result, the very notion of hierarchy – be it patriarchy or indeed matriarchy – is debunked. As Anna declares with stoic but prophetic calm: 'We'll *lave* it so' (meaning both we'll leave it so and we'll resolve the guilt so, lave is also a poetic term for to wash or cleanse).

There can be no definitive conclusion to the *Wake*. It can only end as it begins, in its own endless wake. Redemption for human kind, Joyce suggests, must be sought by embracing, not eschewing, the temporal recurrences and differences of language itself; it must be sought in the woman's word uttered by the washerwomen: 'talk save us!'

It is no accident, finally, that *Finnegans Wake* is largely written about the city of 'doublin' and presents itself as a self-confessed forgery or fake – an 'epical forged cheque' whose 'last word is stollentelling'. The *Wake* teaches us that history is not derived from some preorginal identity which precedes language, but is a multilayered story (the French have the same word, *histoire*, for both history and story), a palimpsest of ever-repeatable textual erasures and revisions. Thus history is revealed to be a text of language; not some linear, causal teleology, but a 'circumbendibus' which, like Vico's road, 'goes round and round to end where time begins'. As Maud Ellmann remarked: 'origin exists only in the wake of its own betrayal … Here instead of presence is a wake: a prelude, a waking – or a wake, an aftermath … The *Wake* is never to be present, but is always *coming into*, or *dying out* of being … The word is literally made flesh: the flesh made literal.'[23]

Joyce gave expression to his anti-phallocentric sentiments when he defended Ibsen's feminist writings to Arthur Power: 'You ignore the spirit which animated him. The purpose of the *Dolls House*, for instance, was the emancipation of women, which has caused the greatest revolution in our time in the most important relationship there is – that between men and women; the revolt of women against the idea that they are the mere instruments of men.' Joyce recognised that any genuine revolution in our socio-political or literary culture would have to begin with a deconstruction of the 'phallogocentric fallacy'. The fact that Joyce was himself a male writer did not in the least disqualify him from participating in such a critique. For one of the crucial tenets of 'woman's reason' is its ability to surpass the old metaphysical oppositions and to champion the creative coexistence of contraries and ambivalences: it knows that truth is *both* female *and* male, nighttime and daytime, Hellenic *and* Hebraic. And this implies in turn, as Derrida notes, that truth is *neither* one *nor* the other. As such, Joyce's 'woman's reason' does not seek to dissolve patriarchy into matriarchy but to unmask the kind of metaphysical thinking upon which such dualistic oppositions rest. As Joyce makes clear, Anna Livia Plurabelle, the 'bringer of plurabilities', is a chiasmus of opposites: 'Every person, place, and thing in the chaosmos of alle … moving and changing every part of the time'.

CHAPTER NINE

Joyce II:
A Tale of Two Cities – Rome and Trieste

'an Irish emigrant the wrong way out ... semisemitic
serendipitist ... Europeanised Afferyank'
Finnegans Wake, 190–1

Roland Barthes ushered in the structuralist era when he proclaimed that 'in narrative no one speaks'. This obituary of the author was soon followed by the elimination of historical time and place as referents for fictional narrative. The text became its own beginning and its own end: a floating island of signifiers. But the structuralist moritorium has, I believe, expired and we now find many of its casualties returning from their graves to reoccupy central, albeit modified, roles in contemporary criticism. In what follows I propose to read Joyce's conception of the father-son story of *Ulysses* in relation to its historical genesis in the author's *Lebenswelt* of Rome and Trieste in the formative exile years of 1906–7.

This reading presupposes a specific method of interpretation – a critical hermeneutics committed to the maxim that a literary work always involves 'someone saying something to someone about something'. Every discourse comprises a four-fold semantic dialectic between author (someone), text (something), reader (someone) and reference (that something about which the text speaks – namely, the time and place of a historical and fictional world). I take my cue here largely from Gadamer and Ricoeur; and in particular the latter's espousal of Freud, Marx and Nietzsche as three key masters of hermeneutic interpretation. Where Freud calls for a reading in terms of the 'unconscious workings' of author/reader, and Marx for a reading in terms of the socio-historical life-worlds of author/reader, Nietzsche reminds us that every literary work can be viewed in terms of the artist's will to self-invention.

During the structuralist purge, such 'relational' or 'referential' models of interpretation were dismissed as humanist or Romantic, but the new historicism and
the emergence of cultural studies has restored the hermeneutic hyphen between
text and world to its rightful place. The new hermeneutics – perhaps best represented by Ricoeur's *Time and Narrative* – argues that if it is indeed the case that
the text 'configures' a new world of meaning, it is also true that the author's
world 'prefigures' this text, and that both in turn serve to 'refigure' the reader's
world. The threefold mimetic cycle of figuration that each text entails reminds
us that the total eclipse of narrative reference is a mistake. Some form of reference, however 'split' or transposed into a second-order of meaning, continues to
operate in the circuit of text and action.

The return of time and place to our critical consideration of texts is
inevitable: a return of the repressed in new, revised and more robust forms,
enlightened and emboldened by the anti-humanist chastisment of structuralism
and other anti-referential methodologies. The reading of Joyce that follows is a
modest attempt to show how such an engaged hermeneutic might interpret at
least one of the subtexts of the greatest novel of the twentieth century, *Ulysses*.

I. Roma

'There is no doubt that *Ulysses* was conceived in Rome where Joyce was
employed as a clerk in the private bank of Nast-Kolb and Schumacher in the
Autumn of 1906.' So claims the great Italian commentator of Joyce, Giorgio
Melchiori, in his book *Joyce in Rome*.[1]

Melchiori bases his claim on the fact that the first mention of *Ulysses* comes
in a letter from Joyce to his brother Stanislaus, dated 13 November 1906. Joyce
writes: 'How do you like the name of the story about Hunter?' The story in
question is *Ulysses*, as Joyce makes clear in the same letter [*Letters* II, 190] and the
Hunter in question refers to a 'dark-complexioned Dublin Jew ... rumoured to
be a cuckold' whom Joyce had met twice in Dublin. Richard Ellmann relates
the following mémoire of one of these reputed meetings in his appendix to the
1968 Penguin edition of the novel: 'On the night of 22 June 1904 Joyce (not as
yet committed either to Nora or to monogamy) made overtures to a girl on the
street without realising, perhaps, that she had another companion. The official
escort came forward and left him, after a skirmish, with "black eye, sprained
wrist, sprained ankle, cut chin, cut hand". Next day Joyce lamented to a friend,
"For one role at least I seem unfit – that of man of honour." He did not mention
what in retrospect evidently became the most impressive aspect of the fracas: he
was dusted off and taken home by a man called Alfred Hunter in what he was
to call "orthodox Samaritan fashion". This was the Hunter about whom the
short story "Ulysses" was to be projected.'[2]

But why should Joyce have thought of writing about a scarcely remembered Dublin Jew, as he sojourned in Rome for seven months and seven days between 31 July 1906 and 7 March 1907? Why should he keep coming back to the story of Hunter in his letters to Stanislaus from Rome?

The first reason appears to be Joyce's fascination with the unfaithfulness of Hunter's wife. (In the same letter of 13 November where he mentions Hunter in relation to *Ulysses*, he is particularly obsessed about 'a Jewish divorce case on last week in Dublin' [*Letters* II, 189, 194].) Joyce himself, as is well known, was driven much of his life by jealous fantasies about Nora – which seemed to have spurred both his mimetic desire and his fictive imagination. These ranged from his jealousy of Michael Bodkin (Nora's childhood lover who died prematurely and was the source for Michael Furey in 'The Dead') and Vincent Cosgrave (whom Joyce suspected at one point of having an affair with Nora, behind his back, serving as a source for the Richard-Bertha-Robert triangle in *Exiles*), to the Trieste journalist acquaintance of Nora who drove Joyce to such fits of envy that he invited him into their home and befriended him. These repetitive obsessions find fictional expression in the 'French triangle' of Anne Hathaway and the brothers Shakespeare in the *Hamlet* discussion of *Ulysses*, as well as in Bloom's later invitation to Stephen to follow him home to Eccles Street and meet his adulterous wife, Molly.[3] The cuckoldry of Hunter certainly connected with something deep and furtive in Joyce's psyche. Were this not so, it would not have become the catalyst for the intended story to be titled 'Ulysses'. 'Although he did not get any farther than the title [while in Rome],' Chester Anderson remarks, Joyce 'kept the character in mind for a time when he could imagine himself cuckolded.'[4]

The second reason for this fascination with Hunter stems, I suggest, from Joyce's identification with the Jew-Greek wanderer in search of a home. This identification was accentuated by his feeling of being an intellectual outsider in the Catholic city of Rome – which itself recalled similar feelings of ostracization in his native Catholic city. His description of Dublin as the city where 'Christ and Caesar go hand in glove', applies as easily to Rome. One of the first things Joyce did upon his arrival in Rome was to visit the Roman forum and St Peter's basilica; shortly after which he wrote: 'Rome reminds me of a man who lives by exhibiting to travellers his grandmother's corpse' [*Letters*, 25 September 1906]. When a bomb was planted in St Peter's on 14 November, Joyce went to visit the church on the same afternoon. And he was also struck, during his stay in Rome, by the huge anticlerical procession in which he participated in honour of Giordano Bruno, burnt at the stake as a heretic in Campo de Fiori in 1600. Joyce was delighted by the phonetic resemblance between Bruno of Nola and the Dublin bookshop Brown and Nolans – a telling instance of his penchant for serendipitous echoes.

Melchiori has this to say about the religious nature of Joyce's identification with the Dublin Jew called Hunter:

In Rome, the centre of Christianity, the Jew was still an alien, in spite of the presence of a large and long-established Jewish community which had been, not long before, released from the confines of the ghetto ... at such a time the separateness of the middle-class Jews in a city permeated and shaped by centuries of Christian culture, civilisation and tradition, must have been particularly evident. And this must have called to mind the plight of the Jew in the other Catholic capital, Dublin.

Melchiori goes on to stress how Joyce's letters during this period draw many parallels between Rome and Dublin.

His daily experience helped out by the papers that he got into the habit of reading – the socialist daily *Avanti!* and the anticlerical satirical weekly *L'Asino* – underlined the condition of frustration that the intellectual outsider felt in either city. The dim memory of Mr Hunter came back to him because ... he recognised in that unremarkable figure moving through the streets of a provincial capital his own present condition as a friendless expatriate small bank clerk in a city whose very architecture celebrated the triumph of a religion he had rejected over an even more splendid past reduced to a state of utter disintegration.[5]

Moreover, Joyce's switch of identification from Christian son (Stephen Dedalus) to Jewish father (Hunter/Bloom) seems to have occurred during his Roman visit at a time when his paternal duties were painfully brought home to him as he struggled to find one accommodation after another for his wife and newly born son, Giorgio. 'Two years earlier he had seen himself as Stephen Dedalus; now that he was a small bank-clerk with a family, with a regular timetable, constantly wearing a tail-coat in order to cover the "two great patches on the seat" of his only pair of trousers, he had already begun to look at Stephen as at a former self.' Or as Carla de Petris puts it in 'Exiles and emigrants': 'Stephen Dedalus and Leopold Bloom, ... Joyce before and Joyce after his Roman exile.' She explains:

It was in Rome that Joyce found himself in the condition of an 'emigrant', instead of a 'voluntary exile'. Therefore Rome had for Joyce an emblematic existential value: instead of the seat of splendid exile, it was for him the shabby background of a humiliating and badly paid job. The striking contrast between reality and dream, everyday life and intellectual life, painfully marks Joyce's stay in Rome; and in fact in times of frustration and anguish Rome was to come back to his mind and memory as the place of struggle between humdrum life and utopia, between Life and Art.[6]

It is surely no coincidence that it was on the day he was ejected with Nora and Giorgio from their lodgings in Via Frattina, that he wrote to Stanislaus requesting more details of Mr Hunter!

Nor is it insignificant that it was in Rome that Joyce first read Guglielmo Ferrero's *Young Europe*, a book about emigrants with a concluding chapter on the Jews – 'this extraordinary race, deprived of fatherland, scattered and persecuted, which has always, obstinately, believed that it possessed the secret of the redemption of mankind'.[7] Joyce enthuses about his intellectual discovery in a letter to Stanislaus of 13 November, where he speaks of his empathy, *qua* Irishman in exile, with the emigrant condition of the Jew. Moreover, it was as a direct echo of Ferrero's final chapter, 'The confrontation between two races', that Joyce years later described *Ulysses* to Carlo Linati as 'the epic of two races: Israel-Ireland'. Indeed it has been argued that it was Ferrero's statement that 'propaganda is ... the greatest creation of the Jewish genius' that prompted Joyce to make Bloom a professional ad man – 'a canvasser of advertisements haunting the newspaper offices'.[8]

But there were other reasons, besides the religious and familial, for Joyce's identification with Hunter/Bloom in the Rome of 1906–7. Joyce's exposure to the political upheavals in Italy during this period recalled and rekindled his interest in the Irish political and literary situation: in particular the politics of dissent. Within a month of his arrival in Rome he had read Wilde's *The Picture of Dorian Gray* (in Italian) and George Moore's *The Lake*. He described himself as an 'intellectual striker' and called Irish writers like Yeats and Colum 'the black-legs of literature'. Joyce was greatly preoccupied by the riots in the Abbey Theatre at the performance of Synge's *Playboy of the Western World* (1–11 February), declaring himself too upset to work. He was also deeply marked by the death in Dublin, on 6 February, of Michael Cusack, founder of the Gaelic Athletic Association (and model for 'the Citizen' in part 12 of *Ulysses*). Dublin continued to haunt and obsess Joyce no matter how distant he was from her. Indeed, the farther he travelled from the city, the nearer she seemed to become.

But it was, arguably, a Dublin ghost of quite a different kind that was to revisit Joyce in his final hours in Rome. Having drunk himself silly probably every night for the last ten days of February, he was mugged on the eve of his departure from the eternal city. On 5 March 1907, after an evening in an *osteria*, he was beaten up and robbed in the street of the last salary and severance money he had collected from the bank.[9] This episode undoubtedly triggered traumatic memories of the above-mentioned incident suffered in Dublin, just three years earlier. This series of events provided the model for the key episode in the concluding sequence of *Ulysses* when Bloom rescues Stephen after his 'skirmish' in Nighttown and brings him back to his home. It also provided the model for the episode in *Exiles* where the young Archie asks his father, Richard Rowan, exiled in Rome for nine years: 'Are there robbers here like in Rome?' Repetition once again. The trivial things of history returning *après coup*. As if Joyce found himself living out in Rome the inchoate patterns of his Dublin pre-existence. Or as he'd put it in *Finnegans Wake*, 'there's no plagues like rome'.

Why the name Bloom? If it was indeed in Rome that Joyce recalled the episode with Hunter as catalyst for his book, what of the name he was to give him? In the midst of his many woes during that final February month in Rome, Joyce sought distraction in a comic opera entitled *Le Carnet du Diable* at the Teatro Nazionale. He reports this in a letter to Stanislaus, on 6 February, where he states that '*Ulysses* never got any forrader than the title' [*Letters* II, 209]. The libretto for that opera – dealing with a cheque-book given by the Devil to a modern Faustus – was by a man called Blum. Yet another example of Joycean epiphany – 'converting the bread of everyday life into something that has a permanent artistic life of its own'?[10]

II. Trieste

If *Ulysses* was conceived in Rome, it gestated in Trieste. It was after his return to Trieste, on 8 March 1907, to rejoin his job at the Berlitz school and the tutelary company of his brother Stanislaus, that Joyce would, in time, find the space and energy to commence writing his 'Jewgreek' book. As Joyce was to confess to Nora: '*la nostra bella Trieste* is the city which has sheltered us. I come back to it jaded and moneyless after my folly in Rome …' [*Letters* II, 249]. Not that Trieste was a heaven after the hell of Rome. Joyce continued to construe himself in the role of mugged and misfortunate outsider – 'poorjoist'. He caught rheumatic fever within months of his return and lost his job at the Berlitz school. Nora was pregnant again and was obliged to give birth to their second child, Lucia, in the pauper's ward of the city hospital, on 26 July 1907. Shortly after the birth they had to move into a cramped flat with adjoining rooms with the two children, beholden once again to Stanislaus for financial assistance.

If Rome had given Joyce nightmares of 'death, corpses, assassinations', Trieste offered him a new life but one that fell far short of beatific resurrection. Joyce was not yet beyond his transitional abyss, the trauma of the backstreet mugging still ghosting him like a bad memory that would not go away. He began to think more kindly of Dublin again, poring over the maps, photographs and histories of his native city, which he had asked his aunt Josephine to send him. *Ulysses* was still evolving embryonically and the identification with the outcast and despised father figure, Bloom, was taking on more flesh and bone.

Joyce was, of course, struck by several similarities between the Triestines and the Irish. Both were labouring under what they considered to be foreign rulers and were fired by an ideology of linguistic nationalism and irredentism. While Joyce never bought into this – in either its Triestine or Hibernian versions – he was nonetheless provoked by the passionate character of this identity quest. And no doubt this had some significant bearing on several episodes of the novel he was writing (in particular, the 'Wandering rocks' and 'Cyclops' chapters).

Just two months after his return to Trieste, Joyce wrote – in a letter dated 19 May – that the 'most powerful weapons that England can use against Ireland are ... those of Liberalism and Vaticanism'. Joyce's exposure to the ferment of Triestine, and more generally Italian, politics is revealed in the series of articles he wrote about Ireland for the Trieste newspaper *Il Piccolo*, between 1907 and 1912, beginning with the famous piece – 'The shadow of Parnell' – where he argued that the Chief was brought down by Gladstone and the Irish clergy, the infamous coalition of British and Vatican imperialism. Other pieces written on his native culture and politics in the immediate aftermath of his return to Trieste include 'James Mangan Ferguson', 'Ireland at the bar', 'Fenianism and Ireland', and 'Ireland, island of saints and sages', all penned in 1907, and three of them delivered as lectures at the Popular University of Trieste.

The first of the Trieste lectures took place on 27 April and was devoted to Irish cultural history. Richard Ellmann and Ellsworth Mason describe the context as follows:

> [Joyce's] Triestine audience was ... attracted by the Irredentist movement which wanted to oust the Austrians and return the city to Italy, but not wholly carried away by it. Joyce had no need to point up the parallel between Ireland and Trieste, both living under foreign domination, both claiming a language distinct from the conqueror's, both Catholic. But he felt compelled to point out that his country had its history of betrayals, of eloquent inactivity, of absurd and narrow belief. His attitude, though he calls it objective, wavers between affectionate fascination with Ireland and distrust of her.[11]

Joyce's opening references to the great diaspora of Irish missionaries between the sixth and ninth centuries were to crop up in several passages in *Ulysses*: 'You were going to do wonders, what? Missionary to Europe after fiery Columbanus'; 'Fiacre and Scotus on their creepystools in heaven split from their pintpots'. Quips at English imperialism abound in the 'Cyclops' episode – e.g. the attack on the German origin of the English royal family and the famous litany of English injustices in Ireland. Compare, among others, the following passage from the Trieste lecture: 'Ireland is poor because English laws ruined the country's industries, especially the wool industry, because the neglect of the English government in the years of the potato famine allowed the best of the population to die from hunger';[12] with this passage from *Ulysses* where the Citizen remarks: 'Where are our missing twenty millions of Irish who should be here today instead of four, our lost tribes? And our potteries and textiles, the finest in the whole world! And our wool that was sold in Rome in the time of Juvenal and our flax and our damask from the looms of Antrim and our Limerick lace.'

But if Joyce appears to anticipate several views advanced by the Citizen/ Cusack character in the 'Cyclops' episode of *Ulysses*, he also reinforces his identification with the wandering exiled Jew, Leopold Bloom. 'No one who has any self-respect stays in Ireland' – Joyce says after his recital of 'centuries of useless struggle and broken treaties' – 'but flees afar as though from a country that has undergone the visitation of an angered Jove'.[13] He also contrasts the sterling service given by the Irish to the building up of the British and American empires, with the total inability of Irish people to help each other at home – 'There must be something inimical, unpropitious and despotic in Ireland's own present conditions, since her sons cannot give their efforts to their own native land.' But such despotism, Joyce insists in this lecture, is not solely a matter of political colonization (what he calls the 'English tyranny'). It is also and more fundamentally a matter of spiritual paralysis – 'the Roman tyranny [which] occupies the palace of the soul'.

Joyce does not end, however, on this despondent note. Having redefined nationality as a hybrid construct that 'transcends … changing things like blood and the human word', he concludes his lecture by looking forward to a time when Ireland might rise from its ashes – a 'bilingual, republican … enterprising island' – and 'resume its ancient position as the Hellas of the north'. Such a view recalls Joyce's description of Irish civilization earlier in the lecture 'as a vast fabric in which the most diverse elements are mingled'. And it prefigures Bloom's inclusive and pragmatic definition of nationality, in his exchange with the Citizen, as 'the same people living in the same place'. If such a revival is to occur, Joyce believes it will not signal a simplistic return to the 'national soul that spoke during the centuries through the mouths of fabulous seers, wandering minstrels and Jacobite poets'. 'Ancient Ireland is dead,' says Joyce, 'just as ancient Egypt is dead.' What the new Ireland would be if it ever came to be, what 'other ideals' would animate its future generation of bards, Joyce does not say. He simply says that no Irish revival, national or otherwise, would occur unless Ireland were, once and for all, to overcome 'failure'. Anticipating the role played by the waking Molly in *Ulysses* and the resurrected Anna Livia Plurabelle in *Finnegans Wake*, Joyce writes: 'If she is truly capable of reviving, let her awake, or let her cover up her head and lie down decently in her grave forever.' And if the resurrection 'play' is to take on political form, it better hurry up, says Joyce, before it is too late. Not that it will effect him either way – for he, like Bloom, 'will have already gone home on the last train'.

One of the most significant things about Joyce's first Trieste lecture of 1907 is the transition it marks between the Gaelic-nationalist-Romantic vision of the Irish Revival movement (represented by Michael Cusack, founder of the GAA, who had died two months earlier) and the postnationalist perspective of the Irish as a hybrid, wandering people (represented by the outsider Bloom/Hunter). When Bloom is ejected from Kiernan's pub as a 'foreigner' at the end of his exchange with the Citizen – because he does not have an Irish name and does not belong to the Catholic religion – Joyce is clearly identifying with the exiled Jew who finds no room at the inn.

The 1907 lectures were not, however, the only ones delivered by Joyce at the Popular University of Trieste. Some six years later, Joyce would return with another series, this time on *Hamlet*. And while this might suggest a distancing of himself from his identification with the Jewish exile, Bloom, the most cursory glance at the National Library episode in *Ulysses*, where *Hamlet* is discussed and Stephen crosses Bloom's path, shows the contrary to be the case. The Shakespeare of *Hamlet* is for Joyce yet another name for Hunter/Bloom/Ulysses.

There are three main obsessions that Shakespeare and Joyce-Bloom share – *banishment, cuckoldry* and *paternity*. Just as Shakespeare, according to Stephen, has been 'banished' from Stratford and compelled to take up exile in London, so Bloom is the wandering Jew banished from his homeland and never quite at home in his adopted land (as the Citizen brutally reminds him). 'The note of banishment, banishment from the heart, banishment from home, sounds uninterruptedly,' says Stephen, throughout Shakespeare's work. As it does, one might add, throughout Joyce's own.

As to cuckoldry, if Shakespeare has been betrayed by his wife, Anne Hathaway, who slept with his brothers Richard and Edmund, so too Bloom had been cuckolded by Molly whose 'adulterous rump' has been offered to Blazes Boylan and others before him. In both cases, we are dealing with the famous theory of the 'French triangle' that dominates Stephen's reading of *Hamlet* in the National Library exchange. And it must not be forgotten that between Joyce's initial interest in the cuckolded Hunter during his stay in Rome and his *Hamlet* lectures in Trieste six years later, Joyce had returned to Dublin for a six week visit in July–August of 1909, where he was devasted by the gossipy claim of his old rival, Cosgrave, that he'd slept with Nora, back in 1904. Joyce believed the story, writing immediately to Nora in Trieste of his despair: 'O, Nora, Nora ... tonight I have learnt that the only thing I believe in was not loyal to me.' This letter was followed several days later by an admission of strange erotic fantasies, strikingly similar to those of Bloom: 'Tonight I have an idea madder than usual. I feel I would like to be flogged by you. I would like to see your eyes blazing with anger. I wonder is there some madness in me. Or is love madness? One moment I see you like a virgin or madonna, the next moment I see you shameless, insolent, half-naked and obscene.'[14]

In the *Hamlet* episode of *Ulysses*, Stephen refers to Shakespeare as the 'cuckold and bawd' who writes the story of his own hidden fantasies into the triangular plot of Ghost-Gertrude-Claudius, in which Hamlet finds himself enmeshed. If Shakespeare was driven by some strange fantasy of 'cuckold and bawd', so was Bloom; and so by all accounts was Joyce. Cosgrave's claim to have betrayed Joyce with Nora, as Chester Anderson comments, precipitated a serious crisis in Joyce's life. For just as he carried ambiguously in the pocket of his second-hand trousers the borrowed money to pay for his own betrayal, so, too, Joyce needed and feared cuckoldry … The fissure caused by this crisis of belief in himself went very deep and revealed sado-masochistic elements which he had not recognised clearly till now.

The only way beyond these fantasies of mimetic rivalry, desire, betrayal and cuckoldry was, it appears, the counter-fantasy of the 'androgynous angel' where, as Stephen puts it in the *Hamlet* sequence, glorified man becomes 'a wife unto himself'. Such a 'glorified' condition would also enable Joyce to escape the equally vicious circle of sacrificial scapegoating and persecution at the hands of his fellow countrymen (Joyce-Stephen is excluded from the literary soirée in the *Hamlet* sequence just as Joyce-Bloom is excluded from Kiernan's pub). Bloom is, of course, the epitome of such a male-female fantasy striving to transcend the cycle of triangular desire and sacrifice towards a condition of 'equanimity' rather than 'envy'.

A third feature that Joyce appears to share with the author of *Hamlet* is the obsession with *paternity*. The kernel of Joyce-Stephen's reading of the play is that Shakespeare identified not only with Hamlet the son but also with Hamlet's father. (Indeed, Shakespeare himself played the part of ghost-father.) Shakespeare wrote the play, we are told, in the months following his own father's death, at a time when he was struggling with the very meaning of paternity for himself as father of his own son, Hamnet. Accordingly, we find in *Ulysses* references to 'fatherhood' as a 'mystical estate', a 'necessary evil', a 'legal fiction' (since no father can be certain he is the father of his son), followed by the question: 'Who is the father of any son that any son should love him or he any son?' All father-hood, we are told, is experienced as a 'sundering' with the son, who in turn is condemned to rivalry and conflict: 'The son unborn mars beauty: born, he brings pain, divides affection, increases care. He is male: his growth is his father's decline, his youth his father's envy, his friend his father's enemy.' Hence the inge-nuity of the Catholic Church, which turned the disease of paternity into a purely spiritual 'apostolic succession' where 'the Father was Himself His Own Son'. The Trinity thus became a strategy to miraculously reconcile the conflict between father and son – so dramatically lived out in Hamlet's relationship to his ghost-father and stepfather (not to mention Joyce's relationship to his own real and symbolic fathers). Shakespeare's drama, according to Joyce-Stephen, is one great imaginative effort to convert the pain of paternity into fictional harmony. Divided between father and son, Shakespeare writes the play of himself in which the 'truth is midway' – namely: 'He is the ghost and the prince. He is all in all.'

The play is thus about Shakespeare's own transition from son to father – 'the boy of act one is the mature man of act five' – just as *Ulysses* is about Joyce's transition from Stephen to Bloom; a transition subtly witnessed in the speechless encounter between Stephen and Bloom in the library scene where Joyce finds himself 'midway' between both. (The 'Wandering rocks' title of this section clearly points to Ulysses' attempt to sail a middle course between Scylla and Charybdis). As Declan Kiberd observes: 'In *Ulysses*, Joyce is Stephen at the start and Bloom at the end ... The Artist, like God in the Trinity, is both father, son and ghost, creator of all including himself (or as Mulligan jokes, "himself his own father"). The whole trajectory of the book is to bring Stephen, a surrogate for the youthful Joyce, into harmony with Bloom, a version of the mature man, so that in this way Joyce can become his own father.'[15] In short, just as God created the play of Himself where he became 'the son consubstantial with the father ... He who Himself begot, middler the Holy Ghost', so too Shakespeare wrote the play of himself called *Hamlet*; and Joyce the book of himself called *Ulysses*.

Is it any wonder then that the narrative of Bloom and Stephen – usurped father and son in search of each other – begins with a reference to a 'theological interpretation' of *Hamlet* as 'the son striving to be atoned with the father', and ends with an image of the traveller at rest: 'manchild in the womb'? And is it any wonder, finally, that the memory of the migrant cuckold Jew, Hunter, which grabbed Joyce's imagination in 1906 in Rome, should have followed him to Trieste and remained with him through his many reveries, letters and university lectures, until it finally found its way onto the pages of *Ulysses*?

'We walk through ourselves,' Joyce-Stephen tells us in the *Hamlet* sequence, 'meeting robbers, ghosts, giants, old men, young men, wives, widows, brothers-in-love. But always meeting ourselves.' Joyce met his robbers on a backstreet in Rome, in repetition of the Dublin incident when Hunter came to the rescue. And he met ghosts in his lectures on *Hamlet*, presented at the University of Trieste. As for giants, old men, young men, wives, widows and brothers-in-love, he met them too during his sojourns in Rome and Trieste, as he did during his youthful years in Dublin. But that is another story.

Conclusion

Joyce rediscovered himself in the Italian cities of Rome and Trieste. He found there a mirror-image of many experiences and encounters he had known in Dublin but had been unable to properly acknowledge until he revisited them in another time and place. In particular, Joyce recollected in the mean streets of Rome the 'generosity' of a Dublin Jew called Hunter, who came to his rescue after a mugging in the streets of his native city. The reactivation of that epiphanic moment of chance kindness was accentuated, I have suggested, by Joyce's mugging in a Roman backlane – where no Hunter came to his rescue. Rome became a *via negativa* to bring Joyce home to Dublin. It turned Dublin into 'doubling' – a city redeemed through *repetition*, relived in exile and emigration, not as farce but as fiction.

Joyce was emboldened in his belief in creative repetition by his reading of the great Italian philosopher, Vico, whose theory of historical *ricorso* was to provide an intellectual scaffolding for his writings in exile. The fact that Vico's name echoed, in the writer's mind, the name of a road in County Dublin where Joyce loved to walk as a young man was, of course, irresistibly serendipitous. The fact that it was a ring road that went 'round and round to end where time begins' was a further felicitous confirmation that the aleatory is the essence of art.

But what Joyce discovered, above all, through his Italian *ricorso* in Rome and Trieste was the difficult lesson of humility. Reading Joyce's letters during that crucial transitional period of 1906–7, we witness him crossing the road from illusion to reality, from defiant filiality to ordinary fatherhood, from great expectations to humble recollections, gradually passing from the mind of Stephen Dedalus to that of Leopold Bloom, the wandering, cuckolded, mortified Jew. It was not just Joyce's severance pay that was robbed in the backstreets of Rome; it was his dream of romantic exile. Bereft of everything, he began all over again, to repeat himself, to recollect his scattered memories, to relive his life: to recreate himself in the story of himself.

The seed for *Ulysses* was planted in Joyce's mind in 1906–7. It was during those bitter days of exile in Rome and Trieste that Joyce began his portrait of the artist as an ageing man. It was then he learnt to 'wither unto truth'. And then that 'poorjoist' became one of the greatest writers of our century.

Chapter Ten

Joyce III: Epiphanies and Triangles

Epiphany was one of the most formative terms of Joyce's aesthetic. It originally derives from the Christian account of the divine manifesting itself to three Magi. What seems to have especially appealed to the young Joyce was the idea that it is through a singular and simple event – the birth of a child – that the sacred claimed to reveal itself to the world. Epiphany signals the traversal of the finite by the infinite, of the particular by the universal, of the mundane by the mystical, of time by eternity. It also signals the fact that truth is witnessed by strangers from afar (as the Gentile Magi were) and that this witness involves at least three perspectives or personas. For Joyce epiphany was to become an operative term in his aesthetics of everyday incarnation. Indeed one of his most moving lyrics went by the epiphanic title of 'Ecce Puer' and ended with the lines:

> Young life is breathed
> On the glass;
> The world that was not
> Comes to pass.
> A child is sleeping: An old man gone.
> O, Father forsaken,
> Forgive your son.

Given the pivotal role played by the father/son idea in *Ulysses* this is, as we shall see, no insignificant sentiment.

I. Epiphany Revisited

It was, by all accounts, in the Pola and Paris Notebooks of 1903 and 1904 that Joyce outlined his early understanding of epiphany. Although it is rumoured that

Joyce first heard the term from one of his Jesuit teachers, Father Darlington, it is probable that he really only developed his own interpretation of this idea as he worked through theories of Aquinas and Duns Scotus during his sojourns in Paris and Pola. From Aquinas he seems to have gleaned an understanding of epiphany as 'whatness' (*quidditas*), meaning an experience of luminous radiance (*claritas*) wherein a particular thing serves to illuminate a universal and transcendental Form. (This is the version offered by Stephen in both *Stephen Hero* and *Portrait*). From Duns Scotus, another medieval metaphysician, Joyce learned of a somewhat different notion of epiphany as 'thisness' (*haecceitas*), namely the revelation of the universal in and through the particular. The distinction is subtle but by no means irrelevant. And this second reading – where the divine descends into the world rather than have the world ascend towards it – is, I submit, the one that the later Joyce favoured in *Ulysses* and *Finnegans Wake*.

The Scotist version lays more stress on the sacramentality of the singular event in its carnal and quotidian uniqueness. It is *this* thing, *this* person, *this* phrase or action itself that serves as an incarnation of the infinite, rather than as a mere pretext for something transcendent that happens to be passing through. *Hic. Haec. Hoc.* It is the very *thisness* here and now that matters. In short, if 'whatness' tends to see the particular as the divine in drag, 'thisness' sees it as divinity in person, that is, in flesh and blood. I suspect it is this radically in-carnational view that Joyce has in mind in *Ulysses* when he has Stephen reply to Deasy's question 'what is God?' with the response, 'That is God … A cry in the street'. And this initial cry in the street anticipates, I will suggest, Molly's ultimate cry of 'yes' in the final chapter.

One of the earliest references to the term epiphany is to be found in chapter 15 of the shadow novel, *Stephen Hero*. Here we find the following definition of Joyce's style of writing around 1904: 'Its soul, its whatness, leaps to us from the vestment of its appearance. The soul of the commonest object, the structure of which is so adjusted, seems to us radiant. The object achieves its epiphany'.[1] Elsewhere in *Stephen Hero* we find epiphany described as a 'sudden spiritual manifestation, whether in the vulgarity of speech or of gesture or in a memorable phase of the mind itself'. Stephen even tells his friend Cranley that 'the clock of the Ballast Office was capable of an epiphany'. And we read here that it is for 'the man of letters to record these epiphanies with extreme care, seeing that they themselves are the most delicate and evanescent of moments'.[2] This telling description relates in turn to another formative account of aesthetic epiphany in *Portrait of an Artist*. Here Stephen defines beauty as radiance or *claritas*, which combines with two other Thomistic aesthetic properties – *integritas* and *consonantia* – to constitute the power of epiphanic revelation, especially as it refers (once again) to ordinary or inconsequential events.

And yet in *Ulysses*, where we might expect this aesthetic to reach its crowning expression, we find only a single usage of the term 'epiphany', and that in the context of an ironic allusion to the vainglorious ambitions of the Romantic artist. The reference occurs in the 'Proteus' chapter where Stephen is unable to seize the moment of mystical insight – the 'secret signature of things' – unlike the hero Menelaus in the original Homeric myth who grasped the slippery figure of Proteus in water. As Stephen negotiates his way over the damp mud of Sandymount Strand in Dublin bay he recalls how, when younger and more narcissistic still, he would bow to himself in the mirror and step forward 'to applaud earnestly, striking face', announcing all the wonderful masterpieces he would write for posterity. At which point, we read this telling sentence: 'Remember your epiphanies written on green oval leaves, deeply deep, copies to be sent if you died to all the great libraries of the world, including Alexandria'. And Stephen adds, extending mock-heroic memory into a future anterior, 'Someone was to read them there after a few thousand years ...' The self-irony could not be more pronounced. Then, immediately, in one quick deflationary instant, we are brought back to the banal nature of Stephen's immediate material environment. The ground is giving way. Our hero is beginning to slide and sink. And as he does so, Stephen thinks of the terrible shipwreck of the grandiose Armada sent to rescue the Irish from British tyranny hundreds of years back. 'The grainy sand had gone from under his feet ... lost Armada. Unwholesome sandflats waited to suck his treading soles, breathing upward sewage breath, a pocket of seaweed smouldered in seafire under a midden of man's ashes.' The hubristic artist rejoins the disenchanted everyday universe of living and dying. Grand illusions are followed by failure and defeat. Epiphany by anti-epiphany.

But this, as it transpires, is not the final conversion for Stephen. It is more like a prelude to the ultimate deflation of Stephen's Promethean ambitions in the National Library sequence which takes place at the very centre of the novel, signalled by the motto: 'the truth is midway'. Here the process of aesthetic demystification will, I suggest, open up a path leading towards a new kind of authorship, and a new kind of epiphany. This second epiphany (epiphany 2), I shall argue, is performative rather than nominative. The text *acts it out* rather than *naming* it.

II. Between 'Whatness' and 'Thisness'

But before proceeding to a detailed reading of Joycean epiphany in the National Library scene let us take a closer look at what Joyce actually understood by the operative metaphysical terms 'whatness' (*quidditas*) and 'thisness' (*haecceitas*). While much has been written about the Thomistic sources of epiphany, insufficient attention has been paid, in my view, to the Scotist sources. Like his predecessor at the National University at Newman House on Stephens Green – Gerald Manley Hopkins – Joyce was very taken by Duns Scotus' teaching about the sacred 'thisness' of things. Scotus understood haecceity to be a concrete and unique property of a thing which characterizes one, and only one, subject. As such, it is the 'last formal determination which makes an individual to be precisely this individual and not anything else'.[3] The haecceity of a thing is that radiance of its internal being as created and apprehended by God. It discloses itself – mystically, poetically, spiritually – in terms of a certain sacred perception. As Hopkins wrote: 'I thought how sadly beauty of inscape was unknown and buried away from simple people and yet how near at hand it was if they had eyes to see it'.[4] For Joyce's 'epiphany', as for Hopkins' 'inscape', haecceity is a way of 'seeing the pattern, air or melody in things from, as it were, God's side'.[5]

But the young Joyce was also reading Aquinas and neo-scholastic journals during his time in Paris. Thus we find Stephen in the *Portrait,* for example, explicitly linking Aquinas' notion of *quidditas* (whatness) with his own aesthetic account of *claritas* (radiance), suggesting that the notion of epiphany is linked to the *causa formalis* or 'essence' of something. But in his book *Joyce and Aquinas,* William Noon concedes that what Stephen seems to mean by *claritas* may have been expressed better by the *haecceitas* of Duns Scotus than by the *quidditas* of Aquinas. Etienne Gilson, an expert on both Aquinas and Scotus, has described the *haecceitas* of Scotus as 'l'extrême point d'actualité qui détermine chaque être réel à la singularité'.[6] Haecceity is, in other words, the noumenal become phenomenal, the sacred perception of things translated into profane perception, in a manner so luminous and unexpected that it appears like an 'explosion out of darkness'.[7] This transfiguration of word into flesh can occur in the most ordinary and demotic of events. And Noon argues that the reason that Joyce later parodies Stephen's 'epiphanies on green oval leaves' in *Ulysses* is because his various books 'with letters for titles', never achieved any existence outside of his own literary mind – they were still figments of his solipsistic fantasy.[8] By the time Joyce writes *Ulysses* and *Finnegans Wake*, he has matured beyond his early view that epiphanies depend on some light within the viewer's mind, to a more ontological or eschatological understanding. He now sees epiphany as coming from the otherness and transcendence of the worldly object – disclosing, as the druid in *Finnegans Wake* puts it, 'the Ding hvad in itself id est', 'the Entis-Onton', the 'sextuple Gloria of light'.[9]

But this transition from an idealist to a more ontological comprehension of epiphany presupposes the traversal of language – the 'sound sense symbol' of literature which allows the inner radiance of a thing's *claritas* to find expression within the 'wold of words'.[10] Central to this process of textual traversal is what Joyce, in one of his unpublished Zurich notebooks, calls 'metaphor', by which he understands not 'comparison' (which only tells you 'what something is like') but the expression of what something 'is'. Noon relates this to the scholastic claim that 'metaphors are poetic vestments of the truth' of things ('metaphorae … sunt quasi quaedam veramina veritatis'), adding that he believes this was not yet fully realized in *Stephen Hero* but would have to await Joyce's mature works.[11] It was, tellingly, during his Paris sojourn in early 1903, when Joyce was steeped in medieval metaphysics, that Joyce penned fifteen short prose snatches which he entitled 'epiphanies'. These served as 'tiny literary seeds' from which whole narratives might issue;[12] they testified to the power of the 'single word that tells the whole story', to 'the simple gesture that reveals a complex state of relationships'.[13] The first of these numbered 'epiphanies' has particular interest for our reading of the National Library episode in *Ulysses*. It reads as follows:

> (Dublin: in the National Library). *Skeffington* – I was sorry to hear of the death of your brother...sorry we didn't know in time...to have been at the funeral...*Joyce* – O, he was very young...a boy...*Skeffington* – Still...it hurts...

It is not clear to what extent Joyce's notion of epiphany ultimately conflates the Thomistic whatness/*quidditas* of radiance with the more Scotist thisness/*haecceitas*. For if radiance/*claritas* is properly speaking a feature of art, epiphany – like haecceity – is also available, it seems, to non-aesthetic sensible experience. This latter and more generic sense of epiphany is likely to have its source in what Oliver St John Gogarty surmises to be an insight imparted by Joyce's teacher, the Jesuit Father Darlington, to the effect that epiphany refers to 'any shining forth of the mind' by which one 'gives oneself away'.[14] But it also appears to derive from a more ontological use of the term in Joyce's early Notebooks to refer, not only to art or literature, but also to non-literary 'moments of spiritual life' when the soul of the commonest object reveals itself by some trivial attitude or gesture, discloses its secret, 'gives itself away'.[15] It may even be the case that Joyce translates the more Thomist interpretation of *claritas* in *Stephen Hero* and the *Portrait* (qua universal form) into a more Scotist interpretation in *Ulysses* (qua individual form). For Stephen in the early works – *Stephen Hero* and *A Portrait* – it could be said that 'not Being but the Beautiful had been the Absolute'.[16] But as we move into *Ulysses* and *Finnegans Wake,* it appears that Stephen is leaving the aestheticism of Mallarmé, Pater and the French symbolists behind him in favour of a more ontological experience of art as inextricably connected to the sensible phenomena of the everyday, that is, radiance in contact with the 'thisness' of things.

If we may say, therefore, that the early Joyce's understanding of epiphany seems to change back and forth between art and experience, the mature Joyce seems to locate it firmly in the 'relation' between the two, a relation that he increasingly understands in terms of the transfigurative power of language. The basic genesis of Joyce's notion of epiphany can be construed accordingly in terms of a 'shift as to the location of radiance (*claritas*), from the actual experience of the spectator in life to the verbal act or construct that imaginatively re-presents this experience in the symbols of language, re-enacts it through illuminating images for the contemplation of the imaginative mind'.[17]

One might rephrase this in more hermeneutic terms to say that the *prefigurative* epiphany of lived experience passes through the *configurative* epiphany of the text before reaching the *refigurative* epiphany of the reader. In short, epiphany is a triadic movement from life to text and from text back to life again – a movement amplified and enriched by the full arc of hermeneutic transfiguration.

III. Epiphany in the Library

The National Library chapter opens with Stephen proclaiming his grand theory about Shakespeare before a band of fellow literary esthetes. From the word go, the tone is set. This is about a 'ghoststory'. Ostensibly Shakespeare's *Hamlet*. But more than that too. When Stephen asks, at the outset, 'what is a ghost?' the answer is telling: 'One who has faded into palpability through death, through absence, through change of manners'. From the beginning of the novel, Stephen has been haunted by the ghost of his own mother, at whose deathbed he notoriously refused to kneel and pray. She returns to him in the form of a recurring guilt – 'agenbite of inwit' – which he tries to dispose of by banishing from his mind the 'mothers of memory'. But these mothers are also of a more collective and cultural nature, constituting that 'nightmare of history' from which Stephen is trying to awake. Motherland (Ireland as Cathleen Ni Houlihan), Mother Church (mariolatrous Catholicism), Mother Tongue (Gaelic). Stephen wants to trade in these unholy ghosts of history for a holy ghost of pure aesthetic mediation. He will seek to reconcile a lost son (himself) with a spiritual father through the medium of Art. And he will look for metaphysical confirmation of this in a certain reading of the Christian Trinity whereby Father and Son are united, 'middler the Holy Ghost'. No women need apply.

But Stephen is not talking in this episode about himself or about Ireland. At least not explicitly. He is talking about Shakespeare who lived through his own crisis of filiality and fiction. According to Stephen, Shakespeare wrote his famous 'ghoststory', *Hamlet,* at the very time he was grieving the loss of his son, Hamnet, and his deceased father, John Shakespeare. The play was composed as some sort of aesthetic compensation for Shakespeare's unbearable confusion as he hovered in the in-between space of fatherless sonhood and sonless fatherhood. The suggestion is that the playwright sought reconciliation through the agency of the ghost (which role Shakespeare actually played in the first London production in the Globe theatre). What is more, Stephen proffers the hypothesis that the incestuous Gertrude is a stand-in for Shakespeare's own wife, Anne Hathaway, who betrayed her husband by having an affair with his brother(s) in Stratford. This is how Stephen enunciates his theory:

> The play begins. A player comes on under the shadow, made up in the castoff mail of a court buck, a wellset man with a bass voice. It is the ghost, the king, a king and no king, and the player is Shakespeare who has studied Hamlet all the years of his life which were not vanity in order to play the part of the specter. He speaks the words... 'Hamlet, I am thy father's spirit' bidding him list. To a son he speaks, the son of his soul, the prince, young Hamlet and to the son of his body, Hamnet Shakespeare, who has died in Stratford that his namesake may live for ever.[18]

Stephen proceeds to suggest that William Shakespeare, in his theatrical perform-ance as King Hamlet's phantom, must surely have been aware that he was playing out his own grief at the loss of his son, Hamnet. 'Is it possible', Stephen asks rhetorically, 'that that player Shakespeare, a ghost by absence, and in the vesture of buried Denmark, a ghost by death, speaking his own words to his own son's name (had Hamnet Shakespeare lived he would have been prince Hamlet's twin) is it possible, I want to know, or probable that he did not draw or foresee the logical conclusion of those premises: you are the disposed son: I am the murdered father: you mother is the guilty queen. Ann Shakespeare, born Hathaway?'[19]

The ghost thus serves to link father (King Hamlet) with son (Prince Hamlet) by displacing the guilty queen Gertrude and replacing her with the 'word of memory' – the story that Hamlet the Prince will eventually release to the world in the final act of the play as he bids Horatio, 'absent thee from felicity awhile to tell my story'. By means of such narrative remembrance, the son shall ulti-mately fulfil the command of the father ('Remember me!) through the spiri-tual-aesthetic agency of the play itself. Shakespeare will be reunited – poetically if not empirically, phantasmatically if not historically – with his lost son (and indeed with his lost father, John Shakespeare). Thus also, we might infer, the ghost may rid Shakespeare of his own 'guilt' by having his story told in this cathartic way. Melancholy gives way to morning as it is 'worked through' in the telling of the 'ghoststory'. So the theory seems to go.

But if Stephen is right, are we not witnessing a curious reversal of Stephen's own history here? Is not the very guilt – 'agenbite of inwit' – that Stephen is seeking to absolve by 'awaking from the nightmare of history' not occasioned by his own lack of proper mourning? In the transposition of his own history to the story of Hamlet, we find a strange transfer of Stephen's guilt about his unmourned mother (Mrs Dedalus in Ulysses) to the opposite guilt of the unmourning mother. Gertrude serves in a perverse sense as the 'guilty queen' (like Anne Hathaway on whom she is based, or Mrs Dedalus and Mrs Bloom whom she represents) whose sexual and spiritual betrayal of her spouse qualify her as a suit-able 'sacrificial scapegoat' whose exclusion from the new trinity of Father-Son-Ghost will, the theory suggests, lead to a perfect artistic purgation and atone-ment. As Pater et Filius are mutually absolved through the medium of the spirit, woman (mother, spouse) is dissolved.

But let's have Stephen speak for himself again. After a few rounds of literary jousting with the librarians Eglinton and Best, Stephen returns to his basic thesis that an artist can recompose the different aspects of his being – including that of father and son – through a work of art. Just as the 'artist weave(s) and unweave(s) his image' in such a way that 'through the ghost of the unquiet father the image of the unliving son looks forth', so too 'in an intense instant of imagination' our past and future can somehow, miraculously, be united into a present moment. This is how Stephen, sitting in the National Library surrounded by his literary peers, looks forward to a time when he will be able to look back at himself as he was in the past and in this very instant: 'that which I was is that which I am and that which in possibility I may come to be. So in the future, the sister of the past, I may see myself as I sit here now but by reflection from that which then I shall be'.[20] In other words, the genius of the artist is to be able to transcend the divisions of existence by means of a spiritual imagination that can subsume the ruptures of our temporality into an aesthetic of eternal redemption. Stephen quotes the poet, Shelley, in this passage, confirming a Romantic sentiment that harks back to Mallarmé's description of Hamlet with which the chapter opens – 'il se promène, lisant au livre de lui-même, don't you know, reading the book of himself'. The fact that this phrase is repeated – in French then in English – in addition to its crucial role of leading off the whole discussion of Hamlet that dominates the chapter, suggests that it is central to the author's meaning.[21] Here is the exemplary paradigm of the Great Book where the contingencies and contradictions of ordinary life may be ultimately transformed.

After several more bouts of repartee about how Shakespeare's dramatic corpus relates to his biography, Stephen returns once more to the theme of father and son in *Hamlet*. We are back with the 'ghost' of King Hamlet on the battlements of Elsinore addressing 'the son consubstantial with the father'. Now the theological idioms of the Trinitarian mystery are explicitly invoked. 'He who himself begot, middler the Holy Ghost, and Himself sent himself, Agenbuyer, between Himself and others…'[22] This passage, beginning with four uses of the term 'himself' and ending with the return of God, now in the person of the cruficied and resurrected Son, to sit at the 'right hand of His Own Self' in heaven, is mock-heroic in the extreme. And, if the reader was in any doubt, the graphic invocation of 'Glo-o-ri-a in ex-cel-sis De-o' to round off the theological parody adds a defining touch of mischievous melodrama.

But this is not all. Stephen comes back to his Trinitarian theory – like a kitten playing with a ball of wool – later in the chapter when raising the question of physical versus spiritual paternity. 'A father', Stephen now opines, is at best a 'legal fiction', at worst a 'necessary evil'. He means of course a biological father who has no real relation to a son apart from the physiological 'instant of blind rut' which engendered him. Paternal and filial affection are therefore, so the theory goes, unnatural, and no son can ever be certain who his father really is (unlike the mother). Whence Stephen's rather cynical quip: 'Who is the father of any son that any son should love him or he any son?'[23]

IV. Trinities and Triangles

So Stephen's overall hypothesis seems to be that in *Hamlet* Shakespeare is replacing the experience of actual fatherhood (his dead father, John Shakespeare) with a spiritual fatherhood that will compensate for all the doubts, uncertainties and rivalries that exist between real fathers and sons (for the male child's 'growth is his father's decline, his youth his father's envy, his friend his father's enemy)'[24] According to Stephen, this 'mystery' of spiritual paternity – represented by the Ghost in *Hamlet* and the Holy Ghost of the Christian Trinity – lies at the very root of the Western church and culture. Here 'fatherhood...is a mystical estate, an apostolic succession, from only begetter to only begotton'.[25] And it is precisely this ingenious fantasy of mystical fatherhood that meant that when Shakespeare wrote *Hamlet* 'he was not the father of his own son merely but, being no more a son, he was and felt himself the father of all his race, the father of his own grandfather, the father of his unborn grandson...etc'.[26] In this manner, Shakespeare contrived to resolve the tragic ruptures of his own life-history (death of his father and son, betrayal by his wife and brothers) by transmuting this history into a mystical story. John Elginton sums up Stephen's metaphysical theory thus: 'the truth is midway...He is ghost and the prince. He is all in all'.[27] And Stephen readily agrees: 'He is...The boy of act one is the mature man of act five'.

The implications of this are extensive. Just as Pater and Filius are miraculously reconciled so too are a host of other human antinomies – 'bawd and cuckold' (being now 'a wife unto himself'), male and female, (united as 'androgenous angel'), possible and actual ('He found in the world without as actual what was in his world within as possible'), and so on. All of which suggests that the solution to life's tragic contradictions and divisions is to be found in the great Trinitarian fantasy – forged by Christian theologians like Sabellius and writers like Shakespeare – in which father and son are reunited through the mediating agency of *Geist*. Is this not what is meant by the summary statement that 'truth is midway' – echoing the earlier allusion, 'middler the Holy Ghost'? This surmise would certainly seem to be born out by Stephen's citation of Maeterlinck's *mot* about Socrates and Judas going forth only to find themselves again. Or as Stephen puts it in his own words: 'We walk through ourselves, meeting robbers, ghosts, giants, old men, young men, wives, widows, brothers-in-love. But always meeting ourselves'.[28] Meaning that if God was the 'playwright who wrote the folio of this world', Shakespeare rewrites the folio of his own world in a play called *Hamlet*. And we might presume, Stephen Daedelus will do likewise when he finally comes to realize his vocation as Romantic Artist par excellence. In other words, if Stephen's theory is correct, art would be the greatest feat of mystical solipsism – Self-Thinking-Thought, Self-Loving-Love, Self-Causing-Cause, Self-Creating-Creation.

But is that the end of the story? Is it simply a matter of converting the mimetic conflicts and sunderings of French 'triangles' into the spiritual sublimity of mystical 'Trinities'? At the end of all the brilliant and grandiloquent discoursing, John Eglinton puts the hard question to Stephen: 'You have brought us all this way to show us a French triangle. Do you believe your own theory?' Stephen replies 'no'. And replies, we are told, 'promptly'.[29] So what are we to make of this sudden recantation? Why such a labyrinthine detour in this august national library, conducted by some of the smartest minds of the young Dublin literati, if we are to end up in a *cul-de-sac*? And why does Stephen go on to claim that the one who helps him to 'believe' in the very theory that he now disowns, is '*Egomen*'? (Egomism is defined in the Shorter Oxford English Dictionary as 'the belief of one who believes he is the only one in existence').

Let us reflect a little more on what exactly might be meant here by the notion of 'French triangle'. A motif running throughout the library episode, as noted above, is that of Anne Hathaway's betrayal of her husband William. This is very much a subtext compared to the central paternity theme but it serves a significant role nonetheless. The terms used to describe Shakespeare's unfaithful spouse are invariably disparaging. She is portrayed as a seductress who tumbles young William in the hay, before going on to do likewise with Shakespeare's brothers (Richard, Edmund and Gilbert), once her husband had left Stratford for London. 'Sweet Ann I take it, was hot in the blood. Once a wooer twice a wooer'.[30] Which is why, according to Stephen, Shakespeare brands Queen Gertrude with 'infamy' in the fifth scene of *Hamlet*. And when Stephen and Eglinton rejoin the discussion of Anne later in the chapter it is in the disparaging context of 'an age of exhausted whoredom groping for its god'.[31] The theological discussion of mystical paternity which immediately follows (discussed above) adds a further nail to the coffin of the tarnished woman. It was on the mystery of the Christian Trinity – and not on the 'madonna which the cunning Italian intellect flung to the mob of Europe'[32] – that the true Church is founded. And this theme resurfaces one last and very telling time as a terminal salvo of Stephen's grand theory, accounting for that singular note of banishment – 'banishment of the heart, banishment from home' – which we are told 'sounds uninterruptedly' from one end of Shakespeare's corpus to the other. The theme of betrayal is not some isolated matter. 'It is in infinite variety everywhere in the world he has created', concludes Stephen. And is further born out by the fact that Ann Hathaway's betrayal repeats itself again in the next generation ('his married daughter, Susan…is accused of adultery'); while Ann herself is refused burial in the same grave as Shakespeare. 'It is between the lines of this last written words', claims Stephen, ' it is petrified on his tombstone under which her four bones are not to be laid'.[33]

Otherwise put, the theme of the infidel woman (wife-mother-daughter) ghosts the entire thesis of spiritual paternity and, Stephen argues, is the real hidden motivation for Shakespeare's invention of a literary 'ghoststory' – a drama where the 'guilty queen' could be sacrificially purged and 'Hamlet *père*' and 'Hamlet *fils*' find themselves ultimately atoned 'middler the holy ghost'. In other words, if the Artist-Author-Creator can become a mystical Father who is 'Himself his own Son' and thereby dispense with the profane mediation of woman ('being a wife unto himself'), then we would seem to have finally hit upon a solution to the cruel sunderings of existence. In this grand finale, Stephen's theory would end where it began – returning to itself in triumphal self-congratulation – that is, with the Romantic vision of the great poet writing and reading the book of himself. The 'playwright who wrote the folio of this world…' echoing the Mallarméan poet *'lisant au livre de lui-même'*.

But, once again, the matter is not so simple. Not only does Stephen revoke his own theory of triangles-supplanted-by-trinities, but he goes on to confront the radical consequences of this disavowal. First, he undermines the metaphysical model of self-thinking-thought as the ultimate guarantor of truth. The mystical paradigm of a self-sufficient-paternity (Trinitarian or other) is now parodied as solipsistic and masturbatory. Mulligan's Dublin ditty about onanistic literateurs – 'afraid to marry on earth/They masturbated for all they were worth' – leads to a send-up of Socratic self-knowledge: 'Jest on. Know thyself'. And this point is further reinforced by Mulligan's proposal of a mock-heroic drama (recalling the earlier theological conceits of self-engendering Trinities and androgenous angels) entitled

Everyman His own Wife
or
A Honeymoon in the Hand
(a national immortality in three orgasms).

This is Mulligan's way of trying to outdo the Irish revivalist movement of Synge, Lady Gregory and Yeats – as well as George Russell who actually participates in the National Library discussion. But Stephen, it now seems, will have none of it. He parts company here with Buck Mulligan and his literary peers. He alone of the Library company is not party to the subsequent reunion in the literary soirée. And this decision to pass beyond the pretentious antics of Dublin's aesthetic coterie – which has preoccupied him up to now – on foot of his renunciation of his grand literary theory, prepares Stephen to meet Bloom. The 'jesuit jew', as Mulligan labels Stephen, is now ready to behold the 'wandering jew', Bloom. 'Jewgreek' crosses paths for the first time with 'Greekjew'. Stephen now definitely renounces his proud presumption to become the great Irish writer to succeed Synge, Shaw and Yeats (all mentioned in the episode). 'Cease to strive', he resolves. And in so doing, Stephen begins the second half of his odyssey. He follows Bloom out of the National Library onto the street of Dublin, a journey which will lead through Nighttown and the cabman's shelter to Bloom's own home in Eccles St, and eventually to Molly. The motto that 'the truth is midway' now takes on another meaning, retrospectively, in so far as Stephen finds a way through the extremes of Scylla and Charybdis to embrace a new aesthetic insight – what I will call the 'epiphany of the everyday'. This is how Joyce describes this crucial traversal of paths:

> About to pass through the doorway, feeling one behind, he (Stephen) stood aside. Part. The moment is now. Where then? If Socrates leave his house today, if Judas go forth tonight. Why? That lies in space which I in time must come to, ineluctably....The wandering jew....A dark back went before them. Step of a pard, down, out by the gateway...[34]

The fact that Stephen will take his departure here from both Mulligan – and Mallarmé – and choose to follow Bloom instead is decisive. He trades in a popular, anti-Semitic literateur for a vagrant, cuckolded ad-man. This is the real turning point in the novel and marks the threshold separating the narcissistic romantic Stephen from the later author of the everyday. And the epiphany that marks this turn? I would suggest it is that instant of recognition wherein Stephen suddenly 'sees' what he had previously been blind to – the Other. The will of another – Bloom the despised and humiliated Semite – that fronts and confronts him humbly and unpretentiously ('bowing, greeting'). The 'other chap', who Stephen confesses presciently helps him to 'unbelieve' his grand theory. In short, that other who will lead him out of the self-enclosed, self-regarding circle of literary solipsism away, back, down, out onto the streets of the ordinary universe. Into a world where the self leads not back to itself – as with Socrates, Judas, Sibellius – but beyond itself towards otherness. A world where time does not subsume space into itself but comes to heed and serve it. 'That lies in space which I must come to...'. And as soon as Stephen accepts this, he sees not only his wayward past illuminated in the instant – 'cease to strive' – but also his immi-nent adventures with Bloom: traversing the roads of Dublin city ('men wandered'), Nighttown ('streets of harlots after') and, finally, Molly ('a creamfruit mellon he held to me').[35] 'You will see', Stephen realizes. This moment of traversal is the epiphany that will change his life.

Moreover, the last lines where the plumes ascending from the chimneys of Kildare Street are compared to the smoke rising from altars in Shakespeare's

Cymbeline, may well allude to the return and resurrection of the sacrificed woman (Imogen-Anne Hathaway-Gertrude-Penelope?) – another pointer to the return of Molly in the last chapter of the book? If this reading is sound, then the throwaway line in the very middle of Stephen's peroration on mystical paternity takes on – retrospectively – another complexion:'*Amor matris*, subjective and objective genitive, may be the only true thing in life'.[36] If so, then Stephen's 'agenbite of inwit' regarding his dead and unmourned mother may itself, at last, be subsiding, the repudiated 'mothers of memory' assuming a more benign visage, the nightmare of history returning as that epiphany of the mundane so faithfully and jubilantly recorded in Molly's final polymorphous poem (itself one sustained coming back of time to space)?

There is still a way to go, of course, from here to there, from the middle of the book to the end. But the tide has turned, and there is no going back. Stephen, it seems, has undergone a profound conversion from belief to unbelief in his own theory. He has died a death and shed his most fundamental delusions. No longer striving to fulfill the Great Expectations of Immortal Art – fostered by his confrères in the Irish Literary Revival as well as by Mallarmé and the symbolists (in a different key) – Stephen is ready to take his lead from a simple adman, Bloom. Renouncing all forms of literary solipsism, Stephen chooses someone who will guide him towards another way of 'seeing' and 'hearing', another kind of art (in the lower case) where father and son do not sacrifice procreation for creation, otherness for selfhood, space for time, female for male, history for mystique, the world of flesh-and-blood for a world of Ghosts and *Geists*. Leaving his grand theory behind him on the shelves of the National Library, Stephen follows Bloom out into a profane universe where divinity is witnessed in a 'cry in the street', in the 'yes' of a woman's desire. 'God: noise in the street: very peripatetic'. This is the truth of epiphany to which Stephen finally comes.

V. Epiphanies – Intra-textual, Extra-textual, Trans-textual

Our account above suggests how we might identify the role of 'epiphany' within the Joycean text. But if Joyce is correct when he claims that 'it would be a brave man would invent something that never happened', is it not legitimate to wonder if Joyce's intra-textual epiphanies might not repeat certain extra-textual experiences in Joyce's own life? Any attempt nowadays – after formalism and structuralism – to relate an author's work to his/her biography is contentious at least. But it is not always unprofitable. Indeed, if we are to give any credence to Stephen's own procedure in correlating Shakespeare's oeuvre with his life – while accepting his disavowal of his own 'theory' about this correlation – we may assume there is more than madness in the method.

I would like to suggest that there are three possible episodes in Joyce's own life which might be said to prefigure crucial epiphanies in the novel.

First, and most obviously, we know from Joyce himself that his first 'going out' with Nora Barnacle on 16 June 1904, lies at the core of the book. This is the very day and date for the setting of the whole story, subsequently commemorated as 'Bloomsday'. If this is so, by the author's own admission, then it is probably fair to conjecture that Molly's climactic phantasia is, in some respects, an epiphanic 'repetition' of this moment – the existential past being given an open future through the *kairos* of the literary moment. Here the human eros of space and time is celebrated in an epiphany of sacredness. 'What else were we given all those desires for I want to know…' Molly reminds us. And as Joyce suggests in a letter to his Paris friend, Valéry Larbaud, we can take Molly at her word: 'Pénélope, le dernier cri'.

Second, it is possible that a particular experience that Joyce had of being rescued after a mugging in Dublin was at the root of his motivation to invent Leopold Bloom. As he relates in a letter from Rome to his brother, Stanislas, dated 13 November 1906, a brutal mugging in Rome in 1906 that left him robbed and destitute, recalled the earlier mugging in Dublin when he found himself rescued by a Dublin Jew called Hunter who took him back to his home and gave him cocoa. The Hunter in question, as Joyce's biographer Richard Ellmann explains, refers to a 'dark complexioned Dublin Jew…rumored to be a cuckold whom Joyce had met twice in Dublin'. In his letter to Stanislas, Joyce reveals that this same Hunter is to be the central character of a planned new story called 'Ulysses'. Ellmann comments: 'On the night of 22 June 1904 Joyce (not yet committed either to Nora or to monogamy) made overtures to a girl on the street without realizing, perhaps, that she had another companion. The official escort came forward and left him, after a skirmish, with 'black eye, sprained wrist, sprained ankle, cut chin, cut hand'…He was dusted off and taken home by a man called Alfred Hunter in what he was to call 'orthodox Samaritan fashion'. This was the Hunter about whom the short story 'Ulysses' was to be projected'.[37] Curiously, however, it was not until the second mugging triggered the forgotten memory of the first that Joyce resolved to create Bloom. Epiphanies seem to have something to do with a certain *anagnoresis* which coincides with a creative repetition or retrieval of some 'inexperienced experience' – a sort of *ana-mnesis* that in turn calls for a particular *ana-aesthesis* of literary epiphany. We might even propose the neologism, *ana-phany*, to capture this curious phenomenon of doubling.[38]

And Stephen? I would hazard a guess that the existential epiphany that lies at the root of the invention of Stephen – if there is one – relates to some pivotal event of awareness-through-sundering which the young Joyce experienced in a Dublin library. Such a moment would most likely have entailed a break with his Dublin literary rivals (for example, Oliver St John Gogarty and Vincent

Cosgrove, who falsely claimed to have slept with Nora) – a break that finally prompted Joyce to take the role of exodus and exile. At least, that is what might be inferred from the National Library exchange which we have analysed above. As Declan Kiberd suggestively remarks about this decisive midway chapter: 'Written in 1918, but dealing with a day fourteen years earlier, this section includes lines which predict its future composition, implicitly uniting the young graduate of 1904 with the mature father and artist of 1918...Already Stephen sets himself at an aesthetic distance from events'.[39] The recurring phrases which young Stephen addresses here in 1904 to his future authorial self – 'see this. Remember' and 'You will see' etc – indicate the criss-crossing of past and future which epitomizes the singular temporality of epiphany (identified by Paul as *kairos* and by Kierkegaard and Heidegger as *Augenblick)*. Moreover, the fact that a key epiphanic moment in *A Portrait* also takes place in a library – Stephen's revelation of the power of words in the famous 'tundish' exchange with the Jesuit Dean of Studies – might further point in this direction. As indeed might the National Library incident in 1903–4 concerning Joyce's exchange with a literary companion (Skeffington) about the untimely demise of his young brother: an incident, let us not forget, that Joyce entered as the first of his fifteen numbered 'epiphanies' recorded in his Paris Notebooks. The place of this epiphany is explicitly stated: 'Dublin: in the National Library'. In this respect, might not young Hamnet's demise, as interpreted by Stephen, be a literary transposition of Joyce's own brother's demise? 'O he was very young...a boy', writes the author. 'Still it hurts', replies Skeffington. The traumatic loss of a young child whose 'hurt' and 'sundering' could only find healing in literature.

All such attempts to link literature to life remain, of course, a matter of conjecture and surmise. Though the fact that pivotal experiences in Joyce's life around the time of 1903–4 – being rescued by Hunter, being separated from his friends in the National Library, being embraced by Norah Barnacle – were later revisited in the text in the form of three epiphanic magi (Bloom, Stephen, Molly) cannot be dismissed as irrelevant. In any case, if one is looking for some kind of historical genesis for Joyce's epiphanies in his own life experience, 1904 would be the year to begin.

Let me conclude with a few supplementary remarks on the *intra-textual* epiphanies of *Ulysses*. Concerning Stephen, the actual proponent of the notion of epiphany in the first instance, we might say that the 'epiphany' of the Library scene is one which mutates and migrates throughout the book, until it reaches its culmination in the 'Part...You will see' intuition. Previous prefigurations of this epiphany are to be found, arguably, not only in the Sandymount Strand scene analysed above ('Wait...Remember'), but already in the opening exchange with Mr. Deasy where Stephen expresses his insight that God is 'a cry in the street'. Such a developmental reading of epiphany – that it emerges within a process of genesis and gestation – would seem to find some support in Stephen Hero's initial description of an object or event 'achieving its epiphany'. The 'radiance' of the 'commonest object' – be it apprehending divinity in a 'street cry' or in the unprepossessing figure of a wandering adman – attests to the traversal of eternity through time. But the eternity incarnate in the instant equally refers back to a past and forward to a future which overspills the moment.

In this sense, we might say that epiphany manifests a paradoxical structure of time which Paul called 'eschatological'. It is exemplified, for example, in the Palestinian formula for 'remembering the one who is still to come' – a phenomenon that numerous contemporary thinkers have called 'messianic' time (Lévinas, Benjamin, Derrida). We are referring here to a singular form of 'anticipatory memory' that recalls the past into the future through the present. A temporal anomaly which Lévinas calls the 'paradox of posterior anteriority'. And which the poet Hopkins – who studied theology and literature in the same Dublin libraries as the young Joyce – called 'aftering' or 'over-and-overing', an ana-esthetic process which enables us to bear witness to the manner in which each simple mortal things 'deals out that being that in each one dwells; selves...crying what I do is me: for that I came...for Christ plays in ten thousand places'('As Kingfishers Catch Fire').[40]

And yet how do we explain that in *Ulysses* Stephen does not invoke the term epiphany except in the ostensibly derogatory sense identified above in the Proteus/Sandymount episode? I think that what we have in *Ulysses* is the mature Joyce translating his – and Stephen's – youthful notion of epiphany into a post-Romantic literary praxis. So that what we witness is not some doctrinal exegesis of epiphany – derived from a grand metaphysical theory – but the *performance* of epiphany in the text itself. It does not have to be named. It is the very process of naming and writing itself. A process which retrieves life through the text and prefigures a return to the life-of-action after the text. Epi-phany as epi-phora and ana-phora: a transferring back and forth between literature and life. Transversality, moving in both directions.

If this is so, then the return of epiphany by performance rather than by name in the Library chapter, might be termed epiphany 2. Such a second epiphany, which dares not speak its name – out of modesty as much as discretion – would be post-Romantic and post-metaphysical, democratic rather than elitist, and deeply demotic in its fidelity to the ordinary universe. Such epiphany we might call *posthumous* to the extent that it resurfaces after the experience of radical parting, powerlessness and loss. For 'there can be no reconciliation', as Stephen learns, 'if there has not been a sundering'.[41]

And what, finally, of the *intra-textual* epiphanies of Leopold and Molly? For Leopold, as for Stephen, one could say that they are multiple, recurring at various key moments in the text (e.g. in Davy Byrne's pub, in the Hollis Street Hospital, in the cab-man's shelter, in Nighttown, when he chooses compassion over violence and hate) – recurrences that seem to 'achieve' their ultimate epiphany in the culminating passage of Ithaca where Bloom, curled up at Molly's feet, embraces a condition of quiet equipoise: 'less envy than equanimity…childman weary, manchild in the womb'. Resisting the path of mimetic rivalry (with Blazes Boylan), jealousy (with Molly), competition (with Stephen) and hatred (with the Citizen and other anti-semitic persecutors), Bloom chooses rebirth.

And Molly's epiphany? The final sequence speaks for itself. Joyce's own verdict, cited above, is not impertinent: 'Pénélope, le dernier cri!'. So that the only remaining question might be: is this one more epiphany amongst a plurality of epiphanies or the ultimate epiphany of epiphanies? Or might we conclude that the entire novel itself is an epiphany from beginning to end, with Stephen, Bloom and Molly serving as three mundane magi – offering us different aspects of a single seed-moment in Joyce's own life: 16 June 1904? Or is it a trinity of such moments (Hunter's rescue, Nora's kiss, Skeffington's phrase) combined into one? One epiphanic time in one epiphanic space? A day in the life of three Dubliners, retrieved, rewritten and resurrected as literature? Not a triumphal literature of closure to be sure, but a textuality of endless receptivity to the events of life as surrendipity, surpise, accident, grace? Joyce leaves it to his readers to decide.

Appendix: Between Molly and the Song of Songs

The three Magi who witness the event of meaning, which epitomizes the epiphanic paradigm, may also be interpreted more textually – or more hermeneutically – as *author, actor* and *reader*. Thus we might say that while a) the lived action of Joyce's world (*le vécu*) 'prefigures' the text, and b) the voice of the narrator-actors (Stephen–Bloom–Molly) 'configure' the meaning in the text, it is we readers who c) complete the function of third witness by 'refiguring' the text once again in our own lived experience, that is, as a world enlarged and epiphanized by the new meanings proposed by the text. This triangular model of epiphany always implies a certain re-birth that constitutes something of a miracle of meaning: the *impossible* being transfigured into the *newly possible*. One thinks of the three angels that appear to Abraham (Gen XVII, 6.8) announcing Sarah's conception of an 'impossible' child (Jacob); the three Magi who bear witness to the 'impossible' child Jesus; or the three persons of the Christian Trinity who bear witness to the birth of a new and 'impossible' kingdom (viz Andrei Rublev's icon of the Blessed Trinity).

This third example, as illustrated by Rublev, brings together the first two and foregrounds the pivotal role of the empty chalice or space (*chora*) at the centre of the triadic epiphany. The movement of the three persons/angels/Magi around the still vacant centre – which the Church fathers named *peri-choresis* or the dance around the open space – may be read, hermeneutically, as the creative encounter of *author/narrator/reader* in and around the locus of language. Moreover this suggests, further, that the triadic model of epiphany always implies a fourth dimension – *chora* understood as the space of advent for the new (Jacob, Jesus, mustard seed etc), the miracle of semantic innovation as an event of language, the transfiguration of the impossible into the possible. That the witness of the three personas is usually met with a celebratory 'yes' (Sarah's 'laugh' in Gen XVII, Mary's 'amen' in the Gospels, Molly Bloom's final 'yes I will yes') is itself significant as an illustration of a *kairological* time that breaks into our conventional chronological time and opens up a surplus of possible meaning hitherto unsuspected and unknown. Epiphany may thus be seen as one that testifies simultaneously to an *event* of meaning (it is *already* here) as well as to an *advent* still to come (it is *not-yet*). In this way, it reenacts the Palestinian formula of the Passover/Eucharist which remembers a moment of saving while at the same time anticipating a future ('until he comes').[42] Indeed, Molly's final cry blends past and future tenses in a typically kairological way – 'I *said* yes I *will* yes'. Her scatological memories are *repeated forward* to the rhythm of eschatological time.

Ulysses may be read as a series of anti-Eucharists or pseudo-Eucharists (Mulligan's black Mass, Stephen's parodic Mass in Nighttown, Bloom and Stephen's failed Mass over a cup of cocoa in Ithica) which ultimately – after a long deconstructive *via negativa* – open up a space where the 'kiss' of the seed cake on Howth Head, as recalled/anticipated by Molly in Penelope, reprises not only the 'kisses of the mouth' celebrated by the Shulamite woman in the opening verse of the *Song of Songs* but also the Eucharistic Passover of Judeo-Christian promise. Molly's remembrance of the 'long kiss' when she gave Bloom the 'seedcake out of [her] mouth' might be thought of as a retrieval of the genuine Eucharistic gift of love after the various deconstructions of failed or inflated Eucharists recurring throughout the novel. In this sense, we might say that Molly's 'yes' epitomizes Walter Benjamin's intriguing notion of messianic time as an openness to 'each moment of the future as a portal through which the Messiah may enter'. This is, in short, epiphany understood as a transfiguring of each ordinary moment of secular, profane time (*chronos*) in terms of sacred time (*kairos*).

It is also worth reiterating here that epiphany implies witnesses that come as strangers from afar – the three angels to Abraham, the three Magi from the East etc. This may be read, hermeneutically, as the event of textual openness to new, alien and unprecedented meanings through the perichoretic textual encounter between *author, narrator* and, above all, *reader*. Reading *Ulysses* as just such an 'open text', Rudolphe Gasche writes of the 'desire to open writing to unforeseeable effects, in other words, to the Other. It is a function of a responsibility for the Other – for managing in writing a place for the Other, saying *yes* to the call or demand of the Other, inviting a response'.[43] In his commentary on Joyce, Derrida invokes Elijah as a sort of messianic model of the reader – as unpredictable Other – who calls the text forth and is called forth by the text. This notion of *Ulysses* as an open textual invitation to 'refiguration' finds confirmation in Joyce's own repeated appeal to the 'ideal reader': a gesture akin to Proust's appeal to his future readers to discover in his novel the book of their own life. One of Joyce's most telling refrains in letters is: 'is there one who understands me?' The metaphor of Eucharistic transubstantiation to convey the miracle of textual composition and reception is also present in Proust, of course, in the epiphany of the Madeleine.[44]

But how are we to read these novelistic repetitions (in Kierkegaard's sense of repeating forward rather than merely recollecting backward) of Eucharistic transformation in Joyce? What is the particular genre, idiom or style that performs such gestures? In Joyce we encounter a certain comic – or as he put it 'jokoserious' – tone. It is clear that Molly is a mock-heroic parody of the elevated and aristocratic Penelope. One only needs to compare Molly's marvellously mundane musings with the following description of Penelope in the last scene of Homer's *Odyssey*: 'So upright in disposition was Penelope the daughter of Icarius that she never forgot Odysseus the husband of her youth; and therefore shall the fame of her goodness be conserved in the splendid poem wherewith the Immortals shall celebrate the constancy of Penelope for all the dwellers upon earth'. This is a far cry from Molly's final cry. Penelope could never say of her spouse what Molly says of hers – 'as well him as another'! And yet it is typical of Joyce's irony that in turning the principle of Homeric epic heroism on its head, his characters curiously maintain the truth of the situation in a kind of creative repetition (not to be confused with Hegelian sublation). Bloom is strangely blessed with his wife (however unfaithful) and does manage to defy his suitors (however indirectly and passively). Molly does not forget Bloom and her ultimate affirmation is 'celebrated' by many 'dwellers upon earth'! In the transliteration of Penelope and Ulysses into Molly and Bloom, Joyce performs an extraordinary act of Eucharistic humour and humility.

Molly's rewriting of Penelope conforms to the basic features of comedy outlined by Aristotle and Bergson, namely: the combining of more with less, of the metaphysical with the physical, of the heroic with the demotic, of death with love. (Recall that *Ulysses* begins with a series of death and burial themes, Stephen's mother, Bloom's son, Dignam's funeral etc. and ends with a call to love: *eros* defying the sting of *thanatos*). Molly's ultimate passing from *thanatos* to *eros* is prefigured several times during her own soliloquy, from fantasies of being buried (e.g. 'well when Im stretched out dead in my grave then I suppose I'll have some peace I want to get up a minute if Im let O Jesus….O Jamsey let me up out of this pooh sweets of sin…') to the climatic cry of eschatological bliss. Here, finally, echoing the Shulamite woman's celebration of wild flora and nature in the *Song of Songs*, Molly affirms that 'we are all flowers all a womans body'. Indeed the culminating Moorish and Mediterranean idioms of sensory ecstasy and excess are deeply redolent of the Shulamite's Canticle – itself styled after the Jewish-Bablyonian nuptial poem or epithalamium. As are the multiple allusions to seeds and trees and waters and mountains and irresistible passions between men and women. 'What else were we given all those desires for..?' Molly asks. If there is something irreducibly humorous in this replay of the *Song of Songs*, there is something deeply serious too. As always in Joyce, the scatological and the eschatological rub shoulders – as do Greek and Jew, Molly and Bloom, life and death – without succumbing to some final synthesis or solution. Joyce's comic transliteration is not the same as Hegelian sublation (*Aufhebung*). He keeps the dialectic open to the end, and beyond.

CHAPTER ELEVEN

Beckett I: The End of the Story?

I. Beckett the Irish Writer: A Contradiction in Terms?

a) Beckett and the Revival

Samuel Beckett considered himself not as an Irish writer belonging to a specifically Anglo-Irish literary tradition, but as an Irishman engaged in the universal
problem of writing. While Yeats, Synge and O'Casey had championed an indigenous literary renaissance and succeeded in founding a national theatre – the
Abbey – Beckett grew up in the secluded Dublin suburb of Foxrock, was
educated at Portora in Northern Ireland, studied French at Trinity College,
wrote convoluted Italianate poetry and dreamt of getting away to Europe. His
early intellectual sympathies were clearly those of 'radicalist modernism'. He
sided with Joycean revolt rather than Celtic Revival.

Beckett bemoaned the insular introspectiveness of most Anglo-Irish literature.
He showed scant sympathy for those who chose to write in their native Gaelic
and derided the triumphalism of the 1916 Rising. Quite typical is his remark that
if all the Irishmen who claimed to be in the General Post Office in Dublin
during the Rising had actually been there, the building would have burst at the
seams. In an early essay, 'Censorship in the Saorstat' (1929), Beckett accused the
Free State government of a 'sterilisation of the mind', exemplified in the removal
of every nude from the National Gallery. Furthermore, those contemporary
writers committed to specifically indigenous concerns frequently earned
Beckett's contempt. He dismissed Arland Ussher's project to translate *Utopia* into
Gaelic as a 'futile exercise'; and Austin Clarke, one of the few Irish poets willing

and able to continue the Yeatsian preoccupation with Celtic mythology and tradition, was ridiculed in Beckett's first novel *Murphy* (1938) as 'Austin Ticklepenny ... a distinguished indigent drunken Irish bard'.[1] 'Not for me all these Deirdres and Maeves and Cathleens,' declares Beckett caustically. And in his critical essay of 1934, 'Recent Irish poetry', the young author is even more unequivocal in his condemnation of the mythologizing that had fired the literary imaginations of the Irish Revival: he pooh-poohs the legends of Cuchulain and Oisín as no more than 'segment after segment of cut and dried sanctity'.

In this same essay Beckett first pronounces, after the manner of Stephen Dedalus, his own aesthetic manifesto: rather than losing himself in antique lore, the artist must cut the cords that tie him to the world that shaped him, to his nation, his family, his tradition. Only by means of such a 'rupture of the lines of communication' can the artist expose and interrogate that 'space that intervenes between him and the world of objects'. Against the *naturalist* thesis that highlights literature's debt to 'objective' environmental factors, Beckett calls in typical modernist fashion for 'the breakdown of the object'. And against the *nationalist* thesis that urged the subordination of the individual subject to a pre-existing mythological tradition, Beckett pleads for a return to the 'existence of the author', to that freedom from any given identity that he calls 'no-man's-land, Hellespont or vacuum'. Henceforth Beckett's writing evinces a systematic suspension of his origins, of that which had determined him at the national, religious or linguistic levels. The Irish Protestant writing in English becomes a nomadic agnostic writing in French. *The vacuum of the author's own interior existence* becomes the singular focus of his work.

A graduate of Trinity College Dublin, Beckett was named *lecteur d'anglais* at the École Normale Supérieure in Paris in 1928. This was to prove Beckett's long-awaited opportunity to follow Joyce into exile and escape the prevailing ethos of cultural revivalism. George Moore, an influential revivalist in his own right, had suggested that 'whoever casts off tradition is like a tree transplanted into uncongenial soil'. And in 1922 George Russell, another leading intellectual of the Revival, declared that 'the Irish genius is coming out of its seclusion and Yeats, Synge, Moore, Shaw, Joyce and others are forerunners. The Irish imagination is virgin soil and virgin soil is immensely productive when cultivated.' Beckett, however, would have nothing of it. The 'virgin soil' of a productive Irish imagination would not be his chosen theme, but the 'uncongenial soil' of his own solipsistic voice. He would write as an inmate in the asylum of the *solus ipse* rather than as an Irishman in his native tradition. His explicit rejection of this national heritage is humorously, if acerbically, evoked in the following passage from *First Love*: 'What constitutes the charm of our country, apart of course from its scant population, and this without the help of the meanest contraceptive, is that all is derelict, with the sole exception of history's ancient faeces. These are ardently sought after, stuffed and carried in procession. Wherever nauseated time has dropped a nice fat turd you will find our patriots, sniffing it up, on all fours, their faces on fire. Elysium of the roofless.'[2] It is little wonder that Beckett refused to return from exile to his native land, preferring 'France in war to Ireland in peace'.

But it would be a mistake to suppose that Beckett rejects *Irishness* in all its aspects. There were many features of the Irish mentality that fascinated Beckett and found comic expression in his writings. What Beckett could not accept was the revivalist idea of a predetermining, inherited identity. Had he been born in France or Germany – or any other nation with an obsessional sense of cultural memory – Beckett would no doubt have been equally impatient with its particular version of cultural nationalism.

b) Beckett and Joyce: Asylum and Exile

Shortly after his arrival in Paris, Beckett was introduced by the Irish poet Thomas MacGreevy to the Joyce circle. In no time, he had become such a devoted disciple that he was referred to by some cynical observers as 'James Joyce's white boy'. Beckett fully acknowledged that his early work had 'adopted the Joyce method … with original results';[3] and he contributed an enthusiastic appraisal of his modernist mentor (entitled, 'Dante … Bruno … Vico … Joyce') to the famous critical collection, *Our Exagmination round his Factification for Incamination of Work in Progress* published in Paris in 1929. But the young protégé soon felt compelled to declare his right to independence. In 1932, Beckett presented Joyce with the poem 'Home Olga' (with its play on *Homo Logos*) in which he announces the termination of his literary apprenticeship. Each line in the poem begins with a letter of Joyce's name and develops an analogy between Joyce and the betrayed Christ. The concluding words 'ecce himself and the picthank agnus' leave us in little doubt as to Beckett's identification with the peccable and ungrateful lamb who abandons the flock of his Saviour-Rabbi (*Ecce Homo*).

Given their shared commitment to experimental modernism, what was it in the Joycean aesthetic that Beckett sought to *avoid*? First, at the level of subject matter, it seems that Beckett wished to surmount the Joycean preoccupation with 'exile' that continued to link the author (albeit in a negative manner) to his national origins. Though written and published abroad, *Ulysses* and *Finnegans Wake* were explicitly concerned with Dublin, Joyce's 'first and only love', and with the local and mythic lore surrounding it. Nor did Joyce ever completely deny his allegiance to Ireland, however radically he modified it for his own aesthetic purposes. This sense of allegiance is candidly stated, for example, in his advice to Arthur Power: 'Borrowed styles are no good. You must write what is in your blood and not what is in your brain … For myself, I always write about Dublin because if I can get to the heart of Dublin I can get to the heart of all the cities of the world. In the particular is contained the universal.'

Beckett too would search for the universal. But his search would not express itself in a fidelity to his native place; and even though some of his prose writings in the thirties – *More Pricks than Kicks* (1934), 'Dream of fair to middling women' (unpublished until 1992) and *Murphy* (1938) – still carry satiric allusions to Irish characters and place names, the movement of interest is clearly away from the historical island of Hibernia and towards the metaphysical island of inwardness. Already in *Murphy*, Beckett voices his own conviction that 'asylum (after a point) is better than exile'. The vertical descent into the void of the self, or non-self, is more challenging for Beckett than the horizontal detour of geographical exile from, and imaginative return to, one's beloved homeland. The Beckettian journey is inner exodus rather than epic odyssey; his anti-hero is styled more on the Hebraic Job than on the Hellenic Ulysses.

In *Finnegans Wake*, Joyce prophesied Beckett's literary vocation as follows: 'Sam knows miles bettern me how to work the miracle … illstarred punster, lipstering cowknucks … He'll prisckly soon hand tune your Erin's ear for you'. While Beckett would indeed fulfil his role as 'illstarred punster', it was not necessarily with a language attuned to 'Erin's ear'. He would write with as much ease and eloquence in French as in English, practising a kind of 'neutralized' language typical of European modernism.[4] The problem of language was truly to be his abiding obsession. But this invariably took the form of a relentless investigation, at once anguished and playful, into the *universal problematic of writing itself*. The questions that haunted Beckett were: How is it possible to continue writing after the 'revolution of the word' that Joyce's radical modernism brought about? What are the conditions of possibility of literary communication given the collapse of traditional systems of meaning that our century has witnessed? Or more particularly, how can modernist writers in the post-war period even begin to express in fictional narrative the insufferable anguish and alienation of contemporary society. 'After Auschwitz, who can write poetry?' asked the German philosopher, Theodor Adorno. This question was also one of Beckett's abiding obsessions. In comparison, all efforts to revive national literatures or purify tribal dialects appeared insignificant, if not insupportable.

c) An Art of Impotence

The difference between the modernist approaches of Joyce and Beckett is, however, perhaps most evident in their respective interpretations of authorial narrative. In his controversial exchange with Israel Shenker in 1956, Beckett is reported to have acknowledged the following contrast between Joyce's writing and his own:

> Joyce was a superb manipulator of material, perhaps the greatest. He was making words do the absolute maximum of work. There isn't a syllable that's

superfluous. The kind of work I do is one in which I am not master of my material. The more Joyce knew the more he could. His tendency is toward … omnipotence as an artist. I'm working with impotence, ignorance. I don't think that impotence has been exploited in the past. There seems to be a kind of aesthetic axiom that expression is an achievement – must be an achievement. My little exploration is that whole zone of being which has always been set aside by artists as something unusable – as something by definition incompatible with art.

Thus while the Joycean aesthetic aspires towards an omniscient narrator (compared in *A Portrait* to 'the god of creation … invisible, refined out of existence, indifferent'), the Beckettian narrator is one who continually acknowledges his own irredeemable failure.

The narrator in 'Dream of fair to middling women', for example, rebukes the author as absolute master and confesses that 'the only unity in this story is, please god, an involuntary unity', for 'the reality of the individual … is an incoherent reality and must be expressed incoherently'. Similarly, in *More Pricks than Kicks*, Beckett cleverly undermines the omniscient stance by making obtrusive critical cross-references from one story to the next. In 'What a misfortune', he introduces Abba Perdue reminding us that 'she was the nice little girl in a "Wet Night"'. And in the same story the author even makes disparaging references to his other unpublished work: 'The powers of evocation of this Italianate Irishman were simply immense, and if "Dream of fair to middling women", held up in the limae labor stage for the past ten or fifteen years, ever reaches the public … we ought to be sure to get it and have a look at it anyway.' Later again he breaks off his narrative in a highly self-conscious aside that affirms that it is 'up to the reader to determine' the meaning; and he includes a footnote to the effect that one of his concluding phrases constitutes 'a most foully false analogy'. This auto-critique of narrative omniscience is further developed in Beckett's novel *Malone Dies* where the hero-narrator frequently intrudes into his own story with such self-deprecating comments as: 'What a misfortune, the pencil must have slipped from my fingers', or 'This is awful', or 'This should all be rewritten in the pluperfect' etc. Malone, the ailing author, rails against the 'whole sorry business, I mean the business of Malone (since that is what I am now called)'.

But nowhere does Beckett express his rejection of the controlling omnipotent narrator more emphatically than in his *Proust* essay of 1931. Here Beckett distinguishes sharply between *involuntary memory*, which gives access to the revelation of being on the one hand, and what he calls *voluntary memory* or 'imagination' on the other. Voluntary memory, Beckett claims, 'is of no value as an instrument of evocation and provides an image as far-removed from the real as the myth of imagination'. Involuntary memory, by contrast, suspends our wilful inventions and brings us face to face with the real *suffering of being*. Whereas the images that convention chooses 'are as arbitrary as those chosen by imagination and are equally remote from reality', involuntary memory constitutes a 'mystic experience' irreducible to the self-projecting subjective will. Just as Swann in Proust's novel decomposes the reality of others in the acid of his fantasizing ego, so too the fiction-writer runs the risk of reducing the *otherness* of reality to his own hermetic imagination. 'Art is the apotheosis of solitude,' Beckett acknowledges stoically. 'There is no communication because there are no vehicles of communication.' Like Proust's Swann, the fiction-writer comes to the realization that the 'art which he had for so long believed the one ideal and inviolate element in a corruptible world [is] as unreal and sterile as the construction of a demented imagination' – 'that insane barrel-organ that always keeps the wrong tune.'[5]

Beckett thus appears, reluctantly, to confirm Proust's conviction that the imagination cannot create without projecting its prejudices onto the world. The creative act, he concedes, tends to dismiss as an intruder whatever cannot be fitted into its preconceived pattern, even though 'the essence of any new experience is contained precisely in [that] mysterious element that the vigilant will rejects as an anachronism.' No amount of imaginative manipulation can recreate a genuine experience of the real world. All fiction is in some sense voluntary and therefore a falsification. The *suffering of being* is as unsayable as it is insurmountable; and art is no more than the 'dream of a madman', finding no solace outside of itself or even within itself. Beckett sums up his attitude of sceptical modernism thus: 'Reality, whether approached imaginatively or empirically, remains a surface, hermetic. Imagination, applied *a priori* to what is absent, is exercised *in vacuo* and cannot tolerate the limits of the real.'

Beckett resolves accordingly to debunk the narrative strategies of omniscient will by exposing the impotence of human consciousness before the void of existence. This necessitates a rejection of the Joycean hegemony of the word. 'I can do anything with language I want', boasted Joyce after the completion of *Ulysses*. By contrast Beckett, in the last of his dialogues with George Duthuit published in *Transition* in 1949, affirmed that the *failure* of his writing is its very *raison d'être*: 'To be an artist is to fail, as no other dare fail, that failure is his world and to shrink from it desertion ... I know that all that is required now ... is to make of this submission, this admission, this fidelity to failure, a new term of revelation, and of the act which unable to act, he makes, an expressive act, even if only of itself, of its impossibility, of its obligation.'

This aesthetic of submission to the suffering of being, with its disclosure of the impotence of language, constitutes the originality of Beckett's writing and signals its departure from Joycean omniscience. Beckett's Malone epitomizes this departure when he begs to be released from the 'gossip of lies' that flows from his fiction-spinning mind.

d) Desophisticating Language

But if Beckett refused the Joycean emphasis on narrative omnipotence, he never-theless recognized in the master's *Work in Progress* a radically new and challenging approach to language. In his 1929 essay on Joyce ('Dante ... Bruno ... Vico ... Joyce'), the twenty-three-year-old Beckett formulated what must be considered one of the guiding principles of his own writing: 'Here is direct expression – pages and pages of it. And if you do not understand it, Ladies and Gentlemen, it is because you are too decadent to receive it. You are not satisfied unless form is so strictly divorced from content that you can comprehend the one almost without bothering to read the other. This rapid skimming and absorption of the scant cream of sense is made possible by what I may call a continuous process of copious intellectual salivation.' To avoid such intellectual salivation, and to appre-ciate properly the force of Joyce's writing, it is imperative, retorts Beckett, not to concentrate on the literal sense or psychological content of writing to the exclu-sion of the writing itself. 'Here form *is* content, content *is* form,' insists Beckett. Joyce's 'writing is not *about* something; it is that something itself.'[6]

As both critic and author, Beckett fully endorsed Joyce's modernist preoccu-pation with language *as language*. If Husserl and the phenomenologists announced a philosophical revolution in the twentieth century with the maxim 'back to the things themselves', Beckett and Joyce announced its literary coun-terpart with the maxim 'back to the words themselves'. But while the modernist 'revolution of the word' (to borrow the *transition* formula) expressed itself in Joyce's writing as a triumphal manipulation of language, it becomes with Beckett, in contrast, a stoical subversion.

It is significant that when the young Beckett wrote about Joyce in 1929, the question of his Irish origin or his position in the Anglo-Irish tradition did not concern him for a moment. The company in which he placed Joyce comprised not Yeats, Synge or Russell but Dante, Bruno and Vico – and these, it must be added, only to the extent that they shed light on Joyce's particular concern with writing. 'Joyce has desophisticated language,' enthuses Beckett. 'And it is worth while remarking that no language is so sophisticated as English. It is abstracted to death.' Beckett's own writing, and particularly his prose, testifies to a similar determination to desophisticate the English tongue. The great lesson he learned from his mentor, Shem the Penman, before taking his French leave, was to show 'how worn out and threadbare was the conventional language of cunning literary artificers,' to expose the very working of words themselves. Such was Joyce's invaluable bequest to Beckett.

But what exactly is the habitual attitude – 'the language of cunning literary artificers' – that Beckett and Joyce were so determined to challenge? This atti-tude is best exemplified by what is known as *classical realism*: a narrative practice employed by most traditional novelists who presumed the literary text to be a medium that carries a message about reality from the author to the reader. This *representational* model, as we noted in our chapter on Joyce, operated on the assumption that there is a given *reality* and that the narrative discourse of the author functions as a mirror reflecting it. The text is thus treated as a definable message for the reader to translate into a paraphrase of 'intended meaning'. The modernist narratives of Joyce and Beckett, by contrast, insist on the breakdown of representation and thereby expose the complex process of language itself that intervenes between the writer and reality. Exploding the realist illusions of 'literary artificers', modernist fiction belies the conventional notion of the text as a transparent object; and, by the same token, it dispenses with the classical realist pretence that the author is an autonomous ego enjoying a privileged hold over reality and deploying the text as a means of transmitting this reality to others. The Joycean or Beckettian texts serve to undo this supposed *correspondence* between the word and the world. Rather than using language to represent experience, they enable us to experience language through a dismantling of representation.[7] Modernist writers put language itself in question. Trojan horses in the city of the Word, they deconstruct it from within.

Beckett, it may be said, replaces the self-sufficient author with the self-differentiating author of plural discourses. The Beckettian narrator discovers that he is nothing more than the sum of his own fictive discourses. Thus the narrator of *The Unnamable* (1958), for example, exclaims: 'All these Murphys, Molloys and Malones do not fool me. They have made me waste my time, suffer for nothing, speak of them when, in order to stop speaking, I should have spoken of me and me alone.' Yet the narrator realizes that the ideal 'me alone' is itself a mere verbal fiction and that as long as he speaks he must always speak in the voice of another, or rather in a multiplicity of voices. For Beckett, as for Rimbaud before him, '*Je est un autre*'. To change one's language, just as to change one's national abode or narrative voice, is not therefore a betrayal of identity – for there is no *identity* to betray. And the very idea of an 'Irish' or 'French' writer is a contradiction in terms, for national identities and traditions are themselves no more than impostures of language. We are the voices that speak us. Language precedes existence. It determines who and what we are. Beckett's entire literary corpus may be seen accordingly as a relentless parody of the fiction of identity which underpins our traditional attitudes to language and, by extension, to literature. But where Joyce chose rebellion, Beckett chose resignation. He has, he believes, no choice in the matter. In the second part of this chapter we offer a detailed analysis of this subversive practice as it progressively unfolds in Beckett's prose writings. (The impact of this practice on his drama is examined separately in an appendix to this chapter.)

II. Beckett and the Deconstruction of Fiction

a) The Early Novels: Beyond the Fiction of Self-Identity

Already in his first published novel, *Murphy* (1938), Beckett satirizes the illusion of self-identity. Beckett's literary and philosophical preoccupations are so intimately connected that one cannot fully appreciate the originality of his writing without some grasp of the metaphysical ideas it rehearses and challenges.[8] Western metaphysics, from Plato onwards (as noted in the epilogue 'Joyce and Derrida: Jewgreek is Greekjew'), has defined the ideal state of Being as a timeless 'presence' that is self-adequate and self-identical. Thus God, the Supreme Being, is referred to as *Ens Causa Sui, Ipsum Esse Subsistens* or *Nunc Aeternum* – an entity existing above and beyond the human world of temporal flux and movement. The intellectual dimension of the human subject is deemed to participate in this Divine Being to the extent that it rises above its mortal physical existence, that is, transcends time so as to become absolutely self-present, at one with itself. This is the essence of the Cartesian attempt to found a self-contained thinking subject (or *Cogito*) that Beckett exposes to ridicule.[9]

Murphy wishes to be alive and dead simultaneously: to be atemporal while existing temporally, to jump out of his own skin. He refers to this post-mortem mortality as his 'Belacqua bliss', alluding thereby to the Dantesque vision of a timeless paradise (a vision that Beckett denounced in his Joyce essay as 'the static lifelessness of unrelieved immaculation'). Thus Murphy aspires to a divine condition of absolute self-sufficiency. Though he is desired and needed by others – Celia, Miss Counihan, Neary, Wylie – Murphy desires and needs no one. For human desire, as Aristotle pointed out, already implies movement beyond the *self* towards the *other*, and Murphy's whole existence is modelled on the Aristotelian ideal of a divine 'Unmoved Mover' (represented by his rocking chair). Murphy wishes to reduce the world to the sealed-off cloister of his own 'ipssimosity'. Hence the appropriateness of his death in a lunatic asylum totally sequestered from the outside world. Murphy's project is to become absolutely present to himself by excluding all that is other than himself. In the nirvana of the isolated ego he expects to accomplish his eternal self-realization.

But Beckett satirically exposes the folly of this endeavour. In chapter 6, Murphy's Leibnizean ideal of splendid self-adequacy is subjected to parody:

> Murphy's mind pictured itself as a large hollow sphere, hermetically closed to the universe without ... Nothing ever had been, was or would be in the universe outside it but was already present as virtual, or actual, or virtual rising into actual, or actual falling into virtual, in the universe inside it ... his mind was a closed system, subject to no principle of change but its own, self-sufficient and impermeable to the vicissitudes of the body.

Beckett introduces the chapter with the heading, *Amor intellectualis quo Murphy se ipsum amat*, an explicit reference to the metaphysical definition of God, in common currency since Augustine, as that Love which is sufficient unto itself (*Amor quo Deus se ipsum amat*). This definition is modelled, in turn, on the Aristotelian ideal of an incorporeal self-thinking thought (*noesis tes noeseos*), an ideal that the author of *Murphy* never ceases to satirically undermine.

In *What Is Literature?* Sartre argued that a writer's style or technique refers us back, implicitly or explicitly, to his metaphysics. This is certainly true of Beckett. Like many of the great modern novelists, from Tolstoy and Dostoevsky to Mann and Camus, Beckett's literary inventions are inseparable from fundamental philosophical projects. His project in *Murphy* is to challenge the traditional doctrine, advanced by the eponymous anti-hero himself, that humans can be identified as timeless, silent and immutable consciousnesses. Already in this first novel, he wittily demonstrates that we are bodily beings bound irremediably to speech, movement and time.

Beckett's assault on the fiction of identity becomes more explicit in his subsequent novel *Watt* (1944). Here Beckett engages in a painstaking, and at times mischievous, critique of the conventional notion of language as a naming process. Language has been traditionally defined as a set of proper names corresponding to a correlative set of univocal objects or essences. Watt's endeavour to establish a fool-proof logic of names reiterates the metaphysical ideal of a perfectly transparent language. But the enigmatic events in Mr Knott's house prove refractory to Watt's naming system. His method for transmuting 'disturbance into words' is far from infallible. By the end of the novel the reader is made painfully aware, even if the tone is playful, of Watt's utter inability to establish language as a self-sufficient totality capable of explaining or containing reality. Language unveils itself as the irreducible reminder of man's tragic-comic fallibility.[10]

As the novel proceeds the comforting illusion that there exists an authorial language able to classify reality is progressively undermined. In Mr Knott's house, for example, Watt discovers a world resistant to the fixities of naming.

> Looking at a pot, for example, or thinking of a pot, at one of Mr Knott's pots, of one of Mr Knott's pots, it was in vain that Watt said, Pot, pot … it resembled a pot, it was almost a pot, but it was not a pot of which one could say, 'Pot, pot and be comforted.'

Mr Knott, as his name suggests, exemplifies that force of nothingness which, as the existentialists have argued, shocks us out of our habitual attitude to things and, filling us with 'dread', reveals the world in all its unassailable otherness. The elusive Mr Knott, like Malone after him, illustrates the enigmatic maxim of Beckettian philosophy that 'nothing is more real than nothing'.[11] The more Watt pursues his goal of explaining the nothingness at the heart of existence, the more he becomes aware of the impossibility of ever finding names for the unnamable. Thus Watt is forced to acknowledge that the self is no more self-contained than the square root of two. Just as the ideal language of mathematics can be exploded from within by the recurring decimal 52.285714 ... , so too the so-called 'identity' of the self is irreparably subject to the haemorrhage of differentiation. The human self bleeds into the void of language.

What we traditionally took to be a pre-established harmony between words and things is in truth, Watt discovers, no more than a 'pre-established arbitrary'. Language itself is a shifting process that we seek to conceal and stabilize by granting it an origin outside of time. But Watt's reflections on the temporal anomalies of the comings and goings of Mr Knott's three servants, Tom, Dick and Harry, brilliantly serve to highlight the tortuous paradox of *time*, the fallaciousness of that eternal 'freedom of indifference' so ardently coveted by Watt, Murphy and other Beckettian narrators. 'It is useless not to seek, not to want' (confesses another of Knott's servants, Arsène) for we are condemned to desire, to exist in time, transcending what we are not (Knott). Thus are we condemned to speak our *failure to be*. In the addenda to the novel, Beckett goes so far in his liquidation of self-identity as to exhort the reader to 'change all the names'. And lest we presume to equate his writing with some fixed symbolic meaning referring to something *outside* of the text, he adds his much quoted caveat: 'no symbols where none intended'.

b) Molloy: *The Demise of the Narrative Ego*

In *Molloy* (1955), the first and most accomplished novel of his trilogy, Beckett intensifies his attack on the classical notion of the authorial subject (thus fulfilling his early promise to explore the problematic 'existence of the author'). Since Molloy, the book's garrulous narrator, is unable to discover a stable ego either in himself or in his fictive pseudo-selves, the whole structure of a traditional plot with a beginning, middle and end has to be abandoned. Molloy's narrative turns in a vicious circle and thereby excludes the possibility of a linear sequence. The end of the novel is in fact the writer writing the beginning: the narrator alone in his room narrating and re-narrating for some unknown author 'who gives him money and takes away the pages'.

Beckett's intention in the trilogy is twofold: to debunk the classical structure of the novel as a linear quest wherein a subject progresses towards the discovery of a real or transcendental self; and to dismantle the idea of a privileged metalanguage (usually that of an omniscient narrator) serving to assess and situate the various other discourses in the text. By parodying Molloy's authorial discourse, Beckett sabotages the standard claim of 'classical realism' to a 'representable' meaning. Words never correspond to reality – Molloy admits that 'what really happened was quite different'.

The narrating ego is thus doomed from the outset. Beckett creates Molloy who confesses to have 'spoken of himself as [he] would have of another'; Molloy creates a sub-self, Malone, who in turn regenerates himself in an endless series of 'vice-existers'. The author, as Beckett demonstrates with his characteristic passion for narrative anarchy, can enjoy no controlling meta-discourse that would permit him to identify himself *outside* of the text as the original source of the story. The author has no identity apart from that of his characters; and his characters have no identity. The writer *is* his writing and his writing is arbitrary, without beginning or end, impotent. The omniscient narrators of the classical novel have had their day, as one of Molloy's vice-narrators complains, 'those old craftsmen whose race is extinct and the mould broken'. Beckett's own confession of authorial impotence to George Duthuit gives us a further chilling insight into this dilemma: 'There is nothing to express, nothing with which to express, together with the obligation to express.'

In something of a love-hate manner, Beckett presents Molloy as an author in search of a story that might furnish him with a new-found sense of selfhood. Through fiction, Molloy hopes to tell the tale of himself, to remember himself, his name, his birthplace, to retrace his existence back to its origins, to his deaf, blind mother Mag, with whom he could only communicate by knocking on her skull ('one knock meant yes, two no, three I don't know, four money, five goodbye'). It is precisely this kind of deflationary humour that flouts the very seriousness of Molloy's enterprise. Moreover, the narrator himself is all too aware that in writing of his origins he is merely spinning an elaborate myth: 'I speak in the present tense, it is so easy to speak in the present tense when speaking of the past. It is the mythological present, don't mind it.'

Furthermore, Beckett doesn't allow us to forget for a moment that Molloy has as many *selves* as he has *stories* to tell of himself, each from a different perspective: 'Chameleon in spite of himself, there you have Molloy, viewed from a certain angle'. Though Molloy's reason for recounting his past is 'to be a little less in the end, the creature you were in the beginning, and the middle', he realizes that the idea of a developing self-identity is itself a mere invention of words. This terrifying realization is expressed in one of the most iconoclastic prose passages composed by Beckett:

> Even my sense of identity was wrapped in a namelessness often hard to penetrate ... there could be no things but nameless things, no names but thingless names. I can say that now, but after all what do I know now about then, now when the icy words hail down upon me, the icy meanings, and the world dies too, foully named. All I know is what the words know, and the dead things, and that makes a handsome little sum, with a beginning, a middle and an end as in the well-built phrase and the long sonata of the dead. And truly it little matters what I say, this or that or any other thing. Saying is inventing.

But to make matters worse – and Beckett simply thrives on making matters worse – it appears that it is not we who invent words but words that invent us. Whether we will or not we are condemned to language. 'You invent nothing, you think you are inventing, you think you are escaping, and all you do is stammer out a lesson, the remnants of pensum one day got by heart and long forgotten, life without tears, as it is wept.'

Beckett's obsession with the *suffering of being* springs from his awareness that language – and more particularly writing – is a process of dying. Language brings us face to face with our own mortality by making us aware that we can never escape from time so as to become fully present to ourselves. We are finite, temporal, decentred beings who are *spoken by* language before we choose to *speak* it.[12] This dissolution of the autonomous humanist subject (or the 'disappearance of man' in Foucault's phrase) into the shifting, impersonalizing structure of language, is what Beckett refers to as the 'deanthropomorphization of the artist'.[13]

c) Malone Dies: *Somewhere in the Void*

In the second novel of the trilogy, *Malone Dies*, (1956) Beckett's chosen theme is, once again, the writer trapped in the purgatory of fiction. Malone, like all the other Beckettian authors, writes in order to absolve himself from the obligation of writing. He speaks in order to stop speaking. But the circle is more vicious here than in any of the previous novels.

Malone begins by telling himself four stories 'almost lifeless, like the teller'. But unlike Molloy before him, Malone is absolutely without illusions. He realizes from the outset that he 'shall not succeed any better than hitherto', and shall only end up finding himself 'abandoned in the dark, without anything to play with'. So no sooner has he begun his first story (about a boy named Sapo) than he retracts it and goes on to the next: 'Already I forget what I have said. That is not how to play ... perhaps I had better abandon this story and go on to the second, or even the third ...' Malone is helpless before the flux of language: 'Words and images run riot in my head, pursuing, flying, clashing, merging, endlessly'. He seeks to get beyond this textual tumult to calm, a silence, a self. This, however, is not permitted for 'when I stop, as just now, the noises begin again, strangely loud, those whose turn it is'. The narrator is unable to represent any credible reality; but he is equally incapable of abstaining from the activity of writing. 'I did not want to write, but I had to resign myself to it in the end', confesses Malone. What is more, Malone is disturbingly aware that he himself is just one *persona* in another narrator's play of words. 'You may say it is all in my head,' he interjects, 'and indeed sometimes it seems to me I am in a head and that these eight, no six, these six planes that enclose me are of solid bone'. Not surprisingly, Malone also revokes his own stories (those of Sapo, the Lamberts, Macmann). 'My stories are all in vain', he repeats, self-consciously rebuffing his own style as 'innumerable babble'. Thus, once more, the classical myth of narrative as an adequate representational correspondence between narrating subject and narrated object is exposed in mock-heroic fashion: 'The subject falls far from the verb and the object lands somewhere in the voice.' And as the illusion of representation dissolves, language itself, as that irrepressible process of signifying, forces itself to the forefront of the reader's attention. Beckett's narrators are perpetual transients of the word, migrants incapable of receding from that endless play of language that Lévi-Strauss has called the 'superabundance of signifiers'.

Subtly undermining our accredited notions of plot, character and even punctuation, Beckett obliges us to acknowledge that meaning is not something originating from an extra-textual world to be subsequently reproduced by text. Meaning can only be produced through the labour of speaking, writing and reading, through the interminable differentiation of signs. Incapable of bringing the Beckettian text to a close the reader discovers that there is no paralinguistic identity to return to. The self covered by the mask of fiction is itself but a mask; each mask being the mask of a mask just as each story is the story of a story. In this way Beckett *implicates* the reader in the text itself; he makes him aware that there is no authentic or 'original' version of a text, only endless translations; no single factual meaning, only interpretations; no truth, only parodies. We are thereby revealed to ourselves, in fear and trembling, *as language*, as continuous dispersion into multiple discourses, as beings who are always *other* than what we say we are, irremediably exposed to the metamorphosis of signs.

To read Beckett is therefore to discover that the meaning of our existence is not *literal* but *figurative*; and this discovery, brought about by the self-disassembling of the Beckettian narrative disrupts our established vision of things. His radical *technics* of formal experimentation – to borrow Sartre's formula – refer us to an equally radical *metaphysics*.[14]

d) The Unnamable: *A Hell of Stories*

The Unnamable (1958) begins where *Malone Dies* left off – with the admission that we can never forestall the disseminating play of language. But the admission has become more vehement and more uncompromising by virtue of its repetition. (And *repetition* or 'supplementarity' is, as Derrida notes, the *modus operandi* of the self-deconstructing writing process). The very *contents* of writing, those vibrant flesh and blood characters and events that make fiction so satisfying, have not survived the purges of the previous novels. Only the metaphysical *problem* of writing remains. 'Whereof I cannot speak, thereof I will be silent', Wittgenstein once asserted. But Beckett, a less quietistic philosopher of language, cannot be silent though he has no longer anything of which to speak. For even if the author stops inventing new stories the old ones repeat themselves. He will go on trying to name the unnamable. 'I seem to speak,' declares the narrator whom

Beckett leaves without a name, 'it is not I, about me ... I shall have to speak of things of which I cannot speak ... I shall never be silent – never.'

This final novel of the trilogy is in fact a never-ending preliminary to a novel that never begins. Here the narrator passes in review all of his previous narrators – Malone, Molloy, Murphy etc. – commenting on their successive failures. Once again we witness a baffling interchangeability of narrator and narrated: 'Malone is there ... He passes before me at doubtless regular intervals, unless it is I who pass before him ... I like to think I occupy the centre but nothing is less certain.' The decentered narrator tries desperately to 'attribute a beginning', a definitive and definable origin, to himself; but he cannot, he remains unnamed and unnamable. And yet he is cruelly condemned to go on *searching* for names, for that ultimate conclusion that would grant him an identity and permit silence. 'I hope this preamble will soon come to an end', exclaims the author after thousands of faltering fine-spun words, 'and the statement begin that will dispose of me'. But in the inevitable absence of such a statement he is doomed to go on – 'murmuring my stories, my old story, as if it were for the first time'. The writer thus finally comes face to face with the brutal metaphysical truth that his world is merely a fiction of language that in turn sustains the fiction of himself as author. The only solution – which of course is no solution – is to accept, with a sort of perverse *amor fati*, the ineluctable 'hell of stories', relinquishing one's will to power, one's will to be oneself. Beckett has rarely expressed the stoic hopelessness of the authorial quest so movingly:

> This voice that speaks, knowing that it lies, indifferent to what it says, too
> old perhaps and too abused ever to succeed in saying the words that would
> be its last, knowing itself unless and its uselessness in vain ... I can't stop it,
> I can't prevent it, from tearing me, racking me, assailing me. It is not mine,
> I have none, I have no voice and must speak, that is all I know ... of what
> I must speak, with this voice that is not mine, but can only be mine ... in
> obedience to the unintelligible terms of an incomprehensible damnation.

e) How It Is: *The Obituary of the Novel*

In 1961 Beckett published his last attempt at a full length novel, *Comment C'est* (published in English in 1964 as *How It Is*). The original French title is an ironic pun on *commencer*, meaning to begin, or in context, to begin all over again. Composing a magnificently poignant and torrential prose, bereft of plot, character, syntax and punctuation, Beckett was to pen here his obituary of the novel form. In a letter to Jack Schwartz in 1959, Beckett admitted that the bottomless pit of *How It Is* is 'as dumb of light as the Fifth Canto of Hell' (an admission that recalls the definition of hell in his early Joyce essay as 'the static lifelessness of unrelieved viciousness').[15]

Here the narrator inhabits the subterranean darkness of a Platonic cave – the original starting point of Western metaphysics; but, in contradistinction to Plato's optimistic allegory, the nostalgic desire for the world of truth 'up there in the light' is forever unfulfilled. This denial is ingeniously expressed in Beckett's very style of writing. The words are meticulously defused by the author and exposed as artifices; they fold back upon themselves and refuse to serve as metaphors pointing beyond (*meta-phorein*) words to some transcendent meaning. In this way the very structure of the narrative belies the traditional illusion of language as a journey *progressing* upwards to an ultimate transcendental meaning (*logos*). By reducing writing to a language without names, without the redemptive magic of transcendence or light (as ultimate metaphysical origin), Beckett pronounces a mordant critique of the 'logocentric' philosophy of Western humanist civilization.

How It Is parodies the classical quest-structure of the novel as a linear journey wherein the hero progresses from ignorance to insight.[16] Beckett achieves this with habitual comic cruelty by portraying the narrator as an abandoned vagabond, crawling through slime and darkness, ten yards at a time, trailing after him a sack of sardine tins (his daily sustenance) and muttering meaningless ditties 'quo qua'. Death would represent a satisfactory termination to this *navigatio* that goes nowhere. But even this, alas, is indefinitely postponed. And so the narrator's discourse turns in a circle, returning to the beginning to end, symmetrically but absurdly, with the pun *comment c'est*. Beckett's deconstructive approach to the traditional novel of quest remains unswervingly consistent from start to finish.

Conclusion

With Beckett the classical forms of fictional narrative, of telling a story with a beginning, middle and end appear to have been utterly negated. It is, one might say, the end of the story. Nothing remains to be represented in the plot and characterization of traditional narration. So why does Beckett go on writing? Why does the reader go on reading?

The answer perhaps lies in the 'postmodernist' appeal of Beckett's literary enterprise. Beckett's writing reveals that the storytelling function of language is not just to relay messages or revive memories but to critically explore and expose the fundamental quest-structure of human existence. This structure, as we pointed out, is an endless transcending towards meaning. The particular character of Beckett's quest-structure is that it leads towards nothing. There is no longer a transcendent meaning that could furnish the narrative self with a fixed identity. The human subject is abandoned to its own devices and desires, marooned on the island of language with no reference beyond itself. In Beckett's texts the metaphorizing of language, therefore, functions less as a means to an end than as an end in itself. And there is, strangely, the power of Beckett's writing. As Geoffrey Hartman has observed in *Deconstruction and Criticism* (1979), the force of modern literature is to reveal 'the priority of language to meaning. Literary language foregrounds language itself as something not reducible to meaning.'[17] Once the transcendental aspirations of language are revealed as misguided – since there is no identifiable transcendence to which it can aspire – the human *quest* is transmuted into *passion* (in the etymological sense of 'patience' and 'suffering', *patior-pati-passus*). Language is exposed accordingly as the *suffering of being*. In this respect, the Beckettian text can be described as *passionate* writing: a writing that insists on waiting for a meaning that refuses to show up, an absent meaning that leaves traces but cannot be traced, signifies but cannot be signified.

In all this Beckett bears an uncanny resemblance to his counterpart from Prague, Franz Kafka. Kafka described the world of writing as a hell with its good moments. For both of these authors language is a labyrinth where the path leads on indefinitely without ever reaching sanctuary. Indeed a Beckettian narrator might well have uttered the exhortation of the accused in *The Trial*: 'Once you have started on a path, stick to it under all circumstances ... And if you fail in the end that is better than if you fail at the beginning, as you certainly would if you retraced your steps ... As long as you don't stop climbing, the steps will not come to an end ...' One is reminded of Beckett's unnameable narrator concluding his monologue with the equally poignant and paradoxical words – 'I can't go on, I'll go on'. Beckett's fidelity to paradox conveys the hope that the hell of language can perhaps have its comic moments, its happy days. There is a serenity in the failure to find meaning that itself constitutes a strange beauty, the beauty of impossibility, perhaps the kind most suited to Beckett's own particular brand of post-war modernism. Far from being an acquiescent nihilist, Beckett traverses human suffering and despair in an obsessive commitment to language as a passionate, if always unrequited, waiting.

Appendix A: Writing Under Erasure

I. Ending Narrative

Beckett's narrator in *Molloy* ends his story where he began, behind his desk, concluding with the same lines that open the story – 'It is midnight. The rain is beating on the windows' – still subordinate to the impersonal dictates of language, to the 'voice telling [him] things'. The only difference is that time has passed and the original meaning has cancelled itself out. The narrator adds – 'it was *not* midnight. It was *not* raining'.

This double strategy of affirmation and denial is what Jacques Derrida calls writing 'under erasure' (*sous rature*). Meaning is cancelled out by the very language that produces it to the extent that it purports to tell us of something existing *before* language – and there is no such thing. There is no *hors texte*. Language itself is disclosed as a self-effacing or self-erasing process which simultaneously points towards and precludes some pre-linguistic origin of meaning. There is no meaning beyond the words that articulate it. For Derrida, as for Beckett, the world is itself a text.

But Beckett, unlike Derrida, will not take no for an answer. He skilfully compels his narrator and reader to go on searching for an absolute origin of meaning *in spite of its non-existence*. His writing thus unfurls sedulously and cunningly, like Penelope's tapestry, weaving and unweaving itself in ever finer, ever more intricate patterns. Indeed, it is a token of Beckett's extraordinary literary talent that he can so deftly spin his web of words as to sustain the reader's interest and excitement in such a self-defeating project.

The narrator of *The Unnamable* persists in reiterating the view of his predecessors that the great metaphysical problem is 'how to get back to me, back to where I was waiting for me'. He reckons that if he can re-establish the genesis of himself, rediscover his family, his birth-place, 'that unthinkable ancestor of whom nothing can be said', then, at last, he will transcend words. Yet the absurd paradox remains that in trying to name his ancestry the narrator is forced to speak with alien, borrowed voices. So that, in desperation, he resigns himself to telling 'another of Mahood's stories and no more about it', to make it his 'last story' so as to bring the whole sorry business to a full stop. No sooner begun, however, than the narrator breaks off and censures his own deceit – 'This story is no good, I'm beginning almost to believe it.' Yet after this interruption, he cannot go on because he has no memory of what he has already said. Consequently the story is suspended in mid-course and he has to begin all over again. Amidst all this confusion and indecision – at once fascinating and frustrating for the reader – all we can know for certain is that 'it all boils down to a question of words – a question of voices'.

And still for all that certainty, the voices keep on trying to deceive the narrator 'till I hear myself saying, myself at last, to myself at last, that it can't be they speaking thus, that it can only be I speaking thus. If only I could find a voice of my own, in all this babble, it would be the end of their troubles, and of mine.' But there is no single voice that he can call his own and be sure that it is his. 'The subject doesn't matter, there is none.'

It also becomes abundantly clear in *The Unnamable* that for Beckett language is naked, utterly devoid of images and things, *incommunicado*. There is no longer any transfer of meaning possible. The words are blank, as the author explains:

That's all words they taught me ... all the words they showed me, there were columns of them, oh the strange glow all of a sudden, they were on lists, with images opposite, I must have forgotten them, I must have mixed them up, these nameless images I have, these imageless names, these windows I should perhaps rather call doors, at least by some other name, and this word man which is perhaps not the right one for the thing I see when I hear it, but an instant, an hour, and so on, how can they be represented, a life, how could that be made clear to me, here, in the dark, I call that the dark, perhaps it's azure, blank words, but I use them … I need them all, to be able to go on, it's a lie.

By describing his imageless names as 'doors' and 'windows', the author is suggesting to himself that they might somehow become referential *meta-phors*, carrying (*phorein*) the self out of (*meta*) itself towards some external reality. 'If only there were a thing somewhere to talk about,' sighs the rueful author. But the 'thing' that metaphor is supposed to talk about is itself no more than a metaphor, a figure of speech, a lie. The so-called window–doors of words are really hollow metaphors referring to nothing beyond themselves. They are quite impotent to carry the self to some higher being and merely 'open on the void'.

The longed for silence of *self-identity*, where language could supposedly 'correspond' with reality or with the subjective ego, is forever deferred.[18] One story leads into another, one narrator into his opposite, and so on *ad vitam aeternam*. This infinite regress of language (towards some non-existent origin) is what Derrida has referred to as a *palimpsest*: behind every text lies another that has been erased or written over, and behind that yet another, etc. Thus Beckett's nameless narrator exclaims that if only he could synchronise these various stories, voices and pronouns into a single 'original' subject, 'then I could stop, I'd be he, I'd be silence, I'd be back in the silence, we'd be reunited, his story, the story to be told, but he has no story he hasn't been in my story, it's not certain, he's in his own story, unimaginable, unspeakable, that doesn't matter, the attempt must be made, in the old stories incomprehensibly mine, to find his …' In the final analysis, there is only language which asserts and then erases itself, boldly exposing itself as a multilayered palimpsest of narratives.[19] The conclusion to *The Unnamable* is an apt statement of such self-erasing exposure: '… Where I am. I don't know, I'll never know, in the silence you don't know, you must go on, I can't go on, I'll go on.'

But the very impossibility of ending the story is itself part of the life-history of narrative. Kermode makes this point in his study of 'schismatic modernism' in *The Sense of an Ending* when he argues that 'crisis is inescapably a central element in our endeavours towards making sense of our world.'[20] The 'shift towards schism', which Kermode identifies with Beckett's subversion of traditional narrativity, retains nevertheless a relationship with narrative para-digms albeit in the form of parody. The schism is devoid of meaning once deprived of all reference to the anterior conditions of narrative: 'The absolutely new is simply unintelligible, even by virtue of its very novelty … novelty itself implies the existence of that which is not new – a past.'[21] In short, the very notion of a radical novelty presupposes the totality of the traditional forms which it seeks to surpass. Nothing, by virtue of a reference to itself only, can ever be *new*. The 'innocent eye sees nothing'. One cannot speak of the *end* of the story without presupposing the prior existence of the story.

Paul Ricoeur develops this point in his philosophical study of the modernist anti-novel in *Time and Narrative*, vol. 2. He argues that whereas the birth of the novel coincided with the security of 'representation realism' (which masked the insecurity of writing itself as a formal process of composition), the end of the novel exposes the insecurity of ordered composition by shattering the traditional conviction that fiction is a mimetic representation of an exter-nally ordered reality. Thus '*L'écriture devient son propre problème et sa propre impossibilité.*'[22] The total refusal of narrative order or coherence would mean the death of the narrative paradigm of storytelling. The end of the story in this sense would signify that modernity has no longer a common experience to narrate. While Ricoeur acknowledges that the anti-novels of Beckett's schismatic 'modernism' or the *nouveaux romans* of postmodernism seem to point towards such an apocalyptic conclusion, he issues the following thought-provoking caveat:

Peut-être, en effet, sommes-nous les témoins – et les artisans – d'une certaine mort, celle de l'art de conter, d'où procède celui de raconter sous toutes ses formes. Peut-être le roman est-il en train lui aussi de mourir en tant que narration. Rien en effet ne permet d'exclure que l'expérience cumulative qui, au moins dans l'aire culturelle de l'Occident, a offert un style historique indentifi-able soit aujourd'hui frappée de mort. Les paradigmes dont il a été parlé aupar-avant ne sont eux-mêmes que les dépôts sédimentés de la tradition. Rien donc n'exclut que la métamorphoses de l'intrigue rencontre quelque part une borne au-delà de laquelle on ne peut plus reconnaître le principe formel de configura-tion temporelle qui fait de l'histoire racontée une histoire une et complète. Et pourtant ... Et pourtant. Peut-être faut-il, *malgré tout*, faire confiance à la demande de concordance qui structure aujourd'hui encore l'attente des lecteurs et croire que de nouvelles formes narratives, que nous ne savons pas encore nommer, sont déjà en train de naître, qui attesteront que la fonction narrative peut se métamorphoser, mais non pas mourir. Car nous n'avons aucune idée de ce que serait une culture où l'on ne saurait plus ce que signifie *raconter*.[23]

II. Ending Play

Having apparently exhausted the traditional resources of the novel, Beckett has had increasing recourse to what may prove to be (along with drama) the most resilient genre of his literary corpus: the shorter prose experiments. Here there is nothing to be proved, nothing to be done; the texts are anti-texts, 'texts for nothing'. In these *écrits manqués*, which Beckett refers to as his *nouvelles* or *residua*, the self-negation of narrative seems capable of persevering indef-initely. The collected shorter prose (1945–66) is entitled, appropriately, *No's Knife* (1967).

The shorter prose texts – ranging from *Texts for Nothing* (1954), *Enough* (1966), *Imagination Dead Imagine* (1965), *Ping* (1967) and *Lessness* (1969) to *Company* (1980) – do not, and cannot it seems, depart from the fundamental Beckettian obsession with the demise of the writing process. The title of *Imagination Dead Imagine* concisely reiterates the essential contradiction involved in fiction's attempt to obviate its own narrative activity. To destroy fiction we must resort to fiction. The word is as inescapable as it is insufferable. Unable to go beyond the paralysing conclusions of *The Unnamable*, Beckett is nevertheless compelled to go on writing, to say and unsay himself again and again. *Company* (1980) is a final reaffirmation of the impos-sibility of discovering some adequate 'correspondence' in or by means of fiction. The first line – 'A voice reaches someone in the dark. To Imagine.' – announces the fiction of companion-ship which the last word of the text – 'alone' – erases. And the text itself is a replay of this unique theme. The 'other', the companion, who might witness the author's existence, justify his narrative quest, and restore his identity, as he lies in the mud, on his back, in the dark, is no more than a ghost of language, one amongst many, a voice uttering a voice uttering a voice ...

In *Waiting for Godot* (1952), his first play, Beckett pursues his deconstruction of the linguistic fictions which hide us from the *suffering of being*. The genre and idiom of drama offered some release from the dwindling resources of the novel form (i.e. fictional narrative). By supplementing words with the actions, gestures and movements of physical characters on a stage, Beckett was afforded a certain distance from the paradigms of verbal narration. But this in its way indicated a departure from his central obsession with the mortality of meaning – the terminal illness of language. In short, the movement from fiction to drama signalled a renewed assault on the strategies of storytelling.

Waiting for Godot shows how language is 'deadened' by human 'habit' so as to preserve the illusion of commonplace meaning. Vladimir and Estragon tell each other stories in order 'to pass the time'. They are terrified by the passing of time, by the process of dying. 'Will you stop tormenting me with your accursed time,' wails Pozzo, reiterating in cogent dramatic terms Beckett's denunciation of the 'time cancer' in his early Proust essay. For time is the reminder that we are transient beings who cannot re-collect our existence into some *original* beginning or *final* end. There is only the passing out – from nowhere to nowhere: the journey is thus transformed into a waiting, an endless, motiveless vigilance. Hence the appositeness of Vivian Mercier's description of *Godot* as a two act play in which 'nothing happens – twice'.

Estragon is the poet who cannot remember. Past events are for him merely traces receding into infinity; they *represent* nothing and might as well be dreams as memories. Pozzo and Godot's messengers deny at each encounter that the previous encounter has taken place. Indeed, all Vladimir and Estragon possess of the past is their story of it. 'To have lived is not enough for them, they have to talk about it.' But they cannot even know if it is really *their* story or merely a repetition of 'all the dead voices' that assail them.

Here again Derrida's palimpsest analogy is helpful for an understanding of Beckett's literary designs. It is not only in Beckett's novels that the phrases and characters refer back to each other in a series of internally receding traces; the plays too participate in this regressive game of superimposition and erasure. Vladimir, for example, repeats phrases from Malone and Molloy; Pozzo's orders reiterate Moran's; Godot is a fourth-generation replica of Manhood, Basil and Youdi; and Lucky's diatribe resumes the Unnamable's endless twaddle. This indicates that the entire Beckettian corpus constitutes a cross-textual play of traces where each text refers to a predecessor. The words spoken by Beckett's protagonists do not refer forward to some *symbolized* extra-textual reality. They refer back to former instances of themselves, previous textual attempts to get beyond the game of language. 'No symbols where none intended.' We must take the author at his word.

This play of language as relentless repetition is alluded to in the Gaelic pun on the name 'Godot' itself, '*go deo*' meaning 'forever' or 'interminable'. The theological parody of the play's title is particularly significant with regard to the theme of deconstructing the word, for as Derrida observes in *De la Grammatologie* (*Of Grammatology*, tr. Spivak, J. Hopkins U.P., 1974): 'The sign and divinity have the same place and time of birth. The age of the sign is essentially theological. Perhaps it will never *end*. Its historical *closure* is, however, outlined' (p. 14). The internal repetitiveness of *Godot* can be read accordingly as a symptom of the 'ending' of the theological model of the sign as a re-presentation of some divine *logos* of meaning. This 'ending' can only express itself as *play*. Derrida explains:

> From the moment that there is meaning there are nothing but signs. We think only in *signs*. Which amounts to ruining the notion of sign at the very moment when, as in Nietzsche, its exigency is recognised in the absoluteness of its rights. One could call *play* the absence of the transcendental signified as limitlessness of play, that is to say as the destruction of onto-theology and the metaphysics of presence. [p. 50]

In the *Phaedrus* Socrates condemned writing as mere play – *paidia* – and saw it as a threat to the self-sufficient speech of the *logos* which was celebrated as 'being its own father', that is, the source of itself as absolute foundation. If Godot is for Beckett the inevitable absence and impossibility of some transcendental signified, then the play, as a play of different and differing signifiers, can only be a waiting without end, a perpetual deferment of accomplishment through time and space. The characters of Beckett's play are all victims crippled by what onto-theology considered to be the 'original sin of language' (Derrida); for language is ultimately a writing which operates as a sign without a signified, that is, a sign which annuls its own *raison d'être* as linear and accumulative movement towards some teleological meaning (*ibid.* pp. 86). Beckett's work is perhaps the most challenging literary instance of this contemporary deconstruction of the sign announced by Derrida:

> 'Signifier of the signifier' describes ... the movement of language: in its origin, to be sure, but one can already suspect that an origin whose structure can be expressed as 'signifier of the signifier' conceals and erases itself in its own produc-tion. There the signified always already functions as a signifier. The secondarity that it seemed possible to ascribe to writing alone affects all signified in general,

affects them always already, the moment they enter the game. There is not a single signified that escapes, even if recaptured, the play of signifying references that constitute language. The advent of writing is the advent of this play; today such a play is coming into its own, effacing the limit starting from which one had thought to regulate the circulation of signs, drawing along with it all the reassuring signifieds, reducing all the strong-holds, all the out-of-bounds shelters that watched over the field of language. This, strictly speaking, amounts to destroying the concept of 'sign' and its entire logic. Undoubtedly it is not by chance that this *overwhelming* supervenes at the moment when the extension of the concept of language effaces its own limits. [*ibid*. p.7]

In *Endgame* (1957), Beckett's second major play, the critique of language as 'sign' becomes even more radical. Here there is not even the pretence of a journey, of linear progress towards truth. The world is reduced to a single cell inhabited by four characters, only one of whom (Clov) is capable of movement. Nagg and Nell, cripples in dustbins, 'tell stories' of their past in order, like Vladimir and Estragon before them, to pass the time. Hamm, the king piece in this stalemate, and his mindless pawn, Clov, both refer back nostalgically to some pre-existence when language had, if they remember correctly, meaning. But now that language is denuded there is no longer even the illusion of communication. There is only the 'suffering of being' and the irrevocable duty, as Clov reminds us, to learn to 'suffer better'. Hamm undoes the play from the inside by making self-conscious critical comments such as 'This is deadly', 'Not an under-plot I trust' or 'I'm warming up for my last soliloquy': comments which express the awareness that he is no more than a chess piece in the endgame of language. It is for this reason that Beckett insisted that the original French title *Fin de Partie* be translated as *Endgame* and not as 'End of the Game' as some suggested. Ending is itself a game. One might even add an *endless* game, to fully savour Beckett's paradox. For Beckett (a keen chess player) is alluding to the technical concept of 'endgame' which is that stage of a chess match where the forces are reduced to such a minimum that stalemate is almost inevitable. Endgame is a game that cannot end, an irresolvable tension between irreconcilable forces.

Endgame is a play within a play: the actors realise that their dialogues are lines written by a dramatist, who is himself merely reiterating his own scenario. Here drama is self-referring, without exit. Beckett admits that in writing *Endgame* he felt 'all dried up, with nothing left but self-translation'. This explains why it is a play 'based on repetitions' and entirely devoid of symbolic references to some ulterior or hidden meaning. As Beckett protested to Alan Schneider after the first French performance in 1957: 'When it comes to journalists, I feel the only line is to refuse to be involved in exegesis of any kind ... If people want to have headaches among the overtones, let them. And provide their own aspirin. Hamm as stated, and Clov as stated, *nec tecum nec sine te*, in such a place, and in such a world, that's all I can manage, more than I could.' In short *Endgame* is impotence, but it is, ironically, perhaps Beckett's most perfectly constructed and experimentally successful drama.

Beckett's subsequent plays are progressively futile – if daring – attempts to justify their own existence. Drama, despite its incarnation in gesture and act – which is undoubtedly the main reason Beckett chose it – proves ultimately no more immune to the mortal disease of language than the novel. And drama, it must be recalled is also a form of language: as Aristotle realised, it is the aesthetic imitation (*mimesis*) of an action. As soon as the action is on stage it is already *re-presented* and *interpreted* by an author, director, actor(s) and audience. Action on stage is itself a *sign*, a semiotic carrier of meaning. Dramatic action is not pure action, pure presence, but is invariably contaminated by the signifying process. Drama too is writing.

Each of Beckett's remaining plays features, in ever diminishing detail, the absurd strategies of different narrator-actors to establish their literal but lost identity, to '*be* again' by obsessively re-telling the story of some illusory existence (what Winnie in *Happy Days* (1961) calls her 'happy days'; what Krapp in *Krapp's Last Tape* (1958) calls his 'never to be forgotten' vision; what the characters of *Play* (1963) refer to as the silence of their pre-existence). They seek an identity which might redeem them from the erosion of time and speech. But their supposedly *literal* identities can only be recaptured through the figurative detour of language, which, of course, amounts to saying they cannot be recaptured at all. Krapp cannot catch up with his past self even with the aid of his numerous tape-recordings; and Winnie's happy days are no more than the fabricated ventriloquist sounds which assail her: 'Yes, those are happy days when there are sounds'.

Beckett has declared that 'the best possible play is one in which there are no actors, only the text' (letter to Deirdre Bair, 1973, quoted in her biography of Beckett, 1978, p. 513). In *Play* the three protagonists are reduced to mouths uttering from urns. In *Breath* (1969) (thirty-five seconds of anti-dramatic, plotless, speechless breathing) there are no protagonists at all; only a voice reduced to a trace of itself, an inarticulate whisper. Here Beckett's art seems to go too far, to reach the apogée of its self-undoing, the prophetic words of his Proust essay being thoroughly vindicated: 'The artistic tendency is not expansive, but a contraction. And art is the apotheosis of solitude. There is no communication because there are no vehicles of communication.' And when the voice hesitantly returns again in *Not I* (1972), it is only to reiterate one last time, during fifteen minutes of meaningless, actorless repetition, that the I cannot represent itself for it is never present to itself: self-identity is nonsense. With *Not I* and the mime plays (*Acts without Words*) in the 1970s and his subsequent TV plays and dance plays for *Süddeutscher Rundfunk* in the 1980s (*Quad* 1 and 2), Beckett's revolutionary crusade to 'de-anthropomorphise' the writing process would seem, as nearly as possible, accomplished.

Appendix B: Beckett and Derrida

Jacques Derrida's notion of language as 'différance' provides us with a valuable key to the understanding of Beckett's critique of writing. Derrida's neologism (difference spelt with an 'a') conveys both the sense of 'differing' and 'deferring' contained in the French verb *différer*. To deconstruct language is, Derrida claims, to discover that it is in fact an endless process of signifying, a 'différance' or differentiation wherein the 'meaning' signified is forever 'different' from itself and forever 'deferred' to some ideal but non-existent source of origin. The traditional metaphysical notion of 'meaning' as a timeless self-identity or presence is itself a myth produced by language and so the quest of language for an original totalizing presence is in truth no more than an endless 'play of differences', a 'temporalizing' by means of ever-receding 'traces':

> Différance is what makes the movement of signification possible for each element that is said to be 'present', appearing on the stage of presence, is related to something *other* than itself ... a trace that relates no less to what is called the future than to what is called the past, and that constitutes what is called the present by this very relation to what is not, to what it absolutely is not. [Jacques Derrida, *Différance in Bulletin de la Société française de philosophie,* vol. 62, no. 3 (1968); *Speech and Phenomena* (Northwestern University Press 1973)]

Every word in language is no more, therefore, than a 'supplementation' or 'substitution' for another word/trace and thus serves to mask and make up for the absence of an original presence. Hence the irony that word-signs *produce* the very illusory presence that they are supposed to *represent*. The differentiating play of traces invents presence and consequently can unmask its imposture. As such it allows for the deconstruction of the metaphysical notion of presence, thereby transforming the traditional semiology of *identity* into what Derrida terms a grammatology of *différance*. Language *is* différance or as Derrida puts it: 'Language preserves the différance that preserves language.' The differential trace itself refers us back to a trace that can never present or re-present itself, that can never appear as such in a transparent phenomenon, in a *name*, in *being*. Each trace functions as a perpetual postponement or deferment of its own origin, as a trace of the effacement of a trace. Derrida concludes accordingly that

> older than being itself, our language has not name for such a differance ... what is *unnamable* here is not some ineffable being that cannot be approached by a name ... what is unnamable is the play (of language itself) that brings about the nominal effects, the relatively unitary or atomic structures we call names, or chains or substitutions for names. In these, for example, the nominal effect of 'différance' is itself involved, carried off, and reinscribed, just as the false beginning or end of a game is still part of the game, a function of the system ... There will be no unique name.

The critical project of Beckett's writing is, I suggest, readily recognizable in terms of this grammatology of unnamable *différance*.

Already in the early *nouvelles*, Beckett's 'deconstructing' scalpel had left its scar. *The Expelled*, written in concise, unsentimental prose, concludes with a statement that annuls its very *raison d'être*: 'I don't know why I told this story. I could just as well have told another.'

The End, stacatto and hesitant from the outset, breaks off just at that point where the narrator discovers that the projected 'story in the likeness of my life' is not the story he has told but a 'story I *might* have told'. And this obsessional search for some original selfhood through language is taken up again in *The Calmative*: 'I'll tell my story in the past none the less, as though it were a myth, or an old fable, for this evening I need another age, that age to become another age in which I become what I was.' In *Texts for Nothing*, (1947–52), one of his more mature prose writings, Beckett pursues his deconstruction with unprecedented ruthlessness. In the first of the thirteen splendidly composed texts, the author establishes the fact that the voices that haunt him are the different time tenses of language, continually overlapping each other and thereby obstructing the quest for an original univocal subject: 'All angles, times and tenses, at first I only had been here, now I'm here still, soon I won't be here yet … I was my father and I was my son.' In the second, the author tries to reconstitute a 'far memory' of his youth which the third text cancels out as 'only voices, only lies'. The futility of the narrator's desire 'to get into my story in order to get out of it' by discovering his true self, becomes patently evident: there is no way out of the vicious circle of language. In the fourth text the author consents to embrace the play of words so as to console himself with some fictional persona; for even as victim of an impersonal voice there is the solace that, at least, 'accusative I exist'. But, remembering his miserable anterior existences as Molloy and Malone, the narrator regrets having allowed his 'figments talk' and convince him to invent a 'story for myself'. It is already too late to escape from his story, nevertheless, or even to decide to end it, for the interminable voice cannot, he realizes, 'be mine'. So that in the fifth text, he resigns himself to the dictates of another's words: 'I'm the clerk, I'm the scribe, at the hearings of what cause I know not,' a Kafkaesque culprit 'not understanding what I hear, not knowing what I write.' The Beckettian narrator is once more driven to confess that the 'phantasms' that appear 'to issue from this imaginary head' are in fact not his own but a stranger's.

In the sixth text, the author suddenly hits upon the quasi-divine art of erasure which allows him to subvert language even while he remains its captive: 'Blot, words can be blotted and the mad thoughts they invent, the nostalgia for that slime where the eternal breathbed and his son wrote, long after, with divine idiotic finger, at the feet of the adulteress, wipe it out, all you have to do is say you said nothing and so say nothing again.' But the seemingly messianic erasure of words – explicitly recalling Christ's action – only produces an illusory silence, 'a silence that is not silence' but rather the inner abyss of language itself: 'This unnamable thing, that I name and name and never wear out, and I call that words.' Whence the author's self-defeating question: 'with what words shall I name my unnamable words?'

The seven remaining texts elaborate this question, scrutinizing it meticulously in all its possible permutations. The unnamable thing is the intangible *I* that the nameless author seeks to reappropriate by means of fiction: 'Fantasies and hope of a story for me somehow, of having come from somewhere and of being able to go back.' If only he could reach this *I* and name it, he could regain his true identity, the neoplatonic *one* that lost itself in giving voice to all its mimetic *vice-existers*: 'I shall know again that I once was, and roughly who, and how to go on, and speak unaided, nicely, about number one and his pale imitations.' (*Text* 10) To name the *I* however is already to invent and such a fictive *I* can be no more than a ventriloquist's medium uttering a ceaseless anonymous language which baulks at self-recovery: 'It is for ever the same murmur, flowing unbroken, like a single endless word and therefore meaningless, for it's the end gives the meaning to words.' Consequently, the author resolves to subordinate his individual will to represent and possess, to the involuntary suffering of being that language imposes. The tone here is at once belligerent and acquiescent, apocalyptic and calm – a prayer uttered in defiance and despair: 'That's right, wordshit, bury me, avalanche, and let there be no more talk of any creature nor of a world to leave, nor of a world to reach, in order to have done, with worlds, with creatures, with words, with misery, misery.' (*Text* 9) By means of such self-effacement, he hopes paradoxically, to be carried beyond (*metapherein*) his suffering state into some 'outer', 'other' redeemed existence beyond the subterranean cave of language. But language has no reality reference to justify a Platonic journey outwards, and so the author finds himself thrown back upon his words lacking 'a body to get there with … and the power to get there, and the way to get there, and pass out, and see the beauties of the skies …' (*Text* 9)

If the voice cannot escape from itself through objective reference or self-effacement, then the last possible resort would seem to be the invocation of a voice that would *at once* speak and be silent: 'a voice of silence'. This ideal of a silent voice constitutes, as Derrida has argued in his remarkable essay 'The voice that keeps silence', one of the fundamental projects of the traditional theory of language. This silent voice would be a voice unbound by time and space, that is, a self-referring presence no longer subject to differentiation or deferment. But the possibility of such a silent voice is of course its very impossibility, for such a voice would have to be 'at the same time absolutely dead and absolutely alive'. Beckett's writings expose the contradictoriness of this ideal voice of presence, or more exactly of immediate at-one-ness of the self with itself. One only appreciates the revolutionary nature of such exposure when one recalls that the contradiction inherent in this mythic voice of presence has remained masked by the Western philosophical definitions of being as an atemporal 'self-originating principle of principles' (*Arche, Ousia,* etc.). Husserl and Heidegger first adverted to this contradiction when they demonstrated that language does not represent some pre-existent presence but rather creates and sustains it. Thus Derrida and others were given the lead to deconstruct the conventional view of language as a transparent signifier whose *signified* would be some silent prelinguistic origin of meaning.

The 'voice of silence' represents the ideal of a timeless and immaterial subject, what Derrida defines as a 'spiritual flesh that continues to speak and to be present to itself'. (Derrida (1967), *op. cit.* pp. 71–87). To acknowledge with Beckett that language (and more explicitly writing) is a material, spatio-temporal process of signifying is to sound the death-knell of the metaphysical fiction of a silent soliloquy of the soul with itself, a fiction that attempts to hide its own *differing activity as signifier* in order to project the 'identity of presence as self-presence' (p. 57). The 'silent voice' signalling the perfect adequation of language and self is impossible, for language always leaves a wake of irrecuperable traces behind it. Language, as Beckett writes in text 13 of *Texts for Nothing,* is 'nothing but a voice murmuring a trace … like air leaves among the leaves, among the grass, among the sand.' The deconstruction of the word into the trace shows us that 'this bending-back is irreductible to presence or to self-presence, that this trace or difference is always older than presence … and prevents us from speaking of a simple self-identity' (Derrida, *op. cit.* p. 58). In fact, the so-called voice of silence is nothing more than 'the voice's breath' which 'breathes in vain' (*Text* 13) since it can never utter the name of presence. Beckett even wrote a fifteen-second play called *Breath* to prove it!

Beckett's writing masterfully deconstructs itself by directing our attention to itself as *writing,* that is as a system of *sounding* signifiers irretrievably at odds with the ideal of a corresponding *silent* signified. It is only by deconstructing the word's pretension to achieve self-adequation by means of silence that we can uncover its hidden self-alienation. The irony that Beckett makes such great play of is, of course, that one is obliged to use language to deconstruct language. We can only undo words by means of words: 'the same lie lyingly denied … no's knife' (*Text* 13). All that the Beckettian author can conclude is that the *I* is *not-I,* that the coveted original *one* is *no-one;* that there is *no-thing* to be said and *no-where* to be journeyed to: 'And it's the same old road I'm trudging, up yes and down no, towards one yet to be named … name, no, nothing is namable, tell, no, nothing can be told, what then, I don't know, I shouldn't have begun' (*Text* 11). The *other I* one seeks to appropriate in words is 'merely a babble of homeless mes and untenanted hims … without number or person whose abandoned being we haunt, nothing' (*Text* 12).

In the 'German Letter', published in *Disjecta: Miscellaneous Writings and a Dramatic Fragment* (Calder, 1983), Beckett makes his deconstructive attitude to language abundantly clear:

> More and more my own language appears to me like a veil that must be torn apart in order to get at the things (or the Nothingness) behind it … As we cannot eliminate language all at once, we should at least leave nothing undone that might contribute to its falling into disrepute. To bore one hole after another in it, until what lurks behind it – be it something or nothing – begins to seep through; I cannot imagine a higher goal for a writer today.

CHAPTER TWELVE

Beckett II:
The Demythologizing Intellect

Beckett's attitude to philosophy, as to almost everything else that obsessed him, is ambivalent. Malone epitomizes the Beckettian intellectual when he concludes some fifty pages of clever metaphysical reflection by dismissing it as 'ballsaching poppycock about life and death' – only to begin all over again. Beckett's personal pronouncements on the subject are equally paradoxical. In his early essays, he warns against the neat identification of the 'analogymongers'[1] and declares that 'allegory ... must always *fail* in the hands of a poet'.[2] Yet Beckett's own works are replete with analogies and allegories and he himself is the first to admit that his writing is a 'fidelity to *failure*'.[3] Similarly, while he affirms in one interview that he 'never read philosophers' and 'wouldn't have had any reason to write novels if (he) could have expressed their subject in philosophic terms',[4] in another he candidly admits that if he were a critic writing on his works he would begin with the metaphysical quotations from Geulincx and Democritus that recur in his novels.[5] Indeed, there is scarcely a work of Beckett's that does not mischievously tease out the questions of some great thinker – Aristotle, Augustine, Descartes, Berkeley, Malebranche, Leibniz, Schopenhauer or Eckhart, not to mention Geulincx and Democritus. The fundamental ambiguity of Beckett's appraisal of philosophy may be understood in terms of Oscar Wilde's maxim that 'a truth in art is that whose contradictory is also true'.[6] So that despite his prevarications, Beckett, perhaps more than any other contemporary writer, succeeded in making philosophy literary and literature philosophical.

It was at *l'École Normale Supérieure* in Paris in 1928 that Beckett discovered Rimbaud's revolutionary plea to abandon inherited certainties and 'become absolutely modern'.[7] This meant for Beckett that modern art must become 'pure interrogation'.[8] It can be said that Beckett himself is absolutely modern to the extent that he compels literature to reflect upon itself, to question the conditions of its own possibility. Modern thought differs from its traditional antecedents in that it no longer assumes the world to be some assured reality to which the self could faithfully conform or correspond. The self becomes the sole critic of existence, putting everything in question, including itself! Beckett argues, accordingly, that the modern writer becomes a critical explorer of that 'rupture of the lines of communication … between himself and the world of objects'.[9] Such critical explorations bring Beckett to the threshold of modern philosophy.

Beckett's writings demythologize some of the oldest and most revered traditions of intellectual identity. They playfully yet pointedly challenge two fundamental concepts of Western culture: the idealist concept of a supreme substance or being (derived from Greek metaphysics) and the theological concept of a divine creator or first cause (derived from a rationalist interpretation of the Judeo-Christian tradition). Beckett's challenge to the former metaphysical tradition takes the form of a parody of idealist thinkers, particularly Descartes and his disciples Geulincx, Leibniz and Berkeley. His challenge to the theological conceptions of God concentrates on the dogmatic definitions of scholasticism as well as simplistic versions of biblical eschatology and mysticism. These major aspects of Beckettian demythologization shall be dealt with in the first two sections of this essay. See the appendix 'The Modern Critique of Being and Language' for a comment on some similarities between Beckett's literary demythologization and the contemporary continental critiques of existence and language.[10]

I. Metaphysical Idealism

In 1926, while still a student in Trinity College Dublin, Beckett discovered the philosophy of René Descartes. This was his first real encounter with the Western tradition of metaphysical idealism. Beckett read Descartes voraciously and filled three notebooks with his own reflections as well as commentaries by biographers and critics. In 1929, as an instructor at *l'École Normale*, he resumed his reading of France's most original thinker. After months of almost total immersion in the life and thought of Descartes, Beckett transmuted his scattered notes into an esoteric ninety-eight line poem entitled 'Whoroscope'. The poem was awarded £10 by the Hours Press and was published in Paris in 1930. 'This long poem, mysterious, obscure in parts,' declared Nancy Cunard who judged the competition, 'was clearly by someone very intellectual …'[11]

'Whoroscope' was a turning point in Beckett's career, not only because it was his first published work, but also because it succeeded in transforming intellectual obsession into literary creation. The punning title alludes to the Greek word for 'hour' – *horo* (the Hours Press prize was for poems about time) and to Descartes' superstitious withholding of his date of birth to prevent astrologers from predicting his death (hence the concluding line – 'starless inscrutable hour'). Curiously, Beckett himself has obscured his own date of birth. Though his birth certificate gives the date as 13 May 1906, Beckett has always insisted that he was born on Good Friday, 13 April, of the same year.

Beckett was fascinated by the Cartesian project to free the thinking self from all external constraints – symbolized in 'Whoroscope' by the determining cycle of the stars and the revolting intrusions of our physical existence. The Cartesian self exists because it thinks – *cogito ergo sum* – and seeks to remain an autonomous substance entirely independent of material reality. The *cogito* aspires to the condition of an eternal and self-sufficient being far removed from corporeal and temporal decay. But the disturbing irony here, as elsewhere in Beckett's work, is that the idealist vision of spiritual freedom is forever confounded by the fact that we are born with bodies. Descartes conjured up all sorts of ways in which the soul might control the body without becoming contaminated by it, eventually concluding that the pineal gland (at the base of the brain) was the secret connection! But if such problems were a source of insufferable metaphysical anguish for Descartes, Beckett seizes upon them as a choice occasion for literary parody. Already in 'Whoroscope' Beckett mockingly juxtaposes Descartes' aspiration for intellectual autonomy with the gross infelicities of his personal biography. Closely following Adrien Baillet's *Life of Descartes*, which he was reading at the time, Beckett ridicules the French philosopher's attempts to transcend his biological ailments in order to achieve a pure spiritual liberty. Hence the ironic pseudo-philosophical question that opens the poem: 'What's that? An Egg?' (referring to Descartes' daily breakfast of ten-day-old 'stinking' eggs). The rest of the poem traces Descartes' biographical itinerary from one episode of physical revulsion to the next. Apart from the titular allusion to whores, there are lurid references to 'stagnant murky blood', 'lashed ovaries with prostisciutto', 'grey flayed epidermis and scarlet tonsils', 'milled sweat' and 'double-breasted turds'. The poem concludes with Descartes' visit to the Swedish court of Queen Christina – 'the murdering matinal pope-confessed amazon, Christina the ripper' – where he perished from lack of sleep and from cold weather. As Beckett explains in his irreverent notes to the poem: 'At Stockholm, in November, [Christina] required Descartes, who had remained in bed till midday all his life, to be with her at five in the morning.'[12]

'Whoroscope' is mined with countless other mock-heroic metaphysical allusions. There is a reference to the 'Brothers' Boot' whose refutation of Aristotle occurred in Dublin in 1640; a pseudo-scholastic send-up of Descartes' 'eucharistic sophistry' when responding to Arnauld's challenge 'to reconcile his doctrine of matter with the doctrine of transubstantiation' – 'So we drink Him and eat Him/And the watery Beaune and the stale cubes of Hovis etc.'; an allusion to Descartes' 'sophistry concerning the movement of the earth' in his contemptuous rejection of Galileo; and a saucy mention of St Augustine's 'revelation in the shrubbery' that culminated in his quasi-Cartesian proof of existence: *fallor ergo sum* (I err therefore I am).

In *Murphy*, his most explicitly philosophical novel, Beckett develops the Cartesian parody adumbrated in 'Whoroscope'. Though his name is Irish, Murphy lives in London and is of indeterminate origin. He seeks the ideal Cartesian state of spiritual freedom beyond the material limitations of time, place, movement and death. The inner chamber of the cogito must accordingly be liberated from the ephemeral outer world: 'Murphy's mind pictured itself as a large hollow sphere, hermetically closed to the universe without.'[13] The nature of outer reality', he affirms, 'remained obscure'. Murphy's favourite occupation is to strap himself to his rocking chair in mimicry of the scholastic definition of the supreme being as an unmoved mover: 'it appeased his body' and 'set him free in his mind ... it was not until his body was appeased that he could come alive in his mind'. Beckett is manifestly obsessed with this Cartesian rupture between mind (*res cogitans*) and body (*res extensa*). Throughout the novel, the coveted liberty of mind is threatened by interferences from the physical world. Murphy's irrepressible lust for Celia, 'the part of him that he hated craved for Celia'[14] – as well as the astronomical determinations of place and time that govern Murphy's every action – suggest that his free volition is in fact a physically conditioned necessity.[15] Even Murphy's final will that his remains be flushed down a toilet bowl in the Abbey Theatre (a mockery of both Yeatsian nationalism and the Cartesian vortex) is ultimately denied him. The cremated ashes are, instead, ignobly scattered over the floor of a pub: 'By closing time, the body, mind and soul of Murphy were freely distributed over the floor of the saloon; and before another dayspring greyened the earth, had been swept away with the sand, the beer, the butts, the glass, the matches, the spits, the vomit.'[16]

Another idealist metaphysician who held a profound fascination for Beckett was the Belgian disciple of Descartes, Arnold Geulincx (1624–69). Beckett first became acquainted with Geulincx's thought in Dublin in the late 1920s. He was particularly impressed by his theory that since man can only secure freedom in the mind one should renounce the will's attempts to master or alter the external world of objects – which includes of course our own body. Murphy refers to 'the beautiful Belgo-Latin of Arnold Geulincx' and enthusiastically cites his quietistic plea for independence from physical volition or desire: *Ubi nihil vales, ibi nihil velis* (where you are worth nothing, will nothing).[17]

Geulincx extrapolates Descartes' idea of the 'freedom of indifference', arguing that the only reasonable approach to one's physical passions is to ignore them, thereby attaining a state of dispassionate neutrality. This notion of passive indifference beyond the terminating cycles of cause and effect, birth and death was to become a key theme not only of *Murphy* – which extols the virtues of 'the freedom of indifference, the indifference of freedom' – but also of the *Proust* essay (1931) where Beckett sees a suspension of the active will (what he calls voluntary memory) as prerequisite to an authentic encounter with the 'suffering of Being' (what he calls involuntary memory). But this metaphysical model of inaction freed from movement and desire, while devoutly to be wished, is usually portrayed by Beckett as a comic impossibility.

Beckett was well aware that the metaphysical ideal of immobility was derived from Parmenidean rationalism. Parmenides, the first of the Greek philosophers to invoke reason and logic to explain reality, held that true being was identical with thought. 'It is the same thing to think and to be,' runs his celebrated maxim. Rational being was considered to exist beyond the sensible and temporal world of becoming. Parmenides' most ingenious disciple, Zeno, employed the reductive arguments of logic to demonstrate that movement was impossible. Beckett refers to Zeno as the 'old Greek' in *Endgame* and makes explicit allusion to his famous *reductio ad absurdum* example of the little heap of millet. This example, which recurs in several of Beckett's other works,[18] runs as follows: If I pour half of a finite quantity of millet grain into a heap and then pour half of the remaining quantity and so on *ad infinitum*, the heap will never be completed, for the remaining quantity, however reduced on each pouring, is infinitely divisible. Similarly, the hare can never overtake the tortoise because the original gap between them, no matter how many times it is halved by the approaching hare, can always be halved yet again. Thus Zeno shows that movement is logically impossible, a mere illusion of the senses. Aristotelian metaphysics refined the Parmenidean position in arguing that only the divine being (*telos*) or reason (*nous*) possessed the qualities of atemporality and immobility, and that mortal beings were condemned, by virtue of their materiality, to time, movement and desire.[19] The only possible escape from mortality was to practise rational contemplation until one participated in the divine condition of the 'self-thinking-thought' (*noeisis tes noeseos*). Aristotle's definition of the divine as a self-thinking-thought was later translated into the Augustinian and scholastic definition of God as a 'self-loving-love' (*Amor quo Deus se ipsum amat*).[20] Beckett pointedly rebukes Murphy's pretentions to divine self-sufficiency by prefacing the Cartesian description of 'Murphy's Mind' with the fake epithet: '*Amor intellectualis quo Murphy se ipsum amat.*'

In the Beckettian universe, no man can shuffle off his mortal coil. We are beings who exist in time; death is inescapable. The 'post-mortem' condition of 'Belacqua bliss' sought by the characters of *More Pricks than Kicks*, *Murphy* and the later novels is perpetually frustrated or deferred. And Beckett's *dramatis personae* are no less unfortunate. 'Have you not done tormenting me with your accursed time?' cries Pozzo in *Waiting for Godot*. 'We are born astride of a grave, the light gleams for an instant then it is night once more.' But it is perhaps in his *Proust* essay, that Beckett first articulates man's failure to transcend his mortality.

Affirming our enslavement to 'that double-headed monster of salvation and damnation – time,' Beckett concludes that 'there is no escape from the hours and the days. Neither from tomorrow nor from yesterday.'[21] It is equally impossible for the self to transcend desire; for we have to desire not to desire and so are invariably tied to the corporeal cycle of existence. As Aèrsene points out in *Watt*:

> It is impossible not to seek, not to want, for when you cease to seek you start to find, and when you cease to want, then life begins to ram her fish and chips down your gullet until you puke, and then the puke down your gullet until you puke the puke and then the puked puke until you begin to like it.[22]

But it is surely in *Murphy* that the Cartesian construction of an immaterial cogito is most pitilessly undone. To Miss Counihan's (a former lover of Murphy) assertion that 'there is a mind and there is a body' the Newtonian Neary replies: 'Kick her arse!' Murphy's own version of dualism is also reduced to comic ridicule:

> Thus Murphy felt himself split in two, a body and a mind. They had intercourse apparently, otherwise he could not have known that they had anything in common. But he felt his mind to be bodytight and did not understand through what channel the intercourse was effected nor how the two experiences came to overlap. He was satisfied that neither followed from the other. He neither thought a kick because he felt one nor felt a kick because he thought one.'[23]

> And so Murphy persists in promoting the idealist fictions of his predecessor Belacqua, 'scoffing at the idea of a sequitur from his body to his mind', content to reside in his 'little internus homo, in the self-sufficiency he never wearied of arrogating to himself.[24]

While Descartes sought to explain the interrelationship of mind and matter by appealing to a pineal gland and a 'divine guarantee', Geulincx formulated the equally implausible, if logically consistent, theory of occasionalism. This theory, espoused by several Beckettian characters from Murphy to Malone, stated that what really happens when the soul and body *seem* to interact is that the movement of one's body and the thought of that movement, as two entirely independent actions, are simultaneously willed by God. In other words, God in his goodness wills us to move at the same time as we desire to move. God's will is the true cause, our will a merely illusory or 'occasional' cause. To clinch the matter, Geulincx provides us with his notorious notion of the mind and body as two parallel clocks whose timing has been perfectly synchronized by a divine clockmaker! The human *cogito* is thus free to the extent that it conforms to the divine will and does not try to interfere with the workings of the material world.[25]

Murphy tries out the dualist theories of Descartes and Geulincx, before finally hitting upon the 'monadological' solution of yet another Cartesian rationalist,

Gottfried Leibniz. In his padded cell in the Magdalene Mercyseat asylum, Murphy believes he inhabits a self-contained monad: 'The compartment was windowless like a monad ... within the narrow limits of domestic architecture he had never been able to imagine a more creditable representation of what he kept calling, indefatigably, the little world.' Leibniz held that every *cogito* is an isolated monadic soul ('little world') with no dependence on sensory perception: '*La monade est sans fenêtre*', as he puts it in *Nouveaux essais sur l'entendement humain*. To enable this monadology to comply with his theory that we live in 'the best of all possible worlds', Leibniz introduced the notion of a 'pre-established harmony' (or 'pre-established arbitrary' as Watt mockingly calls it). By means of such harmonization, God would assure an exact correspondence between the spiritual movement or *conatus* (which Lucky misnames 'conation' during his 'think' in *Godot*) of each monad and the physical movement of the outward universe.[26]

But Beckettian idealists differ from their Cartesian prototypes in that they can have no recourse to a divine Guarantor, Clockmaker or Harmonizer. They can take no solace in a supreme will that might validate their self-thinking thoughts. If there is some pre-established correspondence between Murphy's mind and the astral movements of the universe there is no divine meaning in this correspondence: 'They were *his* stars ... it was *his* meaning'.[27] Murphy is a Cartesian idealist bereft of God, a self alone (*solus ipse*), a solipsistic victim of his own 'precious ipsumossity'. Art, as Beckett affirmed in *Proust*, is the 'apotheosis of solitude. There is no communication because there are no vehicles of communication.'[28] Murphy can find no equivalence in the real world for the fictions of his own mind. The mind's desire is not translatable into correlative objective action. Thus Beckett follows the Cartesian procedure of universal doubt without ever founding the existence of the *cogito* on the existence of God. He takes the doubt and leaves the proof. The Beckettian self is at the mercy of the *malin génie*; he is a sceptic without salvation.

But of all the Cartesian idealists that haunted Beckett, it was perhaps with the Irish philosopher Bishop George Berkeley that he most identified. Born in County Kilkenny in 1685, Berkeley received his BA from Trinity College, Dublin, some two hundred years before Beckett. Interestingly, the definitive edition of Berkeley's works was brought out by Beckett's tutor at Trinity, A.A. Luce. Berkeley has been described as an Irish Cartesian since he subscribes to the metaphysical idealism of Descartes and Malebranche.[29] As Professor Harry Bracken argues: 'Berkeley is neither British nor empiricist. If he must be labelled, he might more accurately be called an Irish Cartesian.'[30] Beckett's reference to Berkeley's '*idealist* tar' (Berkeley's *Siris* is about tar water) in *Murphy* would suggest that he shares Bracken's position. The following are the principal Cartesian characteristics of Berkeley's thought: 1) meaning derives from subjective consciousness rather than the objective world; 2) consciousness is fundamentally dual, divided into perceiver (*percipere*) and perceived (*percipi*); 3) the conscious mind is a free and immortal spirit irreducible to materialistic models of explanation.

In contradistinction to the empiricists who held that genuine knowledge comes from our empirical sensations, Berkeley is a thorough-going immaterialist. He sought to justify a speculative and spiritual vision of the world beyond the limits of the materialistic sciences (which he qualified as 'minute philosophies'). Only a religious sensibility, Berkeley believed, could transcend sensory experience and intuit the supernatural causes of things. The error of the physical sciences is to argue from the visible universe (*visibilis*) to invisible principles of explanation (*invisibilis*), while maintaining that all rests on empirico-metric grounds. Berkeley exposed this error and retorted that it is only when we recognize the strictly material limits of the empirical sciences that we can acknowledge the existence of a higher and irreducible order of spiritual vision.

The material world is the visible world; it *is* because it is *seen*. While the being of matter is to be perceived, the being of mind is to perceive. Or as our Kilkenny luminary put it: *Esse est percipi aut percipere* (To be is to be perceived or to perceive). The table, for example, exists only because I see it existing. But since the world evidently possesses a permanence independent of man's finite and occasional perception of it, it follows for Berkeley that the infinite mind of God must assure its continued existence by perpetually perceiving it. God is the generous and ever-vigilant *percipere* who sustains all things in being. But Berkeley will allow that we can ultimately transcend our passive sensation of the material universe and participate in the active and creative *percipere* of God. It is only by the spiritual vision of our minds, attuned to God's supreme vision, that we may apprehend the secret cause of things. The spiritual 'eye of the mind' transcends the subservient 'eye of matter'. And God's infinite mind is the transcendent cause of both the finite world and our own finite minds.

Beckett's Murphy is Berkeleyian in several important respects. The most unequivocal reference to Berkeley comes when Murphy, through a process of intense mental concentration in a chess game with the mad Mr Endon, mystically surpasses the condition of a material body that is *seen*, towards a quasi-divine *seeing*. In short, he goes beyond empirical sensation (colour, taste, sound, etc.) towards an unadulterated spiritual vision: 'Murphy began to see nothing, that colourlessness which is such a rare post-natal treat, being the absence (to use a nice distinction) not of *percipere* but of *percipi*. His other senses also found themselves at peace, an unexpected pleasure.'[31] Futhermore, Mr Kelly's contemplative efforts to 'determine the point at which seen and unseen meet' by sitting like Murphy in a chair for long periods, is surely an allusion to Berkeley's argument that only a suprasensible vision can apprehend the divine correlation between the *visibilia* of *percipi* and the *invisibilia* of *percipere*.[32]

But it is in Beckett's *Film* that Berkeley's *esse est percipi* argument is pushed to its most extreme conclusion. In the general summary of the script Beckett writes: '*Esse est percipi*. All extraneous perception suppressed, animal, human, divine, self-perception maintains in being. Search of non-being in flight from extraneous perception breaking down in inescapability of self-perception.'[33]

Film shows the muffled figure of Buster Keaton scuttling through laneways and corridors, desperately trying to escape the mortal condition of being seen. In the crowded streets, 'all persons are shown in some way perceiving one another, an object, a shop window, a poster etc., i.e. all contentedly in *percipere* and *percipi*.'[34] And so the one-eyed protagonist, fleeing from the uncritical complacency of the madding crowd, dashes through a narrow street and shuts himself away in a bare room. He takes every possible precaution to avoid being perceived: he drives out his pet animals, covers the bird cage, the gold-fish bowl, a portrait of 'God the Father looking severely at him', the mirror, the windows etc. And finally settles down to sleep in a Murphyesque rocking chair. But he cannot escape the awareness that, in spite of all his precautions, he is *still* not unperceived. The eye of the camera sees the victim even as he flees from all other eyes. And in the end this eye is seen by the horrified protagonist who realizes he can never escape perception of himself self-perceived. The eye of the camera, which opens in full close-up on the eye of the protagonist, cannot be suppressed. We are condemned to be (*esse*) and to be perceived (*percipi*).

Only God could enjoy the privilege of perceiving without being perceived. We mortals, by contrast, can find no refuge from the perceiving other. Hence Beckett's frequent references to Job, Jonah and Moses as witnesses of the Unseen God who sees all. 'Do you think God sees me?' says Estragon to Vladimir in *Godot*. There is, of course, no way of knowing. But what Estragon can be sure of is that Vladimir always sees him. In Beckett's universe the ideal freedom of invisibility inevitably collides with the slavery of visibility, for we can never dispel the presence of the other. Similarly, the ideal of silence is assailed by 'other' voices, be they the voices of conscience and memory (as in *Krapps' Last Tape, Eh Joy, Footfalls* or *Not I*), the voices of the dead (as in *Embers* and *Godot*), the voices of some unnamable other who will not leave us be (*The Unnamable, Texts for Nothing*, etc.), or simply the voices of other all-too-human human beings (as in *Endgame* or *Play*). 'Accusative I exist', confesses the culpable author of *Texts for Nothing* who cannot avoid being seen and summoned. Always accused, always an accusative object of another's sentence, the human self cannot be God. Yet it is satisfied with nothing less.

II. Negative Theology

Beckett's demythologization of enlightenment idealism also expresses itself as a resistance to all attempts to simplify the biblical notion of God in terms of a rationalist theology. He opposes the conventional reduction of the 'God of Abraham, Isaac and the Prophets' (as Pascal put it) to the 'God of the philosophers'. The transcendent God of Judeo-Christian faith is betrayed once it is translated into metaphysical definitions of self-thinking-thought or self-sufficient being (*ens causa sui, ens perfectissimum et realissimum*, etc.). The God of the Bible is, for Beckett, a God of paradox and apocalypse, a *Deus Absconditus* who sends mysterious messengers, perhaps even his son, but never comes himself. Beckett's Godot is an eschatological possibility of the future, a risk and a promise, someone we await in fear and trembling; His existence remains forever in question, in doubt. If Beckett is a sceptic in metaphysics, in theology he is an agnostic. Neither an atheist nor a theist. Hence his refusal to qualify his attitude to God and man as optimistic or pessimistic: 'That would be to judge and we are in no position to judge.'[35]

Beckett's theology, if he can be said to have one, is perhaps best described as a *negative theology*. His writings challenge the presumption of those who would define God in certified or certifiable concepts. His attitude here is, of course, not unprecedented. Kant refuted the traditional proofs for the existence of God, vowing to 'establish the limits of reason in order to make way for faith'. Kierkegaard also rejected the God of speculative metaphysics and maintained that it was only by a 'crucifixion of the understanding' that one could accept the absurd paradox of divine existence. This he called the 'leap of faith', echoing Tertullian's *credo quia absurdum*. But perhaps the most remarkable attempt in recent times to distinguish between the God of reason and the God of faith has been made by Bultmann whose 'theology of demythologization' argues that only by divesting God of the idealist accretions of Greek metaphysics can we recover the original religious experience of the Judeo-Christian scriptures.[36]

Interestingly, most of these demythologizing thinkers are, like Beckett himself, of Protestant origin. Even Berkeley, arguably Beckett's favourite philosopher, displayed his reformational credentials in arguing that the spiritual vision of the divine is essentially a matter of religious intuition or faith removed from abstract, scientific rationalism. (Berkeley differed here from such Catholic philosophers as Descartes or Malebranche.) At the risk of simplification, one could list the more obvious 'Protestant' characteristics of Beckett's portrayal of the God question as follows: 1) God's existence or non-existence is not explicable in terms of the traditional metaphysical proofs of reason; 2) all that we can know about God is what the perplexing parables of scripture tell us; 3) God is totally other and transcendent, absent from the workings of the world; 4) precisely as transcendent, God can only be experienced by a solitary act of faith or by an agonized waiting; 5) God's separation from us is rendered insurmountable by virtue of our inveterate fallibility and fallenness.[37]

But Beckett's borrowings from Protestant theology by no means suggest a sectarian anti-Catholicism. If he indeed explores the 'solitary' nature of faith and the 'absent' nature of God, he also draws from such Catholic mystics as Meister Eckhart (explicitly referred to in *Murphy* and *Dream*) who held that God was a non-being beyond being who can only be experienced by abandoning the light of reason in favour of a patient, purgative waiting (*Abgeschiedenheit*); or St John of the Cross who wrote that God mystically revealed himself through man's encounter with darkness and death, i.e. 'the dark night of the soul' that Winnie calls the 'black night without end'.[38]

Although billed by newspaper journalists as 'the atheist from Paris', Beckett is, I suggest, more accurately described as an agnostic from Dublin. His works show his attitude to theology to be quite as equivocal as his attitude to metaphysics. When Beckett did allow himself to be drawn into a discussion of his religious upbringing, he was either non-committal or mischievously irreverent.[39] The fact that Beckett was brought up in Catholic Ireland to be 'almost a quaker' by an exceptionally devout mother and an Episcopalian father seems, nonetheless, to have been a formative intellectual influence.[40] John Pilling neatly sums up Beckett's singular brand of non-believing belief, 'inescapably attracted to the forms he seeks to subvert', in his study of *The Intellectual and Cultural Background to Beckett*:

> he has continued to be obsessed, personally, by the fundamental religious questions concerning the existence of God, His justice and mercy and the after-life. The excessive literalism of traditional theology, especially of certain thinkers still revered in the Catholic Ireland he has exiled himself from, he is quick to scorn; although his familiarity with it all suggests he was momentarily attracted by it ... What unbeliever would one expect to be familiar with Caugiamila's *Sacred Embryology* and Pope Benedict XIV's Diocesan Synod (quoted in addenda to *Watt*)? At the same time what believer would allow his path to be (even momentarily) halted by the occasional absurdities of Comestor and Adobard (medieval historians referred to by Moran)?[41]

The dissenting character of Beckett's theology approximates at times to a Gnostic view of the world. According to the heretical Gnostics, the creation of the world signified a fall from light into darkness: 'The world is extinguished,' Clov muses, 'though I never saw it lit.' This fall into the cycle of sin and punishment is a conspicuous theme in Beckett's oeuvre. We see, for example, how the Cartesian *cogito ergo sum* and the Augustinian *fallor ergo sum* are ultimately transmuted into a Beckettian *patio ergo sum* (I suffer/wait therefore I am). 'He weeps therefore he lives,' Hamm says of his father, Nagg, in *Endgame*. Quite clearly, in Beckett's world, to be is to suffer for one's sins. Clov repeats this punitive lesson to himself: 'You must learn to suffer better than that.'[42]

This Gnostic-cum-Lutheran suspicion of the fallen, created world is manifest in Beckett's treatment of sexuality and women. Woman as the maternal procreator who perpetuates the corrupt cycle of creation is often reviled by Beckett's male narrators: this is true of Murphy's Celia, Nagg's Nell, Mr Rooney's Mrs Rooney, Malone's mistresses and the Unnamable's mother. 'I look for my mother,' confesses the Unnamable narrator, 'in order to kill her.' One could hardly be further from the Romantic literature of the eternal feminine![43] In *Molloy*, Beckett caricatures human sexuality as the 'fatal pleasure principle' represented by the ludicrous Obidil (an anagramatic inversion of the Freudian Libido).[44] Birth itself is at best a forceps delivery (as in *Endgame*), at worst an aborted mess. ('the old impotent foetus … born in death' of *Malone Dies*). And this revulsion from life's procreative cycle is also manifest in the infanticidal tendencies of several Beckettian characters, notably Hamm, Malone and Mr Rooney.

Several critics have remarked on Beckett's dramatic use of the 'puritanism' he experienced during his days in Portora Royal School in Northern Ireland, and during his early Foxrock childhood with a moralistic mother.[45] 'To be is to be guilty,' says the 'wordshit' narrator of *Texts for Nothing*, whose scatological ridicule of mankind is perhaps equalled only by Beckett's Irish Protestant predecessor, Jonathan Swift. Beckett and Swift both write as disillusioned idealists, once so exigent in their search for a transcendent purity that they now recoil in horror from this decadent world of mortals.[46] Beckett's ailing and excrement-obsessed clowns find their literary ancestry in Swift's Strudbruggs and Yahoos.[47] Moreover Beckett's characters are often so disgusted by the alimentary, sexual and defeca-tory functions of their human condition that they are reduced to sterile impo-tence and immobility: Nagg and Nell are confined to dustbins, the protagonists of *Play* to urns, Murphy to an asylum, Lucky to the end of a rope and the Lost Ones to a hole in the mud. What Hamlet called the 'craven scruple of thinking too precisely on the event' becomes for Beckett's over-intellectualized puritans a source of tortuous paralysis. This iconoclastic view of the human species is comically summed-up in Hamm's suggestion that a post-apocalyptic mankind could be reconstituted from one surviving flea![48]

Some of Beckett's most provocative allusions to religious thought are to be found in his plays. *Waiting for Godot*, as its title suggests, is at once a comic and compassionate portrayal of man's search for God as he 'pines and wastes … towards the great dark' of death. The clowns of *Godot* share the same quest for absolute meaning as the intellectuals of *Murphy*. (Beckett admitted to Colin Duckworth: 'If you want to find the origins of *En Attendant Godot* look at *Murphy*.')[49] The essential difference between the novel of the 1940s and the play of the 1960s is that Beckett's focus has turned from a metaphysical to a theolog-ical perspective. (The Cartesian rationalizations of divine being are hilariously derided in Lucky's 'think' about 'God quaquaquaqua with white beard quaquaquaqua outside time without extension' etc.) *Godot* is, amongst other things, a play about the Judeo-Christian hope for an eschatological God, the waiting for the coming, or second coming, of a Messiah. Several commentators have suggested that Estragon and Vladimir represent Judaism and Christianity respectively;[50] and while remembering Beckett's warning against the 'neat identifications' of the analogymongers it is perhaps unwise to completely dismiss the innumerable theological suggestions to this effect in the play.[51]

Beckett has stated that his use of Augustine's interpretation of the two crucified thieves in *Godot* epitomizes the drama of choice.[52] But if the choices of the Judaic Estragon and the Christian Vladimir are as mutually exclusive as those of the two thieves, the unknown nature of Godot's identity (Jehovah or Christ or simply an absurd joke?),[53] means that both share the same human condition of hoping against hope. Their shared agnosticism is a shared paralysis: they cannot hang each other and yet cannot justify their existence; they cannot communicate and yet cannot go silent; they cannot stay together and yet cannot separate. Their relationship is sustained by the fact that they *both* need Godot: 'In this immense confusion one thing alone is clear. We are waiting for Godot to come – or for night to fall. We are not saints, but we have kept our appointment.'[54]

'Christianity is a mythology with which I am perfectly familiar,' Beckett once confessed to Jack McGowran, 'and so I used it.'[55] *Endgame* is probably Beckett's most concentrated exploration of 'Christian mystology' and certainly his most uncompromising attempt to demythologize some of its more dogmatic interpretations. Now of course *Endgame* operates at numerous levels of meaning, none of which is privileged; and we must take Beckett's comment on the play seriously: 'no symbols where none intended.' Nonetheless, it is undeniable that even the title of the play refers not only to a technical chess position (where play comes to a halt because of diminished forces that cannot culminate in checkmate) but also to the Christian apocalyptic theme of the 'ending of the world'. The play is mined with scriptural allusions – especially to the Book of Revelations – suggesting that Beckett intended a parallel with the eschatological drama between Christ and humanity. Already in *Murphy* Beckett had played with possibilities for such a parallel (the novel is replete with quasi-quotations from Revelations and Murphy himself is cheekily attributed with qualities of the apocalyptic Christ[56]). But it was not until *Godot* and more particularly *Endgame* that these possibilities materialized into a sustained parody.

The first scene of the play may be interpreted as a pseudo-enactment of the crucifixion with Clov as Christ, erecting and mounting his step-ladder crucifix. Clov's opening lines echo Christ's *consummatum est*: 'Finished, its finished, nearly finished, its nearly finished ...' But the tragedy of Golgotha becomes with Beckett a tragic-comedy that can never be terminated or transcended. Clov hopes that despite the 'old Greek's' argument about the grain of millet, time will at last come to an end and sin be fully expiated: 'Grain upon grain and one day, suddenly, there's a heap, a little heap, the impossible heap. I can't be punished anymore.' But the play is precisely a continuation of Clov's punishment, an endgame that cannot be ended.

Hamm (possibly an amalgam of the French *Homme* and the Hebrew *Ha-am*, meaning man or mankind) admits his guilt in having contributed to Clov's (from the French *clou* or nail?) pain and punishment: 'I've made you suffer too much.' But just as Vladimir could not leave Estragon, Clov cannot leave Hamm in spite of his ingratitude and ill-treatment. 'I come ... and go,' says Clov, without ever going. Hamm relates how Clov came in to his house (the world?) as a new born child one 'Christmas eve'. He was brought by his father who begged Hamm to feed and shelter him. But Hamm was irritated by this 'invasion' and mistrusted the millennial promise of Clov's arrival: 'What in God's name do you imagine? That the earth will awake in Spring? That the rivers and seas will run with fish again? That there's manna in heaven still for imbeciles like you?' Now Clov is a grown man and the world is still as unredeemed as ever. A pseudo-eschatological saviour, he acknowledges that he can bring no lasting light into the world ('I see my light dying'); and as the darkness descends, Hamm testifies to the apocalyptic ending of a covenant: 'Then let it end! With a bang! Of darkness! ... It's the end, Clov, we've come to the end. I don't need you any more ... You cried for night; it falls; now cry in darkness.'[57]

The Christ-like Clov is ultimately compelled to acknowledge that his departure from his sepulchre-cell is less a resurrection into light than a return to dust: 'I open the door of the cell and go. I am so bowed I only see my feet, if I open my eyes, and between my legs a little trail of black dust. I say to myself that the earth is extinguished, though I never saw it lit.' Furthermore, Hamm's suggestion that the 'little boy' might be a 'potential progenitor' could be a reference to the symmetrical return of the anti-Christ. His quote from Revelations that 'the end is in the beginning ...', in addition to Clov's mention of the 'brute beast', would certainly seem to confirm such an interpretation. But then again it could also be read as a subversion of eschatological linearity altogether by what Nietzsche, in opposition to Christian eschatology, called 'the eternal return of the same'.[58] Appropriately, it is also impossible to tell whether Clov himself actually leaves the stage, having delivered his farewell address, at the end of the play.[59] Beckett leaves his audience in excruciating doubt. We may choose to recall Dostoyevsky's maxim that 'true faith comes forth from the crucible of doubt'. But then again we may not. It is up to us to wager whether Clov's final 'weeping for happiness' is a token of salvation or despair. Either way, *Endgame* can be interpreted as a further attempt by Beckett to demythologize any lazy or complacent assumptions we may have about Christianity, or any other messianic religion, as panacea to life's suffering.

Theological reference to an unnamable God who sends inscrutable messages to guilt-ridden and uncomprehending humans are also frequent throughout Beckett's novels.

Molloy is a writer who receives orders from an unknown master with a stick, 'who gives (him) money and takes away the pages'. Though rapidly becoming deaf and blind, Molloy feels such punishment to be his due: 'It's my fault. Fault? That was the word.' He ridicules his early fascination for the images of the 'old Geulincx', but still persists in his conviction that 'all things hang together, by the operation of the Holy Ghost.' In the second half of the novel, the master, now named Youdi (a pseudo Yahweh?) sends his 'messenger' Gaber (a pseudo angel Gabriel?; the Greek for messenger being *Angelos*) to another human 'agent', Moran, commissioning him to go in search of his 'protégé' Molloy. Both Gaber and Moran insist that they are 'members of a vast organisation' and refuse to 'conjure away the Chief'; for to do so would be to accept that they are 'solely responsible for (their) wretched existence'.

Moran is tortured by the fear that the Chief and even Molloy are merely his own fictions: 'ready made in my head.' Though he continues to 'obey orders' he cannot be sure whether the voice that utters them is of some transcendent being or his own imagination.[60]

Faithful to this 'ambiguous voice', the novel ends with Moran returning home covered with 'deep lesions and wounds', acknowledging 'the wrong I had done my God, to whom I had been taught to ascribe my angers, fears, desires and even my body'. Moran remains as determined as ever to find Molloy who might help him to understand 'what I had to do, so that Youdi would not punish me'; but his final word remains agnostic, a confession of ignorance: 'I have spoken of a voice telling me things ... It told me to write the report. Does this mean I am freer now than I was? I do not know.'

In the remaining novels of the trilogy, *Malone Dies* and *The Unnamable*, Beckett relentlessly pursues the question of divine existence, but he now approaches it less from the scriptural angle of dogma and revelation than from the mystical angle of a *via negativa*. The mystical way of negative theology operates on the assumption that it is only by divesting God of all anthropomorphic attributes (i.e. by accepting his unnamability) and by divesting our human selves of all desires, fears and hopes, that we may experience the *mysterium tremendum et fascinans* of God. Or, as Beckett put it in his *Proust* essay: 'The wisdom of the sages ... is the wisdom that consists not in the satisfaction but in the ablation of desire.' This mystical way of dispossession is habitually identified with such Christian thinkers as Meister Eckhart, Boehme and St John of the Cross, all of whom Beckett mentions in his works.[61]

In *Malone Dies*, the narrator – Malone – resembles his predecessors in being crippled by religious sentiments of 'punishment and sin'. He is as ignorant of the source of this culpability as he is of the source of its possible remission: 'not knowing what my prayer should be nor to whom'. Yet by narrating one story after another, four in all, each one with new characters (Saposcat, Macmann, Lambert, Jackson, etc.), Malone intends to dispossess himself, to go by the way in which he is not: 'I shall be no more.' Malone cites Democritus' tag that 'nothing is more real than nothing', believing that this *via negativa* will lead to an absolute vision of things. Ironically, one of Malone's fictional characters teaches his parrot to say *nihil in intellectu*, a telling distortion of the Scholastic-Aristotelian dictum *nihil in intellectu quod non prius fuerit in sensu* (there is nothing in the mind, that was not first in the senses).

But the narrator gradually comes to realize that all his stories are no more than an innumerable babble of voices barring access to mystical silence: 'He could make no meaning of the babble raging in his head, the doubts, desires, imaginings and dread.' And so he resolves to renounce all efforts of active will, even 'the last effort to understand … No I want nothing.' If only he can 'die alive', thereby experiencing the nothingness of death, he will achieve illumination. But this paradoxical consciousness-in-unconsciousness is a typical ploy of Beckettian irony. As soon as the narrator thinks he has reached silence, the voices return to plague him. As long as he seeks silence through words he can 'never get dead'. He cannot write himself into silence: 'When I stop, as just now, the noises begin again, strangely loud, those whose turn it is.'

This attempt to reach, through language, some miraculous silence is playfully re-explored in *The Unnamable*. Here the narrator speaks of strange 'delegates' delivering 'lectures' to him about the nature of God: they 'gave me the low-down on God. They told me I depended on him, in the last analysis. They had it on the reliable authority of his agents at Bally I forget what, this being the place, according to them, where the inestimable gift of life had been rammed down my gullet.' The unnamable narrator develops the mystical doctrine that dependency on God is meaningful only when one has ceased to seek, desire, think or speak about him. 'Doubt no more, seek no more,' urges the author. 'Overcome, that goes without saying, the fatal leaning towards expressiveness.' Even hope must be banished – 'none of your hoping here, that would spoil everything.'

The divine, it appears, can only be revealed if our transcendence of ourselves 'opens on the void, on the silence'. Thus the unnamable narrator decides to terminate 'the frenzy of utterances' he has begun. 'If only this voice could stop,' he murmurs, 'this meaningless voice which prevents you from being nothing.' But the search for a verbal means to put an end to speech is of course self-defeating; for it is precisely the search in and through words that obliges the discourse to continue. 'It is impossible,' the narrator admits, 'to speak and yet say nothing.'

Beckett is not unmindful of the implications of this incommunicability of transcendent meaning for scriptural hermeneutics. 'I am Matthew and I am the Angel,' boasts the Unnamable, reminding us that the angels and evangelists before him had also a duty to say the unsayable, or as Beckett puts it 'to eff the ineffable'. The very hermeneutical notions of a 'truth to recover' or a 'labour to accomplish' are themselves symptoms of 'the mad need to speak, to think, to know', symptoms that ultimately subvert the mystical transcendence of the divine. The peace of the biblical God-beyond-being surpasses understanding.

'Dear incomprehension,' declares the ascetic aspirant of non-being, 'it's thanks to you I'll be myself, in the end. Nothing will remain of all the lies they have glutted me with. And I'll be myself at last, as a starvling belches his odourless wind, before the bliss of coma.' Only when, and if, he is 'let loose alone in the unthinkable, unspeakable,' will he be able to encounter God at the heart of darkness.[62]

The God of the unnamable narrator appears to be an absent God who chastises him until, like Job, he becomes a 'worm in the sight of the Lord'. Transposing the traditional version of the *via negativa*, Beckett pens one of his most trenchant parodies of religious optimism:

> The essential is never to arrive anywhere, never to be anywhere ... The essential is to go on squirming forever at the end of the line, as long as there are waters and banks and ravening in heaven and a sporting God to plague his creature, per pro his chosen shits. I've swallowed three hooks and am still hungry? Hence the howls ... nothing to do but stretch out comfortably on the rack, in the blissful knowledge you are nobody for eternity.[63]

But Beckett's explorations of negative theology are nowhere more radical and penetrating than in *Watt*. The novel recounts the sojourn of the rationalist Mr Watt in the house of the elusive Mr Knott, appropriately so named. Mr Knott represents the immutable and immortal condition sought by numerous Beckettian characters: 'nothing changed in Mr Knott's house'. All Watt's attempts to impose a scientific mould on the 'nothingness' he encounters are thwarted and he is forced to the 'mystical' conclusion that true knowledge is non-knowledge, that the truth of being is non-being.[64] A salient theme in *Watt* is, consequently, the demise of rationalism. In his working plans for the novel, Beckett develops the plot by means of Aristotle's ten logical categories and his termination of the text with a note on the pessimistic death-bed words of Aristotle, 'master of those who know', intimates the futility of Watt's invocation of rationalist principles.

Watt cannot fail to see the patent contradiction in his anthropomorphic definitions of nothingness and God: 'the only way one can speak of nothing is to speak of it as though it were something, just as the only way to speak of God is to speak of him as though he were a man, which to be sure he was, in a sense, for a time ...' As the novel progresses, Watt's positivistic endeavour to encapsulate the meaning of Mr Knott in words and names becomes a *reductio ad absurdum* and he finally 'abandon[s] all hope, all fear, of ever seeing Mr. Knott face to face.'

Like Godot, as described by the 'small boy', Mr Knott 'does nothing'. Mr Knott's abode remains an indefinable nothing, an 'empty husk in airless gloom'. So Watt eventually consents to ask no more questions, to 'like the fact that it has no meaning'. He espouses a position of total abandonment: 'this mind ignoring. These emptied hands. This emptied heart. To him I brought. To the temple. To the Healer. To the source. Of nought.' Thus Watt comes to experience the silent infinite spaces, as Pascal put it, of the *Deus Absconditus*. The summary of his stay in Mr Knott's house is, in this respect, expressly equivocal;

> What had he learned? Nothing. What did he know of Mr Knott? Nothing. What remained of his passion to understand? Nothing. But is that not already something? He saw himself as so small and lacking. But is that not already something? So sick, so alone. And now. Even sicker, even more alone, was that not something?

Watt's dealings with nothingness reiterate Murphy's talk of that 'numb peace' that only comes 'when the somethings give way, or perhaps simply add up, to the Nothing, than which in the guffaw of the Abderite naught is more real ... the accidentless One-and-Only conveniently called Nothing.'

Is Beckett suggesting then that the *via negativa* is a valid, possibly the only, way to encounter an incomprehensible God? Or is he simply demythologizing this negative theology as just another desperate leap towards a non-existent God? It is impossible to tell. As Jean Onimus argues in his perspicacious analysis of Beckett's philosophy of religion: 'the revelation of Nothing is ambiguous. According to the instances, it can bring about anguish, anger and despair or the beatific sentiment of liberation.'[65] In a passage in *Molloy*, for example, Beckett infers that silence can indeed be taken as a token of revelation: 'to remain silent and listen, not one being in a hundred is capable of even conceiving what this means. It is however ... beyond the absurd fracas the silence of which the universe is made.' And yet we have been able to cite numerous passages from Beckett's writings where the condition of will-less abandonment celebrated by mystics such as Eckhart is mercilessly ridiculed. (In *Dream* Beckett even goes so far as to dismiss Eckhart as a 'dud mystic'.) Similarly, it is impossible to tell whether the voice that assails Beckett's narrators is simply nihilistic nonsense or the 'still, small voice' of the hidden God that once spoke to Elijah after forty nights in the desert. In short, when a Beckettian character exclaims that he cannot forgive God for not existing, is he affirming or denying Divine existence?[66]

To answer such questions one way or the other would be to betray the unique ambivalence of Beckett's writing. In an interview in 1974 Beckett returns to his favourite example of the two thieves: 'I take no sides ... There is a wonderful sentence in Augustine: Do no despair; one of the thieves was saved: Do not presume; one of the thieves was damned.'[67] And speaking elsewhere of the religious significance of life and death in his work, Beckett elaborates on this impartiality, pronouncing what must be his most conclusive, albeit elusive, word on the subject:

> If life and death did not both present themselves to us, there would be no inscrutability. If there was only darkness, all would be clear. It is because there is not only darkness, but also light that our situation becomes inescapable.

Take St Augustine's doctrine about grace given and grace refused: have you ever reflected on the dramatic quality of this theology? Two thieves are crucified with Christ; one is saved and the other is damned. How can one understand this? In classical drama, such problems do not arise. The destiny of Racine's *Phaedre* is sealed from the beginning ... there is no doubt that she travels towards darkness. That's the play. According to this conception, clarity is possible, but for us who are neither Greeks nor Jansenists, there exists no such clarity. The question would not exist either if we believed in the opposite, in a guaranteed salvation. But where we have at once darkness and light, there we also have the inexplicable. The key word of my work is *perhaps*.[68]

Conclusion

Beckett's entire literary oeuvre embodies a modern critique of traditional notions of 'identity' – whether it concern the self, being, language, God or one's sense of national belonging. His aim, I suggest, is less a nihilistic dissolution of sense into non-sense than a playful wish to expose the inexhaustible comedy of existence. His writing delights in disrupting all hard-and-fast categories and distinctions that seek to simplify experience – including those that would rigidly divide literature and philosophy; it powerfully illustrates how all our rational concepts are ultimately related to an ongoing process of artistic rediscovery and revision. By thus challenging the conventional apartheid that isolated intellect and imagination into mutually exclusive ghettos, Beckett's work might be said to epitomize, to some degree, a peculiarly Irish cast of mind. In Beckett we witness an Irish mind less concerned with self-regarding questions of Irish history and tradition than with the universal concerns of Western humanistic culture as a whole, particularly as it combines the founding heritages of Hellenic idealism and Judeo-Christian theology. Faithful to his specifically Irish experiences of exile, marginality and dissent, Beckett has brought a sense of critical humour to bear on philosophical questions of international import. His writing is testimony to the fact that the Irish mind is no less Irish for dispensing with the mirror of indigenous self-absorption and embarking on the endless quest for the other.

Appendix: The Modern Critique of Being and Language

Beckett's intellectual preoccupations extend beyond the conundrums of Cartesian idealism and negative theology to include a modernist critique of the classical concepts of self-identity. This third dimension of Beckett's demythologizing finds parallels in both the modern philosophies of existence (Heidegger, Sartre, Camus, etc.) and of language (Mauthner, Wittgenstein, Derrida).

As the existentialist or absurdist character of Beckett's work has already been documented by numerous critics, I shall advert to it only in passing. When asked if contemporary philosophers have any influence on (his) thought, Beckett testily quipped: 'I never understand anything they write.'[69] Asked on another occasion about the specific impact of existentialism on his work, Beckett was equally unforthcoming: 'When Heidegger and Sartre speak of a contrast between Being and existence, they may be right, I don't know ...'[70] Yet despite this legitimate resistance to any facile attempt to reduce his complex, playful works to a straightforward philosophical argument, Beckett was clearly familiar with the existentialist philosophy of Heidegger and Sartre. Jean Paul Sartre was at *L'École Normale* in Paris when Beckett lectured there in 1928–30 and Beckett has admitted that they met several times 'without embarrassment'.[71] French existentialism took its inspiration from Martin Heidegger's *Sein und Zeit*, which defined existence as the solitary anguish (*Angst*) of a 'being-towards-death' (*Sein zum Tode*); it was published in 1927 just as Beckett began his travels to Germany and France.

> The principal themes of Heidegger often resemble those of Beckett, [declares Onimus,] both profoundly Christian at the outset, share the same tragic vision of existence. Beckett discovered in the German philosopher the same phenomenology of anguish, nothingness, boredom and finitude, the same conception of the paradoxical reality of lucid existence that is nothing other than a scattering in dread and in time, finally he found there the same horror of life when it is degraded by the inauthentic.[72]

The existentialists radicalized the presocratic and mystical doctrine that Being is intimately related to non-being. In *Was Ist Metaphysik?* (1933), Heidegger argued that 'nothingness is the veil of Being' and that the very formlessness of its experience fills us with dread:

> Nothing is revealed in dread, but not as something that 'is'. Neither can it be taken as an object ... dread finds itself completely powerless in the face of what is as a whole ... Nihilation is not a fortuitous event, but understood as the relegation to the vanishing Being as a whole, it reveals the latter in all its till now undisclosed strangeness as the pure 'other' ... The essence of nothing (*Nichts*) as original nihilation (*Vernichtung*) lies in this: that it alone brings human existence face to face with what is as such.[73]

By thus equating Being with nothingness, Heidegger announced the 'deconstruction' (*Überwindung*) of the traditional metaphysical notions of being as fullness, plenitude and self-sufficiency (e.g. as *ens causa sui*). The truth of Being no longer manifests itself as *what is* (a thing), but rather as *what is not* (a no-thing) or as *what may be* (a possibility). In similar fashion, Sartre affirms in *L'être et le néant* (1944) that 'nothingness lurks at the heart of Being, coiled up like a worm.' He proceeds to define man as a 'useless passion' since all his attempts to impose order on reality are mere aesthetic or imaginary projections. Existence precedes essence, announces Sartre, meaning that we invent our own identity and can rely on no universal system of inherited values. One can see the overlap between this Sartrean solipsism and Beckett's claim in *Proust* that art is absolute solitude.[74] And we might also recall Beckett's own equation of Being with formless nothingness not only in the various passages cited in the previous two sections, but even more emphatically in his 1961 interview with Tom Driver: 'Being is constantly putting form in danger ... I know of no form that does not violate the nature of Being in the most vulnerable manner ... If anything new and exciting is going on today, it is the attempt to let Being into art.'[75]

For art to embrace formlessness is to acknowledge that life is absurd. If human existence is haunted by nothingness then we have no given identity; the very notion of self-identity is itself no more than one of our own inventions with which we can never fully identify. Man is a being who is what he is not and is not what he is, as Sartre formulates it. Consequently, while negative theology interprets the experience of nothingness as a mystical experience of God, the existentialists interpret it as an experience of the anguish or absurdity of Being.[76]

Beckett has described his art as an 'art of failure ... with nothing to express and no means to express it.'[77] To let Being into art, Beckett advises, is to renounce one's will to be oneself and to let the impersonal voices of language speak. The author of *Texts for Nothing* says as much when he confesses that he is 'only a ventriloquist's dummy ... (Who) holds me in his arms and moves my lips'; so that 'it is rare that the sentiment of absurdity is not followed by the sentiment of necessity.'[78] And this sentiment of necessity is precisely that suffering of being which Beckett first championed in his early *Proust* essay as the 'principal condition of aesthetic experience'.[79]

Beckett's answer to our existential anguish is humour. His laughter derives from the recognition of ambiguity, from the impossibility of reconciling juxtaposed opposites – be they hope and despair, logic and folly, presence and absence. 'In the beginning was the pun,' Murphy reveals. The Beckettian laugh is certainly philosophical to the extent that it puts our assured ideas about God or Being in question; but it is also comic for it is a laugh of comfortless wisdom: 'The mirthless laugh is the dianoetic laugh, *risus purus* ... the laugh that laughs – silence please – at that which is unhappy.'[80] Camus, another philosopher of the absurd, exclaimed: '*L'absurde n'a de sens que dans la mesure où l'on n'y consent pas.*' Beckett's laughter of wisdom (Gk. *dianoia*) is perhaps less an uncritical submission to nonsense than a waiting for meaning despite its manifestly absurd presence. This stoic defiance is typified by the Beckettian character in *More Pricks than Kicks* who bravely announces that he 'would arm his mind with laughter as he stepped smartly into the torture chamber.'[81]

Beckett's affinity with the existentialist ethos led naturally to an interest in the modern philosophy of language. Heidegger himself had deconstructed Being not only into nothingness but also into language. 'Language is the house of Being,' he stated in his *Humanismus Brief* (1947) (a singularly pertinent analogy when one thinks of Watt's linguistic experiments in Mr Knott's house). One of the first modern philosophers to capture Beckett's attention was the Austrian logician Fritz Mauthner, from whose major work, *Beiträge zu einer Kritik der Sprache*, Beckett read to the blind but alert Joyce in the 1930s.[82] Mauthner claimed that there is 'no thinking without speaking' and that we could only reach the truth of reality if we transcended the limits of language (which Mauthner considered impossible). The undoing of language requires what Mauthner, in a phrase redolent of Beckettian pathos, termed 'the heavenly stillness and gaiety of resignation and renunciation'. Such a gaiety would occasion the 'suicide of thought' recalling the impossible project of Molloy, Malone, Watt and the unnamable narrator to say the unsayable, to move from speech to silence.

Beckett's critical preoccupation with language also bears a close resemblance to the ideas of another Austrian linguist, Ludwig Wittgenstein. Wittgenstein agreed with Mauthner that there could be no thought without words; and that without words and thought there is only an undifferentiated nothing. The meaning of man's existence is therefore irredeemably linguistic. Since we name and identify our experience through language, our world is commensurate with our words. Beyond words there is only the limitless non-being of silence. Wittgenstein's much quoted conclusion to the *Tractatus* could have been uttered by almost any Beckettian character: 'Whereof one cannot speak, thereof one must be silent.'

It is easy to see the intimate rapport between the philosophical linguistics of Mauthner and Wittgenstein and Watt's futile efforts to reduce Knott's nothingness to his own little world of words. It is 'comforting' for Watt to suppose that if he can name the uncanny events in Mr Knott's house (his dog, his unfinished dinner, his ladder, his stairs, his servants, the comings and goings of his guests, Tom, Dick and Harry, etc.), he can take the harm out of them. But *Watt* is a novel about the dual impossibility of reducing reality to words and of transcending words towards reality. Watt's marathon project to turn 'disturbances into words' by enumerating endless lists of postulates and calculations, is doomed from the start. He soon recognizes the 'old error' of trying to say 'what things were in reality'.[83] Thinking of 'one of Mr Knott's pots', to recite just one of Beckett's hilarious examples, 'it was in vain that Watt said, Pot, pot … It resembled a pot, it was almost a pot, but it was not a pot of which one could say, Pot, pot, and be comforted.'[84] By the end of the novel, Watt has said absolutely nothing of significance about Mr Knott or his world.[85] The terrifying *néant* of Mr Knott's house is refractory to the positivistic claims of reason and language. But as always in Beckett we are left undecided as to whether the timeless, spaceless void beyond language is the portal to a mystical experience (Arsène speaks of the bliss of a 'situation where to do nothing exclusively would be an act of the highest value') or simply the nothingness of the absurd (Watt's 'preestablished arbitrary'). As the author of *Watt* ruefully concludes: 'Know not.'

Beckett's demythologizing of the scientific pretensions of Cartesian idealism, dogmatic theology and linguistic positivism may be seen as a literary counterpart to Jacques Derrida's recent philosophy of *deconstruction*. Derrida develops Heidegger's destruction of the *logos* of Being into a radical deconstruction of the *logos* of language. Heidegger, we observed, dismantled the metaphysical myth of Being as omnipotent presence concluding that its truth can only reveal itself as absence, nothingness or possibility. Following in the footsteps of the master, Derrida sets out to refute the metaphysical myth of language as a transparent *signifier* referring to some meta-linguistic reality (*the signified*). Accordingly, just as being is demytholigized into nothingness, language must be demytholigized into unnamability. Derrida sums up his position in terms that could serve as a gloss to Beckett's entire literary corpus: 'One cannot attempt to deconstruct this transcendence (of the *logos* as original presence) without descending, across the inherited concepts, towards the unnamable.'[86] In other words, Derrida argues that the founding concepts of metaphysics – *Logos, Arche, Eidos, Nous*, etc. – are merely faded linguistic metaphors (of origin, light and presence); he exposes this covert metaphorising at the root of Western philosophy and denounces it as a *white mythology*: 'It is metaphysics which has effaced in itself that fabulous scene which brought it into being, and which yet remains, active and stirring, inscribed in white ink, an invisible drawing covered over in the palimpsest.'[87] Thus Derrida shows that the metaphorizing activity of language, far from re-presenting some extra-linguistic origin of meaning (what he calls the 'transcendental signified'), is no more than the perpetual supplementation of one signifier/word for another. Beyond the words that signify there is *nothing* signified, no presence of subject or object, only an endless series of other signifying traces – more words.

Several of Beckett's prose works can be read as radical literary exercises in such deconstruction. The metaphorizing attempts of Beckettian narrators to transcend language towards some prelinguistic self-identity are continually frustrated. The reality of the self remains forever 'absent' and 'inexpressible'.[88] 'No-one will ever hear me say it, I won't say it, I can't say it … To the voices of language trying to persuade him he "has an ego all of his own", he replies, "I shall not say I again."' At one point he does think he might be able to rediscover himself through a third person, a new fictional character who might serve as a mirror image of his own genesis: 'We must first, to begin with, go back to the beginnings and then, to go on with, follow him patiently through the various stages ... which have made him what *I* am.' But the *I* reached through the detour of the *he* is no more than an imagined self, a trace of itself; the I is always deferred.

The narrative I is a split I, a not–I, forever in pursuit of itself, forever falling short of itself. The Beckettian narrator is a victim of the voices he utters and hears, a prey to language. Thus, for example, Beckett discovers in *Malone Dies* that he cannot disengage his authorial voice from the voice of Malone who, in turn, cannot disentangle himself from the other fictive narrators of Beckett's novels. As long as one lives and speaks, one is a slave to the endless differentiation of language. Only death, it seems, can offer a release from the hell of non-identity: 'Let us leave these morbid matters,' declares the author of *Malone Dies*, 'and get on with that of my demise, in two or three days if I remember rightly. Then it will all be over with the Murphys, Merciers, Morans and Malones, unless it goes on beyond the grave.' But in Beckett's world it does; in the realm of words there is always an after-world. Language is limbo. We can never finally appropriate ourselves for we can never experience our own death as a finality. We can only experience our existence *towards* death (*Sein zum Tode*) or else our imaginary existence *after* it. For Beckett as for Derrida, language is a process of *deferring* and *decentring* the subject, a process that underscores the futility of trying to *be one self*. There can be no last word on the subject.[89]

The modern author, if we are to take Beckett at his word, is a nomad condemned to the alienation of language. But if we lose ourselves in words, we will not, for all that, cease to employ them with joyous abandon and defiance in order to try to recover ourselves. The Beckettian narrators, even though they can't go on, go on – in endless search of themselves.

Chapter Thirteen

A Crisis of Fiction:
Flann O'Brien, Francis Stuart,
John Banville

What was to become of the Irish novel after Joyce and Beckett? How would it be possible to go on writing fiction once its basic narrative quest-structure had been radically overhauled by *Ulysses* and the *Trilogy*? The fact of the matter is that the majority of Irish novelists continued, as did the majority of novelists elsewhere, in the classic tradition of fiction-writing in spite of the challenge issued by the radical modernism of Joyce and Beckett. In this mainstream movement of Irish novelists figure such celebrated authors as Liam O'Flaherty, Sean O'Faolain, Kate O'Brien, Jennifer Johnston, Edna O'Brien, Bernard McLaverty, John McGahern, Brian Moore and Roddy Doyle. These writers broadly conform to the structural requirements of classical realism unflustered by the modernist problematic of fiction (though some did, on occasion, incorporate aspects of its interrogative character).[1] A small number of modern Irish novelists, however, explicitly chose to preoccupy themselves with the modernist critique of writing. In this 'critical' movement of fiction, which we could even call a 'counter-tradition', we might place the experimental works of Flann O'Brien, Aidan Higgins, John Banville and the later Francis Stuart. These authors believe that they can no longer take the novel for granted. Writing in the wake of Joyce and Beckett, they feel compelled to interrogate the very possibility of writing.

In this chapter I want to examine a representative sample of works by some of the major novelists of this Irish counter-tradition – in particular O'Brien, Stuart and Banville. My purpose is to indicate how their writing becomes self-reflexive as it explores fundamental tensions between imagination and memory, narration and history, self and language. In short, I propose to show how these authors share

with Joyce and Beckett the basic modernist project of transforming the traditional narrative of *quest* into a critical narrative of *self-questioning*.

I. Flann O'Brien

Flann O'Brien belongs with Beckett to what might be described as the first
generation of 'critical' Irish novelists. Like Beckett he tended to view Joyce's
deconstruction of the quest-structure of conventional narrative as a total *subordination of reality to imagination.* Writing becomes problematic accordingly in that
the writer appears to be a prisoner of his own fiction. We saw, in the previous
chapter, how this aesthetic reduction of the historical world to the ploys of
imagination posed all kinds of dilemmas for Beckett's narrators as they tried to
break free from the tyranny of their own fiction in order to confront the
'suffering of being'. We also saw how these narrative attempts to undo narrative,
to move from voluntary imagination to involuntary memory, resulted in failure.
Nowhere is this failure more explicit than in Beckett's late short prose piece,
Imagination Dead Imagine.

Here the narration takes the form, significantly, of a monologue, in which the
narrator finds himself trapped inside a plain white rotunda that reduces the
outside world to a hot white light that comes and goes. This rotunda is the imagination itself, and Beckett's point seems to be that even death ('imagination dead')
is no panacea for the solipsism of fiction, which simply goes on imagining. Imagination is the 'eye of prey' that converts all exterior life to its own currency, which
reduces the multifaceted world to its own point of view; and for the writer *there
is no other.* 'No trace anywhere of life, you say, pah, no difficulty there, imagination not dead yet, yes, dead, good, imagination dead imagine ... world still proof
against ending tumult. Rediscovered miraculously after what absence in perfect
voids it is no longer the same, from this point of view, but there is no other.'

In Flann O'Brien's fiction the imagination also reigns supreme; history is no
more than a figment of the narrator's own comic designs. Since imagination
consumes everything it imagines there is no exit from the process of writing itself.
O'Brien's novels – or perhaps post-novels is the more appropriate term – express
their creator's mock-heroic efforts to jump out of his own skin or, like Pygmalion,
to breathe real life into his fictional characters. Narrative becomes for O'Brien, as
for Joyce and Beckett, a questioning of its own conditions of possibility.

O'Brien shares Beckett's modernist dilemma as a practitioner of experimental
fiction. But his 'critical' approach to writing is also informed by his own
profound experience of social alienation and depression in modern urban Irish
society put into quarantine by the Second World War and the isolationist policies of the new Republic. While Beckett depicted the modern ethos of the
absurd within the confines of a nihilistic limbo, O'Brien's novels explore this

ethos in the more localized phantasmagoria of upstart undergraduates, pseudo-intellectual civil servants and eccentric policemen confronted with the squalid inertia of Dublin life in the thirties and forties. Such fictional characters, De Selby remarks in *The Third Policeman*, reside in the 'permanent hallucination known conventionally as "life", with its innumerable concomitant limitations, afflictions and anomalies'.

Joyce hailed O'Brien as a 'real writer, with the true comic spirit'. There can be no doubt that O'Brien inherited the master's iconoclastic approach to the inherited narratives of both classical realism and cultural revivalism. *At Swim-Two-Birds*, published in 1939, is a parody of heroic linear narrative from beginning to end. As with Joyce's *Ulysses* or Beckett's *Trilogy*, the novel here becomes its own critical self-representation, a novel about novel-writing, a narrative that puts itself in question. The opening paragraph is illustrative of this approach:

> Having placed in my mouth sufficient bread for three minutes chewing, I withdrew my powers of sensual perception and retired in to the privacy of my mind, my eyes and face assuming a vacant, preoccupied expression. I reflected on the subject of my sparetime literary activities. One beginning and one ending for a book was a thing I did not agree with. A good book may have three openings entirely dissimilar and inter-related only in the prescience of the author, or for that matter one hundred times as many endings.

The author having thus included himself in his own novel then proceeds to comment upon the 'examples of three separate openings', directing the reader with the obtrusive editorial headings – 'First opening', 'Second opening', 'Third opening', etc.

At Swim-Two-Birds is as much a mimicry of the conventions of the novel as is *Ulysses* or *The Unnamable*. The traditional quest-structure is ridiculed in the aimless wanderings of such Irish legendary heroes as Finn McCool, Sweeney or the pseudo-bardic Pooka Mac Phellimey. By transforming these mythic heroes of cultural nationalism into modernist anti-heroes O'Brien succeeds in under-mining the orthodox structures of realist and revivalist narrative. His various permutating characters slide into each other, self-elide, and ultimately expose themselves for what they are – expendable experiments of the author. Such dismantling of the 'individuated' characterization of the traditional novel together with the recurrence of conspicuous editorial interruptions in the text reminds us that we are witnessing not a story but the problematic creation (and destruction) of a story. We are not permitted to forget that character and plot are but figments devoid of all *rapport* with the real world. Indeed Trellis, the writer, is so attracted by one of his own female creations that he ravishes her and produces a son of a 'quasi-illusory sort'. But the 'literary' son conspires with the other characters and together they revolt against their patriarchal author by writing an alternative fiction in which he is arrested, tortured and put on trial. Rather than cohere in a plausible sequence of events, the diverse characters turn against their own creator – Trellis/Flann O'Brien – and transform him also into a fiction.

The narrator's attempt to reach reality via fiction thus constitutes an infinite regress. At the conclusion of the novel, Sarah the maid discovers that Furriskey and his friends are but inventions of her master Trellis: 'It happened that these same pages were those of the master's novel'. O'Brien's Trellis, like Beckett's Malone, seems to have become a victim of his own inner voices – 'Was Trellis mad? ... Was he a victim of hard-to-explain hallucinations?' Indeed at this point we begin to realize that Trellis himself is but a fictional creation of another author, Flann O'Brien (who is, of course, himself a fictional creation – a pseudonym – of the 'real' author and Dublin civil servant Brian O'Nolan). We thus understand, in retrospect, that the admonitory notice that prefaced the novel is perhaps a self-description of this solipsism of writing: 'All the characters represented in this book, including the first person singular, are entirely fictitious and bear no relation to any person living or dead.'

Flann O'Brien takes Joyce's identification of imagination and reality to mean that writing is all imagination and no reality. Despite countless ingenious strategies, the author cannot make contact with the outside world. The real congeals into the imaginary like Midas' food into gold. The *search-structure* of traditional narrative is therefore shown to be impossible, for the *sought* is identical with the *searcher* from the very outset. In *At Swim-Two-Birds* the snake of fiction curls up and swallows its own tail.

If Flann O'Brien develops the critical legacy of Joyce and Beckett with regard to traditional narrative, he also inherits their irreverent attitude to the Irish Literary Revival. O'Brien's novels are generally set in deromanticized urban contexts and comically undermine the standard revivalist opposition between the country and the city: an opposition that idealized the rural landscape as a timeless and primeval idyll where the noble Irish peasant could live his life uncomplicated by the social and commercial relations of contemporary urban existence. O'Brien's satirical exposure of 'Gaelic nationalist rural pieties' is perhaps nowhere more explicit than in *An Béal Bocht/The Poor Mouth* where he explains, for example, how the inventors of the Revival Myth of the Irish countryside choose not to live there themselves because: '1. The tempest of the countryside was too tempestuous. 2. The putridity of the countryside was too putrid. 3. The poverty of the countryside was too poor. 4. The Gaelicism of the countryside was too Gaelic. 5. The tradition of the countryside was too traditional.'[2]

If *At Swim-Two-Birds* debunks the Anglo-Irish Ireland of Synge and the early Yeats, *The Poor Mouth* parodies the romantic realism of writers like Tomás Ó Criomhthain, Liam O'Flaherty and Frank O'Connor who drew inspiration from the Gaelic culture. Choosing a leitmotif from the elegiac conclusion to Ó Criomhthain's *An t-Oileánach/The Islandman* – 'I do not think that my like will ever be seen again' – O'Brien (writing under the pseudonym Myles na gCopaleen) mocks the plaintive style of such 'native' literature weighed down by a sentimentalism of grievance and loss. Composed originally in Gaelic, this novel is a hilarious language play of puzzles and puns that could be considered a sort of *wake* to the native tongue, an irreverent testimony to the fact that the romantic Ireland of the Gael is dead and gone forever.

But O'Brien believed that the English language was quite as susceptible to 'communication breakdown' as the Gaelic. One of his characters defines the narrative as an attempt to 'unravel Babel' – an echo of Joyce's description of the *Wake* as a retelling of the story of Babel. All of O'Brien's novels from *At Swim-Two-Birds* to *The Third Policeman*, *The Poor Mouth*, *The Hard Life* and *The Dalkey Archive* are replete with logical contradictions of sequence and sense, linguistic absurdities and ridiculous conversations conducted at cross purposes. As with Joyce and Beckett, the conventional temporality of linear narrative is 'dechronologized' (i.e. past, present and future are often confused or even reversed); and the quest-structure is frequently negated (as in the erratic wanderings of Sweeney in *At Swim-Two-Birds* or the assassinated narrator's futile search for the black box in *The Third Policeman*). Moreover, the narratives themselves almost invariably take place *within* the narrator's own head and increasingly abandon any pretence to 'represent' some external action. In O'Brien's fiction, no single perspective or viewpoint is privileged. All things, as the epithet to *At Swim-Two-Birds* announces, 'flee and yield place to each other'. The nameless solipsist of *The Third Policeman* sounds a characteristic Flann O'Brien anthem when he declares: 'I felt my brain cluttered with questions and blind perplexities ... I felt completely alone'. Thus O'Brien debunks the grand illusion of realism with its attendant conventions of characterization, sequential plot, naturalistic setting and fixed authorial viewpoint.[3]

O'Brien's writings also engage, finally, in a play of intertextuality where cross-references are found not just within the framework of the author's own works (characters from one novel crop up in the next) but within the framework of Irish writing generally (e.g. the allusions to Ó Criomhthain in *The Poor Mouth* or to Joyce who actually appears in person in *The Dalkey Archive*). Radical transgressions of novelistic conventions are witnessed in O'Brien's mixing of multiple styles and conflicting plots – in *At Swim-Two-Birds* he uses four separate narratives simultaneously – and his repudiation of the standard norms of psychological verisimilitude. O'Brien's texts might thus be described as anti-novels in Abrams' sense of narratives 'deliberately constructed in a negative fashion, relying ... on annihilating traditional elements of the novel, and on playing against the expectations established in the reader by the novelistic methods of the past.'[4] This self-deconstructive logic reaches its extreme limit in the annihilation of the author himself (as in *At Swim-Two-Birds*). Indeed this strategy is already evidenced in the author's use of different pseudonyms: Flann O'Brien, the Brother, Myles na gCopaleen. The 'real' author, Brian O'Nolan, vehemently denied any knowledge of his pseudonymous creations. In this respect, Roland Barthes' famous account of the 'death of the author' in modern literature provides an apt gloss on the writings of O'Brien and the other Irish modernists:

> Writing is that neutral, composite, oblique space where our subject slips away, the negative where all identity is lost, starting with the very identity of the body writing ... The image of literature to be found in ordinary culture is tyrannically centred on the author, his person, his life, his tastes, his passions ... The *explanation* of a work is always sought in the man or woman who produced it, as if it were always in the end, through the more or less transparent allegory of fiction, the voice of a single person, the *author* 'confiding' in us ... Linguistically the author is never more than the instance of writing ... His only power is to mix writings, to counter the ones with the others, in such a way as never to rest on any of them ... a text is made up of multiple writings, drawn from many cultures and entering into mutual relations of dialogue, parody, contestation.[5]

II. Francis Stuart

The later Stuart belongs with Banville, Higgins and Jordan to the second generation of Irish novelists in the counter-tradition. Like the first generation, Stuart is centrally preoccupied with the dilemma of writing fiction after Joyce; but he tends to read the Joycean 'crisis of imagination' in a different way. Whereas Beckett and O'Brien struggled with the problem of how to get beyond imagination to the reality principle of historical memory, Stuart construes the problem of fiction as an attempt to escape from the oppressive reality of history into some new imaginative order. *A Hole in the Head*, published in the late seventies and perhaps Stuart's most experimental novel, is a self-reflexive narrative that deals both structurally and thematically with the specific problematic of creativity. Here the Joycean identification of imagination with reality is diagnosed as an excess of the reality principle that threatens to annihilate the possibility of fiction altogether. And so we find a reiteration of Stephen Dedalus' project to transform the imprisoning constraints of history into possibilities for imaginative renewal.

Stuart takes the title of *A Hole in the Head* from the legend of a certain primitive tribe who believed that by perforating the skulls of young children they opened them to the influence of good and evil spirits, thus extending their range of knowledge. The hole in the head is Stuart's metaphor for the imagination. The novel details the crisis of the creative psyche of the writer in a contemporary Ireland let loose upon the modern tide of mental and political derangement.

Terrorism and psychosis are for Stuart two fundamental symptoms of a broken and estranged imagination. Barnaby Shane, hero of the novel, is, significantly, a writer trying to come to terms with both these forms of disorder. Shane is haunted by the failure to write creatively, to translate the unruliness of his society into some coherent fiction: 'If only I could think of anything but the one rather hopeless subject – my failure to become the kind of writer I had dreamed of being'. And yet despite the unwieldiness of his surrounding world, Shane refuses to relinquish his conviction that 'nothing of any moment could happen outside of my own imagination'. He flatly denies his psychiatrist's 'distinction between exterior and interior reality'. But such a denial runs the risk of equating creative vision and madness.

In general, Stuart seems to suggest that insanity occurs whenever imagination becomes indistinguishable from reality, no longer capable of discriminating between its own fantasies and fact. 'What is dream-within-dream,' the author asks at one point, 'what plain dream, what drug-induced hallucination, and what the reality at the heart of imagination?' Or again: 'Oh my contradictory yearnings, my confusing fantasies! The mad shuffling between dream and reality'. During the course of the novel, Shane has a relationship with his muse, Emily Bronte, fellow legatee of the troubled Celtic psyche and former inhabitant of the narrator's divided, schizophrenic Ulster (much of the story unfolds in Belbury/Belfast). Stuart suggests that Emily, like the writer-hero himself, was another perturbed imagination prone to violent and psychotic obsessions. On the basis of her own past experience, Emily warns that unless the writer strives patiently towards artistic order, his creative energy will degenerate into hysteria: ' "There's always just one more of anything that we're obsessed and exhausted by. She too knew on a deeper level of reality than my poor fancies, that the imagination, once aroused to this intensity, wanted to roam further and further. One day you'll transform these passions into a legend, but meanwhile bear them in patience and silence".' Shane frequently identifies with Heathcliff's (Branwell's) *dementia*, and on key occasions argues that there is a very thin dividing line between aesthetic and pathological fictions. ' "Hallucinations?" he asks, "optical, auditory illusions? The tilt of an axis shifts and a new reality comes into focus".'

The main worry for Shane is that the creative mind often seems inseparable from the insanity it intends to sublimate. The dilemma is conveyed by the very instability and disjointedness of Stuart's own narrative structures. The uneven, irregular quality of the novel's style, its disruption of normal temporal and psychological patterns, perfectly embodies the crisis of the novel's characters. Folly as content echoes folly as form. But Stuart's whole effort is to show that there is method in this madness, at both levels. Shane is surely speaking the mind of his author when he remarks that:

> Drugs alone could not have induced in me a state in which the puzzle of
> Emily Bronte would have become clear. They played a part but it required

an imaginative, not to say unbalanced temperament like mine, which at the same time felt very close to the subject, to barely solve it. A fiction writer with guilt and obsession of his own knows more about secret and shameful passions than the more sober research worker in the literary field.

Shane dismisses the mediocre conventions of 'medium-mix-fiction' precisely because it lacks all 'energy' and 'obsession'; and Shane's young lover, Claudia, claims that she has been committed to the Kye Sanitorium because like the writer, 'her imagination runs away with her too'. To the Reverend Mother's declaration that Claudia has a 'distorted imagination', Shane replies that the 'very valuable [are] driven to fantasy by their psychology'; and he well might have added, to *crime*. In this work, as in his earlier novel, *Blacklist, Section H*, Stuart is fascinated by what he calls the element of 'criminality in the immensely imagi- native psyche' – that is, the potential for transgression and excess. But the differ- ence between the criminal psychotic and the artist is that whereas the former confounds imagination and reality without knowing that he is doing so, the latter can do so while still being able to differentiate between them. As Shane puts it: 'Imaginative people can resolve inner tensions that keep less gifted ones behind asylum walls.'

Stuart's point seems to be that the imagination is a well-spring of creative energy that, if thwarted, expresses itself as mental derangement or terrorism: 'A flood of energy with nowhere to go except into fighting or clowning, apart from an occasional one of you who tries his hand at fiction or poesie ... fulfilment denied results in violence, yes, but only when fulfilment is desired fiercely enough. Then you have the terrorist, or more rarely, the imaginative artist.' Stuart's writing is a plea for the aesthetic expression of imagination in a world dominated by the 'reality principle' of mediocre politicians. He regrets that 'even a fairly successful writer ranks well below even a minor politician in both parts of this island'; and he proceeds to advocate the need for a 'new mythology'. But for the author Shane, as for Stuart his author, there remains little hope for the creative principle of imagination. If it survives at all it will only do so in the esoteric sanctum of a small minority of poetic seers: 'The new myths, if there be any, in order to redeem will deal with events of utter obscurity'. The relative obscurity of Stuart's own work is indicative of a certain despair before the despotism of contemporary history – a symptom perhaps of the modern Irish imagination?

Stuart would of course reply that the threat to the creative imagination is not some national disorder but a universal symptom of modernity. 'All over the globe,' as the narrator of *A Hole in the Head* remarks, 'a tiny invisible fungus is annulling the nucleic acids which, as we know, are the basis of the imagination.' The contemporary society of Western materialism and consumerism is, for Stuart, so concerned with 'facts' that it produces a kind of collective banality. Under such a dictatorship of the 'reality principle' the only hope for imaginative life is to be found in the esoteric art of the individual. This is a typically modernist stance. But here, as elsewhere, Stuart is closer to the radical modernism of Beckett than to the revivalist modernism of Yeats. As he made plain in a *Crane Bag* interview in 1979, entitled 'Novelists on the Novel', the ideal of a national literary movement offers no real salvation for the modern Irish writer:

> National literature is to my mind a meaningless term. Literature can't be national. Literature is individual. Nationality has nothing to do with it. We have here some outstanding writers. They happen to have been born in Ireland. I don't think they would have been interested in defining a national literature. Let us say there are some writers who are certainly worth discussing as individual writers.[6]

Stuart is no doubt referring here to the Irish writers of the critical counter-tradition. The outstanding writer for Stuart is always outside of the mainstream. He or she is obsessed not with nations or traditions or collective memories but with the artistic processes of language, imagination and creativity. The nightmare of history can only be redeemed, if at all, by the metaphysical magic of the solitary artist. Modernist fiction, Stuart believes, is 'being driven into a corner' by the contemporary craving of Western society 'for more and more facts'. Stuart considers the return of art to itself to be a good thing because the traditional realist novel 'became too spread out and tried to do all sorts of things, to describe and to comment and so on'. Modernist fiction, by contrast, is being 'forced to do the one thing it can do supremely well, better than science and better than any of the other art forms: to delve deeper and deeper into the self, into the human system'. Stuart concludes accordingly: 'I have an obsession with Art as one of the few hopes in a darkening world … I'm not interested in the normal work of fiction … the work that never sets out to do more than tell a story, entertain, give a twist, give facts.'[7]

III. John Banville

Banville also shares the post-Joycean obsession with the possibility/impossibility of writing, and more particularly with the problematic rapport between narrative and history. His central role in the critical counter-tradition becomes quite explicit in his third novel, *Birchwood*, where he parodies the Big House genre that had become the stock in trade of much traditional Anglo-Irish fiction. Agreeing with Stuart's indictment of the 'soft centre' of mainstream Irish fiction as a sort of 'literary knitting', Banville sets out in *Birchwood* to challenge the clichés of traditional narrative. The novel opens with the narrator self-consciously arranging the materials for his story and proclaiming his intention faithfully to record his memories in the form of fiction:

> I am therefore I think. That seems inescapable. In this lawless house I spend the nights poring over my memories, fingering them, like an impotent Casanova his old love letters ... Some of these memories are in a language that I do not understand, the ones that could be headed the beginning of the old life. They tell the story that I intend to copy here, all of it, if not its meaning ...

By inverting the fundamental maxim of Cartesian subjectivity, *I think therefore I am*, Banville's narrator resolves to tell his story *as it really was*. He thus endorses the priority of being (I am) over consciousness (I think), ostensibly subscribing to the claim of classical realism to use fiction as a means of representing reality in a transparent and unproblematic way. But the ensuing narrative confounds this assertion and exposes the impotence of the narrator to go beyond his own fictional reconstruction; the 'secrets' of being are withheld from him. So that by the end of the novel the narrator is obliged to concede that he cannot understand the world or the creatures who inhabit it. 'Intimations abound, but they are felt only, and words fail to transfix them.' The author concludes by citing the admission of Wittgenstein – the modernist sceptic *par excellence* – in the *Tractatus*: 'Whereof I cannot speak, thereof I will be silent.'

Banville's decision to begin and end the narrative of *Birchwood* with allusions to two of the great philosophical practitioners of modern European doubt – Descartes and Wittgenstein – displays not only his preoccupation with the universal problems of modern epistemology but also his determination to dispel the idea of a national Irish literature limited to indigenous concerns. As he explained elsewhere:

> I don't really think that specifically 'national' literatures are of terribly great significance. Perhaps for a country's self-esteem lip-service is paid to the national culture. We go on and on about our great writers but we have very few great writers, perhaps two. Two great writers or even ten great writers don't really make a literature ... The fact that Joyce and Beckett were born in Ireland or even wrote about Ireland is not really important ... There is an Irish *writing*, but there isn't an Irish *literature* ... We can't continue to write in the old way. Most of us do. Most of Irish writing is within a nineteenth-century tradition where the world is regarded as given. Everybody knows what the reality is and people sit down to write stories which occur in the known world with known values. But the modern writer cannot take the world for granted any longer: take Rimbaud's derangement of the senses, take Nietzsche's transvaluation of all values ... I've never felt part of any (national) tradition, any culture even ... I feel a part of a purely personal culture gleaned from bits and pieces of European culture of four thousand years. It's purely something I have manufactured.[8]

Not surprisingly, Banville's next three novels after *Birchwood* turned from Irish to European figures. In *Doctor Copernicus, Kepler* and *The Newton Letter* he explored the great scientific minds of modern Europe. Having dismantled the worn-out narrative patterns of the Big House novel, unravelling its 'literary knitting' with pitiless irony, Banville investigates the highly problematic transition from the medieval to the modern understanding of reality. In these works, Banville rehearses the modernist obsession with the 'crisis of imagination' and its relationship to the 'facts' of the historical world.

Doctor Copernicus opens with the hero's first attempts to put names on things as the child Nicholas Copernicus begins to acquire the use of language. From the outset the central dilemma is posed: how can one know reality if the very words and concepts needed to understand it are themselves ways of creatively transforming reality? As he matures into a scholar of the universe, Nicholas comes to realize that 'the birth of a new science must be preceded by a radical act of creation'. But how is one to reconcile the classical desire to 'save the phenomena', to describe reality as it really is independently of human knowledge, with the discovery that all true knowledge requires an imaginative 'leap of creation'? Put in another way, if all theories are but names, but the world itself is a thing, as the Canon teaches Copernicus, how can the scientist bridge the gap between name and thing? Copernicus gradually discovers that science is a form of 'ritual' or hypothetical 'play acting' which seeks to transmute 'into docile order the hideous clamour and chaos of the world itself'. But this endeavour to flee from the 'terrors of the world' into some miraculous tranquillity of imaginative order, brings with it a dilemma:

> He believed in action, in the absolute necessity for action. Yet action horrified him, tending as it did inevitably to become violence. Nothing was stable; politics became war, law became slavery, life itself became death, sooner or later. Always the ritual collapsed in the face of hideousness. The real world would not be gainsaid, being the true realm of action, but he must gainsay it, or despair. That was his problem.

Copernicus goes on to make his great discovery that the sun is the centre of the planetary universe and not the earth as had been previously taught by Ptolemaic science. But Copernicus is only able to make his 'leap of creation' by replacing the claim of traditional science to 'save the phenomena' (Aristotle) with an act of imaginative faith that transcends the phenomena. In short, science cannot reach towards the truth of reality except through the prism of art. This was the great paradox confronting Copernicus. As Banville himself observed:

The phrase 'to save the phenomena' is a very elegant way of lying. Pre-Copernican science and Copernicus himself were obsessed with saving the phenomena, with producing a theory which would agree with what one saw in the sky but which wasn't necessarily true ... The job of art is not to save the phenomena but to lose them, or to risk losing them.[9]

With *Kepler*, Banville pursues his fictional reconstruction of Europe's great scientific minds. This second novel of the sequence records the particular 'crisis of imagination' suffered by Johannes Kepler, born in southern Germany in 1571, as he confirmed the Copernican revolution in astronomy by discovering that the orbit of Mars is not circular but elliptical. Banville's own elliptical narrative brilliantly juxtaposes Kepler's *inner* world of creative fantasy and *outer* world of everyday contingency. The fragmented narrative techniques, abrupt shifts between first and third person perspectives and reversible time sequences illustrate the dramatic unpredictability and riskiness of Kepler's own quest for cosmic truth. It also serves to render problematic the traditional quest-structure of the novel genre. An early passage offers a masterful description of the clash between inner and outer worlds:

> Johannes Kepler, asleep in his ruff, has dreamed the solution to the cosmic mystery. He holds it cupped in his mind as he would a precious something of unearthly frailty and splendour. O do not wake! But he will. Mistress Barbara, with a grain of grim satisfaction, shook him by his ill-shod foot, and at once the fabulous egg burst, leaving only a bit of glair and a few coordinates of broken shell.
>   And 0.00429.
>   He was cramped and cold, with a vile gum of sleep in his mouth. Opening an eye he spied his wife reaching for his dangling foot again, and dealt her a tiny kick to the knuckles.

The formula '0.00429' salvaged from the wake of his dream is in fact a premonitory cypher for the relationship between the planetary ellipses and their distance from the sun. It is the germ of his great discovery; but it is granted to his waking consciousness merely as a fragment of broken shell. The remainder of the narrative records how Kepler struggles to reconstruct the total shell of his initial dream-intuition shattered by the 'disturbances' of the real universe around him. Kepler's task is to translate his *true fiction* into the world of observable facts so that he may finally dispel the traditional illusion (or *false fiction*) of Ptolemaic astronomy that for centuries had held that it was the sun, not the earth, that moves. But Kepler's alchemical art of translation is constantly threatened by the intrusions of the external world: 'these deformities, the clamour and confusion of other lives, this familiar – O familiar! – disorder ... If he managed, briefly, a little inward calm, then the world without was sure to turn on him.'

And turn on him it does. The narrator's repeated efforts to rehearse in a linear sequence the *essential* events of Kepler's imaginative quest are perpetually frustrated by the *accidental* interruptions of historical existence – the plagues, wars, political upheavals and ecclesiastical intrigues of seventeenth-century Europe, the humiliating banalities of Kepler's domestic grind with his mad witch-mother and fussing wife. These are the daily irritations that the 'Imperial Mathematician and Court Astronomer' labours to overcome in his pursuit of the magic formulae of cosmic harmony. And, of course, there is a price to pay. Having completed his major life-work, the *Somnium*, in 1630, Kepler prepares for death, still struggling to unlock the secret mysteries of the universe and more painfully aware than ever that his dream of intellect has been pursued at the expense of living fully in the 'real world'. Kepler compares himself to a 'dying man searching too late for the life that he had missed, that his work had robbed him of'. Memory (the idiom of history) reinvades imagination (the idiom of dream):

> When he finished the *Somnium* there had been another crisis, as he had known there would be. What was it, this wanton urge to destroy the work of his intellect and rush out on crazy voyages into the real world? It had seemed to him in Sagan that he was haunted, not by a ghost but something like a memory so vivid that at times it seemed about to conjure itself into a physical presence. It was as if he had mislaid some precious small thing, and forgotten about it, and yet was tormented by the loss ... Everything is told us, but nothing explained. Yes. We must take it all on trust. That's the secret.

Banville's own fiction is obsessed with the collision between historical memory and creative imagination. *Doctor Copernicus* and *Kepler* are both strategically suspended between the claims of historical and fictional narrative. And this problematic confusion of genres is a singular mark of their originality. Francis Stuart has accurately identified this central feature of Banville's project:

> Most writers who choose the historical novel as a means of communication do so for such reasons as: long narrative descriptions and scene-setting, a given plot for their story-telling, it suits their particular talents, or, again they may hope to gain popular success by dramatising certain events from the past of the community from which their readers come ... Few writers who have faith in their art as discovery and exploration of areas that lie beyond fact, take it as their medium. Why then are John Banville's last two novels set in the sixteenth and seventeenth centuries? The question does not really arise, as Dr Copernicus and Johannes Kepler are portrayed in that quest for reality that pure scientists and imaginative artists pursue with passion – whether in the past, today, or in the future, up to the final revelation or destruction, as it turns out ... Not the least of Kepler's discoveries was that the solution was not to be found by peering into the heavens at night (he had not a telescope until the end of his life), but in the mind, as Einstein, three hundred years

later, was also to prove: 'It seems to me that the real answers to the cosmic mystery are to be found not in the sky, but in that other, infinitely smaller though no less mysterious firmament contained within the skull.'[10]

In *The Newton Letter: An Interlude*, Banville does not try to tell a story. He interrogates the very nature of storytelling in the double sense of the narrative form of the writing and the imaginative powers of the writer. The narrator is a contemporary historian who attempts to make sense of the nervous collapse suffered by another 'scientific' mind, Isaac Newton, at another point in history, 1693. The only 'factual' evidence he has to go on is an enigmatic letter sent to the philosopher John Locke in which Newton intimates his crisis of faith in the ability of the mind to explain the 'true' workings of the external universe. Scientific facts, Newton seems to suggest, are themselves fictions. The task of the contemporary historian–narrator in the novel is to establish and interpret the 'facts' behind this decisive 'interlude' in Newton's career. Not an auspicious project by all accounts.

The narrator–historian rents a caretaker's cottage on an estate called Fern Hill where he hopes to complete his seven-year research on Newton. The aristocratic estate, itself on the verge of collapse, is anachronistic, an incongruity of history whose inhabitants prove quite as mysterious and impenetrable as Newton himself. While resolved to remain detached and objective, the narrator becomes increasingly obsessed by the inscrutable identities of his landlord neighbours. As he does so he proceeds to construct elaborate fictions in an effort to make some sense of the missing narrative links – or 'interludes' – in their complex interrelationships. (One is reminded of Beckett's Mr Watt in Mr Knott's house). Is Ottilie the mother of the strange child? Or is it Charlotte? And who is the father? Is the narrator in love with Ottilie or Charlotte? Or neither? Or both? (At one moment, indeed, the narrator becomes so confused by the mismatching of names and people that he declares his love for 'Charlottie'.) Trapped in this labyrinth of indecisions and revisions, the narrator essays to resolve his doubts by resorting to fictional interpretations, which invariably turn out to be mistaken. Even his love affair with Ottilie – his one 'real' experience – is, by his own admission, 'conducted through the intermediary of ... a story, a memory History keeps revising, itself in the mind of the creator'.

This historian, not surprisingly, begins his narrative by conceding his own failure of imaginative nerve: 'Words fail me ... I have abandoned my book ... I don't really understand it myself ... I've lost faith in the primacy of text.' The beginning of the novel thus bespeaks the ending; and the entire intervening narrative is written retrospectively in the past tense; that is, in the form of a reminiscence that would explain the narrator's own failed quest for narrative coherence. In *The Newton Letter* the mind is its own prison and history the one possibility of salvation (what its narrator calls the posssibility of 'the innocence of things, their non-complicity in our affairs'). But can the fiction-spinning mind ever dispense with its own interpretations? Can it ever hope to suspend its adulterating inter-ference with the 'innocence of things'? Banville's narrator brings guidebooks on trees and birds with him only to discover that the 'illustrations would not match up with the real specimens'. In similar fashion, the human specimens of Fern House, and indeed the elusive Newton himself, stubbornly defy the historian's code of decipherment just as the truths of the universe defied Newton's scientific blueprints. History thus repeats itself in a timeless pattern of recurrence.

And so the narrator finds himself a prey to his own hermeneutic narratives. 'Look at me, writing history,' he self-mockingly jibes. Even the apparently reli-able evidence of his perceptions capitulates to the seduction of ideas. At one point, for example, the narrator senses something scurrying in the grass: 'I thought it was a blackbird out foraging … but it was a rat. In fact it wasn't a rat. In fact in all my time at Ferns I never saw sign of a rat. It was only the idea.' The author cannot reach reality *in fact*. That is the cruel irony. Finally the narrator is compelled to liken his historical exegesis to the manoeuvrings of an 'artist bliss-fully checking over the plan of a work', whose 'memory gathers its material, beady-eyed and voracious, like a demented photographer'. His entire stay at Ferns is itself transmuted by the act of recollection: 'It has all been lived already and we were merely tracing the patterns, as if not really living, but remembering … the past, immutable, crystalline and perfect.'

The narrator concludes accordingly that only the 'ordinary' and 'common-place' could redeem him from his own myth-making consciousness. Like Newton before him, whose interlude represented a crisis of belief in the mind's ability to reach truth, the historian determines to abandon his writings in order to commit himself to silence (recalling the Wittgensteinian conclusion to *Birch-wood*). The narrator explains his decision by alluding to a *second* letter to Locke in which Newton avowed his preference for a wordless communion with the common mortals of this world – 'the sellers and makers of things' – a non-fictional language 'in which commonplace things speak to me'.

Following Newton's precedent, Banville's historian also signs off with a second letter (the first being the 'confessional' novel itself) in which he celebrates a new-found, non-academic life with ordinary mortals in a mint mine in Iowa. In the same letter, he announces that Ottilie is pregnant by him and that the child's existence will ensure that his delusions ultimately yield to the reality of history. 'The future now has the same resonance that the past had, for me. I am pregnant myself, in a way. Supernumerous existence wells up in my heart.' The question as to whether he will return to Ferns and complete his work on Newton is, significantly, left open.

What then of Banville's narrative – the novel itself? What of the author's own narrative 'interlude' based on his narrator's 'interlude' based on Newton's 'inter-lude'? In an editorial note at the end of the novel, Banville informs us that the second Newton letter to Locke is in fact a fiction! And it requires no great leap of the imagination to realize that the narrator's own final letter is equally fictional. (A realization confirmed by the tell-tale facts that the narrator speaks of the future's resonance *'for me'*; that his own feeling of pregnancy is itself metaphorical; and that the reference to 'supernumerous existence' is a direct literary quote from Rilke's *Duino Elegies*.) The attempt to abandon fiction is thus exposed as fiction. Where Banville went from this, his story of interlude, was, of course, another story.[11]

Conclusion

The representatives of the 'critical' counter-tradition in the Irish novel exemplify a *crisis of imagination*. This crisis, as noted earlier, had been precipitated by Joyce's and Beckett's debunking of the traditional model of narration – i.e. as a transparent representation in *language* of the way things are in *reality*. Traditional novel writing presupposed that these two poles of narration were naturally given and distinct. Once this distinction between *word* and *thing* was flouted by Joyce and Beckett, the *distance* between the narrator's subjective consciousness and the historical world – which motivated the narrator's quest for meaning in the first place – was radically diminished. And so the crucial relationship between language and the real world, between fiction and history, between imagination and memory, became the self-reflexive subject of novel writing. Instead of writing narratives *about* the world, in a straightforward representational manner, the disciples of Joyce and Beckett interrogated the very possibility, or impossibility, of such writing.

Most Irish novelists after Joyce and Beckett by-passed or ignored this crisis of narration. They continued producing traditional novels as if the classical realist model had never been put into question. A small number of Irish novelists did, however, respond to the challenge posed by Joyce and Beckett. Some of these experienced the crisis of fiction as a problematic attempt to recover the realities of historical memory from the solipsistic constructs of imagination; others experienced the crisis in the opposite sense as a struggle to salvage the creative powers of imagination from the oppressive facts of history. We have seen how three such 'critical' Irish novelists – Flann O'Brien, Francis Stuart and John Banville – registered the problem of narration in one or other, or both, of these ways. They are not, however, the only representatives of the post-Joycean counter-tradition. Neil Jordan's *The Past* grapples with similar themes as it recounts the narrator's efforts to reconstruct and resolve the mystery of his mother's *real* past through the *fictional* narratives of his mother's friends' reminiscences, only to discover that historical fact and aesthetic fantasy are inextricably linked. Similarly, Aidan Higgins' innovative novels, ranging from *Langrishe Go*

Down and *Balcony of Europe* to *Scenes from a Receding Past* and *Bornholm Night-Ferry*, focus in a self-reflexive way on the problematic rapport between writing and history. In *Balcony of Europe* we witness the narrator/artist labouring to wrest imagination from the vortex of memory, from that circularity of a recurring past that Stephen Dedalus termed the 'nightmare of history'.[12] *Bornholm Night-Ferry* features an exchange of letters between an Irish novelist (with the mock-heroic name of Finn Fitzgerald) and his foreign lover (a Danish poetess, Elin), which seeks to conjure up an 'opposite land' of fictive refuge denied them in their daily reality, separated as they are by time, place and language.

The authors of the counter-movement in Irish fiction share an obsession with the *crisis of narrative*. Whether the authorial imagination at issue in their critical novels is seen as oppressor or oppressed, it is at all times fundamentally problematic, an imagination that can no longer take writing for granted, but in true modernist fashion, makes it the very theme of writing.

It might be objected that the novelists of the Irish counter-tradition have generally been so preoccupied with the dilemma of narrative and its epistemological rapport with history, that they have tended to ignore the contemporary problems of their own history. The 'critical' novelists have been accused of indulging in an elitist escapism that opts for the international idioms of modernism over the demands of a national literature committed to matters of social and political relevance. Beckett, after all, is more interested in the literature of existentialist anguish than of nationalist revival; Banville writes about the life and times of Nicholas Copernicus not Michael Collins; Stuart invokes Emily Bronte as his muse not Cathleen Ni Houlihan; Higgins chooses the Baltic island of Bornholm as his ideal sanctuary not the lake isle of Inisfree.

Whenever the 'critical' novelists do relate to an Irish context (as O'Brien in *At Swim-Two-Birds*, Stuart in *Hole in the Head* and *Blacklist, Section-H* or Banville in *Birchwood*), it is usually with the purpose of parodying and demythologizing the pieties of national culture in the name of a sceptical individualism of revolt. And so it has been left to those in the mainstream of realist Irish fiction – in particular O'Faolain, Johnston, McGahern, McLaverty and Doyle – to provide narratives of contemporary Ireland's social history. Joyce himself, it could be argued, avoided this alternative by combining an aesthetic commitment to modernist experimentalism with a historical commitment to the modern realities of Irish society. After Joyce, however, these respective commitments appear to have divided into two distinct movements of Irish fiction, the 'critical' and the 'realist'. The attempt it seems, has yet to be made to reunite these opposed commitments in a new post-Joycean synthesis.[13]

CHAPTER FOURTEEN

Heaney and Homecoming

Seamus Heaney is often hailed as Ireland's greatest poet since Yeats. While such praise generally adverts to Heaney's remarkable sense of craft, his verbal and formal dexterity, it frequently betrays another kind of evaluation: one concerned less with Ireland's greatest *poet* than with *Ireland's* greatest poet. Here the emphasis falls on the typically and traditionally Irish quality of Heaney's writing. He is enlisted as the poet of the patria, a home bird, an excavator of the national landscape devoted to the recovery of natural pieties.

Heaney's primary inspiration, we are told, is one of place; his quintessentially Irish vocation, the sacramental naming of a homeland. Hence the preoccupation with images of mythology, archaeology and genealogy, of returning to forgotten origins. This revivalist reading conforms to the paradigm of the 'backward look', which, Frank O'Connor has argued, typifies Irish literature.[1]

This orthodox view would have us believe that while other contemporary Irish poets embraced the more modernist idioms of existential *angst* or the crisis of language, Heaney remained faithful to the primacy of the provincial. He didn't need to take his tune from current trends in continental or Anglo-American poetry; for he had discovered the cosmos, as it were, in his own backyard. Mahon, Montague, Longley, Boland and Kinsella engaged in metaphysical meditations about the problematic rapport between self, language and history. Durcan and Bolger composed biting satires about urban bourgeois hypocrisy and the ravages of advanced industrial capitalism. But Heaney stuck to the home patch. He resisted the modernist impulse and remained, inalienably, 'one of our own'. A true revivalist.

Some commentators have offered a more ideological interpretation of the nostalgia for lost traditions that is said to exemplify the 'native' strain of Irish literature. The harking back to an abandoned, or at least threatened, organic lifestyle still in harmony with all that is best in the national heritage, has been seen as an attempt to reconstruct a cultural unison that would overcome, by overlooking, the actual social divisions that torment modern Irish society. As one critic remarked: 'An emergent Catholic capitalist class espoused a myth of natural pious austerity in opposition to the profane forces of modernity, while the Anglo-Irish déracinés sought harmony with nature and a people characterised by wild, irrational, asocial energies.'[2] Viewed in such an ideological perspective, Heaney's poetic efforts to bring Irish culture 'home' to itself might be dismissed as a conservative return to antiquated mythologies of 'tradition' and 'nature'.

By focusing on the central theme of 'homecoming' in Heaney I propose to show how it involves a complex conflict of sensibility that has little or nothing to do with insular notions of parochial *pietas*. I will analyse Heaney's preoccupation with 'homecoming' less in standard formal terms than in philosophical terms. My aim is to demonstrate that Heaney's treatment of 'homecoming' involves an unresolved dialectic between the opposing claims of home and homelessness. The revivalist reading of his work could do with some debunking. It is time to prise Heaney free from stereotypes.

First, it should be noted that Heaney's poems are not in fact primarily about place at all; they are about *transit*, that is, about transitions from one place to another. One need only look to the titles of some of his major works to see just how fundamental this notion of poetry as transitional act is: *Wintering Out, Door into the Dark, Field Work, Sweeney Astray, Station Island*. One of the central reasons for Heaney's preference for journey over sojourn, for exodus over abode, is, I suggest, a fidelity to the nature of *language* itself. Far from subscribing to the traditional view that language is a transparent means of representing some identity that precedes language – call it *self, nation* or *home* – Heaney's poetry espouses the view that it is language that perpetually constructs and deconstructs our given notions of identity. As such, poetic language is always on the move, vacillating between opposing viewpoints, looking in at least two directions at once.

Heaney has been criticized for refusing to adopt a clear political position, for not nailing his colours to the mast, particularly with regard to the 'national question' (i.e. his attitude to his native North). One Irish politician described him as an 'artful dodger' who displays 'all the skills of the crafty tightrope walker ... sidestepping and skipping his slippery way out of trouble'.[3] Bemoaning the fact that his work is a 'job of literary journeywork', this same critic urges him to 'seek a less ambivalent position'.

The point is, however, that Heaney is a poet, not a party politician. He does not deny that his work has political connotations – for that would be to deny that it is concerned with life as it is lived. But this does not mean that he is compelled to subscribe to a definitive ideological standpoint. His refusal to be fixed, to be *placed*, in any single perspective is no more than a recognition that poetry's primary fidelity is to language as an interminable metamorphosis of conflicting identities. Heaney himself states his position on language as dual or multiple perspective in the following passage from *Preoccupations*:

> When I called my second book *Door into the Dark* I intended to gesture towards this idea of poetry as a point of entry into the buried life of the feelings or as a point of exit for it. Words themselves are doors; Janus is to a certain extent their deity, looking back to a ramification of the roots and associations and forward to a clarification of sense and meaning ... In *Door into the Dark* there are a number of poems that arise out of the almost unnamable energies that, for me, hovered over certain bits of language ...[4]

The poet's commitment to an aesthetic of endless migration is clear.

Heaney's poetry seems to support the idea that literature is essentially about language itself. Mallarmé and Rimbaud made this view the central plank of their modernist programme; as did, in another context, Heaney's compatriots, Joyce and Beckett. This is not to suggest that Heaney approaches literature as some autonomous sphere; nor that his fascination with words degenerates into self-regarding formalism. It is simply to recognize that for Heaney reality as we perceive it is always profoundly informed by the words we use. And these words carry *several* meanings, for language is an endless creation of new worlds; possible worlds that remain irreducible to the univocal slide rule of a one to one correspondence between word and thing. That is why the double-faced Janus is the deity of Heaney's literary 'journeywork'.

Heaney's commitment to the ambivalence of poetic language is, I believe, manifest in his exploration of the pivotal motif of 'homecoming'. Whereas in the early works, Heaney usually talks of home in terms of a personal quest for self-identity, in subsequent collections – and particularly *North* or *Station Island* – he begins to interpret homecoming more in terms of a linguistic search for historical identity. As he himself remarks in *Preoccupations*, words cease to be fingerprints recording the unique signature of the poet and become 'bearers of history'. But if Heaney insists that one of the tasks of the poet is to recover a sense of belonging to a shared past – 'an ancestry, a history, a culture' – he construes this task as a *project* rather than a *possession*, as an exploration of language rather than some triumphalist revival of lost national identity.

Poetry, in short, comes to express the sense of 'home' less as a literal (i.e. geographical, political or personal) property than as a metaphorical preoccupation. Home is something that cannot be taken for granted as present. It must be sought after because it is *absent*. For Heaney, homecoming is never the actuality of an event but the possibility of an advent.

At this point it may be useful to look at some poems in Heaney's collection *North* that deal explicitly with this theme. In a piece entitled 'Homecomings', he would seem to be affirming the experience of home as a *positive* goal. He meditates upon the 'homing' manoeuvrings of a sandmartin as it circles back to its nest:

> At the worn mouth of the hole
> Flight after flight after flight
> The swoop of its wings
> Gloved and kissed home.

The poet sees this instinctual, almost atavistic, homecoming of the sandmartin as an analogy for his own aspiration to return to an originating womb of earth where he may regain a sense of prenatal silence, unity and belonging:

> A glottal stillness. An eardrum.
> Far in, featherbrains tucked in silence,
> A silence of water lipping the bank
>
> Mould my shoulders inward to you.
> Occlude me.
> Be damp clay pouting.
> Let me listen under your eaves.

This experience recalls the opening passage from *Preocccupations* where Heaney invokes the image of the *omphalos* as a hidden underground well of childhood memory. He writes,

> I would begin with the Greek word, *omphalos*, meaning the navel, and hence the stone that marked the centre of the world, and repeat it, *omphalos, omphalos, omphalos,* until its blunt and falling music becomes the music of somebody pumping water at the pump outside our back door ... that pump marked an original descent into earth, sand, gravel, water. It centred and staked the imagination, made its foundations the foundations of the *omphalos* itself.[5]

These positive images of home are identified with nature, mother, earth and childhood. They describe the experience of an Edenesque dwelling in harmony with the natural environment. And, as such, they might be thought to invoke a time before time – before, that is, the arrival of language and self-consciousness. But we must not forget that Heaney's first collection of poems is entitled *Death of a Naturalist*. All of Heaney's writing is informed by an awareness that the poet as a resourceful dweller in language has replaced the naturalist as an innocent dweller in nature. So that if Heaney occasionally seeks to retrieve the experience of the 'naturalist', it is always as a 'post-naturalist': as someone who is, at best, hankering after something that he knows full well is irretrievably *lost*. Homecoming thus becomes a dialectical search for some forfeited or forbidden presence in and through the awareness of its *absence*. We should not be surprised therefore to find Heaney, in a poem called 'Kinship', referring to the *omphalos* as a grave; or to mother earth as the inevitable casualty of autumnal death and decay. Language has now, it seems, adulterated the pristine innocence of nature. The vowel of earth can do no more than 'dream' its root. Home can only be spoken of as some ground from which we have become irreparably uprooted.

In other poems in *North* (the title of this collection itself is a symbol amongst other things, for Heaney's own lost homeland or motherland), the theme of homecoming is submitted to self-questioning. The very attempt to return home is now equated by the poet with necrophiliac nostalgia; it assumes the character of a sacrificial death rite that provokes sentiments of recoil. In a poem called 'Stump', Heaney surmises that his homing instinct may well become a parasite of putrefaction as soon as it contrives to make of home a tribal acquisition. 'I am riding to plague again,' he rebukes himself.

> What do I say if they wheel out their dead?
> I'm cauterized, a black stump of home.

In yet another poem, 'Roots', Heaney's suspicion of necrophiliac impulses reaches even more self-recriminatory proportions. Here he conceives of the tribal hankering after dispossessed origins or 'roots' as a sanguinary death cult bedevilling his Northern province and intruding upon private intimacies. Outside in the terraced streets the earth's 'fault is opening' as the gunshots of the sniper and the sirens of the army scream at each other. Inside in the bedroom, the poet tries to take refuge in love; but his dark bloodletting dreams, echoing the slaughter in the streets, contaminate the lovers' communion and deform it into the image of a mandrake (a poisonous plant whose root is thought to resemble a human form and to shriek when plucked):

> I've soaked by moonlight in tidal blood
> A mandrake, lodged human fork,
> Earth sac, limb of the dark;
> And I wound its damp smelly loam
> And stop my ears against the scream.

Heaney's celebrated 'bog poems' provide arresting examples of the dialectic of homecoming and estrangement. For Heaney the northern bog is a sort of placeless place; it is a shifting palimpsest of endless layers and sublayers, an archival memory of lost cultures. In one of the first of his bog poems – the last poem of *Wintering Out* – Heaney describes how a great elk and a morsel of butter were recovered from Irish bogs having been preserved for centuries in the dark and watery peat. The poem concludes with the following image of interminable excavation for a vanished *omphalos*:

> Our pioneers keep striking
> Inwards and downwards,
>
> Every layer they strip
> Seems camped on before.
> The bogholes might be Atlantic seepage
> The wet centre is bottomless.

Heaney explains that while this bogland motif began as a germ of childhood association it gradually assumed the status of a cultural myth.

> We used to hear about bog-butter, [writes Heaney of his early childhood] butter kept fresh for a great number of years under the peat. Then when I was at school the skeleton of an elk had been taken out of bog nearby and a few of our neighbours had got their photographs in the paper, peering out across its antlers. So I began to get an idea of a bog as the memory of the landscape, or as a landscape that remembered everything that happened in and to it. In fact, if you go round the National Museum in Dublin, you will realise that a great proportion of the most cherished material heritage of Ireland was 'found in a bog'. Moreover, since memory was the faculty that supplied me with the first quickening of my own poetry, I had a tentative unrealised need to make a congruence between memory and bogland and, for the want of a better word, our national consciousness.[6]

But if the bog becomes a symbol of national consciousness, it is not in the manner of an insular, self-righteous nationalism. Heaney is mindful of the fact that the lost homeland is less a territorial locality than an ontological locus whose universal dimensions forever elude the boundaries of a particular nation. The closer we get to home in this sense the more distant it becomes; its very construction is its deconstruction. The wet centre, as Heaney concedes, *is bottomless*. Bogholes of receding memory lead back to a fathomless ocean flow that transcends our contemporary grasp. Homecoming, poetically understood, means therefore that our literal or geographical home is actually de-centred. The very process of homecoming reminds us that we are now displaced, in exile, estranged (*unheimlich*). So that just as the fundamental question of Being, according to Heidegger, can only be retrieved from oblivion by 'de-structing' the pretension of Western metaphysics to represent some unbroken continuous tradition — so too with regard to the more exact question of cultural heritage. Or as another modern thinker, Michel Foucault, puts it: 'In attempting to uncover the deepest strata of western culture, I am restoring to our silent and apparently immobile soil, its rifts, its instability, its flaws; and it is the same ground that is once more stirring under our feet.'[7]

But it would be a mistake to interpret this *defamiliarization* of the experience of tradition to mean that Heaney abandons concern for the plight of his native

Ulster. Heaney insists that his bog poems are also a reaching after 'images and symbols *adequate to our predicament*'. He explains that he felt it imperative to 'discover a field of force in which, without abandoning fidelity to the processes and experience of poetry ... it would be possible to encompass the perspectives of a humane reason and at the same time to grant the religious intensity of the violence its deplorable authenticity and complexity.'[8] In other words, Heaney sees the contemporary conflict in Northern Ireland as, amongst other things, a symptom of a collision between the opposing claims of rationalist order and religious atavism. He makes it quite clear, of course, that he is using the term *religious* not just in the more current sense of sectarian division between Catholic and Protestant, but in the anthropological sense of an ancient enmity between the cults of god and goddess. There is, Heaney observes,

> an indigenous territorial numen, a tutelar of the whole island, call her mother Ireland, Kathleen Ni Houlihan, the poor old woman, the Shan Van Vocht, whatever; and her sovereignty has been temporarily usurped or infringed by a new male cult whose founding fathers were Cromwell, William of Orange and Edward Carson, and whose godhead is incarnate in a rex or caesar resident in a palace in London. What we have here is the tail end of a struggle in a province between territorial piety and imperial power.[9]

By tracing the capillaries of our current political and social ideologies back to their roots in a hidden sublayer of mythologies, Heaney is attempting not to revive these mythologies but to critically explore and expose them.

Nor does Heaney confine himself to Celtic myth. Indeed, one of the most striking emblems of this dialectic between critical distance and mythic belongings is borrowed from the Greek myth of Antaeus and Hercules. Heaney casts Hercules in the role of triumphant reason, 'sky born and royal ... his future hung with trophies'. Antaeus, by contrast, is portrayed as a mould-hugger, clinging to his unconscious terrestrial past. By dispossessing Antaeus of his tribal fixation with ancestral origins, Hercules drags him

> Out of his element
> Into a dream of loss
> And origins – the cradling dark,
> The river-veins, the secret gullies
> Of his strength,
> The hatching grounds
> Of cave and souterrain,
> He has bequeathed it all
> To elegists ...

And so it is, in Heaney's own elegiac bog poems, that the homeless and vanquished Antaeus can only be recovered – if at all – in the suspended animation of his ancient slumber, brought home to us again as a 'sleeping giant/Pap for the dispossessed'. Heaney comments on this key dialectic between rational consciousness and the mythic–religious unconscious as follows:

> Hercules represents the balanced rational light while Antaeus represents the pieties of illiterate fidelity. The poem drifts towards an assent to Hercules, though there was a sort of nostalgia for Antaeus ... This is a see-saw, an advance-retire situation.[10]

To reformulate this position in 'temporal' terms, we might say that the poetics of homecoming require us to juxtapose the *prospective* glance of Hercules and the *retrospective* glance of Antaeus. Otherwise put, it is the Herculean act of estranged detachment that enables us to remember the Antaean origin of 'cave and souter-rain'. To dispense with the distancing detour of elegy would be to diminish the possibility of homecoming as a liberating advent, cultivating it instead as a reactionary return to the past. For it is thanks to the critical challenge of the homeless Hercules that Antaeus' homing instinct may be transformed from tribal nostalgia into an authentic quest for a new cultural community. In this dialectical vacillation between the claims of Herculean reason and Antaean instinct, the *topos* of the past can come towards us as a *utopia* of the future.

Heaney informs us in *Preoccupations* that one of the main sources of his 'bog' motif was Glob's *The Bog People* (a work he first read in translation in 1969, which was 'appositely, the year the killing started' in Ulster). Heaney is under no illusions about the potentially terrifying consequences of the 'quest for home' when this degenerates – as it can – into tribal fanaticism. He offers the following account of how, on reading Glob's work, the various emblems of the 'northern' (Nordic) sacrificial practices came together with the contemporary realities of the 'northern' (Ulster) conflict:

> It was chiefly concerned with preserved bodies of men and women found in the bogs of Jutland, naked, strangled or with their throats cut, disposed under the peat since early Iron Age times. The author, P.V. Glob, argues convincingly that a number of these, and in particular the Tollund Man, whose head is now preserved near Aarhus in the museum at Silkeburg, were ritual sacrifices to the Mother Goddess, the Goddess of the ground who needed new bridegrooms each winter to bed with her in her sacred place, in the bog, to ensure the renewal and fertility of the territory in the spring. Taken in relation to the tradition of Irish political martyrdom for that cause whose icon is Kathleen Ni Houlihan, that is more than an archaic barbarous rite: it is an archetypal pattern. And the unforgettable photographs of these victims blended in my mind with photographs of atrocities, past and present, in the long rites of Irish political and religious struggles.[11]

While recognizing the fecundity of this material for the poetic imagination,

Heaney admits its dangers for political reality. The temptation to fudge the dividing line between a figurative and literal interpretation of this cult is strenuously resisted. Heaney states his critical reservations on this score when he comments on his attitude to the Tollund Man, in another of his bog poems: 'When I wrote this poem, I had a completely new sensation, one of fear. It was a vow to go on a pilgrimage and I felt as it came to me ... that unless I was deeply in earnest about what I was saying, I was simply invoking dangers for myself.'[12] This mention of fear is significant not only in its reference to the traditionally mystic attitude to the sublime or holy as *fascinans et tremendum*, but more directly still in its bearing on the experience of the *unhomely* (see appendix). In 'Tollund Man', Heaney counterpoints the ritual act of returning home with a critical scruple of exile and distance. The poet describes an imaginary pilgrimage northwards to pay homage to an ancestor recovered from a bog still intact after thousands of years and attired in his sacrificial garb of cap, noose and girdle. But it is significant that the northern bog is not in fact in Ulster but in Jutland – and the ancestor in question is not an Irishman but a Tollund man. In other words, Heaney is returning to a home away from home: an *unheimlich* home.

The Tollund victim is described as a 'bridegroom to the goddess', the suggestion being that he has been sacrificed to the earth deity so that she might be sexually regenerated and be preserved in her 'cradling dark' for posterity. In this image of the sanctified scapegoat from the far north, Heaney finds an 'objective correlative' for the near north of his own homeland in Ulster. And the security that the sentiment of homecoming might normally confer is thus offset by a careful awareness of uncanny estrangement.

> Out there in Jutland
> In the old man-killing parishes
> I feel lost,
> Unhappy and at home.

Heaney does not ignore the disobliging implications of such death rites for his native North. In the 'Grauballe Man', he concedes that the perfected memory of the sacrificial bog-victim remains haunted by the present Ulster reality of 'each hooded victim / Slashed and dumped': the poet's response thus hangs in the 'scales with beauty and atrocity'. And elsewhere, in a poem called 'Funeral Rites', Heaney compares the 'slow triumph' of the funeral procession towards the mounds of the ancestral Boyne Valley (considered in Irish legend to be the mystical centre or *omphalos* of the earth)[13] to the ominous winding of a serpent. A similar note of caution is struck in the title poem of *North*, which recounts how the poet had to travel to the 'unmagical' Nordic lands of Iceland and Greenland before he could hear again the voices of his own Viking ancestry in Ireland:

> Ocean deafened voices
> Warning me, lifted again
> In violence and epiphany.

He imagines the swinging tongue of a Viking longship speaking to him 'buoyant with hindsight' of revenge, of 'hatreds and behind backs ... memory incubating the spilled blood'. So that while beckoning the poet to 'lie down in the word-hoard' of his *literary* heritage, this ancestral voice simultaneously warns against a cyclical repetition of past atrocities at the *literal* level of political blood-letting.[14]

Heaney remains mindful of the fact that a culture's 'great first sleep of home-coming' is also a death and a forgetting. The act of poetic remembering must always observe a delicate balance between the opposite risks of belonging to a home and being exiled from this home. To resolve this paradox by opting for either extreme would be to betray the dual identity of his poetry.

It is altogether fitting, finally, that this paradox should find both historical and linguistic correlatives in Heaney's own predicament. Historically, Heaney is aware that the British plantation of Gaelic Ulster in the seventeenth century resulted in the displacement of the Irish language by English (a historical event that found further expression in the early twentieth century with the drawing of a border across the map of Ireland). Part of Heaney's ambivalent predicament is due, consequently, to this maintenance of a notion of himself 'as Irish in a province that insists that it is British'.[15] And this double consciousness is opera-tive at the level of his poetic language where two tongues engage in conflictual dialogue. As Heaney emblematically remarks: 'I think of the personal and Irish pieties as vowels, and the literary awareness nourished on English as conso-nants.'[16] The very words of Heaney's poems bear witness to this aesthetic of dual residence, to a poetic scruple of tireless migration.

This poetic paradox of 'homecoming' is powerfully sustained in *Station Island* (1984), a collection that takes its name from the northern place of pilgrimage, Lough Derg. Here Heaney returns to an exploration of the homing instincts of religious and political reverence, perhaps more explicitly than in any previous work. He self-consciously interprets the fascination with 'home' as a need for tradition, community, memory, mythology, a collective unconscious. In the long title sequence, the poet is assailed by several accusing voices from his past – usually victims of the bloody carnage in his native Ulster. These 'ancestral' ghosts address him in dream or reverie as he rehearses the ritual stations of Lough Derg. Here is a privileged place and time for recollection, for coming to terms with what Joyce's Stephen Dedalus called the 'nightmare of history' – the revivalist claims of motherland and mother church. And here, more than anywhere, is the poet privy to the hauntings of his 'migrant solitude'.

The sequence opens with the poet's alter-ego, Sweeney, shouting at him to 'stay clear of all processions'. But the poet persists on the 'drugged path' of tribal ceremony; he embraces the 'murmur of the crowds', the pious solidarity of the living and the dead. The poet's visitor from beyond the grave is Carleton, another Irish writer who had experienced 'gun butts cracking on the door' and whose rejection of both 'hard-mouthed Ribbonmen and Orange bigots' (tribal northern gangs) had 'mucked the byre of their politics'. The poet confesses that he himself has 'mettle for the angry role' of ancestral revenge; yet he is compelled by Carleton's counsel to 'remember everything and keep (his) head'.

For Heaney, however, as for Hugh in Friel's play *Translations*, to remember everything is also a form of madness. In the first instance, remembrance is racked with guilt — and particularly the poet's guilt about his lack of direct political involvement with the sufferings of his tribe. One visitation from an assassinated childhood friend provokes the poet to seek forgiveness for 'the way (he) has lived indifferent'. And another murder victim, a second cousin, chides the pilgrim for consorting with effete fellow-poets when he first heard the news of his death:

> I accuse directly, but indirectly, you
> Who now atone perhaps upon this bed
> For the way you whitewashed ugliness …
> And saccharined my death with morning dew.

Faced with this litany of ancestral accusations, the author drifts towards repentance. But he also realizes that his primary commitment as a poet is to the exploration of the buried life of *language* — which mediates, records and structures our experience — rather than to the immediate exigencies of political legislation or reprisal: 'As if the eddy could reform the pool'. The hidden truths of language are revealed by poetry to the degree that 1) the poet takes the step back from our familiar use of words as means/end strategies and 2) listens in silence to what language is saying in and through us. The poem is in this way a response, before all else, to the silent voices of language itself. This is what modern thinkers such as Heidegger, Lévi-Strauss and Lacan have taught us. As the latter remarked: 'The subject is spoken rather than speaking … It was certainly the Word that was in the beginning, and we live in its creation, but it is because the symbol has made him man.'[17] Heaney makes this point about his own work when he declares that 'the creative mind is astraddle silence'[18] — an echo perhaps of Beckett's pregnant statement that 'silence is our mother-tongue'.

The final visitation in the Lough Derg sequence of *Station Island* is Joyce's ghost. Joyce, like Carleton, serves as a *literary* conscience. But unlike Carleton's revivalist exhortation to remember everything, he recommends the modernist commitment to writing itself — to 'signatures' of the writer's own frequency. Joyce warns the poet that the obsession with collective guilt and tribal grievance is a mistake:

> That subject people stuff is a cod's game ...
> You lose more of yourself than you redeem
> Doing the decent thing.
> Keep at a tangent.
> When they make the circle wide, its time to swim
> Out on your own and fill the element
> With signatures of your own frequency ...
> Elver-gleams in the dark of the whole sea.

Significantly, the figure of Sweeney Astray – the exiled wandering bard of Irish legend and the subject of a verse translation by Heaney from the Gaelic *Buile Suibhne* – returns in the third section of the book as a symbol of the dissenting and disinherited poet. Sweeney's migratory impulses confirm the Joycean plea. But one of the main strengths of *Station Island* is the refusal to choose between Heaney and Sweeney – between the guilt-ridden pilgrim of history and the carefree *émigré* of the imagination. As the Janus-faced author remarks early in the collection (citing Milosz):

> I was stretched
> between contemplation
> of a motionless point
> and the command to participate
> actively in history.[19]

Heaney's ultimate fidelity to the ambiguity of opposing demands, and to the inner manoeuvrings of poetic language that sustain them, his refusal of any single place or position that would permit the illusion of a final solution, is proof of his tireless transiting between revivalism and modernism. Whether Heaney's continuing 'journeywork' will lead him closer to the radical modernism of Joyce or the revivalist modernism of Yeats remains an open question. Perhaps he will succeed in forging a postmodernist synthesis between the two – what we might call a poetics of perpetual detour?[20] As he observes in a poem called 'Terminus', (*The Haw Lantern*, 1987), dedicated to the god of boundaries and borders:

> Two buckets were easier carried than one.
> I grew up in between.

Appendix: Heaney, Heidegger and Freud – The Paradox of the Homely

Heaney's ambivalent attitude to homecoming – expressed as a double-movement of attraction and recoil, of intense questing and sceptical questioning – bears a certain resemblance to Martin Heidegger's notion of the poet's search for Being as a dialectical passage towards 'home' through the 'unhomely'. And this attitude also corresponds, in several important respects, to Freud's identification of the unconscious with the 'homely/unhomely' paradox.

A comparison between Heaney and these two pioneers of modern thought might prove instructive, I believe, particularly with a view to indicating how Heaney's poetic concerns are not merely Irish but international, not simply parochial but universal. By proposing an anti-revivalist re-evaluation of his work, I hope to scotch the stereotype of Heaney as some latter-day piers ploughman staving off the plague of modernity and guiding us back to a prelapsarian pastureland. The very mention of our supposedly homegrown, tradition-bound Heaney in the same breath as such 'alien' intellects as Heidegger and Freud may strike some as altogether inappropriate. But this is just another token of how pervasive the critical stereotyping of Heaney has become.

I

In a study entitled *Das Unheimliche* (translated as the 'unhomely' or 'uncanny'), Freud explores the paradox that the '*Unheimliche* is the name for everything that ought to have remained hidden and secret and has become visible'.[21] This study, which has become something of a *cause célèbre* for post-structuralist critics,[22] reveals that while the term *unheimlich* refers ostensibly to what is un-familiar or un-known, it also carries the opposite connotation of what is intimately familiar and homely (*heimlich*).

Analysing various extracts from Daniel Sanders' *Dictionary of German Speech*, Freud shows how in certain vernacular usages the *Unheimliche* is precisely that class of the strange which somehow re-evokes what is 'known of old and long familiar'. The etymological links between the terms *heimisch* (native), *Geheim* (secret) and *heimlich* (homely) are highly significant here. For they indicate how that which is *heimlich* can undergo a semantic slippage from its normal connotation of 'homely' (in the sense of being intimately familiar) into another related but ultimately reversed meaning – i.e. that which is so homely that it becomes secretive, 'concealed, kept from sight, so that others do not get to know of or about it, withheld from others'.[23] Hence one finds references to a *heimlich* love affair (surreptitious, prohibited, sinful); a *heimlich* chamber (privy); or a *heimlich* activity (occult, hidden). *Heimlich* is thus revealed to be a highly ambivalent term which can allude *either* to what is congenially accessible *or* to what is so covertly occluded that it actually becomes occult, unspoken or forbidden. The following usage recorded by Sanders is instructive, particularly apropos of our consideration of Heaney's work: '*Heimlich* (is) like a buried spring or dried-up pond. One cannot walk over it without always having the feeling that water might come up there again. We call it *unheimlich*, you call it *heimlich* ... something secret or untrustworthy.' In such wise, *heimlich* comes to mean that which is so intimate and private that it is suppressed from the everyday awareness of the public view. Grimm's dictionary reinforces these implications of semantic inversion by observing that *heimlich* finds its equivalents in the Latin *occultus, divinus, mysticus* and *veraculus*.

Freud contends that *heimlich* may be understood therefore as that which is so withdrawn from our common or conscious knowledge that it becomes, quite literally, *un*-conscious. The *heimlich* becomes an experience that we not only hide from others, but even from ourselves. And in this way, the term, *heimlich* 'comes to have the meaning actually ascribed to *unheimlich* ... Thus *heimlich* is a word the meaning of which develops in the direction of ambivalence until it finally coincides with its opposite, *unheimlich*.' *Unheimlich* is in some way or other a sub-species of *heimlich*.[24]

Identifying this dialectical relation of *heimlich* and *unheimlich* with that of the conscious and the unconscious, Freud goes on to suggest that our experience of the uncanny – especially when accentuated in works of imagination that blur the distinction between reality and fantasy – expresses itself as a doubling or division of the self. While the conscious self follows the sequential, narrative logic of our normal experience, our unconscious self remains haunted by the uncanny recurrence of the same things – 'the repetition of the same features or character traits or vicissitudes, of the same crimes, or even the same names through several consecutive generations'.[25] This splitting of the self into the conscious and unconscious is further explained by Freud in terms of a defence mechanism whereby the ego projects internal impulses and associations outward onto something foreign. 'When all is said and done,' he surmises, 'the quality of uncanniness can only come from the fact of the "double" being a creation dating back to a very early mental stage, long since surmounted – a stage, incidentally, at which it wore a more friendly aspect. The double has become a thing of terror, just as, after the collapse of their religion, the gods turned into demons.'[26]

Considered in terms of the psychic development of the individual, the experience of the uncanny can be attributed to a 'harking-back to particular phases in the evolution of the self-regarding feeling, a regression to a time when the ego had not marked itself off sharply from the external world and other people'. In other words, the uncanny may be seen, in part at least, as a sentiment that is triggered by the involuntary return of an original 'narcissistic' rapport with the world – in the womb or in early childhood – that has been *repressed*, and whose subsequent 'repetition' can strike us therefore as unsettling, estranging, even terrifying. The extension of the linguistic usage of *heimlich* into its opposite, *unheimlich*, is thus explained by the curious fact that the 'uncanny is in reality nothing new or alien, but something which is familiar and of old established in the mind and which has become alienated from it only through the process of repression'.[27]

Freud observes that many people experience this feeling, in the highest degree, in relation to death and the return of the dead in ghostly or ghastly guise. Our experience of death strikes us as uncanny precisely because our primitive feelings and attitudes in this regard have also undergone a repression. 'All supposedly educated people', as Freud remarks, 'have ceased to believe officially that the dead can become visible as spirits, and have made any such appearances dependent on improbable and remote conditions; their emotional attitude towards their dead, moreover, once a highly ambiguous and ambivalent one, has been toned down in the higher strata of the mind into an unambiguous feeling of piety.'[28]

Accordingly, the uncanny is held to be closely bound up with the return of unconscious feelings or primitive desires that were once secretly familiar (*heimlich-heimisch*) but were subsequently repressed. The prefix '*un-*' in *unheimlich* is to be understood less as a logical opposition than a dialectical repression-and-return. And this, in turn, explains why an uncanny effect is often most cogently produced in dream narratives, parapraxis (slips of the tongue), or the symbols and rhetorical tropes of literary works, where the distinction between reality (as a principle of repression) and imagination (as a principle of recall) has been effaced.[29] Indeed, the rapport between poetic language and the unconscious has been explored by several structuralist and post-structuralist critics – most notably, Lacan, Kristeva, Derrida, Cixous and De Man. This approach is summed up in Lacan's famous maxim that 'the unconscious is structured like language'.

Freud's identification of the homely/unhomely paradox with the 'secretive' nature of unconscious experience, finds several echoes in Heaney's poetry. In the second of the Glanmore Sonnets, published in *Field Work*, Heaney describes the words of a poem as 'sensings, mountings from the hiding places/... ferreting themselves out of their dark hutch'. This comparison of poetic energies with subterranean earth creatures emerging from hiddeness, extends into an allusion to the craft of sculpture. The stone, the poet tells us, connives with the artist's chisel, 'as if the grain remembered what the mallet tapped to know'. Such complicity of the materials of art (words for the poet/stone for the sculptor) with the productive activity of the artist (the poet's pen/the sculptor's hammer and chisel) is obliquely equated with the complicity between the unconscious and the conscious, between feeling and knowledge. Heaney concludes the poem by grafting these metaphors of underground and craft onto his own experience of Glanmore in Co. Wicklow as a 'hedgeschool' where he served his apprenticeship, catching his 'voice' from the environment. This is the 'middle voice' of circular reverie, of active passivity: *active* in so far as the poet's words unearth underground sources of feeling: *passive* in so far as this 'other' ground itself opens up hitherto unknown and unnamed dimensions of being: 'Vowels ploughed into other, opened ground,/ Each verse returning like the plough turned round'.

The link between the uncanny return of repressed memories and the 'mythical' or 'vernacular' practice of divination, observed by Freud, is also a key motif for Heaney. Moreover, in Heaney as in Freud, this motif is commonly associated with images of buried springs and wells. We have already adverted to the opening passage of Heaney's selected prose, *Preoccupations*, where he identified his memory of the well/*omphalos* as a 'hankering after the underground side of things'. In this same passage, he goes on to describe this hankering as a desire to reactivate the unconscious energies of words which 'lie deep, like some spirit indelibly written into the nervous system'.[30] Indeed Heaney explicitly invokes the act of 'divination' to poetically retrace our familiar words back to their unfamiliar unconscious origins. 'Poetry as divination', writes Heaney, further expresses itself as 'revelation of the self to the self, as a restoration of a culture to itself'.[31]

Developing this analogy, Heaney imagines the poet's pen to be a diviner's rod sounding out the 'hiding places' of suppressed experience. In Irish custom, the diviner is someone who uses a hazel plant to relocate the concealed water currents from which it was originally nourished. In a poem called 'The Diviner', Heaney writes of this process of poetic recollection:

> Cut from the green hedge a forked hazel stick
> That he held tight by the arms of the V:
> Circling the terrain, hunting the pluck
> Of water, nervous, but professionally
>
> Unfussed. The pluck came sharp as a sting.
> The rod jerked down with precise convulsions,
> Spring water broadcasting
> Through a green aerial its secret stations.

This central image of the diviner – conjoining the classical allusion to the inspiration of the *vates* and the local allusion to the skill of detecting hidden waterflows – becomes Heaney's privileged metaphor for what he terms the 'technique' of poetic creation:

> If I were asked for a figure who represents pure technique, I would say a water diviner. You can't learn the craft of dowsing or divining – it is a gift for being in touch with what is there, hidden and real, a gift for mediating between the latent resource and the community that wants it current and released ... Technique is what allows that first stirring of the mind round the word or an image or a memory, to grow towards articulation: articulation not necessarily in terms of argument or explication but in terms of its own potential for harmonious self-reproduction ... Technique ensures that the first gleam attains its proper effulgence.[32]

While the operative terms of this passage – 'pure', 'divining', 'community', 'memory', 'harmonious', 'proper' – would seem to subscribe to a Romantic rather than a modernist aesthetic, the matter is, as we shall see, not so simple. Although Heaney continues to use the traditional terms of Romanticism, his poems frequently display an ironic and self-conscious detachment from the securities which such terms afforded to his Romantic predecessors. Thus whereas Heaney is close to Wordsworth in many of his sentiments, his self-scrutinising approach to language gives a more modernist inflection to his poetry. If Joyce was a modernist in revolt, Heaney might best be described as a modernist *incognito*.

The images of divining and digging are also, by the poet's own admission, 'sexual metaphors, emblems of initiation ... analogies for uncovering and touching the hidden thing'. Just as Freud located the splitting of the self into conscious and unconscious in the half-forgotten phase of infantile narcissism (where the ego first sees itself mirrored and echoed in mother-nature or other symbols of primary unity), so too in a poem entitled 'Personal Helicon', Heaney reiterates the childhood image of an out-of-bounds well whose very prohibition prompts a return to the repressed:

> As a child, they could not keep me from wells ...
> And old pumps with buckets and windlasses.
> I loved the dark drop, the trapped sky, the smells
> of waterweed, fungus and dank moss.

And in this same poem Heaney describes how his first intimation of self-identity was occasioned by the narcissistic act of contemplating his own image in the dark waters of a well: 'a white face hovered over the bottom' and gave back his own call 'with a clean new music to it'. But while the poet acknowledges that his childhood propensity to 'pry into roots, to finger slime,/ To stare, big-eyed Narcissus, into some spring', is now 'beneath all adult dignity', he also recognizes this phase of 'primary narcissism' (to use Freud's term for the child's original feeling of oneness with the other-than-self) as an indispensable catalyst of self-identification. Without such narcissistic self-discovery, it is possible that the poet would not now be in a position to conclude from a perspective of poetic self-consciousness – 'I rhyme/To see myself, to set the darkness echoing'.[33]

In 'Anahorish' Heaney extends the implications of this retrieval of unconscious experience from individual to cultural self-remembrance. Here Heaney amplifies the notion of language as divination by describing how a meditation upon the lost etymological roots of this local name – 'Anahorish' meaning 'place of clear water' in Gaelic – prises open the congealed contours of the contemporary landscape and unleashes its secret linguistic origin:

> My 'place of clear water',
> The first hill in the world
> Where springs washed into
> The shiny grass
>
> And darkened cobbles
> In the bed of the lane.
> *Anahorish*, soft gradient
> Of consonant, vowel-meadow ...
>
> Those mound-dwellers
> Go waist deep in mist
> To break the light ice
> At wells and dunghills.

But perhaps the most telling example of this paradoxical rediscovery of the unfamiliar (unhomely) in the familiar (homely), is witnessed in Heaney's reflections on the etymological sources of his own Ulster birthplace. 'Our farm was called Mossbawn,' he writes. '*Moss*, a Scots word probably carried to Ulster by the Planters, and *bawn* the name the English colonists gave to their fortified farm-houses. Mossbawn, the Planters' house on the bog. Yet in spite of this Ordinance Survey spelling, we pronounced it Moss Bawn, and *bán* is the Gaelic word for white. So might not the thing mean the white moss, the moss of the bog-cotton? In the syllables of my home I see a metaphor of the split culture of Ulster.'[34]

Such observations give some credence to the claim that Heaney is fundamentally preoccupied with a 'sense of place'. Landscape or local environment can assume the status of a certain 'sacramental' code – 'instinct with signs, implying a system of reality beyond the visible realities'.[35] But such a reality is, for Heaney, fractured and foreclosed. Home is a word that can only be spoken – and desired – because one is *not* there. As Heaney remarks in his 'Open Letter' *Field Day* pamphlet with ironic solemnity:

> My *patria*, my deep design
> To be at home
> In my own place and dwell within
> Its proper name.[36]

We have been concentrating on the more *positive* connotations of the dialectic of home and homelessness in the poetry of Heaney. But Heaney, no less than Freud, is painfully aware of the *negative* or 'uncanny' features of this dialectic. Already in his musings on the buried meanings of his native place name, Heaney offers a hint of the *impossibility* of returning 'home' and rediscovering there some harmonious unity. Mossbawn, as Heaney confides, itself contains a *split* meaning; it thus serves as a reminder of discontinuity, fragmentation and conflict. In his later work, and particularly the 'bog poems' sequence in *North*, Heaney records his encounter with the darker worlds of violence and terror that the return to unconscious energies of the past can evoke. In such poems, as we have seen, Freud's references to the 'return of the repressed' in the guise of necrophiliac obsessions with demon gods or other 'terrifying, estranging and unsettling' phenomena, are graphically registered. We will finally take a brief look at Heidegger's treatment of the 'homely/unhomely' paradox; for the Heideggerian analysis adds another significant modernist perspective – existential *ontology* – to that of Freudian *metapsychology*.

II

Heidegger examines the phenomenon of the 'uncanny' not as a psychic experience of the unconscious, but as an existential experience of Being. In *Being and Time* – a seminal work for such contemporary philosophical movements as phenomenology, hermeneutics and deconstruction – Heidegger isolates the experience of 'uncanniness' as a distinguishing feature of our modern sense of 'uprootedness' and 'estrangement'. Our being-in-the-world is authentic, writes Heidegger, to the extent that it faces up to the 'nothingness' that informs our contemporary relationship to Being. We are no longer at home in our world; we reside between two worlds, being 'too late for the gods and too early for Being'. The ancient experience of Being, in pre-Socratic Greece, for example, as a sacred presence in harmony with the cosmos, has been irretrievably lost. Moreover, any attempt to deny this loss, or to compensate for it by succumbing to the impersonal securities of ideological dogma (what Heidegger terms the 'they' or *Das Man*) is a form of inauthenticity. According to Heidegger, it is only when our existence (*Dasein*) encounters its own inherent anxiety that we are compelled to abandon the everyday illusion that we are 'at home' in the world and to thereby assume our true condition as alienated 'beings-towards-death':

> In anxiety one feels 'uncanny' or 'unhomelike' (*unheimlich*). Here the peculiar

indefiniteness of that which Dasein finds itself alongside in anxiety, comes prox-
imally to expression: the 'nothing and nowhere'. But here 'uncanniness' also
means 'not-being-at-home' (das Nicht-zuhause-Sein).[37]

By contrast, the average awareness of our existence flees from the 'uncanny'. It is thus characterized by the 'everyday publicness of the "they" which brings tranquillized self-assurance' –
'Being-at-home with all its obliviousness'.[38] By fleeing into the 'at home' shelteredness of our
conventional stereotypes, we are in fact fleeing from the reality of not-being-at-home – that is,
from the truth of our ontological relationship to the abyss of Being as it is exposed in the existential awareness of death. Anxiety, as the fundamental human response to the experience of
not-being-at-home, brings us back from our absorption in the world of false familiarity.

In his later writings, Heidegger sees language, and particularly poetry, as the privileged
mode of registering the home/homeless dialectic of contemporary existence. Poetry,
Heidegger claims, unsettles our instrumental approach to everyday speech. By disclosing the
inner nature of language itself, modern poetry reminds us that the genuine words for naming
Being are missing. It thereby reveals that we can only begin to 'come home' to Being by first
acknowledging its absence, by embracing our actual experience of homelessness. Poetry
responds to the call of Being by its vigilant attentiveness to the lost origin of words. This origin
of language is not some transcendental presence existing before or beyond history. It is a
silence or gap in language from which words first emerge into human speech – what
Heidegger calls the 'silent tolling of language' (Das Geläute der Stille). Poetry is described by
Heidegger accordingly as a thinking back (andenken) to the forgotten sources of meaning; a
thinking which serves in turn as a thanking (danken) and remembering (Gedächtnis) of that
summons of Being that, in silence, first gives language. For Heidegger, it is not so much the
poet who speaks language, but language that speaks the poet. In short, poetry 'defamiliarizes'
our taken-for-granted attitude to language; it challenges the role of the human speaker as a
controlling cogito who masters and manipulates words for his own pragmatic ends. To experience language poetically then is to take a 'step back' from our 'natural attitude' which sees
Being as a literal possession or as a mere collection of facts to be passively mirrored and classified by our words.[39]

In a detailed commentary on Hölderlin's elegy, 'Homecoming', Heidegger observes that this
poem is less a celebration of returning to a 'home' than a tragic recognition that such a 'home'
has disappeared. The poet's quest for an ontological home presupposes the absence of a literally
existing one. And this experience of historical loss is attendant upon the awareness that 'the
sacred names are lacking'. The modern world encounters homelessness because our quotidian
language no longer names Being but is reduced instead to the technical and pragmatic transmission of information. 'For the poet', claims Heidegger, 'the assault of techne (as the wilful
manipulation of language, and by extension of the world) is the happening whereby man ceases
to be at home'. But he is careful to insist that it is only 'in his exile from home, that the home
is first disclosed as such'.[40] Poetry is thus construed as an attempt to prepare for a home-coming
by accepting the truth that we are no longer at home in our world.

'Homecoming', in other words, only becomes an ontological possibility when poets take
upon themselves the care (Sorge) for the lost home, for the missing names. And it is by
embodying this 'caring' in poetic language that what is gone may be transformed into what is
yet to come. Consequently, poetic remembrance is not some revivalist nostalgia for an ancient
patria, but the anticipation of new possibilities of home hitherto unimagined. Such remembrance evokes the futurity of homecoming rather than its antiquity. 'Homecoming is the return
into the nearness of origin.'[41] But 'origin' is to be understood here not as a topographical fact
but as an imaginary horizon that is still coming towards us. Poetry as homecoming transforms
the poet and those who listen to his words into a community of questers, and by implication,
questioners. These questioners draw near to the origin because they project a beginning as
opposed to simply repeating one. For the authentic 'home' is a non-present possibility that
can never be revived or re-appropriated once and for all. The neighbourhood of the origin,
into which poetry leads us, 'lets nearness be near and yet lets it be the sought-after, thus not

near … It brings nearness near in that it keeps it away. The neighbourhood of origin is a mystery.'[42] The poetic project of 'homecoming' is, in short, invariably accompanied by the literal awareness of 'homelessness'.[43]

Just as Freud believed that it was in the 'slip of the tongue' (parapraxis), when our conscious defences were unguarded, that the suppressed truths of our unconscious spoke out, so too Heidegger believes that it is when our commonly taken-for-granted discourse is disrupted that the occluded Being of language reveals itself to us.[44] Both agreed that it is the *inhabitual* language of poetry and dream which permits the uncanny or 'unhomely' (*unheimlich*) to come home to us. For poetry demonstrates that listening to the *estranging* call of language, and responding to it, is not a derived form of discourse but the original source of all everyday discourse (which has simply forgotten its origins): 'Authentic poetry is never merely a higher plane of ordinary language. Rather, on the contrary, everyday speech is a forgotten and worn-out, over-worked poem, out of which the call is scarcely audible anymore.'[45]

The most urgent task of the poet in our 'destitute times', Heidegger concludes, is to make us aware of our destitution by reaching into the abyss of human existence – 'the dark of the world's night' – and showing us that the names for Being are no longer available. For Heidegger, as for Brecht, modernist art is characterized by its power of estrangement (*Verfremdung*). By disappropriating us from our conventional approach to words and images, it teaches us that our familiar reality is in fact something strange and alien. Consequently, the unrelenting effort of modernist poets like Trakl, Rilke and Celan to expose the concealed workings of language is in Heidegger's view not some idle self-regard but the self-scrutinizing conscience of our times. 'This is why poetic images', insists Heidegger, 'are imaginings in a distinctive sense: not mere fancies and illusions but imaginings that are visible inclusions of the alien in the sight of the familiar.'[46]

As a footnote to Heidegger's exploration of the poetics of homecoming, it might be appropriate to mention the centrality of this theme in the work of another modernist German poet (considered by Heidegger to be one of the greatest of his generation), Paul Celan. Celan too described his poetry as a 'sort of homecoming'. The silences, dislocations and reversals of normal linguistic usage in his verse reflect the poet's paradoxical awareness – as both a displaced modern European and a post-holocaust Jew – of being an alien in the homeland of the German language. Celan admits the need to 'keep yes and no unsplit', to inhabit the frontier limbo between light and darkness, because 'he speaks truly who speaks the shade'. He pursues this paradox exhorting himself as poet to 'call the shibboleth, call it out/ Into your alien home'. And in a poem called 'Homecoming' (*Heimkehr*), Celan realises that the 'I' – the identity of the poet – can only be 'fetched home into its today' via the interminable detour of white distances 'along the sleigh track of the lost'. Vacillating in a transitional season between silence and speech, the poet hopes against hope that poetic remembrance might forge a daisy-chain between past and present where the claims of loss and presence, discontinuity and continuity, might 'almost' coexist:

> Dumb Autumn smells. The
> Marguerite, unbroken, passed
> between home and chasm through
> your memory.
>
> A strange lostness was
> Palpably present, almost
> You would
> Have lived.[47]

This poetics of homecoming – as outlined by a philosopher like Heidegger and a poet like Celan – bears an obvious relevance to Heaney's preoccupation with home. By juxtaposing our analysis of Heaney with a summary of the Heideggerian poetics, I hope to have suggested the trans-national and singularly modern nature of his literary concerns.

Part Three:

DRAMATIC NARRATIVES

CHAPTER FIFTEEN

The Language Plays of Brian Friel

There has been much discussion in recent times about the *verbal* character of Irish theatre. Some argue that since the Irish are 'great talkers' off stage it is logical that their 'way with words' should be creatively explored on stage. Others claim that the Irish dramatist's preoccupation with language is a curse that hampers the genuine medium of theatre: the immediate, physical presence of actors performing in front of an audience. This criticism of Irish drama could be summed up in the protest: too much talk and not enough action! But what is the significance of this aesthetic opposition between talk and action? How, if at all, does it relate to the conventional wisdom that the Irish facility with words is the indispensable armour of the oppressed? Or how does it relate to Tom Paulin's suggestion in *Field Day* (1984) that 'the history of a language is often the story of possession and dispossession, territorial struggle and the establishment or imposition of a culture'?

I will examine here the verbal nature of Irish theatre with particular attention to Friel's three 'language plays' – *Faith Healer, Translations* and *The Communication Cord*. In so doing, I wish to assess the modernist and revivalist implications of Friel's drama as an exploration of the twin modern crises of *identity* and *language*.

I

Brian Friel's plays in the 1980s were primarily concerned with the problem of language, so much so that they constituted not just a theatre *of* language but a theatre *about* language. Words became both the form *and* content of his dramas. This replay of language within the plays themselves indicated a critical process of self-scrutiny wherein the native movement of verbal theatre was beginning to take stock of itself, to reassess its own assumptions.

Faith Healer (1980) is a story about the art of storytelling. It portrays the attempts made by three characters, a faith healer (Frank), his wife (Grace) and his promotion agent (Teddy) to give order to their shared past by recollecting it in the present. But they cannot achieve a common version of events. Each character is separated by the subjective interpretation he/she brings to bear on his/her experience of the past.

The play, however, is not so much about the characters themselves as the artistic performance in which they are engaged. Coleridge defined the power of 'poetic faith' to transform reality as a 'willing suspension of disbelief'. Friel calls it, simply, *faith*. Frank's 'performance' can only work when the healer and the healed come together in a ritual of magic communion – when they agree to play the language game of faith. The problem arises when the rules of the game are obfuscated, forgotten or interpreted in different ways by different players: in short, when the healing word no longer communicates a common message.

With *Translations* (1981) and *The Communication Cord* (1982), Friel's exploration of the transforming and deforming potencies of the word shifts from a personal to a communal perspective. *Translations* deals with the ways in which the consciousness of an entire culture is fractured by the transcription of one linguistic landscape (Gaelic and classical) into another (Anglo-Saxon and positivist). This loss of a communal continuity of language coincides significantly with the historical demise of the old Gaelic society in the famines of the 1830s and 1840s. *The Communication Cord* features the sentimental contrivings of the modern Irish bourgeoisie to purify the dialect of the tribe and reinstate the antique pieties of a lost culture.

Friel's obsession with the workings of words betrays more than an aesthetic interest in the instruments of his own profession. Though not wishing to minimize the formal problem of language, Friel insists that he is also responding to the contemporary crisis of identity in Irish culture. 'The whole issue of language is very problematic for all of us on this island', he explains. 'I had parents who were native Irish speakers, and also two of our four grandparents were illiterate. It is very close you know. I actually remember two of them. And to be so close to illiteracy and to a different language is a curious experience. In some ways I don't think we've resolved it on this island for ourselves. We flirt with the English language, but we haven't absorbed it and we haven't regurgitated it.'[1]

Friel insists that the *aesthetic* and *cultural* dimensions of the language crisis entail a third and equally fundamental one – the *political*. He is candid in his pronouncements on this aspect of his writing: 'It is back to the political problem – it is our proximity to England, how we have been pigmented in our theatre … with the use of the English language, the understanding of words, the whole cultural burden that every word in the English language carries is slightly different to our burden.'[2] Friel compares his own sentiment of linguistic difference and dissent to Stephen's declaration in *A Portrait* that he cannot, as an Irishman, write or speak the English language without 'unrest of spirit', without holding its words at bay. For the ruled, the lexicon of the ruler remains an adopted one.

But Friel is not only an *Irish* writer; he is more specifically a *Northern* Irish writer. And this geographical distinction accentuates his sense of cultural, political and linguistic alienation. Though he repudiates the colonial identity of Britain, he also feels an outsider in the Republic. This sentiment of permanent dislocation carries with it both a liberty and an urgency to question the prevailing notions of cultural belongingness. 'If you have a sense of exile', Friel confesses, that brings with it 'some kind of alertness and some kind of eagerness, some kind of hunger. If you are in possession you can become placid about things.'[3]

The festering wound of the North is a constant reminder for Friel that the body politic of the nation is deeply haemorrhaged. An amputated Ulster acts as a phantom limb haunting his work. Friel's residence is fundamentally dual, not only because he is an Irish dramatist working in the English language, but also because he is not fully at home either north or south of the Irish border. 'You cannot deposit fealty to a situation like that of the North which you don't believe in,' he declares. 'Then you look south of the border and that enterprise is so distasteful in many respects. And yet both places are home in some way. It may be an inheritance from a political situation.'[4] Friel's *border mentality* epitomizes the dual personality of the Catholic minority in the North. And this duality is undoubtedly amplified by Friel's own formative memories of his childhood in Glenties, the Donegal border town that was to serve as the setting for his language plays (under the pseudonym of Baile Beag).

But while the diagnosis is to a large extent political, the prognosis for Friel is of a cultural order. The divisions within the four political provinces of Ireland may be overcome if and when a fifth province of the imagination is created 'to which cultural and artistic loyalty can be offered'.[5] The creation of this *fifth province* calls for a new vocabulary, a new mode of communication that could acknowledge, and perhaps ultimately mediate, between the sundered cultural identities of the island. A common sense of purpose, or at least the identification of a common problem, which is the *sine qua non* of any genuine community, may, he believes, be retrieved by discovering a common voice. The search for this common voice lies at the heart of Friel's dramatic obsession with words. His language plays are not confined to semantic matters. It is not by ignoring the four political provinces that the fifth province may be produced but by creatively reinterpreting the possibilities of the interrelationship. 'I think that the political problem of this island is going to be solved by language ... Not only the language of negotiation across the table, but the recognition of what language means for us on this island ... Because we are in fact talking about the marrying of two cultures here, which are ostensibly speaking the same language but which in fact are not.'[6] By recognizing the inadequacy and indeed redundancy of the shibboleths that have satisfied and separated us up to now, Friel's plays open up possibilities of finding a 'different voice' that might enable us to understand ourselves in a new way. This linguistic overhaul, he hopes, 'should lead to a cultural state, not a political one ... out of that cultural state, the *possibility* of a political state follows'.[7]

There is, however, yet a further dimension to Friel's dramatic engagement with language. This fourth dimension, which grounds and underpins the other three (aesthetic, political, cultural), may best be described as *ontological* for it concerns the very way in which language determines our innermost being-in-the-world. I employ this existential terminology advisedly, following Friel's own invocation of Heidegger's ontological definition of language in his prefatory program note to *Translations*: 'Man acts as if he were the master of language, while it is language which remains master of man. When this relation of domination is inverted, man succumbs to strange contrivances.' This citation is taken from an essay entitled, 'Poetically Man Dwells', published in Heidegger's major philosophical work on language, *Poetry, Language and Thought*. The passage from which Friel quotes proceeds as follows: 'It is language that speaks. Man begins speaking and man only speaks to the extent that he responds to and hears language addressing him, concurring with him. Language is the highest and foremost of those assents which we human beings can never articulate solely out of our own means.'[8] Heidegger argues here that we can only have a genuine rapport with the Being of the world if we obediently listen to (*ob-audire*) language, abandoning our habitual tendency to master it by reducing words to our own wilful contrivances. Our being-in-the-world becomes authentic when we cease to abuse language as a strategic instrument for the manipulation of people and things and respond to it instead as that which it truly is: the house of Being in which we may poetically dwell. Heidegger warns against the contemporary decadence of language evident in the prevailing habit of taking language for granted as a mere tool for conveying information and representing objects. This modern eclipse of the original vocation of language to reveal the poetic gift of Being has provoked a crisis of human alienation of unprecedented proportions. A conversion in our historical or cultural being can never occur, Heidegger insists, without a prior conversion in that innermost region of our existence, which is nothing less than our ontological rapport with the very essence of language itself.

> It is because language is the house of Being, that we reach what is by constantly going through this house. When we go to the woods, we are already going through the word *woods*. When we go to the well, we are always already going through the word *well* ... All beings are, qua beings, in

the precinct of language. This is why the return from the realm of objects and representation into the innermost region of the heart's space can be accomplished, if anywhere, only in this precinct.[9]

It is surely within this perspective that we should read Friel's caveat to those who seek to reduce his plays to political propaganda tracts. Of *Translations*, he writes: 'I don't want to write a play about Irish peasants being suppressed by English sappers ... The play has to do with language and only language.' And Friel adds that since he is determined that his drama should avoid being equated with 'public questions, issues for politicians', he will concentrate more on 'the exploration of the dark and private places of individual souls'.[10]

Friel's trilogy of language plays – *Faith Healer, Translations* and *The Communication Cord* – constitute a sustained attempt to bring about a conversion in our ontological attitude to language.

II. Faith Healer

In *Faith Healer*, Friel's probings of language focus primarily on its *aesthetic* power to recreate reality in fiction. His choice of the dramatic medium – a faith healer's performances – as the subject of the play, reflects Friel's critical concern with the *modus operandi* of his own professional activity as a playwright. The word-player is holding a mirror up to himself, examining his own conscience.

Friel does not shy away from these implications of the play. He freely concedes that *Faith Healer* is 'some kind of metaphor for the art, the craft of writing ... and the great confusion we all have about it who are involved in it. How honourable and dishonourable it can be.'[11] Since writing is a pursuit that requires one to be introspective, it can lead to great selfishness. So that the natural impulse to pursue one's own creative talents is constantly invigilated by the 'third eye' of self-consciousness. But this in turn, Friel admits, can be a dangerous thing, because in some way 'it perverts whatever natural freedom you might have, and that natural freedom must find its expression in the written word. So there's an exploration of that element of the charlatan that exists in all creative work.'[12]

In *Faith Healer* Friel's attitude to the creative work vacillates between the despondency of a sceptic and the ecstasy of a believer. The play teases out that subtle knot in which religious and aesthetic faith are intertwined. It is not so much a matter of rehearsing anthropological theories about the origins of drama in primitivistic ritual as a keen sounding of that deep psychic need for marvel and miracle to which both religion and theatre have always responded in their distinctive ways. *Faith Healer* has a perennial ring about it.

The play begins with Frank Hardy's incantation of a list of paltry towns in which he has performed his art of healing: Aberarder, Aberayron etc. The names are reeled off like an ancient pilgrim mindlessly reciting his rosary beads of memory. The assonantal place names are repeated, Frank tells us, for their purgative powers of 'mesmerism and sedation'. They serve as 'relics of abandoned rituals' in a secular age. Frank is the high-priest of his own imagination, recruiting the lingering pieties of senescent rural communities where despair is beginning to replace orthodox religious belief. He is a hybrid creature possessing both the compassion of a messianic healer devoted to the infirm and the commercialism of a meretricious mountebank. He is an artist in straits, the evangelist of a message that has fallen into disrepute. Frank describes his own art of faithhealing accordingly as a 'craft without an apprenticeship, a ministry without responsibility, a vocation without a ministry'.

But while acknowledging that his art is obsolescent, Frank still clings to the conviction that it responds to an ineradicable need in himself and in his audience to be made 'whole and perfect', to be released from what they *are* into what they *might* be. People still hunger for the fiction of a life transformed. And so the show goes on. One half of Frank knows that he is a con man of many masks; but the other remains faithful to the suspicion that he is endowed with a unique and awesome gift that compels him to put it to the service of others. 'Was it chance? – or skill? – or illusion? – a delusion?' he asks himself bemusedly. 'Precisely what power did I possess? Could I summon it? When and how? Was I its servant? Did it reside in my ability to invest someone with faith in me or did I evoke from him a healing faith in himself? … Faith in faith?' Put in the terms of existential ontology, Frank's equivocations amount to the fundamental question: Am I the manipulative master or the obedient servant of the healing word?

Faith Healer is a play in four acts that records this crisis of faith as it is experienced by three characters – Frank, the Irish miracle worker, and his two English travelling companions: Grace his mistress and Teddy his stage-manager. All three deliver monologues in which they bear witness like modern-day gospellers to the wandering, homecoming and sacrifice of the Fantastic Frank Hardy.

Grace recounts how Frank performed his art 'in such complete mastery that everything is harmonised for him … that anything is possible'. Her 'proud testament', as she half ironically terms it, pays reverence to his hypnotic play with words – 'releasing them from his mouth in that special voice he used only then, as if blessing them or consecrating himself'. But Grace's testimony is also tinged with resentment. She is jealous of the way in which Frank's single-minded quest for artistic completion erased her from his orbit of concern as he withdrew into the sanctum of his 'private power'. This memory of exclusion prevents Grace from invoking the litany of place names with the same impersonal devotion as Frank. She halts at the name Kinlochbervie. In this tiny sequestered village in

Scotland their stillborn child – a tangible symptom of their diseased life – was brought into the world and buried. Though she may grant to Kinlochbervie its ritual fitness in the aesthetic scheme of things – 'a nice name, a complete sound' – she cannot dispel the tragic reality that it connotes. This is where Grace's narration of the past parts company with Frank's. The gruesome memory of her child's death resists the healing power of fiction. Frank's faith, by contrast, can only survive intact by obliterating this memory from his mind.

The bitter intrusion of the past causes Grace's faith to lapse. For a few brief moments she casts a cold eye on Frank's addiction to his own narrative. She recalls how Frank would humiliate her by constantly changing her name and rearranging the facts of her life (where she was born, how they met, etc.) to suit his own scenario. His talent for healing others on stage was evenly matched by his talent for hurting her in life. He had chosen, in Yeats's phrase, perfection of the work over perfection of the life. Not content to fictionalize only the characters of his performance, Frank dragged all of his family and friends (father, mother, wife, child, Teddy) into the quarrel between himself and his art. Each person became grist to his fictional mill.

Grace concedes this painful fact; but she cannot wholly consent to it. Indeed, her account of her tortuous wanderings with Frank gives us a good idea of how Synge's Pegeen Mike might have mused to herself had she left her homeland of Mayo and taken to the roads with her storytelling playboy:

> It wasn't that he was simply a liar – I never understood it – yes, I knew that he wanted to hurt me, but it was much more complex than that, it was some compulsion he had to adjust, to refashion, to re-create everything around him. Even the people who came to him … yes, they were real enough, but not real as persons, real as fictions, his fictions, extensions of himself that came into being only because of him. And if he cured a man, that man became for him a successful fiction and therefore actually real … But if he didn't cure him, the man was forgotten immediately, allowed to dissolve and vanish as if he had never existed.

Teddy is the third member of the performing trinity. He is described by Grace as a 'dedicated acolyte to the holy man'. But Teddy's apostolic posturings are tempered by his clowning humanity. The cockney comic in him keeps the religious votary in check: and if Teddy canonizes Frank it is not as a member of the ancient communion of saints but of the new communion of stage-and-screen idols that includes Fred Astaire, Lillie Langtry, Laurence Olivier, Houdini, Chaplin and Gracie Fields. Teddy is the odd man out, an Englishman bemused by Frank's 'Celtic temperament' and bewildered by his turbulent exchanges with Grace. As entrepreneurial mediator between Frank and his fictions, Teddy is determined to remain aloof and uninvolved, following his chosen thumb rule that friends is friends and work is work and never the twain shall meet. But

Teddy's entire monologue belies his own rule and testifies to his incapacity to separate his professional commitment to Frank and Grace from his personal commitment to them as real people. Life and art are as inextricable for Teddy as for Frank and Grace.

Friel deftly underscores the discrepancies between the three narrators' accounts of their shared past. The conflict of evidence is particularly obvious in their different versions of the death and burial of the stillborn child. We witness how fiction is deployed by each character as a strategy of survival. Friel's juxtaposition of the three diverging testimonials reveals how each is caught up in a fictive re-enactment of the past, condemned to a stage performance. The monologue format is here ingeniously exploited by Friel as an exact correlative of their solitary confinement. They have ceased to communicate with each other; the confessional mode of private address has become the last resort of their language play.

By means of this play-within-a-play technique, Friel reiterates one of the cardinal themes of modernist theatre developed by Pirandello, Genet, Sartre, Beckett and others: the performer can never be released from his performance and his very existence as a player of roles depends on both author and audience keeping faith with his fiction. Theatre is an *interpretative* art whose very interpretation involves mediation. The final words of Grace's monologue are directed not solely to Frank but to Friel and the spectator as well – 'O my God, I'm one of his fictions too, but I need him to sustain me in that existence.' There is, as Sartre would say, *no exit* …

Faith Healer terminates with Frank, in the last of the monological testaments, deliberating on his first and final performance of the 'miracle' in his native townland of Ballybeg in Donegal. Frank had intended his return from exile to be a glorious homecoming, the ultimate fulfilment of his promise – 'a restoration … an integration, a full blossoming'. Frank's valedictory speech is replete with mock-heroic allusions to the New Testament. He talks of those rare performances when he could have moved mountains; of how only one of the many that were cured came back to thank him; of Grace's father, the disbelieving Yorkshire judge, dismissing his faith-healing as chicanery; of the triumphal homecoming to Ballybeg; the miracle of the healed finger performed with the wedding party in the pub; and the Gethsemane reckoning, with Grace and Teddy asleep, in the year when he prepared for his sacrifice, 'both awed and elated … as if he were entering a church'.

The apocalyptic overtones of Frank's portrayal of himself as a lamb being led to the slaughter are unmistakable. As he walks towards his faithless executioners, a prophet unrecognized in his own country, Frank speaks of being possessed of a strange intimation that 'the whole corporeal world – the cobbles, the trees, the sky, those four malign implements – somehow had shed their physical reality and had become mere imaginings, and that in all existence there was only myself and the wedding guests.' This intimation gave rise in turn to a still deeper sentiment:

even we had ceased to be physical and existed only in spirit, only in the need we had for each other. And as I moved across that yard towards them and offered myself to them, then for the first time I had a simple and genuine sense of home-coming ... and the maddening questions were silent.

This passage is a veritable *tour de force*, the pathos it evokes extending to the deepest reaches of symbolic association. Apart from its manifest biblical connotations, the speech also sends reverberations through the Irish literary subconscious. One thinks of Yeats's 'Second Coming' or the enigmatic lines in 'Ben Bulben' that invoke the transfiguring potency of apocalyptic violence:

> Know that when all words are said
> And a man is fighting mad,
> Something drops from eyes long blind,
> He completes his partial mind,
> For an instant stands at ease,
> Laughs aloud, his heart at peace.
> Even the wisest man grows tense
> With some sort of violence
> Before he can accomplish fate ...

One is also reminded of the 'terrible beauty' symbolism of the Irish nationalist ideology of martyrdom and blood-sacrifice (e.g. Pearse's appeal to bloodshed as a 'cleansing and sanctifying thing'). Viewed in this perspective, the complex relationship of conflict and complicity between Frank, Grace and Teddy might even be construed as a veiled allegory of Anglo-Irish relations. And it is perhaps useful – apropos of such a reading – to recall Friel's statement in 1972, that Irish theatre must be prepared to respond to the major crisis of faith in contemporary Irish politics and culture:

> The future of Irish drama ... must depend on the slow development of the Irish mind, and it will shape and be shaped by political events ... I do not believe that art is a servant of any movement. But during the period of unrest I can foresee that allegiances that have bound the Irish imagination – loyalty to the most authoritarian church in the world and devotion to a romantic ideal we call Kathleen – will be radically altered. Faith and Fatherland, new definitions will be forged, and then new loyalties and then new social groupings ... The Irish imagination – that vivid, slovenly, anarchic, petulant, alert to the eternal, impatient with the here and now instrument – will have to set about shaping and interpreting the new structure in art forms.[13]

Friel's casting of Frank as a hapless *salvator mundi* retains, however, its primary function as a metaphor for the self-destructive impulses of the creative artist over-obsessed with his own art. The storyteller who sacrifices life to fiction, Friel suggests, risks becoming the victim of his own script, the dummy of his own ventriloquism. Placed in the context of the Irish dramatic tradition, *Faith Healer* may be read accordingly as a cautionary tale in response to the romantic optimism of Synge's *Playboy*. For if the belief in the power of a lie made Christy into a likely gaffer in the end of all, it makes Frank into a mutilated corpse.

And yet one cannot escape the feeling that Friel's verdict on his own aesthetic profession is equivocal. A tentative plea of not guilty is lodged somewhere between the final lines. We are left with a sneaking admiration for these possessed players ready, quite literally, to lay down their lives for their faith. Nor are we allowed to easily forget that if nine times out of ten Frank failed to perform the miracle, one time in ten he *did* succeed in making the crippled whole, the faithless faithful. In these exceptional moments of dramatic magic, the healing touch worked. It is not − as Beckett's Didi commented of the two crucified thieves in *Godot* (one of whom was saved) − 'a reasonable percentage'. But it is a percentage nonetheless. And one sufficient to sustain Friel's faith in his own writing and the audience's faith in the power of his dramatic lie.

III. Translations

With *Translations* Friel's exploration of language play takes a new turn. He moves beyond the critical examination of his own aesthetic conjuring with words to the broader question of the socio-cultural role of language in the historical evolution of a community.

Translations begins where *Faith Healer* ends − in the Donegal town of Ballybeg. Only now it goes by its original Gaelic name of Baile Beag. Friel has wound the clock back a century, recreating the life and circumstances of this small Donegal community as it faced into the social upheaval provoked by the Great Famine of the 1840s. The year is 1833 and the old Gaelic language and culture are enjoying their last lease of life. The play relates the fortunes of a hedge schoolmaster, Hugh − Frank Hardy's spiritual and tribal ancestor − and his motley crew of scholarly disciples: the sixty-year-old 'infant prodigy', Jimmy Jack, fluent in Latin and Greek; Hugh's son and assistant, Manus; and the quasi-illiterate peasant pupils, Sarah, Máire and Doalty. The hedge school fosters a harmonious compound of Gaelic and Classical cultures. 'Our own culture and the classical tongue', boasts Hugh, 'make a happy conjugation'. Athene and Gráinne, Apollo and Cúchulainn rub shoulders here with unaffected ease. The poetic imagination still reigns supreme, roaming from Baile Beag to Athens and Rome in the breath span of a single verse.

But this cultural sanctuary is abruptly threatened by the arrival of a detachment of Royal Engineers from the British Army sent to make an Ordnance Survey map of the local landscape. This military mission is disguised as a benign exercise in geographical linguistics, its ostensible purpose being the transcription of Gaelic place names into English equivalents. Friel's play documents the consequences that this seemingly innocuous administrative project has upon the indigenous community. Special attention is given to the role played by Owen, the school master's second son. Recently returned from the anglicized capital, Dublin, Owen enlists in the survey project as translator and mediator between the two languages, only to find himself spiritually spreadeagled in the collision of loyalties.

The play opens with two crippled beings struggling towards communication: Manus, the master's lame and loyal son, is trying to teach a local dumb girl, Sarah, to speak. After much encouragement, she succeeds in repeating the sentence – 'my name ... is Sarah'. Manus hails this miraculous act of speech as the unlocking of a hidden landscape of consciousness. 'Marvellous,' he expostulates, 'soon you'll be telling me all the secrets that have been in that head of yours all these years.' While Manus is shepherding Sarah into speech, Jimmy Jack is reciting, chorus-like, the Greek legend of the goddess Athene magically touching and transforming Ulysses with her wand. Friel provides us here with a Hellenic tale of faith-healing that subtly counterpoints the reciprocal act of communication whereby Manus and Sarah cure each other of the paralysis of solitude that their respective forms of crippledom embodied. Jimmy's facility with languages is a token of his attunement to the original harmony between word and world – what the Greek philosophers called the *harmonia* of the *logos*. We are told that for him the world of the gods and ancient myth is 'as real and as immediate as everyday life in the townland of Baile Beag'. Jimmy represents that declining old order where people still felt at one with the divine (he talks of gods and goddesses 'as if they lived down the road') and where language was still a cohesive rather than a divisive force. For Jimmy speech equals communication equals community.

The other characters in the opening act of the play are also defined in terms of their attitude to language. The first we hear of the master, Hugh, is that he is off at a christening, helping to choose a name for a baby. The choice of name is impatiently awaited by the community as a means of deciding the dubious identity of the child's father! Hugh is thus casually introduced as a minister of names and, by extension, a guarantor and guardian of the community's cultural identity. Moreover, by professionally imparting to his students the scholarly art of translating Gaelic words into Latin and Greek, Hugh permits the community to converse with cultures other than its own. It is of course significant that the classical tongues cultivated by the master represent *past* civilizations, now dead and gone: a hint of what is in store for his own Gaelic tongue and civilization. Hugh's vision is sighted on a vanishing kingdom. He is an inquisitor of origins and etymologies who speaks in the past tense. He is backward-looking for the simple reason that the future holds no hope for his language.

When Hugh finally arrives on stage, he proudly announces the identity of the child disclosed at the 'ritual of naming' – or *caerimonia nominationis* as he hastens to add. He then proceeds to quiz his pupils on the Greek and Latin etymologies of the word baptise – *baptizein*, to dip; *baptisterium*, a bath etc. And when his pupils apprise him of the departure of one of his students from the school he extends the importance of the naming motif with the humorous quip: 'Nora Dan can now write her name – Nora Dan's education is complete!'

But Nora Dan may well be one of the last graduates of Hugh's hedge school. English – the new colonial language of commerce and maps – is already making incursions into the old system of learning. Several of the young peasants greet the arrival of this tongue as holding out the promise of a new beginning. Máire is one such peasant pupil seduced by the allure of English words. She only knows three snatches that an aunt has taught her to recite by rote. Though still not having an idea what the words actually mean, she is prepared nonetheless to trade in her limited knowledge of the classics for more of the same: 'I don't want Greek, I don't want Latin … Fit me better if I had that much English.' Máire belongs to the emerging generation of aspiring peasants tired of treading the mudtracks of oppressed Gaeldom. She dreams of finer things to come, citing the opinion of Dan O'Connell, the 'Liberator', that the sooner 'we all learn to speak English the better … The old language is a barrier to progress'.

Máire has secured passage money to the New World and knows full well that the only *useful* language for her now is English. She sits on the hedge school floor excitedly scanning the map of America for the English place names of her future abode. But the lens of her youthful fascination soon focuses on a more literal map nearer home. The British soldiers 'making the maps' for the Ordnance Survey in the neighbouring fields have not escaped her attention. Máire's enthusiasm for the arrival of the Royal Engineers is, however, offset by two discreet allusions to the threat that their colonial culture represents to the native Gaelic-speaking community. First, we are casually informed that the hedge school is to be replaced by a progressive national school where every subject will be taught through English. And second, we learn of the imminent danger of a potato blight: 'just beyond where the soldiers are making the maps – the sweet smell was everywhere'.

The next character to make an appearance at the hedge school is the master's second son, Owen. He is something indeed of a prodigal son returning from his travels with a reputation of great business successes. (Máire claims she heard stories that he owned 'ten big shops in Dublin'.) Owen is accompanied by two English officers – Captain Lancey and Lieutenant Yolland – in whose employ he is engaged as a 'translator'.

(Hugh has already prepared us for the arrival of the English speakers. Having met with Captain Lancey on his return from the baptism, Hugh had pointed out to the Royal Engineer that his alien tongue 'couldn't really express us' and was only employed in the community on rare occasions for 'purposes of commerce'

– a use, Hugh comments with jocular disrespect, to which the English language 'seemed particularly suited'. Hugh mischievously informs the officers that his people are not familiar with their English literature: feeling 'closer to the warm Mediterranean. We tend to overlook your island.')

Owen arrives first at school – like an Indian scout preparing the way for the ensuing cavalry. He greets his father, brother and the local pupils with genuine camaraderie. It is, after all, his first homecoming to Baile Beag. And it is no less festive than that of Frank Hardy a century later. Owen immediately enters his father's game of translating Irish into Latin and vice versa, thus reminding his people that he is still one of them, still familiar with the rules of their language game. Owen is a master of what Patrick Kavanagh called 'the wink and elbow language of delight'. There follows a particularly poignant exchange between Owen and Sarah. Echoing the earlier act of communication between his brother (Manus) and the dumb girl, Owen asks her name. When she falteringly replies that it is Sarah Johnny Sally, he spontaneously adds: 'Of course! From Bun na hAbhann! I'm Owen Hugh Mor from Baile Beag.' Owen thus subscribes to the password of the tribe, uttering once again that communal dialect that identifies its members at birth according to their origins – the name of their parents and local birthplace.

Owen does not try to hide the fact that he is on the payroll of the Ordnance Survey expedition. On the contrary, he announces his brief as civilian interpreter with good-humoured candour: 'My job is to translate the quaint, archaic tongue you people persist in speaking, into the King's good English.' Owen then introduces the two officers who have been waiting in attendance. Captain Lancey is a hardnosed military expert with little or no culture. He mistakes Jimmy's Latin for Gaelic and is only interested in language in so far as it may prove a useful instrument in the colonial conquest of a landscape by means of a mechanistic mapping system. Lancey's attitude epitomizes the British empiricist philosophy of language as a pragmatic reductionism of things to signs. 'A map is a representation on paper', he explains, subverting Hugh's pedagogical role. 'His Majesty's Government has ordered the first ever comprehensive survey of this entire country – a general triangulation which will embrace detailed hydrographic and topographic information and which will be executed to a scale of six inches to the English mile.' Nor does Lancey leave us in any doubt that this apparently inoffensive task of cartographical translation involves an ulterior purpose – the colonial and commercial exploitation of the native community as a whole. He blandly reveals:

> This enormous task has been embarked on so that the military authorities will be equipped with up-to-date and accurate information on every corner of this part of the Empire ... and also so that the entire basis of land valuation can be reassessed for reasons of more equitable taxation.

Lancey shows himself to be a patronizing hypocrite, however, when he presents the entire exercise as a token of British altruism, undertaken to 'advance the interests of Ireland'. The Irish people are privileged, he affirms, since no such survey will be undertaken in England! In short, Lancey's formal address exposes the devious uses to which his language is being put as an imperial ploy to patronise, deceive and conquer.

But Friel's depiction of the adversary resists the temptation of crude caricature. If Lancey is cast as a cheerless servant of the Crown, his subordinate officer, Yolland, impresses immediately as a sensitive and romantic youth. Yolland is a 'soldier by accident' whose birthplace was only four miles away from that of William Wordsworth – a signal, as it transpires, of his own spiritual identity. He takes his note from the temper of his environment across the water: an imaginative disposition that enables him to empathize with this strange Gaelic culture into which he has been dispatched. Yolland is a hibernophile enamoured of the local people and perturbed by his inability to understand their language. Struggling for words, in a manner reminiscent of Sarah's stammering towards speech, Yolland's opening address is in stark contrast to that of his military superior. 'I – I – I've nothing to say – really ... I feel very foolish to – to – to be working here and not to speak your language ... I hope we're not too – too crude an intrusion on your lives.'

In all this, Owen plays a double language-game, commuting with ease between the two parties. But the ease is no more than apparent. In reality, Owen's linguistic duality entails a fundamental duplicity. He mistranslates Lancey's message, winnowing off its mercenary implications in order to make it more palatable for the locals. Yet at the same time Owen is sufficiently circumspect to withhold his real name (and by extension, *identity*) from the English officers, operating under the pseudonym of Rolland. Owen is both a mistranslator and a misnomer, double-timing, as it were, in his efforts to keep in with both sides of the colonial schism. In response to his brother's objection that there is nothing incorrect about the existing Gaelic place names, he declares – 'They're just going to be standardised ... where there's ambiguity, they'll be anglicised.' Owen's description of this linguistic transportation is in fact a self-description, accurately foreshadowing his own fate. Friel touches here, with characteristic irony, on the crisis of cultural ambiguity that hallmarks the modern Irish psyche. *Tradition* can only survive by being 'handed over' (*tradere*) from one historical generation to the next; but this 'handing over' frequently requires a *translation* or 'carrying over' (*transfere-translatum*) that alters the original order of meaning even as it releases it into a new historical duration. The survival of tradition by means of translation from one language to another can thus be construed as 'a subversion or perversion of tradition conceived as *continuity*'.[14] Owen, the privileged *translator* who 'double-crosses' over and back between the old Gaelic idioms and the new English ones, is also a *traducer* who trades in one linguistic currency for another.

In the second act of the play, Friel provides us with two dramatic instances of translation. The first is a translation of labour (between Owen and Yolland); the second a translation of love (between Yolland and Máire).

The act opens with Yolland and Owen, bent over a Name Book and large map. They are embarked upon their task of transposing the Gaelic toponymy of Baile Beag into an English alternative. The translation of names also involves a translation of namers – the roles of colonizer and colonized are reversed, as Yolland and Owen undergo an exchange of identity.

While Owen is patently engrossed by the mapping process, Yolland is lost in a world of dreams, savouring each Gaelic word upon his tongue, reluctant to 'traduce' it into its Anglo-Saxon equivalent. So that when Owen offers the practical suggestion of rendering, *Bun na hAbhann* (in Irish, mouth of the river) as *Burnfoot*, Yolland's reaction is one of protective deference towards the original: 'Let's leave it alone. There's no English equivalent for a sound like that.' But it is not just the sound that is at stake. It is the stored heritage of local history that each Gaelic name recollects and *secretes*. The translation of these place names closes off rather than discloses their mnemonic secrets, distorts their former meaning.

Yolland describes his first encounter with the Gaelic language as a quasi-mystical revelation. The linguistic divide is experienced by him as a threshold demarcating fundamentally heterogeneous modes of consciousness. He speaks of discovering a new continent of feeling, one belonging to 'a totally different order. I had moved into a consciousness that wasn't striving nor agitated, but at its ease and with its own conviction and assurance.'

But the threshold is also a frontier. It cannot be crossed with impunity, as Yolland will discover to his cost. Already he has intimations of the impenetrable barrier of words that no translation, however well-intentioned, can traverse. 'Even if I did speak Irish,' concedes Yolland, 'I'd always be an outsider here, wouldn't I? I may learn the password but the language of the tribe will always elude me, won't it? The private core will always be … hermetic, won't it?' Owen's reassuring rejoinder – 'you can learn to decode us' – has an ominous ring, its scarcely veiled sarcasm reflecting his private complicity with his own native tribe. In short, the commercial collusion between Planter and Gael cannot be immunized against the cultural-linguistic conflict that opposes them.

If language unites people by permitting communication, it divides them by cultivating the possibility of separate tribal identities. This paradox is a heritage of the *felix culpa* of our first parents: their fall from the Edenesque *logos* that enabled God and humans to speak with one voice. And this original sin of language – the sin of speaking in a multiplicity of conflicting tongues – finds its ultimate nemesis in the subsequent biblical account of the Tower of Babel.

(In *After Babel*, George Steiner writes of the literary history of translation as a series of attempts to build bridges between the disparate tongues of our fallen humanity. Friel has been deeply impressed by Steiner's disquisition and succeeds in *Translations* in dramatically extrapolating some of its scholarly insights. In an appendix to this study, we provide a short inventory of several key passages from *After Babel* that Friel has reworked in his own original idioms. What is of interest in this creative partnership of minds is the way in which Friel brilliantly contrives to refashion Steiner's academic research in a drama concretely situated in his own native cultural context. Friel's play serves in this respect as a fine example of how literary theory may be reclaimed by literature, of how criticism may be retranslated back into imaginative practice.)

Yolland cannot help recognizing that the whole business of toponymic translation constitutes an 'eviction of sorts': an 'erosion' of the traditional Gaelic pieties in the name of imperial progress. But Yolland's disapproval is counterbalanced by his naïve belief that there might exist an ideal system of translation where the obstacles thrown up by tribal dialects could be transcended. Yolland is hankering after a prelapsarian naming, similar to that of Adam when he named the animals, capable of achieving an exact correspondence between word and thing. When Owen finally confesses to Yolland that his real name is not *Rolland* but *Owen* – or better still *Oland* by way of a perfect compromise between the nominal differences of Irish (Owen) and English (Yolland) – they celebrate their newfound confraternity of naming:

> *Owen*: A christening! …
> *Yolland*: A thousand baptisms! Welcome to Eden!
> *Owen*: Eden's right! We name a thing and – bang! – it leaps into existence!
> *Yolland*: Each name a perfect equation with its roots.
> *Owen*: A perfect congruence with its reality. Take a drink.
> *Yolland*: Poteen – beautiful.
> *Owen*: Lying Anna's poteen.
> *Yolland*: Anna na mBreag's poteen … I'll decode it yet.

Once again, Friel reminds us that the magical equation of word and world is achieved by the power of a lie! The fact that Owen and Yolland consecrate their new transliterate unity (as *Oland*) with Anna's illusionist brew is itself a hint of the disillusioning reality to follow.

Friel juxtaposes this 'translation of labour' sequence between Owen and Yolland with a scene featuring a 'translation of love' between Yolland and Máire. In this second exchange Friel highlights the impossibility of attaining an ideal system of language capable of decoding semantic differences into some common transcultural identity. Yolland and Máire meet at the local dance. Ever since Yolland arrived in the village they have been admiring each other from a distance. Now at last together they try to transcend this distance, stealing away to the fields so that they might communicate their mutual love. But if their love is mutual their dialect is not. Máire begins by speaking Latin, which Yolland mistakes for Gaelic. Then she stammers forth the only three English words in her possession – water, fire, earth. But even though Yolland congratulates Máire on her 'perfect English', his lie of encouragement cannot alter the fact that they continually misunderstand each other's words. Finally they do appear to reach some level of communication by lovingly reciting to each other the litany of Gaelic place names. The irony is of course that this source of semantic agreement is precisely the issue that so divides their respective tribes. Their commonly uttered words still consign them to separate worlds; as Friel indicates in a textual note: 'Each now speaks almost to himself/herself'. (One recalls Frank's and Grace's equally discrepant invocation of place names in *Faith Healer*.) As each name is intoned by one lover and antiphonally echoed by the other, they move closer and embrace. This climactic touch serves as a leitmotif reiterating the opening exchange between Manus and Sarah. The order is reversed, however, in so far as speech now becomes touch whereas in the former scene touch had become speech.

When Yolland and Máire finally kiss, their moment of loving silence is no more than a provisional reprieve from the decree of language. Sarah enters and, shocked by what she witnesses, rushes off calling the name of Máire's suitor – 'Manus!' Thus in a twist of dramatic fortunes, Sarah's transition from silence to speech – her initiation into the naming process in the opening love scene between herself and Manus – becomes the condition for the betrayal of love.

According to the local code, Máire has been promised to Manus and this tacit tribal contract cannot be gainsaid or 'decoded' by an outsider – even in an act of love. As Jimmy Jack explains in his final speech, enunciating his own fictitious betrothal to the Goddess Athene: 'The word *exogamein* means to marry outside the tribe. And you don't cross those borders casually – both sides get very angry. Now, the problem is this: Is Athene sufficiently mortal or am I sufficiently godlike for the marriage to be acceptable to her people and to my people?' Whatever about transgressing the mythological boundaries between the human and the divine, the real boundaries between one human code and another cannot be ignored with impunity. Yolland is assassinated by the Donnelly twins – renegade pupils from the hedge school; and Captain Lancey promises retribution on the whole community: he orders their livestock to be slaughtered and their abodes levelled.

Friel's irony excels itself at this point: Lancey's threat to destroy the very locality that his own Ordnance Survey was proposing to civilize and advance renders the whole 'translation' process null and void. Nominal eviction has been replaced by its literal equivalent. This reversal of plot also extends to a reversal of character. Summoned before a local gathering, Owen is now compelled to give a literal translation of Lancey's punitive intentions, his compromising role as go-between now made embarrassingly plain. For the dubious benefit of his own tribe, Owen is forced to *retranslate* Lancey's English rendition of the names of the local villages to be destroyed back into their Gaelic originals. Owen's own labour of words has backfired; he is hoist with his own petard.

Máire also becomes a victim of this reverse play of language. Exposed in the abrupt polarization of the two rival tribes, she can no longer feel at home in her own community and yet has no other home to go to now that Yolland is dead. Employing again his dramatic technique of reverse repetition, Friel reinvokes the idiom of mapping to emphasize Máire's dilemma. Tracing out an imaginary map on that very spot on the hedge school floor where Owen's Ordnance Survey map had been spread, she lists off the place names of Yolland's native Norfolk which he had taught her to recite during their love-duet the previous night – Winfarthing, Barton, Bendish, Saxingham, etc. 'Nice sounds,' she muses, as Yolland had done before her with reference to Gaelic names, 'just like Jimmy Jack reciting Homer.' But there is a fundamental difference between the recitation of Jimmy Jack and that of Máire and Yolland. Since the Greeks had no historic quarrel with the Gaels their two tongues could peaceably conjugate in a way that English and Gaelic cannot. In one particularly striking moment, Máire recalls that Yolland's parting message to her was in fact a mistranslation: 'He tried to speak in Irish, he said – "I'll see you yesterday" – he meant to say, "I'll see you tomorrow".' This mistranslation is a poignant signal of the fact that in the colonial conflict between England and Ireland the time was out of joint. In such a context, linguistic discrepancies are the inevitable consequence of historical ones.

These reversals of *plot*, *persona* and *time* are reinforced by a more generalized reversal of *perception*. The disarticulation of language brought about by the various abortive attempts at translation also expresses itself at the level of the characters' distorted perceptions of the world about them. The last scene of the play is littered with misidentifications, on a par with the most convoluted comedies of Wilde or Shakespeare. Manus, who flees to Mayo, is mistaken for the assassins (the Donnellys); the fumes from the burning army tents are mistaken for the sweet smell of potato blight; Doalty is mistaken for the arsonist; a bacon-curing schoolmaster from Cork is mistaken for the village schoolmaster, Hugh – the national school replacing the old hedge school; and the anglicized Owen is mistaken for (in the sense of taking over from) his inveterately Gaelic brother, Manus, as faithful son to their father, Hugh.

All these instances of displacement consolidate Friel's message about the mistaken substitution of Irish by English. But Friel, like Hugh, recognizes that this mistake is an irreversible, if regrettable, inevitability of history. 'We like to think we endure around truths immemorially posited,' Hugh explains with rueful wisdom, 'but we remember that words are signals, counters. They are not immortal. And it can happen … that a civilisation can be imprisoned in a linguistic contour which no longer matches the landscape of … fact.' The rich mytho-poetic resources of the Gaelic tongue, Hugh adds, were themselves a response to the painful historical circumstances that conditioned its development: 'Yes, it is a rich language ... full of mythologies of fantasy and hope and self-deception – a syntax opulent with tomorrows. It is our response to mud cabins and a diet of potatoes; our only method of replying to ... inevitabilities.' Thus in stoical acknowledgment that what is done cannot be undone, Hugh determines to make a virtue of necessity by creatively refashioning the English language so as to make sense of the new landscape of historical fact. At one point Owen tries to revoke the repercussions of translation, dismissing the whole sorry business as '*my* mistake – nothing to do with us'. But Hugh has had enough of self-deception. Pointing to the Name Book, he counsels his community to reclaim in and through the English language that which has been lost to it. 'We must learn those new names,' he soberly challenges, 'we must learn to make them our own, we must make them our new home.'

If history has deprived the Irish of their native tongue, this will not prevent them from reinterpreting their identity in a new tongue. Speaking in his capacity as poet, Hugh bequeaths to his community a legacy of challenge, the challenge of an Irish literature written in English, the challenge to persist in an aesthetic reconquest of that cultural self-image vanquished by the *empirical* fact of colonization. We the audience recognize of course that the entire modern tradition of Irish writers of English – extending from Synge, Yeats and Joyce to Friel himself – has emerged in response to just this challenge. We know that for the Irish writer this is his *heritage now*. The fatality of dispossession has not condemned the Irish imagination to dumb show. Our best writers have masterfully reworked their adopted language and also the images of their cultural past. Indeed *Translations* is itself a paramount example. Hugh outlines a blueprint for this poetic retrieval of lost ground when he appeals for a discrimination between the laws of history and imagination, or if you wish between the laws of empirical necessity and cultural freedom. 'It is not,' he insists, 'the *facts* of history, that shape us, but *images* of the past embodied in language ... We must never cease renewing those images; because once we do, we fossilise.' Jimmy Jack, the otherworldly poet of the old order, has fossilized precisely because he was unable to make that discrimination. The poets of the new order cannot afford the luxury of such indifference.

But Hugh's lesson in aesthetics also serves as a history lesson. Friel would seem to be cautioning us against the temptation of becoming political prisoners to historical fact. 'To remember everything is a form of madness', Hugh warns, implying a preference for a more discerning use of memory capable of distinguishing between the past that liquidates by a narrow obsession with revenge, and the past that liberates into new possibilities of recollection. Recalling the rebel uprising of 1798 when himself and Jimmy went forth to battle, with pikes in their hands and Virgil in their pockets, Hugh confesses that after several miles of marching they got drunk in a pub before staggering unheroically home. He admits to the feeling of 'perception heightened … and consciousness accelerated' that the prospect of violence induced in them. But in a precise inversion of Frank's apocalyptic vision at the end of *Faith Healer*, Friel shows Hugh opting for an alternative homecoming, an option for a more domestic and poetic form of survival. 'Our *pietas* was for older, quieter things,' Hugh recounts, 'the *desiderium nostrorum* – the need for our own.' If Frank suffers the capitulation of words to violence, Hugh averts violence in the name of the recreative power of words.

To rephrase this alternative in terms of a Yeatsian parallel, we might say that while *Faith Healer* mirrored the apocalyptic tones of 'Ben Bulben', *Translations* moves closer to the ancestral solace of *A Dialogue of Self and Soul*:

> Why should the imagination of a man
> Long past his prime remember things that are
> Emblematic of love and war?
> Think of ancestral night that can …
> Deliver from the crime of death and birth.

A cultural fidelity to the *images* of the past, Friel seems to suggest, is not necessarily reducible to the *facts* of the past. There may be other, more complicated, ways of recovering what has been lost and settling one's score with history. One of these ways is the poetic possibility of forging a new language, of recreating a new home. Any attempt at such a cultural transition is, of course, fraught with risk and danger: the risk of losing everything, the danger of self-annihilation. But given the ominous alternatives, it may be a risk worth taking. Perhaps this is why Hugh agrees at the end of the play to teach Máire English. He concedes the necessity for change, telling Máire that the word 'always' is a silly one. But Hugh cannot guarantee that her acquisition of the art of translation will permit her to transport the secret heritage of the old culture into the new. His parting verdict promises neither too little nor too much. 'I will provide you with the available words and the available grammar,' he assures Máire, 'but will that help you to interpret between privacies? I have no idea.'

IV. The Communication Cord

The Communication Cord is in many respects the logical sequel to *Translations*. Friel has made plain his wish that the two plays be considered 'in tandem',[15] as consecutive forays into the border-lands of our language culture.

If *Translations* set out to chart the transition of a language from the mythological past to the pragmatic present, *The Communication Cord* operates in reverse order: it portrays the attempt to retrace language from contemporary contingency back to pristine ancestry. Both plays conspire to present us with a genealogy of the process of human speech, the ways in which we use words to progress or regress in history, to find or lose ourselves, to confuse or to converse. The fact that the former play is composed in *tragic* tones, while the latter is written as a *farce*, is in itself an indicator of Friel's tragic-comic realization that there is no going back on history; that the best that can be achieved is a playful deconstruction and reconstruction of words in the hope that new modes of communication may become possible.

Both plays situate the conflict of language models in the specific context of Irish culture. *Translations* deals with pre-Famine Ireland bracing itself for the final translation of Gaelic into English. *The Communication Cord* takes up the story more than a century later. It shows us modern Ireland taking stock of its linguistic identity and attempting to recover the ancient pieties of its pre-famine heritage. While one play features the old language looking forward to its ominous future, the other features the new language looking back to its dispossessed origins.

The scene of the action in *The Communication Cord* – a 'restored' thatched cottage in Ballybeg – is an inverted replica of the 'condemned' schoolhouse of Baile Beag. In similar fashion, Tim Gallagher, the central character of the play – a university lecturer in linguistics preparing a Ph.D. on communication – serves as a mirror-image of his ancestral prototype, Hugh. Both are displaced scholars without tenure; both teach that the transmission of communal wisdom cannot be divorced from the ontological power of language. In fact, Tim is attempting to prove what was still self-evident for Hugh: that words that function as positivistic units or linguistic maps based on agreed codes are, at root, derived and often distorted forms of ontological 'response cries'. To put it in Heidegger's terms, Tim is resolved to return from the language of objects and representation (Owen's modern legacy) to the ultimate origin of words in the interiority of the heart's space (Hugh's lost legacy).

The ersatz character of the refurbished cottage betokens the futility of any literal quest for the grail of a vanished past. Adorned with the antiquarian accoutrements of churn, creel, crook, hanging pot, thatched roof and open hearth, the cottage is described by Friel in a stage note as 'false ... too pat ... too authentic'. It is, in short, an artificial reproduction, a holiday home of today counterfeiting the real home of yesterday. Moreover, Friel's scenario is perhaps also parodying the folksy rural Romanticism of the Abbey tradition.

This play about communication begins, significantly, with a failure of communication. Tim is saying that the door to the cottage is open, while Jack McNeilis, his friend, misunderstands him to say that it is locked. From the outset their language is at cross purposes. If Owen was Manus's alter-ego in *Translations*, Jack is Tim's. Jack is a successful and self-assured barrister from Dublin. He possesses all those qualities of the modern Irish bourgeoisie which Tim lacks –

efficiency, sexual confidence and above all (since language remains the key) a remarkable felicity with conversational repartee.

Jack's *nouveau-riche* family bought the cottage in Ballybeg and revamped its rustic charms in order to experience the 'soul and authenticity of the place'. Jack's description of this revivalist return to the land is presented as a saucy parody of Hugh's *pietas*. 'Everybody's grandmother was reared in a house like this', Jack quips, claiming it to be the 'ancestral seat of the McNeilis dynasty, restored with love and dedication, absolutely authentic in every last detail … This is where we all come from. This is our first cathedral. This shaped our soul. This determined our first pieties. Yes. Have reverence for this place.' Jack's way of revering his 'father's house' is, ironically, to recite a tedious inventory or map of all the objects contained in the cottage (fireplace, pot-iron, tongs, etc.). He employs naming according to the model of utilitarian representation in order to classify each thing as a use-item. For Jack, language is not a house of being but a filing cabinet of objects.

But if Jack and Tim's ultimate concern is with words, their ostensible concern is with women. They have come to the cottage for the purpose of amorous exchange – Tim with the girl of his fancy, Susan; Jack with his latest catch, Ivette Giroux from the French Embassy in Dublin. When Tim tries to express genuine reservations about his feelings for Susan, Jack reassures him that it's a 'perfect match'. He means of course a perfect *commercial* match: 'you're ugly and penniless, she's pretty and rich'. One of the central themes of the play is thus discreetly announced – the conflict between Tim's view of communication as an ontological *response cry* and Jack's view of communication as a *commercial contract*.

Friel has Tim expound his linguistic thesis in the opening act of the play, thereby establishing the conceptual co-ordinates for the subsequent unfolding of the plot. Tim argues that language operates on two levels – as *information* and as *conversation*. At the first level, words function as messengers transmitting information from a speaker to a listener. Language becomes a process of encoding and decoding messages. Where a common code exists messages can be exchanged, where not there is misunderstanding. Echoing the terms of Lévi-Strauss, Tim explains that 'all social behaviour, the entire social order, depends on communicational structures, on words mutually agreed on and mutually understood. Without that agreement, without that shared code, you have chaos.' It is surely no coincidence that the example Tim chooses to illustrate his point is the absence of a common code of *translation* between two speakers of different languages.

At the second and more fundamental level, language transcends its pragmatic function as a formal transmission of information and seeks a more profound sharing of interpersonal experience: 'You desire to share my experience – and because of that desire our exchange is immediately lifted out of the realm of mere exchange of basic messages and aspires to something higher, something much more important – *conversation* … a response cry!' Response cries bespeak the existential interiority of the heart's space. They are by definition 'involuntary', Tim observes, in that they forgo all strategies of wilful manipulation or commerce. But the difficulty is how to discriminate between genuine response cries that speak straight from the heart and the mere pretence at such speech. How is language to escape from the insincerity of role-playing (or as Wittgenstein would put it, the ploys of 'language games')? Tim's inability to resolve this dilemma is not only the reason why he cannot complete his thesis or decide whom he truly loves; it is the very *raison d'être* for the play itself. It is the importance of being earnest all over again. Indeed Friel's debt to Wilde's comic genius is perhaps nowhere more evident than in *The Communication Cord*.

The entire action of the play may be seen as an experimental testing of Tim's hypothesis of reconnecting the modern positivistic model of language to its ontological origins. The plot unfolds accordingly as a farcical rewind of *Translations*.

Tim is not only a recast of Hugh but also of Manus, the schoolmaster's sincere and penurious son. He is, as Jack jibes, 'worthy and penniless – all nobility and no nous'. Just as Manus remained implacably opposed to Owen's translation project, so too Tim denounces Jack's abuse of language as a transmission of financial and erotic messages as 'damned perfidious'. Like Owen, Jack is a dealer in identities, mediating between the cunning locals (he recognizes his neighbour Nora Dan to be a 'quintessential noble peasant – obsessed with curiosity, greed and envy') and the mercenary outsiders (Senator Donovan from Dublin and the German blow-in eager to purchase a property in the locality – Barney the Banks). Jack is at once adept in the communal game of *pietas* – as when, in mock-Heideggerean fashion, he goes to 'the well for a bucket of the purest of pure spring water' – and a master of modern pragmatism. The *map* of translation is replaced here by the *watch* of time-keeping: the new symbol of progress. Appropriately, Jack can mastermind the plot by virtue of the expert timing of his watch, whereas Tim, whose watch keeps stopping, has no control whatsoever over all the comings and goings.

Other characters in the play may also be seen as comic reincarnations of the *dramatis personae* in *Translations*. Claire, Tim's former girlfriend and the true love of his heart, recalls both Sarah and Máire. She is described as 'open and humorous' and is bravely determined to communicate her love to Tim, come what may. The German prospector of property recalls the Royal Engineers. And Nora Dan recalls her eponymous forebear who left the hedge school as soon as she had learnt her name. The modern day Nora Dan, in a pastiche of the patrilinear nomenclature practised in *Translations*, explains her double name to Tim as follows: 'I get the Dan from my father – that's the queer way we have of naming people around here.' Nora Dan is a peasant who, Friel tells us, 'likes to present herself as a peasant'. She is a stage Irish-woman who has perfected her stagecraft.

Lastly, Senator Donovan is cast as a sort of modern antitype of Jimmy Jack. He is an 'amateur antiquarian', a self-made man full of his own importance as both doctor and politician, who extols the 'absolute verity' of the cottage. Donovan is a caricature of all that is sentimental and sententious in the modern bourgeois Republic. He represents cultural revivalism at its worst. His speeches are reeled off like fatuous travesties of Hugh's and Jimmy's *desiderium nostrorum* – the sacramental longing for older, quieter things. Arriving in Ballybeg he pretentiously muses: 'This silence, this peace, the restorative power of the landscape … this speaks to me, this whispers to me … and despite the market place, all the years of trafficking in politics and medicine, a small voice within me still knows the *responses* … This is the touchstone … the apotheosis.'

Donovan's version of the response cry traduces Tim's own prediction of this term. And his interpretation of love play with pretty women, as another means of moving from word representation to wordless response, is a further falsification of Tim's real meaning. 'When you're as young and as beautiful as Madame Giroux,' opines the lusty Senator, 'language doesn't matter does it? Words are superfluous aren't they?' The radical difference between Tim's and Donovan's respective attitudes to language becomes clear in their dramatic exchanges. While Donovan pursues his pseudo-cultural cant about getting back 'to the true centre' of spiritual renewal in the heart of rural Ireland, Tim confesses that he 'hates all it represents'. Similarly though Donovan tries to negotiate the sale of the cottage with Tim (mistaking him for the owner), Tim simply cannot make the cap of commercial proprietor fit. He cannot bring himself to conform to the language-game of mercantile deceit.

Donovan's misidentification of Tim, a symptom of his misuse of language, is multiplied in the countless mistaken identities of the other characters: Claire is mistaken for Ivette; Donovan for Dr Bollacks; Barney the Banks for Jack and for a fictitious wife-beater; Nora Dan for a local scrambling champion, and so on. Friel seems to be suggesting that his confusion of each character with the other is a logical consequence of the historical translation, documented in *Translations*, of the native Irish language and culture into the contemporary babel of the International European Community (Donovan commutes between Dublin and Brussels as an EC Senator). This mix-up of cultural and linguistic identities (Irish, English, German, French) epitomizes the absence of a shared code of communication that characterizes life in *Ballybeg* one hundred and fifty years after its translation from *Baile Beag*.

While exploiting to the full the conveniences of modern multinational society, Donovan still clings to the illusion that nothing has changed, that Romantic Ireland is alive and well in a restored Donegal cottage waiting to be purchased by the highest bidder. In other words, Donovan would have it both ways. He is hypocrisy incarnate, a symbol of the very *discontinuity* in Irish cultural history that he refuses to acknowledge. But Donovan's charade of *pietas* is finally scotched when, invoking the shibboleth of Ireland as the 'woman with two cows', he actually chains himself to an antique cow harness in the cottage and is unable to extricate himself. The myth becomes literal. As his rantings become more desperate, the entire stage is plunged into darkness. All the characters lose their bearings and stagger about in farcical mimicry of the cultural-linguistic disorientation that has befallen them.

When the light returns the truth begins to dawn; the aliases are de-bunked and the artifices of the confounding language-games exposed. This enlightenment of consciousness is nowhere more evident than in the concluding love scene between Tim and Claire. Their masks removed and their feelings made plain, the lovers move towards the most authentic form of language – the response cry of silence. As Tim explains: 'Maybe the units of communication don't matter that much ... We're conversing now but we're not exchanging units ... I'm not too sure what I'm saying ... Maybe the message doesn't matter at all then ... Maybe silence is the perfect language.' The positivist model of communication as the circulation of word-units in the symbolic form of *women* (Susan/Ivette/Claire) or *commodities* (Donovan, Barney, Jack and Nora Dan are all engaged in negotiations for the purchase of the cottage) is shown to be hopelessly inadequate. The employment of language for the exchange of women and property between the different individuals or tribes in the play (Irish, German and French), does not produce either communication or community (see Appendix C). The ontological secrets of the heart's space cannot, Tim and Claire discover, be disclosed through the verbal exchange of informational units, but only through 'reverberations' occasioned by a genuine 'response' of feeling. Responding to Claire's response cry – 'Kiss me' – Tim embraces her. As he does so, the lovers lean against the fragile upright beam of the cottage causing it to collapse around them in a flurry of apocalyptic chaos. The local tower of babel is demolished in one loving stroke. And even Jack, the wizard of word-play, is compelled to resort to a response cry – 'O my God'.

Conclusion

What do Friel's plays say about language? More specifically, what do they tell us about their author's attitude or contribution to the native Irish tradition of verbal theatre? Are Friel's plays trojan horses in the citadel of this tradition, contesting its conventions of storytelling from within and pointing towards the possibility of more immediate, non-verbal modes of expression? Are the apocalyptic endings to his language plays symptoms of a crisis of faith in the power of words? Does Friel subscribe in the final analysis to a theatre of the Word or to a theatre of the Senses?

This formulation of the question is perhaps inadequate. Friel's work ultimately resists the facility of such an either/or. The conclusion to *The Communication Cord* is, for instance, disquietingly equivocal. The hint of some salvation through silence (recalling Heidegger's notion of a mystical 'tolling of silence' at the heart of language) is counteracted by the literal unleashing of darkness and destruction. While the abandonment of speech spells loving communion for Tim and Claire, it spells the collapse of the community as a whole. Silence is a double-edged sword heralding *both* the beginning of love and the end of society. While the departure from language may well lead to love, it may equally lead to violence. So Friel's ontological optimism with regard to silence as the 'perfect language' appears to go hand in hand with a pessimistic, or at least sceptical, appraisal of its socio-historical implications. The term 'cord' itself conveys this double sense of a bond and an alarm signal.

Seen in conjunction with *Translations*, the ambiguity of Friel's conclusion becomes even more explicit. If *Translations* tended to mythologize language, *The Communication Cord* demythologizes it. While the former showed how language once operated in terms of a cultural rootedness and centredness, the latter de-centres all easy assumptions about the retrieval of lost origins. One displays the original fidelity of language to a timeless ontological piety of *nature*; the other affirms the irreversibility of *history* as an alienation from the natural pre-history of words: and this very affirmation exposes the impotence of language to save a community from the corrosive effects of time, from the mixed blessings of modern progress.

Seamus Deane, one of the directors of Friel's Field Day Theatre Company, states this dilemma in his preface to *The Communication Cord*, 'Nostalgia for the lost native culture – so potent and plaintive in *Translations*', writes Deane,

> appears ludicrous and sham … Real communication has begun to disappear the moment you begin to isolate it as a problem and give degrees in it. Friel has presented us here with the vacuous world of a dying culture. The roof is coming in on our heads … There is little or no possibility of inwardness, of dwelling in rather than on history.

Situating this crisis of language in the more specific context of Irish cultural history, Deane adds:

> Irish discourse, especially literary discourse, is ready to invoke history but reluctant to come to terms with it … So we manage to think of our great writers as explorers of *nature*, as people who successfully fled the historical nightmare and reintroduced us to the daily nature we all share, yet this feeling is itself historically determined. A colony always wants to escape from history. It longs for its own authenticity, the element it had before history came to disfigure it.

By refusing to flee from history and from its complex rapport with language, Friel's drama is political; but in a sense radically opposed to political propaganda. Friel's drama is political in the manner in which it protests against the abuse of language by covert political ideologies. Moreover, Friel's insistence that *Translations* and *The Communication Cord* be considered 'in tandem', suggests that the respective claims of mythologization and demythologization, of the old Gaelic-classical culture and the emerging Hiberno-English culture, are *both* valid. The tension between their different approaches to language is in itself creative. (It has certainly proved conducive to some of Friel's finest dramatic work.) It is perhaps in this context that we should read Hugh's remark that 'confusion is not an ignoble condition!'

But the implications of this dialectic extend even further, calling into question the received notions of what 'culture' actually means. Friel refuses to accept the conventional policy of treating the cultural and the socio-historical as entirely separate spheres of discourse. His language plays represent a powerful evocation of the ways in which our cultural use of words determines our society and is determined by it in turn. Friel regards culture, in F.S.L. Lyons's phrase, as 'everything from the furniture in men's kitchens to the furniture in their minds'. Hence Field Day's determination to foster a new dialectical rapport between language and history. Such a dialectic, if successful, might not only project new possibilities for the future development of Irish culture, but might also liberate the dramatic tradition of storytelling from its more encrusted orthodox moulds. The fact that the six directors of Field Day include both poets (Seamus Deane, Seamus Heaney, Tom Paulin) and non-poets (Stephen Rea, a performer, and David Hammond, a musician) may well be an indication of Friel's own desire, as dramatist, to combine both the verbal and non-verbal resources of his art. As the prefatory note to *The Communication Cord* intimates:

> if a congealed idea of theatre can be broken then the audience which experiences this break would be the more open to the modification of other established forms. Almost everything which we believe to be natural or native is in fact historical; more precisely, is a historical fiction. If Field Day can breed a new fiction of theatre, or of any other area, which is sufficiently successful to be believed in as though it were natural and an outgrowth of the past, then it will have succeeded. At the moment, it is six characters in search of a story that can be believed.

Friel, like Christy Mahon in *The Playboy*, is asking his audience to make his fiction true. He is asking that the promise of Field Day be made real by the power of a lie. Unlike Christy, however, and the Irish dramatic movement that produced him, Friel holds out the possibility of a new kind of storytelling, one more cognizant of history and more attentive to those forms of expression that reach beyond the word.

Appendix A: The Native Tradition of Verbal Theatre

In addition to our analysis of Friel's language plays it might be useful i) to rehearse the main lines of argument concerning the 'verbal' character of traditional Irish drama and ii) to enumerate, in this light, some major objections to Friel's language plays on the grounds that his supposedly 'nationalist' bias distorts the relationship between historical facts and dramatic fiction.

The indigenous movement of verbal theatre boasts an august lineage extending from Goldsmith, Wilde, Shaw, Synge, Yeats and O'Casey to such contemporary dramatists as Murphy, Kilroy, Leonard and Friel. All of these authors share a common concern with the play of language; they have created plays where words tend to predetermine character, action and plot. Oscar Wilde stated his own commitment to language where he wrote:

> It is very much more difficult to talk about a thing than to do it.
> There is no mode of action, no form of emotion that we do not
> share with the lower animals. It is only by language that we rise
> above them ... (Action) is the last recourse of those who know not
> how to dream.[16]

Synge confirmed this predilection for words when he argued that 'in a good play every speech should be as fully flavoured as a nut or an apple'. The *Playboy* proves his point. This drama is a powerful example of native language resources brought to full fruition in the speeches of its characters. But it is a language play in another sense also. The *Playboy* is a drama about the power of words to transform oneself and one's world. 'By the power of a lie' – that is, by his fantastic story of fictional parricide – Christy Mahon ceases to be a 'stupid lout' subservient to his tyrannical father and becomes instead the 'only playboy of the western world'. Deploying words in an imaginative way Christy persuades himself and others to believe in his fiction; and the fiction recreates reality according to its own image. By playing out his fantasy of heroic rebel, Christy actually *becomes* a great lover and a great athlete. When his father eventually intrudes upon the scene, the verbal fiction is momentarily shattered. Christy is accused by Pegeen Mike of being a fake who in reality possesses 'no savagery or fine words in him at all'. The accusation is highly significant for it epitomizes Pegeen's own failure of imaginative nerve before the discrepancy between word and world. 'A strange man is a marvel with his mighty talk', says Pegeen, 'but there's a great gap between a gallous story and a dirty deed.'

Christy resists such scepticism however. His fall from grace is no more than provisional. Tenaciously reaffirming the triumph of fiction over fact, he proclaims himself a hero in spite of Pegeen's rebuke. 'You've turned me into a likely gaffer in the end of all,' he retorts. Father and son set off on the roads to have 'great times ... *telling stories* of the villany of Mayo and the fools is here.' The marvel of 'mighty talk' vanquishes the daily treadmill of mediocrity. And Pegeen is compelled to acknowledge that what she has lost is not the 'small, low fellow, dark and dirty' that Christy *was*, but the playboy of the western world he has *become* through the power of a lie.

Synge's portrayal of the transfiguring power of the word is representative of the mainstream of the Irish dramatic movement. In a study entitled 'Anglo-Irish Playwrights and the Comic Tradition', Tom Kilroy, another Irish dramatist of the verbal school, argues that the indigenous fascination with the play of language is a direct response to the Anglo-Irish experience of a displaced or de-centred cultural identity. Writing of Goldsmith, one of the inaugurators of the native dramatic tradition, Kilroy remarks that his works are informed by an interplay between two contrasting *styles* of language: a 'low' style imbued with natural integrity and imaginative feeling and a 'high' style marked by pretentiousness, hypocrisy and snobbery. The tension between these opposing cultures of language provides his plays with their singular verbal intensity. Goldsmith, he concludes, 'had an acute ear for the way in which language betrays a distortion of personality and a benevolent discernment of how metropolitan culture produces such artificiality. The perspective from which he perceived this is that of a figure off-centre, personally awkward in a society which measured correct bearing with calibrated accuracy, feckless in a society dedicated to thrift and efficiency.'[17]

In recent decades there have been several attempts to challenge the primacy of verbal theatre in Ireland. Tom Mac Intyre's experiments with mime, dance and gesture in *Doobally/Blackway, The Great Hunger, The Bearded Lady, Rise up Lovely Sweeney* and *Dance for Your Daddy*, are, in large part, motivated by the conviction that the Irish preoccupation with verbal theatre has neglected the more fundamental aspects of dramatic art – namely the rituality of performance and the carnal immediacy of movement. Mac Intyre believes that these latter qualities provide better means of expressing the root dimensions of human emotion – the subterranean 'black way' of our proverbial and preconscious experience. He describes his theatre as 'collaborative, pictorial and gestural' in defiance of the verbal tradition. 'We are not interested', states Mac Intyre apropos of *Rise up Lovely Sweeney*, 'in the theatre of discourse but in the theatre of experience. We're not putting arguments to the viewer but events that are highly charged and which we ask viewers to receive on terms that they themselves largely create.'[18]

This plea for a more *embodied* form of drama gained considerable momentum in Ireland with the emergence of performance art and such experimental theatre groups as Red Rex, Operating Theatre and The Dublin Mime Company. These groups were committed to a drama of the senses. As Roger Doyle explained with respect to the work of Operating Theatre: 'Theatre is freeing itself from the bondage of the word ... The communication is now in the actors not in the words they speak. The idea is to bring visual life back into the theatre. Theatre does not have to be a written medium. Too often the word is mistaken for the actor. This creates a block in the audience's perception of the performance. There has been too much emphasis on declaiming lines and not enough on the rhythm of word sounds.' Olwen Fouere, another member of this group, explains their innovatory project as follows: 'Words may even distract from the inner life of the show ... They are such a limited way of communicating. They reach an audience only through the intellect. The body and the voice *without any words* have much more potency on stage.'[19] It is surely significant that this alternative model advanced by Operating Theatre draws from the combined resources of a visual artist (Coleman), an actress (Fouere) and a musician (Doyle).

This challenge to the hegemony of verbal theatre in Ireland is perhaps most cogently formulated by David McKenna, the director and critic, in a manifesto entitled *The Word and the Flesh – A New View of Theatre as Performance*. He opens with this salvo: 'Irish theatre began with the word, the word, unfortunately, of a Great Poet (W.B. Yeats) and it has been dominated by the word ever since.'[20] McKenna decries the fact that in Ireland the writer has invariably been considered the 'unique starting point of the process' of drama. This prejudice, he submits, has been the major cause of the 'lack of attention paid to the performer in Irish theatre, an oversight which has produced a stagnant and repetitive relationship between actor and audience.' Adverting to the ways in which theatre has been developing internationally in terms of experimental performance – largely due to the pioneering work of Stanislavsky, Artaud, Piscator, Brecht and Brook – the author regrets that 'in Ireland we have been *telling stories*'. McKenna attributes much of the blame to Yeats's underestimation of the pre-verbal 'dionysian spirit' and 'sensual exchange', which he believes are the very flesh and blood of powerful drama. As one of the most decisive and formative influences on modern Irish theatre, Yeats 'left the field to the story-tellers. These people produced charming tales, mostly of rural life, ranging from the whimsical and commercial to the magical and superstitious. The Abbey Theatre was their hearth ...' The manifesto concludes by indicting the Abbey's legacy of 'processing well-spoken automatons ... shrouded, hobbled, muffled, and untrained in those gestures which create a tangible dramatic world'. (To be fair to Yeats, however, it must also be remembered that he was not only a poet of words but an experimental playwright whose Noh plays introduced dance, ritual, music and gesture into Irish drama).

While Friel's language plays are not explicitly identified by these critics, they are exemplary instances of verbal theatre – albeit in a high self-questioning mode.

Appendix B: Friel and Nationalism

Considerable controversy has surrounded the political implications of Friel's concern with cultural identity. This is well illustrated in the following description of *Translations* by the critic Brian McEvera: 'I find *Translations* [and to a certain extent the stance of *Field Day*] deeply worrying ... By the time the play had ended I was having doubts. I felt manipulated. Obviously, I sensed that the play was lop-sided, that traditional nationalist myths were being given credence. I was uneasy at the whole notion of the shift from Irish to English as a form of cultural suppression ... The play actually shores up a dangerous myth – that of cultural dispossession by the British – rather than what I take to be the historical actuality, the abandonment of the language (by the Irish people themselves) ... Friel's work is directly political in its implications; and its "awareness" is one-sided. The "shape" observed is a nationalist one – and a limited partial view of nationalism at that.' McEvera ends his critique by declaring his hope that either 'the more overt political element will disappear from [Friel's] work', or else that he will 'confront directly in his work those aspects of nationalist violence which have so far been submerged'.[21] Edna Longley makes a similar point when she accuses Friel and his Field Day group of repeddling nationalist myths of a pre-lapsarian past destroyed by British colonialism. 'Does *Translations* itself renew "images of the past", or does it recycle a familiar perspective?' she asks. Her answer: 'The play does not so much examine myths of dispossession and oppression as repeat them.'[22] Citing the particular moment in *Translations* when the soldier/survey officers use unhistorical bayonets after Lieutenant Yolland is murdered, Longley argues that Friel's real, though unacknowledged, subject is 'the behaviour of British troops in the Catholic ghettos of Belfast and Derry during the nineteen-seventies'. And she goes on to observe that at the end of the play Owen, who has 'collaborated' with the survey, reverts to potentially violent tribal loyalty. Rather than confronting the contemporary realities of Northern Irish politics, Friel and Field Day are charged with chasing the dream of a political impossibility: the return to 'a mythic landscape of beauty and plenitude that is pre-Partition, pre-Civil War, pre-famine, pre-plantation and pre-Tudor'.[23] Longley concludes that Friel's drama has become fossilized because 'he explores the ethos of a particular community exclusively in relation to British dominion over the native Irish. No perspective discriminates between past and present, nineteenth-century Ireland and twentieth-century Northern Ireland. There is simply equation ... *Translations* refurbishes an old myth.'[24]

These objections to the political content of Friel's plays are frequently related to the charge that he abuses the criteria of historical truth and fails, for ideological reasons, to observe the way things really were – the *facts*. In a *Crane Bag* exchange between Friel and Professor J.H. Andrews, author of a scholarly book on the Ordnance Survey of Ireland, entitled *A Paper Landscape* (which by Friel's own admission was a major source of inspiration for *Translations*), Andrews isolates some empirical inaccuracies in the play. These range from Friel's anachronistic reading of the nineteenth-century Ordnance Survey in terms of a Cromwellian policy of plantation, to more particular details such as the survey officers prodding the ground with bayonets which they were not in fact allowed to possess.[25]

These objections to Friel's drama are, I believe, largely beside the point. The charges of political nationalism and historical inaccuracy mistake the primary intent of Friel's work by reading it as a sociological tract. The author's primary intent, as I hope to have shown, is to dramatically interrogate the *crisis of language* as a medium of *communication* and *identity* – a crisis that is an indispensable ingredient of contemporary Irish culture. Moreover, Friel's preoccupation with language does not simply conform to the mainstream Irish tradition of verbal 'storytelling' (See Appendix A), but puts this very tradition into question by high-lighting the *problematic* functioning of language itself.

Appendix C: The Conflict of Language Models (Ontology versus Positivism)

Friel's work explores two basic linguistic models – one ontological, the other positivistic. The former treats language as a house of Being; the latter treats it as a mechanical apparatus for the representation of objects.

As we had occasion to remark above, Friel's ontological approach to language is, philosophically speaking, akin to that of Heidegger. Here language is celebrated as a way to truth in the Greek sense of the term, *a-letheia*, meaning un-forgetfulness, un-concealing, disclosure. Language tells us the truth by virtue of its capacity to unlock the secret privacies of our historical Being (the 'interiority of the heart's space'). In *Translations* Friel identifies this ontological vocation of the Word with the Gaelic and classical languages. It manifests itself in the local community's use of naming to release the secret of their psychic and historical landscape or in Hugh's excavations of Latin and Greek etymologies. Friel dramatizes Heidegger's claim that language is the house of Being, not only in so far as it permits us to dwell poetically in our world but also in that it grants us the power to recollect our past, to divine our forgotten origins. (It is perhaps not insignificant that Friel's collection of stories published just two years after *Translations* was called *The Diviner*.) Language houses Being by recalling things from their past oblivion, thus attuning us once again to our lost identities, enabling us to re-member (*an-denken*) our alienated, dismembered selves. Poetic words are not, Heidegger teaches us, 'copies and imitations'; they are 'imaginings that are visible inclusions of the alien in the sign of the familiar'.[26]

Friel opposes this ontological model of language to the positivist use of words as agents of pragmatic progress. This alternative positivist model is perhaps most closely associated with the philosophy of British Empiricism, which served in recent centuries as the ideological mainstay of British colonialism; though it has found a more contemporary ally in the scientific structuralism of Lévi-Strauss and others. Positivism maintains that words are mechanically given (*positum*) – objects in a world of similar objects. They are eminently unmysterious entities to be used as instruments for the representation, mapping or classification of reality. And the reductionist goal of positivism is to produce an exact decoding of the world by establishing a one-to-one correlation between *words* and the *facts* of empirical experience. Language is thus reduced to a utilitarian weapon for the colonisation of Being. It murders to dissect.

John Locke was one of the most notable proponents of British Empiricism. He believed that only such a philosophy of perception and language could prevent our thoughts from straying 'into the vast ocean of being', could remove the metaphysical 'rubbish from the way of knowledge'. A keen defender of the right of proprietors – which he saw as an inalienable right of man and an essential prerogative of any gentleman's son – Locke construed language according to an equally proprietorial epistemology. He promoted the ideal of a perfectly transparent language resulting from the accurate mapping of words onto empirical sensations. The domestication of reality by means of this rigid conformity of words to sensory objects would lead, he believed, to a rigorously scientific knowledge. Naturally there was to be no quarter given to poetic or ontological language in this scheme of things. And in *Thoughts Concerning Education*, Locke advises parents who were unfortunate enough to have children born with a poetic propensity, to 'labour to have it stifled and suppressed as much as may be'. This empiricist view of language is caricatured by Friel in *Translations* as the reduction of a living ontological landscape to the practical proportions of a six-inch map. The following comment from Lord Salisbury, which Friel places alongside his quotation from Heidegger in the prefatory notes to the play, clearly reveals the author's satiric intentions: 'The most disagreeable part of the three kingdoms is Ireland; and therefore Ireland has a splendid map.' Once exposed to the linguistic lens of empiricism, the landscape ceases to be and becomes merely *useful*: language as *evocation* is replaced by language as *information*.[27]

Another (more flexible) positivist model of language to have gained widespread currency in recent years is linguistic structuralism. The two most influential exponents of this model are Ferdinand de Saussure and Claude Lévi-Strauss. The structuralists may be classed as 'positivistic' to the extent that they attempt to reduce language to a mechanistic system of formal substitutions, to a skeletal logistics of signs. 'Language is a *form* not a *substance*', ran Saussure's celebrated maxim. And it was on the basis of this maxim that structuralist linguists could argue that the entire complex of language be considered as an impersonal system of coded relations between its constituent units (semantic or phonetic), with no ontological rapport whatsoever with nature, history or the human subject. Words are thus treated as neutral objectified units of exchange in an abstract network of coded messages. The ontological question of the *authenticity* of language as a disclosure of personal and historical meaning no longer arises. The flesh of *subjectivity* – the 'interiority of the heart's space' – has been stripped away to leave the clean bare bones of *structure*.

Lévi-Strauss' original contribution to structuralism lay in his equation of the codes of the language system (as an exchange of structural units) with the codes of kinship systems (as an exogamous exchange of women – or by extension, other consumer commodities – between different tribes). This primitive model of kinship as a mechanism of utilitarian and commercial substitution is, Lévi-Strauss believes, the determining structure of all languages. In a passage remarkably apposite for a reading of Friel's language plays, Lévi-Strauss claims that we should regard 'marriage regulations and kinship systems as a kind of language, a set of processes permitting the establishment, between individuals and groups, of a certain type of communication' (*Structural Anthropology*).[28] That the mediating factor, in this case, should be the *women* of the group, who are circulated between classes, lineages, or families, in place of the words of the group, which are circulated between individuals, does not at all change the fact that the essential aspect of the phenomenon is identical in both cases. This structuralist model of language bears particular relevance to Friel's third language play, *The Communication Cord*.

Appendix D: Friel and Steiner

The following is a list of key passages from George Steiner's essay 'Understanding and Translations' (contained in *After Babel: Aspects of Language and Translation* [Oxford University Press 1975], pp. 1–50), which served as a major critical and philosophical source for Friel's language plays.

1. 'In certain civilisations there come epochs in which syntax suffers, in which the available resources of live perception and restatement wither. Words seem to go dead under the weight of sanctified usage: the frequency and sclerotic forces of clichés, of unexamined similes, or worn tropes increases. Instead of acting as a living membrane, grammar and vocabulary become a barrier to new feeling. A civilisation is imprisoned in a linguistic contour which no longer matches, or matches only at certain ritual, arbitrary points, the changing landscape of fact.' (p. 21)

2. 'We have histories of massacre and deception, but none of metaphor ... Such figures (i.e. metaphors) are new mappings of the world, they reorganise our habitation of reality.' (p. 23)

3. 'No semantic form is timeless. When using a word we wake into resonance, as it were, its entire previous history. A text is embedded in specific historical time: it has what linguists call a diachronic structure. To read fully is to restore all that one can of the immediacies of value and intent in which speech actually occurs.' (p. 24)

4. 'The schematic model of translation is one in which a message from a source-language passes into a receptor-language via a transformational process. The barrier is the obvious fact that one language differs from the other, that an interpretative transfer sometimes, albeit misleadingly, described as encoding and decoding, must occur so that the message "gets through". Exactly the same model – and this is what is rarely stressed – is operative *within a single language.*' (p. 28)

5. 'What material reality has history outside language, outside our interpretative belief in essentially linguistic records (silence knows no history)? Where worms, fires of London, or totalitarian regimes obliterate such records, our consciousness of past being comes on a blank space. We have no total history, no history which could be defined as objectively real because it contained the literal sum of past life. To remember everything is a condition of madness. We remember culturally, as we do individually, by conventions of emphasis, foreshadowing omission. The landscape composed by the past tense, the semantic organisation of remembrance, is stylised and differently coded by different cultures.' (p. 29)

6. 'The metaphysics of the instant, this slamming of the doors on the long galleries of historical consciousness, is understandable. It has a fierce innocence ... But it is an innocence as destructive of civilisation as it is, by concomitant logic, destructive of literate speech. Without the true fiction of history, without the unbroken animation of a chosen past, we become flat shadows. Literature, whose genius stems from what Eluard called *le dur désir de durer*, has no chance of life outside constant translation within its own language ... In short, the existence of art and literature, the reality of felt history in a community, depend on a never-ending, though very often unconscious, act of internal translation.' (p. 30)

7. 'Languages conceal and internalise more, perhaps, than they convey outwardly. Social classes, racial ghettos speak at rather than to each other.' (p. 32)

8. 'When anti-theatrical meanings are forced upon the same word (Orwell's newspeak), when the conceptual reach and valuation of a word can be uttered by political decree, language loses credibility.' (p. 34)

9. 'At any given time in a community and in the history of language, speech modulates across generations.' (p. 34)

10. 'Eros and language mesh at every point. Intercourse and discourse, copula and copulation, are sub-classes of the dominant fact of communication. They arise from the life-need of the ego to reach out and comprehend, in the two vital senses of 'understanding' and 'containment', another human being. Sex is a profoundly semantic act. Like language, it is subject to the shaping force of social convention, rules of proceeding, and accumulated precedent.' (p. 38)

11. 'Hence the argument of modern anthropology and the incest taboo, which appears to be primal to the organisation of communal life, is inseparable from linguistic evolution. We can only prohibit that which we can name. Kinship systems, which are the coding and classifi-cation of sex for purposes of social survival, are analogous with syntax. The seminal and semantic functions (is there, ultimately, an etymological link?) determine the genetic and social structure of human experience. Together they construe the grammar of being.' (p. 39)

12. 'Under extreme stress, men and women declare their absolute being to each other, only to discover that their respective experience of eros and language has set them desperately apart.' (p. 45)

13. 'Lévi-Strauss's contention is that women and words are analogous media of exchange in the grammar of social life.' (p. 45)

14. 'It is not as "translators" that women novelists and poets excel, but as declaimers of their own, long-stifled tongue.' (p. 45)

15. 'Any model of communication is at the same time a model of trans-lation, of a vertical or horizontal transfer of significance. No two historical epochs, no two social classes, no two localities use words and syntax to signify exactly the same things, to send identical signals of valuation and inference. Neither do two human beings. Each person draws, deliberately or in immediate habit, on two sources of linguistic supply: the current vulgate corresponding to his level of literacy, and a private thesaurus. The latter is inextricably a part of his subconscious, of his memories so far as they may be verbalised, and of the singular, irreducibly specific ensemble of his somatic and psychological identity. Part of the answer to the notorious logical conundrum as to whether or not there can be a 'private language' is that aspects of every language-act are unique and individual ... The concept of a normal or standard idiom is a statistically-based fiction (though it may have real existence in machine-translation). The language of a community, however uniform its social contour, is an inexhaustibly multiple aggregate of speech-atoms, of finally irre-ducible personal meanings ... We speak to communicate. But also to conceal, to leave unspoken. The ability of human beings to misinform modulates through every wave-length from outright lying to silence.' (p. 46)

16. 'Thus a human being performs an act of translation, in the full sense of the word, when receiving a speech-message from any other human being. Time, distance, disparities in outlook or assumed reference, make this act more or less difficult. Where the difficulty is great enough, the process passes from reflex to conscious technique. Intimacy, on the other hand, be it of hatred or of love, can be defined as confident, quasi-immediate trans-lation ... With intimacy the external vulgate and the private mass of language grow more and more concordant. Soon the private dimension penetrates and takes over the customary forms of public exchange ... In old age the impulse towards translation wanes and the pointers of reference turn inward. The old listen less or principally to themselves. Their dictionary is, increasingly, one of private remembrance.' (p. 47)

17. 'Interlingual translation is ... an access to an inquiry into language itself. "Translation", properly understood, is a special case of the arc of communication which every successful speech-act closes within a given language ... The model "sender to receiver" which repre-sents any semiological and semantic process is ontologically equivalent to the model "source-language to receptor-language" used in the theory of translation ... In short, *inside or between languages, human communication equals translation.* A study of translation is a study of language.' (p. 47)

Tom Murphy's
Long Night's Journey into Night

Tom Murphy's *The Gigli Concert*, premiered at the 1983 Dublin Theatre Festival, confirmed his reputation as an innovative force in modern Irish drama.[1] *The Irish Literary Supplement* hailed it as 'one of the finest Irish plays of the decade', while *Theatre Ireland* declared it to be 'the most significant event in European theatre since the première of *Waiting for Godot* in Paris in 1953'. In this chapter, we will analyse how this play represents a dramatic challenge to the mainstream tradition of Irish theatre rooted in the Irish Literary Revival.

While Brian Friel's Field Day company represented a particularly Northern response to the fundamental problems of tradition, history, language and identity confronting contemporary Irish culture,[2] Murphy's work could be said to represent the most significant Southern counterpart to such a critical movement. The Field Day Theatre company has been perceived, in general, as an exploration of the more *historical* dimension of cultural displacement (particularly as it found explicit expression in the conflict of Northern Ireland where Field Day originates). Murphy's work, by contrast, focused on the *existential* malady of inner displacement and division to which, he believes, the inhabitants of the Southern, ostensibly more 'settled', provinces were singularly prone.

Murphy has probed the dark recesses of modern Irish experience with unrelenting obsessiveness. In a Murphy drama, the border that truncates and polarizes is *within*: it marks more of a metaphysical rupture between self and self than a geographical/historical partition between one community and another (Northern/Southern, Irish/British etc.). The metaphor of the 'wall' that recurs throughout Murphy's plays signals a confinement to our solitary, divided selves. As Malachy puts it in *On the Inside* (1974): 'Self-contempt is the metaphysical key. How can you, I ask myself, love someone, if first you do not love yourself?' 'My spirit is unwell too', declares Harry in *The Sanctuary Lamp* (1976), as he wrestles with the angel of his own 'holy loneliness', keeping demonic vigil over his deceased loved one (Teresa) and his deceased God (the play takes place within a church: Nietzsche's 'madman' was also carrying a 'sanctuary lamp' when he announced the 'death of God').

In all of his plays, Murphy seems to be saying that we are still, always, *on the outside* (the title of his first play, 1959) even, and most agonizingly, when we are *on the inside*: that is, even when we contrive to escape the alienating circumstances of modern existence by seeking asylum in the sanctuary of our own inner selves. It is perhaps Michael, in *A Whistle in the Dark* (1961), who most poignantly sums up this condition of existential disease when he utters his cry of self-contradiction: 'I want to get out of this kind of life. I want ... I want us all to be – I don't want to be what I am ... But I can't get out of all this ... What's wrong with me?'

This metaphysical experience of the dark abyss of self-division (most of Murphy's plays take place at night), confessionally registered yet comically resolved, is the abiding motif of Murphy's *oeuvre*, which includes over fifteen plays. It suggests that his work shares less with the native *folk* concerns of Synge, Yeats or Molloy, than with the existentialist explorations of such dramatists as Ionesco, Sartre or Beckett. As Christopher Murray has observed: 'All of Tom Murphy's work is a "whistle in the dark", an exultant cry of triumph over the facts of death and history. The subject matter can be serious, but the struggle to establish a self, a personality free from the subtle determinants of society, is presented with comic vigour, with what Nietzsche ... called metaphysical delight.'[3]

Murphy's drama departs from the indigenous tradition of the well-made folk-drama and embraces, with Friel and Beckett, the modernist obsession with the crisis of human communication and identity. While his plays ostensibly conform to the Irish norm of 'verbal' theatre, they substantially modify this norm, concentrating more on the *mood* or *tone* of feeling created by language than on the narrative plot or storyline as such. Murphy's characters tend to tell stories about themselves rather than play out a role in a story told about them (by the author). The action develops in the actors rather than the actors in the action. Brian Friel has described Murphy as the 'most distinctive, restless and obsessive imagination working in the Irish theatre today'. There is little doubt that Murphy's many experiments with form and dialogue (especially in the surreal and stylized later plays) testify to a sense of dramatic *navigatio*, of tirelessly attempting to articulate the inarticulate, to sound the unconscious, or as Beckett once put it, to 'eff the ineffable'.

I

Murphy belongs to a counter-tradition in Irish drama to the extent that he poses a direct challenge to both the naturalism and Romanticism of the Literary Revival. While this Revival was largely created in a metropolitan context for a metropolitan audience it promoted an idealized image of rural Ireland that corresponded to the emergent culture of Irish nationalism. In drama, the revivalist movement was particularly associated with the work of the Abbey Theatre. In their 1906 manifesto entitled *Irish Plays*, Yeats and Lady Gregory equated the best in Irish life with the rural peasants and their legendary landscape. These dramatists maintained that they had 'taken their types and scenes direct from Irish life itself'. This life, they added, 'is rich in dramatic materials, while the Irish peasantry of the hills and coast speak an exuberant language and have a primitive grace and wildness due to the wild country they live in, which gives their most ordinary life a vividness and colour unknown in more civilised places.'[4] This revivalist identification of national life with rural life led to a theatre often dominated by the pull of the past where a displaced modern individual sought to recover an identifiable place in a traditional community usually associated with his or her peasant ancestry.[5]

The plays of Tom Murphy explode the myths of revivalist drama. *On the Outside, Famine, A Whistle in the Dark, Conversations on a Homecoming* and *Baile-gangaire* expose the pieties and pretences of rural folklore. Moreover, Murphy's deromanticization of the established canons of folk drama corresponds, at the level of form, to his increasing use of *non-naturalistic* scenery, characterization and dialogue, exemplified in the almost surrealist idioms of *Morning After Optimism* and *The Gigli Concert*. Indeed, in the latter, Murphy has succeeded in reversing the revivalist transposition of urban to rural, introducing the disillusioned rural 'Irishman' directly into the modern metropolis of social and existential crisis.

II

The Gigli Concert works at several levels. It highlights the dramatic collision between tradition and modernity, between rural and urban values, between the cultures of the Gael and the Planter. But it does so in a way that circumvents political stereotypes. The two main characters of the play are an anonymous self-made 'Irishman' whose ambition it is to sing like the great Italian opera singer Beniamino Gigli and the English-born J.P.W. King who postures as a native psychotherapist capable of resolving our most turbulent desires. The allusion to the old chestnut of Anglo-Irish relations is obvious – and there is even a northern mistress called Mona to make up the triangle. But one of the singular strengths of Murphy's writing is to avoid cliché and confound predictable expectations. Murphy goes straight for the jugular of psychic confrontation. He presents his drama as an existential psychodrama where the claims of historical fact and subjective fantasy overlap with mischievous ease. The key to the whole problem, he suggests, is in the intimate relation between language and illusion. He compels us to recognize how we use words to lie to ourselves, to invent myths, to conceal what we are and create what we might be.

The Gigli Concert is – along with Friel's 'language plays' – verbal theatre in its most accomplished form. Rarely has an Irish dramatist so convincingly exposed the role that language plays in the unconscious world of our fears and aspirations. Several of the drama's dialogues are unrelenting. But Murphy refuses to compromise. He compels his characters to work with language until its surface meanings collapse into silence (the impossibility of communication) or music (the epitome of communication). Either way, *The Gigli Concert* reminds us that we cannot take words for granted, that they are never innocent and rarely mean what they *appear* to mean. Murphy suggests that by feeding the heart on fantasies, words can become as loaded and destructive as time bombs. Appropriately, King describes his philosophy as 'dynamatology' – a double reference to explosives and to the Greek term for the hidden world of 'possibility' (*dunamis*) opened up by the imaginative resources of language. Dynamatology, in its author's words, promises 'to project you beyond the boundaries that are presently limiting you'. If this is 'political' theatre, it is not so in any ideological sense, but in the sense indicated by Seamus Heaney when he says that 'the *imagined* place is what politics is all about. Politicians deal in images.'[6] It is in fact by exposing the imaginative underworld of our political stereotypes and clichés, turning them inside out and tracing their origin back to the buried fears and aspirations of the psyche, that Murphy shows how the worlds of public and private experience feed off each other. In this way, Murphy grafts a 'drama of society' onto a 'drama of character', as Patrick Mason, the director of the Abbey première of *The Gigli Concert*, observes:

> Murphy's theme is the brokenness of spirit and the strange demons that lie in the Irish psyche. The hero in this play who is the magician and poet is an Englishman. The Irishman is the corrupt, self-made building contractor who has sold his soul. It's an interesting antagonism, a reversal of the traditional stereotypes, which makes the play absolutely fascinating. Murphy is not a writer who deals in a naked political dialectic. The play also has a universal theme of what use is beauty. In a world that is increasingly corrupt and factual, what do you do about those inner urges that just won't go away and every now and then burst out into some kind of expression? Obviously the whole business of wanting to sing like Gigli is an extreme but extraordinary expression of that creative need.[7]

III

The Gigli Concert is not so much a play within a play as a psychodrama within a psychodrama. It stages a turbulent exchange between its central characters. One is from the 'outside', J.P.W. King, the middle-aged Englishman masquerading as a 'resident' psychotherapist (he claims he had a Tipperary grandmother) with messianic pretentions to help people realize their secret dreams. The other is from the 'inside', an 'Irishman' (as the script describes him) with no name, address or telephone number, posturing as a musically gifted cobbler's son from the Italian town of Recaniti who wants to sing like the great opera singer Beniamino Gigli. The drama unfolds as a sort of life and death struggle between these *frères ennemis*, whose complicity of mutual misunderstanding suggests at times that they are more similar than they pretend, perhaps even alter-egos of each other (as James and Edmund in Murphy's earlier play, *The Morning after Optimism*, 1971). J.P.W. and the Irishman are psychic doubles of a divided self seeking the completion of a possible unity. As such, they might be viewed as dramatic approximations of Seamus Heaney's poetic dialectic between the two extremes of the Irish imagination in his 'Hercules and Antaeus' poem in *North*. Of this dialectical opposition, Heaney wrote:

> Hercules represents the balanced rational light while Antaeus represents the pieties of illiterate fidelity. The poem drifts towards an assent to Hercules though there was a sort of nostalgia for Antaeus ... This is a see-saw, an advance-retire situation. There is always the question in everybody's mind whether the rational and humanist domain which produced what we call civilisation in the West, should be allowed full command in our psyche, speech and utterance ...[8]

But what is the precise nature of the opposition between Murphy's protagonists? J.P.W. represents the intellectually 'progressive' future-oriented ethos of English and European Enlightenment; he claims to be a 'dynamatologist' sent over to Ireland by the movement's founding-father in order to propagate a new method for helping people to realize their 'potential' (*dunamis*). By contrast the 'Irishman', or Beniamino as J.P.W. insists on calling him, ostensibly represents the native West-of-Ireland ethos of cunning instinct, memory and tradition; he has experienced this ethos as fundamentally repressive and has sought to escape from it, first by becoming a *nouveau-riche* 'operator' in the building trade, and finally by seeking a form of perfection beyond the materialist idols of power and wealth – the sublimity of music. Though he prides himself on being a no-nonsense self-made man who knows far more about life than any professional philosopher, Beniamino feels compelled nonetheless to procure the therapeutic 'self-realising' services of an 'intellectual' such as J.P.W.

Beniamino is an Irishman thoroughly disabused with the cult of bourgeois opportunism and careerism of which he is a victim. (This cult was brought about, in part, by the modern transition from de Valera's vision of pastoral piety to Lemass's hardnosed ideology of commercial 'rising tides' and political fundraising development schemes). Thus, while he may invoke the authority of facts and figures, Beniamino ultimately wishes to escape from the constraints of such empirical necessities into the 'possible and possibilising' world of pure art. He wants to trade-in fact for fiction, his self-made man success story having degenerated into a nightmare of despair. Delinquent itinerants, he complains, have overrun his domestic 'territory'; and instead of communicating with his wife and nine-year-old son, he can now only utter a 'roar of obscenity'. The centre can no longer hold. And so Beniamino wants to transmute the dark energies of that roar within him into music. He wants, quite simply, to sing like Gigli.

As the play unfolds, we gradually learn that the differences between the two characters are more apparent than real. If the Italianate Beniamino is no more than a pseudonym for the nameless Irishman, the messianic-sounding 'dynamatologist' is itself no more than a pseudonym for the hapless, narcotic-and-vodka crazed mess of broken dreams that J.P.W. really is. (Both characters admit at different times that they 'do not know how [they] will get through the day'.) Far from being able to 'make all things possible', as his professional title and philosophy profess, J.P.W. King is no *salvator mundi*; while he chides Beniamino for believing that the 'Romantic Kingdom is of this world', it transpires that he himself is neither king of this world nor of any other. In short, the analyst is just as screwed up as the analysand.

J.P.W. claims that his dynamatological theory will replace the oppressive 'I am who I am' model of divine power (the *Yahweh* God who cast Adam and Eve out of Eden into *Angst* because they ate of the forbidden fruit of imagination, i.e. acquired the Creator's knowledge of good and evil) with a new 'I Am Who May Be' model capable of realizing the divine potentialities of each human being. But J.P.W. has *in fact* been no more successful in realizing his own possibilities than his deceiving and self-deceiving client. He has squandered his potential for love in unrequited infatuation for an intangible 'Helen' who finally dismisses him as little more than an 'obscene telephone caller'. And his proud story of domestic happiness – an idyllic wife and house with clematis growing round the doorway – is itself exposed as just another self-incarcerating fantasy. In reality, the one woman who *truly* loves him, the down-to-earth, plainspeaking, physical Mona, is taken for granted until it is too late. (The moment J.P.W. comes to realize that Mona had longed all these years to have a child with him – a *real* potentiality for life that J.P.W. had entirely ignored – is the same moment that he learns that she is dying from cancer). The time is out of joint for this modern day prince of Kierkegaardian Denmark; no amount of fanciful subterfuge can put it right.

The final bombshell to explode J.P.W.'s dynamatological illusions comes, ironically, in the shape of Beniamino himself. He returns in the last act to announce that his desire to sing like Gigli was not in fact some life-long ambition to transcend misery, as he had pretended, but a desperate obsession provoked by one of his many recurring depressions. In other words, J.P.W.'s own Faustian dream of enabling others to realize their *dreams* founders on the rocks of factuality. In one fell swoop, both he and his client are exposed as frauds. Thus while presented as polar opposites in the early scenes, the roles of the two protagonists are now exchanged – a transitional operation enacted on stage as the analyst-behind-the-desk swaps places with the analysand and begins to pour out his own story of childhood trauma. In this overlapping process, both are seen to inhabit the same circle of darkness and despair which, as J.P.W. prophetically spoofs, is 'where the battle must be fought', and to share the same desire to translate their self-destructive obsessions into a Gigli song. Benianimo's initial claim that the 'only way to communicate is to sing' has now become J.P.W.'s own credo. Gigli's operatic scores have invaded not only his office/apartment (where Beniamino has installed a hi-fi system) but also his very soul ('Gigli is a devil' who possesses one's entire being, Beniamino had warned). As Beniamino finally returns to 'normality', a sort of Dorian Gray reversal occurs whereby it becomes J.P.W.'s turn to rave and rant and reach out for the impossible possibility of a perfected music.

Impotent to realize the quasi-mystical promise of what he terms the 'quiet power of the possible' (a phrase used by the existentialist philosopher Martin Heidegger),[9] J.P.W.'s belief in dynamatology degenerates into a caricature of itself (with all the destructive connotations implied by the allusion to dynamite). The final explosion is not that from the barrel of Beniamino's putative pocket-gun, which it transpires was merely another strategy, but from the break-up of J.P.W.'s own professional illusions. 'Mama, do not leave me in the dark', cries the dynamatologist from the depths of his Faustian dream. (Indeed the Faustian theme is also echoed in J.P.W.'s relation with the Gretchen-like Mona and the use of Boito's *Faust* as one of the scores in the play). His ultimate cry into the dark falls somewhere between the sigh of Goethe and the howl of Ginsberg.

And yet from the darkness a hint of redemption emerges. For a few brief moments, it seems that J.P.W. does in fact sing like Gigli. It is no more than a glimpse, a possibility. It might be just another illusion, one last psychic twist of self-deception resulting from an overdose of alcohol. But then again, it might not. There is at least a suggestion that the very tenacity of J.P.W.'s new-found 'act of faith' to sing like Gigli has yielded not just another artifice, but genuine art. It is no more than a *maybe*. But that is as much as can be expected from the heretical God of the Possible – the I Am Who May Be who has supplanted the I Am Who Am (i.e. the old paternalistic God hostile to the Adamic presumption that the human imagination is capable of projecting possibilities of a new creation).

Thus it transpires that Beniamino's imposture has, ironically, infused J.P.W.'s hitherto 'spiritless being' not only with the audacity of despair but also and more importantly, with the 'longing to soar': the audacity to believe in his own belief, to transform his obsessive fantasies into creative fiction, to realize the impossible possibility of pure Being. In a conclusion reminiscent of the final scene in Synge's *Playboy*, when Christy departs triumphantly from the stage having become 'a man by the power of a lie' (the fiction of parricide), J.P.W. packs his bags and exits – exultant in the belief that his dream has been, or at least *may be*, realized. He leaves behind him a society of dreamless pragmatists who, as Beniamino has warned, would 'kill him if he stayed'. Perhaps after all, in the shadow of the deceased Father-God, a son has been born.

IV

One of the most conspicuous features of Murphy's work is its ability to transcend, while reflecting, its local setting and thus assume a stature of international proportions. For while at one level the exchanges between J.P.W. and Beniamino can be interpreted as emblems of the age-old conflict between England and Ireland – with the Northern Mona as a sort of neglected go-between: the woman victimized by the male-dominated struggle for power – they also represent the problematic opposition between two universal value systems: the future-oriented Enlightenment versus past-oriented traditionalism; humanist intellect versus native instinct; utopian idealism versus pragmatic materialism.

Murphy's capacity to amplify the parochial into the universal by going beyond the conventions of folk Irishry is a hallmark of his drama. In *The Gigli Concert* we witness an author grappling with native concerns yet fully cognizant of the fascination that modern European culture – from Gigli to the existentialists – exerts upon 'the native mind'. To take just one comparative example, it is interesting to observe the parallels between Beniamino's desire to sing like Gigli in order to escape the mess of everyday existence and Roquentin's desire, in Sartre's *Nausea*, to reach the condition of pure Being symbolized by the song of a negress:

> *It* does exist … if I were to get up, if I were to snatch that record from the turn-table which is holding it and if I were to break it in two, I wouldn't reach *it*. It is beyond – always beyond something, beyond a voice, beyond a violin note. Through layers and layers of existence, it unveils itself, slim and firm, and when you try to seize it you meet nothing but existents, you run up against existents devoid of meaning. It is behind them: I can't even hear it. I hear sounds, vibrations in the air which unveil it. It does not exist, since it has nothing superfluous in relation to it. It *is*. And I too have wanted to *be*. Indeed I have never wanted anything else.

Sartre contends that the greatest power of the song is that it projects an aesthetic world of pure possibility 'cleansed of the sin of existing'. Murphy's view of things is in this respect strangely akin to that of the existentialists. Life, for both, is absurd, chaotic, insane; it can only be redeemed, if at all, by a stoical belief in the transforming power of imagination. All truth is an artefact, taught Nietzsche, but one that we could not survive without. The only way to combat the absurdity of existence is, therefore, to keep on believing in meaning in spite of everything, like Sisyphus rolling his rock to the top of the hill in the belief that he will eventually reach the summit; even if he doesn't, the struggle itself – the act of faith in the possible – justifies the effort. Or as Beckett's 'unnamable' narrator put it, if 'I can't go on, I'll go on'. Indeed, Murphy's misfits bear a striking resemblance to Beckett's in that both succeed in representing the universalist dimensions of 'existentialist man' in recognizable localized settings. Perhaps Beckett's move to Paris and Murphy's ten year sojourn in London (where he worked at *The Royal Court* and *The Old Vic*, and wrote and staged his first plays) helped both to bring 'outside' perspectives to bear on their indigenous experience.

V

If one examines the implications of this universalist existentialism in the Irish context of Murphy's plays a slightly unsettling assumption emerges. The message that Murphy's angst-ridden characters convey is that the mainstream traditions of Irish society are moribund. In *On the Outside*, set at the doorway of an Irish dancehall, it is the small-town provincialism of moral *resentment* and begrudgery that the author exposes. In *A Whistle in the Dark*, it is the psychic paralysis produced by introverted family competitiveness. In *On the Inside* and *The Sanctuary Lamp*, Murphy turns his satirical attention to the life-denying oppressiveness of Irish Jansenism. 'Holy medals and genitalia in mortal combat with each other', as Malachy remarks in the former, 'is not sex at all'. Murphy caricatures this jansenistic God of devotionalism in *The Sanctuary Lamp* as a necrophiliac 'metaphysical monster' whose supposedly 'real presence' of consolation (symbolized by the lamp) is little more than a mask for the 'violence-mongering furies' of a moribund deity. Abandoned to their own self-destructive solitude, Murphy's godless but god-obsessed 'orphans' resort to the last possible refuge – the sanctuary of insanity: 'Do you think madness must at least be warm,' muses Harry, 'I don't mind admitting I keep it as standby in case all else fails.' In *Famine* and *The Blue Macushla*, Murphy indicts the chauvinistic and pseudo-patriotic hypocrisy that, he believes, has so contaminated political life in Ireland. The latter play is a trenchant send-up of narrow Irish nationalism, from the highest of government ministers to the lowest of paramilitary fanatics (the *Éireann go Brách* splinter group of a splinter group!); it recounts how such forces conspire to rob Eddie

O'Hara of his 'person' (his sense of self as biographically detailed in the opening soliloquy of the play) and ultimately of his life. 'Wearing patriotism on your sleeve like gold cufflinks', Murphy suggests, is more conducive to the spread of a contagious national disease than to one's sense of personal integrity. Lastly, in *The Gigli Concert* Murphy unleashes his iconoclastic ire on the consumerist bourgeoisie who resent any deviant flight of creativity, force many of their artists into exile, and, as Beniamino admonishes (and he should know as he was once one of them), try to destroy those who remain.

This angry, at times apocalyptic, attitude to contemporary Irish society has made, in Murphy's case, for charged drama. The exuberance of form and language – sometimes straining at the seams – that Murphy's uncompromising *non serviam* has produced cannot be underestimated. And yet one is tempted to ask if his global repudiation of Ireland's social, religious and political institutions does not run the risk of excessive caricature, even falling back, at times, into the cliché of the *poète maudit*: the solitary artist guarding the last flame of vision within his breast against the benighted hostility of the community at large. Kierkegaard dismissed the anonymous masses that threatened the creative individual as the 'Crowd', Nietzsche as the 'Herd', and Sartre as '*les salauds*'. Murphy's heroes do not usually give an explicit identity to this social collectivity; it has contaminated the very air they breathe; it is witnessed in the visible scars of their failure; it is quite simply that faceless omnipresent 'they' invoked by Beniamino when he warns J.P.W. that there's kindness in the world but '*they'll* kill you if you stay over here'. Murphy's response to this threat of the collective is invariably one of fierce individualism, recalling Swift's savage indignation at the 'yahoo' mentality.

In Murphy's world, the individual is the agent of liberation; the collectivity – and its idioms of history, tradition, authority, politics, nationalism – an agent of coercion. Nearly all his plays are centred around an individual's struggle for self-realization against the constraints of his/her social environment. Whether it be Eddie O'Hara in *The Blue Macushla*, John O'Connor in *Famine* or J.P.W. in *The Gigli Concert*, in each case the line of demarcation between spiritual salvation and social insanity is perilously thin. Ireland remains Murphy's first and only love, where genius and lunacy go hand in glove.[10]

Murphy's plays declare war on the paralysing forces in our society, compelling us to sound out our most hidden fears and encouraging us, where possible, to transcend them in humour and faith. For these above all are the characteristic virtues of Murphy's dramatic enterprise – the laughter that emancipates and the leap of faith towards new *possibilities* of experience, more perfect, more creative, more human. Murphy will not stop writing until we are all singing like Gigli.[11]

Part Four:

VISUAL NARRATIVES

CHAPTER SEVENTEEN

Modern Irish Cinema: Re-viewing Traditions

Since its inception in the early part of this century, Irish cinema – by which I mean films made in or about Ireland – has been dominated by a number of stereotypes. These include the portrayal of Ireland in terms of a romanticized past, a mythical landscape and a mystical rapport between the national mother-land and her violent heroic sons. So pervasive has this cinematic representation of Ireland been that any attempt to break free from it ran the risk of being read back into the tradition it sought to subvert. I wish to examine here two Irish films – Neil Jordan's *Angel* (1982) and Pat Murphy's *Maeve* (1981) – which to my mind succeeded in critically exposing the stereotypes and explored new ways of representing contemporary Irish society. But before proceeding to a detailed analysis of these films, I will briefly review some examples of the stereotyping of celluloid Ireland.

It is arguable that several of the cinematic clichés of Irish national character were promoted by a romantic sentimentalism eager to project an exotic image of Ireland both at home and abroad. *Rory O'More* (1911), *Guests of the Nation* (1934), *Dawn* (1935), and *The Rising of the Moon* (1957), or a film like *Ryan's Daughter* (1970), were instances of this. As one contemporary critic, Kevin Barry, remarked:

> One of the depressing consequences of an Irish film industry has always been the re-enforcement of stereotypes of Irish character, history and landscape: the cinematic versions of women in red shawls, upright yet drunken men, senti-mental nationalism, the sheepdog in the lane, the heifer in calf, the school-teacher in trouble, the pastoral western retreats from social and political conflict. *Ryan's Daughter* has had too many fathers and too many sons. And it is clear that the native productions, insofar as there have been any in our cinema history, have offended no less than the international productions.[1]

But if sentimental nationalism, as fostered by the more romantic strain of the cultural revival, was one source of the stereotypes of celluloid Ireland, it was not the only one. Indeed it could reasonably be argued that this stereotyping had a lot to do with the *absence* of any indigenous Irish film industry. This absence meant that the representations of Ireland were largely subject to the commercial and ideological designs of American and British film companies. In other words, the export market for Irish films frequently involved the prior import of stock views of Ireland from abroad. Thus we find Ireland being used by several multi-national film companies as a folkloric landscape for stage-Irish narratives that distorted the realities of Irish history. This was particularly evident in the portrayal of Irish violence.

In *Cinema and Ireland*, the first comprehensive book on Irish film, John Hill writes of 'Images of violence'. Analysing a variety of Irish films, ranging from early works like *Odd Man Out, The Gentle Gunman* and *Shake Hands with the Devil* to subsequent representations of violence in *Hennessy, The Long Good Friday, Angel* and *Cal*, Hill seeks to identify the influence of American and British models of violence. The Hollywood version of the Irish hero portrayed violence according to the frontier paradigm of the self-made man asserting his virility and prowess against the forces of convention. Violence was here celebrated as a form of heroic resolution. For its part, the British model tended to conserve Irish violence in terms of fatalism, i.e. as a motiveless malignity, an aboriginal curse or freak side-show that dramatically obstructed the order of reason and law. 'Violence', writes Hill, 'was not to be accounted for in terms of a response to political and economic conditions, but simply as a manifestation of the Irish "national character". By this token, the proclivity for violence was simply an inherent characteristic in the "nature", if not the blood, of the Irish natives.'[2] In short, while American companies patronized and romanticized Irish violence, British companies tended to criminalize it.

Hill's analysis is illuminating in several respects – but not in all. Having isolated a partial truth, he tries to totalize it. He pushes his argument too far, exaggerating the force of filmic stereotypes of Irish violence to the point where he sees them at work everywhere. Neil Jordan's *Angel* is a case in point. Hill describes this film as follows:

> Jordan's preoccupation with 'pure' violence requires a suppression of social and political specifics … As with *Odd Man Out*, the attempt to create a 'universal' drama, while maintaining a recognisable Irish setting, only helps to confirm a view of the 'troubles' as unintelligible. 'We know where the madness is,' one of the assassins tells Danny. So, too, will the film's audience. For by rendering political relations and motivations irrelevant, it is only the 'madness' of Northern Ireland which *Angel* permits us to see …[3]

Hill then proceeds to level an even more serious charge against *Angel*. He maintains that the neglect of political specifics does not free the film from political implications, but actually promotes a policy consistent with the British view of things. 'By denying its political origins and motives ... paramilitary violence is simply represented as criminal. By the same token, if the film's use of a de-contextualising aesthetic strategy necessarily undermines the "legitimacy" or rationale of political violence, so it also adds to the legitimacy of the State by depoliticising its activities as well.'[4]

I. Jordan's Angel

By suggesting that *Angel* subscribes to the commercial and ideological stereo-types of Irish violence (i.e. as criminal and irrational), Hill is ignoring the subversive and experimental power of Jordan's film. I would argue that there is a new generation of Irish film makers emerging – including Neil Jordan, Pat Murphy, Cathal Black, Pat O'Connor, Ciaran Hickey, Jim Sheridan and Joe Comerford – who are successfully challenging the inherited cinematic stereo-types and paving the way for a critical Irish film culture. The two examples I focus on here are Jordan's *Angel* and Murphy's *Maeve* – both of which, in my view, brush against the grain of traditional Irish cinema and propose alternative modes of narrative. In so doing, they challenge the viewer to reassess the dominant myths of Irish violence – that is, *both* the native myths of revivalist nationalism *and* the commercial and colonial ones imported from Britain or America.

Angel debunks the orthodox portrayal of Irish political violence. It deroman-ticizes several of its stock motifs – most notably that of the national hero at arms. Rather than conforming to any specific ideology, this film exposes the hidden unconscious forces that animate ideological violence, whether they be repub-lican, loyalist or British imperialist. Jordan's cinematic exploration of the psychic roots of violence permits him to cut through ideological conventions and disclose that world of inner obsession and desire which, he believes, is a key source of both our political and poetic myths.

If the artist is someone with an educated nervous system, then *Angel* is an instance of genuine art, functioning as it does to educate the viewer's inner sensibility, to enable us to experience the unconscious that informs our everyday actions and perceptions. As Jordan himself explains: 'What I get the greatest pleasure out of is trying to make manifest how ... a perceiving eye can see and feel the world. I suppose really that fiction or any art is like sensual thinking. It's like thinking through one's senses ... [which] is deeper, more valuable than abstract thinking.'[5] In this respect, Jordan has learned much from his mentor, John Boorman (with whom he worked as creative consultant during the making of *Excalibur*). Jordan shares Boorman's determination to investigate the pre-conscious powers of collective or personal mythology that continue to motivate much of our social existence.

But while Jordan would seem to subscribe to the conviction that myths play a central role in the *formation* of a national consciousness, he is equally aware that they can contribute to its *deformation*. Moreover, he explores the mythical not in terms of ancient legend but in terms of contemporary experience. His approach is *critical* in that it brings ethical scruples to bear on the exploration of the mythic unconscious; in so doing, he discloses how it can as easily lead to destructive fanaticism as to creative renewal.

Angel tells the story of a saxophone player, Danny, who encounters paramilitary violence and eventually becomes seduced by it. It is set, significantly, in Northern Ireland and opens with a band playing in a rural ballroom. The initial sequence introduces three women into Danny's orbit of performance: Deirdre, the lead singer in the band; a deaf-mute teenager named Annie; and a young bride in white who asks Danny to dance but is quickly snatched away by her jealous husband. Danny is drawn to each in turn. But it is with the mute Annie that he makes love after the dance in a shelter outside the ballroom. Though their encounter is almost accidental, it is far from manipulative. In a love scene accompanied by the elegiac score of Verdi's *Requiem*, the spectator glimpses a tale of fleeting innocence. Then, from the shelter, Annie and Danny see a car drive up to the ballroom. Four masked men exit and proceed to murder the manager of the showband because they believe he has paid protection money to a rival paramilitary group. When the unsuspecting Annie leaves the shelter to approach the killers they shoot her also. The gang escapes just before the ballroom, which they have mined with explosives, erupts into flames. Thus begins Danny's first encounter with the horror that will lead him to the heart of darkness. Romantic Ireland is irrevocably dead and gone.

This episode of violence unfolds with arresting rapidity, each image of mounting brutality cutting in upon the next. But amidst this traumatic sequence of terror, Danny fastens upon the stark image of an orthopaedic shoe worn by one of the killers. This frame is to become an indelible memory for Danny, repeated in successive flashbacks as he plummets towards an ever-deepening obsession with revenge.

Recovering from shock in a Belfast hospital, Danny is visited by two police detectives (presumably RUC or Anti-Terrorist Squad) called Bloom and Bonner. He tells them less than he knows and says nothing of the central clue – the orthopaedic shoe. The violence has become so *internalized* for Danny that he is determined to investigate it for himself. Danny chooses to explore this evil at a psychic level beneath the legal logic of politics and police. But he soon becomes entranced by the malignity he seeks to destroy. Danny's inordinately personalized quest for revenge eventually assumes the proportions of an impersonal obsession.

And so begins Danny's gradual substitution of violence for art. This transition is epitomized by Danny's departure from the band and his musical/love partner, Deirdre, as he removes his saxophone from its case and replaces it with an armalite. Indeed Deirdre's plaintive singing of the heroic Irish ballad 'Danny Boy' becomes ironically, and despite her intentions, a mock-heroic call to arms! The exchange of musical instrument and gun is a decisive scene. It occurs in Danny's childhood bedroom at his Aunty Mae's house. Employing sombre, dreamlike images, Jordan shows Danny undergoing here what psychoanalysis has described as a 'transfer of unconscious desires', as he switches from one 'transitional object' (the sax) to another (the machine gun). The transfer is patently a regressive one, conveyed in a trancelike sequence without the use of words or abstract theorizing.

Jordan offers the following account of this crucial psychic transition from artistic creativity to violent destruction:

> When you begin to work artistically you throw yourself to a certain extent into chaos, into the area of your mind and experience which is very volatile, even in some cases dangerous. The attraction of art, and perhaps the beauty of it, is that it can encapsulate all the beauty of sensual experience and at the same time allow you to meet this chaos and the darker side of your personality in, perhaps, the most meaningful way. Now violence to me – the attraction of violence – is the polar opposite to that. It does throw one into contact with chaos, with the darker side of human experience, with evil, and it does so, obviously, in the most brutal way imaginable.[6]

But while stressing the difference between art and violence as two ways of responding to the 'dark side' of the psyche, Jordan is equally aware, as is clear in *Angel*, of the uncanny similarities they possess:

> I think the lure of art for people is that very often it will give their lives a pitch of intensity they don't normally have. The lure of violence is quite similar, because it gives them this pitch of excitement, this visceral drive, and results in the decay of the human person ... In Danny, I wanted to posit a very innocent character who plays the saxophone and is obsessed with his instrument the way any musician is. It's interesting, by the way, that a lot of musicians call their instruments their axe. It's a strangely violent image. But there's a mechanic-of-the-arts thing about him; he's at home with his instrument, he knows how the key works, he could mend it himself even, and the first time he sees the gun, the appalling paradox of it is that on that basic mechanical level – a child's fascination with how the thing works – it has the same draw for him as the saxophone.[7]

One of the strengths of *Angel* is its precise ability to focus on this 'basic mechanical level' of reflex attraction and recoil, symptomatic of the workings of the subconscious. In this way Jordan investigates that fundamental nexus between aesthetic creativity and violence that has become one of the most frequented stamping grounds of modern art. One thinks of Yeats's 'Ben Bulben', Heaney's *North*, D.M. Thomas's *The White Hotel*, Visconti's *The Damned*, and perhaps most of all, Thomas Mann's *Dr. Faustus*. This last work examines the complex relationship between invention (the atonal symphonies of Schoenberg) and political barbarism (Nazism). And Mann, like Jordan, concludes with an impassioned plea for the recognition of the artist's ethical responsibility: 'One does wrong to see in aesthetics a separate and narrow field of the human. It is more than that, it is at bottom everything; it is what attracts and repels … Aesthetic release or the lack of it is a matter of one's fate, dealing out happiness and unhappiness, companionship or helpless if proud isolation on earth.' Mann's conclusion could well serve as an epilogue to *Angel*. Unable to find aesthetic release through his music, due to his psychic paralysis after Annie's murder, Danny resorts to the alternative 'play' of destruction (i.e. that which ironically occasioned his paralysis in the first place). Though initially motivated by the desire to avenge his lover, he soon finds himself embroiled in an inexorable spiral of blood-letting.

After he leaves hospital, Danny succeeds in tracking down one of the killers, thanks to the cleft-foot clue and a chance encounter. He executes the paramilitary with the same mechanical ease with which he formerly played his instrument; and from then on it's simply a question of tracking down the other three members of the gang. As Danny progresses in his new vocation of avenging angel, he discovers that the assassins he has pledged to assassinate have private lives just like himself. This theme of the 'double' is heightened by the fact that each revenge-shooting is preceded by a scene where Danny confronts his paramilitary opponent in the intimacy of the latter's domestic existence. The first two assassins are confronted by Danny in the secluded privacy of their homes, the third in his sequestered forest love-nest. And the fourth gang-leader – who in a surprise denouement turns out to be the police inspector, Bonner – is finally tracked down in his birthplace: Bonner dies, gripping Danny in a desperate love/hate embrace, with the words – 'Stay with me, I grew up around here.' Moreover this same phrase, 'stay with me', was also uttered by the second assassin after he had been shot by Danny, thereby functioning as a refrain to reinforce the sinister collusion between Danny and the killers. Before each execution, Danny feels compelled to enter the inner circle of the victim's life, to find out his name, to understand his secret loves and hates. 'I want to know everything he ever did,' Danny says of one of the killers. It is this unnerving interplay between the public outer-world of the thriller plot and the private inner world of psychic motivation that hallmarks *Angel* as an original cinematic exploration of Irish political violence. What the film really seeks to detect is the psychological and social motivation that can transform the hero, Danny Boy, from an angel into a psychopath (a point echoed by the young bride of the dancehall scene who warns Danny that 'men start out as angels but end up as brutes').

To this end, Jordan juxtaposes the surface-structure of the 'detective' narrative, full of fast-moving suspense, with a deep-structure of psychic probing. This latter structure exposes the underworld of unconscious obsession that preconditions the action of the 'political' plot (i.e. the gang's assassination of Annie, Danny's assassination of the gang, and the police hunt for both the gang and Danny). The psychic deep-structure of the film lies beneath the 'police story' (as the detective, Bloom, says to Danny: 'You can go places where I can't go'), and operates according to a radically different temporality. Borrowing the terms of structural linguistics, we might say that while the deep-structure unfolds 'synchronically' by repeating key visual and sound motifs, the surface-structure progresses 'diachronically' according to the standard conventions of a sequential plot. It is the deeper (synchronic) structure that expresses the poetic, ethical and psychological dimensions that most interests Jordan:

> Given that the film is a thriller, and given that I wanted to speak about morality and questions of good and evil and the soul, I didn't want to make it with the speed, and the glitter, and the distractions with which action films are normally made. I wanted to do precisely the opposite of that. When someone is holding a gun on somebody else I wanted him to be actually asking the question of what they're like. I wanted all the time to polarise and contrast the act of violence with the actual poetic dimensions of people's lives.[8]

Perhaps the most effective example of deep-structure in *Angel* is the use of *defamiliarizing* images. These introduce a mood of reflective stillness that cuts across and punctuates the high-speed action of the surface-plot. One might cite such scenes as the highly surreal montage of the asylum sequence that precedes the second execution; the elegiac scene with the Salvation Army band on the Bray waterfront that follows the second assassination; the mountain landscape of uncanny silence that serves as sequel to Danny's execution of the third killer in her car; and the final faith-healing rite between Danny and the child that preludes the execution of Bonner.

These framing episodes are synchronic to the extent that their stylized unreality interrupts the linear melodrama of the narrative, turning our attention to a deeper level of awareness. With this 'alienation' device, Jordan's vertical images serve to freeze the flow of the action, frustrating our common explanations and heightening our critical perception. Jordan thus makes the viewer reflexively aware of his/her own responses. By disrupting the realist conventions of cinematic representation, he exposes the way in which the very process of fictional narrative operates. This technique enables the viewer to delve beneath the tribal clichés of Ulster violence, so conditioned by daily newsreel, to its 'unconscious' or 'unseen' dimensions. It lets us glimpse what goes on behind the scenes.

One of the most important consequences of this disruption of linear narrative in *Angel* is the film's refusal to allow the spectator to identify passively with the avenging hero. The legendary national stereotype of Danny Boy (that incidentally served as the title for the film on its release in America) is debunked both formally and thematically. *Angel* may be considered accordingly as a deromanticization of the cult of heroic violence – a cult that has fuelled sentimental nationalism in many of its traditional and contemporary guises.

II. *Murphy's* Maeve

If Neil Jordan's *Angel* disputes the cinematic stereotype of the national hero in arms, Pat Murphy's *Maeve* dismantles the corresponding stereotype of the national heroine in alms, i.e. Irish woman as a perpetual Deirdre of the Sorrows. This latter stereotype had dominated film portrayals of Irish women not only in the early cinema of the cultural revival but also in much contemporary cinema. In a study entitled 'Aspects of Representation of Women in Irish Film', Barbara O'Connor states the problem thus:

> Among the most powerful tools of women's ideological oppression, is their media representation. These images of women have contributed in no small way to a patriarchal hegemony in which the real class and gender relations of women in society have been replaced by myths. Cinema, as one of the mainstream media, has been instrumental in the repression of a woman's discourse ... Film production in the early decades of the new Irish State was characterised by a choice of theme whose aim was the consolidation of this state (exemplified by strict censorship). The consequences of this for the representation of women was that they were either absent from a screen which was concerned with the epic deeds of the male heroes of Irish history or cast in the role of mother or sweetheart of these same heroes. Turning from a celebration of Irish customs and traditions to a critique of many aspects of our way of life, the 'New Wave' of film makers opened up some space for women to re-emerge into history.[9]

Perhaps the most important figure in this new wave of film makers to challenge the mythic representations of Irish women is Pat Murphy. *Maeve* is a film that rescues the mythological Queen Maeve from her ideological distortion in the revivalist version of Irish history and restores her, 'demythologized' as it were, to the contemporary context of war-torn Ulster. Murphy achieves this rewriting of orthodox myth by advancing an avant-garde cinema whose object is 'the deconstruction of the forms of dominant cinema, which are seen as essentially patriarchal, and their replacement with new "feminine" forma.'[10]

The forms of dominant cinema are, however, pervasive. Apart altogether from such internationally produced melodramas as *Rory O'More* or *Ryan's Daughter*, there have also been a large number of 'home produced' films that continue to cast Irish women in the stock roles of passive romantic heroine or helpless victim. Recent examples of what we might call the 'Deirdre of the Sorrows' myth (in contrast to the 'Maeve' anti-myth) are to be found in the portrayal of women in such films as Wynne-Simmons' *Outcasts*, Kieran Hickey's *Attracta* and Edward Bennett's *Ascendancy*, all of which cast their heroines as hapless spiritual casualties of political crisis. Most of these films not only conform to the traditional typecasting of Irish women; they also subscribe to the cinematic conventions of naturalist narrative.

Pat Murphy's *Maeve* runs directly counter to this mainstream. Made by an Irish woman to champion the cause of women's liberation in Ireland, this film is also set in modern Ulster and takes as its central heroine a Belfast girl suffering from the tribal conflicts of male aggression. (Maeve and her family are abused by the British army, and her boyfriend is a member of the Provos.) But Pat Murphy radically shifts the emphasis of her portrayal so that her heroine moves from the passivity of paralysis to the activity of protest. She departs from the mythology of Deirdre of the Sorrows in order to embrace the opposing mythology of Maeve as a figure of resistance and revolt. Maeve not only suffers but acts. To the military and patriarchal ideology of men she opposes the liberation struggle of the female body. The war of the sexes replaces the war of the tribes. As Luke Gibbons has remarked:

> Sexuality … as represented by powerful female figures such as Maeve, had to be written out of Irish history, a task for which a heightened narrative impelled by violent action was eminently suitable. It is hardly surprising then that the return of another Maeve to Ulster should bring about a direct confrontation with this mythic version of the past. The only difference is that now the drama is taking place on the streets.[11]

The process of writing powerful women out of Irish history had already begun with Standish O'Grady, one of the major influences on the national cultural revival. In order to provide appropriate heroic narratives of 'gods and fighting men', O'Grady felt compelled to alter certain parts of the *Táin Bó Cúailnge* saga where Ulster is invaded by the warrior Queen of Connaught, Maeve. Maeve's rebellious spirit and 'loose morality' were so out of keeping with O'Grady's Romantic ideology that he felt compelled to exclude them. As Philip Marcus observes in his book on O'Grady,

> The treatment of Maeve was perhaps most at variance with the source materials. O'Grady tried to make her seem more 'feminine', to endow her with some of the personality traits traditionally associated with the 'weaker sex', and at times the proud amazon of the sources seems more like the delicate fainting heroines of the nineteenth-century novel.[12]

Maeve decomposes not only the stereotype of Romantic heroine but also the traditional relationship in Irish cinema between mythic landscape, male heroism and linear narrative. The Romantic tradition of Irish cinema used the rural landscape as a reminder of the lost heroic age, of what O'Grady called the 'early Irish tales that cling around the mounds and cromlechs'. This reduction of historical time to a kind of eternal landscape was, in O'Grady's words, able to evoke legends 'believed in as history ... and drawing (their) life from the soil *like a natural growth*'.[13]

Murphy (like Jordan) uses flashback techniques to dispel the *natural* appearance of linear narrative. Several of these flashbacks show us the young child, Maeve Sweeney, accompanying her father from their home in urban Belfast on visits to the ancient stone monuments of the surrounding landscape. Her father, like O'Grady and other exponents of the Revival, sees the ruins of the past as bearers of national *myths* which he has come to believe in as *realities*. The landscape thus serves to identify political history with the magical power of nature. As they contemplate the legendary countryside, Maeve's father narrates the tales of the nationalist Revival. But Murphy strategically dislocates the normal flow of naturalistic narrative by decentering the traditional relationship between male (as controlling centre) and female (as passive background). Using various distancing devices, Murphy compels us to recognize that the images before us on the screen – no less than the 'stories in stones' that Maeve's father recounts – are constructs. This negates the desire of the paternal author to mask his own dominant role in the narrative by presenting it as if it were as natural as the stones in the landscape. In *Maeve* we are never allowed to forget that the inherited versions of history – as narrated by Maeve's father and boyfriend for example – are governed by a male vision of things. There are several scenes in which the controlling narrative of the father is exposed:

> the extent to which this continual appropriation of history removes women to the periphery is suggested in one striking later sequence in which Martin loses himself in an even more drawn out narrative than usual, while the young Maeve hovers in the background, edging herself along the circular walls of a ring-fort. As she reaches the centre of the frame, directly behind Martin, she alights from the stone wall of the fort thereby parting company with the dominant conception of history. Martin's authority has been displaced, a fact which is expressed cinematically in both of the storytelling sequences in question by the manner in which he is prevented from assuming the role of an invisible, omniscient narrator, and is forced instead to relate history in the form of a direct address to camera. By drawing attention to the authorial presence of the camera, and reminding the audience that they are in fact looking at a visual construction of reality, one of the main conditions of classical illusionistic narrative is undermined ...[14]

We witness a similar debunking of naturalist narrative in a later sequence where Maeve engages her republican boyfriend, Liam, in a long political argument about the use of violence in contemporary Ulster. During this exchange, which takes place on a hill overlooking Belfast, Liam's controlling narrative is subverted by Maeve's insertion of fragmented word-associations that disrupt the illusion of realist dialogue. By means of this estrangement technique, Liam's ideology is exposed as a patriarchal myth masquerading as reality. 'Whatever way you look at it,' as Pat Murphy explained in an interview in *Iris*,[15] 'the language of republicanism is patriarchal.' (And the film also features scenes, it must be noted, which expose the equally patriarchal character of the loyalist and British colonialist ideologies.) Brushing the realist conventions of visual and verbal narrative against the grain, Pat Murphy discloses how ideological myths – of whatever political persuasion – are fabrications of the mind, not facts of nature (as they pretend to be). Her shift of emphasis from the content of the storyline to the form of cinematic storytelling serves to remind the viewer that our political culture – like the film *Maeve* itself – is a *construct*, not a given. The film and the character of Maeve are, therefore, also myths of a kind. But they are *self-critical* myths that expose the very process whereby myths are made and unmade. Unlike ideologies, which lie to hide the truth, they are, as Maeve reminds Liam, 'lies which tell the truth'. This self-exposure of the devices of cinematic representation is witnessed not only in the self-conscious use of direct address to camera, of protracted non-naturalistic monologue and of flashback sequences that interrupt the forward flow of the story, but also in a number of pointed allusions to the *television medium* as a means of insulating people from their surrounding social environment. Here again Luke Gibbons provides a perceptive commentary:

> In the opening scenes of the film television violence competes for attention with the real life threat of the bomb-scare outside the front window, allowing Martin to retreat to the back-kitchen to compose the letter to Maeve which initiates the action of the film. The feelings of security generated by representations, which place the spectator at one remove from reality are shattered, however, in a subsequent scene (a flashback to the past) in which Maeve's family, watching July 12th celebrations on television, are abruptly brought back to earth by a brick coming through the window of their front room. In a later episode, the use of television as a security monitor in a Republican pub shows how representations no longer merely simulate but actively participate in the violence they portray, the image becoming an accomplice in, rather than a refuge from, the propaganda of the deed. In a similar manner, it is suggested, Martin's stories and fictions no longer serve to prevent his immersion in reality, a point illustrated to stark effect in one strange, almost surreal sequence, in which he is forced by a squad of British troops to unload a consignment of televisions from the back of his van onto the street, their screens silent, blank and ineffectual.[16]

By traditional standards, Maeve is very much an anti-heroine. She refuses the Romantic roles of sentimental girlfriend, domestic daughter and long-suffering victim. The rebel Maeve defies both the female stereotype of the sorrowing Deirdre and the male stereotype of the armed warrior. Yet while she critically dissociates herself from the Romantic myth of national heroine devoted to her military hero or tribal landscape, Maeve never resorts to indifference. She remains aware of the immense social and moral responsibility resulting from the discovery that national myths are historical constructions. But this sense of responsibility leads her to commit herself not to a patriarchal movement of resistance through ideology, but to an opposing female movement of resistance through the body. 'When you're denied power,' as she explains to Liam during their final exchange, 'the only form of struggle is through your body.'

Maeve seems to suggest that one of the most effective ways of divesting history of the ideological myths of the dead past is to affirm the positive powers of desire and sexuality. Over and against the sectarian violence of Ulster, domi-nated as Maeve puts it by the ideology of 'purity and death', the solution lies not in some escapist return to the haven of family domesticity – for this would simply be to reinforce the traditional gender stereotypes that oppose the public world of male action to the private world of female passivity – but in the asser-tion of the body as a site of political struggle where private and public coincide. Rescuing the female body from the dominant representations of Romantic nationalism, Maeve resolves to liberate republicanism from its male-dominated mythology. So doing, she transcends tribal factionalism in the name of a universal solidarity between all those oppressed by patriarchal ideologies. This new found solidarity is illustrated in the hospital scene where the Catholic Maeve finds herself side by side with an old Protestant woman who sings 'Abide with me'. The concluding scenes of the film offer a vivid summary of the central implications of Maeve's revolt:

> Many of the film's key concerns – landscape and memory, history and narra-tive, male discourse and female solidarity – converge in the penultimate scene set in the Giant's Causeway, one of the most important antiquarian sites in Ireland. The total disintegration of the male controlling voice is evident in the figure of the ranting orator, hurling the rhetoric of the Ulster covenant at the sea while Maeve, Roisin and Eileen find refuge behind the rocks, sharing jokes and confidences and experiencing a new collective identity.[17]

Angel and *Maeve* are both innovative films that debunk some of the stereo-types that have dominated not only mainstream Irish cinema but the national cultural revival as a whole. Both films are set in deromanticized urban contexts and deal with themes of contemporary relevance: the violence in Ulster; the modern popular culture of dancehall, pub gigs and television; the sexual and psychological relations between men and women. Both films also succeed, at a formal level, in subverting the uniform narratives of classical realism that encourage the viewer to passively identify with heroic characters in an unbroken linear plot. Such realist narratives are easy to follow, using techniques that ensure unbroken continuity of action, so that with the final 'closure' of the plot the viewer is also 'closed', i.e. satisfied and unquestioning.

Neil Jordan and Pat Murphy are two young directors who have been deeply marked by the formal experimentalism of the radical new wave of modern European cinema and have responded accordingly by dismantling many of the old narrative conventions that in Irish cinema so faithfully served the ideology of revivalism. Their respective critiques of the orthodox typecasting of national hero and heroine have not just focused on what is portrayed but also and more importantly on how it is portrayed. In short, the shift in content has been accompanied by a corresponding shift in form. Jordan and Murphy are not content with merely telling stories; they critically expose the way in which stories are constructed by means of camera work, cinematic narrative, framing devices and flashbacks: and, in so doing, they remind the viewer that highly complex structures are at work in the visual telling of a story, or at a broader level, in the making of a myth. Jordan and Murphy have set radical precedents for future experimental projects in Irish cinema. They have proved that it is possible to penetrate beneath the surface of visual and verbal ideologies and to expose the processes whereby myths and stereotypes are constructed.

CHAPTER EIGHTEEN

An Art of Otherness:
A Study of Louis le Brocquy

Le Brocquy's journey as a painter has been marked by two overriding and inter-related obsessions – the phenomenon of whiteness and the image of the head. What appears most to fascinate the painter about these two subjects is their basic refusal to be represented in terms of a single perspective. They are for le Brocquy an invitation, above all else, to an *otherness of perception*.

I

The colour white has been a frequent obsession of artists. Malevich, the revolu-tionary Russian painter, made his controversial tableau *White on White* (1917) the centrepiece of the avantgarde Suprematist movement. Whiteness was the ulti-mate statement of Suprematism as a search, through the material of paint, for the 'infinite intangible' – the matrix where the visible intersects with the invisible. It was for similar reasons that Herman Melville, the American novelist, chose the elusive whiteness of the whale as a central theme in *Moby Dick* describing it as 'not so much a colour as the visible absence of colour, and at the same time the concrete of all colours ... a dumb blankness, full of meaning ... a colourless all-colour.' From *The Blue Door*, one of his earliest works painted in 1932, to his *Presences* sequence in the 1950s and 1960s, to his more recent studies of heads emerging from white backgrounds, le Brocquy has pursued his exploration of the essential *ambivalence* of whiteness as colourless all-colour. In all of these paintings, white serves as the hidden dimension from which forms emerge and recede, an absence which presences, an interplay of light and shadow in which

298

substance – devoid of circumstance – dissolves. John Russell, the American critic, has described le Brocquy as a painter who 'lays siege to whiteness'.

In his series of head images, begun in the mid-1970s, le Brocquy makes a partly white face emerge from a white background and at the same time recede back into it:

> It is the play between the different areas of white which makes the paintings go taut with energy. The face which looms up leads us to sense the presence of the person in the white surrounds. Yet these surrounds elicit at the same time a feeling of absence, of a void. This void enters the face through the white areas of the latter. We look again and again at this face which leads us once more into the white background. And so a circulation of glances (or energies) is set up and it is this circulation which produces the characteristic ambivalence (presence/absence, passing/timelessness, animation/coldness) of the portraits, their 'spiritual' energy.[1]

Le Brocquy's preoccupation with the face or head image appears to have a double focus. On the one hand, it draws its inspiration from the ancient practice of stone headcarving that dates back to the very origins of Western art. 'The heads themselves in the high-relief sculpture of Celto-Ligurian Entremont', writes le Brocquy, 'and the heads within the "plummet-measured face" of Romanesque Clonfert (are) at once persons and stone bosses, both durable and timeless, forever emerging and receding.'[2] Le Brocquy maintains that what most interests him about these ancient heads is their ability to signify 'a profound paradox – a succession of presents spread out before us, without beginning or end'.[3] On the other hand, le Brocquy's fascination with the head image has resulted in a series of portrait studies of modernist artists – both Irish (Joyce, Beckett, Yeats) and non-Irish (Strindberg, Bacon, Lorca). These portraits seek to represent the artists' spiritual consciousness through the material medium of paint. And this attempt to give palpable expression to the modernist consciousness through the primitive idiom of the head image involves le Brocquy in a fundamentally ambivalent probing of different and often conflicting planes of time and space. The result is an endless series of inconclusive representations that bear witness to the essential *otherness* of human experience: that is, its refusal to be represented in a single image of identity.

Le Brocquy's *120 Studies towards an Image of Joyce* are a good case in point. This series epitomizes the painter's commitment to the multifaceted nature of perception. The quality of open-endedness ensures that no one image can be isolated from the sequence and accorded a privileged status. Like Joyce's own disclosure of the multiple meanings of words in *Finnegans Wake*, le Brocquy's multiple representations of the Joyce head reveal that the goal of a definitive identity forever eludes us. The potentially interminable character of the series as 'studies *towards* an image ...' may be seen as a sort of visual palimpsest, a painter's witness to the impossibility of freezing creative consciousness in a fixed perspective. The recognized Joyce is thus rendered unrecognizable, his familiar identity defamiliarized. And in this respect, we might say that le Brocquy is being faithful to one of the most basic impulses of modernist art: the disclosure of the pluri-dimensional character of human consciousness. His work may be viewed in terms of Cézanne's resolve to *éclater la perspective*, Rimbaud's call for a *dérèglement systématique des sens*, or indeed Joyce's discovery that language is a 'bringer of plurabilities'. Le Brocquy provides us with the best guide to the understanding of his own work in the following description of what he calls the 'multiple identity' of the Joyce heads:

> Ever since I rediscovered for myself the image of the head, I have painted studies of James Joyce ... Thus almost 120 studies towards an image of James Joyce have emerged in one medium or another. It remains an unending task. For to attempt today a portrait, a single static image of a great artist like Joyce seems to me futile as well as impertinent. Long conditioned by photography, the cinema and psychology, we now perceive the human individual as faceted, kinetic. And so I have tried as objectively as possible to draw from the depths of paper or canvas changing and even contradictory traces of James Joyce ... I myself therefore see these studies rather as an indefinite series without beginning or end and thus perhaps in tendency counter-Renaissance, as in a sense was also Joyce himself.[4]

Modernism, as we have noted in preceding chapters, revolted against the Renaissance convention of classical realism that promoted the illusion of a single controlling perspective. Joyce's dismantling of classical (linear) narrative and le Brocquy's refusal of classical (perspectival) representation both attest to their counter-Renaissance impulse. Le Brocquy's head series shatters the illusion of orthodox portraiture and introduces an arresting sense of *otherness*. One of the consequences of this formal experimentalism in his studies of the canonized figures of Irish national literature – Yeats, Joyce, Beckett – is to oblige the spectator to view these familiar faces in an unfamiliar way, revealing a disturbing *alien* quality that forbids the security of immediate appropriation.

Roland Barthes, a French philosopher, speaks of the inability of bourgeois realism to 'imagine the other'. Once the bourgeois realist is confronted with the other, 'he blinds himself, ignores and denies him, or else transforms him into himself. In the petit-bourgeois universe ... any otherness is reduced to sameness.'[5] Le Brocquy's paintings are, in this sense, a rebuke to the norms of bourgeois realism. By resisting our uniform modes of perception, they refuse to reduce the other to the same. We thus witness the images of the great modernist artists self-destruct before our eyes, exposing the art product as an endless

production of meaning. We, the spectators of these images, are denied any dominant position from which to tally the representation with some supposed 'original'. Le Brocquy's portraits of the artists implicate the onlooker in the artistic
process itself. As a perpetual dissemination of traces they cannot be retraced to
some 'real' model existing outside of the series of representations. Thus le
Brocquy's images of Joyce reveal that Joyce's identity as an artist is as elusive as
the art that he created and in which, in his own words, 'the forms multiply
themselves indefinitely'.[6] Unable to *possess* the image we are compelled to
imagine it, and indeed ourselves, as other. For as le Brocquy explains, 'art is
neither an instrument, nor a convenience, but a secret logic of the imagination.
It is *another* way of seeing, the whole sense and value of which lies in its
autonomy, its distance from actuality, its *otherness*.'[7]

II

Some might view this modernist preoccupation with the otherness of art as a
symptom of elitism, even obscurantism. But the matter is not so simple. There
are many who argue the opposite, viewing the aesthetic of otherness as a form
of radical, even revolutionary, consciousness. Thus we find the Marxist playwright Bertolt Brecht championing the alienation or estrangement (*Verfremdung*) effects of modernist theatre. Brecht's own experimental drama renounced
the tendency of bourgeois audiences to passively identify with the language, plot
or characters on stage through an uncritical process of psychological realism.
Brecht affirmed that the major task of art was to challenge our preconceived
assumptions and enable us to see the world in a new way. 'A work which does
not exhibit its sovereignty *vis-à-vis* reality', Brecht wrote, 'and which does not
bestow sovereignty upon the public *vis-à-vis* reality is not a work of art.' And
Joyce, it might be recalled, made a similar point when he explained that he
wrote the nighttime language of *Finnegans Wake* 'because a great part of every
human existence is passed in a state which cannot be rendered sensible by the
use of wide awake language'.[8]

In his last published work, *The Aesthetic Dimension* (1979), the German philosopher Herbert Marcuse defends the radical potential of art's 'distance from actuality'. Challenging all forms of aesthetic realism (be it the socialist realism of
orthodox Marxism or the classical realism of bourgeois conformism), Marcuse
argues for a recognition of the arresting strangeness of art:

> The radical qualities of art, that is to say, its indictment of the established
> reality and its invocation of the beautiful image (*schöner Schein*) of liberation
> are grounded precisely in the dimension where art *transcends* its social deter-
> mination and emancipates itself from the given universe of discourse and

behaviour ... The world formed by art is recognised as a reality which is suppressed and distorted in the given reality. This experience culminates in extreme situations (of love and death, guilt and failure, but also joy, happiness and fulfilment) which explode the given reality in the name of truths normally denied or even unheard. The inner logic of the work of art terminates in the emergence of another reason, another sensibility, which defies the rationality and sensibility incorporated in the dominant social institutions.[9]

What Marcuse refers to here as the inner logic of the aesthetic dimension is what le Brocquy calls the secret logic of imagination. This logic subverts actual worlds in the name of possible worlds; it refuses to subscribe to the everyday exigencies of social pragmatism in order to disclose hitherto occluded dimensions of meaning. Le Brocquy insists upon the necessity of such aesthetic transcendence with uncompromising candour: 'In the context of our everyday lives, painting must be regarded as an entirely different form of awareness, for an essential quality of art is its alienation, its otherness. In art at its most profound levels, actuality – exterior reality – is seen to be relevant, parallel, but remote or curiously dislocated.'[10] In other words, art must keep the established reality – be it social or perceptual – at arm's length. For only by thus alienating itself from reality can it liberate the alienated dimensions of reality. Le Brocquy's work is, by his own admission, an attempt to give '*possible* form to that which is impalpable and interiorised' by revealing that 'reality is that which is possible, conceivable and not merely what is actual and phenomenal'.[11]

This is not, of course, to consign modernist painting to a reactionary creed of art-for-art's sake. The alienation of art should not be misconstrued as an *indifference* to social well-being. On the contrary, as Marcuse reminds us, the autonomy of art contains the categorical imperative – *things must change*.[12] It is precisely the aesthetic dimension of transcendence that keeps us perpetually dissatisfied with the established order of things. The *difference* of art reminds us that the world too can be *different*, that there is always something *more*. So that if le Brocquy's images are not immediately familiar to orthodox one-dimensional consciousness, this is not an argument against these images but against the existing orthodoxy.

The modernist aesthetic of otherness therefore has radical social implications. By refusing to conform to the officially accepted paradigms of perception, art revolts against the social order that it is supposed to submissively represent. Modernist art protests against the suppression, however subtle, of *alternative* ways of viewing our world; it explodes the norms of conventional communication and response: 'Art has its own language and illuminates reality only through this *other* language.'[13]

III

There have been attempts to undermine the otherness of art. Both the Agitprop and Performance Art movements in the West and the Socialist Realist movement in the East have, in their different ways, sought to subordinate art to the existing social reality. Performance art, for example, breaks down the barriers separating the aesthetic and the everyday by presenting art as an immediately consumable commodity. The performance artist works to demolish the distance between the art object and its audience, as for example during the 1980 Rosc exhibition in Dublin when street bystanders were invited to devour a Joyce-tower made of locally baked brown bread. The purpose of this *happening* was clearly to annihilate the notion of art as some autonomous activity displayed in galleries or museums. But it could be argued that by collapsing the divide between the otherness of art and the sameness of our consumer society, the performer divests his work of its radically estranging and therefore emancipating power. Once art entirely abandons its distinctly aesthetic dimension does it not endorse the formless reality that it presumably wishes to indict? Such exercises in anti-art as this Rosc performance or Andy Warhol's famous line of Campbell's soup tins may well be self-defeating to the extent that they succumb to the everyday world of consumer exploitation that radical art intends to subvert. As Brecht warned, the total repudiation of aesthetic form and distance leads all too often to a regressive banalization of experience.

While le Brocquy's paintings alter aesthetic form, they do not abandon it. They remain essentially liberating in so far as they disassemble outworn forms of representation, not in order to sanction formlessness, but in order to reconstruct *different* forms. Le Brocquy's art reinterprets our everyday way of seeing, transforming meaning as it has *already been expressed* into meanings *yet to be expressed*. In this sense, it is an uncompromising indictment of the perceptual, and by implication social, status quo. For once our inner vision changes we realize that the outer world can also change. Aesthetic transformation may thus serve as a prelude to social transformation, but it can only do so by insisting on the *difference* between the worlds of art and reality: that is, by refusing to become a weapon of propaganda or a commodity of consumerism. In short, it is precisely the otherness of art that reminds us that the world as it is can be made *other* than it is.

If we look towards the East, we find the official aesthetic of Socialist Realism obliging artists to compose works that faithfully reflect the 'genuine social reality'. The irony here is that it is the party propagandist, not the poet or painter, who ultimately decides what is 'genuine', what is 'social' and what is 'reality'. As Leonid Brezhnev remarked in his address to the 1981 Soviet Party Congress: 'The Party encourages ... art's active intervention in the solution of our society's problems ... The heroes of works of art should not withdraw into trivial affairs but live with the concerns of their country at heart.' Brezhnev went on to champion a literature devoted to the heroic life of the socially committed worker, be it 'a building team leader, a collective farm chairman, a railway worker or army officer'. Nor did he make any bones about affirming the Party's duty to monitor the 'ideological orientation of art' and to ensure it remained 'active in the building of communism'. But is there not a patronizing benevolence in this glorification of the factory-floor in the name of the collective good? Does it not amount to saying that the toil, suffering and exploitation of the worker (East or West) is an aesthetic model of experience (which it patently is not)?

Le Brocquy's art could certainly not be described, by any stretch of the imagination, as an 'active intervention in the solution of society's problems'. But his unflagging commitment to the exploration of visual *inwardness* may be seen as a disclosure of an aesthetic dimension that refuses the misery of exploitation and manipulation. By sustaining an irreducible distance, one might even say antagonism, between the interiority of art and the exteriority of the social universe, le Brocquy's work testifies to the fact that the present world of domination can never fully eliminate the potential world of freedom. The basic thesis that art must be a factor in changing the world, as Marcuse has observed, 'can easily turn into its opposite if the tension between art and radical praxis is flattened out so that art loses its own dimension for change ... The flight into inwardness may well serve as a bulwark against a society which administers all dimensions of human existence. Inwardness and subjectivity may well become the inner and outer space for the subversion of experience, for the emergence of another universe.'[14]

Le Brocquy maintains that there is a deep connection between the aesthetic dimensions of *inwardness* and *otherness*. As he explained in an interview with Harriet Cooke: 'I often think of painting as being a kind of personal archaeology, I feel one is digging for things and suddenly something turns up which seems to be remarkable; something apparently outside oneself, which one has found in fact within oneself.'[15] By means of palpable paint, le Brocquy is groping towards an impalpable interiority of meaning, what he calls 'the inner reality of the human presence beyond its merely external appearance'.[16] But when le Brocquy speaks of the primacy of subjective inwardness he is not for a moment advancing the romantic supremacy of the individual will or cogito (which typified both Cartesian subjectivism and bourgeois individualism). Le Brocquy has repeatedly affirmed that his painting is not primarily self-expression, but the exploration of an interior dimension of otherness that explodes our assured personal identity and suspends our controlling will. (It is what Beckett, in his Proust essay, called the revelation of involuntary imagination.) Le Brocquy defines subjectivity accordingly as 'an interior invisible world', an 'autonomous disseminated consciousness surpassing individual personality'.[17] He believes that the painter must await the emergence of the image without imposing his own voluntary projections:

> When painting I try not to impose myself. Discoveries are made – such as they are – while painting. The painting itself dictates and although the resultant image seems rhetorical to some, it appears to me to be almost autonomous, having emerged under one's hands not because of them … *Invention* for me is *discovery*.[18]

By embracing the polyvalent stream of inwardness, the artist strives to overcome his centralizing cogito in order to 'discover, uncover and reveal'.[19] Seamus Heaney has written perceptively of this aspect of le Brocquy's archaeology of painting as an emergence of the *other* through the inner dissolution of the mastering *self*:

> Yet that hand does not seek to express its own personality. It is obedient rather than dominant, subdued into process as it awaits a discovery. What it comes up with will sometimes feel like something come upon, a recognition. Like a turfcutter's spade coming upon the body on the bog, the head of the Tollund Man, ghostly yet palpable, familiar and other, a historical creature grown ahistorical, an image that has seized hold of the eye and will not let it go.[20]

IV

How, if at all, does le Brocquy relate to his own culture or to those other Irish authors and artists whose work we have been examining in the preceding chapters? True to the paradox of the artistic consciousness as a dialectic between sameness and otherness, le Brocquy maintains that, like Joyce before him, it was only after his departure from Ireland and subsequent encounter with 'foreign' cultures that he became deeply obsessed by his native culture.

> Although I was born in Dublin in the year of the Rebellion, [he writes] and brought up entirely in Ireland, I do not remember being conscious of being particularly Irish … None seemed to me less manifestly Irish than that small family whose name I bore. Then one day in my 21st year, I precipitously sailed from Dublin into a new life as a painter studying in the museums of London, Paris, Venice and Geneva … Alone among the great artists of the past, in these strange related cities, I became vividly aware for the first time of my Irish identity to which I have remained attached all my life.[21]

But le Brocquy strenuously resists the dangers of what he terms 'self-conscious nationalism'. He believes that art betrays itself as soon as it subscribes to cultural insularism. While admitting that the 'flowering of our imagination is nourished by roots hidden in our native soil', le Brocquy opposes the manipulative use of self-righteous national identity.

The art critic Dorothy Walker maintains that le Brocquy's preoccupation with head images and cyclical structures is a distinct borrowing from the Celtic heritage.[22] This debt to Celtic visual motifs combines with le Brocquy's modernist commitment to innovative forms of representation that run counter to the Renaissance conventions of classical realism and centralized linear perspective. Le Brocquy himself has argued that we are currently witnessing a revolutionary transition from an essentially *perceptual* and outward-looking art to a new decentralized art that rediscovers the source of meaning 'within the mind and within those *conceptual*, interiorised images of a world transformed'. While the perceptual era, devoted to exterior surface phenomena, held sway from the Renaissance up to the turn of the twentieth century, in recent decades 'the painter has been insistently aware of those renewed conceptual tendencies characteristic of painting in our time'.[23] Le Brocquy suggests that it was Joyce's enthusiasm for this counter-Renaissance tendency that accounts for his profound interest in the Medieval and Celtic universes of nighttime consciousness (a suggestion confirmed by Arthur Power who was told by Joyce that 'the Renaissance and its return to classicism was a return to intellectual boyhood').[24] We thus find le Brocquy surmising that the plural identity of his own images of Joyce 'may represent a more medieval or Celtic viewpoint, cyclic rather than linear, repetitive yet simultaneous and, above all, inconclusive.'[25]

In his fragmented and polymorphous images of Joyce, le Brocquy succeeds in evoking the fundamental ambivalence of time, space and emotion that so typify the world of *Ulysses* and *Finnegans Wake*. The pluralizing interiority of consciousness tends to produce, le Brocquy notes, 'an ambiguity involving a dislocation of our individual conception of time (within which coming and going, beginning and end, are normally regarded) and confronts this *normal* view with an alternative, contrary sense of simultaneity or timelessness, switching the linear conceptions of time to which we are accustomed to a circular concept returning upon itself, as in *Finnegans Wake*'. And le Brocquy adds his conviction that his alternative mode of vision can be reproduced in a certain paratemporal dimension of painting, a dimension that manifests itself in a double role 'involving a transmogrification of the paint itself into the image and vice versa'.[26] 'In my own small world of painting,' he writes, 'I myself have learned from the canvas that emergence and immergence − twin phenomena of time − are ambivalent: that one implies the other and that the state or matrix within which they coexist apparently dissolves the normal sense of time, producing a characteristic *stillness*.'[27] This is certainly an accurate description of that enigmatic confluence of presencing and absencing that le Brocquy's studies of the head embody. Indeed le Brocquy explicitly relates the visual paradoxes of his own paintings to the verbal paralogisms of Joyce's writing, simultaneously day-consciousness and night-consciousness, 'like Ulysses and Finnegan, or like a living human head image of the whole in the part, the old synecdochism of the Celt'.[28]

Is this, le Brocquy asks finally, 'the underlying ambivalence which we in Ireland tend to stress ... the indivisibility of birth and funeral, spanning the apparent chasm between past and present, between consciousness and fact?'[29] It may well be. But if it is, such a Celtic prototype offers le Brocquy and Joyce not the solidarity of some antiquarian repossession but the solitude of modern dispossession: less a Celtic Twilight than a Celtic darkness, an encounter with an inwardness that remains so irretrievably other that it abrogates any triumphalist tenure within a continuous tradition.[30] When Stephen Dedalus talked of forging the conscience of his race he significantly reminded us that it was still *uncreated*. Cultural identity, like national identity, is not something presupposed; it remains an open-ended task, an endless narrative to be reinterpreted by each artist in his own way. The time-space ambivalence of consciousness that manifests itself in le Brocquy's art is so different from our given modes of perception that it shatters rather than substantiates any centrist notion of identity. As another contemporary painter Patrick Collins remarked, one of the most consistent features of Irish art has been its propensity to erase any suspicion of a stable or unchanging tradition. In the best works of modern Irish art, Collins claims, the poet or painter brings himself 'to the point where he eliminates himself' and, by extension, the orthodox tradition from which he derives.[31] So if the Irish hero Finn becomes Finn-again in Joyce's writings, or the Irish writer Joyce becomes Joyce again in le Brocquy's paintings, it is only in both cases by becoming radically other.

Le Brocquy's dual fidelity to the *otherness* of both ancient Celtic and modern experimental art suggests that his work may be appropriately located in the tension between the revivalist and modernist impulses of contemporary Irish culture.

Appendix: Le Brocquy and Ballagh – A Postmodern Dimension?

Le Brocquy's work may be usefully compared and contrasted with that of another contemporary Irish painter who seeks to negotiate a passage between tradition and modernity – Robert Ballagh.

Whereas le Brocquy's work celebrates the otherness of art, Ballagh is more concerned to demystify it. He likes the idea of his art being *used*. Hence his decision to make stamps for the Irish postal system, posters for the trade unions, colour screens for the student cafeteria in University College Dublin and pop portraits for such patrons of the nation as Brendan Smith and Charlie Haughey. Ballagh is proud of the possibility that in years to come his stamps may be considered more important than his paintings. He refuses the view that socially useful or commissioned works are a betrayal of art. And he has little time for the argument expressed by Clement Greenberg, the high priest of modernist abstraction, that painting has nothing to do with anything other than itself. Even those who defend the autonomy of art cannot escape, says Ballagh, the investment speculations of the gallery-dealer system.

Art has always been linked to commercialism and developments in technology, Ballagh points out in reply to those who dispute his use of techniques drawn from popular culture and the mass media. There has, he insists, never been anything immaculate about the conception of art: 'Artists are fooling themselves and everyone else if they fuss about at the edge of society saying "I'm pure, I'm a virgin, I won't sully my hands"(quoted in *Robert Ballagh* by Ciaran Carty, *Magill*, 1986). For Ballagh, the artist is just as conditioned by the society in which he/she lives as any other kind of worker; and painting, like every other mode of production, is the expression of a specific place and time in history. A child of the contemporary age of comic strips, movies and rock music, Ballagh endorses the collapse of the old dichotomy between High Art and popular culture. He sees his New Realist portraits as pop posters designed to speak to the many rather than the few – their purpose being communication rather than contemplation.

Ballagh considers this set of preferences as an option for the more populist impulse of postmodernism over the elitist formalism of modernism. In this respect, as in many others, he would appear to be radically different from le Brocquy. But the matter is not so simple. Le Brocquy and Ballagh have more in common than first meets the eye. Both would share the postmodern credo (announced by architect Philip Johnson) that 'you cannot *not* know history'. Both believe that the consciousness of the artist is deeply informed by a particular set of cultures and traditions. And both reject the modernist cult of the Briefly New – the illusion that every art movement must be a Giant Leap Forward for Mankind, a total break with everything that preceded it – preferring to 're-connect' (Ballagh's phrase) with the discarded traditions of Western art. Moreover, this postmodern desire to 're-connect' has for Ballagh, as for le Brocquy, nothing to do with a revivalist program of reactionary restoration. In contradistinction to the conservative habit of *imitation*, the postmodern tendency in Ballagh and le Brocquy functions according to the radical method of *quotation* – the belief that art opens onto the future by quoting its own past, rewriting and reinventing itself in a paradoxical and often parodic fashion. Postmodernism sees history less as *continuity* than as *collage*. The modern aesthetic of inevitable novelty and progress is replaced by a postmodern mixing of multiple styles and images drawn from past and present.

Le Brocquy's head series might be described as postmodern in this sense. They represent a curious blending of the old and the new, the ancient and the modern. At one level, they depict the great minds of modern art – Yeats, Joyce, Beckett, Bacon, Lorca. Yet at another, they look back (as le Brocquy informs us) to the ancient sculpted heads of Celto-Ligurian Entremont and Romanesque Clonfert. The end of Western art is thus superimposed on its beginning. Linear chronology is deconstructed into an ambiguous coexistence of different time-frames. This double vision, this temporal ambivalence, is not something invented *ex nihilo* by le Brocquy. It is discovered within the very consciousness of those he portrays. In Beckett's work, for example, he discovers that 'going is confounded with coming, backwards with forwards'. And in Joyce he discovers the convergence of dayconsciousness and nightconsciousness, of the modern-day Finnegan and the mythological Fionn MacCumhaill – 'spanning the apparent chasm between past and present'.

Ballagh also espouses the postmodern view of art as a collage of quotations drawn from diverse traditions of the past. 'Art cannot escape the past and the traditions that are ingrained in our consciousness,' observes Ballagh. 'We have to see where we come from. We have to recognise that we go further back than the modernist experience' (quoted in *Robert Ballagh*, op. cit.). But where le Brocquy used quotation as *paradox*, Ballagh uses it as *parody*. We could cite here, for example, his series of contemporary pastiches of classic masterpieces by Goya, Delacroix and David, or his mocking allusions to Velasquez and Vermeer in his own parodic self-portraits *Winter in Ronda* and *The Conversation*.

Another postmodern feature that le Brocquy and Ballagh share – despite the differences of their aesthetic practices – is a determination to dismantle the Renaissance and Romantic cult of the 'unique image'. This determination is exemplified in several contemporary works (e.g. the philosophies of Derrida and Baudrillard, the writings of Calvino and Pynchon, the films of Lynch or Tarantino), works that undermine their own status as original, isolated or finished objects. This is generally achieved by setting an open series of images into motion that expose their own lack of originality by alluding to other texts that have preceded them and preconditioned their meaning in some manner. Ballagh's parodies of the classical and Renaissance art-images and his use of pop poster reproduction techniques do this in an obvious way. But le Brocquy's work also testifies to a postmodern desire to debunk the fetish of the *unique image*. As noted, the multifaceted character of his head images refuses the Renaissance cult of an original, centralizing image. The multiplication of the image into an indefinite series of traces without beginning or end is essentially counter-Renaissance for le Brocquy, allowing for a mode of vision that is recursive rather than unique, inconclusive rather than fixed. But, by le Brocquy's own insistence, this counter-Renaissance tendency is not just a re-connection with pre-modern paradigms of Celtic and medieval art; it is also, and fundamentally, a reflection of the fact that we belong to a postmodern era of technical reproduction. 'Long conditioned by photography and the cinema,' le Brocquy affirms, 'we now perceive the human individual as faceted, kinetic.'

The works of le Brocquy and Ballagh compel us – in very different ways – to question the conventional rapport between images and their originals. By reproducing an almost endless series of reproducible images, they disinherit our received assumptions about representation. They undermine the modern cult of the authentic original and render the relationship between image and reality, copy and model, radically undecidable. In this postmodern gesture, le Brocquy and Ballagh find common ground.

Chapter Nineteen

Exchanging Memories:
New York Famine Memorial

I

In this paper I want to explore the relation between poetics and ethics as it pertains to the remembrance of time through place. I take as my guide here the hermeneutic model of 'exchanging memories' advanced by my friend and mentor Paul Ricoeur.[1] So doing, I will suggest that certain topographical memorials of historical trauma can epitomize an ethics of hospitality, flexibility, plurality, transfiguration and pardon. My chosen example will be the Irish Hunger Memorial in Battery Park in New York City, an interactive monument designed and installed by Brian Tolle in 2001 to commemorate the Great Irish Famine of the 1840s and the subsequent immigrations to North America.

First, a word about the memorial itself. The installation basically consists of a stone cottage transplanted from the west coast of Ireland to Battery Park at the very heart of downtown New York, not far from where the Twin Towers once stood.[2] The memorial does not attempt some nostalgic retrieval of a quaint Irish past – so often represented by picture postcard versions of the traditional thatched cottage. On the contrary, it seeks to re-imagine the past in its present condition of destitution and ruin. As such, Brian Tolle's installation might best be described as a hybrid construct that serves as both 1) a commemoration of the Great Irish Famine of the nineteenth century and 2) a site-specific art installation in metropolitan New York in the third millennium marking the on-going tragedy of world hunger. This double fidelity to separate moments in time provokes a sense of disorientation that prevents the act of memory regressing to some kind of sentimental fixation with the past (what Ricoeur calls 'blocked memory').[3] By the same token, it also prevents the exhibit from serving simply as an exotic curiosity of tourist voyeurism in the present.

This is a famine memorial with a difference. Whereas most conventional commemorations of the Famine featured 'people without land' (usually leaving on ships from Ireland or arriving off ships in the new world), we are confronted here with an uncanny experience of 'land without people'. Though the installation is located at the very heart of one of the world's most populous cities, there are no human beings represented here. As such it recalls the 'deserted village' of Slievemore on Achill Island, County Mayo, which was one of the artist's primary sources of inspiration for the work, where a haunting depopulated row of abandoned and decayed stone huts stand facing out towards the Atlantic. And it is reminiscent in its way of other monuments of historical rupture and ruin – e.g. the bare walls of Machu Picchu in Peru or the floating hulk of the *Marie Celeste*. It is a far cry in any case from the idealized portraits of rural Irish cottages by romantic landscape painters like Paul Henry or James O'Connor.

Tolle's installation resists mystification and mystique by presenting us with a powerful and disturbing sense of material 'thereness'. As we enter the site we are confronted with a fieldstone cottage, transplanted stone by stone from Ireland, and here reconstructed on its own quarter acre of soil in New York City. But it is impossible to feel at home here. This could never be a dwelling for us, contemporary visitors to the cottage. The most obvious reason for this is no doubt its location at the core of a bustling metropolitan cityscape where it is clearly *out of place*, misplaced and dislocated literally and symbolically. And the fact that the cottage and surrounding potato drills are themselves planted on a suspended limestone and concrete base doubly confirms the sense of not belonging. This sentiment of spatial disorientation provokes us, in turn, to reflect on the paradox that our sense of identity and placement in the world often presupposes an acute sense of loss and displacement. As when the Irish Captain MacMorris asks 'What is my nation?' in Shakespeare's *Henry V*, his question betraying the fact that he is preoccupied with his national identity precisely because he has *forfeited* it – he is speaking in the English language and wearing an English army uniform. Likewise, it has often been noted by Irish critics such as Declan Kiberd, Roy Foster and Luke Gibbons that Irish tradition is in many respects an *invention* by modernity,[4] just as our sense of the past is almost always constituted and reconstituted by our present historical consciousness.

This sense of spatial and temporal inversion is compounded here by the fact that the roofless cottage remains un-restored and is exposed to local weather conditions. Unlike most works of art, this installation is half construct and half nature – it is an artificially contrived synthesis of 'real' stone and soil and architectural-sculptural design. The underground tumuli and passageways, by which one enters the cottage from beneath, are further reminders that the cottage has

a dark and buried history – recalling not only the neolithic Irish burial cham-
bers of Newgrange, Knowth and Dowth in County Meath but also the unmarked
mass graves of thousands of famine victims in Ireland and elsewhere. The fact
that these subterranean passageways are themselves panelled with glass panes
covered in various texts and subtexts – historical, political, fictional, rhetorical,
spiritual, apologetic, testimonial – further adds to the sense of a plurality of
voices and interpretations. Tolle's memorial refuses to yield any quick fix. There
is no single, assured access to this placeless place, this timeless time. It cannot be
'naturalized' in the sense of celebrating some literal recovery of a landscape. Yet
it cannot be explained away either as a purely 'aestheticized' sculpture residing
in some museum space – for the site alters continually with the surrounding
weather and climate, one season covered with weeds, potato shoots and wild-
flowers, another with snow or mud, and at all times registering the odours,
reflections, shadows and sounds of the surrounding city. We are thus palpably
reminded of the passing of time, of historical fluidity and transience that no
monumental fixation can bring to a full stop. The myth of an eternal Celtic-Mist
landscape is demystified before our very eyes.[5]

Not that there weren't efforts by certain officials and politicians to perpetuate
the myths. On opening the site, for example, Governor Pataki of New York
spoke of the opportunity offered here 'to touch the sod of our heritage'; while
Mayor Giuliani concluded his inaugural speech with the words: 'May this beautiful Memorial, like Ireland itself, be forever free, forever green.' And some
members of the Irish tourist board praised the installation's capacity to evoke the
'rolling hills of old Ireland' – conveniently forgetting that the quaint potato field
is planted over a slab of concrete and surrounded by high rises! Certain Irish-
American societies and groups were also quick to contribute their own gloss to
this sentimentalizing process. Even the Irish government weighed in at one
point offering an authentic 'stone' from every county in Ireland (thirty-two in
all), along with an ancient pilgrim standing stone. While Tolle initially resisted
such appropriations he soon came to acknowledge that these readings should
not simply be dismissed as inappropriate or misguided. Instead he realized that
any *interactive* installation of this kind must learn to incorporate such views into
the actual process of the work itself as an open text of interpretation and reinterpretation.[6] Tolle decided, accordingly, to inscribe the deep aspiration of
many visitors to relocate the old counties of Ireland by accepting the stones and
then placing them at random throughout the landscape. The stones scattered
throughout the site thus serve to reiterate the role of the stones in the walls and
lintels of the cottage itself – that is, to function as 'indices' for the lost meanings
and bearings of forgotten dwellers rather than as 'icons' that claim to restore the
fetish of an original presence.

Tolle's installation is an invitation to 'mourning' (acknowledging that the lost
object is lost) rather than 'melancholy' (refusing to let go of the lost object by

obsessively fixating on it).[7] By soliciting visitors' active involvement with the site, as part of an on-going drama of semantic and symbolic reinvention, Tolle manages to ensure that the work remains a work in perpetual progress, inter-textually open and incomplete by definition. The fact that new readings and reactions are regularly included onto both the audio soundtrack of voices (which visitors hear as they traverse the underground tunnels) and the visual inscriptions on the glass panels, is a powerful token of Tolle's determination to maintain a process of active and responsible memory. Robin Lydenberg captures this radically hermeneutical sense of Tolle's design in her essay 'From icon to index: Some contemporary visions of the Irish stone cottage':

> Tolle designed the memorial to invite and incorporate the viewer's active engagement with the land and its history rather than with vague nostalgia or the iconography of fixed and sentimentalized stereotypes. One entrance into the memorial leads visitors through an underground passageway up into the ruined cottage ... The walls of the passageway are constructed of alternating sedimented bands of stone and frosted glass on which official and unofficial testimonies from those who experienced the Famine are cast in shadows. This sculptured layering evokes the geologically and historically sedimentary aspect of the Irish landscape. Hunger is not naturalized or aestheticized here but contextualized historically and politically, giving forceful articulation, for example, to the failure of British officials to alleviate massive starvation. Entering the quarter acre of Ireland through this buried history, viewers cannot simply delight in the landscape as idealized icon: the cottage interior is cramped and exposed, the 'rolling hills' are the remnants of uncultivated potato furrows. Visitors may also enter the installation by stepping directly onto the sloping earth and climbing up through the landscape to the ruined cottage and its prospect; there they discover, belatedly, the textual history buried below. Whether the memorial is entered from above or from below, the charm of the landscape and its violent history exist in productive tension.[8]

By deterritorializing the stone cottage from rural Ireland and reterritorializing it amidst the alien urban bustle of New York, Tolle is reminding us that the place of trauma is always haunted by a no-place of mourning. Such mourning calls for a letting go of the literal landscape of the past in order to give this past a future, in order to open it to new possibilities of interpretation. In this we could say that the artist is conjuring up the emancipatory potential of the 'Fifth Province'. Ireland, as everyone knows, has four provinces – Munster, Ulster, Leinster and Connaught – but the Irish word for province is *coiced*, meaning a fifth. So where, one might ask, is the fifth fifth since there are only four actually existing as geographical places? The Fifth Province is a placeless place, a place of disposition rather than of position, of detachment rather than attachment. And it has been acknowledged since the beginnings of Irish myth and folklore that it is precisely this Fifth Province that provides a dimension of peace, wisdom and catharsis to the otherwise warring parts of Ireland.[9] Tolle's memorial might thus be said to remind us that all our lives – whether we are Irish or not, emigrants or natives, survivors or victims – are always haunted by an irretrievable sense of absence and loss, ghosted by a longing for some 'irrecoverable elsewhere'.[10]

Tolle attests to the Fifth Province by ensuring that his poetical text – the site as work of art – remains answerable to an ethical context of responsibility. And he brings this about by turning his famine memorial into an intertextual play of multiple readings and perspectives. The hold of a single Meta-narrative of Irish history is thus loosened and liberated into a polyphony of discontinuous and competing narratives. Tolle juxtaposes, in both the written and audio commentaries, statistics about the Irish Famine with equally perturbing facts and figures about other famines and world hunger generally. He mixes snatches of Irish history and politics with snippets of song and poetry. He blends together a variety of vernacular and postmodern art styles – naturalism, folk craft, conceptual art, hyperrealism, landscape architecture, theme sculpture, pop art, earth art, etc. Moreover, the fact that the installation can grow and mutate – thanks to the use of climatically sensitive organic materials, and to the deployment of flexible, alterable texts (silk-screened onto strips of clear plexiglas) – illustrates Tolle's conviction that historical memorials are themselves subject to change according to the addition of new and alternative perspectives. As Lydenberg writes:

> This memorial makes no claim to enlighten visitors with a totalizing narrative of the Irish Famine; the texts create a mixture of facts, political propaganda, and personal experience – the imaginative work of fantasy, desire, and hope. Tolle's design offers a transitional passageway through fragmented, often anonymous, voices in the embedded texts and an accompanying audio collage, both of which will be revised, updated and expanded periodically in response to continuing crises in world hunger. The narrative is discontinuous, full of gaps and silences; Tolle teases out multiple meanings by placing fragments in shifting juxtapositions rather than in fixed narrative sequence. A heritage industry presentation of history as a recoverable and repeatable past to be fixed 'like a fly in amber' is displaced here by ... a 'preposterous history' that multiplies uncertainty and doubt. This alternative mode of history calls for an alternative mode of memorial, one that would ... defy easy readability and consumer satisfaction to communicate instead dissatisfaction, complexity, and a sense of loss.[11]

The transatlantic exchange between Mayo and New York, between abandoned stone cottage and postmodern concrete megapolis, solicits a response of profound questioning and curiosity in most viewers to the site, reminding us that if we pass *from action to text*, in entering this memorial, we return from text to action again as soon as we exit the installation – bringing the heightened poetics of remembering, which we experience in this placeless place, to bear on our ethics of remembering in the real life world around us.

Finally, we might add that if Tolle's memorial is an intertext in so far as it brings together the diverse idioms of poetics and ethics, and the diverse disciplines of history and geography, it also functions intertextually by relating to a number of what might be termed 'counter-texts' in the immediate or not so immediate environment.[12] One thinks of Ellis Island and the Statue of Liberty visible to the south of the waterfront memorial – both symbols of aspiration and expectation for so many Irish emigrant survivors of the Famine. One thinks of the giant Twin Towers, in whose shadow in lower east Manhattan the memorial was originally constructed and in whose wake it now stands vigil in commemorative commiseration. One thinks of Irish Famine memorials in Boston and other emigrant ports of North America, so different and so similar; or the memorials to other historical traumas and tragedies from the Holocaust to Vietnam – in particular the Museum of Jewish Heritage: A Living Memorial to the Holocaust also housed in Battery Park; or Maya Lin's famous Washington monument to the Vietnam War dead. One might, indeed, even extend the scope of intertextual reference to include the fictional testimonials of writers like Tomas O'Flaherty and Tom Murphy; or of film makers like Scorcese whose representation of Irish emigrant warfare in *Gangs of New York* reminds us that within earshot of Battery Park stood the old site of tribal conflict called the Five Points, a notorious battleground where blocked, fixated memories of vengeance and obsession played themselves out in bloody conflict in the 1860s – Nativists and Hibernians locked in hatred, impervious to the work of mourning, catharsis and forgiveness. It is just such a process of therapeutic working-through (*Durcharbeitung*) which, I would argue, memorials like the Battery Park Famine installation solicit.

In sum, Tolle's memorial serves, I submit, as a model for a healing exchange of memories. The exchange in question here involves that between indigenous and emigrant, Irish and Irish-American, Irish-American and Anglo-American, Irish-American and non-Anglo American (Asian, African, Middle-Eastern, Hispanic, etc.). It also involves an exchange between home and abroad, between the old world and the new, between Achill Island and Manhattan Island. And of course, to move from geography back to history, it involves an exchange – in both directions – between past and present. By refusing to either naturalize or aestheticize memory, Tolle keeps open a crucial critical 'gap' that prevents history from collapsing back into a frozen past. His memorial resists being obsessively reified and replicated. Instead, Tolle preserves the gap between Now and Then, Here and There, enabling both poles to transit back and forth between the everyday reality of New York life today and an imaginary place in the minds of those Famine emigrants who left it behind over a century and a half ago. It is in this 'between' that contemporary visitors to the site may experience what we might properly call a *poetical ethics of memory.*

II

So how might we relate the case of the Irish Hunger Memorial in New York to a specifically hermeneutic paradigm of memory exchange, mentioned at the outset? In an essay entitled 'Reflections on a New Ethos for Europe', Paul Ricoeur outlines just such a paradigm. He shows, first, how this can provide a basis for an *ethic of narrative hospitality* that involves 'taking responsibility in imagination and in sympathy for the story of the other, through the life narratives which concern the other'.[13] In the case of memorials like Tolle's this takes the form of an exchange between different peoples' histories so that we practice an art of transference and translation that allows us to welcome the story of the other, the stranger, the victim, the forgotten one.

Second, Ricoeur shows how this calls in turn for an ethic of *narrative flexibility*. Memorials face the challenge of resisting the reification of a historical event into a fixed dogma by showing how each event may be told in different ways by different generations and by different narrators. Not that everything becomes relative and arbitrary. On the contrary, acts of trauma and suffering call out for justice, and the best way of achieving this is often to invite empathy with strangers and adversaries by allowing for a plurality of narrative perspectives. The resulting overlap may thus lead to what Gadamer calls a 'fusion of horizons' where diverse horizons of consciousness may at last find some common ground,[14] a reciprocal transfer between opposite minds. 'The identity of a group, culture, people or nation, is not that of an immutable substance', writes Ricoeur, 'nor that of a fixed structure, but that, rather, of a recounted story.' A hermeneutic exchange of stories effectively resists an arrogant or rigid conception of cultural identity that prevents us from perceiving the radical implications of the principle of narrativity – namely, 'the possibilities of revising every story which has been handed down and of carving out a place for several stories directed towards the same past'.[15]

This entails, by implication, a third ethical principle – that of *narrative plurality*. Pluralism here does not mean any lack of respect for the singularity of the event narrated through the various acts of remembering. It might even be said to increase our sense of awareness of such an event, especially if it is foreign to us in time, space or cultural provenance. '*Recounting differently* is not inimical to a certain historical reverence to the extent that the inexhaustible richness of the event is honored by the diversity of stories which are made of it, and by the competition to which that diversity gives rise.'[16] And Ricoeur adds this critical point: 'The ability to recount the founding events of our national history in different ways is reinforced by the exchange of cultural memories. This ability to exchange has as a touchstone the will to share symbolically and respectfully in the commemoration of the founding events of other national cultures, as well as those of their ethnic minorities and their minority religious denominations.'[17]

This point applies as much to events of pain and trauma (like that commemorated in the Famine memorial) as to events of triumph and glory.

A fourth aspect of the hermeneutic exchange of memories is the *transfiguring of the past*. This involves a creative retrieval of the betrayed promises of the past, so that we may respond to our 'debt to the dead' and endeavour to give them a voice. The goal of memorials is, therefore, to try to give a future to the past by remembering it in the right way, ethically and poetically. A crucial aspect of reinterpreting transmitted traditions is the task of discerning past promises that have not been honoured. For 'the past is not only what is bygone – that which has taken place and can no longer be changed – it also lives in the memory thanks to arrows of futurity which have not been fired or whose trajectory has been interrupted'.[18] In other words, the unfulfilled future of the past may well signal the richest part of a tradition; and the emancipation of 'this unfulfilled future of the past is the major benefit that we can expect from the crossing of memories and the exchange of narratives'.[19] It is especially the founding events of a community – traumatic or dramatic – that require to be reread in this critical manner in order to unlock the potencies and expectancies that the subsequent unfolding of history may have forgotten or travestied. This is why any genuine memorial involves a certain return to some seminal moment of suffering or hope, to the original events and textual responses to those events, which are all too often occluded by official history. 'The past is a cemetery of promises which have not been kept,' notes Ricoeur. And memorials can, at best, be ways of 'bringing them back to life like the dry bones in the valley described in the prophecy of Ezekiel'.[20]

A fifth and final ethical moment in the hermeneutics of memory-exchange is *pardon*. If empathy and hospitality towards others are crucial steps in the ethics of remembrance there is something *more* – something that entails moving beyond narrative imagination to forgiveness. In short, the exchange of memories of suffering demands more than sympathy and duty (though these are essential for any kind of justice). And this something 'extra' involves pardon in so far as pardon means 'shattering the debt'. Here the order of justice and reciprocity can be supplemented, but not replaced, by that of 'charity and gift'. Such forgiveness demands huge patience, an enduring practice of 'working-through', mourning and letting go. But it is not a forgetful forgiveness: amnesty can never be based on amnesia. It remembers our debt to the dead while at the same time introducing something other, something difficult almost to the point of impossibility, but something all the more important for that reason. One thinks of Brandt kneeling at Warsaw, Havel's apology to the Sudeten Germans, Hume's preparedness to speak with the IRA, Sadat's visit to Jerusalem, Hillesum's refusal to hate her hateful persecutioners. All miraculous moments where an ethics of reciprocity is touched by a poetics of pardon. But I repeat: one does not replace the other – *both* justice *and* pardon are equally important in the act of remembering past trauma. 'To the degree that charity exceeds justice we must guard against substituting it for justice. Charity remains a surplus; this surplus of compassion and tenderness is capable of giving the exchange of memories its profound motivation, its daring and its momentum.'[21]

It is not difficult to see how this hermeneutical model of memory-exchange relates to the Irish Hunger Memorial in New York, which we analysed in the first part of this paper. The one thing to add perhaps is that memorials that are located in places far removed from the original trauma serve the extra purpose of seeking pardon not only from the victims and survivors of that particular event, but from all visitors to the site. This is where a poetics of narrative fantasy may usefully complement a politics of historical judgment. For when we dare to visit the memorials dedicated to other peoples and communities (not our own), we are suddenly all Famine sufferers, we are all Holocaust victims, we are all casualties of the Vietnam War. At least for a special, impossible, fleeting moment.

Part Five:

DIALOGUES

CHAPTER TWENTY

Migrant Minds: Bono, Paul Durcan, Neil Jordan, Robert Ballagh (1988)

Introductory Note

The following statements by Bono, Durcan and Jordan are edited versions of a lengthy conversation that we conducted together on an afternoon in May 1988. The contribution by Ballagh, who could not be present at the original session, was written as a response and subsequently inserted. Each of the participants represents a different art form – Bono (music), Durcan (poetry), Jordan (cinema) and Ballagh (painting). But despite their different media, there are some telling convergences of mind.

We are talking about a new generation that grew up in Ireland between the sixties and eighties – a changing culture where television, cinema and popular music exercised a more formative influence than the traditional pieties of revivalist Ireland. This was the 'blank generation' of revolt and experimentation: a new breed of urbanized and internationalized youth determined to wipe the slate clean, to start again from scratch. Sons busy burying their fathers. Daughters desperate to escape the mothers of memory.

There is much said about journeying. Each posits the virtue of a migrant mind tired of the old ideologies and hungry for some 'other place', some utopia where they could meet strangers who would let them be, be themselves. But this postmodern model of cultural migration differs from the inherited patterns of Irish emigration in that it affirms the option, or at least the possibility, of return. The journey is a two-way ticket. And its virtue lies in the fact that on returning home you know that you will never be totally at home. The old ideologies of fixed national identity or insular salvation can never suffice again. Once bitten by the tooth of exile, the migrant mind recognizes that 'homecoming' is an imaginative quest, not a literal event.

The discovery that one is always something of an outsider or misfit – at home as well as abroad – grants a certain liberty to rediscover and recreate what is most valuable in one's own tradition. Having taken one's distance from the 'home-land', physically or mentally, you can return to it and find there something of immense and lasting value. Traditions of myth and music can be explored again with a newfound and non-fanatical freedom.

This is where modernity's obsession with absolute novelty and rupture – its frequent repudiation of historical memory – is tempered by an awareness that we cannot afford to *not* know our past. Rupture is complemented by remembrance. Creation *ex nihilo* gives way to the more playful practice of recreation. We are more ready to acknowledge that the waters are muddied; that the established ideologies of purity and identity have often proved demeaning or destructive; that the future is not guaranteed by some ineluctable destiny; that history is a healthy confluence of tenses – past traditions mingling fruitfully with present crises and future aspirations. The postmodern mind also resists the modernist contempt for the so-called mass media; it democratically celebrates the confounding of distinctions between 'high' art and 'popular' culture. Thus, in the conversations that follow, we find that Bono, one of the most popular singers of this decade, invokes the poetic exemplars of Heaney and Kavanagh, while the poet, Durcan, invokes the popular exemplars of Dylan, the Stones, Duke Ellington and Van Morrison. Jordan blends a literary admiration for Yeats and Joyce with a fascination for the electronic media of cinema, TV and video, in which he now works. Ballagh produces visual art that mingles themes drawn from the great classical traditions with motifs taken from the popular contemporary techniques of comic strip, poster portrait and newsreel documentary.

Disillusioned with the 'hard ideologies' that have defined us according to a single, unadulterated 'identity' (nationalist, unionist, Catholic or Protestant), this new generation of Irish artists affirms the positive value of confusion, uncertainty, homelessness, migrancy, questioning, questing for 'another place'. This does not amount, in any sense, to a repudiation of their Irish culture, or indeed to a denial of a specifically 'Irish thing' about their work. On the contrary, each acknowledges a fundamental sense of belonging and fidelity to a 'native place'. It is, to be sure, not the nation-state in any official sense. It is a place more local than the nation, more personally and communally experienced – one not circumscribed by abstract statutes or boundaries. A place where the old antagonism between the native and the alternative ceases to apply. A place of recreation only disclosed when one has ventured out in search of the no-place (*u-topos*) that is always elsewhere. Here we understand that we can be Irish *and* citizens of the world without contradiction.

The Irish thing surfaces, almost in spite of oneself, when the obsession with a unique identity is abandoned. The reason we could not find it was perhaps that we were looking too hard, too self-consciously, too fanatically. Now, as we are rediscovering ourselves through our encounter with others, reclaiming our voice in our migrations through other cultures and continents – Europe, Britain, North America – we are beginning to realize that the Irish thing was always there. We could not recognize it for as long as we assumed we were at home with ourselves, sufficient unto ourselves, slaves to the illusion that we were masters on our island, Robinson Crusoes of a land apart. It takes the migrant mind to know that the island is without frontiers, that the seas are waterways connecting us with others, that the journey to the other place harbours the truth of homecoming to our own place.

– Bono: The White Nigger –
Paul Hewson

How does the music of U2 relate to our being Irish? I come to this question as someone who does not know who he is. There are people out there who know who they are ... I like to meet these people ... But I am not one of them. When I was growing up I didn't know where I came from ... I didn't know if I was middle class, working class, Catholic, Protestant ... I knew I was from Ballymun, Dublin, but I didn't know what that meant. I didn't know I was Irish until I went to America. I never actually thought about it. One of the reasons I want to contribute to this discussion now is that I've become interested in these questions lately. But I come to it with no set point of view.

It is curious that U2 are seen as this 'Irish' thing. So much emphasis is placed on it. And we ourselves emphasize it. But if you look at the surface level of music – its obvious contents – there's maybe nothing very Irish about it. It comes from a suburban blank generation culture which I grew up in, watching cartoons on TV, Thunderbirds and Hanna Barbera and designer violence. That was the real world: concrete, grey, kicking footballs and admiring English football stars. That's the culture I came from, and that's what our music reflects, on the surface at least. It is very 'un-Irish' in the accepted sense.

However, I now realize that beneath the surface there are certain Irish characteristics to the music ... even the choice of words. Our producer, Brian Eno, said that he thought that I was a better poet than a songwriter ... what I think he meant by that was the sound, rhythm and colour of the words seem at times as important as the meaning. The love of language *for its own sake* and not just as a vehicle to comment on or describe events, seems to me to be very Irish – you grow up reading Joyce for God's sake or Beckett, and they seem to abuse and therefore use the English language in new and interesting ways.

With U2, people often point to a song like 'Sunday, Bloody Sunday' as an example of our Irishness, but for me it's not, and in retrospect it didn't succeed in making its point. We had this highfalutin' idea to contrast or make the connection between the blood of the crucifixion on Easter Sunday and the blood of the victims in Derry on Bloody Sunday. The idea of Jesus dying to save us from death is a painful irony to both Catholic and Protestant in the light of the Troubles. Anyway, now when I look at the words, all I see is a description of that day as a tragedy in the tradition of Peggy Seeger or American folk:

> And the battle's yet begun
> There's many lost but tell me who has won
> The trenches dug within our hearts
> Mothers, children, brothers, sisters torn apart.

To me the sound and colour of the language in a song like 'A Sort of Home-coming' is more Irish:

> The wind will crack in wintertime
> A lightning bomblast waltz
> No spoken words ... just a scream ...
> See the sky the burning rain, she will die and live again
> Tonight, we'll build a bridge across the sea and land.

This is not American folk or blues. The words are much more influenced by poets like Heaney or Kavanagh ... than say, Woodie Guthrie.

I used to think U2 came out of a void, a black hole; we seemed completely rootless. Though we had many influences, our version of rock 'n' roll didn't sound like anyone else's in the present or in the past. I met Bob Dylan for the first time backstage at Slane Castle '85. He sat there talking about the McPeeke Family ... this Irish group I'd never even heard of ... and how he used to hang around backstage at Makem & Clancy concerts – 'Yeah,' I said, 'I remember they used to be on the *Late Late Show*!' ... and then I began to listen more carefully to the bold and bald sound of Irish folk singers ... I recall listening to Paul Brady kick up more of a storm with an acoustic guitar than most people could do with a rock band. I told Dylan and Van Morrison, who was there at the time, that I felt we didn't belong to any tradition, it was like we were lost in space, floating over many traditions but not belonging to any one of them. It then struck us that there was a journey to be undertaken. There was something to be discovered.

We started looking back into American music, Gospel, Blues, the likes of Robert Johnson ... John Lee Hooker. Old songs of fear and faith. As I said when we first started the band, we felt like outsiders to rock music but these themes were very much inside U2, they were also very Irish, so even though there isn't an obvious Irishness in a song like 'Bullet the Blue Sky' (a U2 song about military interference in El Salvador), there is something Irish about the subject of oppression and also, I think, about the language I used to paint the picture:

> In the howling wind comes a stinging rain
> See them driving nails into souls on the tree of pain
> You plant a demon seed, you raise a flower of fire
> See them burning crosses see the flames higher and higher.

I feel there is a strong link between American and Irish traditional music. So you see we found the 'Irish thing' through the American – Gospel, Blues, Robert Johnson, Bob Dylan – these became passports home.

Though we had grown up on it, for some reason we also felt outsiders to the English rock 'n' roll scene. At the time it all seemed surface with nothing behind the surface. We were up there – scruffy, soaked in sweat, unpoised – not concealing but revealing ourselves, what was on our minds and in our hearts. I began to realize how alien this was to the white, stiff-upper-lip syndrome which I still find in UK music criticism ... They seemed to find any kind of passion hard to take, they prefer a mask of *cool* ... unless you're black. That is interesting, because though this passion is to me an Irish characteristic, in American blacks it's called *soul*. I was called a 'white nigger' once by a black musician, and I took it as he meant it, as a compliment. The Irish, like the blacks, feel like outsiders. There's a feeling of being homeless, migrant, but I suppose that's what all art is – a search for identity. The images of our songs are confused, classical, biblical, American, Irish, English, but not in a negative sense. The fight, the struggle for a synthesis is what's interesting about them. The idea of an incomplete, questioning, even abandoned identity is very attractive to me.

Our journey to America eventually turned us back to where we came from. It brought up musical questions and also political questions. During Bobby Sands' hunger strike we had money thrown onto the stage because we were Irish ... you couldn't but be moved by the courage and conviction of this man ... yet we struggled with the question, is that the right way? Is violence inevitable? Is it the only answer to partition in Northern Ireland? Again there was a parallel between the Irish and the blacks. In the sixties the black civil rights movement led by Martin Luther King Jr. had resisted a bloody upsurge. I've read Dr King's *Strength to Love* and was inspired by his movement of aggressive but non-violent resistance. Here was a man who believed enough in his cause to give his life, but would never take a life ... an 'armed struggle' seems cowardly in comparison. I know it's not that simple, but we must get beyond confrontation, beyond a revolution where ideas matter more than people ... surely we are coming out of that period where we believed that just one bang of the door and it would swing open ... it's just not like that. I mean, I'm from the South and relatively uneducated about the situation, but if war in Northern Ireland is what it means to be Irish then we must redefine Irishness. There was a time when political thinkers could tolerate violence as a way forward, but this a different time … the old ideologies of the Right and the Left – as promising a final solution – are redundant. The microchip will dwarf the machine in its impact on our lives; multinational corporations don't need people in their workforce anymore – just people to sell to … we have a new problem, we need a new solution.

Even in music and art there's a changing of the guard; it's the end of the 'cold wave' and hopefully of the hardness associated with modernism, where chaos is not challenged just reflected … like a mirror.

There's a warmth and humanity in Irish music that I don't see in the big city music of London or New York. What kind of music will people be listening to in the future? Machine music? Sophisticated noise of a New York dance club? I don't think so. I feel the music that people will be holding under their arms like holy books or treasures will be much more traditional, be it Irish, American, soul, reggae, cajun – these musics may be reinterpreted by the new technology but as we are more dehumanized, urbanized, corralled into confusion, surely we will turn to simplicity, to 'the pure drop' of Seamus Ennis, the voice of Van Morrison. The anger of U2 is not cold or cynical; I hope an ambition to 'kick the darkness till it bleeds daylight' will have its place.

Maybe we Irish are misfits, travellers, never really at home, but always talking about it. I met a fisherman who told me we were like salmon: it's upriver all the time, against the odds, the river doesn't want us … yet we want a way home … but there is no home. Religious minds tell us *exile is what having eaten the apple means*, that 'home' is a spiritual condition. We in Ireland already know this, not because we've been exiles, but because hardships, be they economic or political, have forced us to be less material … I don't swallow the Church's idea of 'pie in the sky' when we die either! That's the worst of religion … accept the crap now, we'll have diamonds later. I much prefer the notion of 'Thy Kingdom Come on Earth as it is in Heaven'. Some Heaven on Earth right now would be nice – they should preach that! I mean we get some glimpse of it in music, painting, the West of Ireland, Donegal, people, sex, conversation … a few pints, a glass of whiskey. Even if it's been a cause of bitterness and has on occasion been warped by organized religion, our Christianity, our sense of the spirit, is valuable, especially right now when a hard, empirical approach to things is beginning to give way to a more open metaphysical questioning. Belief in God does not necessarily imply a lack of belief in men.

I don't know, maybe Romantic Ireland is dead and gone. If the America I love only exists in my imagination, maybe the Ireland I love is the same. Dublin, I mean, everybody gives out about Dublin and there's lots of things to give out about … unemployment, what the planners have done to the people of Tallaght and Ballymun, the architects who have defaced what was a beautiful city, these are the real vandals … but still we love the city …

I met a U2 fan in Switzerland recently who said to me: 'Jazus Bono, I can't wait to get home and throw some litter on the ground!' – I think I know what he meant.

– Passage to Utopia –
Paul Durcan

When Bono began by saying he doesn't know who he is – well that's exactly how I feel. I want to approach the question about a future Ireland without frontiers in terms of a journey. I want to talk about the experience of energy received from moving about. The journey moves between two main poles – opposite poles – violence and utopia. But I will return to this.

Here I am, thinking self-consciously about myself. A thing I don't normally do. Looking back on my life as a practising artist I see it as a journey, or a series of journeys. My work as a poet has always been a searching for the *other place*. The notion of 'utopia' is fundamental to something about myself, and I think, about human nature. It is a theme which has cropped up again and again in my recent readings of Primo Levi, the Italian Jew whose books bear witness to his time in a Nazi concentration camp; Leonardo Boff, the Latin American theologian of liberation, and Richard Kearney. Utopia, for me as for them, does not mean harking back to a 'lost Eden'. All my life I have been looking for a Mont Sainte Victoire. And it is no accident that most of my books have the names of places in them. I see Cézanne sitting there looking over at this mountain. And one way or another I think that all of us who are artists are doing this.

Some eighteen months ago, I wrote a poem called 'O Westport in the Light of Asia Minor' and later again I wrote a poem called 'Going Home to Russia'. What I would like to do here is to read the journey between these two poems in search of an 'other place' in terms of a travel diary. I use the term journey both in the sense of a poetic composition and in the more literal sense of moving about between harbours and airports and railways. The whole thing is a matter of connections. And these connections, with all their strange accidents and coincidences, are in turn a matter of metamorphosis.

I want to concentrate here on one particular journey – a journey to Italy and back which I made recently with Richard Kearney. We were participating in a conference in Turin on the question of Celtic identity. I was especially struck by a seminar there conducted between Kearney and the Italian 'postmodern' philosopher, Gianni Vattimo. It was a revelation to me. Vattimo spoke humorously and with energy of the strength to be gained from a recognition of the 'feebleness of one's identity' and of the 'casual role of the self'. These phrases, heard in a foreign place, connected with things Patrick Kavanagh had been saying several decades ago – and that I've been mulling over for years. In particular, I think of his celebration of what he called the art of 'complete casualness'.

Turin was also very important for me as the city of Primo Levi. This survivor of Auschwitz who endured so much violence lived to tell the tale and finally committed suicide. I was deeply aware of his presence in this place of his birth. I did a reading of 'Going Home to Russia' at the conference and after it a woman came up to me and said: 'I feel very sorry for you. We Italians and Continentals have been through that journey ourselves.' This was not an isolated view. Some days later in Rome I met a doctor who is a committed member of the Italian Communist Party and he spoke to me of Pier Paolo Pasolini and his disillusionment with the 1968 movement. Pasolini was, of course, also a committed communist but he caused great controversy when he published an essay denouncing the hatred he had seen in the eyes of fanatical students in the student revolution of the sixties. He contrasted the violence of the students to the beleaguered and bewildered faces of the policemen from the country, concluding that he had no doubt with whom he identified.

At the Turin conference on Celtic identity there was a Scottish poet, George MacBeth, and a Welsh poet, Danny Abse. Though the participants in the conference were ostensibly in search of some kind of common identity, what struck me most was the crucial differences which distinguished their childhood memories and mine. They both read poems about their experiences of the Second World War – of roofs tumbling in during a bombing raid, of the family in fear and threat of invasion. And I thought, by contrast, of our cosy insularity in Ireland. Then and now. And I recalled Primo Levi's warning that it could happen again. At that moment I saw my own country not as a neutral defender of peace unaffected by the 'outside' world, but as harbouring its own fascism with its own brand of violence.

After Turin and Rome, I visited Assisi. I can still see the painting of St Francis – a man of peace – by Cimabue. And I recall looking across the valley at Assisi from Perugia one evening – and seeing the town hanging there in the sky. And again the image of Mont Sainte Victoire came back to me. The other place. Utopia. The home away from home.

After the reading that evening in Perugia I was asked by a TV interviewer whether it was possible to be a poet in a world of mass media. I replied that it was precisely because it was a mass media society that it was more possible than ever to be a poet. He was surprised. But I believe it. The old division between art and popular culture is happily disappearing. And as I thought more about it a number of instances came to mind. I though of Christy Moore singing Jimmy McCarthy's 'Ride On' in the National Stadium in Dublin – an occasion and a place which for me were full of the aroma of poetry. I though of the Russian poet Bulat Okudzhava's phrase that 'poetry is a way of giving us back to ourselves'. I thought of the marvellous audience that I had during the first day of the Belfast Workers' Festival in the late eighties. Without that kind of audience hungry for music and poetry there can be no work of art, either factually or metaphysically. And I thought of Trafalgar Square – one of the most crowded and democratic places in the world – and a visit I made to the National Gallery to see the floor mosaic by the Russian *émigré* Boris Anrep. It is called *Compassion* and features the poet Anna Akmatova lying naked with angels guarding her against the demons of war. The painting is inspired by David's *The Death of Marat* (the fourteen-year-old boy shot dead for shouting 'Vive le roi'). And finally, I thought of two films which I saw with my daughter, Sarah, during a visit to Paris – *Down by Law* by Jim Jarmusch (about solidarity and humour between prisoners in the US) and *Sacrifice* by Tarkovsky (about an act of love which saves the world from a nuclear holocaust). Thinking of all these examples of art expressing itself through popular and democratic media, struggling with the horror of violence, I was reminded of the power of music and poetry. A power greater than the power of armies and scaffolds and bombs.

It's not that I'm an optimist. I agree with Primo Levi when he says that we must keep on remembering what happened. So that it can never happen again. I believe that violence is at the end of every question. That it is not confined to the Nazis but can happen in any society, in our own society. When I see a photograph or a TV image of a body on the side of a road in Northern Ireland with a head hanging out of it covered in blood and full of bullets, I find it so difficult to cope with this terrifying reality. But there are less dramatic things about our day to day living here which frighten me. The way some of our legal and medical professionals speak in a way that dehumanizes the people they are dealing with. The use of terms like 'access to children' after the breakdown of a marriage. The manner in which divorce is often regarded as a moral evil thereby ignoring the suffering that certain couples are actually living through. Violence can be sensed in the very way words are used to deny the fact that people are human beings. For me the most obvious examples of this in Ireland are the ways in which people tend to speak of war and nationalism (be it republican or loyalist). As a child, I fed myself on comics about the war between the Nazis and the British. I even had recurring nightmares about being chased by the Gestapo and being agonized by whether I would talk or not. But I now know that the violence can happen here too. It is not confined to the Nazis. I often worry about what Ireland will be like for our children in the next century.

One of the things I brought back with me from Turin was Vattimo's injunction to rejoice in the 'feebleness of our identity'. This is his motto for the new postmodern era, his hope for an end to ideological war and violence. Sometimes I am accused of betraying the nation because I don't support the traditional sense of nationalist identity. The very word nationalism sometimes fills me with disgust. This does not mean that I reject the local place of origin. I respect Kavanagh's statement that it takes a lifetime to get to know the corner of a field, that there is a valid pride of place – what he calls the 'parish' rather than the 'province'. When Bono speaks of his generation coming from the 'void', I feel like quoting Angelo Roncali after he was made patriarch of Venice in the 1950s – 'like any other man I come from a particular family and a particular place'. This feeling about place is very important. As far back as I can remember, journeys to places were powerful experiences. Travelling to Mayo or Portrane there was a sense that there were no fences, no boundaries, each step along the way was a kingdom, with its own story.

I don't want to debunk nineteenth-century nationalism. But for my generation things have changed a lot. I recall an incident in 1966 when a British journalist in a pub asked me what 1916 meant to me. I told him quite honestly that it was very remote for me. That I was more interested in what Patrick Kavanagh was saying in his poems. Patrick Kavanagh and I shared a common interest in Jack Kerouac, the Rolling Stones and Bob Dylan. (I even wrote out all the words of Dylan's 'Desolation Row' for Kavanagh – all 200 of them.) The British journalist just couldn't understand this; he felt I was betraying the Irish cause.

If only I could imagine people being as moved by utopia as by what they believe nationalism to be! Duke Ellington means more to me as an exemplar than William Butler Yeats. I have this image of him travelling around the world in a dressing gown composing these beautiful numbers. And this is what I find so attractive about Bono's idea of the Irish black man. I can just picture him – a great jazzman or saxophonist wandering around Europe. He wouldn't be a 'bucklepper', a stage Irishman jumping up on counters and fitting into the revivalist image. Kavanagh denounced this cliché as a 'pure-bred English lie'. The whole business of Kavanagh's life was not to have an identity. His was a philosophy of 'not caring'. For him the 'incompleteness of the self' was a virtue. He called for a sense of repose, beyond the obsession with identity, of being open to the world of the now. 'To look on is enough in the business of love,' he once put it. How difficult it is, this way of dispossession, getting out of oneself and listening. Even when one goes to see a play or a film sometimes one realizes how easy it is to be caught up inside oneself. That's why Kavanagh's favourite words were 'abandon', 'gay', 'explosive'. You can imagine what an extraordinary revelation it was for me to come across a postmodern philosopher in Turin, called Vattimo, saying the same thing as Kavanagh was saying in the sixties, advocating that we abandon the obsession with identity. And surely Vattimo is close to Kavanagh when he claims that it is in poetry rather than in politics that we can find a free, non-fanatical, postmodern attitude to our myths.

I feel very divided on the question of home. On the one hand I yearn for some kind of home, some place where emotion can be recollected in tranquillity, where I can rest. On the other, I think of the protagonist of the New Testament – the acceptance of loss and death, the refusal to take out insurance policies, the challenge to all of us to leave home, to go on journeys.

At the end of every question, there is the problem of violence. Art is one way of responding to this. 'The end of art is peace' – to take a quote from Heaney's poem 'The Harvest Bow'. The reason Primo Levi took his own life one year after the publication of his last book, *The Drowned and the Saved*, was that he felt it was all going to happen again. One must keep on giving witness all the time. This is what my journey to Italy taught me. And also my journey to Russia. Violence is not an alternative in personal, national or international behaviour. The lesson of all my journeys has been that utopia is peace. And that pacifism is not an option but a necessity. To believe in utopia is to believe that there is some kind of homecoming in the 'other place'. Asia Minor. Russia. Turin. The quest for the 'other place' – whether it take the image of Mont Sainte Victoire or the village of Assisi hanging in the sky – enables us to be freer, no longer captive to our island. It also encourages us to struggle for peace in our first and literal home. You see things when you return from the journey that you had not seen before. You are filled with new outrages, new dreams.

– *Imagining Otherwise* –
Neil Jordan

When I started writing I felt very pressured by the question: How do I cope with the notion of Irishness? It meant almost nothing to me. I was, of course, profoundly moved by the Irish literature I encountered as a student – Yeats and Joyce. But how was I to write about the experience I knew, as someone born in Sligo and growing up in the suburban streets of Dublin in the sixties? The great books of Anglo-Irish literature had very little to do with this; they had no real resonance at this level. My most acute dilemma was – how to write stories about contemporary urban life in Ireland without being swamped in the language and mythology of Joyce. Indeed I recall the contemptuous response of one of my professors in UCD when I suggested we have a course on contemporary Irish writing: 'How dare you presume that your experience measures up to that of our great literary tradition.' The first real story I wrote was about an Irish labourer who cut his wrists in a London baths. Almost every work of fiction I've indulged in has been an escape to an alternative landscape – to a space or time not associated with the traditional themes of great Irish literature. (And it *is* great – whatever one might think of the Young Ireland movement, revivalist nationalism or Joyce's obsession with his homeland.) The primary questions for me were: Who am I? What do my experiences mean? What am I – a person here and now who puts pen to paper to express himself – in relation to the huge pressure of tradition?

The only identity, at a cultural level, that I could forge was one that came from the worlds of television, popular music and cinema which I was experiencing daily. Applied to literature this seemed strangely disembodied. It didn't have the surety of something handed down by tradition or my parents. It was with this problem in mind that I wrote a novel called *The Past*. The narrator is someone trying to retrace the life of his parents, to find out what lay behind the great mythological mystery which shrouded their past. And there were analogies with de Valera and the heroes and heroines of Irish nationalism. This held a fascination for me whose experience seemed so suburban and mundane – great in its own way, but not graced by any of these senses of belonging.

For me, to make films was to escape from these questions, these hankerings. In the world of cinema, none of these questions existed; there had never been an 'Irish' cinema. My mother and my sisters are painters. And I share with them the sense that the visual is free from the constraints and pressures of our literary tradition. The Irish question is – how to get rid of it. There are more interesting questions than the crippling one about 'Irish identity'. The encounter with other worlds – be it the world of cinema or painting, which have no past for us – delivers a different sense of oneself. Once one succeeds in shaking off the paralysing question of self-conscious identity, one discovers that there are certain specifically Irish features to your imagination. It's a funny journey. I had a strange experience when I first went to America. It was with the Sheridan brothers – Jim and Peter – and a theatre company we had just formed. We were struck by the fact that almost all the little artefacts of landscape we came across – highways, skyscrapers, desert scenes etc. – were even more familiar to us, thanks to the media of popular culture, than the typical landscape associated with Ireland – a crumbling castle, a green hill, a village church. The American landscape was what we were looking at every day of the week in TV serials and Hollywood movies. And I said to myself: Wouldn't it be wonderful to make your own landscape as resonant and familiar to other people as this landscape was to me? That's why I used shots of the Sally Gap and Bray beach in *Angel* and a ruined old manor in *High Spirits*.

What I found most liberating when I first started working in cinema was that there was no set of assumptions and associations specifically related to being an Irish director. But having worked in it now for several years, I find the Irish thing is emerging. When I go to Italy or France or the States and I'm asked what I feel about belonging to the new movement in British cinema, I reply rather weakly, 'Well, I'm not British, you know.' I find myself resisting being defined in terms that have nothing to do with me. The importance I give to the emotional articulation of my world and work is not something typical in British cinema. The attempt to imagine another state of living, another way of being, is I believe very Irish. It's difficult to say what exactly underlies this or why it should be so. It's something to do with the quest for another place, another manner of thinking. It's a dissatisfaction with the accepted and scientifically approved explanations of the world.

Lucien Freud's paintings are typically British. They are perfect expressions of his class and society – easeful, graceful, comfortable. By contrast, the very inarticulacy with which the Irish explain their world is actually a virtue in a strange way. There's a sense that the reality is too large, that it doesn't fit the language. And this awareness of the inadequacy of language is perhaps why we are so fascinated by it, so good at reworking it in new and original ways. I think this is what Friel meant in *Translations* when he has one of his characters say that 'confusion is not an ignoble condition'. He is also talking about a certain nobility of failure. The failure of Hugh Mór to get to Glenties and stick his pike into a British soldier. In one way, failure can be a great liberator, can't it? If we could only begin from the recognition that we are 'failed'. If we could only see the virtue of this. The great stupidity of Irish history has been the pretence to be a self-enclosed and unconfused nation.

Ireland is confused. But at least the confusion is a reality. My film *High Spirits* is basically about a man (Peter O'Toole) who runs an unworkable enterprise, who inherits an ungovernable fact – a hotel which nobody will come to. This is an experience which everybody in Ireland has experienced: living in an unworkable society, a state which never quite became a state, which feels itself to be the drab sister of other nation-states: the hotel owner just can't make it work. But then he gets this idea – he will make the break by pretending his ruined castle is haunted and thus attract people. People come to the hotel, but it's a disaster. And then, in spite of himself, it happens. The magic happens. The disaster becomes a triumph. There is something of the Oscar Wilde comedy about it.

Our mistake was to assume that we could be at home in a single nation. We fed ourselves on ideologies of violence and instant salvation, the illusion that history is a continuum moving forward to its perfect destiny. We thus forgot that we can never be at home anywhere. Perhaps it is one of the functions of writers and artists to remind the nation of this. To expose the old ideologies. To feel in exile abroad and also when one returns home. To remain faithful to the no-place (*u-topos*) in us all. As a film maker I feel bereft in Ireland – like a shoemaker without his leather – and yet I always remain something of an 'outsider' in other countries. I think it is only when you accept the condition of being a transient, when you realize that home is impossible, that you find a certain peace.

– *Responding* –
Robert Ballagh

Richard Kearney speaks of a convergence of minds between the invited participants, yet I must confess to feeling slightly at variance with some of the stated views. In trying to flesh out this divergence my gaze settled on his phrase, 'all speak of the critical experience of growing up in the new Ireland between the sixties and eighties'. Since my own formative years were spend in the fifties perhaps this accounts for some difference, after all the passage from the fifties to the sixties in Ireland was marked by changes more radical and perhaps more contradictory than others felt since the foundation of the state. In the Ireland that I grew up in, cultural life was dominated by a vision of Ireland that was narrow, exclusive and deeply conservative. The 'true' Ireland was viewed as being Gaelic, rural and Catholic, explicitly defined in de Valera's gospel of 'frugal self-sufficiency'. Education for the majority was authoritarian, in that it was dominated by a rigid, bigoted Roman Catholic orthodoxy, and brutal, since corporal punishment was still an integral part of the system. Today it is difficult to imagine that, in the fifties, the Catholic Archbishop of Dublin stated publicly it was a sin to watch Yugoslavia, a communist country, playing football; yet this did happen. It was against this reactionary background that most of my ideas and attitudes were formed.

However, instead of articulating an opposition in exile like so many others I decided to stay in Ireland, to attempt not only to build a career as an artist but also to try to participate in efforts to change Irish attitudes. In fact others, far more influential than I, were beginning to accept that de Valera's dream of a rural arcadia based on protecting the native entrepreneur could not sustain the nation. A way of life that had once been extolled as the authentic base upon which the nation securely rested was no longer considered viable. In 1959 de Valera was replaced by Seán Lemass and new economic policies were set in train that opened up the country to international capital, beginning a process of dependency that continues to this day. This remarkable volte-face by the Fianna Fáil government was achieved with the intellectual integrity of the 'with one bound he was free' solution to the dilemma of the doomed hero at the end of each serial or 'follier-up' that we as kids eagerly watched each week in the local flea-pit. Also this action was made possible by the total absence of any serious ideological basis to Irish political life. Just as nature abhors a vacuum so too any ideological vacuum in society will be quickly filled. Consequently, I am convinced that our present difficulties cannot be resolved through the abandonment of so-called 'hard' ideologies. The real task is to oppose conservative attitudes with radical progressive ideas.

The kind of society set in train in the early sixties and reinforced in the seventies and eighties by our accession to the EC has created a situation of dependence. We seem to have become totally reliant on others to provide the answers to our many problems. Our own institutions appear to have failed us completely. Someone once wrote, 'The shape of Irish society (and institutions) fits the Irish people like a badly tailored suit: we do not acknowledge the suit as our own, we do not feel at home in it, but we tolerate it as we have always tolerated everything.' There is a real irony in the way James Molyneaux so easily re-routed C.J. Haughey's oft-repeated barb about the North being a 'failed political entity' in a more southerly direction. In this context I note, with interest, Neil Jordan's *High Spirits* and its analogy between Peter O'Toole's unworkable hotel and Ireland's failed condition as a modern state. It seems to me that in the present debilitated situation where Yeats's feared 'greasy till' rules the roost and where Irish political life is devoid of vision, our artists can play a significant role. Brian Friel, the playwright, noted that 'you've got to produce documents, sounds and images in order to make yourself distinctive' and that 'if there's a sense of decline about how the country is, it's because we can't readily produce these identification marks'. So the problem is one of identity, after all 'documents, sounds and images' abound in Ireland today, yet how many are like the afore-mentioned ill-fitting suit – fashioned by others, for others, and then adopted, second-hand, by us. Therefore, the creation of documents, sounds and images that relate to our experience becomes much more than simply an aesthetic issue, it becomes a political imperative. Unfortunately it remains a vexed question as to the exact nature of what we are prepared to accept as an Irish cultural iden-tity. When I began to work as an artist I remember being infuriated by criticisms that suggested I was 'un-Irish', that I was importing an alien culture into Ireland. I was angry because I felt that my work was an honest response to my own urban background, formed from many influences including the movies, comic books and popular music. Of course many urban people in Western society share a similar background and consequently a common visual language, yet I felt that there was something essentially different in my work to that produced by other artists from other countries.

It was in 1975 that the nature of this difference became apparent to me. At the time I was commissioned to paint some pictures for a restaurant in Clonmel, County Tipperary, with the proviso that they be of local interest. After searching to find a suitable theme I finally settled on the eighteenth-century author Laurence Sterne, who was born in Clonmel in 1713; afterwards he lived in Carrickfergus, Mullingar, Dublin and Annamoe until he left for schooling in Halifax and further education in Cambridge. I read his famous book *The Life and Opinions of Tristram Shandy, Gentlemen* for the first time in 1975 and was immediately struck by what I felt to be a common sensibility, even though we were separated in time by over two centuries. I first felt that we simply shared a common artistic purpose but slowly it occurred to me that the book was steeped in what I can only call an Irish sensibility. The conversational style of the writing, the sense of humour and irony, the use of parody and the 'frisky digres-sions' all go to create a book that, however un-Irish it may appear on the surface and however much Sterne may be categorized as an English writer, has at its core, incontestably, a real Irishness. In my opinion, Laurence Sterne quite natu-rally absorbed these characteristics during his formative years in Ireland. I now sensed that an Irish identity is not something that can be superficially imposed on a work of art, for example through the application of Celtic ornament, but rather that it is something that goes much deeper and is, in essence, difficult to define. It could be summarized possibly as an attitude to life or more accurately

335

a way of dealing with life, consisting of, perhaps, a preponderance to irony, satire or metaphor, a sense of humour (often dark), an enjoyment of parody and, above all, a healthy scepticism. These attributes are not uniquely Irish, but nonetheless the Irish do possess them in abundance. And there are sound reasons as to why this should be the case. After all Irish history, being a history of colonialism, oppression and marginalization, has meant that whenever subversive ideas were to be communicated it became necessary to employ some sort of disguise – for example, poets frequently used metaphor to communicate their feelings when a direct statement would have been considered treasonable. Over the years this predilection for subverting dialogue has become second nature to the Irish. A problem, however, is that since these attributes are indeed second nature to the Irish, often we can fail to take full notice of them. Frequently it can be an outsider who draws our attention to these 'Irish' characteristics.

I believe that earnestly questing for an Irish cultural identity can be counter-productive. I am certain that a distinctive identity will surface quite naturally if the artist speaks with his/her own voice about his/her own experience and environment. I remain convinced that filling empty modernist vessels with 'Irish' contents or inscribing Celtic decoration on modern art objects or the slavish adoption of international styles can only substitute a specious counterfeit for the 'real' thing.

CHAPTER TWENTY-ONE

Dialogue with Borges and Heaney:
Fictional Worlds (1982)

Joyce and Borges: Modernism and the Irish Mind
(Richard Kearney and Seamus Heaney
in conversation with Jorge Luis Borges)

The following interview took place in Dublin on 16 June 1982, Bloomsday. Borges had been invited to Dublin by the Joyce Centenary Committee to honour Ireland's most famous writer one hundred years after his birth. Borges first read Joyce when a friend presented him with a first edition copy of *Ulysses*. In 1925 he published a remarkable essay on Joyce and a translation of a fragment from this work in the Argentine journal *Proa*, entitled 'El *Ulises* de Joyce: Traducción de James Joyce, La última hoja del *Ulises*'.

For some sixty years Borges had, as he puts it, 'walked the imaginary landscape' of Dublin portrayed by Joyce in *Ulysses*. He had experienced Dublin as the exiled Joyce had fictively recreated it – not as a literal but as an imaginative presence. Now that he finally set foot in this labyrinthine city, 'at the ripe old age of 82', he was blind, still compelled to represent its visual contours in his mind, tip-tapping his way through its streets with his probing stick like the blind man of the 'Sirens' episode. Here he was, reliving Dublin just as the ageing Joyce had done – as a blind man's memory. 'Maybe my trip to Ireland is just a dream,' he mused. Borges savoured the irony of this impish, almost Joycean, coincidence.

But the similarity between Borges and Joyce does not end, nor begin, with this Bloomsday coincidence. Both are modernist masters of the word, avant-garde non-conformists who pioneered new forms of literary creation (the compressed, parabolic fiction of Borges, the expansive, epic prose of Joyce); both promoted the paradox that an international literary consciousness may be forged from the vernacular and lived experiences of its authors; and both believed in a cyclical metaphysics of time, convinced that the worlds of reality and fiction continually intertwine, the meaning of human history revealing itself like the Vico road in *Finnegans Wake*, turning round and round 'to end where time begins'. Finally, Joyce and Borges both subscribed to the notion of the artist as *émigré*. Borges insists on the importance of his extended journeys abroad as a young man, and particularly his sojourn in Geneva (1914–21) where he first discovered Conrad, Baudelaire and Joyce and joined, as he put it, the 'international modernism of letters'. This discovery of European culture was, he insists, really a rediscovery of himself as an 'expatriated European'. His own experiments in writing, he decided, would try to remain faithful to the rich multiplicity of European culture as experienced by the European-in-exile that he considered himself to be. If something specifically Argentine remains in his work, it is, he reminds us, because he believes, as Joyce did before him, that the universal can best be reached by an abiding, if not always apparent, fidelity to the genesis-glance of the particular.

Kearney: I think it would be appropriate, since today is Bloomsday and since you are here in Dublin for the Joyce Centenary celebrations, if you could begin by talking about your literary relationship with Joyce. In 1925 you declared yourself proud to be the 'first Hispanic adventurer to undertake the conquest of James Joyce'. How would you describe this adventure?

Borges: Let us go back to the early 1920s. A friend of mind gave me a first edition of *Ulysses* which had just been published by Sylvia Beach in Paris. I did my best to leaf through it. I failed, of course. However, I did recognize from the beginning that I had before me a marvellously tortuous book. But a book of what? I asked myself. Every time I thought of *Ulysses*, it was not the characters – Stephen, Bloom or Molly – that first came to mind, but the words which produced these characters. This convinced me that Joyce was first and foremost a poet. He was forging poetry out of prose. My subsequent discovery of *Finnegans Wake* and *Pomes Penyeach* confirmed me in this opinion. When I consider novelists such as Tolstoy, Conrad or Dickens, I think of their powerful characters or plots, of the content matter of their narratives. But with Joyce the focus has shifted to the forms and words of the language itself, to those unforgettably musical sentences that strive towards the condition of poetry. Looking back on my own writings sixty years after my first encounter with Joyce, I must admit that I have always shared Joyce's fascination with words, and have always worked at my language within an essentially poetic framework, savouring the multiple meanings of words, their etymological echoes and endless resonances. My own characters are often no more than excuses to play with words, to enter the fictional world of language. Joyce's obsession with language makes him very difficult if not impossible to translate. Especially into Spanish – as I discovered when I first translated a passage from Molly's soliloquy in 1925. The translations of Joyce into the Hispanic or Romance languages have been very poor to date. His symphonically compound words work best in Anglo-Saxon or Germanic languages. Joyce uses prose to produce poetry and I think all of his works should be read as poetry.

Heaney: I have often wondered about what constitutes the difference between Joyce's use of language in his poems, *Chamber Music* for example, and in his prose works, *A Portrait* or *Ulysses*. It seems to me that in the former Joyce is approaching language as a sort of ventriloquist: he remains its obedient servant; he rehearses a note caught from literature. Whereas in the prose, something cuts loose and comes alive in a new way. Whenever he tried to approach verse directly he seems to have been hampered. Yet it was the inveterate struggling poet in him which enabled him to play with prose in unprecedentedly creative forms.

Kearney: In an essay in 1941 you praised Joyce for having written some of the 'most accomplished pages in matters of style'. Do you think Joyce has influenced your own style as a writer?

Borges: I was very struck by the way in which Joyce dared in *Ulysses* to write each chapter or episode in a different style. My own work also uses a plurality of styles. I'm not sure, however, that there is a direct influence here. Or if there is it is an unconscious one. The writers whose literary influence I consciously assimilated were Stevenson, Chesterton, Kipling and Shaw, authors I read when I was still a young boy growing up in Buenos Aires and spending a considerable amount of my time in my father's library, which contained a remarkable collection of English books. I spent my childhood dreaming with these authors, with Kipling in India, with Coleridge in Kubla Khan, with Dickens in London. This is perhaps where I first experienced literature as an adventure into an endless variety of styles. The library was like a single mind with many tongues. I have been fascinated by libraries ever since (as have many of my fictional characters). I longed, for instance, to work in the National Library of Buenos Aires which possesses over 900,000 volumes. But the year in which I was finally appointed director of this library – 1955, after the fall of Peron – was the year I went blind. There I was surrounded by books I could no longer read. Sometimes I used to pretend I could still see. Even to this day, I occasionally go into a bookshop and buy some volumes so as to deceive myself that I can still read. But I feel uneasy when talking about influences on my 'writing' for I do not consider myself as a writer. I don't write very good stuff and whatever I do write I cannot bear to reread. Nor have I ever read a commentary on my work. My library does not contain one such commentary. I have become famous, it seems to me, in spite of what I've written, not because of it. There must be some mistake, I say to myself. Perhaps people mistake me for somebody else, for some other writer?

Heaney: Perhaps it is Borges rather than you who writes your works?

Borges: Perhaps indeed! There seems to be two of us, at least. The shy, private man and the celebrated, talkative, public man.

Kearney: In *The Argentine Writer and Tradition* you said you felt yourself to be an author 'outside of a cultural mainstream'. Joyce expressed a similar sentiment when he described 'home, fatherland and church' as restrictive nets he would try to fly by, or when he had Stephen admit that he could never feel at home in the English language, that he could never speak or write its words 'without unrest of spirit'. Do you experience such a cultural or post-colonial alienation in your use of the Spanish language?

Borges: It is true that as an Argentine I feel a certain distance from the Spanish mainstream. I was brought up in Argentina with as much familiarity with the English and French cultures as with the Spanish. So I suppose I am doubly alien – for even Spanish, the language I write precisely as an outsider, is itself already on the margin of the mainstream European literary tradition.

Heaney: Do you think there exists such a thing as a Hispanic-American tradition – accepting the fact that all traditions have to be imagined before they emerge?

Borges: It is true that the notion of tradition involves an act of faith. Our imaginations alter and reinvent the past all of the time. I must confess however that I was never very convinced by the idea of a Hispanic-American tradition. When I travelled to Mexico, for example, I delighted in their rich culture and literature. But I felt I had nothing in common with it. I could not identify with their cult of the Indian past. Argentina and Uruguay differ from most other Latin-American countries in that they possess a mixture of Spanish, Italian and Portuguese cultures which has made for a more European-style climate. Most of our colloquial or slang words in Argentine, for instance, are of Italian origin. I myself am descended from Portuguese, Spanish, Jewish and English ancestors. And the English, as Lord Tennyson reminds us, are themselves a mixture of many races: 'Saxon and Celt and Dane are we.' There is no such thing as a racial or national purity. And even if there were, the imagination would transcend such limits. Nationalism and literature are therefore natural enemies. I do not believe that there exists a specifically Argentine culture which could be called 'Latin-American' or 'Hispanic-American'. The only real Americans are the Indians. The rest are Europeans. I like to think of myself therefore as a European writer in exile. Neither Hispanic nor American, nor Hispanic-American, but an expatriate European.

Heaney: T.S. Eliot spoke of the 'whole mind of Europe'. Do you feel you have inherited something of this mind through the Spanish detour?

Borges: In the Argentine, we have no exclusive allegiance to any single European culture. We can draw, as I said, from several different European languages and literatures – perhaps even from the 'whole mind of Europe', if such a thing exists. But precisely because of our distance from Europe we also have the cultural or imaginative freedom to look beyond Europe to Asia and other cultures.

Kearney: As you do in your own fiction when you frequently invoke the mystical doctrines of Buddhism and the Far East.

Borges: Not to belong to a homogeneous 'national' culture is perhaps not a poverty but a richness. In this sense I am an 'international' writer who resides in Buenos Aires. My ancestors came from several different nations and races – as I mentioned – and I spent much of my youth travelling through Europe, particularly Geneva, Madrid and London, where I learned several new languages: German, Old English and Latin. This multinational apprenticeship enabled me to play with words as beautiful toys – to enter, as Browning put it, the 'great game of language'.

Heaney: I find it very interesting that your immersion in several languages in early childhood – and particularly Spanish and English – gave you that sense of language as a toy. I know that my own fascination with words was keenly related to my learning of Latin as a young boy. And the way words travelled and changed between languages, the Latin roots, the etymological drama; all that verbal phantasmagoria in Joyce also seems to be deeply involved with his conventional classical education.

Kearney: Are there other Irish writers, besides Joyce, that you particularly admire?

Borges: When I was still a young man in Buenos Aires I read George Bernard Shaw's *The Quintessence of Ibsenism*. I was so impressed that I went on to read all of his plays and essays and discovered there a writer of deep philosophical curiosity and a great believer in the transfiguring power of the will and of the mind. Shaw possesses that typically Irish sense of mischievous fun and laughter. Oscar Wilde is another Irish author who had that rare ability to mix humour and frivolity with intellectual depth. He wrote some purple passages, of course, but I believe that every word he wrote is true ...

Kearney: Wilde once said that a 'truth in art is that whose contrary is also true'.

Borges: Yes, this is just what I meant by *comic truth*, the truth of fiction which is able to tolerate cyclical and contradictory representations of reality. This is why I say that every word that Wilde wrote is true. I too believe in comic truth. Perhaps it is no accident that my first literary venture as a young man was a translation of Wilde's fairy tales. But there is another Irishman who also fired my imagination at an early age – George Moore. Moore invented a new kind of book, a new way of writing fiction, nourished by anecdotal conversations which he overheard in streets and then transformed into a fictive order. I learned from him too.

Kearney: And what of Beckett – perhaps Joyce's closest Irish literary disciple? He seems to share with you an obsession with fiction as a self-scrutinizing labyrinth of the mind, as an eternally recurring parody of itself.

Borges: Samuel Beckett is a bore. I saw his *Waiting for Godot* and that was enough for me. I thought it was a very poor work. Why bother waiting for Godot if he never comes? Tedious stuff. I had no desire to go on to read his novels after that.

Kearney: Your works are peppered with metaphysical allusions and reflections. What is your relationship with philosophy?

Borges: For me Schopenhauer is the greatest philosopher. He knew the power of fiction in ideas. This conviction I share, of course, with Shaw. Both Schopenhauer and Shaw exposed the deceptive division between the writer and the thinker. They were *both* great writers *and* great thinkers. The other philosopher who fascinated me greatly was George Berkeley – another Irishman! Berkeley knew that metaphysics is no less a product of the creative mind than is poetry. He was no civil servant of ideas, like so many other philosophers. Plato and the pre-Socratic thinkers knew that philosophical logic and poetic mythologizing were inseparably linked, complementary partners. Plato could do both. But after Plato the Western world seems to have opposed these activities, declaring that we either dream *or* reason, use arguments *or* metaphors. Whereas the truth is that we use both at once. Many hermetic and mystical thinkers resisted this opposition; but it was not until the emergence of modern idealism in Berkeley, Schelling, Schopenhauer and Bradley (whose wonderful book *Appearance and Reality* actually mentioned me in its foreword: I was so flattered to be taken seriously as a thinker!) that philosophers began to explicitly recognize once again their dependence upon the creative and shaping powers of the mind.

Kearney: How did you first become interested in Berkeley's metaphysics?

Borges: My father introduced me to Berkeley's philosophy at the age of ten. Before I was even able to read or write properly he taught me to think. He was a professor of psychology and every day after dinner he would give me a philosophy lesson. I remember very well how he first introduced me to Berkeley's idealist metaphysics and particularly his doctrine that the material or empirical world is an invention of the creative mind: to be is to be perceived/*esse est percipi*. It was one day after a good lunch when my father took an orange in his hand and asked me: 'What colour is this fruit?' 'Orange' I replied. 'Is this colour in the orange or in your perception of it?' he continued. 'And the taste of sweetness – is that in the orange itself or is it the sensation on your tongue that makes it sweet?' This was a revelation to me: that the outside world is as we perceive or imagine it to be. It does not exist independently of our minds. From that day forth, I realized that reality and fiction were betrothed to each other, that even our ideas are creative fictions. I have always believed that metaphysics, religion and literature all have a common source.

Kearney: Berkeley insisted that his idealism was not to be confounded with British empiricism and protested against Locke: 'We Irish think otherwise.' Yeats hailed this phrase as 'the birth of the national intellect'. Do you think it is just a happy accident that your early discovery of the creative power of the mind coincided with your admiration for Irish writers and thinkers such as Berkeley, Shaw, Wilde and Joyce, who had also made such a discovery? How would you account for this shared empathy?

Borges: Perhaps nothing is an accident? Perhaps all such coincidences obey some hidden law, the unfolding of some inscrutable design? The principle of Eternal Return? Of a Universal *logos*? Of a Holy Ghost? Who knows. But as an outsider looking on successive Irish thinkers I have sometimes been struck by unusual and remarkable repetitions. Berkeley was the first Irish philosopher I read, from the *Principles* and the *Three Dialogues to Siris*, and even his messianic poem about the future of the Americas: 'The course of Empire takes its sway … etc.'. Then followed my fascination for Wilde, Shaw and Joyce. And finally there was John Scotus Eriugena, the Irish metaphysician of the ninth century. I loved to read Eriugena, especially his *De Divisione Naturae*, which taught that God creates himself through the creation of his creatures in nature. I have all of his books in my library. I discovered that Berkeley's doctrine of the creative power of the mind was already anticipated by Eriugena's metaphysics of creation and that this in turn recurred in several other Irish writers: in the last two pages of the foreword to *Back to Methuselah* we find Shaw outlining a philosophical system remarkably akin to Eriugena's system of things coming from the mind of God and returning to him. In short, what Shaw calls the life-force plays the same role in his system as God does in Eriugena's. I was also very struck by the fact that both Shaw and Eriugena held that all genuine creation stems from a metaphysical nothingness, what Eriugena called the 'Nihil' of God, which resided at the heart of our existence. I doubt that Shaw ever read Eriugena; he certainly showed very little interest in medieval philosophy. And yet the coincidence of thought is there. I suspect it has less to do with nationalism than with metaphysics.

Kearney: Your own writing displays a continuous obsession with the world of fiction and dream, a universe of subconscious labyrinths. So dream-like is it on occasion that it becomes impossible to distinguish between the author (yourself), the characters of the fiction and the reader (ourselves).

Heaney: This interplay between fiction and reality seems central to your work. How does the world of your dreams affect your work? Do you consciously use dream material?

Borges: Every morning when I wake up I recall dreams and have them recorded or written down. Sometimes I wonder whether I am awake or dreaming. Am I dreaming now? Who can tell? We are dreaming each other all of the time. Berkeley held that it was God who was dreaming us. Perhaps he was right. But how tedious for poor God! To have to dream every chink and every piece of dust on every teacup and every letter in every alphabet and every thought in every head. He must be exhausted!

Kearney: Several characters in your fictions suggest the possibility of a single Divine mind or Alphabet which conjures up the universe as an author conjures up his imaginary world. In *The Aleph*, for example, you seem to be challenging the conventional notion of an individual ego or subject, implying that all human beings may be no more than the *dramatis personae* of a universal play. The hero of this fiction declares at one point: 'I have been Homer ... shortly I shall be all men'. And in *Tlön, Uqbar, Orbis Tertius* it is even stated that 'it has been established that all works are the creation of one author who is atemporal and anonymous'.

Borges: Schopenhauer spoke of '*die traumhaft Wesen des Lebens*' – the dreamlike being of life. He wasn't referring to some oneiric unconscious sublimation as modern psychology might like us to believe. He was referring to the restless mind in its search for imaginative fulfilment. Though I discovered this metaphysical doctrine in Berkeley and Schopenhauer, I later learned, on reading Koeppea's *Die Lehre des Budda*, that it was a central teaching of Eastern philosophy. This Buddhist teaching that reality is the recurring dream of a godhead prompted me to write 'Circular Ruins'.

Heaney: I would like to come back to the relationship between your dreams and your fictions. Does your dream world actually nourish your writing in a direct fashion? Do you actually borrow and transpose the *content* of your dreams into literature? Or is it a narrative skill that gives the images their shape and form?

Borges: The fictional retelling brings an order to the disorder of the dream material. But I cannot say whether the order is imposed or is already latent within the disorder merely waiting to be highlighted by its repetition in fiction. Does the writer of fiction invent an entirely new order *ex nihilo*? I suppose if I could answer such questions, I would not write fiction at all!

Heaney: Could you give us some actual examples of what you mean?

Borges: Yes. I will tell you of a recurring dream which interested me greatly. A little nephew of mine, who often stayed with me and told me his dreams every morning, experienced the following recurring motif. He was lost and then came to a clearing where he saw me coming out of a white wooden house. At that point he would break off his summary of the dream and ask me, 'Uncle, what were you doing in that house?' 'I was looking for a book,' I replied. And he was quite happy with that. As a child he was still able to slide from the logic of his dream to the logic of my explanation. Perhaps that is the way my own fictions work.

Heaney: Is it then the *mode* rather than the actual material of dreams that primarily inspires and influences your work?

Borges: I would say that it is both. I have had several recurring dreams over the years that have left their imprint on my fiction in one form or another. The symbols often differ, but the patterns and the structures remain the same. I have frequently dreamt, for example, that I am trapped in a room. I try to get out. But I find myself back in a room. Is it the same room? I ask myself. Or am I escaping into an outer room? Or returning to an inner one? Am I in Buenos Aires or Montevideo? In the city or in the country? I touch the wall to try to discover the truth of my whereabouts, to find an answer to these questions. But the wall is part of the dream! So the question eternally returns, like the questioner, into his room. This dream provided me with the motif of the maze or labyrinth which occurs so often in my fictions. I am also obsessed by a dream in which I see myself in a looking glass with several masks or faces each superimposed on the other; I peel them off successively and address the face before me in the glass; but it doesn't answer, it cannot hear me or doesn't listen, impossible to know.

Heaney: What kind of truth do you think Carl Jung was trying to explore in his analyses of symbols and myths? Do you think the Jungian archetypes are valid explanations of what we experience in the subconscious worlds of dream and fiction?

Borges: I have read Jung with great interest but with no conviction. At best he was an imaginative, exploratory writer. More than one can say for Freud: such rubbish!

Kearney: Your suggestion here that psychoanalysis has worth as an imaginative stimulant rather than as a scientific method reminds me of your claim that all philosophical thought is 'a branch of fantastic literature'.

Borges: Yes, I believe that metaphysics is no less a product of imagination than is poetry. After all, the ontological idea of God is the most splendid invention of imagination.

Kearney: But do we invent God or does God invent us? Is the primary creative imagination divine or human?

Borges: Ah, that is *the* question. It might be both.

Heaney: Did your childhood experience of the Catholic religion nourish your sensibility in any lasting way? I'm thinking more of its rites and mysteries than its theological precepts. Is there such a thing as a Catholic imagination, which might express itself in works of literature, as it did in Dante, for example?

Borges: In the Argentine, being a Catholic is a social rather than a spiritual matter. It means you align yourself with the right class, party or social group. This aspect of religion never interested me. Only the women seemed to take religion seriously. As a young boy, when my mother would take me to Mass, I rarely saw a man in the church. My mother had a great faith. She believed in heaven; and maybe her belief means that she is there now. Though I am no longer a practising Catholic and cannot share her faith, I still go into her bedroom at four o'clock every morning – the hour of her death four years ago (she was ninety-nine and dreaded being a hundred!) – to sprinkle holy water and recite the Lord's Prayer as she requested. Why not? Immortality is no more strange or incredible than death. As my agnostic father used to say: 'reality being what it is – the product of our perception – everything is possible, even the Trinity'. I do believe in ethics, that things in our universe are good or bad. But I cannot believe in a personal God. As Shaw says in *Major Barbara*: 'I have left behind the Bride of Heaven.' I continue to be fascinated by metaphysical and alchemical notions of the Sacred. But this fascination is aesthetic rather than theological.

Kearney: In *Tlön, Uqbar, Orbis Tertius*, you spoke about the eternal repetition of chaos gradually giving rise to, or disclosing, a metaphysical pattern of order. What did you have in mind?

Borges: I enjoyed myself very much in writing that, I never stopped laughing from beginning to end. It was all one huge metaphysical joke. The idea of the eternal return is of course an old idea of the Stoics. St Augustine condemned this idea in the *Civitas Dei*, when he contrasts the pagan belief in a cyclical order of time – the City of Babylon – with the linear, prophetic and messianic notion of time to be found in the City of God, Jerusalem. This latter notion has prevailed in our Western culture since Augustine. But I think there may be some truth in the old idea that behind the apparent disorder of the universe and the words we use to speak about our universe, a hidden order might emerge – an order of repetition or coincidence.

Kearney: You once wrote that even though this hidden cyclical order cannot be proved it remains for you 'an elegant hope'.

Borges: Did I write that? That's good, yes, very good. I suppose that in eighty-two years I am entitled to have written a few memorable lines. The rest can 'go to pot', as my grandmother used to say.

Heaney: You spoke of laughing while writing. Your books are certainly full of fun and mischief. Have you always found writing an enjoyable task or has it ever been for you a difficult or painful experience?

Borges: You know, when I still had my sight, I loved writing, every moment, every sentence. Words were like magic playthings that I would toy with and move about in all sorts of ways. Since I lost my sight in the 1950s, I have not been able to exult in writing in this casual manner. I have had to dictate everything, to become a dictator rather than a playboy of words. It is hard to play with toys when one is blind.

Heaney: I suppose that the physical absence of pen and being hooped to the desk makes a big difference …

Borges: Yes, it does. But I miss being able to read even more than being able to write. Sometimes I treat myself to a little deceit, surrounding myself with all sorts of books – particularly dictionaries – English, Spanish, German, Italian, Icelandic.

They become like living beings for me, whispering to me in the dark.

Heaney: Only a Borges could practice such an act of fiction! Your dreams have, quite obviously, always been important to you. Would you say that your capacity or need to inhabit the world of fiction and dream was in any way increased by your loss of sight?

Borges: Since I was blind all I have left is the joy of dreaming, of imagining that I can see. Sometimes my dreams extend beyond sleep into my waking world. Often, before I go to sleep or after I wake up, I find myself dreaming, babbling obscure and inscrutable sentences. This experience simply confirms my conviction that the creative mind is always at work, is always more or less dimly dreaming. Sleeping is like dreaming death. Just as waking is like dreaming life. Sometimes I can no longer tell which is which!

CHAPTER TWENTY-TWO

'The Stones in the Midst of All':
Interview with Anne Madden (1983)

Kearney: Does the fact that women are intimately linked as you say with the 'fathomless past' of the collective unconscious mean that their artistic expression will be in some sense different from the artistic expression of men? Joyce spoke about the possibility of a specifically 'feminine' writing; do you believe that there is such a thing as a specifically 'feminine' painting?

Madden: No, I do not. What I mean is that both men and women tap this unconscious source when they are creating. I think that when Joyce spoke of a 'feminine' writing he believed that this would be as possible for a man as for a woman to the extent that both are capable of drawing from the female principle of the psyche, which has been suppressed for so long in our Western culture dominated by male values, forced back as it were into the realm of the subconscious and only rarely able to find expression in the form of dream or in the creative process.

Kearney: So you would disagree with the traditional 'essentialist' doctrine that male and female have two separate natures from birth?

Madden: It seems to me they are obviously separate and complementary, but both men and women possess a dual psychic structure, a male and a female principle; and in artistic or symbolic expression these two principles are in different degrees present. This means that a male poet or artist is he who is open to the feminine side of his psyche, breaking out of the conventional male ghetto mentality. Keats recognized this when he said that the poet must develop a feminine sensibility. Similarly, the genuine female poet or artist is she who is prepared to reconcile, in symbol or image, word or paint, both her suppressed female and male psychic possibilities (what Jung called the *anima* and *animus*). Artistic expression represents therefore the possibility of releasing the male as well as the female from the stereotyped and 'sexist' roles of 'man' and 'woman' imposed upon them by Western culture. The artist is in this sense a transformer and a liberator.

Kearney: So you would disagree with Simone de Beauvoir when she maintains that woman must separate herself from man, at both the sexual and social levels, in order to assert herself authentically as a woman?

Madden: Yes, I cannot agree with her in this. We cannot and must not separate ourselves from each other; to do so is merely to become alienated from our innermost psychic unity, which is precisely what has tended to happen over the centuries with men and women being slotted into narrowly and dogmatically defined 'male' and 'female' pigeon holes. The artist, drawing from the entirety of his or her being, has always represented a challenge to this kind of simplistic separatism, and still does. We are now entering a new era in which the woman is at last in a position to control the nature of her biological role and in which she has won the possibility, still unrealized of course, of being creative in nearly all domains, including art. I was struck by Anton Ehrenzweig's suggestion in *The Hidden Order of Art* that the relationship between the artist and his oeuvre approximates in many respects to the transferences of 'undifferentiated scanning' between mother and child. It's a very complex question and I don't pretend to have any clear understanding of the implications involved, but I do believe that the recognition of this feminine part of the psyche will be just as revelatory for men as for women.

Kearney: Do you see artistic expression as a sort of psychoanalysis of this hidden psyche?

Madden: No, for we cannot prove meaning or have any purely logical interpretation of it. We interpret the world and our relation to it through myth and symbol, through personal and abstract devotions and though art, which is the expression of this deep stream of consciousness, the creator of myth, of dream, of God – wherein experience is transformed into images and where lies the most important area of consciousness, because it reflects the consciousness of being. And it is this hidden level of being that founds the possibility of communion between male and female consciousness. It is like a deep stream which has its own source of nourishment, like a river whose surface water hides and nourishes, through infiltrations, the underground river, the subterranean layer. All we can hope for is to be given or develop a maximum capacity to 'dream' and turn it into ourselves, and ourselves into it, thus making it real.

Kearney: You already mentioned that maternity came to rock your boat when you were already on your way as a painter and that you did not find it easy to sail under these two conflicting winds. You are now an internationally recognized painter and a mother of two children. How in fact did you manage to reconcile the exigencies of maternity and creativity?

Madden: I think it's important to mention two things here. First, I was fortu-
nate enough to have already had several years of discipline and devotion to my
work before I had children, which meant that a precedent of professional
activity had been firmly established and was not to be easily abandoned.
Secondly, and perhaps the major reason why I was able to combine being a
mother and a painter is largely *economic*. This is an essential point and one often
overlooked. I was lucky enough to have always been able to afford help. I
worked in a studio in my own home which meant I was a presence for my
children – something I've always considered very important – but if I'd had to
look after my children completely, I think it would have been virtually impossible for me to have painted professionally, at least for a considerable number
of years. For those women who find themselves in an economic or social situation where they cannot arrange to have help with their children, it must be
extremely difficult, if not impossible, to pursue their creative vocation. Indeed
it is possibly because women found themselves historically in a dependent
economic situation that there have been more male than female artists. I think
that those Western thinkers, like Plato or Nietzsche, who claimed that men are
intrinsically more creative than women have served to propagate an unjust and
discriminatory fallacy. In pre-Platonic civilization, woman was recognized as a
sacred guardian of culture and art. Sappho was just one known example. That
history denied woman this creative status is due almost entirely to the fact that
history forced her into a subservient economic role.

Kearney: Both you and your husband, Louis le Brocquy, find yourselves in the
unique situation of both being professional painters working in the same
studio in your home in the south of France. Does this lead to conflictual or
complementary working rapport?

Madden: Complementary. I think it is probably rare that such situations work
out, but I am convinced that Louis and I are mutually helpful to one another
by a happy chance rather than merely by goodwill. The fact that our painting
is so very different is an advantage; it means that we can bring to each other's
work a very 'fresh eye' whenever momentary blindness or despondency seems
to paralyse either one of us.

Kearney: Much of your work appears to be influenced by ancient Irish motifs,
as several of the titles of your monolithic diptychs and triptychs suggest –
'standing stones', *Menhir*, *Megalith*, etc. You spent much of your childhood in
the barren and boundless landscape of the Burren in County Clare. To what
extent would you consider yourself an Irish painter by inspiration as well as
by origin?

Madden: All my formative years were spent in County Clare, where I grew up
amidst the local megalithic stone monuments, pillar stones, dolmens, menhirs
and so on. These forms lived within me even though they found no explicit

artistic expression until very many years afterwards, in fact only after I'd left Ireland and come to live in France. After a long and painful rupture in my work, these images of my childhood finally emerged in pictorial form and have determined the main body of my work ever since in large, human-scale canvasses. In a sense it was perhaps important to have left Ireland behind before these forms could be internalized and then finally reappropriated from a distance. I did not, however, choose to leave Ireland for this reason and cannot know whether I would have discovered the same 'distance' if I had stayed in Ireland. But it would certainly have been more difficult to distil these forms had I stayed, as then the landscape might have rather served to distract by its immediacy.

Kearney: Could you say more about your fascination, perhaps even your obsession, with these megalithic stone forms?

Madden: Stone has always meant a great deal to me instinctively. I have suitcases and shelves filled with stones. As a young child, from the age of eight or nine, I used to spend hours every day breaking open stones to discover their marvellous secrets, their hearts. I was convinced that my brain was in my fingertips and that I could only discover the hidden reality of the world through my hands. Stone was to neolithic man (and is to me) one of the most enduring realities. Mircea Eliade has observed that stone always remains itself, abides and endures, thus showing man something that transcends his humanity. The great stones of Newgrange, Stonehenge, Carnac, mark the division of space between the ordinary and the divine. These megaliths represent the first monumental expression of our attitude to death. They are to me elegiac in the same sense as Rilke's *Duino Elegies*, in so far as they are an attempt to conjugate death and life, or re-conjugate them. Indeed Rilke visited Carnac in January 1911 and wrote to his wife – I will read the letter: 'A calyx column stands there like a lone survivor and you don't encompass it because it stands far out beyond our life; only together with the night somehow, can you comprehend it, take it along with the stars where for a second it becomes human – human experience.' These death/life preoccupations I speak of reside in me and lie behind the paintings. But painting is born of painting and conforms to and breaks its own rules. It is ever expandable and I believe in the limitless and potent possibilities of painting as a means of reinventing the world and itself simultaneously. The images in my work refer back to the myths and symbols of a non-verbal and non-representational culture which contains our origins and which enacted both the anguish and hope of a people in the rituals performed in the stone edifices of Newgrange, etc. I felt an exciting and intuitive recognition since childhood of the symbolic power and hidden secrets of our origins in the stone circles, menhirs and tumulae. I think there is an affinity and continuity between the artist today and his primeval counterpart, in so far as the former's main task in his or her own short lifespan is essentially the same as that of the palaeolithic artist, that is his striving to come to terms with the invisible forces around and within him. Painting and sculpture are essentially the artist's psychic reflection of the visible world. I think the artist is above all a transformer of what is beyond sight and appearance – of the essence of things. In this sense I think that all great art is ontological. The artist is faced by something which demands to be made by her into a work. She is concerned with an act of being if she carries it through, wherein the effective power operates and the work arises. She has to wait for the will, the attentive will which is directed towards the effective power. The act necessitates sacrifice and risk. All must be given and risked. The work demands this and if the artist does not serve it right it is broken or breaks her.

Kearney: The Irish critic Brian Lynch has pointed out that your paintings also express a very specific landscape of cloud and sea, of turbulent light on rock, conveyed by reddish browns and blacks, a certain representation of the Irish seascape or weather which he terms an exteriorization or 'objective correlative' of an 'inner weather' of emotion and anguish. Do you see your work as a correspondence between inner and outer scapes?

Madden: Well, all art is an attempt, very often a desperate attempt, to reconcile the inner with the outer world. Even the megaliths embody this attempt in its first primitive expression for they stand exposed to the harsh outer elements of the world but at the same time they incarnate and symbolize our fears and hopes concerning that inner cycle of life and death. In 1969, personal tragedies caused a rupture in my painting. It came to a halt. I was unable to paint. However I did make a series of serigraphs on perspex, which were shown here and there, including New York in November 1971 where I went for the exhibition. On my return I found I was able to paint again, after nearly two years. But the work had changed: the great megalithic tombs now presented themselves to me as images – linked I suppose with my own confrontation with death – and I began a series of large vertical paintings. They tended to be dark tonally, reflections of grief, of the Irish landscape, of an instinctive search to find or extract light from darkness: elegies of personal grief but also to the terrible and tragic events in Northern Ireland.

Kearney: Dominique Fourcade, the French poet, has written: 'What emerges from behind onto the surface of Anne Madden's canvas is neither dolmen nor menhir but paint, paint which asks to be recognised as such.' Would you agree?

Madden: Yes, yet the image remains important to me; though it may not seem to be as it emerges in its own pictorial terms. The American movement of Abstract Expressionism in the 1950s did of course influence me and give me encouragement, for I recognized in the paintings of Jean-Paul Riopelle and Sam Francis some of my own preoccupations with paint. In a sense the essential constituents of all great art are abstract: so in this sense for me there is no intrinsic difference between say Matisse's *The Moroccans* and Piero della

Francesca's *Baptism of Christ*. As you know there has been a whole school of painting since the beginning of the fifties – Abstract Expressionism, Lyrical Abstraction, etc. – and these labels have been stuck on me, implying that I also denied the image completely in order to insist on the language of paint alone. What is significant in this movement towards abstraction, witnessed in literature also, is that it reflects a divorce from society and an increasing dependency on the individual and the autonomy of his medium. It undermines the conventional correspondence of form to reality and tries to create new forms on the basis of the medium alone. While I identified with this movement to a large extent, I continued to lean emotionally on the image. The image of stone in particular remained for me an integral part of the work. Some other Irish painters, including Louis, seem to have felt a similar fidelity to the image. In my own case, while incorporating the image, I have felt impelled to divide my work formally into separate panels, diptychs or triptychs. Maintaining the image for me demands a physical separation between its various parts. After photography and film, I can find no other way to render the multiple aspects of reality. Then, once I begin to paint, to commit the image to the canvas, the language of paint takes over completely, and the work is realized in purely pictorial terms. Of course there is always the question in the end as to whether it has been entirely transformed in paint in the process, and revealed in a purely plastic space.

Kearney: You would not see your work as committed to any specific spiritual or social vision?

Madden: Many people have said to me that the paintings have a certain gravity or graveness about them. They see them in churches, and do I intend this? The answer is no, I don't intend them *for* anywhere or anybody unless the work is commissioned for a specific place. The intent and content is contained within the work itself. I suppose if there is any religious sense in them it is an instinctive sense of the 'sacred' in all things which is reflected in them maybe. (Though my formal Catholic upbringing nearly managed to unseat this sense!) But I hope that when I say that my paintings are not intended for anyone or anywhere that this will not be taken as an arrogant attitude. It is meant as the very opposite. I believe the artist is confronted by and is alone with his or her art. It may or may not *be* or *become* significant to others. But those who proclaim they are making their poems or paintings for the working classes or the bourgeoisie are being patronizing! Even should he proclaim he is freely celebrating a political ideology the artist tends to make himself a prisoner. Above all he must remain free within himself. I do not think that this precludes profound social or religious convictions, as long as these remain the artist's *own* convictions. The proclamation of individual consciousness can be the only role of the artist, because that is what he or she is fundamentally doing. Thus political commitment is largely irrelevant to the work. Nevertheless, sociologically speaking there are some disturbing questions all artists face. For instance, can the painter or poet prevent or mitigate human barbarity? No, but nonetheless we will continue to make our poems and our paintings – in the knowledge that they are useless to society. It is a difficult position to face: to remain integral while necessarily living in isolation from society. The question of spiritual and religious commitment is perhaps a little more flexible. For instance stone, to return to our example, contains an inherently religious symbolism, be it pagan, Christian or alchemical. As M-L von Franz has pointed out, the alchemists considered stone as a symbol of eternity and compared it to the mystical experience of God in the human soul. It was believed that only prolonged suffering could burn away the superfluous psychic elements concealing the 'stone', the profound inner core of our being. The fact that this symbol of the human self is an object of inorganic matter points to a deeper and as yet unknown correlation between the unconscious and what we call 'matter'. Psychosomatic medicine is an attempt to grapple with this enigma. Is it possible that the psyche and matter are the same phenomenon, one seen from within and the other from without? The suggestion in all this is that religious symbolism very often operates at a level which precedes any conscious interpretation or commitment.

Kearney: The motif of the void in your work has struck many people. Fourcade has written that 'the canvas is a space to which Anne Madden lays claim as her own void, a desert over which she presides, as each of us does in his own way. Impelled to set down this desert, to project the volume of its abyss, she surveys it, drawing from its depths as she draws from within herself. For it is within this desert, this void, that the reverberations of paint echo.' Your painting has been described as a 'surface hungry for paint', 'a reality craving for light', 'a fugue towards light that is also darkness'. How does this motif of the void or of the interplay of light and darkness operate in your work?

Madden: Fourcade is talking metaphorically about the process of painting as such. When I paint, I spread the canvas horizontally on the ground and in this sense it serves as a two-dimensional blank space corresponding to a void within, which seeks to be experienced and bodied forth in paint. The interplay of light and darkness is another metaphor for this process of transforming an invisible inner absence into the luminous visibility of painting: the absence is the floor of our being, the hidden darkness or silt which remains amorphous and formless until exteriorized into paint. The light cannot exist without darkness, just as the world of the *anima* cannot exist without the world of the *animus*. Perhaps art is a way of consummating this dialectic of mutual hungers?

Chapter Twenty-Three

Interview with James Coleman (1982)

To enter into the work of James Coleman is to embark on a journey through the intricacies of experience itself; those processes by which we identify and create relationships to the objective world and with ourselves as 'author' are suppressed in the interests of the 'text', whose emphasis is on the active participation of the spectator. Thus, the work does not come into flower until the viewer enters into an imaginative collaboration with it; and it is through its carefully orchestrated choice of media and the atmosphere of its space that its perceptual and psychological meaning begins to emerge.

Coleman's earlier installations, such as *Flash Piece* (1970), *Slide Piece* (1973) or *Two Seagulls or One Seagull Twice* (1973/4), situate us in the imaginary realm of immediate perceptual experience in which the object tends to separate out into an entity independent of relationships. Through disorientating spatio-temporal transformations, he directs our attention, not only to what we are experiencing, but to how we are experiencing it, severing our habits of seeing, making us aware of ourselves as perceiving subjects, and the ways in which we invest objects with meaning.

Coleman uses time as a primary signifying element referring directly to our perceptions. His 'text' unfurls and reveals itself in the real time of our involvement. Conceived as a continuous cycle, it is an endless repetition, inaugurated at whichever point we enter the cycle. Thus, unlike conventional narrative, there is no satisfying closure; no resolution of those contradictions that are the contingent reality of 'real life', no gratification of that desire for unity with the other that eludes us, and that is the lure of traditional narrative. In *Box* (1977), we catch glimpses of the boxers circling the ring into eternity. Tunney, like Sisyphus, is trapped in a perpetual repetition in which he must forever play out the fantasy of mastery over the other, in constant fear of his own mortality. The visual and acoustic space of *Box* encloses us (as if) in the mind and body of the boxer, rendering Tunney's anxiety as our own: we are both voyeur and participant in an essentially erotic struggle with our own other.

Clara and Dario (1975) represents the artist's first complete expression of perceptual experience becoming integrated into a social life: the navigation into symbolic exchange that replaces the subject in the wider context of human relationships. Through changing patterns of sequences and re-ordered repetitions, Clara and Dario's interdependent responses reveal how the self is not a 'wilful' entity but is intimately bound to the other; in the temporal shifts between a wistful nostalgia and the present, we begin to understand how far we romanticize and fictionalize our past lives. *Clara and Dario* is related thematically to two subsequent works, the video installation, *So Different … and Yet* (1980), and the live performed work, *Now and Then* (1981), both of which are concerned additionally with the projected image of the self: our desire for social recognition manifested through the cultural codes of 'style' and gesture, and our relationship to media representations of ourselves.

The psychological implications of the 'projected image' are central to the artist's later works. In *Strongbow* (1978), the tragedy of Tunney's fragile sense of self revealed behind his public face as 'champ' becomes translated into a historical dimension in terms of the symbolic function of the cultural 'hero'. In this installation, the silent effigy of the Norman knight emerges from the shadows of the historical past as an emblem of an authoritative (social) order, yet ironically impassive to the drama enacted in his presence (the present) by the clapping orange and green hands. As with the intensely disturbing *A-Koan* (1978), we are caught in a dialogue between remembrance of the past and the anticipation of the future in which, as in life, we cannot reunite the self with itself, or the self with a mythic identity to the past.

In building the spectator's role into the work, Coleman does not conceal the meanings inherent in the language of representation itself. In so doing, the work retains a power to reveal the ideological framework at the root of social intercourse, drawing us out of our apathetic unawareness of the meanings it contains. Coleman's work is 'political', not in the conventional sense, but in the fact that it challenges the very basis of ideology: those relative, socially determined values projected and reinforced through the images and symbols of culture that ensnare us in a system of pre-determined meanings and relationships that, because familiar, seem 'natural' and therefore unquestionable.

(Synopsis of the monograph of James Coleman by Jean Fischer, Exhibition catalogue, The Douglas Hyde Gallery, Dublin 1982, Arts Council of Northern Ireland, Belfast. Presented by the Ulster Museum.)

Kearney: Why did you choose to abandon the conventional medium of painting in favour of more complex innovatory media incorporating video, slide projections, sound, music, narrative and acting?

Coleman: You know, I never did feel I did abandon painting ... picturing ... maybe. Long before I ever began to introduce other media into my work – When I gradually began to lose interest in a simple retinal reality I began to sense a feeling that I needed to take cognizance of the psychological dimension. To do this I initially used film to document, later on as a device of expression. I realized that my medium was also part of things as much as my eye or mind was. My first installation, working directly with 'time' (1968) was really no more than my painting ideas expanded into time. I believe painting or the static form is a device like any other. Some artists feel it's the best medium for what they want to do – and they do it very well or badly. Others use sound and achieve what they want to do well or not so well. I have absolutely nothing against painting or sculpture. I'm bewildered about the media-anxiety some have. To label an artist as a 'video artist' is just as crazy as being labelled as a 'pencil artist' just because one uses a pencil!

Kearney: Is your intention to 'free' the spectator from traditional and stereotyped ways of looking and listening? If so, how do you understand such 'freedom'? Is it a question of liberating the spectator from the constraints of habit – or is it also a question of liberating the spectator for something new, for new possibilities of creating or imagining?

Coleman: I'd imagine all art functions to free the spectator in some way; but my primary concern is not to be didactic or prescriptive. Any quest for conscious freedom must be about knowledge. Knowledge (in particular its communicative function) has an aesthetic dimension. In my work I try to be conscious of an aesthetic/knowledge relationship. Let me put it in the form of an ancient Eastern legend. Walking one evening along a deserted road, Mullah Nasrudin saw a troop of horsemen coming towards him. His imagination started to work; he saw himself being captured and sold as a slave, or forced into the army. Nasrudin bolted, climbed a wall into a grave, and lay down in an open tomb. Puzzled at his strange behaviour, the men – honest travellers – followed him. They found him stretched out, tense and quivering. 'What are you doing in that grave? We saw you run away. Can we help you?' 'Just because you can ask a question does not mean there is a straightforward answer to it,' said the Mullah, who now realized what had happened. 'It all depends on your viewpoint. If you must know, however, I am here because of you, and you are here because of me.'

Kearney: That reminds me of Joyce's phrase about the aesthetic enigma of 'intermisunderstanding minds'. But to change track a little, could you say something about your preoccupation with temporality in your work? In *Being and Time*, Heidegger argues that there can be no isolated meaning in an abstract present, that to be human is to exist in time because the human imag-ination is intrinsically temporal and historical, invariably interpreting its present experiences in terms of its past or its future: we carry the past with us into the present even as we project ourselves towards our future possibilities. Heidegger's aim is to deconstruct the traditional notion of being as a timeless, objectified presence. Why do you introduce temporality into your works (e.g. *So Different … and Yet*)? Do you see any parallels between Heidegger's project for modern philosophy and your own aesthetic project in this respect?

Coleman: Yes, there may be parallels of 'form'; but our intentions would be different. I think Heidegger strove to establish a methodology to enable us to understand the truth of Being. My art has no such aim. Art embraces science and philosophy but similarities can be deceptive. In the work you mention, *So Different … and Yet*, narration is proposed as a form for reading and conceiving a presented reality, not for establishing a structure on which to construct a true reality. My work is not about true or false realities, it's about consciousness of shifting realities. Narration is not intended to produce truth, though it may propose a form for conceiving or locating it. The narrative structure in my work questions linear sequence, and tries to create ambiguity between temporality and causality – to nudge events and states of feeling between ideas of the past and the possible. For example, the narrative in *So Different … and Yet* juxtaposes such different time references as: 'it happened …' and 'you are about to hear …' etc.

Kearney: The question of time in your work leads logically to the related ques-tion of the important role played by *memory*. You seem to deal with memory not just in terms of the personal unconscious or past (e.g. Clara and Dario's recollection of childhood) but also in terms of revising and responding to the cultural and political history that has shaped us and made us what we are. The Tunney-Dempsey film projection exposes the ways in which the media of Western culture make collective heroes out of tortured split-personalities (for example, the soundtrack of Tunney's interior monologue).

Coleman: Very true. In fact as good a title might have been *Hit and Myth!* The work offered lead-ins on different levels starting from a simple visual and aural reaction to more contemplative and maybe even active participation by unfriendly spectators! The whole memory thing is so inextricably bound up with one's personal and shared experiences. I must tell you the story of an experience I had some years ago. It happened that I was paying weekly visits to a psychiatric hospital with an ex-patient to gather information for a project (never realized), when one day he recounted a strange experience. He had a heavy drinking problem and suffered hallucinations. Once he claimed he saw two tigers sitting on top of a bus. He attributed the event to his hallucination, and all was fine until some time later when he was cured and out of hospital, he happened to see a photograph in an old newspaper of two tigers perched on top of a bus – some publicity stunt in the same town (Milan) around the time he believed himself to have had the famous hallucination. The photograph had a very negative effect on him. He was convinced, up to the time he had seen the photograph, that his vision was hallucinatory and described it to everyone as such. Like any good patient he wished to put his problem behind him and for a while simply related the experience as a hallucinatory event. But because of his contemplative nature he began to get worried and perplexed about whether or not he ought now to describe the event as a 'memory'. I got him books from the library and together we got deeply into the problem as potential material for an aesthetic project. Once he saw I was as perplexed as himself, and shared his dilemma, his sense of self-security began to return.

Kearney: Experiencing some of your multimedia works (*Strongbow, Now and Then, So Different … and Yet*) I was reminded of Beckett's description of his own work as a 'breakdown of the object', an attempt to rupture the lines of communication between the subject (creator or spectator) and the naturalistic object. Beckett's manifesto is a variation on Rimbaud's appeal to the artist to be 'absolutely modern' by 'destroying the senses' (i.e. our normal way of seeing, hearing, reading, feeling, etc.). Do you see a parallel between this literary attack on the conventional modes of perception and what is being achieved in the contemporary visual arts – in particular your own experimental work?

Coleman: Rimbaud's 'destroying the senses' or Beckett's 'breakdown of the object' seems a very severe reductionist method of working, which might, I feel, lead nowhere but into an aesthetic black-hole (though Beckett himself avoids the suction). In art, innovation has been achieved by artists wandering along many lanes bringing with them qualities which (to me) are important: personal expression, confession, the collective. I try to project and reflect questions of ideology, tradition, and how what we do relates to the production of meaning. Whatever else, making art is no joke, though it's like one in that if taken asunder you ruin it.

Kearney: How do you see the rapport between the literary and visual motifs in your work? Do they work with, or against, each other?

Coleman: Every image is to some extent a scripto-visual phenomenon. Seeing is obviously not arrested at the retina, and when we look at an image it becomes interrelated in a complex web of knowledge on the rational and on the subconscious level. It is at this level that the visual and the literary-narrative work can play together; and my work frequently explores the ways in which this game can continue.

Kearney: Dorothy Walker, the Irish art critic, has described your recent work as an attempt to 'clarify how historical images become symbols' – would you agree?

Coleman: I would agree that her interpretation is a sensitive response to how I would like to see my work interpreted.

Kearney: In *Strongbow* and *A-Koan* the recollection of times past makes explicit reference to Irish political unity. The former features a tomb of Strongbow (emblem of the Anglo-Norman conquest of Ireland) with a colour video of two hands – orange and green – at first clasped in a prayerful gesture and then breaking into a strident clapping movement. The second work (*A-Koan*) is an image of the Irish flag furling and unfurling with loudspeakers emitting repetitive tones and a child's voice calling plaintively for its mother. Both works appear to communicate a sense of conflict or contradiction in Irish history and culture. Do you intend these works as statements about Irish nationalism?

Coleman: I see 'Irish nationalism' as a crème-de-ment-al, relished for its green colour, syrupy sweetness or heady stimulation. Oh sure, I love to indulge in it be-times!

Kearney: Do you consider your work to be specifically Irish in any way: in content, form or in inspiration? What of the rapport, for example, between your work and Irish landscape and history?

Coleman: I used to live for periods in the Connemara Gaeltacht and the Aran Islands, and this landscape in particular had – and still has – a very emotional effect on me. Maybe if I tell you about a recent experience I had when I tried to draw the landscape I might begin to answer your question. While I sat sharpening my pencil and contemplating the job that lay ahead of me, I decided that whatever I did, the drawing should not be too 'abstract'. That whatever shapes and lines I put down on paper should also offer an accessible account of my subject to any local passer-by who cared to look over my shoulder. I took a long hard look at what was around me. The landscape began to assume a posture – it gradually became a sign of its past and present culture – a culture I could never totally share nor belong to. The landscape became a kind of parody – more a mimesis – of all those forms through which I had gained access to its culture: music, poetry, and in particular painting. I realized that the works that came to my mind were mostly created by extraneous interpreters and observers of the indigenous culture I somehow wished to represent in my work. This began to weigh on me as a constraint and a responsibility. I did not wish to alter or change – more to continue, in a pertinent way – a culture I had come to respect and love. As I sat there contemplating the difficulties of the task I had set myself, I realized that I had all this time been making marks on my paper. Forms and shapes had spontaneously come into being influencing new forms and shapes. At first I was bothered about how 'abstract' it looked. Then, cautiously, I began to wonder: perhaps these shapes and lines might conceal a secret and hidden perspective, a point in space and cultural time from which they could be viewed and interpreted as a true and faithful representation of all that I secretly wanted to achieve. I began to show the drawing to people. They took the drawing in their hands and began holding it back to the side and tilting their heads in different ways, searching for a way to read and interpret it – this was a good beginning.

Kearney: Like many other Irish artists – Louis le Brocquy, Anne Madden, Michael Farrell and Eithne Jordan, etc. – you have lived and worked abroad, in London, Paris and Milan. Have you found working abroad particularly helpful in any way?

Coleman: Yes, working and exhibiting outside one's immediate cultural environment is a challenge which forces an artist to be objective about his or her work, culture and self. The experience has been very formative for my work.

Kearney: While you were working abroad during the sixties were you influenced by the 1968 attempt to break down the barriers between the artist and society? Was your installation on the public railway bridge in Milan using mirrors influenced by what was taking place in art during this period?

Coleman: Very much so. I was attending college in Milan at the time and we spent one full year sitting in and discussing work. I motivated a group of students to do some projects involving group activities outside the then rather hot-house atmosphere of the academy. The railway footbridge was one such project. It started off as grist for our revolutionary mill when I was arrested for photographing the bridge (it's still forbidden under Italian law to photograph around a railway station). We studied the bridge from a sociological viewpoint and carried out interviews with those who used the bridge – mostly working people who also had to drag their bicycles over dangerous steps. We took into consideration the formalistic urban-architectural dimension and finally decided to put a park-bench on the bridge for the tired passers-over to sit and rest on. In front of the bench was a mirror which reflected the sitter and the bridge. A second mirror reflected the other people passing along and their gazes. Our purpose was to establish an observational relationship of the man/woman on the bridge to their environmental structures. It was a time when we were very unified in the smug security of knowing exactly what was wrong with society. We did manage to keep the project outside the institutional art space context for some time. Then the TV came and did a film of it! But I'm very glad to have been a student then. It made me conscious of the fact that art can never simply be reduced to a concept of simple acts of self-expression.

Kearney: Do you think, therefore, that art can break down the frontiers separating it from the everyday world of socio-political activity without ceasing to be art? In his last work entitled *The Aesthetic Dimension* (1978), Herbert Marcuse argued that when art becomes too involved in socio-political affairs it loses that essential dimension of difference, distance and strangeness – what he calls aesthetic transcendence – which identifies it as art and distinguishes it from the contingency of our one-dimensional ordinary experience. Marcuse maintains that art is the final refuge of the two-dimensional experience, the 'authentic utopia'. Do you agree with these sentiments? To what extent do you see parallels between socio-historical and aesthetic movements? What of your own endeavours to introduce an 'ideological' dimension into your work?

Coleman: The history of art shows that parallels between the socio-historic and aesthetic movements do exist. However, it is the way art keeps a distance from the real – 'reality principle' – which gives it an 'aesthetic' dimension. Except in societies which officially sponsor a 'socialist realist' concept of art there is a widespread and tacit assumption that art does have some *intrinsic* value which is not dependent wholly upon its relationship to its extrinsic environment. This would seem to account for its 'extraordinariness', its 'otherness'. But I do not accept the either/or approach. Even though the political is a more conceptual business than art (generally more sensible), the political shares with art a *communicative* dimension (however unrefined), and I believe that any form of communication has some 'aesthetic' level. This is not to deny that there are essential differences between the 'political' and the 'aesthetic'. The political is supposed to be about specific things like asking precise questions, and solving specific problems. Politicians are busy providing us with laws and strict codes of behaviour – an ethic about how to achieve political aspirations. We should therefore be able to judge the 'political' dimension (and its politicians) on how it actualizes or achieves these aspirations. The political will always require something like a 'Utopia'; it must have something to reach for beyond its own preservation as a system. But does art need a Utopia? From my understanding of the 'aesthetic', I would say it doesn't – at least not of the kind the political needs. But are we not taught that the 'aesthetic' dimension of art is a value which distinguishes itself from other realities (including the political). The 'aesthetic' is not understood as being subordinate to any value other than its own – and this is precisely its 'dimension of difference', its 'otherness'. If the aesthetic has any need for an ethic – which I doubt – it must surely be a horse of a different colour from the kind that the political ought to possess. If a work of art is 'good and perfect', it must surely be good 'in itself' (contain its own built-in Utopia). But there is, I believe, a level at which art as a *practice* is similar to the political, and that is at the level where the political and art must possess some respective code of behaviour. The meaning of a work of art does not lie merely in its origin, but also in its destination, and as such it can never totally dispense with, or be outside, the political dimension. But to say that the value of art should lie in the fulfilment of a function which could be performed in some other way is theoretically to allow that art is expendable. To the extent therefore that works of mine have legitimately been perceived as 'political', I would say this: subject matter is not the same as content (or form) in art. To cite an artist yet to be accorded the esteem his work deserves – J.M. Synge – 'there are, it may be hinted, several sides to it'. (This statement was made following the *Playboy* riots.)

Kearney: You mention Synge. You are obviously interested in the theatrical/ dramatic tradition and work in relation to it. Would you perhaps consider any of your performed works – such as, for example, *Now and Then* – to be within the area of 'performance art'?

Coleman: No, I do not consider my performed work to be 'performance art'. The work you mention, *Now and Then*, and a subsequent piece, *Ignotum per Ignotius* (done in conjunction with Operating Theatre), were specifically conceived for a theatre and planned to be performed on a stage. However, it's difficult to define 'performance art'; it is a form that has been characterized by shifting values and rules. It's curious how its rapport to theatre has traditionally been a rather detached affair. I've noticed that performance artists rarely, if ever, go to the theatre – even hate the theatre. They often are, used to be, suspicious of the term itself, because they believed it threatened to subvert their work's integral relationship with the visual arts. In my works to-be-performed it is my intention to work from the theatrical.

CHAPTER TWENTY-FOUR

Between Conflict and Consensus:
Response to Sheeran and Witoszek (1985)

In their challenging and provocative article, 'From explanations to intervention', Pat Sheeran and Nina Witoszek reproach *The Crane Bag* for succumbing to a sense of grievance. They identify this with the masochistic desire of the slave for self-flagellation and self-scrutiny. Instead of indulging in Hamlet-like introspection or else looking to the false trinity of *modernism, Europeanism* and *Enlightenment rationalism* for a solution to the problem of Irish culture, our critics submit that Irish intellectuals in general, and *The Crane Bag* in particular, should be celebrating our privileged status as a 'secondary culture'. Moving beyond our obsession with the critique of native ideologies (epitomized by Yeats's Literary Revival, the dominant role of the Catholic Church and the pervasive influence of tribal mythologies), we are counselled to become active celebrants of 'soul, transcendence and myth'. Sheeran and Witoszek contend that these latter qualities constitute the true trinity of Irish culture – a spiritual heritage that Enlightenment Europe has forgotten or ignored to its detriment. Instead of working for the pluralization of Irish culture and the abandonment of provincialism, we should be turning 'our anachronisms to a virtue' and practising a definite brand of 'heretical aggression'. In short, rather than belatedly turning to Enlightenment Europe for emancipation we would do better to recognize that Europe is now beginning to turn to us, that is, to return to those very properties of 'soul, transcendence and myth' of which Ireland is still in privileged and proud possession. 'One way out of our dilemma,' our critics suggest, 'is not to abandon the Romantic agenda (as *The Crane Bag* recommends) but to complete it.'

There are several points I wish to make by way of a brief reply. First, *The Crane Bag* is not, and has never been, the mouthpiece of some like-minded self-appointed intellectual elite. (In fact, there are not two members of our editorial board who could be guaranteed to agree on any subject.) We do not operate in terms of a pre-established ideology of 'solutions', but seek to cultivate a creative conflict of interpretations. *The Crane Bag* is non-aligned (in the sense of being unaffiliated to any particular political party, religion, tribe or educational establishment in this country). This does not of course mean that it is non-committed. It is deeply so. But its commitment is first and foremost to questioning, to the creation of a form of critical debate that speaks from and to the contemporary conditions of Irish culture in which it is situated. For we believe that no thinking worth its salt can function in a vacuum. All critical questioning emerges within a specific time and place.

The Crane Bag is also committed to a sense of community, to the achievement of consensus (or what, in our first editorial, we called a 'fifth province'). But this can only occur if we start by acknowledging existing divisions and conflicts, that is, a plurality of perspectives. Despite the assumptions of our critics, we do not *begin* from some transcendental vantage point of common understanding, but seek in and through the indispensable detour of conflicting viewpoints to work towards such an understanding as a *goal*. Genuine consensus is not, we hold, an inherited possession but a teleological project.

This conflict of perspectives is most obviously represented by the diversity of contributions to our journal – to give a random sample of political contributors, it would be difficult to maintain that John Hume, Andy Tyrie, Conor Cruise O'Brien, Seamus Twomey, Noam Chomsky, Herbert Marcuse, Garret FitzGerald, Michael D. Higgins or Desmond Fennell are all of one mind! But the conflict also exists, at a more general level, between the different issues of *The Crane Bag*. Indeed it is perhaps significant that while Sheeran and Witoszek criticize *The Crane Bag* for repudiating 'soul, transcendence and myth' (e.g. 'the mystique of Irishness, rural piety, Romanticism, nationalist myth, provincialism and tradition'), we have also been criticized for the very opposite: an over-assertive cultural nationalism. (I am thinking in particular of Edna Longley's critique.) I would suggest that both criticisms tend towards caricature by selecting certain aspects of the overall conflict of interpretations at the expense of others. Moreover, I would like to think that our being accused of both extremes – anti-nationalism and nationalism – is in itself an indication that we must be doing *something* right.

This commitment to intellectual pluralism raises larger issues in the particular cultural context of this island. We are not concerned here with pluralism for pluralism's sake (i.e. publishing anything that comes along just to be 'broad-minded'), but with a conviction that critical contestation and dissent have been conspicuously lacking in contemporary Ireland. This was not always the case, as the proliferation of radical cultural journals in the early decades of the twentieth century testifies – e.g. *The United Irishman* edited by John Mitchell and Arthur

Griffith, *An Claidheamh Soluis* edited by Patrick Pearse, *Workers' Republic* edited by James Connolly, and the *Irish Statesman* and *Irish Homestead* edited by George Russell and Horace Plunkett. All of these journals were committed, in their different ways, to a fundamental debate about the kind of culture and society that had created us and that we might wish in turn to create. Questioning was sustained by the quest for a new sense of social and cultural consensus. Since the establishment of partition, however, such journals disappeared (with the notable exception of *The Bell*) and were replaced by more specialized journals of either an exclusively political or exclusively literary nature. Culture became narrowly identified with literature and society with party politics. One of the major casualties of this ideological partition was the provision of an ongoing intellectual debate. Anti-intellectualism took root, and any attempt to contest the partitionist stereotypes of Gaelic-Catholic nationalism south of the border and British-Protestant unionism north of the border was treated with irritation. Each society settled into its own simplified notion of a homogeneous monolithic culture that muffled its respective minority voices. The attitude of 'what we have we hold' prevailed in both camps. In such a climate of insular conformism and mistrust it was not surprising that the expression of an internal conflict of opinion became virtually synonymous with subversion.

The typecasting of the Gael as a feckless, fanciful, thoughtless romantic and of the Planter as a hard-nosed, industrial, Enlightenment empiricist has not just been imposed on us by the colonizer. We have internalized these very stereotypes within us (as the founding ideologies of our two partitionist states testify, e.g. Craigavon's Protestant parliament for a Protestant people and de Valera's Catholic constitution – in parts at least – for a Catholic people). We have done this, I believe, in order to simplify our existence; in order not to have to think about, or resolve, the complexities of our contemporary society. It is this tendency towards facile polarization that *The Crane Bag* has endeavoured to challenge. And if it is true that we have borne too much resemblance, at times, to Hamlet's critical scrutinizing, this is perhaps because our society has, all too often, borne too much resemblance to Polonius' self-deception. Where ideological simplification has been the order of the day, a dose of creative conflict and complexity may be an appropriate, if provisional, remedy.

The danger, it seems to me, is to give credence to a series of supposedly irreconcilable oppositions: Gael versus Planter, native versus foreigner, Romanticism versus Enlightenment, myth versus reason, tradition versus innovation. Surely it is not a question of either/or but of both/and. We do not, and we should not, feel compelled to choose between a reactionary return to the traditions of the past and a jettisoning of the past altogether, Pol-Pot style, out of obsessive devotion to some postmodernist *tabula rasa* of the future. A healthy dialectical tension is requisite here. Instead of blindly rejecting all our traditions out of hand, therefore, might it not be wiser to detribalize and renew the contents of our cultural heritage – particularly where they have congealed into incarcerating stereotypes? And does this not require a critical discrimination between the differing ways in which the past relates to the concrete realities of our present condition? Alasdair MacIntyre has recently challenged the conservative habit (derived from Burke) of contrasting the stability of tradition with the free-floating destructiveness of critical reason. 'All reasoning,' he argues,

> takes place within the context of some traditional mode of thought, transcending through criticism and invention the limitations of what had hitherto been reasoned in that tradition; this is as true of modern physics as of medieval logic (and one might add, of modern Ireland). Moreover, when a tradition is in good order it is always partially constituted by an argument about the goods the pursuit of which gives to that tradition its particular point and purpose ... Traditions when vital, embody continuities of conflict.

MacIntyre insists that such a position is the very opposite of 'conservative antiquarians', or the *laudator temporis acti* mentality. It is rather the case, he concludes, that 'an adequate sense of tradition manifests itself in a grasp of those future possibilities (those not-yet-completed narratives) that the past has made available to the present'. Here we find, I believe, a good retort to those who condemn Irish intellectuals and artists for continuing to debate about the meaning of our history and traditions. There is no meaning that exists in splendid isolation from its social, historical and cultural contexts. And tradition itself is a narrative construct, not some invariant, timeless 'essence'. Every meaning is part of a narrative and requires an ongoing process of reinterpretation.

This raises, finally, the crucial question of translation, of negotiating and mediating between opposite extremes. As Hugh Mór, the schoolmaster in Friel's play *Translations*, observes: 'We like to think we endure around truths immemorially posited ... [but] it can happen ... that a civilisation can be imprisoned in a linguistic contour which no longer matches the landscape of ... fact.' Hugh goes on to suggest accordingly that 'we must never cease renewing those images [of the past embodied in language], because once we do we fossilise.' Jimmy Jack, the otherworldly bard of the old order, and the Donnelly twins who brutally assassinate Lieutenant Yolland of the Ordnance Survey commission, have both fossilized (the former into benign escapism, the latter into malign hatred) because they failed to renew their images. Hugh, by contrast, comes to realize that a mindless enslavement to the native pieties of the past is condemned to destruction. 'To remember everything', he affirms, 'is a form of madness.' He urges instead that we discriminate between 1) the past that liquidates by spawning a narrow obsession with revenge, and 2) the past that liberates us into new possibilities of self-understanding. Any attempt at such cultural translation and transition is, of course, freighted with risk. But given the ominous alternatives, it is a risk worth taking. Perhaps this is why Hugh agrees at the end of the play to teach Máire English. He frankly concedes the necessity of change, telling Máire that the word 'always' is a silly one. But Hugh cannot guarantee that Máire's acquisition of the art of translation will permit her to transport the secret heritage of the old culture (the heritage of the 'soul, myth and transcendence') into the new one. His parting verdict on translation promises neither too little nor too much. 'I will provide you with the available words and the available grammar,' he assures Máire, 'but will that help you to interpret between privacies? I have no idea.'

Perhaps the most that *The Crane Bag* can hope for is to help provide such a grammar of translation. What it cannot do is offer premature certainties and hard-and-fast remedies. Our society has suffered from too many easy answers and not enough hard questions. In this context, perhaps it is wise to recall Hugh Mór's conviction – and it was Hamlet's in another context – that 'confusion is not an ignoble condition'. *The Crane Bag*, in short, is not a programme of propaganda; it is – at best – a promissory note.

The temptation to propagandize is always present – and never more so than when one is charged with 'interpreting' the world rather than 'intervening' and changing it. But I tremble to think what a constitution rewritten on the magical principles of 'soul, myth and transcendence' would realistically imply for our society. Practical action usually involves a resolute singleness of purpose and a willingness to devote oneself to one particular vision. This is tantalizingly attractive to intellectuals. But it is not the business of editors to impose one specific point of view (their point of view) on the contributors or readers of their journal. We are not party whips.

This does not require that we turn our backs on history; nor that we renounce the struggle for social justice in favour of some transcendental even-handedness or eclecticism. What it certainly does require is an unswerving commitment to a radical critique that will unmask the ideological motivations that inform our contemporary society. Such a critique of ideology – and our final issue of *The Crane Bag* concentrates on this specific theme – operates out of an awareness that no viewpoint, no matter how culturally quarantined, is absolutely 'neutral'. Things as they are *must change*, for they are simply not good enough. Such an awareness presupposes, of necessity, a fundamental desire for a more just, equitable, liberated and creative society. Interpretation here calls for intervention, but it is certainly not identical with it. And it is presumptuous folly to claim otherwise. This position is a far cry from that trendy, but ultimately self-deluding, liberalism that sees a disengaged equipoise of opposing attitudes to be the end of social and cultural conflict. Mere 'disinterestedness' of this bland variety fosters submission to the political status quo and is a recipe for intellectual inertia. It is conservatism masquerading as liberalism.

The kind of consensus that *The Crane Bag* seeks to promote, by contrast, is not one that would dissolve real differences into some magical harmony; it takes the existing, and usually concealed, oppositions of the historical moment as its starting point. As such it is an ideal project that may or may not be realized. But it is one that cannot be permanently abandoned either. For to do so would be to accept the way things are here and now. That is why *The Crane Bag* has sought to occupy a critical position between conflict and consensus, between the clashing demands of politics and art.

Chapter Twenty-Five

Dialogue with Georges Dumézil (1982)

Kearney: There is still some debate as to how exactly your work should be situated and classified. Is it primarily philosophical, sociological, anthropological, theological or linguistic? After 1938 you begin to define your study of ancient myths and religions as 'the comparative study of the Indo-European religions' or simply 'Indo-European civilization' in contradistinction to the earlier title of 'comparative mythology'. How does this change in nomenclature describe your specific approach to myth and religion?

Dumézil: My work is primarily linguistic, or to be more precise philological. That is, the classification and interpretation of ancient myths in terms of textual structures or types. My first concern was to discover what the earliest texts of the various Indo-European civilizations might have in common, what similarities of *function* might exist in different mythic or religious orders to suggest a shared source. Eventually I discerned the 'ideology of the three functions' – Sovereignty, Force and Fecundity – firstly in texts representative of diverse layers of Vedic, Germanic and Roman civilization. And this led me to ascertain that there existed a specific conception of the three functions in all of the Indo-European cultures from India to Ireland. So that my original philological preoccupation to better understand the texts of Indian and classical poets, for instance, developed into a passion to understand the unrevealed ways of thought of their common ancestors. In short, *philology* enabled me to posit the existence of an underlying Indo-European *ideology*.

This development meant of course that my work could no longer be accurately termed 'comparative mythology' since the ideology of the three functions proved to be one of the chief characteristics of Indo-European civilization as a whole; it is not, for example, present in any articulate way in African, American-Indian, Chinese or even Biblical texts, and if they are present to a degree in the 'Aniki' tradition of Polynesia, that probably results from very ancient and strong action of some Indian component. Moreover, 'mythology' itself became too limited a rubric, for the ideology of the three functions was also to be found in the religious, literary, philosophical and even at times social structures of Indo-European societies.

Kearney: How does this approach differ, for instance, from the 'anthropological' method of Claude Lévi-Strauss or the 'comparative phenomenological' method of Mircea Eliade?

Dumézil: Both Eliade's and Lévi-Strauss' readings of the world of myth are very different from my own. Eliade's approach to myth strikes me as being primarily that of a man of letters. He interprets myth as a poet might in terms of its inexhaustible mystery and sacredness. To see this, one only has to read his reflections on the myths of cyclical time and eternal return. But he differs of course from the ordinary poet in that he is a philosophizing poet. He is concerned with the comparative study of the myths and rituals of different world civilizations in order to identify what he would see as the universal characteristics of man as a *homo religiosus*.

Lévi-Strauss, on the contrary, is before all else a philosopher. His philosophy is essentially a *critical* philosophy: that is, a critical interrogation of the systems and structures which enable men to understand their world. Hence the term 'structuralist', which is applied to him.

Kearney: If you differ from Eliade and Lévi-Strauss in terms of *method* – philological rather than poetic or philosophical – is it not true that you also differ in respect of *subject matter*?

Dumézil: Certainly. Eliade, though he began as a specialist of Eastern European culture (which he knew intimately as a Romanian) and Indian folklore (of which he also had firsthand acquaintance from his visits there in the thirties), analyses material from all or most of the world religions. He was also a talented philologist and linguist; but his overriding interest is a 'comparative phenomenology', that is a reflective description of 'essential meaning' of the totality of ancient myths, rituals and symbols still available to modern research.

Lévi-Strauss, for his part, specializes in the study of the religions of peoples *without writing*. This is what he calls 'savage thought' (*la pensée sauvage*) with no derogatory intent, because it precedes and precludes historical transposition into a developing or evolving literature (what he calls 'diachronic' culture). Lévi-Strauss's principal subject matter is, accordingly, the culture of the Latin-American Indian where the symbolic and ritual structures have resisted time and change, remaining the same throughout the centuries ('synchronic').

To put it briefly, I differ from Eliade in that my research is confined to the ideological structures of Indo-European civilization, and from Lévi-Strauss in that this Indo-European civilization is a historically developing and diachronic one in direct contrast to the *pensée sauvage* of the American Indians. That said,

I must point out that there is absolutely no conflict between our three approaches; they operate on three heterogeneous planes without collision. I have great respect for the work of both Eliade, with whom I have been associated, and of Lévi-Strauss, who so kindly received me at *l'Académie française* and whose work I see as wholly compatible with my own, though some of his disciples have claimed otherwise.

Kearney: What would you consider to be the relationship between the ideology of the three functions and history? Would you consider yourself a historian?

Dumézil: I like to think of myself as a historian of sorts, though many historians would object to this. The study of Indo-European ideology does not exclude the study of history. On the contrary, I believe that history as we know it is ultimately founded on an *ultra-history*. This ultra-history consists of an interpretation of the historical facts; to be more precise, it comprises the tripartite ideological functions which structure the historical facts available to us. For what is the ideology of the three functions but the way in which the Indo-Europeans *explained* their world, giving the facts of existence an explicit meaning, order or coherence. Thus historical facts, as rendered or recorded in Indo-European texts, are already conceptual interpretations of history. For example, in the last six songs of the *Aeneid*, the articulation of Aeneas, Tarchon and Latinus is given coherence by being modelled on the tripartite structure of Romulus (the religious sovereignty of the proto-Romans), Lucumon (the warrior force of the Etruscans) and Tatius (the wealth and the gift of the Sabines), which had been itself produced as an expression of the tripartite scheme. But these ideological divisions exist not only in mythic and literary structures but also in the *ensemble* of religious, social and philosophical structures of a society. They cut right through a culture and give it its specific sense of order. Thus when I speak of ideology I do not mean it in the habitual sense of a 'theory of illusions' opposed to the reality of history; I mean rather the comprehensive sense of a body of structural formations and functions to be found in a society's myths (mythology), deities (theology), ideals (philosophy) and even at times in the organization of its social history. In this respect, I would say that my homeland of research resides somewhere between the philologists and the historians, somewhere between the text and the historical facts that are being conceptualized or harmonized in the text – their ultra-history.

Kearney: But how does this ultra-historical ideology of a culture correspond to its empirical or sociological institutions? Lévi-Strauss's 'social anthropology' indicates a direct connection between sociological and mythological structures. In your own work what is the rapport, if any, between ideology and sociology?

Dumézil: This is an extremely complex question. First, one must remember that every form of ideology – be it mythological, theological or philosophical – is somehow a response to social reality. However, while in some Indo-European societies, for instance the Indian, one can detect a clear correlation between the tripartite ideology and the real tripartite division of that society into priests, warriors and labourers, this is not always the case in other societies. Indeed, I would be tempted to say that where such a correspondence does exist it is but one amongst other applications of the ideology. In other words, social organization conditions the ideology less than it is conditioned by it. I say this because I was struck by the fact that in many cultures the ideology of the three functions can survive at the level of religion, or myth, or literature, without any corresponding social organization. This is true of the Scythien, the Ossetes or the Celts. For example the tripartite ideology is manifest in the old Welsh legend of the Mabinogi of Math (eleventh century) even though the tripartite division no longer operated in the social practices of the Welsh people. Similarly, as Jean-Pierre Vernant and others have demonstrated, the tripartite ideology perdured in Greece even though its social instantiation had virtually disappeared. The same is true of Rome, where ideology represented by the three gods – Jupiter (the sacred), Mars (the military) and the more complex Quirinus (partially the productive) bears no relation to the binary social division into Patricians and Plebians. One could argue, accordingly, that the tripartite ideology teaches us that there can be a realm of values and explanations beyond the purely economic order.

Kearney: So you would hold that the tripartite ideology can go beyond socio-economic facts and become autonomous?

Dumézil: I believe that the ideology of truth can ultimately free itself from the social or economic determinations of a society. This does not mean that at one time the ideological and sociological structures were synonymous. Nor, on the other hand, does it mean that ideology ceases to function as a structural interpretation of man's biological, social or existential needs. I am convinced that the tripartite ideology corresponds to three fundamental biological needs which every human group must satisfy in order to survive: every man has a brain, hands and a mouth which correspond to his natural needs for control (sovereignty), protection (force) and nourishment (fecundity and plenty). Even animals and insects must operate according to the three basic functions as soon as they begin to organize in groups; one can see this by examining a bee hive or ant colony. So it is undeniable that the tripartite ideology has some basis or beginning in nature. The natural needs of nourishment, power and survival are at the root of the ideology of the three functions and constitute its 'primary matter'. But there is a radical difference between the material needs of nature or human society, from which the three functions may originate, and the formulated ideology of these functions, which can go beyond material needs and enjoy considerable autonomy. The three functions always operate as natural needs, but it is only in the old Indo-European cultures that they assume an *explicit conceptual form* by means of which a society can provide itself with an ideological *raison d'être*.

Kearney: But how would you account for this distinction between the three functions as biological needs and ideological forms? What enables the human spirit to make this leap from nature to culture; from the real to the ideal? I noted, for example, that in *Mythe et epopée* you speak of myths as 'dreams of mankind', as 'creations that testify above all to the fertility of the human mind'. You seem to suggest that the ideology of myth cannot be exhaustively explained in terms of its biological, socio-economic or unconscious origins (what Paul Ricoeur calls the 'archaeological' or reductive hermeneutic). Do you believe then that ideology can be seen as a creative projection or invention whereby man expresses his desire to transcend the given facts of existence towards a more coherent or perfect model of explanation which often has no place (*u-topos*) in the world of historical contingency? This latter interpretation is what Ricoeur calls the 'teleological' hermeneutic of hope, meaning that myths, dreams or symbols can be read as signs of man's striving towards a future goal (*telos*) rather than as mere symptoms of a determining past or origin (*arche*). In short, is myth the product of social and biological determination or of a creative and utopian imagination?

Dumézil: These are really questions for the philosophers. It is true that in my youth I experienced the enthralment and enthusiasm of philosophy, particularly the philosophy of Bergson. This early experience is one that I have attempted to both assimilate and suppress. And in so far as I have assimilated it, I would say that Bergson's notion of the *élan vital* always tempted me to suppose the existence of a teleological dimension, in addition to an archaeological one, in the creation of ideology. I think that both dimensions exist. But these are things which we can never scientifically prove or demonstrate; we can only 'dream' about them.

Kearney: Your conviction that ideology can sometimes transcend the conditioning empirical facts of history and society would certainly seem to corroborate the teleological interpretation. But I would like to tackle the relationship between ideology and philosophy from another angle. In the preface to *Mythe et epopée* you describe the ideology of the three functions as a 'philosophy' and affirm that 'these reflections of the old thinkers merit this name [philosophy] just as much as the speculations of the pre-Socratics'. What do you mean exactly by such a comparison?

Dumézil: I am taking philosophy here in its largest and most generous sense to mean the explanation of human experience in terms of conceptual structures. Therefore, just as the pre-Socratics explained their experience of nature and the cosmos in terms of the cycle of the four elements – air, fire, water, earth – or in terms of dialectical pairings such as love/hate or light/darkness, the ideology of the three functions proffers an equally coherent structuring of experience with its division into 1) the sacred, 2) the martial and 3) the productive. Thus in Greek mythology we find an interpretation of the world quite as ordered and complex as the pre-Socratic explanation of things. In the description of the Judgement of Paris, to take just one example, we witness the ideology of the three functions represented by Hera (sovereignty), Athena (victory) and Aphrodite (love). And this ideological division survives in Greece even though the tripartite social division into priests, warriors and producers had disappeared. Even Plato, the speculative philosopher *par excellence*, drew on this ideology of the three functions in his ideal partition of society in *The Republic*. So the line separating 'speculation' and 'ideology' is not always a clear one.

Kearney: Did the Indo-European ideology disappear in France with the demise of the Gallo-Roman Empire?

Dumézil: Probably. But there has been something like a re-insemination of the tripartite ideology in the ninth century in France when the three functions reappear in the Latin texts as *Oratores/Bellatores/Laboratores* and later again the three orders of the middle ages: namely, Clergy, Nobility and the Third Estate (*Tiers État*) of productive labourers and peasants. Indeed, as Joël Grisward showed in a recent book, in the thirteenth century one finds that the legendary cycle of Emery of Narbonne (in the south of France) presents the same form of tripartite structure as the Indian legend of Yayati and his sons. There are three possible ways in which the Indo-European ideology found its way back into France. First, it could have come through the Germanic, especially Visigoth, invasions; second, it could have come through the Anglo-Saxon channels of influence; or third, through Irish monasticism which contributed much to the intellectual renaissance in Europe (e.g. John Scotus Eriugena who spearheaded the Palatine school at Laon in the ninth century). For early Christianity, as Proinsias McCana and others have remarked, tolerated and often preserved the Celtic ideology of the three functions by means of the creative coexistence of the pagan Druid and *File* with the Christian monk.

Kearney: How does the tripartite ideology as such relate to monotheism? Some critics have argued that it is the exclusive preserve of polytheistic paganism. Would you agree?

Dumézil: It is unquestionable that the rise of Judeo-Christian monotheism in Europe did much to dispense with the necessity of the Indo-European explanation of things. Naturally, monotheism insisted on the all-powerfulness of the one God rather than apportioning the divine functions to different deities. In 1959, John Brough wrote a study entitled 'the tripartite ideology of the Indo-Europeans and the Bible: an experiment in method' in which he tried to demonstrate that the tripartite ideology operated in the Bible also. The complete failure of his demonstration at every level (e.g. the qualifications of the God of the Bible, of the twelve tribes of Israel, of Solomon, etc.) suggests that Judaic theology has no need to transpose the three natural necessities of sovereignty, force and abundance into a corresponding tripartite ideological system. Yahweh is the one and only God, and such a monotheistic explanation of the world is hardly likely to accommodate a pluralistic ideology of functions. This also applies to Islamic and Christian monotheism. Attempts to read the Christian trinity in terms of the tripartite Indo-European ideology are meaningless. (It was once suggested to me that the Holy Spirit represented the third function of phallic fecundity!) However, the impossibility of reducing monotheistic theology to the Indo-European ideology does not mean that monotheistic and Indo-European elements cannot coexist within the same culture or society.

Kearney: We have already mentioned the compatibility of Celtic paganism and Christianity in ancient Ireland. Do you believe that the Indo-European ideology can have a positive significance for contemporary society?

Dumézil: I think it can, so long as it remains at the philosophical or aesthetic level, as part of our collective or communal memory, as the stuff of our dreams. However, it cannot and should not be inserted into contemporary politics because the modern social organization of Western man is alien to a tripartite hierarchy of priests, warriors and workers. The ideology of the three functions is something of the past; but precisely as such it has *descriptive*, not at all *normative* value. To suggest that the ideology could be revived in order to serve as the blueprint for a new political order is most dangerous. We know what happened in Nazi Germany when the ideology of the warrior-hero was rehabilitated and deformed in order to mislead an entire people.

Kearney: So the Indo-European ideology is not some 'privileged dream' which, as the New Right like to believe, might denote the superiority of one culture or people over another?

Dumézil: Absolutely not. As I mentioned, the three natural necessities of human survival constitute the 'primary matter' of all ideologies – be they theological, sociological or mythological. Consequently, every culture or society – Indo-European or not – could *de jure* formulate an ideology of the three functions. So that the ideological formulation of the three functions is potentially universal qua 'primary matter'. However, *de facto* it was only the Indo-European peoples who achieved such a formulation, who transposed the tripartite natural structure of human needs into a corresponding conceptual one. But this formulation is only one of the many possible explanations of human existence: the Hebrew, the Chinese, the Babylonian and the American-Indian, to name but some, offered very different conceptual ideologies. Though all cultures share the same material and biological necessities, they 'dream' differently. And no culture or civilization has the right to declare its dream a privileged one.

CHAPTER TWENTY-SIX

Philosophy at the Limits of Reason Alone (2006)

While visiting the Institute of Philosophy at Leuven University, Belgium, Professor Kearney kindly took the time to give an interview for the Newsletter. *The interview took the form of a conversation between Professor Kearney and several of our doctoral students: Niall Keane, Francisco Lombo de Leon, Michael Funk Deckard and Sonja Zuba. One of our alumni, Dr James McGuirk, also participated.*

James McGuirk: *First of all, Professor Kearney, I'd like to start by welcoming you to Leuven University. By way of getting the ball rolling, perhaps you could tell us a little bit about your own current philosophical project.*

Well, my current project is an attempt to articulate a 'philosophy at the limit', which is the overall title of my recent trilogy. The three books are attempts to say the unsayable, think the unthinkable, and imagine the unimaginable. In the case of *The God Who May Be* (2001), it is the question of God; in the case of *On Stories* (2002), it is the question of the unnarrated trauma, which is something so painful and intolerable that it is blocked from memory, and hence we deploy stories in order to try to unlock and unblock those repressed memories and to find some healing. Basically I deal with how repressed narratives need to be retrieved and retold, be it in relation to stories of empire, i.e. conquerer stories, and then on to various other case histories of the survivors of trauma. I also talk about literature as a form of narrativity that deals with some secret, gap or enigma in an author's life which needs to be worked out through fiction. In *The God Who May Be* I am trying to zoom in on one limit experience of the unsayable, namely, what is called the divine. In *Strangers, Gods and Monsters* (2002), there is a more pluralist approach to the unsayable in terms of the question of the limit experience of good and evil. I deal specifically with the question of good and evil in relation to strangers and monsters. This book attempts to amplify the phenomenology of the sacred so as to cover non-monotheistic religions, something I believe is vitally important for the hermeneutics of dialogue and which I call 'diacritical hermeneutics'. With this diacritical hermeneutics I am trying to chart a middle course between apophatic and cataphatic extremes: between, on the one hand, the cult of silence – sublime speechlessness, for example – which can lead to paralysis, and, on the other, the standard metaphysical definitions of God which often say *too much*. This latter temptation is what William Desmond calls 'excessive speech', in which everything must be immediately converted into talk, categories, substances and so on. So, if the latter kataphatic tradition leads to excessive speech – Marion's 'conceptual idolatry' – the other apophatic tendency leads to aphasia and, all too often, to inaction. Basically I'm trying to find a middle way through the two poles.

Francisco Lombo de Leon: *Could you say a little bit more about your own formation and how you may have moved beyond your earlier position?*

Curiously enough, when I was working with Ricoeur in Paris in the seventies, he thought that I was much too influenced by Lévinas, Derrida, and of course, Heidegger. So we used to have great dialogues on these grounds. Ricoeur was very much an Aristotelian: he was always defending metaphysics against the charges of Heidegger, Lévinas and Derrida, who said that metaphysics was totalizing and onto-theological. Hence, my thesis under Ricoeur, entitled *Poétique du Possible*, was actually a work which Ricoeur felt was not very loyal to his own hermeneutic path. He respected it very much and we had good conversations about it, but it was a conversation between two voices coming from very different perspectives in that I worked as much with Lévinas and Derrida as I did with Ricoeur.

Nowadays, in fact, I would say that I am closer to Ricoeur than to any other philosopher that I know. But I'm not a 'disciple' of Ricoeur's, so to speak. One of the reasons for this is that his whole hermeneutic philosophy is about a fecund *conflict* of interpretations and he has a huge suspicion of a hermeneutics of closure. Hermeneutics, as Ricoeur kept reminding us, is itself the impossibility of closure, an infinite openness to new textual readings. Thus, because of Ricoeur's own hermeneutics it was impossible for him ever to have a school as such, and because of this there are no 'Ricoeurians' around. He taught his students to think for themselves. In addition, I was always more interdisciplinary than Ricoeur; I would introduce literature, politics, and theology into philosophy more readily than he would. For him Derrida was always too literary and Lévinas was always too religious. Unlike Ricoeur, I never minded crossing borders and transgressing boundaries.

However, my inspiration for diacritical hermeneutics, as I try to develop it in *Strangers, Gods and Monsters* and *The God Who May Be,* did come largely from Ricoeur, and also from Gadamer's hermeneutic tradition, and by implication from the Socratic practice of *dialegein*. They were my mentors in that they emphasized the Platonic dialogue as a model for philosophy, as that space where different points of view work their way towards a new point of view. Therefore, there is always a surplus of meaning (*un surcroît du sens*) which points towards something still to come in the text. But I would also say that my experience of growing up in Ireland between two cultures, two religions and two languages, two poles of North and South, was also very formative for me. I realized that if I am without dialogue, then I am somehow forced to align myself with one side against another. So for reasons of personal history too, I was trying to open up a third way.

Michael Funk Deckard: *You have tried in your work to bring together Irish philosophy, literature and ethics. One particular passage that you have used is taken from the work of James Joyce, which you quoted to us in your lecture the other night. It is taken from the very long hallucinogenic Circe chapter in* Ulysses *when Stephen's cap speaks to him. The cap says, 'Woman's Reason. Jewgreek is Greekjew. Extremes meet. Death is the highest form of life. Bah!' In taking your impetus from Lévinas and Derrida, is Joyce's passage here just a humorous tool as found in its original context or can it be used as the basis for a deconstructive ethics? If you support the latter, what is the content of such an ethics?*

Neither Derrida, who cites that line in his essay on Lévinas (*Violence and Metaphysics*), nor Lévinas himself, would adhere to the sentiment expressed in that phrase. I don't think Lévinas even knew about Joyce's phrase until he read it in Derrida, but the substance of it, the content of it, is very operative in Derrida and also in my own work, at a much more modest level of course. Lévinas is one of the main contemporary thinkers to put forward the idea that there is an Abrahamic path of exodus, a path traversing the desert and moving towards the infinite, in contrast to the Odyssean path of circumnavigation which leaves from itself and returns to itself, which he identifies as Greek ontology and totality. Thus, Lévinas sets up a pretty neat opposition, and yet as Derrida points out, the very process of writing *Totality and Infinity*, as a working through of Western metaphysics, means that he cannot avoid ontology and phenomenology, which is the Greek language of presence and totality.

I wanted to restore the robustness of the two voices of Jew and Greek instead of separating them out as Lévinas tried to do. I was trying to find a way between Derrida's complete mixing and collapsing of the two by using the language of mutual contamination, and Lévinas's attempt to keep the two separate. The result of this is a diacritical hermeneutics where there is a mutual openness of Jew to Greek and Greek to Jew. I like that about Joyce. Yet I think it's not just to be found in Stephen's cap, but also in Molly, who takes up where Stephen's cap leaves off, in that she represents woman's reason where Greekjew and Jewgreek come together, the Jew being Bloom and the Greek being Stephen. Hence, there is a coming together of both, but not in such a way that there is a co-mingling or collapsing of the two into each other. It is more a question (as the Calcedonian formula goes) of a crossing-over or community without total separation or without total confusion. One consequence of this is, I think, an openness to inter-religious dialogue with non-Western discourses and wisdom traditions. In recent years, I have found it personally and academically fruitful to try to expose myself to the narratives of the Upanishads and the Bhagavad Gita, and to Buddhism and Taoism. I know all too little about these wisdom traditions, but I am interested in exploring possibilities of 'other voices', apart from the Jew and the Greek, of opening further the space between.

Sonja Zuba: *You used the term 'between' just now. Do you have any specific philosophers in mind when you use it? Do you perhaps have William Desmond in mind? If so, where do you differ from William Desmond?*

Well, I am very indebted to my friend and compatriot, William Desmond, for his intriguing notions of *metaxu* and metaxology. But I have also borrowed this idea of a middle or medial way from Plato, Aristotle and Ricoeur, and from the Buddha, and from Martin Buber. It has a long and noble lineage. The 'diacritical method' I outline in *Strangers, Gods and Monsters* also plays on the diagnostic connotations of the term, *diacrinein*, which means to distinguish, discriminate, discern the *juste milieu* between extremes. Hence the more technical usage today in grammar of diacritical signs or marks that distinguish different sounds or values of the same letter – for example, *diaeresis*, cedilla or accents like circumflex or acute, etc. (ê é è ù à). These tiny and almost imperceptible inflections of sound or sight, of hearing or reading, can make a significant difference in sense. French captures this well when it uses the same verb, *entendre,* for both acts of reception (to hear and to understand). But the term *diacrinein* also has a rarer and older sense of medical diagnosis. And this diagnostic and therapeutic sense is one which interests me greatly, as I agree with Wittgenstein that critical philosophy – as a practice of attentive, vigilant, careful discernment – can also be a form of healing.

While William Desmond and I agree fundamentally on the mextalogical role of the 'between', there is one point, perhaps, at which I felt William was more Hegelian than I would have been; though in his recent publications he has most definitely moved beyond the Hegelian model, just as Ricoeur at one point moved beyond Hegel as well.[1] And it is here that we realize that 'the middle' is not just a synthesis of opposites which leads to closure or totalization. Here the middle actually opens out onto a new path by reintroducing the *metaxu* of Socrates and Plato. Now if we understand this to be a diacritical method, a way of accenting differences, of placing a stress or inflection upon this or that, then we can see that discernment is what is called for. Hegel to me is not a genuine call for discernment. The mediating middle of Hegel leads to a final synthesis that ends in absolute consciousness, whereas diacritical hermeneutics would want to keep that constantly open to the further discernment of Spirit such that you never actually reach the end, so that you are always coming back and asking new questions and every concept becomes a sign which calls for a new concept. There is a hermeneutical way of rereading Plato's *metaxu*, as Desmond suggests, which rescues him from the charge of onto-theology and totalizing presence. I owe a lot to William on this score. But whereas I tend to draw more from contemporary continental philosophy – phenomenology and hermeneutics in particular – William seems to me to be more indebted to great classic thinkers like Plato, Aristotle, and Hegel. In other words, he would be more a defender of 'metaphysics', while I have always been more an iconoclast of metaphysics. However, I feel William's work of late is moving more and more beyond metaphysics, whilst I, on the other hand, am moving more and more back to metaphysics. So perhaps we'll meet somewhere in the middle!

Niall Keane: *You have been clearly inspired by Heidegger's well-known critique of onto-theology in the Western philosophical tradition, and you seem to follow his lead, to some extent at least, by addressing the issue of a possible God in a post-metaphysical sense. However, doesn't one run the risk, as Heidegger most certainly did, of ignoring the complexity and profundity already to be found in traditional or standard metaphysics by calling for a diacritical or hermeneutical metaphysics?*

Onto-theology is a caricature or summary selection of these reified conceptual moments which have forgotten the fundamental dimension of things – Being, God, Eschaton, etc. What one means by a hermeneutic retrieval that comes after metaphysics – that is, post-Platonism, post-Aristotelianism, post-Cartesianism, post-Hegelianism – does not amount to saying one is post-Plato, post-Aristotle, post-Descartes, or post-Hegel. It is a question of trying to retrieve what has very often been occluded in the texts themselves. When Heidegger actually reads Aristotle – the source of his hermeneutics of facticity being the *Rhetoric*, the *Ethics*, and the *Poetics* of Aristotle – he is more interested in opening up new dimensions of Aristotle, the originary questions, which were very often covered over for those of us schooled in Scholasticism. That is how I would qualify what I mean by the 'God after metaphysics', or what I prefer to call an eschatological God. This God is already inscribed in the great metaphysical thinkers and texts, but there has been a tendency to privilege certain concepts at the expense of others, for instance actuality over possibility, speech over writing, perhaps Being over becoming or non-Being. We could go through a series of examples. The one that I was concerned with retrieving in *The God Who May Be*, and perhaps to some extent reversing, was the priority of the actual over the possible. The point was not to deny that there are aspects of actuality within the divine but to ask whether there are aspects of *dunamis* also within the divine. It is simply a question of de-reifying doctrines and re-imagining concepts, not of inventing something absolutely *new*, for everything has always already been said. There is ultimately a necessary iconoclastic, self-transfiguring motivation within philosophical and religious thought, and this is clearly evident in that all the great thinkers are perpetually starting all over again. That is all I am attempting to explore.

Niall Keane: *Whilst I agree with the perpetual necessity to start all over again, what is also essential, however, is the carefulness and exactitude with which we start all over again. For example, Heidegger is definitely a more arresting thinker than Gadamer, yet Gadamer is clearly more careful with the philosophical tradition. How important, in your opinion, is it to be philosophically careful?*

Well, everyone who starts all over again, at the beginning at least, is not very careful because they usually start by saying 'let's imagine that nothing has been thought'! Here, there is a necessary methodological bracketing out of the conversation that has been going on for thousands of years, and this gives people a certain sense of simplicity. Yet Gadamer, like Ricoeur, begins quite humbly in the *middle* of a conversation by quoting other people. We also need this approach, so as to be interpreters who mediate the tradition, working like Himalayan Sherpas who know the way up and down the mountain and who are constantly serving others. But this is not to take from those more 'original' thinkers who set out to discover new continents: the pioneers. The guys who actually made it to the top of Everest. I think Husserl and Heidegger did this when they called for phenomenology to be a rigorous science. That kind of instinct for originality, the striking out for something new, is always required if philosophy is to continue on its course. Whereas the Gadamers and the Ricoeurs of this world are hermeneutic mediators who are always modestly helping us to unravel things. They really do not have the same impact as those who come out with revolutionary-sounding statements.

James McGuirk: *Regarding this question of the complexity of the tradition, I wanted to ask about your employment of Heidegger's notion of onto-theology as a way of characterizing the tradition in* The God Who May Be. *You say, 'If the tradition of onto-theology granted priority to Being over the good, this counter-tradition of eschatology challenges that priority.'[2] I find it interesting that inasmuch as the notion of onto-theology is accepted uncritically, it also seems to mean whatever we want it to mean. For here, the point is distinctly Lévinasian/Derridean and so Heidegger is a part of, and as guilty as, the dominant tradition of Western thought. Do we not risk, then, making the term onto-theology dangerously imprecise or inaccurate?*

Well yes, I could see that as a danger. But it can be avoided if we recognize that this is a methodological move. If we acknowledge that onto-theology is a caricature, a schema, or a paradigm which is representative of a decline of thought from its original moments. It's a way of telling a good story! Heidegger located what he calls the 'originary moment' of thinking in the pre-Socratics, after which followed two thousand years of forgetfulness that was ultimately broken by the phenomenological revolution. Now that is a very exciting story, as if some philosophical Rip Van Winkle had gone to sleep for two thousand years and now he's back! It is more interesting and arresting than saying that the question had never been forgotten. However, when Heidegger starts doing the phenomenological *Destruktion*, the retrieval of metaphysics, that is exactly what he finds: the question had never been forgotten, and every time someone experiences *Angst* they are simultaneously experiencing the question of Being and non-Being. I see the notion of onto-theology mainly as a methodological ploy which Heidegger himself eventually moves beyond. This is how I like to read both Heidegger and Derrida.

Niall Keane: *The eschatological dimension of your project is quite evident in your work and along with that you appropriate many Heideggerian categories along the way, for example,* Jemeinigkeit *and* Entwurf *to name but two; however, I'm interested to know, following a recent comment by Jean Greisch on your work, where exactly Heidegger's notion of* Geworfenheit *or 'thrownness' fits into your project? Do you run the risk, as Greisch has indicated, of 'forgetting or shading out what Heidegger calls* Geworfenheit'?[3]

I think that's a very relevant point and actually Ricoeur makes a very similar observation in his review of my work in *Philosophy Today*, where he says that the narratives I deploy and promote are basically very enabling, eschatological narratives. Yet he asks, 'What about tragedy?', which is another name for the *shade*, that which resists translation or transfiguration into the eschatological. Here he is pointing to the intractable nature of *Geworfenheit*, that which cannot be transformed by narrative imagination or by any form of working through. It is that which is irredeemable, that which we must be silent about in living with the pain. So yes, I take your point and I take the point from my interlocuters, Ricoeur and Greisch, on that one too.

Yet my response would be something like this: one of the things that worried me about traditional metaphysics, at least as I imbided it in a very Scholastic manner at University College Dublin in the seventies, is that philosophy was realism and realism was truth. What disturbed me about that was that everything was already acquired; truth was always a systematic given and it was there to be learned from Creation onwards; it was spoken by Jesus Christ and then published by St Thomas Aquinas: the system as perfect synthesis. Hence, my philosophy grew out of a hunger for the 'possible' and it was definitely a reaction to my own philosophical formation. Yet that wasn't my only reaction. I was also reacting to what I considered to be the deep pessimism, and even at times 'nihilism' of the postmodern turn. What interests me most in the whole postmodern debate about metaphysics is to see if we can still return *from text to action*. I am interested in the possibility of an eschatology of action, and that is what fascinates me about the 'possible'. My philosophical position is a reaction to both Scholasticism and postmodernism. But like every reaction it tends to go to the other extreme, in that one forgets the shadow or shade and the limits that are always already set. That is why my trilogy is called 'Philosophy at the Limit', where even though I'm attempting to say the unsayable, I'm still trying to deal with those 'limit experiences', as Jaspers called them. By contrast, in early works like *Poétique du Possible* or *Poetics of Imagining*, I wasn't really dealing with limit experiences. It seemed the world was wide open. Imagination was there to blaze new paths of discovery. From that point of view, I think Ricoeur and Greisch were right to suggest I redress the balance. The poetics of the possible always needs to acknowledge the ethics of the real.

Sonja Zuba: *In your work you speak about God as 'possible'. Yet God is usually defined as eternal, so can we, in fact, talk adequately about God in terms of time and in terms of possibility?*

Absolutely not. I believe we are compelled to speak and simultaneously to acknowledge the limits of our speaking. Now this means that when we talk about the futurity or the possibility of God – as I do in *The God Who May Be* and *Strangers, Gods and Monsters* – we are always talking in terms of human phenomenological categories, that is, hermeneutic constructs. We are not talking about the ontological substance of God, the 'in itself' of God. And, curiously enough, in the wisdom traditions the very unnameability of God, the fact that the eternal cannot be reduced to time, itself allows for, and in fact calls for, a multiplicity of names, figures, tropes, and metaphors. For if you confine the divine to a few terms and sacralize those few, and turn them into doctrines and dogmas, then you are really reducing God to our terms, which you claim are the only true terms. That for me is the true danger of idolatry. The danger does not reside in having a hundred different names for God, but in presuming to have only one! Hinduism and Buddhism have much to teach us here. The more images, figures and faces of the divine you have, the more you are respecting the inability of any one of them to adequately represent the divine. Thus I would concur with Stanislas Breton when he suggests that the truth of monotheism, in any of the wisdom traditions, is polytheism. Now, in *The God Who May Be*, I do speak of the futurity of God, but I would not want to do so at the expense of the presentness or pastness of God. These three temporal aspects have to be maintained. Eschatological futurity is only one of these, but the one in my view that has been most occluded in the official history of Western metaphysics.

James McGuirk: *When you speak of moving 'from text to action', do you intend this in a Marxist sense (i.e. the mission to change rather than interpret the world)? And secondly, given your sense of the openness of diacritical hermeneutics, do we not risk descending into a 'pure openness' that becomes unable to discern between good actions and bad?*

Well, I have never had an explicit reckoning with Marxism, but Marx would have had a greater influence on me as a student than Hegel did – not doctrinally of course, as I was never drawn by any Marxist movement, but I was very taken by philosophers who were influenced by Marx, namely, Marcuse, Bloch, Horkheimer and Adorno. Or thinkers like Ricoeur, Lévinas and Michel Henry who spoke very respectfully about Marx. Basically from the very beginning I was drawn towards various philosophies of radical action. I was never drawn at all by speculative and abstract philosophy. I found Aristotle's *Metaphysics* unreadable; I found the *Summa theologiae* unreadable; I found Hegel's *Encyclopaedia* unreadable; even Kant's *Critique of Pure Reason* was unreadable to me. I did read them, but without relish. Thus, I loved Kierkegaard after reading Hegel; I loved reading Rousseau after Kant; and I loved rereading Plato's dialogues after Aristotle. Therefore, I was always drawn towards the existential tradition, which I see as going back to Socrates and resurfacing again in Augustine and Pascal and then leading to the nineteenth- and twentieth-century existentialists. My difficulty with Marx's work was that it always had the tendency to become Marx*ism*. The problem I kept encountering was Marx's closure to the question of transcendence and poetics, which for me were necessary critical chaperones for politics. Without the questions of God and imagination, political economy risked losing the run of itself and taking itself for the only game in town.

Now to come back to your second interesting question about a pure openness to the possible: firstly, the eschatological model that I propose is an emphatic acknowledgment that the divine is not reducible to the human. In other words, eschatologically and in the order of eternity, God remains unconditionally a call, a solicitation, and a summons. But in the order of history and phenomenology, where human beings reside, God – unless we endorse the God of theodicy, which I do not – has created the Seventh Day where we give flesh, or do not give flesh, to the divine call. It is actually the incarnational call, the summons of perpetual embodiment (*ensarkosis*). Here I approve the Scotist idea that creation is going on *in every moment* and working its way towards the eschaton. But the eschaton may never happen in history. There is a promise that it will, and there is an invitation and a desire, both human and divine, that it should. But we can also pull the trigger. We have the liberty to destroy the world of history as we know it, in which case there will be no Second Coming for this world since we will no longer be here. If we are *not* free to say no to God, then the incarnation is a rape, it is a violation, and so is every form of good and evil. According to such a model (theodicy) – which I utterly reject – God wills what is good or evil and ethics has really nothing to do with us. This is where I remain a steadfast existentialist! I believe that human freedom is indispensable and I resist any divinity that threatens that.

This brings me to the other part of your question: whether or not we run the risk of becoming so open that we become indiscriminate. In *Strangers, Gods and Monsters*, my main scruple, recurring throughout, is an ethical and hermeneutical scruple about discrimination. This was my main difference with Derrida at the three Villanova conferences and in various written texts – namely, that deconstruction was so open in that 'every other could be every other'. I just want to suggest that we need *some* guide-rails as we traverse the abyss. Now Derrida does say that we have to act against evil, we have to act for justice. But where do we find the criteria for good and evil, for justice and injustice? That is the problem for Derrida. Of course, Derrida's always been on the side of the good and the just, I've never known Derrida to support a malign cause. He has always defended the oppressed of the world. But for Derrida there are no hermeneutical criteria for reading the signs. I would like to keep those criteria pretty variable. I like the idea, in diacritical hermeneutics, of a plurality of narratives. Diacritical hermeneutics strives to preserve a balance between unity and difference, between dogmatism and relativism.

Niall Keane: *But isn't Gadamer's application or appropriation of Aristotelian* phronesis *essentially the deliberative and discriminating tool which you are calling for?*

Well it is, and you're right in a way. But my quarrel with Gadamer, the other face of hermeneutics, is that for him *phronesis* is fundamentally grounded in ontology; it is a practical understanding grounded in the voice of Being, an interior ontological voice that is primarily found in the Greeks. Gadamer certainly took a step beyond Heidegger in opening a debate with plurality, but I don't think he went far enough. For even when he admits to a certain alienation or slippage of the text, to the necessity of estrangement and the play of to and fro, he does so always with a view (shared by Heidegger) to finally arriving at some kind of *Aneignung* or reappropriation, some sort of 'fusion of horizons'. By contrast, diacritical hermeneutics does not aim to return from the other to the same. It works towards an overlapping of concentric circles, where the overlap will always be very small *vis-à-vis* the space of difference. Here it is a question of emphasis, if you will. Gadamer's hermeneutics – and I am deeply indebted to it – inclines more towards convergence, consensus, unity, oneness and, to some degree, sameness. That is not what I'm doing. With diacritical hermeneutics I'm trying to find a middle way between ontological fusion and ethical difference. Diacritical hermeneutics aims at this 'way between' the one and the many. A very age-old project indeed!

CONCLUSION

CONCLUSION.

CHAPTER TWENTY-SEVEN

Myth and the Critique of Ideology

One must preserve the tension between tradition and utopia. The problem
is to reanimate tradition and bring utopia closer.

Paul Ricoeur

A major question arising from our studies of the transitional tension between
tradition and modernity is that of the role of *myth*. The modernist break with
the rhetoric of revivalism usually took the form of a *demythologizing* project.
While this project provides a corrective to the conservative apotheosis of tradition, it can also be pushed to extremes. Careful discrimination is necessary.

In the field of contemporary aesthetic theory, the 'textual revolution' has
occasionally yielded excessive versions of formalism, subjectivism and even
nihilism. And in the human sciences, the impulse to deconstruct tradition at all
costs and in every context has been known to result in precipitate celebrations
of the 'disappearance of man'.[1] In the process history itself, as the life-world of
social interaction between human agents, is often eclipsed. Reduced to a 'prison
house of language' (i.e. to an endless intertextual play of signifiers), the very
concept of history is drained of human content and social commitment. It is
deprived of its memory. It falls casualty to the amnesia of the absolute text.

In the sphere of politics, the project of demythologization has also led, at
times, to a full-scale declaration of war against the past. Marx anticipated such a
move in *The Eighteenth Brumaire* when he distinguished between the revolution
that draws its inspiration from the past, 'calling up the dead upon the universal
stage of history', and the revolution that creates itself 'out of the future',
discarding the 'ancient superstitions' of tradition and letting the 'dead bury the
dead in order to discover its own meaning'.[2] Roland Barthes, in *Mythologies*,
pushes the latter model even further when he canvasses the view that the political critique of myth must be motivated by 'acts of destruction'. The genuine

demythologizer, he says, is one who knows not what he is for but what he is *against*. For him, 'tomorrow's positivity is entirely hidden by today's negativity'.[3]

The danger of demythologizing occurs when it is pressed into the service of a self-perpetuating iconoclasm which, if left unchecked, liquidates the notion of the past altogether. Modern consciousness may thus find itself liberated into a no-man's-land of interminable self-reflection without purpose or direction. It is not enough to free a society *from* the 'false consciousness' of tradition; one must also liberate it *for* something. This raises the question of *myth* as a potentially emancipatory project. By myth we mean a collective act of symbolic narration: a story which, in Liam de Paor's felicitous phrase, a society tells itself about itself in order to describe itself to itself – and to others.[4]

The attempt to erase historical remembrance altogether provokes a new kind of enslavement (i.e. to the blind immediacies of the present, or to abstract dreams of the future). It is a mistake to schismatically oppose the utopian impulses of modernity to the recollective impulses of tradition. For every culture invents its future by reinventing its past. And here we might usefully contrast Nietzsche's 'active forgetting' of history with Benjamin's more subtle notion of 'revolutionary nostalgia' – an active remembering that reinterprets the suppressed voices of tradition in critical relation to modernity.[5] This latter notion entails the development of an *anticipatory memory* capable of projecting future images of liberation drawn from the past. The rediscovery of the subterranean history of the past as a 'presage of possible truth' may thus disclose critical standards tabooed in the present. And in this event, recollecting the discarded projects of tradition triggers a liberating return of the repressed. The *recherche du temps perdu* becomes the vehicle of future emancipation.[6] Herbert Marcuse spells out some of the radical implications of this *anticipatory memory* as follows:

> The Utopia in great art is never the simple negation of the reality principle (of history) but its transcending preservation (Aufhebung) in which past and present cast their shadow on fulfillment. The authentic utopia is grounded in recollection. 'All reification is a forgetting' ... Forgetting past suffering and past joy alleviates life under a repressive reality principle. In contrast, remembrance spurs the drive for the conquest of suffering and the permanence of joy ... The horizon of history is still open. If the remembrance of things past would become a motive power in the struggle for changing the world, the struggle would be waged for a revolution hitherto suppressed in the previous historical revolutions.[7]

I

How does this relate to the dialectic of tradition and modernity that our studies have been exploring in the context of Irish culture?

In a commemorative address for Thomas Ashe (the 1916 patriot who died on hunger strike a year after the Easter Rising), Seán MacBride accused 'many of our so-called intellectuals' of devaluing the 'concepts of Irish nationality and even the principles upon which Christianity is founded'. MacBride deplored the absence of idealism and the erosion of moral standards, which were causing young people in Ireland to despair and be cynical. Our national pride, he observed, was being corroded by the emergence of an insidious double-talk and the resurgence of the slave mentality that existed prior to 1916. 'It seems to me', MacBride concluded, 'as if we are at a crossroads at which the choice has to be made between idealism and possibly sacrifice or betrayal and an abandonment of our national traditions and goals.'[8]

MacBride was quite justified in counselling intellectuals to respect the positive heritage of their tradition. He was also no doubt correct in warning against the fashionable tendency to dismiss summarily the very concepts of nationality, religion and cultural identity as so many outworn ideologies. (Indeed as the critic Frederic Jameson remarked, 'a Left which cannot grasp the immense Utopian appeal of nationalism, any more than it can that of religion … must effectively doom itself to political impotence'.)[9] MacBride was labouring under a misapprehension, however, if he rebuked intellectual attempts to question or reinterpret tradition as thinly veiled forms of perfidy. Tradition can only be handed over (*tradere*) from one historical generation to the next by means of an ongoing process of innovative translation. And if tradition inevitably entails translation, it equally entails transition. The idea that there exists some immutable 'essence' of national identity, timelessly preserved and impervious to critical interrogation, is a nonsense. Traditions are transmitted by means of multiple translations, each one of which involves both critical discrimination and creative reinvention.

Gone are the days, fortunately, when intellectuals were expected to serve the nation by parroting simplistic formulae such as 'Up the Republic' and 'Keep the Faith' – or, north of the border, 'No Surrender' and 'No Pope Here'. Gone also, one would hope, are the days when Irish intellectuals could be branded by a government minister as 'pinko liberals and Trinity queers', or have their works banned because they raised questions that were better not discussed (a sorry phenomenon that prompted one commentator to cite 'anti-intellectualism' among the seven pillars of Irish political culture).[10] Irish intellectuals have been accused of almost everything,

> from elitism to indifference and from subversion to being drunk and refusing to fight … Frequently these charges were trumped up because people in general, and their leaders in particular, did not take kindly to the idea of arguing with awkward customers about issues which, in the interests of peaceful existence, ought to be left alone. For the politicians and the

Churches, such people were particularly troublesome … and the label 'intellectual' was tied to their names to show that they were at best boring and at worst dangerous.[11]

The need to perpetually re-evaluate one's cultural heritage raises, once again, the central question of narrative. Narrative – understood as the universal desire to make sense of history by retelling the story of ourselves – relates to tradition in two ways. By creatively reinterpreting the past, narrative can serve to release new, and hitherto concealed, possibilities of understanding one's history; and by critically scrutinizing the past it can wrest tradition away from the conformism that is always threatening to overpower it.[12] To properly attend to this dual capacity of narrative is, therefore, to resist the polarized alternative between the eternal verities of tradition, on the one hand, and the exercise of critical imagination, on the other. Every narrative interpretation, whether it involves a literary or political reading of history, 'takes place within the context of some traditional mode of thought, transcending through criticism and invention the limitations of what had hitherto been reasoned in that tradition … Traditions, when vital, embody continuities of conflict.'[13] This implies that the contemporary act of rereading (i.e. re-telling) tradition can actually disclose uncompleted narratives that open up new possibilities of understanding. No text exists in isolation from its social and historical contexts. And tradition itself is not some sealed monument, as the revivalist orthodoxy would have us believe; it is a narrative construct requiring an open-ended process of reinterpretation. To examine one's culture, consequently, is also to examine one's conscience – in the sense of critically discriminating between rival interpretations. And this is a far cry from the agonizing inquest conducted by revivalists into the supposedly 'unique essence' of national identity. Seamus Deane is right, I believe, when he pleads for the abandonment of the idea of essence – 'that hungry Hegelian ghost looking for a stereotype to live in' – since our national heritage, be it literary or political, is something that has always to be rewritten. Only such a realization can enable a new writing and a new politics, 'unblemished by Irishness, but securely Irish'.[14]

II

What is the philosophical context of the demythologizing project that so powerfully informs modern thinking? Most contemporary critics of myth have focused on its *ideological* role as a mystifying consciousness. Their approach has been termed a 'hermeneutics of suspicion' in that it negatively interprets (Gr. *hermeneuein*) myth as a masked discourse that conceals a *real* meaning behind an *imaginary* one.[15]

The modern project of unmasking myth frequently takes its cue from the investigative methods developed by Marx, Nietzsche and Freud – the 'three masters of suspicion', as Ricoeur calls them. Nietzsche advanced a genealogical hermeneutic that aimed to trace myths back to an underlying will to power (or in the case of the Platonic and Christian myths of otherworldly transcendence, to a negation of this will to power). Freud developed a psychoanalytic hermeneutic that saw myths as ways of disguising unconscious desires. Thus in *Totem and Taboo*, for example, Freud identified the origin of myth as a primitive form of compensation for prohibited experience. As such, religious myths were said to represent a sort of collective 'obsessional neurosis' – a concealment of libidinal drives – through mechanisms of inhibition and sublimation. And thirdly, there was Marx, who proposed a dialectical hermeneutic of 'false consciousness' aimed at exposing the hidden connection between ideological myths (superstructures) and the underlying realities of class domination exemplified in the struggle for the ownership of the means of production (infrastructures). Thus for Marx, the myth of an ideal transcendental fulfilment – whether it is formulated by religion, art or philosophy – is in fact an ideological masking of socio-economic exploitation.

Marx shares with Nietzsche and Freud the suspicion that myth conceals itself as an imaginary projection of false values. It is 'myth' precisely in the sense of illusion: that is, a deceptive inversion of the true priority of the real over the imaginary, of the historical over the eternal. Hence the need for a negative hermeneutics of unmasking. The critique of myth is described accordingly as 'the categorical refusal of all relations where man finds himself degraded, imprisoned or abandoned'.[16] And in this respect, Marx's denunciation of the mythico-religious character of the money fetish in the first book of *Capital* constitutes one of the central planks of his critique of ideology. Moreover, it is this equation of myth with the fetishization of false consciousness that animates Roland Barthes' famous structuralist critique of bourgeois 'mythologies' (where he argues that myth is an ideological strategy for reducing the social process of history to timeless commodities of nature).[17]

What all these exponents of the hermeneutics of suspicion have in common is a determination to debunk the ideological masking of a true meaning behind a mythologized meaning (see appendix on 'Ideological functions of myth' below). While confirming the necessity for such a demythologizing strategy, we may ask if this critique is not itself subject to critique. So doing, we may recognize perhaps another more liberating dimension of myth – the genuinely *utopian* – behind its negative *ideological* dimension. Supplementing the hermeneutics of suspicion with a hermeneutics of affirmation, we discern the potentiality of myth for a positive symbolizing project.[18]

III

Myth is an ideological function. But it is also *more* than that. Once a hermeneutics of suspicion has unmasked the alienating role of myth as an agency of ideological conformism, there remains the task of a positive interpretation. Hermeneutics thus has a double duty – both to *suspect* and to *listen*. Having demythologized the ideologies of false consciousness, it labours to disclose utopian symbols of a liberating consciousness.

Symbolizations of utopia pertain to the futural horizon of myth. The hermeneutics of affirmation focuses not on the origin (*arche*) behind myths but on the end (*eschaton*) opened up in front of them. It thereby seeks to rescue mythic symbols from the gestures of reactionary domination, to show that once the mystifying function has been exposed, we may discover genuinely utopian anticipations of peace and justice. A positive hermeneutics offers an opportunity to salvage myths from the abuses of doctrinal prejudice, racist nationalism, class oppression or totalitarianism. And it does so in the name of a universal project of freedom – a project from which no creed, nation, or individual is excluded. The utopian content of myth differs, then, from the ideological in that it is inclusive rather than exclusive; it opens up human consciousness to a common goal of liberation instead of closing it off in the inherited securities of the status quo.

Where the hermeneutics of suspicion construed myth as an effacement of some original reality (e.g. will to power, unconscious desire, the material conditions of production or domination), the hermeneutics of affirmation operates on the hypothesis that myth may not only conceal some pre-existing meaning but may also reveal new horizons of meaning. Thus instead of interpreting myths solely in terms of a first-order reference to a predetermining cause hidden *behind* myth, it discloses a second order reference to 'possible worlds' *beyond* myth. It suggests, in other words, that there may be an *ulterior* meaning to myths in addition to their *anterior* meaning – a horizon that looks *forward* as well as a horizon that looks *back*. Myth is not just nostalgia for some forgotten world. It can also constitute 'a disclosure of unprecedented worlds, an opening onto other possible worlds which transcend the established limits of our actual world'.[19]

The *epistemological* distinction between two different horizons of myth also implies an *ethical* one. Myths are not neutral as Romantic ethnology would have us believe. They become authentic or inauthentic according to the 'interests' that they serve. These interests, as Habermas recognized in *Knowledge and Human Interests*, can be those of utopian emancipation or ideological domination. Thus, for example, the religious myths of a Kingdom of Peace may be interpreted either as an opiate of the oppressed (as Marx pointed out) or as an antidote to such oppression (as the theology of liberation reminds us). Similarly, it could be argued that the myths of Irish republicanism can be used to enhance a community or to incarcerate that community in tribal bigotry. And the same would apply to a critical reading of the Ulster loyalist mythology of 'civil and religious liberties'. Moreover, our own century has also tragically demonstrated how Roman and Germanic myths – while not in themselves corrupt – have been unscrupulously exploited by fascist movements.

IV

The *critical* role of hermeneutics is therefore indispensable. But this does not mean that we simply reduce mythic symbols to literal facts. It demands rather that we learn to unravel the concealed intentions of myth so as to distinguish between, on the one hand, their role of ideological 'vindication' (which justifies the status quo in a dogmatic or irrational manner) and, on the other, their role of utopian 'exploration' (which challenges the status quo by projecting alternative ways of understanding our world). *Demythologizing*, as an urgent task of modern thought, must not be confused here with *demythizing*, which would lead to a reductionist impoverishment of culture.[20]

The crisis of modernity is characterized by a separation of myth and reality: a separation that has led to the desacralization of tradition. But precisely because of this we need no longer be subject to the ideological illusion that myth *justifies* reality. We should no longer expect myth to provide a *literal* account of our historical environment. Indeed it is the very demythologization of myth in this sense that permits the rediscovery of myth as a *symbolic* project.[21] Having eliminated the inauthentic function of legitimating how things *are*, we are free to reveal the authentic function of myth as an exploration of how things *might be*. We begin to recognize that the very value of myth resides in its ability to contain *more* meaning than a scientific description that is, objectively speaking, true. This is what Ricoeur calls the *saving of myth* through demythologizing. As he points out in my *Dialogues with Contemporary Continental Thinkers*:

> We are no longer primitive beings, living at the immediate level of myth. Myth for us is always mediated and opaque ... Several of its recurrent forms have become deviant and dangerous, e.g. the myth of absolute power (fascism) and the myth of the sacrificial scapegoat (anti-Semitism and racism). We are no longer justified in speaking of 'myth in general'. We must critically assess the content of each myth and the basic intentions which animate it. Modern man can neither get rid of myth nor take it at its face value. Myth will always be with us, but we must always approach it critically ... Only then can we begin to recognise its capacity to open new worlds.[22]

What is required, then, is a hermeneutic dialectic between a critical *logos* and a symbolic *mythos*. Without the constant vigilance of reason, *mythos* remains susceptible to all kinds of perversion. For myth is not authentic or inauthentic by virtue of some eternal essence *in itself*, but by virtue of its ongoing reinterpretation by each historical generation. Or to put it another way, myth is neither good nor bad but interpretation makes it so. Every mythology implies a *conflict of interpretations*. And this conflict is, in the final analysis, an ethical one. It is when *mythos* is conjoined with *logos* in a common project of liberation for *all* mankind that we can properly speak of its utopian dimension. Whenever a myth is considered as the founding act of one particular community to the exclusion of all others, the possibility of ideological perversion immediately arises:

> The original potential of any myth always goes beyond the limits of any single community or nation. The *mythos* of a community is the bearer of something which extends beyond its own particular frontiers; it is the bearer of other *possible* worlds … Nothing travels more extensively and effectively than myth. Whence it follows that even though myths originate in a particular culture, they are also capable of emigrating and developing within new cultural frameworks … Only those myths are genuine which can be reinterpreted in terms of liberation, as both a personal and collective phenomenon. We should perhaps sharpen this critical criterion to include only those myths which have as their horizon the liberation of mankind *as a whole*. Liberation cannot be exclusive … In genuine reason [*logos*] as well as in genuine myth [*mythos*], we find a concern for the *universal* emancipation of man.[23]

We best respect the universalist potential of myth by ensuring that its utopian *forward look* is one that critically reinterprets its ideological *backward look* in such a way that our understanding of history is positively transformed.[24] The proper dialectic of *mythos* and *logos* observes both the need to 'belong' to the symbolic representations of our past and the need to critically 'distance' ourselves from them. Without the critical 'distancing' of the *logos* we would not be able to disengage the genuine utopian promise of each myth from its ideological perversions. If *mythos* is to guarantee its *utopos*, it must pass through the purgatorial detour of *logos*. But a due recognition of our sense of 'belonging' (i.e. that our understanding always presupposes a culturally situated pre-understanding) is also necessary. Without such recognition, critical reason may presume some kind of totalizing knowledge beyond the limits of human understanding. All objective knowledge about our position in a social community or cultural tradition is based on a relation of prior belonging from which we can never totally extricate ourselves. The claim to total truth is an illusion. Before we ever achieve critical distance, we belong to a history, to a nation, to a culture, to one or several traditions. In accepting this prior belonging, we accept the mediating function of mythic self-representation.[25] To renounce completely the cultural situatedness of the *mythos* is to lapse into the lie of a *logos* elevated to the rank of absolute truth. When reason pretends to dispense thus with all mythic mediations, it risks becoming a sterile and self-serving rationalism – an ideology in its own right, and one indeed that threatens to dominate in our modern age of science and technology. Left entirely to its own devices, *logos* suspects everything but itself. And this is why the rational critique of myth is 'a task which must always be begun, but which in principle can never be completed'.[26]

V

We return, finally, to the crucial question of *national myth*. How may we demythologize tradition while saving its myths? How may we concretely distinguish between their ideological and utopian functions? While it is absolutely essential to subject our mythology to a hermeneutic of suspicion – as several of the studies in this book have attempted – it would be foolish to conclude that every national myth is *reducible* to the ideological function of mystification. As Tom Nairn rightly advises, even the most elementary comparative analysis shows that 'all nationalism is both healthy and morbid. Both progress and regress are inscribed in its genetic code from the start.'[27] In the *political unconscious* of Irish nationalism there also exists a utopian project that it is unjust and unwise to ignore.[28] But this utopian dimension is only legitimate to the extent that it is capable of transcending all sectarian claims (i.e. to be the one, true and only ideology) in a gesture that embraces those whom it ostensibly excludes. At a political level, one might cite, first, the readiness of the Forum for a New Ireland (to which all parties of Irish constitutional nationalism subscribed) to go beyond many of nationalism's 'most cherished assumptions' in order to respect opposing traditions and identities.[29] By thus demythologizing the myth of a United-Ireland-in-the-morning-and-by-whatever-means, it was possible to preserve the genuine utopian aspiration of the 'common name of Irishman' – a project that pledged to cherish all the children of the nation equally. But this project found more radical and inclusive expression in the Good Friday Agreement of 1998, to which both nationalists and unionists subscribed.

At a literary level, we have the exploratory narratives of many contemporary Irish authors who demythologize the insularist clichés of Irish culture in order to remythologize its inherently universalist resonances. Once a myth forgoes its power of ideological dissimulation, once it ceases to be taken literally as a force of domination, it ceases to *mystify*. Myth then no longer serves as a monolithic doctrine to which the citizens of the nation submissively conform; it becomes a symbol bearing a plurality of meanings. It is precisely the *symbolic* nature of a myth's reminiscences and anticipations that commits it to a *multitude* of interpretations.[30] No one version of a myth is sacrosanct. The worlds it discloses are possibilities to be explored rather than pre-established possessions to be restored. The universality of myth – which enables it to migrate beyond national boundaries and translate into other cultures – resides, paradoxically, in its very multiplicity. Here we are touching on a new understanding of myth: one we might best term *postmodern* by way of distinguishing it from both the *revivalist* apotheosis of myth as unitary tradition and the *modernist* rejection of myth as mystifying dogma. A postmodern approach to myth construes it as a two-way traffic between tradition and modernity, rewriting the inherited as a project of the imagined.

Joyce was no doubt one of the first to anticipate this postmodern dialectic in his reworking of the national myth of Finn. *Finnegans Wake* invites us to have 'two thinks at a time'; and as the title itself informs us, Joyce's narrative refers both to Finnegan's death (the term wake in Ireland means a funeral ceremony) and to his rebirth (that is, Finn-again-awake). Joyce deconstructs the monolithic myth of Finn, the hero of Ireland's founding mythological saga, into an infinite number of myths. (Joyce calls the *Wake* his 'messonge-book'; and he thereby acknowledges that the 'national unconscious' that expresses itself in his dreams (*mes songes*) of the legendary hero, may be interpreted either as an ideological *mensonge* or as a utopian message). The Celtic myth of Finn and the Fianna had been invoked by the Irish Literary Revival and by many of the leaders of the new Republic to provide a renewed sense of cultural identity for the Irish people. Joyce knew the great power of such myths to animate the national unconscious. But he also recognized the possibilities of abuse. Joyce had little time, as we noted above, for the sanctimonious romanticizing that characterized aspects of the Celtic Revival. He disliked its tendency to turn a blind eye to the lived experience of the present out of deference to some fetish of the past. And he fully shared Beckett's disdain for a 'Free State' that erected a commemorative statue of a dying Celtic hero in its General Post Office (where the Easter Rising began) at the same time as it introduced censorship laws that banned many of its living writers. The recital of myths of the motherland to legitimize a new intellectual orthodoxy was to be treated with scepticism; for such a practice was unlikely to foster a pluralist culture respectful of the diversity of races, creeds and dialects that existed in the nation. It was in defiance of chauvinistic stereotypes of the motherland that Joyce reinterpreted the ancient Celtic heroine, Anna, as Anna Livia Plurabelle – the 'Everliving Bringer of Plurabilities'.[31] He thus opposed the multi-minded logic of utopian myth to the one-minded logic of ideological myth. *Finnegans Wake* contains not one dominant personage but many interweaving personae, not a single totalizing plot but a play of narrative metamorphosis. Similarly, Joyce's book explores not just one but many languages (he exults in its 'polyguttural' complexity), not just one but many cultural myths (alongside the Celtic and the Judaeo-Christian we find the Hellenistic, the Babylonian and the Chinese, etc.) In both its form and its content, *Finnegans Wake* is a 'mamafesta' of multiple meaning. It is an open text that looks beyond the either/or antagonism of tradition versus modernity, memory versus imagination, towards a postmodern collage where they may coexist.

There are many other instances of a postmodern attitude to myth to be found in recent Irish culture. To isolate just one example, one could cite how the old Irish legend of Sweeney has been reinterpreted in a wide variety of ways by writers like Flann O'Brien, Heaney, Friel and Mac Intyre as well as by the film maker Pat Murphy (in *Maeve*). Far from recycling some immutable national vision, these various rewritings of the Sweeney myth manifest a rich diversity of narratives. The retrospective allusion to indigenous mythology opens onto the prospective horizon of multiple identities. It is because our contemporary consciousness no longer *believes* in myths as ideological creeds that we can freely *reinvent* them as utopian metaphors. Without disbelief there can be no 'willing suspension of disbelief'. Without demythologization, no remythologization.

Postmodern myth invites a plurality of viewpoints. It encourages us to reread tradition, not as a sacred and inviolable scripture, but as a palimpsest of creative possibilities that can only be reanimated and realized in a radically polyphonous culture.

The narratives that I selected for analysis in this book share, with few exceptions, a common capacity to journey beyond the frontiers of Ireland while retaining the birthmarks of their origins. The works of Joyce, Beckett, Flann O'Brien, Banville, Heaney, Friel, Jordan, Murphy and le Brocquy have all responded in their particular ways to the transitional crisis of Irish culture; and they have done so while simultaneously translating this crisis into the larger idioms of 'world culture'. Is this not, indeed, one of the primary aims of all narrative – to navigate back and forth between the familiar and the foreign, the old and the new, tradition and utopia, reinterpreting one's own history in stories that address the challenge of mutation?

Appendix: The Ideological Functions of Myth

There are three main ideological functions of myth – *integration, dissimulation* and *domination*. It is only by exposing the ideological idols of myth that we can begin to let its utopian symbols speak. No contemporary consideration of myth can dispense with the critique of ideology.

Myth as Integration. Ideology expresses a social group's need for a communal set of images whereby it can represent itself. Most societies invoke a tradition of mythic idealizations that provide a stable, predictable and repeatable order of meanings. This process of ideological self-representation frequently assumes the form of a mythic reiteration of the founding-act of the community. It seeks to redeem society from the contingencies or crises of the present by justifying its actions in terms of some sanctified past, some sacred Beginning.[32] One might cite here the role played by the Aeneas myth in Roman society, the cosmogony myths in Greek society, or indeed the Celtic myths of Cuchulain and the Fianna in Irish society. And where an ancient past is lacking, a more recent past will suffice: e.g. the Declaration of Independence for the USA, the October Revolution for the USSR and so on.

Ideology thus serves to relate the social memory of a historical community to some inaugural act that founded it and that can be repeated over time in order to preserve a sense of social integration. The role of ideology, as Ricoeur has explained, is not only to extend the conviction beyond the circle of founding fathers, so as to make it the creed of the entire group, but also to perpetuate the initial energy beyond the period of effervesence.

> It is into this gap, characteristic of all situations *après coup*, that the images and interpretations intervene. A founding act can be revived and reactualised only ... through a representation of itself. The ideological phenomenon thus begins very early: for domestication by memory is accompanied not only by consensus, but also by convention and rationalisation [in the Freudian sense]. At this point, ideology ... continues to be mobilising only insofar as it is justificatory.[33]

The ideological recollection of sacred foundational acts has the purpose therefore of both integrating and justifying a social order. While this may accompany a cultural or national revival, it can also give rise to what Ricoeur calls a 'stagnation of politics' – a process where each power reiterates an anterior power: every prince wants to be Caesar, every Caesar wants to be Alexander, every Alexander wants to hellenize an Oriental despot.[34] Either way, ideology entails a process of schematization and ritualization, a process that stereotypes social action and permits a social group to bind itself together in terms of rhetorical maxims and idealized self-images.

Myth as Dissimulation. If the schematic 'rationalizations' of ideology bring about social integration, they do so, paradoxically, at a 'pre-rational' level. The ideology of foundational myths operates behind our backs, as it were, rather than appearing as a transparent theme before our eyes. We think *from* ideology, rather than *about* it. And it is precisely because the codes of ideology function in this indirect manner that the practice of distortion and dissimulation can occur. This is the reason for Marx denouncing ideology as the falsifying projection of 'an inverted image of our own position in society'.[35] Ideology is by its very nature an *uncritical instance* and thus easily susceptible to deceit, alienation – and by extension – intolerance. All too frequently, ideology functions in a reactionary or at least socially conservative fashion. 'It signifies that what is new can be accommodated only in terms of the typical, itself stemming from the sedimentation of social experience.'[36]

Consequently, the future – as opening up that which is unassimilable and unprecedented *vis-à-vis* the pre-existing codes of experience – is often translated back into the stereotypes of the past. This accounts for the fact that many social groups display traits of ideological orthodoxy that render them intolerant towards what is marginal or alien. Pluralism and permissiveness are the *bêtes noires* of social orthodoxy. They represent the intolerable. This phenomenon of ideological intolerance arises when the experience of radical novelty threatens the possibility of the social group recognizing itself in a retrospective reference to its hallowed traditions and pieties.

But ideology can also dissimulate the gap between what *is* and what *ought* to be, that is, between our presently lived reality and our idealized self-representations.[37] By masking the gulf that separates contemporary historical experience from mythic memory, ideology often justifies the status quo by presuming that nothing has really changed. This self-dissimulation expresses itself as a resistance to change, as a closure to new possibilities of self-understanding. Whence the danger of reducing the challenge of the new to the acceptable limits of an already established heritage of meaning.

Myth as Domination. This property of ideology raises, finally, the vexed question of the hierarchical organization of society – the question of authority. As Max Weber and later Jürgen Habermas observed, social systems tend to *legitimate* themselves by means of an ideology that justifies their right to secure and retain power.[38] This process of legitimation is inherently problematic, however, in so far as there exists a disparity between the nation/state's ideological *claim* to authority and the answering *belief* of the public. Ideology thus entails a surplus of claim over response. If a system's claim to authority were fully and reciprocally consented to by those whom it governs, there would be no *need* for the persuasive or coercive strategies of ideological myths. Ideology operates accordingly as a 'surplus-value' symptomatic of the assymetry between the legitimizing *ought* of our normative traditions, on the one hand, and the *is* of our lived social existence, on the other. It is when there is no transparent coincidence between those governing and those governed that ideological myths are deemed necessary to preserve the *semblance* of unity.

Notes

– Introduction –
The Transitional Paradigm

This is a revised and updated version of the original Introduction to the author's Transitions: Narratives in Modern Irish Culture *(Wolfhound Press/St Martins Press 1988).*

1. As the French philosopher Paul Ricoeur argues: 'The ultimate problem is to show in what way history and fiction contribute, in virtue of their common narrative structure, to the description and redescription of our historical condition. What is ultimately at stake ... is the mutual belonging together of narrativity and historicity.' 'The Narrative function' in *Hermeneutics and the Human Sciences* (Cambridge University Press 1981), p. 274. For a more detailed analysis of the hermeneutic philosophy of narrative and interpretation see Paul Ricoeur, *Time and Narrative* (University of Chicago Press 1984); Hans-Georg Gadamer, *Truth and Method* (Sheed and Ward 1975); Alasdair MacIntyre, *After Virtue* (Duckworth Press 1981); and Frederic Jameson, *The Political Unconscious: Narrative as a Socially Symbolic Act* (Methuen 1981). See also Roland Barthes' comprehensive definition of narrative in his 'Introduction to the Structural Analysis of Narratives': 'The narratives of the world are numberless. Narrative is first and foremost a prodigious variety of genres, themselves distributed amongst different substances – as though any material were fit to receive man's stories. Able to be carried by articulated language, spoken or written, fixed or moving images, gestures, and the ordered mixture of all these substances; narrative is present in myth, legend, fable, tale, novella, epic, history, tragedy, drama, comedy, mime, painting, stained glass windows, cinema, comics, news items, conversation. Moreover, under this almost infinite diversity of forms, narrative is present in every age, in every place, in every society; it begins with the very history of mankind and there nowhere is nor has been a people without narrative. All classes, all human groups, have their narratives, enjoyment of which is very often shared by men with different, even opposing, cultural backgrounds.' *Image-Music-Text* (Fontana 1977), p. 79.

    On the relationship between narrative and the transitional crisis of a culture see Hannah Arendt's *Between Past and Future* (Penguin 1977) – the French title is, significantly, *La Crise de La Culture* (Gallimard 1972).

2. Desmond Fennell, 'Wanted: A project for Ireland', *The Irish Times* (July 1985). See also the same author's more comprehensive treatment of this theme in *Beyond Nationalism* (Ward River Press 1985). My own discussion of revivalism in this introduction is indebted to his work.

3. Seamus Deane, *Celtic Revivals: Essays in Anglo-Irish Literature* (Faber and Faber 1985), p. 15.

For a brilliant and illuminating critique of the Irish revivalist aesthetic see also Declan Kiberd, 'The war against the past' in R. Garrett and A. Eyler (eds), *The Uses of History* (University of Delaware Press 1987) and *Inventing Ireland* (Random House 1999).

4. See Frank Kermode's useful discussion of different kinds of modernism in *The Sense of an Ending: Studies in the Theory of Fiction* (Oxford University Press 1966), pp. 113–20, and particularly his distinction between the traditionalist modernism of Yeats and the 'schismatic' modernism of Beckett.

5. Deane, *Celtic Revivals*, p. 13.

6. Paul Ricoeur, 'Universal civilisation and national cultures' in *History and Truth* (Northwestern University Press 1965), p. 277.

7. See our Introduction to *The Irish Mind: Exploring Intellectual Traditions* (Wolfhound Press/Humanities Press 1985) and also 'The Irish mind defended' in *The Sunday Independent* (26 May 1985).

8. See Edward W. Said's proposal of a critical 'program of interference' in 'Opponents, audiences, constituencies' in *Postmodern Culture*, edited by H. Foster (Pluto Press 1985), pp. 156–7: 'Non interference means laissez-faire: "they" can run the country, we will explicate Wordsworth and Schlegal … Instead of noninterference and specialisation, there must be *interference*, crossing of borders and obstacles, a determined attempt to generalise exactly at those points where generalisation seems impossible to make. One of the first interferences to be ventured, then, is a crossing from literature, which is supposed to be subjective and powerless, into those exactly parallel realms, now covered by journalism … that employ representatives but are supposed to be objective and powerful.' Against this division of intellectual labour, Said proclaims the necessity of a 'sustained, systematic examination of the coexistence of and the inter-relationship between the literary and the social, which is where representation – from journalism, to political struggle, to economic production and power – plays an extraordinarily important role' (p. 153).

– Chapter One –
Towards a Postnationalist Archipelago

This is a revised version of an article that first appeared in The Edinburgh Review, *103 (2000).*

1. Colley, 'Britishness and otherness', *Journal of British Studies*, no. 31 (1992), p. 72.
2. *Ibid.* p. 76.
3. Jürgen Habermas, *The Postnational Constellation* (Polity 2001), p. 70.
4. 'Sovereignty' in *Encyclopaedia Britannica*, vol. 11, p. 57.
5. *Manchester Guardian* (December 1921).

– Chapter Two –
The Irish Mind Debate

This is a revised version of the Introduction to the author's edited volume, The Irish Mind: Exploring Intellectual Traditions *(Wolfhound Press/Humanities Press 1985).*

1. There have been several significant studies of Irish cultural history, in particular *The Celtic Consciousness*, edited by R. O'Driscoll (Dolmen Press 1982) and M.P. Hederman and R. Kearney (eds), *The Crane Bag Book of Irish Studies* (Blackwater Press 1982), but neither of these works focuses specifically on the speculative, conceptual or philosophical achievements of the Irish mind. They are primarily, though not exclusively, concerned with the

Irish imagination rather than Irish thought *per se*. The present publication hopes to supplement and complement these works.

2. This stereotype of the imaginative, thoughtless Celt has been frequently challenged by such critics as Desmond Fennell and Seamus Deane.

3. One of the earliest records of a colonial campaign to promote a strategic stereotype of the 'mindless' Irish was that of Giraldus Cambrensis, *History and Topography of Ireland*. This work was written *c.* 1187, two years after the author had visited Ireland in the entourage of Prince John. Although he praises Ireland's temperate climate and admires its inhabitants' ability to play musical instruments and recount fanciful tales of miracle and magic, his overall judgement is a damning one: 'They are a wild and inhospitable people. They live on beasts only, and live like beasts. They have not progressed at all from the primitive habits of pastoral living … For given only to leisure and devoted only to laziness, they think that the greatest pleasure is not to work and the greatest wealth is to enjoy liberty.' (Giraldus Cambrensis, *History and Topography of Ireland*, trans. John O'Meara [Dolmen Press 1982].) In *Celtic Leinster: Towards an Historical Geography of Early Irish Civilisation AD 500–1600* (Irish Academic Press 1983), Dr Alfred Smyth has successfully challenged this view that early Irish society was exclusively pastoral and demonstrates that agriculture played an essential part in the early economy. But one should not be surprised by the historical inaccuracy of the details of Giraldus Cambrensis' *Topography*, for one of its primary ideological purposes was to vindicate a programme of political invasion. As the Irish historian Dr Art Cosgrove has observed: 'The picture drawn by Gerald was unflattering; the Irish were economically backward, politically fragmented, wild, untrustwothy and semi-pagan, and guilty of sexual immorality. Doubtless the picture was much influenced by the need to justify conquest and dispossession.' (Art Cosgrove, 'Seeing Ireland first', *Books Ireland*, no. 71 [1983].)

4. Cf. G.J. Watson, *Irish Identity and the Irish Literary Revival* (Croom Helm 1979), pp. 16–17. I am grateful to Timothy Kearney for bringing these passages to my attention.

5. Seamus Deane in D. Dunn (ed.), *Two Decades of Irish Writing* (Carcanet 1975), p. 8.

6. Seamus Heaney, *Preoccupations* (Faber and Faber 1980), p. 104.

7. Garrett Barden, 'Image', *The Crane Bag*, vol. 1, nos 1 and 2 (1978), pp. 140–1.

8. W.B. Yeats, *Uncollected Prose* (Columbia University Press 1970), p. 172.

9. Frank O'Connor, *The Backward Look* (Macmillan 1967), p. 5.

10. Sean O'Faolain, 'Living and dying in Ireland', *London Review of Books*, vol. 2, no. 14 (1981). I am grateful to Nuala O'Farrell for bringing this article to my attention.

11. Seán Ó Tuama, 'The Gaelic League idea', A *Thomas Davis Lecture* broadcast by RTÉ in 1969 and published in 1972. Apart altogether from the important contributions to these fields of conceptual thought documented in this book, one could also mention here the original and influential publications in these areas by such modern Irish philosophers and thinkers as Conor Cruise O'Brien (*Writers and Politics*), Arland Ussher (*Journey through Dread*), Enda McDonagh (*Towards a Christian Theology of Morality: Gift and Call*), Patrick Masterson (*Atheism and Alienation*), John Bernal (*The Social Function of Science*), Eiléan Ní Chuilleanáin (*Irish Women: Images and Achievements*), James Whyte (*Church and State in Modern Ireland*), Denis Donoghue (*Ferocious Alphabets*), Anthony Cronin (*Heritage Now*), Seamus Deane (*Essays in Anglo-Irish Literature*), John Maguire (*Marx's Theory of Politics*), Bernard Cullen (*Hegel's Social and Political Thought*), Oliver MacDonagh (*States of Mind*) and many others.

12. See also the debates on the role of the intellectual in Irish culture – Declan Kiberd, 'Aosdána: A comment', *The Crane Bag*, vol. 5, no. 1 (1981), pp. 44–6; and Desmond Fennell, 'Making Aosdána what it's meant to be', *Sunday Press* (18 April 1982), 'Everyone is agreed that the Aosdána scheme [set up by the Irish government and Irish Arts Council in 1981 to assist and promote Irish creative writers] is excellent in principle, but it has one serious defect which could make it, in practice, a botched job, surrounded continually by embarrassing controversy … The trouble lies in that absurd definition of literature – limiting it to fiction, plays and poetry – and partly in the exclusion of all works of creative thought,

no matter how brilliant, original or inspiring ... This discrimination will maintain and intensify the poverty of creative thought in modern Irish culture ... It will make us continue to live up to the colonial stereotype of the *imaginative, thoughtless Celts.*'

13. This logic expressed itself according to the following three principles: 1) A is A (the principle of Identity); 2) A is either A or non-A (the principle of the Excluded Middle); 3) If A is A it cannot be non-A (the principle of Contradiction).

14. Thomas Kinsella, 'The divided mind' in *Irish Poetry in English* (Mercier Press 1972), particularly the first chapter; and Declan Kiberd, 'Writers in quarantine? The case for Irish Studies', *The Crane Bag*, vol. 3, no. 1 (1977), pp. 11 ff.

15. Vivian Mercier, *The Irish Comic Tradition* (Faber and Faber 1962), cf. Andrew Carpenter, 'Double vision in Anglo-Irish literature' in *Place, Personality and the Irish Writer* (Colin Smythe 1979), pp. 173–91.

16. Cf. Richard Ellmann, 'An Irish European art', *James Joyce Centenary Issue of Ireland of the Welcomes*, vol. 31, no. 3 (1982), pp. 5–6.

17. John Montague, 'Jawseyes', *The Crane Bag*, vol. 2, nos 1 and 2 (1978), pp. 9–10.

18. Seamus Heaney in an interview with Seamus Deane, 'Unhappy and at home', *The Crane Bag*, vol. 1, no. 1 (1977), pp. 61 ff. and in M.P. Hederman and R. Kearney (eds), *Crane Bag Book*. Brian Friel affirms a similar position of double allegiance with regard to Irish theatre. Referring to his own work as an Irish dramatist he speaks of being at once 'in exile' and 'at home' and relates this feeling of dislocation to the problem of writing of the Irish experience in the English language: 'It's our proximity to England, it's how we have been pigmented in our theatre with the English experience, the use of the English language, the understanding of words, the whole cultural burden that every word in the English language carries is slightly *different* to our burden.' (Interview with Fintan O'Toole, *In Dublin*, no. 165 [1982], pp. 20 ff.)

19. Derek Mahon, 'Lettre ouverte à Serge Fauchereau', *Digraphe*, no. 27 (June 1983), p. 20.

20. Louis le Brocquy, 'A painter's notes on awareness', *The Crane Bag*, vol. 1, no. 2 (1977), pp. 68–9.

21. See Dorothy Walker, 'Traditional structures in recent Irish art', *The Crane Bag*, vol. 6, no. 1 (1982), pp. 41 ff.

22. K. Scherman, *The Flowering of Ireland: Saints, Scholars and Kings* (Gollancz 1981), also Heinz Löwe, *Die Iren und Europa im Früheren Mittelalter* (Klett-Cotta 1982).

23. The early Irish missionaries called this voluntary journey into exile a *peregrinatio pro Christi*. The celebrated *Navigatio Sancti Brendani*, St Brendan's tale of maritime adventure in search of the Isles of the Blest, gave rise to the Gaelic literary genre called *Immram*. Another thinker who might be mentioned here is Pelagius, the fifth-century secular monk and heretical theologian who disputed the orthodox Roman doctrine of original sin, affirming that man, like Adam, is created innocent by God and becomes good or evil by his own free will. Pelagius' theory of the essential goodness of human nature, summed up in his teaching: 'Man can live without sin' (*Hominem posse esse sine peccato*) was vigorously attacked by St Augustine (*De Gestis Pelagii*) and by St Jerome (*Dialogi adversus Pelagianos*). His writings, particularly *De Libero Arbitrio*, were condemned as heresy by Pope Innocent I in 417 and again by the Second Council of Orange in 529. 'Pelagius' means 'son of the open sea', a name derived from the original Celtic 'Morgan'. There is some debate about his origins, some scholars arguing that he was born in Britain or Brittany, others that he was Irish (H. Zimmer, *Pelagius in Ireland*, and St Jerome, who referred to him as an 'Irish heretic bloated with porridge'). In general, however, Pelagius was never considered to be a representative Irish thinker in the same manner as Eriugena or Berkeley. But it is fair to say that he did share with these Irish philosophers a distinctive proclivity towards unorthodox speculation, and certainly matched Eriugena's record as a travelling scholar (arriving in Rome in 400 and North Africa in 412: he died in Jerusalem). Cf. F.L. Cross (ed.), *The Oxford Dictionary of the Christian Church* (Oxford University Press 1958), p. 1040, and *The Catholic Dictionary* (Addis and Arnold 1959), p. 631.

24. Seamus Deane, 'The literary myths of the Revival: A case for their abandonment' in J.

Ronsley (ed.), *Myth and Reality in Irish Literature* (Wilfred Laurier University Press 1977), pp. 317–29.

25. W.B. Yeats, *Essays and Introductions* (Macmillan 1961), p. 402, quoted in Deane, 'Literary myths of the Revival'.

26. Richard Kearney's interview with Paul Ricoeur, 'Myth as the bearer of possible worlds', *The Crane Bag*, vol. 2, nos 1 and 2 (1978), in particular the following passage, p. 114: Paul Ricoeur, 'You have hit here on a very important and difficult problem: the possibilities of a perversion of myth. This means that we can no longer approach myth at the level of naivety. We must always view it from a critical perspective. It is only by means of a selective reappropriation that we can become aware of myth. We are no longer primitive, living at the immediate level of myth. Myth for us is always mediated and opaque. This is not so only because it expresses itself through a particular apportioning of power functions but also because several of its recurrent forms have become deviant and dangerous, e.g. the myth of absolute power (fascism) and the myth of the sacrificial scapegoat (anti-Semitism and racism). We are no longer justified in speaking of "myth in general". We must critically assess the content of each myth and the basic intentions which animate it. Modern man can neither get rid of myth nor take it at its face value. Myth will always be with us, but we must always approach it critically. And I think it is here that we could speak of the essential connection between "critical instance" and the "mythical foundations". Only those myths are genuine which can be reinterpreted in terms of liberation. And I mean liberation in any sense of the word, personal or collective. Or we should perhaps extend this critical criterion to include only those myths which have as horizon the liberation of mankind as a whole. Liberation cannot be exclusive.' For more detailed analysis of this question see R. Kearney, 'Myth and terror', *The Crane Bag*, vol. 2, nos 1 and 2 (1978), pp. 125–40, and *Poétique du Possible* (Beauchesne 1984), and also 'Myth and motherland', *Field Day*, 5 (1984).

27. Terry Eagleton, *Walter Benjamin or Towards a Revolutionary Criticism* (Verso Editions and New Left Books 1981), p. 59. I am much indebted to Eagleton's analysis.

28. Historiography is hermeneutic in at least three ways: 1) the events are interpreted in terms of an *aesthetic* narrative or plot; 2) the events are interpreted in terms of an *ideological* paradigm of a socio-political or cultural nature; 3) the events are interpreted in terms of an *ethical* choice that determines how the narrative and ideological strategies of shaping the past can be seen as serving a liberating and progressive role in relation to contemporary problems. Hannah Arendt succinctly identifies the ways in which every historical hermeneutic operates when she observes that 'tradition puts the past in order, not just chronologically but first of all systematically in that it separates the positive from the negative, the orthodox from the heretical, and that which is obligatory and relevant from the mass of irrelevant or merely interesting opinions and data.' (Introduction to *Illuminations* [Jonathan Cape 1970], p. 44). For a more detailed analysis of this precise question see Paul Ricoeur, 'L'histoire et le recit' in *Temps et recit* (Éditions du Seuil 1983), pp. 137 ff.

29. Mircea Eliade, *Myths, Dreams and Mysteries* (Fontana 1968), pp. 23–39.

30. Deane in Ronsley, *Myth and Reality*, p. 326.

31. Marx himself seemed to have recognized this fundamental point in several of his writings, in particular *The Paris Manuscripts* of the 1840s and the opening chapters of volume 1 of *Capital*, where he analyses the fetishistic nature of commodities and the labour theory of surplus value, or in his analysis of the role of ideology in *The German Ideology*, cf. on this question, C. Castoriadis, *L'institution imaginaire de la Société* (Éditions du Seuil 1975). Deane's literalistic hermeneutic displays its dualist assumptions once again when he praises Kavanagh and other contemporary Irish poets for their 'modesty in relation to history', their refusal 'to play games with history' or to invent 'traditions … to liberate the mind'. Deane's conclusion reveals that the ultimate aim of his literalist-dualist interpretation of Irish intellectual history is to corroborate a hermeneutic of discontinuity: 'It is perhaps more honest and sensible to admit the discontinuity which marks the various achievements of those Irish authors who wrote in the English language during these

centuries. Continuity is the invention of the revival ... Our present dilapidated situation has borne in upon us more fiercely than ever the fact that discontinuity, the discontinuity which is ineluctably an inheritance of colonial history, is more truly the signal feature of our condition ... For it is the intractability of our situation, the impossibility of converting it ... into myth which has at last begun to free poets from the aesthetic and heroic vocabularies of the revival.' (Deane in Ronsley, *Myth and Reality*, pp. 325–7). Deane's conclusion is entirely legitimate, but his method and means of reaching it are not always so.

32. O'Connor's translations included *Cúirt an Mhéan-Oíche, Cill Cais* and *A Golden Treasury of Irish Poetry, AD 600–1200*, in collaboration with David Greene.

33. Proinsias MacCana, 'Review of *The Backward Look*', *Studia Hibernica*, no. 8 (1968), pp. 153 ff.

34. Frank O'Connor, *The Backward Look* (Macmillan 1970), p. 8.

35. Nor is it claimed that all those Irish intellectuals who managed to surmount the divide between critical and poetic reason always acknowledged this fact. Deane's analysis has already been referred to in this regard. Mention was also made, at the outset, of O'Connor's statement in *The Backward Look* that the Irish chose imagination rather than intellect – an ironic preface to a work of imaginative intellect that belies just this opposition! As MacCana remarks: 'Here is the creative mind looking for the significant substructure and inner meaning of a tale. He does take cognisance of the philosophical facts; but it is his own artistic intuition which finally counts' ('Review of *The Backward Look*', p. 153). The point is simply that such inconsistencies or exceptions do not disprove the general rule that some of Ireland's finest intellectuals display, on occasion, a singular ability to synthesize qualities of the human mind commonly opposed in Western culture.

36. Are not the characteristics of *decentredness, paradox, exodus* or *otherness* equally recognizable features of the Jewish mind, a mind that also resisted in large part the hegemony of Greek logocentrism? Contemporary Jewish thinkers such as Lévinas, Buber, Scholem, Benjamin or Derrida, would certainly suggest that this is so. Indeed, this is perhaps one of the reasons why Joyce felt such an affinity with the Jewish Bloom and chose him as the nomadic wanderer to parody his Greek prototype in *Ulysses*. Compare also in this regard our observations on Joyce as a cultural and linguistic exile above, with the following passage in which Franz Kafka describes the Jewish writer's approach to the German language as an 'overt or covert or possibly self-tormenting, usurpation of an alien property, which has not been acquired but stolen, (relatively) quickly picked up, and which remains someone else's possession, even if not a single linguistic mistake can be pointed out.'

37. Sean O'Faolain, 'Living and dying in Ireland', *London Review of Books*, vol. 2, no. 14 (1981). As an example of the 'underground stream', O'Faolain cites the 'lethal practice' of hunger-striking, which has survived in Ireland and India, 'the two peripheries of the Indo-European world'.

38. Quoted by Seamus Deane, *The Crane Bag*, vol. 3, no. 1 (1979), p. 8. Deane concludes his editorial with the following significant admission: 'The idea of an Irish tradition ... is not easily dismissed since it has provided a basis for much of the political and cultural activity of this century.'

39. Walter Benjamin, *Illuminations*, trans. H. Zohn, edited by H. Arendt (Fontana 1973), p. 57.

40. Arland Ussher, *The Journal* (Raven Arts Press 1981).

41. Walter Benjamin, *One Way Street*, trans. E. Jephcott and K. Shorter (New Left Books 1979), p. 359; cf. Eagleton, *Walter Benjamin*, pp. 43 ff.

42. T.S. Eliot, 'Tradition and the individual talent' in *Selected Essays* (1919), p. 150.

43. Benjamin, *One Way Street*, p. 362, quoted by Eagleton in *Walter Benjamin*.

44. *Ibid.* p. 314. See also Heidegger's hermeneutic blueprint in *Kant and the Problem of Metaphysics*, trans. J. Churchill (Indiana University Press 1962), p. 207: 'It is true that in order to wrest from the actual words (myths or images) that which they intend to say, every interpretation must necessarily resort to violence. This violence, however, should not be confused with an action that is wholly arbitrary. The interpretation must be animated and

guided by the power of an illuminative idea. Only through the power of this idea can interpretation risk that which is always audacious, namely, entrusting itself to the secret *élan* of a work, in order by the *élan* to get through to the unsaid and attempt to find an expression for it. The directive idea itself is confirmed by its own power of illumination.' I would like to think that the hermeneutic plan followed in this work could combine the leisurely probings and trial-and-error searchings of Benjamin with the more assertive thrust towards essential, illuminative principles advanced here by Heidegger.

– *Chapter Three* –
Myth and Martyrdom: Foundational Symbols in Irish Republicanism

This is a revised version of an essay that first appeared in The Crane Bag, *edtied by Richard Kearney and M.P. Hederman, 2, 1–2 (1978).*

1. Paul Ricoeur, 'Universal civilisation and national cultures' in *History and Truth* (Northwestern University Press 1965), pp. 271–86.
2. These passages are quoted by David George, 'These are the Provisionals', *The New Statesman*, no. 19 (1971).
3. M.P. Hederman, 'An interview with Seamus Twomey' in *The Crane Bag*, vol. 1, no. 1 (1977); reprinted in M.P. Hederman and R. Kearney (eds), *The Crane Bag Book of Irish Studies* (Blackwater Press 1982), pp. 107–13.
4. See Conor Cruise O'Brien, *States of Ireland* (Panther 1974), p. 287: 'And in Padraig Pearse's mind and those of some other notable Irish patriots, the sufferings of the Irish [Catholic] people were in a particular sense one: the sacrifice of Irish patriots was analogous to the sacrifice of Christ; and the resurgence of the national spirit that such a sacrifice could set in motion was analogous to the resurrection of Christ. The timing of the rising for Easter was no coincidence.' Unfortunately Dr Cruise O'Brien does not go on to analyse the *meaning* of the analogy.
5. Eamonn MacCann, *War and an Irish Town* (Pluto Press 1980), pp. 9, 13.
6. Mircea Eliade, *Myths, Dreams and Mysteries* (Harper & Brother Publishers 1960).
7. Oliver MacDonagh, *States of Mind: A Study of Anglo-Irish Conflict, 1780–1980* (Allen and Unwin 1983), p. 13.
8. See Redmond Fitzgerald, *Cry Blood, Cry Erin* (Vandal Publications 1966), p. 112. The title of this popular history of the Rising is itself representative of the widespread conception of this event in terms of a 'blood-letting' myth. For the other references and quotations in this section see in particular Roger McHugh's comprehensive anthology, *Dublin 1916* (Arlington Books 1966). See also G.F. Dalton's critique of the symbols of the Irish tradition of blood sacrifice in 'To the goddess Eire', *Studies* (Winter 1974), pp. 343–54.
9. See Augustine Martin's detailed discussion of this symbol in 'Reflections on the poetry of 1916: To make a right rose tree', *Studies* (Spring 1966); and Dalton, 'To the goddess Eire', pp. 349 ff.
10. Daniel Corkery, *The Hidden Ireland* (Gill 1967). See also the preface by Thomas Kinsella and Seán Ó Tuama to their translation of *An Duanaire: Poems of the Dispossessed 1600–1900* (Dolmen Press 1981).
11. Quoted by Edgar Holt in his *Protest in Arms* (Putnam 1960), p. 141.
12. Lennox Robinson, *Four Aspects of Change* quoted in McHugh, *Dublin 1916*, pp. 338–50.
13. Quoted in Martin, 'Reflections'. See also Joyce Kilmer's 'Easter Week': 'There was a rain of blood that day, / Red rain in gay blue April weather. / It blessed the earth till it gave birth / To valour thick as blooms of heather ... / Romantic Ireland is not old. / For years untold her youth will shine/ Her heart is fed on Heavenly bread, / The blood of martyrs is her wine.'
14. W.B. Yeats, *The Trembling of the Veil* (Werner Laurie 1922), pp. 53–4.

15. *Ibid.* pp. 145–50.

16. See also the final stanza of Yeats's verse-play *The Death of Cuchulain*: 'Are those things that men adore and loathe / their sole reality? / What stood in the Post Office / with Pearse and Connolly? / What comes out of the mountain / where men first shed their blood? / who thought Cuchulain till it seemed / he stood where they had stood?' Similarly, in Eoin Neeson's biography of Michael Collins we hear this republican hero praised as one 'who has been admitted to the company of heroes stretching from Cuchulain to Hugh O'Neill and Parnell'.

17. Yeats was by no means an isolated 'poetic' spokesman of this mythic dimension of the republican movement. In a poem called 'Situations' George Russell proclaimed that Pearse has 'turned all life's water into wine' and that MacDonagh had been 'by death redeemed'; he concluded his panegyric with the sententious claim that 'Life cannot utter things more great / Than life can meet with sacrifice'. Eva Gore-Booth, writing of another Easter hero, Francis Sheehy-Skeffington, declared that he was not alone when he died, 'for at his side does that scorned Dreamer stand / Who in the Olive Garden agonised'. And in the same vein, Sean O'Casey caricatured the mythological trappings of the uprising as follows: 'Cathleen Ni Houlihan, in her bare feet is singing, for her pride that had almost gone is come back again. In tattered gown and hair uncombed she sings, shaking the ashes from her hair, she is singing of men that in battle array ... march with banner and fife to the death, for their land ... The face of Ireland twitches when the guns again sing, but she stands ready, waiting to fasten around her white neck this jewelled story of death, for these are they who will speak to her people for ever; that Spirit that had gone from her bosom returns' (Sean O'Casey, *Autobiography*). See also Frank O'Connor's recognition of the mythic nature of the Rising in *An Only Child*: 'It was only in the imagination that the great tragedies took place ... the impossible and only the impossible was law ... then the real world began to catch up with fantasy' (quoted in McHugh, *Dublin 1916*).

18. Sean O'Faolain, *Vive Moi!* quoted in McHugh, *Dublin 1916*, pp. 369–86.

19. Hederman, 'Seamus Twomey'.

20. Jürgen Moltmann, *Theology of Hope* (SCM Press 1967). Rudolph Bultmann argues in a similar vein in *Theology of the New Testament*: 'To understand Jesus' fate as the basis for a mythic cult, and to understand such a cult as the celebration which sacramentally brings the celebrant into such fellowship with the cult-divinity that the latter's fate avails for the former as if it were his own – that is a *Hellenic* mystery idea.' Rudolph Bultmann, *Theology of the New Testament* (SCM Press 1952).

21. Mircea Eliade, *Patterns in Comparative Religion* (Sheed and Ward 1958). For an analysis of the 'reactualising myths' of blood-sacrifice, see Eliade, *Myths, Rites, Symbols: A Mircea Eliade Reader*, vol. 1 (Harper 1975), pp. 253–5. For a feminist critique of the sacrifice myths see: M. Condren, 'Death and patriarchy' in Valver and Buckley (eds), *Women's Spirit Bonding* (Pilgrim Press 1984). See also N. Jay, 'Sacrifice as remedy ...' in C. Buchanan (ed.), *Immaculate and Powerful* (Beacon Press 1985); Edna McDonagh, 'Dying for the cause: An Irish perspective on martyrdom' in *Between Chaos and New Creation* (Gill & Macmillan 1968).

22. Eugen Fink, *Spiel als Weltsymbol* (Kohlhammer 1960).

23. Paul Ricoeur, *The Symbolism of Evil* (Beacon Press 1969), pp. 162–3.

24. Max Scheler, *Ressentiment* (Schocken Books 1972).

25. See Jean-Paul Sartre, *Sketch for a Theory of the Emotions* (Metheun 1962) and *The Psychology of Imagination* (Citadel Press 1972); see also my analysis of Sartre in *Modern Movements in European Philosophy* (Manchester University Press 1985).

26. Ricoeur, *Symbolism of Evil*, p. 5. See also Mircea Eliade, *Myths, Dreams and Mysteries* (Fontana 1968), p. 27: 'It seems that myth itself, as well as the symbols it brings into play never quite disappears from the present world of the psyche – it only changes and disguises its operations.' We might add at this point that the credibility of our attempt to identify a mythological dimension in Ulster terrorism does not presuppose a belief in a

Jungian collective unconscious, Herderian Racial Memory or Yeatsian *Anima Mundi*. Mythic archetypes of behaviour and thought are as likely transmitted by means of actual and narrated experience as by some form of transhistorical or innate inheritance. It is enough for the Provisionals to have known and heard of the 1916 martyrs, and these to have known and heard of the Fenian rebels, and these of the heroes of ancient Ireland etc. for the mythic experience of sacrificial terror to perdure and recur.

– Chapter Four –
The Triumph of Failure: The Irish Prison Tradition

This is a revised version of an essay that first appeared in The Crane Bag, *edtied by Richard Kearney and M.P. Hederman, 4, 2 (1980).*

1. Bobby Sands, *One Day in My Life* (Pluto Press 1983), pp. 117–18.
2. *Ibid.* Seán MacBride, Introduction, pp. 7–21.
3. See, for example, reports, by Cardinal Tomás Ó Fiaich and Tim Pat Coogan, author of *On the Blanket* (Ward River Press 1980).
4. H-Block Christmas Document (1979), compiled by Dennis Faul and Raymond Murray (whose defence of the prisoners never prevented them from continually condemning the IRA's use of violence). In this document the authors make the following plea: 'Let all the Irish family … respond to this new threat of hunger by Britain with loud and endless protests against British tyranny' – the allusion here being to the great Irish famine of the 1840s and 1850s where millions died due to the continued exportation of grain by the British after the potato crops had failed.
5. Coogan, *On the Blanket*, p. 15. I am indebted to Mr Coogan's detailed research on the republican prison campaigns for much of the material in the following analysis.
6. Quoted in Coogan, *On the Blanket*.
7. Quoted in Coogan, *On the Blanket*.
8. Garret FitzGerald's famous 'flawed pedigree' attack on Mr Haughey on the eve of his election as Taoiseach in 1980 merely reinforced this curious status in allowing Haughey to play the coveted dual role of leader and victim. This ambivalence which appeals so much to the Irish political psyche, is perhaps the secret of Charles Haughey's success. If our minds gave assent to the moral reasoning of Conor Cruise O'Brien, our hearts ran with the dark horse 'Charlie'. Which went some way to explaining why Dr O'Brien failed to be re-elected and was soon editing the *Observer* 'over there' while Mr Haughey decided our political future 'over here'. Charles Haughey's term as scapegoat greatly contributed to his earning a term as prime minister of the Irish Republic. It might also be remembered that Neil Blaney, a Fianna Fáil colleague of Mr Haughey also accused in the arms trial, went on to be elected as a European Deputy several years later. Moreover, it is possible that the Peace Movement's inability to maintain their initial momentum and support stems from the fact that they rapidly became *prize winners* of prestige and success thereby forfeiting their original *sacrificial role as victims of violence*.
9. Quoted in Coogan, *On the Blanket*.
10. *Ibid.* See also Seán MacBride, Introduction to Sands, *One Day*, pp. 14–16, and the Faul and Murray H-Block document, where the authors write: 'The problem of prisoners is the problem of peace in Northern Ireland. The evidence of the growth in the number of prisoners, from 712 in 1969 to 3000 prisoners in 1979, is due to the political conflict involving Northern Ireland and Great Britain. The British handling of H-Block has blighted hopes for peace for years to come …'
11. Quoted in Coogan, *On the Blanket*, pp. 177–8.
12. Quoted by Seán MacBride in Sands, *One Day*, pp. 11–12.
13. *The Irish Press* (22 January 1979).

14. Paul Durcan in *The Cork Examiner* (2 September 1980).
15. See the statement of the former IRA leader, Seamus Twomey, 'From all wars peace has sprung. Peace has never been built on anything else but violence.' M.P. Hederman, 'An interview with Seamus Twomey', *The Crane Bag*, vol. 1, no. 1 (1977); reprinted in M.P. Hederman and R. Kearney (eds), *The Crane Bag Book of Irish Studies* (Blackwater Press 1982), pp. 109.
16. Statement by IRA Army Council spokesman talking to Ed Maloney in *Magill* (September 1978), p. 27.
17. For further analysis of this sacrificial logic see my 'Myth and motherland', *Field Day*, 5 (1984); and 'Terrorisme et sacrifice, Le cas de L'Irlande de Nord', *Esprit* (April 1979).
18. See Ed Maloney's interview with IRA Army Council Spokesman, *Magill* (September 1978). It is surely no accident that several bombing campaigns followed immediately after statements by the British government to the effect that the terrorists had been effectively quashed. See *Magill* article on the IRA (September 1980), p. 27: 'We have not managed to match last year's performance this year … But we are totally confident that we can overcome these short-term problems. The British are sliding into their 1977 mistake of predicting our defeat. They're fighting a statistical war, we're not. We're fighting a political war. The Brits are saying the Provos are beaten, operations are down, there's less poundage of explosives used, four soldiers less have died this year, etc. That's a false confidence and that's OK with us because we will wreck it when we choose to'. See also the statement by Gerry Adams, IRA leader: 'In December Mason said he would squeeze out the IRA like a tube of toothpaste. The IRA replied with a bombing offensive and the toothpaste congealed.' *Hibernia* (December 1978), p. 25.
19. Seán MacBride in Sands, *One Day*, p. 14.
20. For legal and statistical details see Seán MacBride in Sands, *One Day*, pp. 14–20.
21. For a detailed analysis of the myths and ideologies of the Protestant tradition in Ulster see the third set of *Field Day* pamphlets (nos 7, 8, 9; 1985) by Terence Brown, Marianne Elliott and Robert McCartney; and Desmond Bell's 'Contemporary cultural studies in Ireland and the problem of Protestant ideology' in *The Crane Bag, Irish Ideologies*, vol. 9, no. 2 (1985). Bell offers the following reservations: 'Loyalism as an ideological *practice* amongst the Protestant working class does not primarily take the form of an unswerving electoral support for political representatives who proclaim a conditional loyalty to a British state seen as defending Protestant interests via various political guarantees and policies. Rather its potency resides in a set of cultural practices – to which the Orange parade is central – concerned with the public display of the symbols of Protestant identity. This display is often interpreted as being solely triumphalist in intent. These marches are, as they always have been, about the staking of symbolic claims to territory i.e. where you can or cannot "walk". But, they are also about the celebration of a sense of belonging. The names of the bands inscribed on the colourfully decorated drums of the marchers proclaim a loyalty to community and Ulster Protestant identity, rather than to any distant polity.'
22. The flaming straw dummy of Lundy was annually suspended (on 18 September) from the statue of the victorious governor Walker overlooking the subordinated Catholic Bogside. The rite still continues despite the fact that the provisional IRA exploded the loyalist memorial to the victorious Walker. It should also be mentioned that if extreme loyalist ideology and rhetoric occasionally invoke the theme of Christian martyr (as, for example, Ian Paisley's naming of his Belfast church 'The Martyr's memorial'), it is 'martyr' taken in its literal etymological sense of 'witness' to the power, glory and wrath of God, rather than to his suffering and passion.
23. Manuel de Diégeuz, reply to my 'Terrorisme et sacrifice'.

– Chapter Five –
Faith and Fatherland

This is a revised version of an essay that first appeared in The Crane Bag, *edtied by Richard Kearney and M.P. Hederman, 8, 1 (1984).*

1. For details and statistics on these changes in the religious attitudes of Irish youths, see Peader Kirby, *Is Irish Catholicism Dying?* (Mercier Press 1984); John J. O'Riordan, *Irish Catholics, Tradition and Transition* (Veritas 1980); Liam Ryan, 'Faith under survey', *The Furrow* (January 1983); Ann Breslin and John Weafer, 'Survey of senior students' attitudes towards religion, morality, education 1982' (available from the Council for Research and Development of the Irish Bishops' Conference, Maynooth, Co. Kildare); and Bernadette MacMahon, 'A study of religion among Dublin adolescents' in *Religious Life Review,* vol. 23, no. 107 (1984).

2. See Patrick Corish, 'The origins of Catholic nationalism' in *A History of Irish Catholicism,* vol. III, no. 8 (Gill 1968), p. 57.

3. James McEvoy, 'Catholic hopes and Protestant fears', *The Crane Bag, Forum Issue,* vol. 7, no. 2 (1983), pp. 90–105.

4. Quoted by Padraig O'Malley, *Uncivil Wars* (Blackstaff Press 1983).

5. Lévi-Strauss, *Tristes Tropiques* (Antheneum 1971). See also on this subject of religious myths and nationalism my 'Myth and motherland', *Field Day,* 5 (1984).

6. Uinseann MacEoin, *Survivors* (Dublin 1980), p. 242; quoted by Margaret O'Callaghan, 'Religion and identity: The Church and independence', *The Crane Bag, Forum Issue,* vol. 7, no. 2 (1983), pp. 65–76. I am indebted to Margaret O'Callaghan for several of the quotations and arguments used in this chapter.

7. O'Callaghan, 'Religion and identity'.

8. *Ibid.*

9. *Ibid.*

10. *Ibid.*

11. Quoted in Terence Brown, *Ireland: A Social and Cultural History 1922–79* (Fontana 1981).

12. See Dermot Moran, 'Nationalism, religion and the education question', *The Crane Bag, Forum Issue,* vol. 7, no. 2 (1983), pp. 77–85.

13. See John A. Murphy, 'Further reflections on nationalism', *The Crane Bag,* vol. 2, nos 1 and 2 (1978); reprinted in M.P. Hederman and R. Kearney (eds), *The Crane Bag Book of Irish Studies* (Blackwater Press 1982), pp. 304–12.

14. 'Minorities in Ireland', report prepared by the Irish Council of Churches advisory forum on Human Rights. See *The Irish Times* (5 September 1985).

– Chapter Six –
Between Politics and Literature: The Irish Cultural Journal

This is a revised version of an essay that first appeared in The Crane Bag, *edtied by Richard Kearney and M.P. Hederman, 7, 2 (1983).*

1. For the research material used or quoted in the first section of our study I am indebted to Barbara Hayley's exhaustive study of the journals of this period, 'Irish periodicals from the union to the nation', *Anglo-Irish Studies II* (1976), pp. 83–103. See also Patrick Rafroidi's comprehensive list of Irish nineteenth-century journals in *Ireland and The Romantic Period* (Colin Smythe 1980).

2. Hayley, 'Irish periodicals'.

3. As Hayley also points out it was the professional, clerical and university *intellligensia* who produced these journals, however popular their base of support. An illustrative case in point is the resounding success of the *Dublin University Magazine*, founded by Trinity College graduates in 1833 and surviving for over forty years. Hostile to any hint of pro-Catholic liberalism on the part of its fellow Protestants, the manifesto of this journal was uncompromisingly provocative and bellicose: 'We are conservatives: and no feeble vacillation shall dishonour our steady and upright strength. We cannot assent to the suspicious friendship that would counsel an impotent moderation, where vigour and intrepid activity point to rough collision' (cited in Hayley, 'Irish periodicals').

4. Seamus Deane in D. Dunn (ed.), *Two Decades of Irish Writing* (Carcanet 1975), p. 8.

5. Another noteworthy cultural journal that combined non-sectarian politician and literary interest in the pursuit of a cross-communal national identity was the *Irish Monthly Magazine of Politics and Literature*, founded in 1833, which addressed its new generation of enlightened readers as follows: 'We come not to support Whig or Tory ... We shall, in our philosophy, in our politics, in our fun, even in our vituperation and satire, be Irish – and purely Irish ... [our] cause is that of the Nation – not of sect or party, but of the entire people of Ireland' (cited in Hayley, 'Irish periodicals').

6. Hayley, 'Irish periodicals', p. 93.

7. F.S.L. Lyons, *Ireland Since the Famine* (Wiedenfield and Nicolson 1971), p. 244.

8. *Ibid.* p. 46.

9. Terence Brown, *Ireland: A Social and Cultural History 1922–79* (Fontana 1981), pp. 120–9. I am indebted to Brown's extensive research for much of the material in this section.

10. For a detailed analysis of the cultural debates between *The Irish Statesman* and D.P. Moran and the *Catholic Bulletin*, see Margaret O'Callaghan's thesis on 'Language and identity: The quest for identity in the Irish Free State 1922–1932' (University College Dublin Press 1981).

11. Quoted in Brown, *Ireland*, p. 121.

12. Brown, *Ireland*, p. 205.

13. Quoted by Ronan Fanning, *The Four-Leaved Shamrock. Electoral Politics and National Imagination in Independent Ireland* (University College Dublin Press 1983).

14. Editorial, *The Crane Bag*, vol. 1, no. 1 (1977), reprinted in M.P. Hederman and R. Kearney (eds), *The Crane Bag Book of Irish Studies* (Blackwater Press 1982), p. 11. For further analysis of the new cultural journals emerging in Ireland in the eighties see my 'Postmodern Ireland' in M. Hederman (ed.), *The Clash of Ideas* (Gill and Macmillan 1987).

15. Walter Benjamin, 'The story teller, reflections on the works of Nikolai Leskov' in *Illuminations* (Jonathan Cape 1970), p. 87.

16. *Ibid.* p. 89.

– *Chapter Seven* –
Yeats and the Conflict of Imaginations

This is a revised version of an essay that first appeared in The Crane Bag, *edtied by Richard Kearney and M.P. Hederman, 3, 2 (1979).*

1. See the analysis of the historical philosophies of imagination in the introduction to my *Poétique du Possible* (Beauchesne 1984).

2. Elizabeth Cullingford, 'The unknown thought of W.B. Yeats's in R. Kearney (ed.), *The Irish Mind: Exploring Intellectual Traditions* (Wolfhound Press/Humanities Press 1985), p. 232.

3. Seamus Deane, prefatory note in the Field Day Theatre Company programme for Brian Friel's *The Communication Cord* (1983).

4. Seamus Deane, 'Yeats, Ireland and revolution' in M.P. Hederman and R. Kearney (eds),

The Crane Bag Book of Irish Studies (Blackwater Press 1982), pp. 139–48; and also in Deane's *Celtic Revivals: Essays in Anglo-Irish Literature* (Faber and Faber 1985).

5. W.B. Yeats, *Selected Prose*, edited by A. Norman Jeffares (Macmillan 1964), pp. 85–7.

6. *Ibid.* p. 85. This conflict of interpretations, as Yeats fully realized, goes as far back as Plato, the founding father of Western metaphysics. Plato was the first to recognize the existence of two distinct and ostensibly opposed types of imagination – the 'mimetic' and the 'ecstatic'. The 'mimetic' imagination was identified with the shaping activity of the human psyche. It was treated with deep suspicion to the extent that it presumed to invent a world of images out of its own desire. This imaginary world was termed 'mimetic' because of its anthropomorphic nature, that is, because the imagination that fashioned it was deemed a threat to the authority of the Divine Demiurge who, according to Plato, was the only legitimate shaper of the world. Artists who think they are creating a new order are mistaken. In fact, they are merely 'imitating' (*mimesis*) in idolatrous fashion the divine activity of the Demiurge who first modelled nature on the Transcendental Forms (which exist beyond our historical world of time, space, matter and movement). The 'mimetic' imagination of the creative artist was condemned accordingly to Plato in the tenth book of the *Republic*. Its greatest offence was to seek to emulate the divine order of Forms with a human order of fantasies.

In some of the later mystical dialogues such as the *Phaedrus* or *Timaeus*, however, Plato acknowledged a radically different kind of imagination that he called 'ecstatic'. This imagination was attributed to the visionary poet or holy seer. It did not invent images but received them from a sacred source beyond human experience. It was termed 'ecstatic' because it permitted man to stand outside himself (*ek-statis*) serving as a receptacle for transcendent visions. Rather than vainly desiring to create a new world in historical time, the ecstatic imagination chose to *remember* the timeless world of Divine Forms, which the soul inhabited in its 'pre-existence' before it was born into this temporal world. In short, while the mimetic imagination was committed to *desire (Eros)*, the ecstatic imagination was committed to *recollection (Anamnesis)*.

7. Denis Donoghue, *Yeats* (Fontana 1971), p. 19.

8. *Ibid.* While it may appear strange at first to couple the terms 'mimetic' and 'romantic' – in opposition to the standard reading of Yeats's Romanticism, by Abrams and others, as a replacing of *imitation* (the mirror) with *expression* (the lamp) – this equation is in fact justified when we consider the original Platonic identification of *mimesis* with human 'images of desire', which lay claim to an autonomous life in defiance of the original source of light in the Transcendental Forms. It is this sense of Romantic 'mimesis' that Yeats himself invokes when he endorses Mallarmé's image of the Hérodiade's defiantly self-referential mirror dance: 'All about me lives but in mine own / Image, the idolatrous mirror of my pride'; or again when he writes: 'Mirror on mirror mirrored is all the show'. Moreover, as Jonathan Culler has argued in *The Pursuit of Signs: Semiotics, Literature, Deconstruction* (Routledge and Kegan Paul 1981), pp. 162–5, the strict opposition between mirror (as derivative light) and lamp (as self-generating light) that Abrams promotes as a central motif of Romanticism is ultimately unsustainable, a token of what Culler terms its 'self-deconstructive logic'.

9. 'Anima hominis' in W.B. Yeats, *Selected Criticism*, edited by A. Norman Jeffares (Macmillan 1964), p. 173.

10. Jeffares (ed.), *Selected Prose*, p. 64.

11. Quoted in Richard Ellmann, *Yeats: The Man and the Masks* (Faber and Faber 1949), pp. 19–20.

12. *Ibid.* p. 141. This attitude is typical of Phase 16 as outlined by Yeats in *A Vision* (Macmillan 1937; Gill and Macmillan 1988), pp. 138–9; 'There is always an element of frenzy, and almost always a delight in certain glowing and shining images of concentrated force.' It is this strident, querulous aspect of imagination that Denis Donoghue defines as the 'hysteria of imagination' in his *Yeats*, p. 126. The opposite Phase is 14, which Yeats has Robartes describe at that time when 'The soul begins to tremble into stillness, / To die

into the labyrinth of itself!' It is represented by the 'mind moving upon silence', by sacramental 'visions deeper than reverie or sleep' (Donoghue, *Yeats*, p. 60).

13. W.B. Yeats, *Essays and Introductions* (Macmillan 1961), p. 529.

14. Quoted in Ellmann, *Yeats*, p. 20.

15. Allan Wade (ed.), *The Letters of W.B. Yeats* (Rupert Hart-Davies 1954), pp. 582 ff.

16. *Ibid.* p. 583.

17. W.B. Yeats, *The Trembling of the Veil* (Werner Laurie 1922), p. 197.

18. W.B. Yeats, *Per Amica Silentia Lunae* (Macmillan 1919), p. 133.

19. 'Autobiographical writings' in Jeffares (ed.), *Selected Prose*, p. 194.

20. This is a typical statement of Romantic idealism. See chapter 4 of my *The Wake of Imagination* (Hutchinson 1987).

21. Jeffares (ed.), *Selected Prose*, p. 130.

22. Jeffares (ed.), *Selected Prose*, p. 113; cf. on Yeats's and Mallarmé's theory of the Eternal Imagination, Hugh Kenner, *The Pound Era* (University of California Press 1972), p. 109.

23. This is 'an Ireland / The poets have imagined, terrible and gay'. As such it proved eligible for Yeats's doctrine of the Mask: 'I, that my native scenery might find imaginary inhabitants, half-planned a new method and a new culture.' Quoted in John Unterecker, *Yeats* (Prentice Hall 1963).

24. Jeffares (ed.), *Selected Criticism*, pp. 133–4. It was this ability to assimilate the products of history to the designs of an erotic imagination that Pound satirized in Yeats when he wrote of him stopping to 'admire the symbol with Notre Dame standing inside it'.

25. Yeats, *Trembling*, p. 206.

26. Jeffares (ed.), *Selected Prose*, p. 86.

27. *Ibid.* p. 86.

28. Yeats, *Trembling*, p. 207. Yeats finds precedents for this passive and involuntary aspect of the sacramental imagination in the examples of the priesthood of Apollo who acquired great powers from the religious meditation of his 'divine Image'; the citizens of ancient Egypt who 'assumed in contemplation, the images of their gods'; or the case of Gemma Galgani who in 1889 caused deep wounds to appear in her body by contemplating her crucifix: *Hodos Camelionis* in Yeats, *Trembling*, p. 150.

29. *Ibid.* p. 136.

30. *Ibid.* p. 136.

31. *Ibid.* p. 235. And this conviction takes on even more significance when we recall Yeats's much-quoted belief that 'the Celt is a visionary without scratching', for the Irish people's 'hatred of abstraction' made them deal more easily in 'visions and images', Jeffares (ed.), *Selected Prose*, p. 159.

32. Yeats, *Trembling*, p. 143.

33. *Ibid.* p. 149.

34. 'Now image called upon image in an endless procession, and I could now always choose among them with any confidence, and when I did choose, the image lost its intensity, or changed into some other image.' *Ibid.* p. 150.

35. *Ibid.* p. 152. This statement of disaffection from the Romantic imagination, made in 1922, was already prepared for some thirty years earlier when Yeats held that in various sessions with such occult spiritualists as Mathers and Madame Blatvastsky, there rose before him 'mental images which [he] could not control'. Already then in the 1880s Yeats was forced to ask the question: 'What certainty had I that [these images] which had taken me by surprise could be from my own thought?'

The following passage from *Hodos Camelias* is representative of Yeats's mystical impulse: 'When a man writes any work of genius, or invents some creative action, is it not because some knowledge or power has come into his mind from beyond the mind? It is called up by an image ... but our images must be *given to us*, we cannot choose them deliberately.' *Ibid.* p. 153.

36. Jeffares (ed.), *Selected Prose*, p. 77.

37. Jeffares (ed.), *Selected Criticism*, p. 81 ('Magic'); p. 162 ('Poetry and tradition').

38. Jeffares (ed.), *Selected Prose*, p. 82.

39. *Ibid.* p. 84. And mythology, we must remember, is for Yeats no 'mere vanity' invented by the will but a portal to the 'Unknown' beyond the will: 'Introduction to the Words upon a Window Pane' in Jeffares (ed.), *Selected Prose*, p. 214.

40. Jeffares (ed.), *Selected Criticism*, p. 34.

41. Yeats, *Trembling*, p. 219.

42. Jeffares (ed.), *Selected Prose*, p. 234. Blake is also numbered amongst the mystic company. Yeats was particularly admiring of the prophetic poems and was, he admits, tempted to give credence to Blake's own claim that their 'author was in eternity' (Jeffares [ed.], *Selected Criticism*, p. 86). The visionary, as opposed to the Romantic, in Blake was one of those rare poets receptive to the 'memory of nature that reveals events and symbols of distant centuries … the things of eternity' (p. 89); one of that sacramental company who followed the way of the saint, abandoning themselves to the 'wilderness to so waste the body, and to so hush the unquiet mind that, still living, they might pass the doors the dead pass daily' (pp. 89–90). It was as a representative of the sacramental imagination that Yeats rapturously praised him: 'Blake represented the shapes of beauty haunting our moments of inspiration: shapes held by most for the frailest of ephemera, but by him for a people older than the world, citizens of eternity, appearing and reappearing in the minds of artists and of poets, creating all we touch and see by casting distorted images of themselves …' (p. 23). This passage constitutes perhaps Yeats's clearest concession to the sacramental view that imagination received images created elsewhere and is not itself their creator. In fact, analogies between the 'ecstatic' imagination of the poet and the saint are not infrequent. Speaking of Gérard de Nerval, Yeats observes that in an earlier time 'he would have been of that multitude whose soul's austerity withdrew … from desire and regret' in order that they might 'reveal those processions of symbols that men bow to before altars, and woo with incense and offerings' (p. 51). Another example is witnessed in Yeats's appeal for a new art that would do away with the 'invention of the will' and turn instead towards more 'meditative, organic rhythms' that are the embodiment of that imagination, which 'neither desires nor hates, because it has done with time' (p. 52). Morris, Bunyan, Dante and Paracelsus were, for Yeats, also just such 'religious artists'. The beauty of their poetry was intended to 'set us at peace with natural things', rather than creating quarrels between man and his world as would be expected of the Romantic imagination. They deployed a symbolism 'by which the soul when entranced … communes with God and with angels' (pp. 109, 126). It was through repeated meditation on the works of such sacramental poets that Yeats became sufficiently emboldened to formulate the notion of a supernatural artist who revealed himself in poetic or visionary images. Even so typical a Romantic as Shelley was deemed to have partaken, on privileged occasions, of that religious Ecstasy of the Saint where the self abandons itself to a truth higher than its own creative will. Yeats begins his essay 'The Philosophy of Shelley's Poetry' by confessing that whereas he once believed that the world's destiny could best be discovered by words that gathered up the heart's desire, 'since then I have observed dreams and visions very carefully, and am now certain that the imagination has some way of lighting on the truth'; and furthermore, that its commandments are only 'delivered when the body is still', that is, when the *heart's desire* is appeased in sacramental 'vision of the divine order': that order which Shelly's platonism led him to denote as the Intellectual Beauty (p. 55).

43. See Terry Eagleton, 'Politics and sexuality in W.B. Yeats', *The Crane Bag*, vol. 9. no. 2 (1985), p. 139.

44. *Ibid.* pp. 139–41.

45. Supportive of such a reading is the much quoted passage in *Anima Hominis* where Yeats argues that whereas the saint or sage follows the straight line to truth, the artist and poet must follow the path of the serpent that winds from desire to weariness and back to desire again. According to this view, sacramental vision could only occur when we renounce the circular self of desire and are taken up into a 'clear light and are forgetful

even of our own names and actions'. (Jeffares [ed.], *Selected Criticism*, p. 178).

46. See for example the passage in Jeffares (ed.), *Selected Criticism*, p. 87, where Yeats talks of the imagination '*creating* or *revealing* for a moment what I call a supernatural artist'. See also when he wonders whether 'it is *we* or the *vision* that creates the pattern' (p. 179).

47. Jeffares (ed.), *Selected Prose*, p. 115. In a letter to Olivia Shakespeare in 1926, Yeats states that the tragic attitude most befits the ageing man: 'I suppose to grow old is to grow impersonal, to need nothing and to seek nothing for oneself.'

48. *Ibid.* p. 115.

49. Jeffares (ed.), *Selected Criticism*, p. 163. This means, Yeats concludes, that the tragic-comic poet is 'known from other men by making all he handles *like himself*, and yet by the *unlikeness to himself* of all that comes before him in a pure contemplation' (p. 163).

50. *Ibid.* p. 164. The twin pillars of civilization, as Yeats explains, are 'creativity/culture' and 'holiness' (p. 116).

51. Quoted in Ellmann, *Yeats*, p. 129.

– *Chapter Eight* –
Joyce I: Questioning Narratives

This is a revised version of a chapter that appeared in the author's Transitions: Narratives in Modern Irish Culture *(Wolfhound Press/St Martins Press 1988).*

1. Desmond Ryan (ed.), *Collected Works of Padraig Pearse*, p. 65. Quoted by Seamus Deane in 'Joyce and nationalism' in *Celtic Revivals: Essays in Anglo-Irish Literature* (Faber and Faber 1985), p. 94.

2. Seamus Deane, 'An example of tradition', *The Crane Bag*, vol. 3, no. 1 (1979), p. 47.

3. See Colin McCabe, *James Joyce and The Revolution of the Word* (Macmillan 1978).

4. See Joseph O'Leary, 'Joyce and the myth of the fall', *The Crane Bag*, vol. 2, nos 1 and 2, (1978).

5. Mikhail Bakhtin, *Problems of Dostoevsky's Poetics* (Manchester University Press 1984). See Paul Ricoeur's discussion of Bakhtin's concept of the 'dialogical imagination' in the modern 'polyphonic novel' in *La configuration dans le récit de fiction (Temps et Récit, II)* (Éditions du Seuil 1984), pp. 144–8 and Denis Donoghue in *We Irish* (Knopf 1986).

6. See M.P. Hederman's analysis of this 'nighttime consciousness' in 'The mind of James Joyce' in R. Kearney (ed.), *The Irish Mind: Exploring Intellectual Traditions* (Wolfhound Press/Humanities Press 1985). See also Sheldon Brivic, *Joyce: Between Freud and Jung* (Kennikat Press 1980) and *Joyce the Creator* (University of Wisconsin Press 1985). For Jung's own most explicit statement on Joyce's use of the language of the unconscious see his essay '*Ulysses*: A monologue' in *The Spirit in Man, Art and Literature* (AFK 1984), pp. 109–35, in particular the following passages: 'The book can be read just as well backwards, for it has no back and no front, no top and no bottom. Everything could easily have happened before, or might have happened afterwards ... Objective and subjective, outer and inner, are so constantly intermingled that in the end, despite the clearness of the individual images, one wonders whether one is dealing with a physical or with a tran-scendental tape worm ... *Ulysses* wants to go on singing its endless tune into endless time ... What seems to be mental abnormality may be a kind of mental heath which is inconceivable to the average understanding: it may even be a disguise for superlative powers of mind ... The distortion of beauty and meaning by grotesque objectivity or equally grotesque irreality is, in the insane, a consequence of the destruction of the personality; in the artist it has a creative purpose ... In the destruction of the criteria of beauty and meaning that have held till today, *Ulysses* accomplishes wonders. It insults all our conventional feelings, it brutally disappoints our expectations of sense and content, it thumbs its nose at all synthesis ... It is not a matter of a single thrust aimed at one definite spot, but

of an almost universal 'restratification' of modern man, who is in the process of shaking off a world that has become obsolete ... He worked on *Ulysses* in many foreign lands, and from all of them he looked back in faith and kinship upon Mother Church and Ireland. He uses his foreign stopping-places merely as anchors to steady his ship in the mainstream of his Irish reminiscences and resentments. Yet *Ulysses* does not strain back to his Ithaca – on the contrary he makes frantic efforts to rid himself of his heritage ... *Ulysses* shows how one should execute Nietzsche's 'Sacrilegious backward grasp' ... Prophets are always disagreeable and usually have bad manners, but it is said that they occasionally hit the nail on the head ... like every true prophet, the artist is the unwitting mouthpiece of the psychic secrets of his time, and is often as unconscious as a sleep-walker ... All the Dedaluses, Blooms, Harrys, Lynches, Mulligans, and the rest of them talk and go about as in a collective dream that begins nowhere and ends nowhere, and takes place only because 'no-man' – an unseen Odysseus – dreams it ... Joyce's inexpressibly rich and myriad-faceted language unfolds itself in passages that creep along in tapeworm fashion, terribly boring and monotonous, but the very boredom and monotony of it attain an epic grandeur that makes the book a *Mahabharata* of the world's futility and squalor ... the transformation of eschatology into scatology proves the truth of Tertullian's dictum: *anima naturalita christiana* ... O *Ulysses*, you are truly a devotional book for the object-besotted, object-ridden, white man! You are a spiritual exercise, an ascetic discipline, an agonising ritual, an arcane procedure, eighteen alchemical alembics piled on top of one another, where amid acids, poisonous fumes, and fire and ice, the homunculus of a new, universal consciousness is distilled!'

7. Deane, 'Joyce and nationalism' in *Celtic Revivals*, p. 98.

8. Georg Lukács, *The Theory of the Novel* (Merlin 1971); R. Girard, *Mensonge Romantique et Vérité Romanesque*, (Grasset 1961); L. Goldmann, *Pour une Sociologie du Roman* (Gallimard 1964). See, for instance, Goldmann's statement that the novel 'is the transposition on the literary plane of the everyday life in the individualistic society created by market production' (p. 7).

9. Milan Kundera, 'Encore sur le Roman', *Lettre Internationale*, no. 4 (Spring 1985), pp. 3–7.

10. Deane, 'Joyce and nationalism' in *Celtic Revivals*, p. 93. On the distinction between 'egology' and 'ecology' see Robert Scholes, *Structuralism in Literature* (Yale University Press 1974), p. 183.

11. See Jean-Michel Rabaté, 'De la Hauteur à laquelle l'autorité se noue (Joyce, Hegel et la philosophie)', in *La Littérature dans la philosophie* (Presses Universitaires de Lille 1979) p. 66–8. Jung also observed in his '*Ulysses*: A Monologue' in *The Spirit in Man*, p. 114: 'We behold the disintegration of Joyce's personality into Bloom, *l'homme moyen sensuel* and the almost gaseous Stephen Dedalus, who is mere speculation and mere mind. Of these two, the former has no son and the latter no father'.

12. See S.L. Goldberg, *Joyce* (Oliver and Boyd 1962): 'For the *Portrait*, more than an autobiographical novel, or even a study of artistic alienation, is that peculiar twentieth-century phenomenon: a work of art which is at once a representative fable ... a kind of demonstration of its own significance as a work of art ... (the artist) expresses the external world as he understands it and at the same time expresses the very form of his understanding' (p. 51–2). But as Goldberg remarks Joyce 'could not dramatise more of the deeper vision to which Stephen is groping than is embodied in this groping itself. Hence the need for a sequel, *Ulysses*' p. 62. In *Time and Narrative* (University of Chicago Press 1984), Paul Ricoeur comments on the movement from the traditional novel to the modern (anti-) novel as follows: 'It is the reader who completes the work inasmuch as ... the written work is a sketch for reading. Indeed, it consists of holes, lacunae, zones of indetermination, which, as in Joyce's *Ulysses*, challenge the reader's capacity to configure what the author seems to take malign delight in defiguring. In such an extreme case, it is the reader, almost abandoned by the work, who carries the burden of emplotment' (p. 77).

13. The 'light' extinguished in Bella Cohen's brothel reappears in Molly's bedroom window as 'as a visible luminous sign', a sort of Dantesque vision, at the end of the chapter. See

W.Y. Tindall, *A Reader's Guide to James Joyce* (Thames and Hudson 1959), p. 220. Molly's unequivocal affirmation of reality is an answer to Stephen's espousal of life-excluding art: 'In woman's womb word is made flesh but in the spirit of the maker all flesh that passes becomes the word that does not pass away'. Indeed, this rejection of Stephen's quest was cogently prefigured in the 'Oxen of the Sun' episode where, as we noted, the fecundity of Mrs Beaufoy-Purefoy's child's nine-month embryonic development is contrasted with the sterility of the nine-part chronological parody of the styles of prose writing, from Sterne and Swift to Carlyle and Dickens, and the final decay of literature in America confusion and Billy Sunday. 'Agendath is a wasteland' as Bloom comments. Joyce seems to be suggesting that the principle of artistic creation must not ignore or despise the principle of gestatory creation. See also René Girard's critique of what he calls the *'mensonge romantique'* of desire which seeks to exclude the other and all forms of commitment to social or historical meditation, in *Mensonge Romantique et Vérité Romanesque* (Grasset 1961), pp. 29–31, 42–3, 53–4.

14. Jacques Derrida, *Writing and Difference* (University of Chicago Press 1978). See also Derrida's essay in C. Jacquet (ed.), *Ulysse, Grammaphone L'ouie-dire de Joyce* in *Genèse de Babel* (Éditions du Centre National de la Recherche Scientifique 1985)
15. Hederman, 'The mind of James Joyce' in Kearney (ed.), *Irish Mind.*
16. Jacques Derrida, *Dissemination* (Athlone Press 1981), p. 167.
17. *Ibid.* p. 92.
18. *Ibid.* p. 93.
19. See Sheldon Brivic, 'Synchronicities in *Ulysses*' in *Joyce the Creator* (University of Wisconsin Press 1985), and *Joyce Between Freud and Jung* (Kennikat Press 1980).
20. Colin MacCabe, *Joyce and the Revolution of the Word* (Gill and Macmillan 1979), p. 147.
21. I am indebted, for several of these references, to Deborah Reid's MA Thesis on Joyce 'Never start to finish' (Unpublished thesis, University College Dublin 1980).
22. Cf. Hederman, 'The mind of James Joyce' in Kearney (ed.), *Irish Mind.*
23. See Maud Ellmann's paper on Joyce's 'Allegory of the Fall in *The Wake*', delivered at the Zurich International Joyce conference, 1980.

– Chapter Nine –
Joyce II: A Tale of Two Cities – Rome and Trieste

This was originally delivered as a paper in Dublin in 1992 and later at the Joyce International Summer School, 1997 (unpublished).

1. Giorgio Melchiori, 'The genesis of *Ulysses*' in Melchiori (ed.), *Joyce in Rome* (Bulzoni Editore 1984), p. 37. I am indebted to Melchiori for many of the citations from Joyce's letters from Rome.
2. Quoted in *ibid.* p. 38.
3. For a gloss on Joyce's fascination with the 'French triangle' model of mimetic desire and rivalry, see René Girard, ' "Croyez-vous vous-même à votre théorie?": James Joyce, *Ulysse*' in *Shakespeare: Les feux de l'envie* (Grasset 1990), pp. 313–30, also published in English by Oxford University Press as *A Theater of Envy: William Shakespeare* (1991).
4. Chester Anderson, *James Joyce and his World* (Thames and Hudson 1967), p. 65.
5. Melchiori (ed.), *Joyce in Rome*, pp. 40, 41.
6. Carla de Petris, 'Exiles and emigrants' in Melchiori (ed.), *Joyce in Rome*, pp. 84, 93.
7. Cited in Melchiori (ed.), *Joyce in Rome*, p. 44.
8. *Ibid.* p. 49. See also p. 50: 'Ferrero's book, *L'Europa Giovane,* and the ideas, the attitudes, the personality itself of the author came at exactly the right moment to provide the elements and the ideological background for a story that Joyce had begun to plan a few weeks earlier. They found a fertile ground in Joyce's mind because the first two months

he had spent as a bank clerk in Rome had prepared him for them: he had discovered a new approach to politics and to the human condition of the disinherited, the expatriate and the rootless. Ferrero acted as the catalyst, but without his Roman experience Joyce would never have conceived the story of Mr Hunter.'

9. Melchiori, 'Chronology' in *Joyce in Rome*, p. 22. Joyce's bout of heavy drinking during this time was probably brought on by news of the rejection of *Dubliners*, received on 21 February 1907.

10. Letter to Stanislaus, cited by Anderson, *Joyce and his World*, p. 52.

11. R. Ellmann and E. Mason (eds), *The Critical Writings of James Joyce* (Faber and Faber 1959), p. 153.

12. James Joyce, 'Ireland, island of saints and sages' (Trieste Lecture 1907) in Ellmann and Mason (eds), *Critical Writings*, p. 167.

13. Joyce, 'Ireland, island of saints and sages', p. 171 ff.

14. Anderson, *Joyce and his World*, p. 73.

15. Declan Kiberd, note to *Ulysses: Annotated Student's Edition* (Penguin 1992), p. 1013.

– *Chapter Ten* –
Joyce III: Epiphanies and Triangles

This paper was originally delivered as a keynote lecture at the International Society of Anglo-Irish Literature at Charles University, Prague, in 2005 and in its present revised form as a lecture at the University of Madras, 2006 (unpublished).

1. I wish to thank Amanda Gibeault for bringing this and other such texts to my attention. The full passage from *Stephen Hero* reads: 'First we see that the object is *one* thing, then we see that it is an organized composite structure, a *thing* in fact: finally, when the relation of the parts is exquisite, when the parts are adjusted to the special point, we recognize that it is *that* thing which it is. Its soul, its whatness, leaps to us from the vestment of its appearance etc...' (*Stephen Hero* [New Directions 1963], p. 213). Stephens speaks these words to his friend, Cranley, to explain how even the most demotic of objects – in this case the clock of the Ballast Office – can achieve an epiphany. So from this earliest consideration of epiphany in Joyce's work we realize that it involves 1) a sensible response to an external stimulus in the world (rather than a merely intra-mental insight) and 2) a certain interpretative response on the part of the viewer (or by extension, reader). In *Stephen Hero*, as later in *A Portrait*, this discussion is followed by a Thomistic account of the properties of aesthetic beauty. Though already in *A Portrait* Joyce appears to be taking a certain ironic distance from his early 'theory' of epiphany, though not, I would contend, of the phenomenon of epiphany itself which remains central to Joyce's developing aesthetic – in practice if not in name – in both *A Portrait* and *Ulysses*. I shall introduce the terms epiphany 1 and epiphany 2 below to mark this important distinction between the early and later Joyce. While the former seeks to force essences out of their everyday vestments, the later Joyce seems to acknowledge that the essences are to be found within the everyday events themselves, no matter how trivial or insignificant. In what follows, I am grateful to my colleagues in the Joyce-Proust Reading Seminar and 'Phenomenology of Fiction' seminar at Boston College, and especially Andy Van Hendy and Kevin Newmark, who introduced me to so many intriguing aspects of Joyce which I would otherwise have ignored.

2. James Joyce, *Stephen Hero* (New Directions 1963), p. 211.

3. Gerard Casey, 'Hopkins', *Studies,* vol. 84, no. 334, p. 163.

4. Cited William Noon, 'How Culious an Epiphany' in *Joyce and Aquinas* (Yale University Press 1927), p. 61. See also Hans Urs Von Balthazar's revealing chapter 'Hopkins: Oxford, Ignatius and Scotus' in *The Glory of the Lord: A Theological Aesthetics,* edited by Joseph

Fessio and John Riches (Ignatius Press 1986).

5. Cited in Casey, 'Hopkins', p. 164. See also the more developed analysis of this subject in Philip Ballinger, *The Poem as Sacrament: The Theological Aesthetic of Gerard Manley Hopkins* (Peeters Press 2000), chapter 3, especially pp. 193–8. See also here Fran O'Rourke's analysis of Joyce's debt to the related scholastic notion of 'quidditas' as derived from his studies of Thomas and Aquinas in his Paris and Pola Notebooks of 2003–2004: F. O'Rourke, *Allwisest Stagyrite: Joyce's Quotations from Aristotle* (National University of Ireland 2006).

6. Noon, 'How Culious an Epiphany' in *Joyce and Aquinas*, p. 51. For more detailed presentations of this Scotist idea of '*haecceitas*' as a principle of divine individuation see *Jean Duns-Scot ou La Revolution Subtile*, edited by Christine Goémé (FAC editions 1982), pp. 25–9, 32–6 and Etienne Gilson, *Jean Duns Scot* (Vrin 1952), pp. 460–6.

7. *Ibid.* p. 61.

8. *Ibid.* pp. 61–2.

9. *Ibid.* pp. 62–3.

10. *Ibid.* p. 63.

11. Noon demonstrates how Aquinas, whom Joyce studied in some depth along with his reading of Aristotle in the Paris Notebooks (1903) and Pola Notebooks (1904), gave a prominent role to the symbolic and sacramental power of language. As he wrote in the *Summa Theologica*: 'The illumination of the divine ray of light in this present life is not had without the veils of imaginative symbols, since it is connatural to man in this present state of life that he should not understand without an imaginative sign....The signs which are in the highest degree expressive of intelligible truth are the words of language'(ST, II-II, q 174, a 2–4).

12. Noon, 'How Culious an Epiphany' in *Joyce and Aquinas*, p. 75.

13. Harry Levin, *James Joyce*, p. 28.

14. Oliver St John Gogarty, *As I was Going Down Sakeville Street* (Reynal and Hitchcok 1937), pp. 293 ff.

15. Joseph Prescott notes this in 'James Joyce's Epiphanies', *Modern Language Notes*, 64 (May 1949), p. 436; cited and commented by Noon, 'How Culious an Epiphany' in *Joyce and Aquinas*, p. 70. I think that the French philosopher, Maurice Merleau-Ponty, offers a suggestive gloss on this phenomenon of epiphanic perception in the *Phenomenology of Perception* (Routledge 2002), pp. 246–8. He writes: 'Just as the sacrament not only symbolizes, in sensible species, an operation of Grace, but *is* also the real presence of God, which it causes to occupy a fragment of space and communicates to those who eat of the consecrated bread, provided that they are inwardly prepared, in the same way the sensible has not only a motor and vital significance, but is nothing other than a certain way of being in the world suggested to us from some point in space, and seized and acted upon by our body, provided that it is capable of doing so, so that sensation is literally a form of communion'(p. 246). Merleau-Ponty goes on to elaborate on this Eucharistic power of the sensible as follows: 'I am brought into relation with an external being, whether it be in order to open myself to it or to shut myself off from it. If the qualities radiate around them a certain mode of existence, if they have the power to cast a spell and what we called just now a sacramental value, this is because the sentient subject does not posit them as objects, but enters into a sympathetic relation with them, makes them his own and finds in them his momentary law'(p. 248).

It is difficult to read these passages without thinking of how Joyce performs literary transubstantions between the sensible and the sacramental, and vice versa. Indeed Joyce explicitly invokes idioms of transubstantional mutation at several key points in his texts as noted above.

16. Noon, 'How Culious an Epiphany' in *Joyce and Aquinas*, p. 68. Noon elaborates as follows: 'The poet, the literary artist, is the manipulator par excellence of the symbol, or metaphorical signs; he is the craftsman of the phantasmata, the contriver of the meditative verbal image that suggests, reveals, "epiphanises" ... The Joycean epiphany in litera-

ture may be described as a formulation through metaphor or symbol of some luminous aspect of individual human experience, some highly significant facet of most intimate and personal reality, some particularly radiant point to the meaning of existence'. We may thus see Joyce's work as a series of efforts to find 'vital symbols at the verbal level, capable of interpreting the ineffable epiphanies of experience, and of making these "sudden spiritual manifestations" permanently available through words for the apprehension of other minds'(p. 70).

17. *Ibid.* p. 77.

18. James Joyce, *Ulysses* (Penguin 1968), pp. 188–9.

19. 189.

20. 194.

21. This citation from Mallarmé comes from a passage on Hamlet in Mallarmé's *Divagations* which reads as follows: 'The play, a pinnacle of the theater, is, in the work of Shakespeare, transitional between the old multiple plots and the future Monologue, or drama of Self (*avec Soi*). The hero....he walks, no more than that, reading in the book of himself, high and living Sign; he denies the others attention'. The fact that another line from this same Mallarmé passage – 'sumptuous and stagnant exaggeration of murder' – turns up a few sentences later as part of Stephen's own interior monologue, *unattributed to Mallarmé*, that is, without inverted commas or quotes, suggests that the Mallarmé take on Hamlet as a solipsistic self-reading Self is close to Stephen's own stance at this point in the scene. The various references, later in the chapter, to the library as a place of death and ghostliness (e.g. 'Coffined thoughts around me, in mummycases, embalmed in spice of words') adds to the suspicion that Stephen needs to move beyond this enclosed world of mummification if he is to live and write as a real author, free from the deadening hold of a reified literary and intellectual tradition. The fact that Bloom leads Stephen beyond the National Library – as does Mlle de Saint Loup lead Marcel beyond the Guermantes library – towards a life and literature still to come, is a curious parallel between the two novels. The solipsistic Selves they leave behind them in the library are, arguably, Stephen Hero (for Joyce) and Jean Santeuil (for Proust) respectively – the Romantic narrators whom they have to shed in order to find their own voice.

22. 197.

23. 207.

24. 208.

25. 207.

26. 208.

27. 212.

28. 213.

29. 213. See also here René Girard's intriguing reading of this passage in '"Croyez-vous vous-même à votre théorie?": James Joyce, *Ulysse*' in *Shakespeare: Les feux de l'envie* (Grasset 1990), pp. 313–30, also published in English by Oxford University Press as *A Theater of Envy: William Shakespeare* (1991).

30. 202.

31. 206.

32. 207.

33. 212.

34. 217.

35. It is telling that these allusions hark back to Stephen's anticipatory dream in the Proteus chapter where he speaks of a 'street of harlots' and a certain Haroun al Raschid, an 8th century caliph of Baghdad who disguised himself as a commoner and wandered among his people to find out who they really were and what they really needed. In his dream, Stephen follows the man who offers him a mellon ('creamfruit smell') just as in the Library chapter Stephen will follow Bloom who holds out a 'creamfruit mellon' to him, a reference which anticipates the final fruits of the 'mellonsmellonous' Molly in the Penelope episode. This convoluted temporality of forward reprise or anticipatory

memory typifies the experience of epiphany which is never just a 'once off' isolated moment, but a multivalent present (*kairos/Augenblick*) traversed by both past and future. Commenting on this phenomenon, Amanda Gibeault writes: 'Stephen's enjoinder to remember the scenes leading up to the epiphany take on accrued importance: without the memories, the epiphany will cease to have an anchor in the world of the text and will appear an ad hoc combination of words. The conclusion we can draw from this is that an epiphany is only genuinely a revelation if it includes the context of description of the revelation – that is, if it is actually embedded in a narrative with a temporal unfolding….This means that the reader must do the work of reconstruction to reach a full understanding of Stephen's epiphany'('Epiphany in Joyce and Narrative Identity', Presented at Boston College 'Phenomenology of Fiction' Seminar, November 2004).

36. Joyce, *Ulysses,* p. 207.

37. R. Ellmann, appendix to the 1968 Penguin Edition of *Ulysses*, p. 705.

38. For more on our theory of ana-aesthetics see our 'Epiphanies of the everyday: Towards a micro-eschatology' in *After God: The Religious Turn in Continental Philosophy* (Fordham University Press 2005).

39. See Declan Kiberd's very informative note to the Penguin Annotated Students Edition of *Ulysses* (Penguin 1992), p. 1013.

40. The analogies with Hopkins, also a Jesuit priest, are not meant to suggest that Joyce's reading of epiphany was in any way exclusively Christian. He no doubt first learnt of the Christian feast in his own early Catholic upbringing and education, and certainly seems to have refined it in his readings of two major Christian philosophers, Scotus and Aquinas. But the way Joyce reworks the notion of epiphany in his own aesthetic clearly extends the notion to other religions, in particular Bloom's Judaism, but also (in *Finnegans Wake*) to Eastern and Vedic wisdom traditions (e.g. the reference to the 'Ding hvad in itself id est' in note 9 above). If anything I would suggest that Joyce's aesthetics of epiphany is trans-religious, though some might argue that it is a thoroughly secularized version of an originally religious notion. I have attempted to develop the philosophical and theological connotations of the Joyce-Hopkins notion of epiphany in 'Epiphanies of the everyday' in *After God* and 'Epiphanies in Joyce and Proust' in *Traversing the Imaginary: Encountering the Thought of Richard Kearney*, edited by Peter Gratton and John Manoussakis (Northwestern University Press 2006).

41. This phrase occurs in the National Library scene. Joyce, *Ulysses* (Penguin 1968), p. 195.

42. See our discussion of the eschatological temporality of the Palestinian formula in both Judaic and Christian messianism in 'Hermeneutics of the Possible God' in *God and Giveness*, edited by Ian Leask and Eoin Cassidy (Fordham University Press 2005).

43. *Inventions of Difference: On Jacques Derrida* (Harvard University Press 1994), p. 230. Gasché is here elaborating on Derrida's reading of Joyce in 'Ulysses Gramophone' in *Acts of Literature*, edited by Derek Attridge (Routledge 1992). Derrida offers a useful gloss on the language of Molly/Penelope in an intriguing footnote to his commentary on the relationship between Greek and Jew in Emmanuel Lévinas, 'Violence and Metaphysics: An Essay on the Thought of Emmanuel Lévinas' in *Writing and Difference* (University of Chicago Press 1978), pp. 320–1. Commenting on a phrase in *Ulysses* – 'Jewgreek is greekjew. Extremes meet' – Derrida attributes this not only to 'woman's reason', as in Joyce's text, but he also identifies Joyce here as 'perhaps the most Hegelian of modern novelists' (p. 153). The implication here seems to be that the discourse of 'feminine logic', associated with Molly/Penelope, is one which, for Lévinas at least, suggests an 'ontological category' of return and closure: namely, Ulysses returning to Penelope in Ithica, Stephen and Bloom returning to Molly in Eccles Street where they may find themselves 'atoned' as father-son, jew-greek, greek-jew etc. It is not quite clear where Derrida himself stands towards Joyce in this early 1964 text, though it is evident that he thinks Lévinas would repudiate the Joycean formula as overly Hegelian and Greek (that is, not sufficiently respectful of the strictly Jewish/Messianic/eschatological need for a radically dissymmetrical relation of self and other). In his later essay, 'Ulysses Gramaphone', first

delivered as a lecture to the International Joyce Symposium in Frankfurt, 1984, he makes it clear that the 'yes' of Molly/Penelope marks an opening of the text beyond totality and closure to an infinite and infinitely recurring 'other'. Even if it is a response to oneself, in interior dialogue, 'yes' always involves a relay through an other. Or as Derrida cleverly puts it, *oui-dire,* saying yes, always involves some form of *oui-dire* or hearsay. 'A yes never comes along, and we never say this word alone' (p. 300). With this relay of self through the other, this willing of yes to say yes again, 'this differing and deferring, this necessary failure of total self-identity, comes spacing (space *and* time), gramophoning (writing *and* speech), memory ...' (p. 254). And this 'other' clearly implies a reaching beyond the text of *Ulysses* itself to the listener, the reader, an open call for our response. I think Derrida makes a similar point in 'Two Words for Joyce' when commenting on the last lines of Book 2, chapter 2, of *Finnegans Wake:* 'The final 'Mummum', maternal syllable right near the end, could, if one so wished, be made to resound with the feminine 'yes' in the last line of *Ulyssses,* the 'yes' of Mrs Bloom, of ALP, or of any 'wee' girl, as has been noted, Eve, Mary, Isis, etc ...' (in *Post-Structuralist Joyce,* edited by Derek Attridge and Daniel Ferrer [Cambridge University Press 1984]). Derrida's point seems to be that the feminine yes in both of Joyce's masterpieces defies the 'phallogocentric' system and opens onto new beginnings and birthings of meaning.

In this sense we would say that *Ulysses* is a deeply anti-Hegelian book. Molly's finale does not represent some great teleological reconciliation of contradictions in some absolute synthesis of Spirit, but an ongoing affirmation of paradoxes, struggles, contraries, contingencies in a spirit of humor and desire. 'What else were we given all those desires for ...?' asks the polymorphously perverse Molly, a far cry from the Hegelian triumph of Identity. We may conclude therefore that the story of struggle and trouble does not end when Stephen follows Bloom out of the library, it only begins. And by the same token, Molly, when she finally arrives, does not put paid to Trinities as such, she simply reintroduces us – along with Stephen and Bloom – to another kind of trinity, one without a capital T and more inclusive of time, movement, natality and desire (all those things banned from the Sabellian Trinity of self-enclosed Identity). And one might add, more inclusive of the reader. For like any epiphany, Molly's too calls out to an open future of readers.

44. On this later point see Julia Kristeva, *Time and Sense: Proust and the Experience of Literature* (Columbia University Press 1996), pp. 3–22.

– *Chapter Eleven* –
Beckett I: The End of the Story?

This is a revised version of a chapter that appeared in the author's Transitions: Narratives in Modern Irish Culture *(Wolfhound Press/St Martins Press 1988).*

1. Cf. Deirdre Bair, 'Samuel Beckett's Irishness', *The Crane Bag,* vol. 1, no. 2 (1977), in particular pp. 16–19. Bair's argument is succinctly summed up in the following statement: 'Beckett had no pride in his Irishness, national identity meant nothing to him.'
2. Cf. Seamus Deane, *The Crane Bag,* vol. 3, no. 1 (1979), p. 7.
3. This reference and several others were brought to my attention by a paper, 'Samuel Beckett, James Joyce's "Illstarred Punster"', delivered by S.E. Gontarski at the Joyce International Congress in Zurich, 1979.
4. For a detailed account of this 'neutral' writing see Roland Barthes' analysis of modernist literature, *Writing Degree Zero* (Jonathan Cape 1967).
5. Samuel Beckett, *Proust* (Grove Press 1931). See also the passage in this essay where he equates solitude with the impossibility of authentic personal communication: 'Even on the rare occasions when word and gesture happen to be valid expressions of personality

(i.e. the ego) they lose their significance on their passage through the cataract of the personality that is opposed to them. Either we speak and act for ourselves – in which case speech and action are distorted and emptied of their meaning by an intelligence that is not ours, or else we speak and act for others in which we speak and act a lie ... We are alone. We cannot know and cannot be known'.

6. Beckett's essay on Joyce appeared in the collection *Our Exagmination round his Factification for Incamination of Work in Progress* (Shakespeare and Company 1929), pp. 3–22.

7. For the guidelines to such an analysis see Colin MacCabe, *Joyce and the Revolution of the Word* (Gill and Macmillan 1979). Following MacCabe I first attempted to employ such a method in 'Joyce on language, women and politics', *Screen*, vol. 20, no. 3/4 (1980), pp. 124 ff.

8. See chapter 12, 'Beckett II: The demythologizing intellect'.

9. For a more detailed analysis of the central role of Cartesian metaphysics in Beckett's novels see the first section of chapter 12, 'Beckett II: The demythologizing intellect'.

10. See Richard Coe, *Beckett* (Oliver and Boyd 1964), p. 4.

11. For an analysis of Beckett's use of Democritus' phrase see section two of chapter 12, 'Beckett II: The demythologizing intellect'.

12. See Michel Foucault, Lévi-Strauss and also the 'post-structuralist' analysis of Jacques Derrida, *La Voix et le Phénomène* (Presses Universitaries de France 1967), translated by D.B. Alison as *Speech and Phenomena* (Northwestern University Press 1973), pp. 102, 93.

13. Quoted in Deirdre Bair, *Samuel Beckett, A Biography* (Jonathan Cape 1978), p. 191. In part two of *Molloy*, Beckett pushes this alarming argument further. Moran, a second pseudo-self of the author, is yet another writer-narrator who serves as 'agent' to some unknown and unknowable 'master' (Youdi, later to become Godot) who sends meaningless orders through his 'messenger' Gaber. Moran is commissioned to assassinate Molloy; but they cannot meet for, as Moran acknowledges, Molloy is merely his own protean fiction: 'I had invented him, I mean found him ready made in my head'. The total absence of some extra-textual space where 'Moran could bend over Molloy' is all too evident. Such an illusory space was the prerogative of the omniscient narrators of the classical novel. It is of just such a timeless, meta-linguistic omnipotence that Moran wistfully dreams of when he asks: 'would we all meet in heaven one day, I, my mother, my son, his mother, Youdi, Gaber, Molloy, his mother, Yerk, Murphy, Watt, Camier and the rest?' Moran himself is, however, the first to admit his inability to narrate a story capable of uniting and identifying his different pseudo-selves: 'What a rabble in my head, what a gallery of moribunds. Murphy, Watt, Yerk, Mercier and all the others. I would never have believed that – Yes, I believe it willingly. Stories, stories, I have never been able to tell them. I shall never to able to tell this one.'

14. Jean Paul Sartre, *Qu'est-ce que la littérature?* (Gallimard 1948).

15. In the same essay, 'Dante ... Bruno ... Vico ... Joyce' in *Our Exagmination round his Factification for Incamination of Work in Progress* (Shakespeare and Company 1929), p. 23, Beckett contrasted this definition of hell to the 'purgatorial' writing of Joyce which he defined as a 'flood of movement and vitality'. Here again one is reminded of the radical difference between the 'impotent writer' Joyce – 'the more he knew the more he could' – and the 'impotent writer' Beckett – 'all I can manage more than I could' (Letter to Alan Schneider in 1973).

16. See Lucien Goldmann, *Pour une Sociologie du Roman* (Gallimard 1964); this theory has also been developed by Georg Lukács, *The Theory of the Novel* (Merlin 1971), and René Girard, *Mensonge Romantique et Vérité Romanesque* (Grasset 1961). See also discussion of this theme in our preceding chapter on Joyce.

17. Geoffrey Hartman, *Deconstruction and Criticism* (Routledge and Kegan Paul 1979), p. VIII.

18. See Derrida's exposition of this concept of 'différance' in *Writing and Difference* (University of Chicago Press 1978) and *Speech and Phenomena* (Northwestern University Press 1973); see also chapter 12, 'Beckett II: The demythologizing intellect'.

19. This notion of the 'palimpsest' of writing is developed by Derrida in *De la Grammatologie* (Les Editions de Minuit 1967), *Marges de la Philosophie* (Les Editions de Minuit, 1972) and *La*

Dissémination (Éditions du Seuil 1972). See Paul Ricoeur's discussion of Derrida's thesis on 'La Méta-phore et la Méta-physique' in *La Métaphore Vive* (Éditions du Seuil 1975), translated by R. Czerny as *The Rule of Metaphor* (University of Toronto Press 1977), pp. 280 ff.

20. Frank Kermode, *The Sense of an Ending, Studies in the Theory of Fiction* (Oxford University Press 1966), p. 94.

21. Kermode, *Sense of an Ending*, pp. 116–17.

22. Paul Ricoeur, *Temps et Récit (vol. II): La Configuration dans le Récit de fiction* (Éditions du Seuil 1984), p. 42.

23. *Ibid.* p. 48. See also Ricoeur's analysis of the dialectical rapport between the modern anti-novel and traditional narrative in *Time and Narrative*, vol. I (University of Chicago Press 1984), pp. 68–70 as quoted in note 12 of chapter 27, 'Myth and the critique of ideology'.

– Chapter Twelve –
Beckett II: The Demythologizing Intellect

This is a revised version of a chapter in the author's edited volume, The Irish Mind: Exploring Intellectual Traditions *(Wolfhound Press/Humanities Press 1985).*

1. Samuel Beckett, 'Dante ... Bruno ... Vico ... Joyce' in *Our Exagmination round his Factification for Incamination of Work in Progress* (Shakespeare and Company 1929).

2. Beckett, *Proust* (Chatto and Windus 1931).

3. Beckett, 'Three dialogues with Georges Duthuit', *Transition*, no. 5 (1949).

4. G. d'Aubarède, 'Waiting for Beckett', *Trace*, no. 42 (1961).

5. Interview with Lawrence Harvey, quoted by John Pilling in *Samuel Beckett* (Routledge and Kegan Paul 1976), p. 124.

6. Quoted by Vivian Mercier, *Beckett/Beckett* (Oxford University Press 1977).

7. Deirdre Bair, *Samuel Beckett, A Biography* (Jonathan Cape 1978), p. 91.

8. Beckett, 'Dennis Devlin', *Transition*, no. 27 (1938), p. 289.

9. Beckett, 'Recent Irish poetry', *The Bookman*, no. 86 (1934).

10. It is worth noting from the outset, however, that if Beckett attempted to demystify some of the key philosophical 'myths' that underwrote the Western sense of identity, he was never motivated to secure an alternative tenure in some indigenous Celtic tradition. The Celtic lure of self-identity was considered by Beckett to be no less mythic or mystificatory than its Hellenic and Hebraic counterparts. Beckett had no time for the native nostalgia of the Celtic Twilight and found here a further fetish for his demythologizing intellect. In his essay 'Recent Irish poetry', Beckett contrasts the 'altitudinous complacency of the Victorian Gael', promoted by the 'antiquarian' writers of the Irish Revival, with 'other' Irish writers such as Joyce (and presumably Brian Coffey, Denis Devlin, Thomas MacGreevy and of course himself) who took their cue from the European literary models of critical interrogation. Yeats, Clarke and Corkery represent the former 'antiquarian' category. Beckett was singularly harsh on Yeats, whom he accused of a 'flight from self-awareness'. In the Yeatsian universe of Celtic myth and lore, the 'self is either most happily obliterated or else so improved and enlarged as to be mistaken for the décor' (Beckett, 'Recent Irish poetry'). See also the preceding essay on Beckett, particularly the section 'Beckett the Irish writer: A contradiction in terms' and also J.C.C. Mays, 'Mythologised presences: *Murphy* in its time' in J. Ronsley (ed.), *Myth and Reality in Irish Literature* (Wilfred Laurier University Press 1977), pp. 202–3: 'The staking out of critical principles and of a relationship to the traditions he inherits or is aware of is an almost inevitable preliminary to any Irish writer's career, and one that at the same time involves him in predicaments of national and personal identity ... his understanding of the situation in more than national terms, in feeling the alternative to Yeats lies not in realism but, following the example of Joyce, in European writers of a quite different ambience.'

In pointed contrast, Beckett places the work of Jack Yeats – W.B.'s brother – in the 'other' category of Irish artists and compliments him for his exploration of '*le plus secret de l'esprit*' as follows: 'The artist who plays his being is from *nowhere*. And he has no brothers' (April 1954, '*Hommage à Jack B. Yeats*', *Les Lettres Nouvelles*, p. 619, quoted in Mays in Ronsley [ed.], *Myth and Reality*) Furthermore, Beckett is prepared to give O'Casey the benefit of the doubt in his shifting attitudes to Irish identity. He was particularly sympathetic to O'Casey's anti-nationalism in *Juno and the Paycock,* judging it to be his finest work in so far as it communicates the 'dramatic dehiscence' of insular identity: 'mind and world come asunder in irreparable dissociation – "chassis".' ('The essential and the incidental', *The Bookman,* no. 87 [1935]).

In his first novel, *Murphy,* Beckett continues his critical exposure of the Irish Revival pretensions and particularly its claim to a fixed national identity. He lampoons the patriotic efforts of Austin Clarke to found a literature on a national Hibernian heritage. He calls him 'Austin Ticklepenny', the 'pot poet from the country of Dublin' and derides the 'class of pentametre that Ticklepenny felt it his duty to Erin to compose … bulging with as many minor beauties from the Gaelic prosodoturfy as could be sucked out of a mug of Beamish's porter' (Beckett, *Murphy* [Routledge and Kegan Paul 1938], p. 63). In an equally mischievous vein, Beckett's portrayal of Neary's Cork chauvinism 'mocks the narrow literary nationalism emanating from Munster and upheld by Daniel Corkery' (Mays in Ronsley [ed.], *Myth and Reality*, p. 208: '[Beckett's] satire is at random at the expense of all things Irish, from Junior Fellows to Irish virgins, as well as at life at large'). Of course Beckett did not hesitate to use Irish material for his own literary needs. *More Pricks than Kicks, Murphy* and *Molloy* are peppered with local allusions and the majority of Beckettian characters bear conspicuously Irish names. But his fondness for home-made material is largely to facilitate his parody of self-righteous or sentimental claims to a native literary identity. If contemporary European culture was undergoing a crisis of modernity typified by its art of 'pure interrogation', the Celtic hinterlands were not to be coveted as an alternative. Such an Ireland, Beckett believed, could offer no legitimate refuge from the 'filthy modern tide' of alienation. That is why he followed Joyce and MacGreevy to Paris, preferring 'France in war to Ireland in peace' (Interview with Israel Shenker, *New York Times* [6 May 1956]).

11. Bair, *Samuel Beckett,* p. 104.
12. On Beckett's references to Cartesianism cf. J. Onimus, *Beckett* (Desclée de Brouwer 1968), pp. 40 ff.; Pilling, *Samuel Beckett,* pp. 112 ff; E. Levy, *Beckett and the Voice of Species* (Gill and Macmillan 1980), pp. 18 ff.; Richard Coe, *Beckett* (Oliver and Boyd 1964), pp. 20 ff.
13. Beckett, *Murphy,* p. 107.
14. *Ibid.* p. 8.
15. See Bair, *Samuel Beckett,* p. 220: 'All Murphy's seemingly random actions are set within a specific period, and every date is presented with information about the heavenly bodies … the reader knows exactly what time and date it is throughout the novel.' The frequent allusions to chess and mathematical calculations further confirm the sense of predetermined unfreedom in the novel.
16. Beckett, *Murphy,* p. 275. Joyce so admired this passage that he committed it to memory.
17. *Ibid.* p. 178. See Bair, *Samuel Beckett,* p. 92: 'Geulincx's philosophy had the most powerful and lasting effect on Beckett of anything he had read to date. So impressive was it that he made it the key of his novel, *Murphy,* written in 1935.'
18. The Zeno example also recurs in *Lost Ones* and *Happy Days;* cf. Pilling, *Samuel Beckett,* p. 125.
19. For Aristotle's critique of Zeno see *Metaphysics,* p. 160b, *De Sophisticis Elenchis,* pp. 172a, 179b and *Physics,* vol. 5, pp. 204a, 206a.
20. Pilling, *Samuel Beckett,* pp. 89, 136, 167; and Levy, *Beckett,* pp. 64–5, 77–9. In *More Pricks than Kicks* Beckett mocked Duns Scotus' definition of the divine being as a 'haecceity of puffect love'.
21. Beckett, *Proust,* p. 1.

22. Samuel Beckett, *Watt* (Grove Press 1959), p. 48.

23. Beckett, *Murphy*, p. 109.

24. Samuel Beckett, *More Pricks than Kicks* (Calder 1934), pp. 31, 41.

25. Several of Beckett's characters suffer from a total lack of synchrony between thought and action; they will to do one thing but in fact do the opposite, e.g. Estragon and Vladimir, Malone, Molloy, Moran and Clov.

26. See Pilling, *Samuel Beckett*, on Beckett and Leibniz, p. 185.

27. Beckett, *Murphy*, p. 185

28. Beckett, *Proust*, p. 64

29. Berkeley met Malebranche in Paris and Beckett refers to him by name on several occasions, e.g. Beckett, *How It Is* (J. Calder 1964) p. 33; cf. also Pilling, *Samuel Beckett*, p. 116.

30. H. Bracken, *Berkeley* (Macmillan 1974), p. 18.

31. Beckett, *Murphy*, p. 276.

32. *Ibid*, p. 190. For other commentaries on the influence of Berkeley on Beckett see V. Mercier, *Beckett/Beckett*, pp. 101, 161, 194; Pilling, *Samuel Beckett*, pp. 2, 116, 117.

33. Samuel Beckett, *Film* (Faber and Faber 1972), p. 11.

34. *Ibid.* p. 12; cf. Alec Reid, 1977, 'Beckett, the camera and Jack MacGowan' in Ronsley, *Myth and Reality*, p. 224.

35. Quoted by Mercier, *Beckett/Beckett*, p. 175.

36. See Kant, *Critique of Pure Reason* (1781; William Pickering, London 1838), preface; Kierkegaard, *Fear and Trembling* (1843; trans. Walter Lowrie, Princeton University Press 1954).

37. For the most suggestive analysis of the influence of Protestant thinking on Beckett's writing, see Onimus, *Beckett*, pp. 88–98: 'Lorsque le dualisme cartésien vient s'articuler sur une théologie aussi tragique que de Luther, Dieu s'éloigne. La sensibilité et l'imagination (qui jouent en ce domaine un rôle si important) s'accoutument à un "extrincésisme" séparateur qui exile Dieu par delà tout horizon. Dieu n'est *plus que* le 'Tout Autre', l'étranger par excellence, celui qui est radicalement en dehors (p. 88). Qui sait si les supplices de la dépossession, de l'impuissance, de la claustration ne sont pas des tentatives de l'au-delà pour entrer en communication avec ses créatures? … Peut-être l'engloutissement de Winnie par une suffocante chaleur est-il un bien – comme la marche errante de Molloy et la longue agonie de Malone? Peut-être le malheur même est-il orienté vers une plénitude – comme cette foule misérable qui, dans *l'Innomable*, avance lentement par bonds dérisoires, dans la boue, mais avance quand même, obstinément en direction de l'Orient, vers la lumière du matin (pp. 92–6) … Le Tout n'est séparé du Rien que par un *presque*, un *peut-être*, l'espace d'une hésitation. Mais toute l'oeuvre de Beckett n'est-elle pas faite de cette hésitation?' (p. 98).

38. On Beckett and negative theology see Onimus, *Beckett*, pp. 111–20; Coe, *Beckett*, pp. 12–34; H. Deyle, *Samuel Beckett* (Aix-en-Provence 1960), pp. 27–71; S. Kennedy, *Murphy's Bed* (Bucknell University Press 1971), particularly on the negative theology of the Pseudo-Dionysius, pp. 38–40, 58–9, 83–4, 93–4, 155–6, 163–4, 294–5. One should also keep in mind the similarities between Beckett's exploration of nothingness and the negative theology of Meister Eckhart who claimed that the mystical experience returns us 'to the calm desert, the bottomless abyss of God in which we must eternally submerge ourselves, as one nothingness to another nothingness.' (*Deutsche Werke*, vol. 1, p. 281).

39. 'My family was Protestant,' says Beckett, 'but for me it was only a nuisance and I left it … Irish Catholicism is not seductive but it is more profound. When an Irish bus passes a church all hands make a quick sign of the cross. One day, the dogs in the street will do likewise, perhaps even the pigs.' (Interview with Tom Driver in *Columbia University Forum*, 1961).

40. Onimus, *Beckett*, p. 19. Beckett's description of Belacqua Shuah as a 'low-down Low Church Protestant' of Huguenot stock (*More Pricks than Kicks*) may be a comic reference to himself.

41. Pilling, *Samuel Beckett*, pp. 117–18. It is also worth noting that Beckett frequently makes

humorous allusions to several dogmas of traditional Catholic theology; in *Whoroscope* and *Watt*, for example, he parodies the 'Jesuitasters' teaching of the 'real presence' of Christ in the Eucharist; in *First Love* he mocks at the Irish Catholic ruling on censorship and contraception, and so on.

42. On the theological motif of suffering and sin in Beckett, see Deyle, *Samuel Beckett*, pp. 27–47; and Onimus, *Beckett*, pp. 102, 108–9: 'Dieu est en dehors; son action sur les consciences ne peut s'excercer que de loin et pour ainsi dire mécaniquement. Il n'y a pas de "co-naissance" possible entre des êtres si totalement étrangers. Dieu a été rejeté sur l'autre versant de l'existence, le versant infernal, et Beckett rejoint spontanément la vieille gnose pour qui le monde ne peut être que l'oeuvre du Malin: tout ce qu'il comporte de positif est, en profondeur, négatif, puisque les êtres n'existent que pour pouvoir se dégrader et souffrir; le désir de vivre, qui est toujours un besoin d'absolu, mène fatale-ment au désir du néant et à la haine de soi ... Pour que le mal soit lié à ce point à l'ex-istence on en vient naturellement à croire que l'existence est elle-même une faute, la conséquence d'une erreur, et que l'on paie toute sa vie cette erreur d'être né. Beckett notait déjà une telle angoisse dans son *Proust* et y parlait du péché d'être né.'

43. See H. Deyle's analysis of Beckett's treatment of women, *Samuel Beckett*, pp. 62 ff: 'Beckett assimile la femme au piège de la vie qui nous détourne du grand néant. Joyce identifie A.L. Plurabelle à la vie fluide et féconde.'

44. For Beckett's attitude to the psychoanalysis of Freud and Jung, whom he read and admired, see Bair, *Samuel Beckett*, pp. 166–78, 208–12. Beckett attended a lecture of Jung's in 1935 and was fascinated by his theory that consciousness was an illusion and that the complexes of the unconscious could form 'little personalities' of their own until 'they appear as visions (and) speak in voices which are like the voices of definite people' quoted in Bair, p. 208.

45. See Deyle, *Samuel Beckett*, p. 27. One might add that the Jansenistic Catholicism current in Ireland during Beckett's youth was no less 'puritanical' than its Irish Protestant coun-terpart; one only has to read Joyce or Flann O'Brien to be reminded of this.

46. Cf. Deyle, *Samuel Beckett*, pp. 52 ff.; and Mercier, *Beckett/Beckett*, pp. 141, 193–4, 207.

47. The clowns in *Godot*, for example, suffer from swollen feet, diseased prostrates, syphillis, etc., while Molloy and Malone are constantly preoccupied by their bowel movements.

48. Cf. Beckett, *Watt*, p. 84.

49. Quoted in Mays in Ronsley (ed.), *Myth and Reality*, p. 214.

50. See for instance Daniel Stempel, 'History electrified into anagogy: A reading of *Waiting for Godot*' in *Contemporary Literature*, vol. 17 (Madison 1976), pp. 266–9. Stempel contends that Estragon and Vladimir represent Judaism and Christianity respectively in a dying Europe. Estragon, he points out, is a type-name referring to both tarragon – in French *estragon* – the 'bitter herb' of the Jewish passover supper, and the Spanish-Jewish city of the same name where Christians and Jews debated in 1414 the question of whether the Messiah had come or was yet to come. (Interestingly, in the original manuscript of the play, Estragon is called by the archetypally Jewish name Lévy.) Vladimir, Stempel argues, refers to Duke Vladimir of Kiev who was the first Russian converted to Christianity and to the last famous Russian theologian Vladimir Soloviev whose *War and Christianity* ends with a discussion of the apocalypse to be expected in decadent modern Europe and frequently alludes to the two thieves crucified with Christ (a recurring motif in *Godot*). On the theological motifs of *Godot*, see also Onimus, *Beckett*, particularly pp. 80 ff., 99 ff.

51. Stempel, 'History electrified', p. 8. Estragon admits that he cannot recall when he last read the Bible but vividly revisualizes the map of Holy Zion: 'The dead sea was pale blue ... that's where we'll go on our honeymoon' (p. 56). The elder of the two protagonists, Estragon, only quotes Jehovah as an invisible all-seeing eye and interrupts Vladimir's story of the two thieves crucified 'at the same time as our Saviour' to ask – 'our what?' Whereas Estragon calls the plant where Godot promised to meet them a 'bush' (recalling the burning bush in which Yahweh appeared to Moses), Vladimir insists that it is a 'willow tree' (a crucifix that may serve as a gibbet of despair or a 'little leaved' flowering of hope).

The temporal axis of Estragon's theology is the Godot of the past – he observes that they were waiting in exactly the same place the 'day before'; Vladimir's, by contrast, is the Godot of the future. To Estragon's statement that they are 'tied' to Godot (the French *lier* meaning 'to tie', having the same root as alliance or covenant), Vladimir retorts 'not yet'. Estragon as the Wandering Jew has sore feet after all his travelling and wants to go barefoot as his fellow Jew, 'Christ did'. But Vladimir is irritated by such a sacrilegious analogy: 'Christ! What has Christ to do with it: you're not going to compare yourself to Christ!' Estragon replies, however, that he has compared himself to Christ all his life, taking solace from the idea that 'they crucified quick' and adding: 'The best thing would be to kill me, like the other.' In short, it can be argued that Estragon, who is beaten every night by unknown assailants, identifies with Christ only as a fellow human victim, unlike Vladimir who sees him as a resurrected Saviour who will return. Perhaps this is why Vladimir is so shocked when Godot's messenger informs them that the Master's beard is 'white' rather than 'blond' for it hints that Godot might indeed be the distant Father of the Old Testament rather than the redemptive Son of the New: 'Christ have mercy on us,' exclaims Vladimir on hearing the news. On the other hand, Pozzo's allusion to the unexpected arrival of darkness reinforces the apocalyptic notion of Christ returning like a thief in the night: 'Behind this veil of gentleness and peace night is charging and will burst upon us pop! ... just when we least expect it.' This would also explain why Vladimir enthuses at the prospect of a Redeemer-Godot arriving: 'It's Godot! We're saved,' while Estragon reacts: 'I'm in hell.' For if Christ *is* God then Vladimir is the thief who is saved and Estragon the one who is damned.

52. On Beckett and the Augustinian image of the two thieves (Beckett read Augustine's *Confessions* in 1935) see Bair, *Samuel Beckett*, p. 386 and Mercier, *Beckett/Beckett*, pp. 172–3.

53. Godot is the epitome of unknowability as Beckett made quite clear when he replied to critics that if he knew who Godot was he would have said so in the play!

54. On the conflicting theistic and atheistic readings of *Godot* see Deyle, *Samuel Beckett*, p. 90.

55. Bair, *Samuel Beckett*, p. 386.

56. *Murphy* opens with a paraphrase of the Book of Ecclesiastes: 'The sun shone on the nothing new' and is replete with references to Revelation, e.g. 'There should be time no longer' (Revelations 10:6) and 'the beginning and the end' (Revelations 21:6) as well as constant allusions to the image of the apocalyptic 'nihil' of time as the Anno Domini. This apocalyptic theme of the ending of time is strengthened by pointed astrological and calendar references to such Judeo-Christian feasts as Passover and Holy Week. Several other biblical references identify Murphy as a mock-messiah: Friday is called a 'day of execution, love and fast'; the epithet of chapter 9 announcing Murphy's entry to the Magdalen Mental Mercy seat: 'Il est difficile à celui qui vit hors du monde de ne pas rechercher les siens,' is reminiscent of John 1:2 ('He came into his own and his own received him not.') Furthermore, Bom Clinch sees Murphy as a Christ-like fool and the narrator develops the parallel as follows: 'Admire Bom feeling dimly for once what you feel acutely so often, Pilate's hands rustling in his mind. Thus Bom ... delivered Murphy to his folly.' There are also the quasi-quotations from the New Testament which summarise Murphy's relationship with Celia; 'The hireling fleeth because he is a hireling' (John 10:13) and 'What shall a man give in exchange for Celia' (Mark 8:37); as well as echoes of Job 17:16 and Revelations 21:16, 23, all well documented by Kennedy, *Murphy's Bed*, pp. 245 and 265: 'In Revelations 21:16, 23 the City of God is described as standing "foursquare" with "no need of the sun, neither of the moon, to shine on it." As Cooper rushes away from the supposed deathbed of Murphy, he sees a vision not unlike that of St John. Before him, standing "foursquare" is a "glowing gin-palace ... that had no need of the sun, neither of the moon, to shine in it" (p. 120).'

57. I wish to acknowledge my debt here to T. Eisele's informative essay, 'The Apocalypse of Beckett's *Endgame*', *Cross Currents*, vol. 26, no. 1 (1976), pp. 11–32. As Eisele puts it: 'This play offers the most sustained portrayal of Beckett's religious sensibility' (p. 12). He goes on to argue as follows: 'The Apocalypse of Beckett's *Endgame* is the revelation of the

coming of the Anti-Christ and the leaving of Christ. With that event the world of Christianity ends. So while Beckett's play recalls the New Testament's Book of Revelation in its imagery, it produces a startlingly new twist to that iconology. Christianity does not triumph as it does in the New Testament, but dies' (p. 22). The Anti-Christ is presumably the 'small boy' seen by Hamm in the deluged ('under water') and 'corpsed' wasteland outside his window at the conclusion of the play. The ending of Christianity is heralded by the ending of Clov's relationship with Hamm. Clov declares that he has done his 'best to create a little order' in Hamm's house, while Hamm concedes that Clov's arrival 'was the moment I was waiting for'. Clov's departing speech, with its subtle parodying of Christ's mission, can be read as a statement of disillusionment with the evangelical message of loving sacrifice: 'They said to me, that's love, yes, yes, not a doubt … They said to me, Here's the place, stop, raise your head and look at all that beauty. That order! They said to me, Come on, you're not a brute beast, think upon these things and you'll see how all comes clear. And simple! They said to me, What skilled attention they get. All those dying of their wounds … I say to myself – sometimes, Clov, You must learn to suffer better than that if you want them to weary of punishing you – one day … It'll never end, I'll never go. Then one day, suddenly, it ends, it changes, I don't understand, it dies, or it's me, I don't know, I don't understand that either.' There have also been commentaries on the eschatological themes in *Endgame* by such diverse critics as Cavell, Esslin, Cohn and Sheedy: for bibliographical references see Eisele, 'Apocalypse of *Endgame*', pp. 31–2.

58. Eisele, 'Apocalypse of *Endgame*', p. 31. Clov hovers between the hell of Anti-Christ and the heaven of Christ; he inhabits the purgatory of incertitude and repetition. But is it the Dantesque purgatory of orthodox redemption or the Joycean purgatory, which Beckett defined in his *Exagmination* essay as 'the absolute absence of the absolute'? Whereas Dante's purgatory ends in salvation, Joyce's is an endless repetition of the human quest for salvation: 'Dante's is conical and consequently implies culmination,' explains Beckett, 'Joyce's is spherical and excludes culmination.' As Mercier comments in *Beckett/Beckett*, p. 178: 'Purgatory is another theological concept that Beckett found extremely useful for structural purposes.'

59. Still with Dostoyevsky, we could as easily construe *Endgame* as an enactment of the nihilist's statement in *Notes from the Underground* that 'man is a frivolous and incongruous creature who like a chess player loves the process of the game, not the end of it!'

60. 'I am still afraid, but simply from force of habit. And the voice I listen to needs no Gaber to make it heard. For it is within me and exhorts me to continue to the end the faithful servant I have always been, on a course that is not mine, and patiently fulfil in all its bitterness my calamitous past … And this was with hatred in my heart, and scorn, of my master and his designs. Yes, it is rather an ambiguous voice and not always easy to follow in its reasonings and decrees … And when it ceases, leaving me in doubt and darkness, I shall wait for it to come back', *Molloy* (Picador 1955), p. 121. Pursuing his nomadic journey 'in obedience to Youdi's command,' Moran suddenly embarks on a comic mimicry of the theological dogmas of divine creation. 'Certain questions of a theological nature preoccupied me strangely,' says Moran. 'What value,' he asks, 'is to be attached to the theory that Eve sprang not from Adam's rib, but from a tumour in the fat of his leg (arse?)?' Or: 'How much longer are we to hang about waiting for the Anti-Christ?' Or again: 'What was God doing with himself before the creation?' (p. 153). Moran's blasphemous buffoonery reaches its climax in his inversion of the 'quietest' Our Father: 'God is no longer in heaven, nor on earth, nor in hell, I do not wish nor desire that Your Name be hallowed' … etc.

61. See references to Boehme in *More Pricks than Kicks,* to Eckhart in *Dream*, to St John in *Malone Dies*, etc. As Coe points out in his analysis of Beckett's mysticism (*Beckett*, p. 20): 'To confront the limits of the human condition is not only the equivalent of facing up to the philosophical basis of the scientific attitude, it is also a profound mystical experience.' In *Four Quartets* T.S. Eliot expressed *the via negativa*, which he felt best corresponded

to modern man's critical quest for the absolute, in terms frequently echoed in Beckett's mature writing:

> ... the mind is conscious but conscious of nothing –
> I said to my soul, be still, and wait without hope
> For hope would be hope for the wrong thing; wait without love
> For love would be love of the wrong thing; there is yet faith
> But the faith and the love and the hope are all in the waiting,
> Wait without thought, for you are not ready for thought:
> ...
> ... In order to arrive there,
> To arrive where you are, to get from where you are not,
>   You must go by a way wherein there is no ecstasy.
> In order to arrive at what you do not know
>   You must go by a way which is the way of ignorance.
> In order to possess what you do not possess
>   You must go by the way of dispossession.
> In order to arrive at what you are not
>   You must go through the way in which you are not.
> And what you do not know is the only thing you know
> And what you own is what you do not own
> And where you are is where you are not.

62. Onimus, *Beckett*, pp. 75 ff.: 'Parler de Dieu dans l'oeuvre de Beckett c'est parler d'un absent. L'absence est tout autre chose que l'inexistence: on pense à un absent, on peut fictivement s'adresser à lui, on l'attend, on le désire, on ressent même sa présence comme un manque, un vide pénible, une blessure ... c'est la contemplation d'un *Dieu-néant*, d'un être qui, à force de la torturer, a fini par épuiser chez sa créature les réserves d'angoisse qui lui donnaient prise sur elle – et l'abandonne hébétée, le regard figé sur le Rien [p. 76] ... Nous sommes nés en état d'expectative – peu important nos croyances: nous attendons la plénitude et nous ne pouvons vivre sans elle [p. 81].'

63. Of course, the fundamental irony in Beckett's treatment of this negative theology is that even if one succeeds in suspending one's own interfering will, one is still prevented from attaining the silence of non-being since there are always *other* voices to speak and name us: 'Feeling nothing, knowing nothing, he exists nevertheless, but not for himself, for *others*, others conceive him and say, Worm is, since we conceive him, as if there could be no being but being conceived ... One alone turned towards the all-important, all-nescient, that haunts him, then *others*.' The Beckettian purgation of the Unnamable differs from the biblical purgation of Job in that it is without issue. Unlike Eliot's fideistic assurances in *Four Quartets* that our salvation lies in the 'rigid purgatorial fires of which the flame is roses and the smoke is briars,' Beckett's purgatory is endless, its roses and smoke devoid of mystical redemption: 'They mentioned roses. I'll smell them before I'm finished. Then they'll put the accent on the thorns. What prodigious variety: the thorns they'll have to come and stick into me, as into their unfortunate Jesus. No, I need nobody, they'll stand sprouting under my arse, unaided ...' And so the narrator of *The Unnamable* concludes with the horrifying supposition *à la* Hamlet that even the silence of death will be tormented by dreams, by further words: 'Perhaps it's all a dream ... I'd wake in the silence and never sleep again ... dream of a silence, a dream silence, full of murmurs, I don't know.' And not knowing, and knowing that he'll never know, he simply vows to go on without end. 'I'll go on, you must say words, as long as there are any, until they find me, until they say me, strange pain, strange sin, you must go on ...'.

64. Cf. Mercier, *Beckett/Beckett*, p. 167: 'I find two dominant philosophical patterns in *Watt*: one ontological, the other epistemological. Watt at Mr Knott's house experiences, however dimly, both the difference between being and non-being, and the difference between knowing and not-knowing ... The philosopher's quest for "truth" ... is the

comic image that underlies many pages of *Watt* and gives the book whatever unity it possesses.'

65. Onimus, *Beckett*, p. 114.

66. Cf. Coe, *Beckett*, p. 15.

67. Interview with Alan Schneider, 1974, quoted by Mercier, *Beckett/Beckett*, p. 163.

68. Interview with Tom Driver; cf. Onimus, *Beckett*, pp. 178–9.

69. Interview with G. d'Aubarède.

70. Interview with Tom Driver.

71. Cf. On Beckett and Sartre: Levy, *Beckett*, pp. 87, 127;. Pilling, *Samuel Beckett*, p. 129; V. Mercier, *Beckett/Beckett*, pp. 84, 161. Sartre himself has adverted to his common cause with Beckett as a dramatist of 'scandal' aiming at a 'decentralisation of the subject' (cf. Jean Paul Sartre, *Politics and Literature* [Calder Press 1973], pp. 63, 66). Sartre's description of the modernist movement in literature is also particularly relevant to Beckett: 'It pushed contestation to the limit, even to the point of contesting itself; it gives us a glimpse of silence beyond the massacre of words ... it invites us to emerge into nothingness by destruction of all myths and all scales of value; it discloses in man a close and secret relation to the nothing.' (Jean Paul Sartre, *Literature and Existentialism* [Citadel Press 1969], p. 146).

72. Onimus, *Beckett*, p. 88.

73. Martin Heidegger, *What is Metaphysics?* trans. W. Brock, in *Existence and Being* (Vision Press 1949), pp. 368–69. On the relationship between Beckett's writing and existentialist phenomenology see Eugene F. Kaelin, *The Unhappy Consciousness: The Poetic Flight of Samuel Beckett. An Inquiry at the Intersection of Phenomenology and Literature* (D. Reidel Publishing 1981).

74. Beckett, *Proust*, p. 47

75. Pilling, *Samuel Beckett*, p. 22 citing interviews with L.E. Harvey, 1962, and interview with Tom Driver.

76. Beckett's leanings towards the existentialist philosophy of the absurd were certainly nurtured by his reading in the early thirties of Nietzsche and Schopenhauer, two progenitors of modern existentialism. Nietzsche's declaration that 'God is dead' and that the world is really an 'eternal return of the same', and absurd and nihilistic repetition, had a profound impact on Beckett; he also appears to have been deeply attracted by Schopenhauer's pessimistic doctrine that wisdom only comes when we accept that there is 'no will: no idea, no world ... only nothingness'. Language itself, Schopenhauer believed, is condemned to nothingness and can aspire to 'being' only by going beyond words towards the mystical condition of music. It is perhaps no accident that both Beckett's *Murphy* and Sartre's *Nausea* culminate with an invocation of the *being* of music beyond the absurd nothingness of words.

77. Interview with Alan Schneider.

78. Beckett, *Watt*, p. 146.

79. Beckett, *Proust*, p. 16.

80. Beckett, *Watt*, p. 53. On Beckett's humour see Deyle, *Samuel Beckett*, pp. 75–8.

81. Beckett, *More Pricks than Kicks* (Chatto and Windus 1934), p. 236. This comic stoicism is also typified by Malone's routine cultivation of potted plants in his dark and airless basement even though he knows their survival is against all the odds.

82. Bair, *Samuel Beckett*, p. 90; Pilling, *Samuel Beckett*, pp. 126–9.

83. Beckett, *Watt*, p. 250.

84. *Ibid.* pp. 88–9.

85. Watt soon recognizes the 'odd error' of trying to discover 'what things were in reality' (Beckett, *Watt*, p. 250). Beckett may be thinking here of Leibniz's famous attempt to establish an ideal alphabet – *caracteristica universalis* – that might englobe all of reality, or of the logical positivist formulation of an equally foolproof *Begriffschrift* advanced by Frege and the early Wittgenstein. I refer the reader here to Coe's excellent analysis of Watt as 'a living incarnation of the theories of Fritz Mauthner and of Ludwig Wittgenstein' (*Beckett*, pp. 39–45). As Coe observes, 'Watt is the first incarnation of what is to be

one of the primary themes of Beckett's later work: the failure of man, in his search for the significance of either himself or of the cosmos, to penetrate the barrier of language' (p. 41). Cf. also Levy, *Beckett*, pp. 27, 33.

86. Jacques Derrida, *La Voix et le Phénomène* (Presses Universitaries de France 1967), translated by D.B. Alison as *Speech and Phenomena* (Northwestern University Press 1973); as Derrida explains, 'The prerogative of Being cannot withstand the deconstruction of the word' (p. 74).

87. Derrida, 'La mythologie blanche,' *Marges de la philosophie* (Editions de Minuit 1972), pp. 247 ff. Derrida bases his argument that the deconstruction of the metaphysical notion of language as a metaphorizing transcendence from absence to presence, on Heidegger's doctrine that 'the metaphorical exists only within the metaphysical.' Cf. P. Ricoeur's lucid critique of this Heidegger-Derrida thesis in 'La méta-phore et la méta-physique' in his *La Métaphore Vive*, translated by R. Czerny as *The Rule of Metaphor* (University of Toronto Press 1977), pp. 280 ff.; for a more detailed analysis of the motifs of metaphor and palimpsest in Beckett see my 'Myth and motherland', *Field Day*, 5 (1984).

88. Thus Beckett debunks our habitual approach to language as a representational 'expression' (*Ausdruck*) of some self-present subject and reveals it as a perpetually self-deferring 'signification' (*Anzeigen*) irreducible to presence. 'All speech,' Derrida contends, 'which does not restore the immediate presence of the signified content, is inexpressive ... all these "goings-forth" effectively exile this life of self-presence in signification. We know that signification ... is the process of death at work in signs' (Derrida, *La Voix et le Phénomène* , trans. Alison, p. 40). The temporality of signification cannot be reduced to the expression of a self-identical subject 'precisely because it cannot be conceived on the basis of a present or the self-presence of a present being; time defers the presence of self to self *ad infinitum,* which means that 'my death is structurally necessary to the pronouncing of the I' (p. 86). Accordingly, 'only a relation to my death could make the infinite differing of presence appear' (p. 102). Elsewhere, Derrida is even more explicit on this point: 'Constituting and dislcoating it at the same time, writing is other than the subject ... Writing can never be thought under the category of the subject ... And the original absence of the subject of writing is also the absence of the thing or the referent' (Derrida, *Of Grammatology* [Baltimore; London: Johns Hopkins University Press 1976], pp. 68–9). It is not difficult to see the relevance of Derrida's analysis to the life/death, absence/presence dilemma of the Beckettian narrator.

89. It is remarkable how close Beckett is here to Heidegger's doctrine that the subject is not the master but the servant of language (e.g. 'man is the shepherd of language', *Humanismusbrief,* 1949), or to Lévi-Strauss's theory that language is not an 'epistemology' enabling the subject to know truth but a 'mythology' which dispenses with the subject as a magisterial author: 'les mythes n'ont pas d'auteur ... ce n'est pas l'homme qui pense les mythes mais les mythes qui se pensent dans l'homme' (*Mythologiques*, vol. 1 [1964]). 'I'm in word, made of words, other's words,' howls Beckett's unnamable narrator, 'I'm all these words, all these strangers, this dust of words with no ground for their settling.' And as Beckett thus dissolves and ruptures the 'I' into a 'bloody flux' of words, he significantly compares the writer to both a Prometheus and a Job (Worm) beholden to the anonymous voices of language; in choosing these two examples Beckett is perhaps inferring that the tragic comedy of language is inscribed into the two traditions of Western civilisation – Hellenic and Hebraic. One is also reminded of the affinity between Beckett's attempt to 'deanthropomorphise' the subject through language (Bair, *Samuel Beckett*, p. 191) and Michel Foucault's theory of the 'deanthropologising' role of language in the twentieth century (*The Order of Things* [Random House 1973]); Foucault argues that while in the Renaissance *things resemble things*, and in the classical age and nineteenth century *words represent things*, in the twentieth century *words speak themselves* (with no reference to things or ideas beyond themselves) thus undoing the habitual notion of man as the centre of language. Lastly, one might mention the relevance of another French thinker of Beckett's generation, Maurice Blanchot, who holds that language has become a neutral, impersonal,

interminable voice that expresses itself in modern literature as an 'enigmatic space of repetition' (see *L'entretien infini* [Gallimard 1969], particularly p. 504 where Blanchot speaks explicitly of Beckett). In short, all these contemporary thinkers, including Derrida, share Beckett's determination to expose the *logos* of language as a mere *mythos*, an endgame heralding not only the 'end of philosophy' and the 'end of the subject' but also 'the end of history' as we have known it.

– Chapter Thirteen –
A Crisis of Fiction: Flann O'Brien, Francis Stuart, John Banville

This is a revised version of an essay that first appeared in The Crane Bag, *edtied by Richard Kearney and M.P. Hederman, 3, 1 (1979).*

1. See in particular Brian Moore's *Answer From Limbo* and John McGahern's *Leavetaking*, both of which exemplify aspects of critical 'self-consciousness' and 'self-reflexivity'. I discuss the latter in my article 'The crisis of imagination', *The Crane Bag*, vol. 3, no. 1, (1979), pp. 64–6; reprinted in M.P. Hederman and R. Kearney (eds), *The Crane Bag Book of Irish Studies* (Blackwater Press 1982).
2. See Fintan O'Toole, 'Going west: The country versus the city in Irish writing', *The Crane Bag*, vol. 9, no. 2 (1985).
3. See Rudiger Imhof (ed.), *Alive Alive O: Flann O'Brien's At Swim-Two-Birds* (Wolfhound Press 1985), and Tess Harson's 'The making of a good wake', *The Sunday Tribune* (8 December 1985).
4. M.H. Abrams, *A Glossary of Literature* (New York; London: Holt, Rinehart and Winston 1981), p. 114, quoted by Anthony Curtis in 'An essay on the novels of Brian O'Nolan' (unpublished). Curtis describes O'Nolan appropriately, as a 'reluctant modernist … a home based exile of vast polarities and firm dichotomies'. Curtis argues that O'Nolan/O'Brien shared with Beckett and Joyce an uncanny ability for 'literary punning, distorted autobiography (use of persona), satire, exaggeration and expansive imagination'. I am much indebted to Curtis' analysis.
5. Roland Barthes, 'The death of the author' in *Image-Music-Text* (Fontana 1977). See also Tony Tanner, 'Thomas Pynchon and the death of the author' in *Thomas Pynchon* (Methuen 1982).
6. 'Novelists on the novel' (an interview with Francis Stuart and John Banville by Ronan Sheehan), *The Crane Bag*, vol. 3, no. 1 (1979), pp. 76–84. See also Stuart's article on 'Literature and Politics', *The Crane Bag*, vol. 1, no. 1 (1977), pp. 72–6. (Both are reprinted in M.P. Hederman and R. Kearney (eds), *Crane Bag Book*).
7. *Ibid.* p. 80.
8. 'Novelists on the novel', *The Crane Bag*, vol. 3, no. 1 (1979), pp. 76–80.
9. *Ibid.* p. 79.
10. 'Sweet harmony' by Francis Stuart in *The Sunday Tribune* (8 February 1981), p. 26.
11. I contrast this analysis of Banville's *The Newton Letter* to Bernard MacLaverty's traditional quest-novel, *Cal*, in a review article entitled 'The nightmare of history', *The Irish Literary Supplement,* vol. 2, no. 2 , 1983, pp. 24–5. See David McCormack, 'John Banville; literature as criticism', *The Irish Review*, 2 (1987).
12. See my analysis of this novel as an example of the 'critical' counter-tradition of the Irish novel in 'The crisis of imagination', *The Crane Bag*, vol. 3, no. 1 (1979), pp. 69–70.
13. John Banville subsequently published *Mefisto* (Secker and Warburg, 1986). It is seen by some as the fourth and final part of a tetralogy on the scientific imagination. Certainly there is a continuity of theme running from the Copernicus, Kepler, Newton series to *Mefisto*: viz. the complex rapport between memory and imagination, history and artifice. Gabriel Swan, the narrator-author, is, like his Proustian prototype, committed to the

retelling of his life-history. The problem for Gabriel however is that 'times past' cannot actually be remembered except through the grid of fictional reinvention. Memory, as a faithful recorder of things as they really happened, is thus transformed into a form of narrative imagination that surpasses the plausible limits of history. When queried about the reality of what he recounts, Gabriel retorts: 'It's what I remember, what does it matter whether it's possible or not?' The act of fiction, as storytelling, repeatedly comments upon its own fictitiousness – as when having described a nun with a head-dress and ledger, the narrator self-consciously confesses: 'No, there was no nun. I invented her.' In *Mefisto*, as in his preceding triad of novels on the scientific imagination, Banville endeavours to deconstruct the accredited distinction between scientific fact and poetic invention. And yet he remains wholly aware of the vexed nature of such a deconstruction. If *Mefisto* is the guiding spirit of the modern Faustian project to invent a new order of creation, he is also an emblem of demonic destruction. Banville leaves the precise identity of his contemporary Mefisto suitably undecided.

– Chapter Fourteen –
Heaney and Homecoming

This is a revised version of a chapter that appeared in the author's Transitions: Narratives in Modern Irish Culture *(Wolfhound Press/St Martins Press 1988).*

1. Frank O'Connor, *The Backward Look* (Macmillan 1970). For an informed critical discussion of this revivalist reading of Heaney see Mark P. Hederman, 'Seamus Heaney: the reluctant poet', *The Crane Bag*, vol. 3, no. 2 (1979), pp. 61–71; Blake Morrison, *Seamus Heaney*, (Methuen, 1982); Tony Curtis (ed.), *The Art of Seamus Heaney* (Poetry Wales Press 1982); Edna Longley, 'Stars and horses, pigs and trees', *The Crane Bag*, vol. 3, no. 2 (1979), pp. 54–60, and 'Poetry and politics in Northern Ireland', *The Crane Bag*, vol. 9, no. 1 (1985), pp. 26–41; Timothy Kearney, 'The poetry of the North: a post-modernist perspective', *The Crane Bag*, vol. 3, no. 2 (1979), pp. 45–54; and finally Maurice Riordan, 'Eros and history: on contemporary Irish poetry' in *The Crane Bag*, vol. 9, no. 1 (1985), pp. 49–56. The last of these essays offers perhaps the most explicit critique of the 'mythologizing impulse' in Heaney's work. Riordan gives a historical interpretation of this impulse as a carry-over from the aesthetic of the Irish Literary Revival. In accordance with political efforts to establish Ireland as a nation with a distinct identity, Irish poets, Riordan argues, have frequently sought to 'restore to the national imagination an image of the greatness of the past'. This 'mythologizing tendency', he claims, 'has persisted in Irish poetry, though perhaps its explicit political-ideological function has diminished'. The basic motivation remains largely that of evoking the 'spirit of Ireland as a sustaining power, usually in the form of a goddess who is bride of the poet's imagination'. Riordan links this motivation to the historical fact that the writers of the Revival 'drew their force from the ideological preparation for a patricide ... a colonial patriarchy is rejected for the sake of the motherland'. Relating this theme to the powerful poetic motif of Cathleen Ni Houlihan, Riordan observes that 'the glimpse of, the desire for, an originary amplitude and innocence is bodied forth in a myth of Ireland as an exalted entity – to be reverenced and known, and, above all, to be reclaimed by her royal sons and heirs'. Riordan concludes that Heaney's poetry conforms to this basic traditional aesthetic of re-fusing history in forms of myth: 'it opposes to the usurping historical characters, a mythological entity ... as if to suggest that history were the intruder'. And even where Heaney's poetry does not ignore history, it is 'hard pressed by it ... its summons is to be the sacred ground beyond history. It is nostalgic and melancholic, sporadically ecstatic, in its hunt for lost origins, for the lost site of bliss, where the self would feel its wholeness and potency. It is, in a word, Rousseauistic, a nationalistic mutation of romanticism'.

Against this mythologizing nostalgia, Riordan advocates a modern Irish poetry 'prepared to embrace the varied adventure of its becoming, the gay responsibility of making, rather than remaking, history'. I will argue that a modernist or postmodernist reading of Heaney's work exposes an irony and ambiguity in his approach to mythology; and that this approach, far from being a Rousseauistic nationalism or Romanticism, does succeed in *making* rather than simply *remaking* history – the two options being, in the final analysis, inseparable.

2. Terence Brown discussing C. Curtin, M. Kelly and C. O'Dowd (eds), *Culture and Ideology in Ireland* (Galway University Press 1984) in *The Crane Bag*. vol. 9, no. 1 (1985), p. 90.

3. Jim Kemmy, *New Hibernia* (November 1984).

4. Seamus Heaney, *Preoccupations: Selected Prose 1968–1978* (Faber and Faber 1980), p. 52.

5. Heaney, *Preoccupations*, pp. 17–20.

6. *Ibid.* p. 55.

7. Michel Foucault, *Language, Counter-Memory and Practice* (1977).

8. Heaney, *Preoccupations*, p. 56.

9. *Ibid.* p. 57.

10. Seamus Heaney in an interview with Seamus Deane, 'Unhappy and at home', *The Crane Bag*, vol. 1, no. 1 (1977), p. 63; and in M.P. Hederman and R. Kearney (eds), *The Crane Bag Book of Irish Studies* (Blackwater Press 1982).

11. Heaney, *Preoccupations*, p. 57. Another major source for Heaney's bog poems was Anne Ross's study, *The Religion of the Pagan Celts*, in which the author identifies the emblem of the severed human head as a 'kind of short-hand symbol for the entire religious outlook of the pagan Celts' (p. 59). Indeed this Celtic motif of the severed head was also to provide the Irish painter and friend of Heaney – Louis le Brocquy – with the predom-inant theme for his 'head series' (of Joyce, Beckett and others) in the seventies and eighties. Le Brocquy claims that the severed 'human head, the mysterious box which contains the spirit, consciousness', is the 'deepest and most persistent of all Celtic images' ('A painter's notes on awareness' in *The Crane Bag*, vol. 1, no. 2 (1977). Numerous schol-arly researches have been conducted on this bizarre head cult of the Celts pointing up its sacrificial import. Of particular note is the study by the French anthropologist, Clémence Ramnoux, entitled *La mort sacrificielle du roi* (1954), in which the author docu-ments instances in several Celtic myths of how the tribal communities sought to resolve their periodic crises by resorting to rites of sacrificial bloodletting (*La mort sacrificielle du roi in Ogham,* tradition Celtique, 1954). And it is not difficult to adduce more contem-porary examples of this cult of sacrificial martyrdom in the recent history of Irish repub-licanism (See chapter 3 of this book, 'Myth and Martyrdom').

12. Heaney, *Preoccupations*, p. 58.

13. In 'Funeral Rites', Heaney sees the burial tombs of the Boyne – Knowth, Dowth and Newgrange – as offering the possibility of a tribal home for his 'dead relations'. The Boyne Valley mounds were considered legendarily to be at once the *omphalos* of the earth – its *axis mundi* – and the sacred centre of Ireland itself: the valley is situated in Meath, in Gaelic *Midhe* or middle.

14. When another poetic persona, Friel's Frank Hardy in *Faith Healer* 'returns' home in a literal sense, he discovers that such homecoming entails his own destruction. Heaney's paradoxical response to the 'terrible beauty' of the ancestral cults of blood-sacrifice is nowhere more poignantly expressed, however, than in a poem called 'Punishment', when he compares the ancient ritual practice of sacrificing young maidens to tribal deities by drowning them in bogs to the contemporary Ulster rite of tarring and shaving girls who have associated with the enemy:

> My poor scapegoat,
> I almost love you
> But would have cast, I know,
> the stones of silence ...

Who would connive
In civilised outrage
Yet understand the exact
And tribal, intimate revenge.

In a poem called 'Strange Fruit', which immediately follows 'Punishment' in *North*, Heaney adapts the anti-lynching elegy of Billie Holiday, to repudiate his own reaction to tribal revenge: 'Murdered, forgotten, nameless, terrible/Beheaded girl, outstaring axe/And beatification, outstaring/What had begun to feel like reverence'.

15. Heaney, *Preoccupations*, p. 35.
16. *Ibid.* p. 37.
17. Jacques Lacan, *Ecrits* (Éditions du Seuil 1966).
18. Heaney, *Preoccupations*, p. 78; see Blake Morrison's analysis of the theme of 'silence' in Heaney's poetry in *Seamus Heaney* (Methuen, 1983).
19. This characteristic tension in Heaney's work between the sanctity of home and the scepticism of homelessness is perceptively summed up by his fellow northerner Seamus Deane: 'The poet turns, entering into conversations with his family, his friends, his dead, his various personae ... asking for manumission from his enslavement to reverence, and fearful that it will be granted. As always with Heaney, there is a paradox here. Even in his caution there is risk, and one of the delights of his poetry is to see the variety of ways in which he can pungently embody the opposing attitudes ... 'a cunning middle voice' learns to negotiate between the known and the foreign, the dialect of the local and the *lingua franca* of the world. Even in berating himself for his caution, he recognizes that he enhances the feeling of veneration for everything that is private, love-worn, ancestral by the very act of suspecting it, of chastening its easily available consolations. On the other hand, this suspicion allows him to bring in the voice of the other, peremptory world of the present, with its political crises and its alien immediacies. *Station Island's* three parts are phases in the intricate debate thus established'. Seamus Deane, 'A noble startling achievement', *The Irish Literary Supplement* (Spring 1985), pp. 1, 34.
20. It might be noted that Heaney's notion of homecoming as an endless circling around an origin that is no-longer or not-yet, an absent centre, a siteless site, is in tune with the basic postmodernist emphasis on cultural discontinuity and heterogeneity – what has been termed the 'crisis in cultural authority' (by Craig Owens in *Postmodern Culture*, edited by H. Foster [Pluto Press 1983], p. 57). Heaney's overriding obsession with idioms of nomadic pilgrimage – while paying passing tribute to Romantic notions of 'sacred contemporaneity' (the cultural project of uniting past and present in some quasi-mystical epiphany) – also works in the opposite direction: his poems often serve as ironic self-parodies of the orthodox Irish cultural aesthetic, with its concern to retrieve a sacred, mythic motherland. Yet Heaney is equally determined to avoid the modernist cult of aesthetic individualism. Here one finds certain parallels with the postmodern philosophy of Derrida and Foucault, the postmodern literature of Ashbery and Pynchon, or the postmodern cinema of Wenders – in particular the self-parodying homecoming motifs of *Paris, Texas*. Like Travis in *Paris, Texas*, Heaney's poetic *personae* carry with them faded photographic memories of their ancestral origins (the film's title refers to a plot of land in Paris, Texas, where Travis was conceived), but never succeed in returning home. The very quest for the lost origin is the very impossibility of ever arriving there. We have here a poetics of perpetual detour – perhaps the most signal feature of Heaney's contemporary journeywork.
21. Freud, 'The Uncanny', *New Literary History*, vol. VII, no. 3 (1976), p. 623.
22. See in particular the commentary of Freud's essay by Hélène Cixous, 'Fiction and its phantoms', *New Literary History*, no. 7, (1976), pp. 525–48.
23. Freud, 'The Uncanny', p. 622.
24. *Ibid.* p. 624.
25. *Ibid.* p. 630.

26. *Ibid.* p. 631.
27. *Ibid.* p. 634.
28. *Ibid.* p. 635.
29. Freud also offers the following personal example of his experience of the 'uncanny' as a 'repetition of the same thing': 'As I was walking one hot summer afternoon through the deserted streets of a provincial town in Italy which was unknown to me, I found myself in a quarter of whose character I could not long remain in doubt. Nothing but painted women were to be seen at the windows of the small houses, and I hastened to leave the narrow street at the next turning. But after having wandered about for a time without enquiring I suddenly found myself back in the same street, where my presence was now beginning to excite attention. I hurried away once more only to arrive by another detour at the same place yet a third time. Now, however, a feeling overcame me which I can only describe as uncanny ... Other situations which have in common with my adventure an unintended recurrence of the same situation, but which differ radically from it in other respects, also result in the same feeling of helplessness and of uncanniness' (*ibid.* p. 631).
30. Heaney, *Preoccupations*, p. 20.
31. *Ibid.* p. 212.
32. *Ibid.* pp. 47–8.
33. It is useful to recall, in this regard, that in the original Greek myth, Narcissus was not seen as a victim of his own egoism, but as an emancipator of the aesthetic potencies of both nature and his own creative eros. Herbert Marcuse puts this point well in his *Eros and Civilisation*: 'The spring and the forest respond to Narcissus' desire ... Narcissistic Eros awakens and liberates potentialities that are real in things animate and inanimate, in organic and inorganic nature – real but in the un-erotic reality suppressed ... In the Narcissistic experience of the world ... the opposition between man and nature, subject and object, is overcome. Being is experienced as gratification, which unites man and nature so that the fulfilment of man is at the same time fulfilment, without violence of nature. In being spoken to, loved, and cared for, flowers and springs and animals appear as what they are – beautiful ... the things of nature become free to be what they are' (Herbert Marcuse, *Eros and Civilisation* [Beacon Press 1955], pp. 165–6). In 'Eros and history', Maurice Riordan offers the following controversial account of the relation between sexuality and poetry in modern Irish literature: 'The sexual relationship between the poet and his subject, moreover, is not incidental or merely a conceit; on the contrary, the poet frequently uses erotic language when broaching such subjects as cultural identity, history or landscape. It is surely strange that eroticism should arise at all in relation to such subjects; that it should do so consistently seems to imply not just the political incompleteness of the nationalist revolution, but a psychological incompleteness as well (...) Heaney's poetry carries this eroticisation of the landscape a step further ... enacting an identity between the psyche and landscape. (Heaney's bog poems) draw up their exotic strange fruit from the bog; the deeds of men are restored to light in an assuaging rhetoric, in the voluptuous auto-erotic ease of a language that flows in vowel and consonant over tongue and tooth'. (pp. 49, 54).
34. Heaney, *Preoccupations*, p. 35.
35. *Ibid.* p. 132.
36. Heaney, 'An open letter', *Field Day* (1983).
37. Heidegger, *Being and Time* (1927), para. 40.
38. *Ibid.*
39. Heidegger, *Poetry, Language, Thought*, trans. A. Hofstadter (Harper and Row 1971), p. 91 ff.
40. *Ibid.*; see also Heidegger, *Introduction to Metaphysics* (1973), pp. 127 ff., and *Commentaries on Hölderlin* (1971), pp. 23–31.
41. Heidegger, *Commentaries on Hölderlin*. But we should not forget that for Heaney, as for Heidegger, there is also a *positive* side to the religious and mythological dimensions of poetry. The poet names what is holy, according to Heidegger, in the measure that he

seeks to relocate things in the ontological play of the world's fourfold – earth, sky, mortals and gods. Heaney makes a similar point, I suggest, when he contends that poetry aspires towards a 'sacramental apprehension of things' (*Preoccupations*, p. 90). Such an apprehension does not serve to reinforce some racist cult of ancestral supermen; it works in the opposite direction to forestall any such fascist deification of a pure, preoriginal race by enabling us to come to terms with our unconscious atavisms and thereby transform them. It demystifies the past in order to preserve its essential mystery for the present. Hence, rather than incarcerating us in the old myths of superstition and bigotry, it strains to renew myth into a liberating dimension of experience. This is surely what Heaney intends when he ratifies Patmore's maxim that 'the end of art is peace'. And this is also why Heaney's poetic reworking of local idioms – e.g. place names – assumes a significance that extends beyond the locale itself. Without such a reformation of his communal, national or cultural origins it is hard to imagine how Heaney's work could have communicated so effectively to other nations and cultures – the Anglo-American in particular. Heaney's foregrounding of the sacramental dimension of poetry is to be understood, therefore, not in the sense of some triumphalist bigotry that would sacrifice the humble things of this earth for the sake of an otherworldly kingdom in the future or an antediluvian golden age in the past. For Heaney to say that poetry can have a sacramental role is to say that it can help restore things to their sacred uniqueness in the present play of the world's fourfold dimensions. In an essay on art, Heidegger disclosed the way in which a simple jug could poetically re-enact this cosmic play. In *Station Island,* Section x, Heaney evokes this same restorative power of the *logos* – the play of language as a language of play. The poet writes here of an inconspicuous mug that had remained on a shelf in his home for many years, 'unchallenging and unremembered', no more significant that the 'thud of earthenware on the common table'; 'still as a milestone' – by two actors who borrowed it as a prop for a play. Beholding the actors as lovers on a stage kissing the mug and calling it their 'loving cup', the poet feels estranged from his domestic possession for the first time. But by the same token, by means of this very estrangement, he also sees the mug in all its strangeness for the first time – translated and redeemed, as it were, by the language of play:

> Dipped and glamoured from this translation
> It was restored with all its cornflower haze
> Still dozing, its parchment glazes fast –
> As the other surfaced once with Ronan's psalter
> Miraculously unharmed, that had been lost
> A day and a night under lough water.
> And so the saint praised God on the lough shore.
> The dazzle of the impossible suddenly
> Blazed across the threshold, a sun-glare
> To put out the small hearths of constancy.

This poem could be interpreted in Heideggerean terms as a translation of the unholy into the holy. The poet's act of remembrance would be understood as releasing the mug from its inauthentic existence as an anonymous object amongst objects into its own authentic 'inscape' as a play of the fourfold. The poem would then be seen as bringing together the habitually opposed claims of earth (the earthenware on the common table) and sky (the blue-eyed haze and the sun's glare), mortals (the transfiguring act of the players) and gods (the saint's celebration of the divine miracle). In this way, the creative re-play of actor and poet can be construed as liberating the mug from its familiar home into the *unheimlich* dimension, which allows it to be restored to its unfamiliar, because forgotten, home – 'it reappeared ... back in its place'. In other words, by entering the play of the poetic *logos*, the mug undergoes a sea-change into something strange and precious; it is allowed poetically to dwell.

Section x of the *Station Island* sequence exemplifies in a concrete and unpretentious manner the main sacramental attributes of poetic language as outlined by Heidegger – remembrance, homecoming, the naming of the Holy, the piety of thinking, the presencing of the strange and the play of the fourfold. The ultimate end of such poetic language is peace. Not just the private ease of the poet, but the well-being of the entire community. For the final aim of poetry is, Heaney insists, 'to be of service, to ply the effort of the individual work into the larger work of the community as a whole' (*Preoccupations*, p. 106).

42. Heidegger, *Commentaries on Hölderlin*.

43. Hence the curious fact that the 'joy' of homecoming is at all times tempered by 'serenity'. If, therefore, Heidegger speaks of poetry allowing us to come home, he means it not in the sense of some triumphalistic revival of the past (*Heimkunft*), but rather in the sense of an arriving that can never finally arrive: a perpetual arriving (*Heimkommen*) that preserves itself in the serene expectancy of an advent (*Ankunft*). Moreover, this problem is not confined to the individual consciousness of the poet. The poet cannot inaugurate a homecoming by himself; he needs others to listen to his language as a caring for the hidden dimensions of Being, and to take the burden of that caring upon themselves. 'Once spoken, the word slips away from the guardianship of the caring poet', affirms Heidegger, 'and so the poet must turn to the others, so that their remembrance can help the poetic word be understood, with the result that the homecoming self-appropriately transpires for each in his destined way' (*Commentaries on Hölderlin*). Poetry thus reveals itself as a *social* as well as *aesthetic* responsibility. And the fact that it informs society with scruples of care, serenity and anxiety ensures that all revivalist assumptions that 'home' is some pre-existing, secure tenure are exploded.

44. In contradistinction, therefore, to an exclusively utilitarian view of language, poetic thinking allows the beauty and originality of language to come to light as it is in itself. Rather than deploying words as mere instruments or strategies, the poet invites us to dwell in language by listening to it speak. He dares language to be itself. Silence thus reveals itself as an essential dimension of language in so far as it resists all possibility of objectification. Though we can use language to objectify things in words, the Being of language itself can never be objectified in words. And this is why it is often when words fail us, when language withholds itself in silence, that we are compelled to break off our total preoccupation with things and attend to language itself as that which allows things to be in the first place. 'Where is language itself brought to word?' asks Heidegger. 'Strangely enough, there where we cannot find the right word for something which concerns us ... Thus, we let that which we mean or intend acquiesce or rest in the unspoken and thereby, without properly reflecting about it, pass through moments in which language itself has touched us, fleetingly and from afar, with its presencing' (*On The Way to Language*, 1971).

45. Heidegger, *On the Way to Language*, p. 152. See also L. M. Vail, *Heidegger and The Ontological Difference* (1972), pp. 169 ff.

46. Heidegger, *Poetry, Language, Thought*, p. 226. In a study entitled 'Language in the Poem', Heidegger expands his analysis of 'homecoming' as poetic estrangement in a commentary on Georg Trakl's verse, 'Something strange is the soul on the earth'. He makes quite clear that he understands the term 'strange' (*fremd*), not in the sense of occult escapism, but as a concrete existential experience open to all human beings who specifically seek to dwell poetically in the innermost, and for that reason frequently unknown, being of things: 'The word we are using – the German *'fremd'* ... really means – forward to somewhere else, underway toward – onward to the encounter with what is kept in store for it. The strange goes forth, ahead. But it does not roam aimlessly, without any kind of determination. The strange element goes in its search toward the site where it may stay in its wandering. Almost unknown to itself, the 'strange' is already following the call that calls it on the way into its own. The poet calls the soul 'something strange on the earth'. The earth is that very place which the soul's wandering could not reach so far. The soul only *seeks* the earth; it does not flee from it. This fulfils the soul's being: in her wandering

to seek the earth so that she may poetically build and dwell upon it, and thus may be able to save the earth *as* earth (*On the Way to Language*, p. 163). See also Heidegger's analysis of Trakl on 'Language' in *Poetry, Language, Thought*, pp. 187–210; and his analysis of Rilke in 'What are Poets for?' in *Poetry, Language, Thought*, pp. 89–142.

47. All quotations from Celan are from Michael Hamburger's translation *Paul Celan: Poems* (Carcanet 1980).

– Chapter Fifteen –
The Language Plays of Brian Friel

This is a revised version of a chapter that appeared in the author's Transitions: Narratives in Modern Irish Culture *(Wolfhound Press/St Martins Press 1988).*

1. 'The man from God knows where', interview with Brian Friel by Fintan O'Toole, *In Dublin,* no. 165 (October 1982), p. 21.

2. *Ibid.* p. 21.

3. *Ibid.* p. 22.

4. *Ibid.* p. 20.

5. *Ibid.* p. 21. See M.P. Hederman and R. Kearney (eds), *The Crane Bag Book of Irish Studies* (Blackwater Press 1982), pp. 10–12.

6. *Ibid.* p. 23.

7. *Ibid.* p. 23.

8. Heidegger, *Poetry, Language, Thought*, trans. A. Hofstadter (Harper and Row 1971), p. 215 ('Poetically man dwells').

9. *Ibid.* p. 134 ('What are poets for?').

10. Friel's diary entries for 29 May and 1 June 1979, quoted by Richard Pine in *The Diviner: The Art of Brian Friel* (The Lilliput Press 1988).

11. O'Toole, 'Man from God knows where', p. 22.

12. *Ibid.* p. 22.

13. Quoted by Pine, *Diviner.*

14. Quoted by Pine, *Diviner.*

15. O'Toole, 'Man from God knows where', p. 23.

16. *Complete Works of Oscar Wilde* (Collins 1949), p. 1023.

17. T. Kilroy, 'Anglo-Irish playwrights and the comic tradition', *The Crane Bag,* vol. 3, no. 2 (1979).

18. Interview with Tom Mac Intyre by Ciaran Carty in 'Arts Tribune', *The Sunday Tribune* (8 September 1985).

19. *Dialogue* by Ciaran Carty, Arts Page, *Sunday Independent* (24 October 1982).

20. D. McKenna, 'Word and flesh: A view of theatre as performance' , *The Crane Bag,* vol. 6., no. 1 (1982).

21. Brian McEvera in *Fortnight* Magazine, no. 215 (March 1985), pp. 19–21.

22. Edna Longley, 'Poetry and politics in Northern Ireland' in *Contemporary Cultural Debate, The Crane Bag,* vol. 9, no. 1 (1985), p. 28.

23. John Wilson Foster, 'The landscape of the Planter and the Gael', *Canadian Journal of Irish Studies,* vol. 1, no. 2 (November 1975), quoted in Longley, 'Poetry and politics'.

24. Longley, 'Poetry and politics', p. 29.

25. John Andrews and Brian Friel, '*Translations* and *A Paper Landscape:* Between fiction and history' (with a preface by Kevin Barry), *The Forum Issue of The Crane Bag,* vol. 7, no. 2 (1983), pp. 118–25.

26. Heidegger, *Poetry, Language, Thought*, p. 226 ('Poetically Man Dwells').

27. In part III of the *Essay*, entitled 'Words of language in general', Locke used his 'historical,

plain method' of empiricist rationalism in order to overcome the artifice, fallacy … and cheat of words' (III, x) caused by the traditional notions of a natural or ontological language, and to replace it with a pragmatic interpretation of language based on the commonsense correlation of words with empirical sensations. 'All words', Locke argued, 'are taken from the operations of sensible things' (III, I). He maintained that these operations were best appreciated by 'those minds the study of mathematics has opened' (Locke, *Works*, vol. VIII). Language can be exploited in the domination of the *logos* of Being by the logic of science, for 'the making of *Species* and *Genera* is in order to generalise names' (III, VI). Locke wished to abolish the confusion of uncertainty spawned by mystical or metaphysical doctrines of language (e.g. Boehme's belief in the 'signatures of things', the 'language of nature … which is a secret, a mystery granted by the grace of God'). He promoted instead a *conventionalist* theory of naming, which argues that there is no essential or intrinsic relationship between being and words, only an arbitrary rapport *imposed* by men for reasons of ease, order, efficacy and utility – what he called 'the improvement of understanding'. Rejecting all ontological models of naming in favour of a representational model, Locke insisted that 'the same liberty also, that Adam had of affixing any new name to any Idea, the same has one still … But in communication with others, it is necessary, that we conform the ideas (i.e. common sensible ideas) we make the Vulgar Words of any language stand for, to their known proper significations, or else to make known what new signification we apply to them' (III, v). 'The signification of sounds', Locke affirms accordingly, 'is not natural, but only imposed and arbitrary' (III, IV). Locke's exclusive emphasis on scientific objectivity compelled him to jettison the ancient doctrine that some etymological alliance could obtain between language and nature; he had no time for the etymologist's reverence for language as a remembrance of the hidden *origins* of meaning or community (See Hans Aarsleff, *From Locke to Saussure, Essays on the Study of Language and Intellectual History, Athlone* [London Athlone 1982], pp. 66–9, 82–3). For Locke, language was merely a tool for the attainment of certain and certifiable knowledge. Words were legitimate in so far as they were useful and useful in so far as they enabled men to 'range (things) into sorts, in order of their naming, for the convenience of comprehensive signs … so that we may truly say, such a manner of sorting things is the Workmanship of Men' (III, VI). Speaking of how such Enlightenment positivism serves to reduce man's rich sense of temporal and historical being to a manageable 'picture', William Spanos, the Heideggerean critic, talks appositely of 'a flattened out, static and homogeneous Euclidean space – a totalised and ontologically depthless system of referents (a *map*) – if the objectifying consciousness is positivistic …' (See V. Leitch, *Deconstructive Criticism* [Hutchinson University Library 1983], p. 74).

28. *Anthropologie Structurale* (Plon 1958); see also John Sturrock (ed.), *Structuralism and Since* (Oxford University Press 1979).

– *Chapter Sixteen* –
Tom Murphy's Long Night's Journey into Night

This is a revised version of a chapter that appeared in the author's Transitions: Narratives in Modern Irish Culture *(Wolfhound Press/St Martins Press 1988).*

1. Cf. Tom Murphy, *Collected Plays*, vol. I (Gallery Books 1983).
2. See my article on 'Language play: Brian Friel and Ireland's verbal theatre', *Studies* (Spring 1983), pp. 20–56.
3. Christopher Murray, 'The art of Tom Murphy' in the Abbey Theatre Program to *The Gigli Concert* (September 1983). I am also grateful to Murray for several of the above quotations. See also Murray's informative article on Tom Murphy in 'The contemporary Irish writers series', *Ireland Today*, no. 997 (April 1983); and his specially edited issued of

The Irish University Review (Spring 1987) devoted to the work of Tom Murphy. This issue includes very illuminating articles by Fintan O'Toole and Patrick Mason on *The Gigli Concert*.

4. Quoted Fintan O'Toole, 'Going west: The country versus the city in Irish writing', *The Crane Bag*, vol. 9, no. 2 (1985).

5. *Ibid.* Fintan O'Toole offers the following commentary on the central role played by the Abbey Theatre in this revivalist project:

> The notion of the peasant and of the country which the peasant embodied was not a reflection of Irish reality but an artificial literary creation, largely made in Dublin, for Dubliners. It was a political image of the countryside which helped to create a sense of social cohesion in a country which was trying to define itself over against England. Since the Revival centred around the Abbey Theatre it was not enough to simply create peasants of the mind, creatures of the imagination. The Abbey had to literally create a company of peasants to act the peasant plays which made up two thirds of its early repertoire. It had to create an imagined country in the heart of the city. It had to turn Dublin clerks and civil servants into western peasants.

The dramatic transposition of urban to rural life required that modern Dubliners had to be convinced that what they were viewing on the Abbey Stage were *real* peasants (and not simply idealized fictions). And this resulted in the Abbey's use of ultra-naturalistic scenery featuring *real* three-legged stools, creels of turf or spinning wheels beside the fireside. The pretence that the Abbey was a theatre of real peasants in the heart of the city meant that 'for a Dublin audience, which was often no more than a generation removed from the countryside, a visit to the Abbey was a travelogue into its collective past'. But this pretence also served, ironically, to re-enforce certain colonial stereotypes of the Irish peasant as a charming and fanciful Celt, 'a dreamer of dreams' unadulterated by the pressures and exigencies of modern urban existence. By continuing to romanticize the golden age of rural peasantry, the national Literary Revival thus occasionally interiorized, despite itself, the patronizing imperial views of the former British colonizers: 'The charm and naturalness seen by the (Revival) writers in the Irish west is in its turn reproduced as a literary creation and is recognised at the heart of the Empire as the genuine essence of Ireland. The Irish identity which has been 'revived' over and against England is an identity which fits in well with one aspect of colonial paternalism. The Abbey presented itself in such a way as to allow it to be patronised, creating a strong identification between the peasant and childishness, and, for England, an identification between Ireland and childishness ... Their language is the language of the British imperialist talking about the wild savages of the jungle – naive, animal-like, part of the landscape, outside of history – and the fact that it was not seen as such is a mark of how effectively the Revival had nationalised colonial attitudes, internalising a process which belonged to the colonial mentality and selling it back to the outside world as a reflection of Irish reality. The appeal of the peasant-as-child was an appeal to an imagined past, freezing and fossilising the country as an unreal category, a safe and conservative myth'. Fintan O'Toole shows how Tom Murphy's play *Bailegangaire* (1985) serves to parody and subvert such stock revivalist motifs in his review article of the play (Gallery 1986) in *The Irish Review*, 2, 1987.

6. Lecture at the Royal Dublin Society, 1984, quoted by Richard Pine in *The Diviner: The Art of Brian Friel* (The Lilliput Press 1989).

7. Quoted by Claudia Harris in *The Irish Literary Supplement* (Spring 1985), p. 39.

8. Seamus Heaney in an interview with Seamus Deane, 'Unhappy and at home', *The Crane Bag*, vol. 1, no. 1 (1977), p. 63; and in M.P. Hederman and R. Kearney (eds), *The Crane Bag Book of Irish Studies* (Blackwater Press 1982).

9. See my 'Heidegger and the possible', *Philosophical Studies*, vol. XXVII (1980), pp. 176–95;

'Heidegger, le possible et Dieu' in *Heidegger et la question de Dieu*, R. Kearney and J.S. O'Leary (eds) (Grasset 1980), pp. 125–68; and my *Poétique du Possible* (Beauchesne 1984).

10. Perhaps even Murphy's uncompromising defence of the three-hour duration of *The Gigli Concert* against those 'condescending, begrudging' critics (his terms) who recommended it be cut by an hour, itself revealed the author's conviction that the artist is, almost by his very nature, condemned to challenge the conformist expectancies of 'public opinion'. Murphy particularly resented the assumption that plays be written according to a standardized two-hour formula (with time 'for a quick dinner beforehand and a drink afterwards'). The work of art, he retorted, has its own laws of time and space. Of course, Murphy's turbulent relation with his critics is incidental to the nature of his work. But since everything Murphy writes – and *The Gigli Concert* is certainly no exception – is written, after the manner of O'Neill or O'Casey, from the 'blood, sweat and tears' of the author's personally felt experience, this relation is perhaps not altogether irrelevant an analogy for the defiant Murphyesque anti-hero incorrigibly at odds with society. (Moreover, these remarks on Murphy's individualistic repudiation of the collectivity are in no way intended to diminish his fidelity to the theatrical community itself. Directors, actors and audiences have all borne witness to his deep commitment to the communal act of collaboration – be it with the Druid or Abbey companies – which is the hallmark of great drama).

11. Since the completion of this article Murphy wrote *Bailegangaire* (1985) a play which develops many of the themes of *The Gigli Concert* and his early dramas: in particular, the soul destroying constraints of contemporary Irish society and the power of creative fiction and storytelling to conquer in spite of all.

– Chapter Seventeen –
Modern Irish Cinema: Re-viewing Traditions

This is a revised version of a chapter that appeared in the author's Transitions: Narratives in Modern Irish Culture *(Wolfhound Press/St Martins Press 1988).*

1. Kevin Barry, *The Furrow* (1985).
2. John Hill *et al.*, *Cinema and Ireland* (Syracuse University Press 1988), p. 149.
3. *Ibid.* pp. 179–80.
4. *Ibid.* p. 180.
5. *In Dublin*, no. 152.
6. *Ibid.*
7. *Ibid.*
8. Neil Jordan, *Irish Times* interview, 11 May 1982.
9. Barbara O'Connor, 'Aspects of representation of women in Irish film', *The Crane Bag,* vol. 8, no. 2 (1984).
10. *Ibid.*
11. Luke Gibbons, 'Lies that tell the truth: History and Irish cinema', *The Crane Bag,* vol. 7, no. 2 (1983).
12. Philip Marcus, *Standish O'Grady* (Burknell University Press 1970), p. 35.
13. Standish O'Grady, *History of Ireland* (1881).
14. Gibbons, 'Lies that tell the truth'.
15. Interview with Pat Murphy, *Iris* (June 1984).
16. Gibbons, 'Lies that tell the truth'.
17. *Ibid.*

– Chapter Eighteen –
An Art of Otherness: A Study of Louis le Brocquy

This is a revised version of a chapter that appeared in the author's Transitions: Narratives in Modern Irish Culture *(Wolfhound Press / St Martins Press 1988).*

1. Conor Joyce, 'Louis le Brocquy', *Circa*, no. 22 (May/June 1985), p. 32.
2. Louis le Brocquy, 'A painter's notes on ambivalence', *The Crane Bag*, vol. 1, no. 2 (1977), p. 69; reprinted in M.P. Hederman and R. Kearney (eds), *The Crane Bag Book of Irish Studies* (Blackwater Press 1982), p. 152.
3. Le Brocquy, 'A painter's notes on ambivalence'.
4. Louis le Brocquy, 'Notes on painting and awareness' in Dorothy Walker (ed.), *Louis le Brocquy* (Ward River Press 1981), pp. 151–2.
5. Roland Barthes, *Mythologies*; quoted by Denis Donoghue in *The Arts Without Mystery* (BBC 1983), p. 137.
6. Quoted Richard Ellmann, *James Joyce* (New York; Oxford: Oxford University Press 1982), p. 393. As Joyce remarks in *Finnegans Wake*: 'every person, place and thing in the chaosmos of Alle was moving and changing every part of the time'; so that the text constitutes a multiplicity of 'forged palimpsests'.
7. Louis le Brocquy, 'A painter's notes on his Irishness', *The Recorder*, vol. 42 (1981), pp. 24–6.
8. Quoted in Ellmann, *James Joyce*, p. 597.
9. Herbert Marcuse, *The Aesthetic Dimension* (Beacon Press 1978).
10. Le Brocquy, 'Notes on painting and awareness', p. 135.
11. *Ibid.* p. 146.
12. Marcuse, *Aesthetic Dimension*, p. 13.
13. *Ibid.* p. 22. Marcuse's spirited defence of the otherness of art was shared by several of his humanist-Marxist colleagues in the Frankfurt School of Social Research – in particular Adorno and Horkheimer. This defence has been most cogently developed in recent years by the art critic Peter Fuller who has consistently attacked all attempts by both orthodox Marxism and bourgeois conservatism to reduce the aesthetic dimension of art to the utilitarian functions of ideology or consumerism. Further sums up his position in a manifesto entitled 'towards a materialist Aesthetic': 'The aesthetic dimension which I uphold implies the rejection of ... the simplistic equation of art with the so-called technologising ethos of modern times. It calls for the refusal of the visual ideology of contemporary capitalism – the publicity syndrome – which is also frequently evidenced in certain left-wing ideologies of art. This refusal affirms the existence of a reality *other-than-this-one* which I believe is anticipated by the 'aesthetic dimension' which can find expression in authentic painting, sculpture and design'. Peter Fuller, 'Towards a Materialist Aesthetic' in *Penser L'Art Contemporain: Bulletin de la Biennale de Paris*, 1980, p. 158. One might also note here some curious similarities between le Brocquy's paintings and the modern continental philosophies of Heidegger, Merleau-Ponty and Derrida, which attempt to reinstate the alterity and ambivalence of meaning that the logocentric bias of traditional Western thought consigned to oblivion. Logocentrism is to philosophy what classical realism is to art – that is, an attempt to reduce the multiplicity and mystery of being to a single centralizing and controlling perspective (the *logos*). Heidegger seeks to deconstruct this logocentric prejudice of classical thinking, based on the reduction of human experience to a linear non-contradictory consciousness, in order to rediscover the essential strangeness (*Unheimlichkeit*) of Being as a presencing that absences, as a giving (*Es Gibt*) that recedes. Indeed, it is significant that Heidegger looks to modern poets and painters as the best guides or witnesses to this suppressed dimension of ontological otherness. Derrida also urges philosophy to take its 'deconstructive' lead from modern literature and art in its disclosure of the disseminating character of language as an endless play of multiple meaning. And Merleau-Ponty, another exponent of Heideggerian

Destruktion, concludes his celebrated study of paining, *Eye and Mind*, by suggesting that what we call artistic inspiration should be understood as a response to the irreducible ambivalence of being: 'There is truly inspiration and expiration of Being, action and passion so scarcely discernible that one no longer knows what sees and what is seen, what paints and what is painted. One says that a man is born at that instant when that which was but a virtual visibility at the heart of the maternal body makes itself visible for itself and for us. The vision of a painter is a perpetual birth'. Merleau-Ponty, 'Eye and Mind' in John O'Neill (ed.), *Phenomenology, Language and Sociology: Selected Essays of Merleau-Ponty* (Heinemann 1974), pp. 28–312. Le Brocquy's paintings are powerful aesthetic testaments to this dual inspiration and expiration of Being that defy our accredited modes of perception.

14. Marcuse, *Aesthetic Dimension*, pp. 35, 39.
15. Le Brocquy, interview with Harriet Cooke in *The Irish Times,* quoted in Walker (ed.), *Louis le Brocquy*, p. 69.
16. But le Brocquy is not the only modern painter to speak about this enigmatic reciprocity of aesthetic interiority and otherness. Max Ernst declared that the task of the painter is to 'discern that which sees itself through him'. Similarly, Paul Klee described how he used to experience the trees of a forest perceiving him and speaking to him as he painted them, concluding: 'I think that the painter should be transpersed by the universe rather than wish to transperse it ... I wait to be submerged and to submit; and I paint in order to emerge'. See my essay, 'Phénoménologie et Peinture', *Penser l'Art Contemporain, Bulletin de la Biennale de Paris* (1980), pp. 117–29.
17. Le Brocquy, 'Notes on painting and awareness', p. 139.
18. *Ibid.* pp. 147–9.
19. Quoted by John Russell in his introduction to Walker (ed.), *Louis le Brocquy*, p. 16; See also le Brocquy's remark to Harriet Cooke: 'Where an artist is concerned his own personality should not be imposed but overcome', p. 39.
20. Seamus Heaney, 'Louis le Brocquy's Heads' in Walker (ed.), *Louis le Brocquy*, p. 132. Referring specifically to his Joyce images, le Brocquy elaborates as follows on this paradox of painting as an emergence of the *other* through the suspension of the *self*: 'Is there an archaeology of the spirit? Certainly neither my will nor my skill has played any essential part in these studies. For the fact is that many of them emerged entirely under my ignorant left hand – my right hand being for some months immobilised in plaster. So it would appear that no dexterity whatever was involved in forming these images, which tended to emerge automatically, so to speak, jerked into coherence by a series of scrutinised accidents, impelled by my curiosity to discover something of the man and, within him, the inverted mirror-room of my own experience'. (Quoted in Walker [ed.], *Louis le Brocquy*, pp. 59–60).
21. Le Brocquy, 'A painter's notes on his Irishness'.
22. See Dorothy Walker's essay in *Louis le Brocquy*, pp. 44–5. She writes: 'Two aspects of Celtic culture may still be said to inform Irish art in the twentieth century: one is the head image and the other is the cyclical abstract linearity of form and structure. Le Brocquy's head images, although single images centrally placed on the canvas, have nothing to do with a Renaissance centrist order. On the contrary, the image defies its central placing by floating in an indeterminate space between planes. This effect is sometimes accentuated by the artist's device of placing the central image within two faintly delineated squares, one unfinished at the top and the other unfinished at the bottom. The artist has invested this nebulous space not just with the memory or recreation of one man, but with one man from time immemorial. In the barely palpable evidence of a human image, a human presence moves slowly forward to the surface of the painting from unimaginable depths of time'.
23. Le Brocquy, 'Notes on painting and awareness', pp. 147–9.
24. Quoted Vivian Mercier, 'James Joyce as medieval artist', *The Crane Bag*, vol. 2, nos 1 and 2 (1978), p. 11; reprinted in M.P. Hederman and R. Kearney (eds), *Crane Bag Book*, pp. 161–7.

25. Le Brocquy, 'Notes on painting and awareness', p. 152.
26. *Ibid.* p. 139.
27. Le Brocquy, 'A painter's notes on ambivalence', p. 69.
28. *Ibid.*
29. *Ibid.*
30. Walker (ed.), *Louis le Brocquy*, p. 45.
31. Patrick Collins, 'A celtic art?', interview with Aidan Dunne, *The Crane Bag*, vol. 5, no. 2 (1981), reprinted in M.P. Hederman and R. Kearney (eds), *Crane Bag Book*, pp. 920–5.

– *Chapter Nineteen* –
Exchanging Memories: New York Famine Memorial

This paper was first delivered as a lecture at the State University of Arizona in 2004 (unpublished).

1. Paul Ricoeur, 'Reflections on a new ethos for Europe' in *Paul Ricoeur: The Hermeneutics of Praxis* (Sage 1996), pp. 3–14.
2. I am very grateful to my Boston College colleague, Robin Lydenberg, for her illuminating and instructive essay on this work, 'From icon to index: some contemporary visions of the Irish stone cottage' in *Eire/Ireland*, edited by Vera Kreilkamp (McMullen Museum, Boston College, 2003), pp. 127–33. Lyndenberg also kindly brought my attention to the following relevant and informative literature on the topic: Philip Nobel, 'Going hungry', *Metropolis Magazine* (November 2002); Margaret Kelleher, 'Hunger and history: Monuments to the great Irish Famine'; Yvonne Moran, 'Taking Mayo to Manhattan', *The Irish Times* (1 September 2001); David Dunlap, 'Memorial to the hunger', *The New York Times* (15 March 2001); Marita Sturken, 'The wall, the screen and the image: The Vietnam Veterans Memorial' in *The Visual Culture Reader*, edited by Nicholas Mirzoeff (Routledge 1998); Daniel Libeskind's 'Jewish Museum in Berlin: The uncanny arts of memorial architecture' in *Jewish Social Studies*, vol. 6, no. 2 (2001); Vivian Patraka, 'Spectacular suffering: Performing presence, absence and witness at U.S. Holocaust museums' in *Spectacular Suffering* (Indiana University Press 1999).
3. Ricoeur, *La Memoire, L'histoire, L'oubli* (Éditions du Seuil 2000), p. 82 ff.
4. Declan Kiberd, *Inventing Ireland* (Vintage 1996); R.F. Foster, *The Irish Story: Telling Tales and Making it up in Ireland* (see especially his critique of Famine heritage parks and the cult of 'Faminism' for foreign export, p. 23 ff.) (Allan Lane 2001); and Luke Gibbons, *Transformations in Irish Culture* (Cork University Press 1996).
5. Lydenberg, 'From icon to index', p. 131.
6. It is worth noting here that discontinuous readings of the Irish Famine in terms of rupture and trauma are always dialectically linked to continuous readings of the Famine in terms of an unbroken historic past that is still somehow present, or at least representable. Whereas Romantic interpretations tend to stress the latter approach and post-modern interpretations the former, most contemporary memorials (including Tolle's) signal some sort of balance or tension between the two.
7. Sigmund Freud, 'Mourning and Melancholy' in *The Pelican Freud Library*, vol. 2 (Penguin 1984), pp. 251–68.
8. Lydenberg, 'From icon to index', p. 131.
9. See 'The Fifth Province' in R. Kearney, *Postnationalist Ireland* (Routledge and Kegan Paul 1997), pp. 99–100: 'Modern Ireland is made up of four provinces. And yet, the Irish word for a province is *coiced*, which means fifth. This fivefold division is as old as Ireland itself, yet there is disagreement about the identity of the fifth. Some claim that all the provinces met at the Stone of Divisions on the Hill of Uisneach, believed to be the mid-point of Ireland. Others say that the fifth province was Meath (*mide*), the "middle". Both traditions divide Ireland into four quarters and a "middle", though they disagree about the

location of this middle or "fifth" province. Although Tara was the political centre of Ireland, this fifth province acted as a second centre, which if non-political, was just as important, acting as a necessary balance. The present unhappy state of our country would seem to indicate a need for this second centre of gravity. The obvious impotence of the various political attempts to unite the four geographical provinces would seem to warrant another kind of solution … one which would incorporate the 'fifth' province. This province, this place, this centre, is not a political or geographical position, it is more like a disposition'. For an illuminating application of this concept of the Fifth Province to contemporary Irish-British literature and politics, see Aidan O'Malley's doctoral dissertation 'In other words: Coming to terms with Irish identities through translation' (European University Institute at Florence 2004), especially pp. 20–41.

10. Lydenberg, 'From icon to index', p. 132.
11. *Ibid.* p. 131.
12. I am grateful to Joel Gereboff of Arizona State University for this notion of 'counter-text'.
13. Paul Ricoeur, 'Reflections on a new ethos for Europe' in *Paul Ricoeur: The Hermeneutics of Praxis* (Sage 1996), p. 7.
14. Hans-Georg Gadamer, *Truth and Method* (Sheed and Ward 1975).
15. Ricoeur, 'Reflections on a new ethos', p. 7.
16. *Ibid.* p. 8.
17. *Ibid.* p. 9.
18. *Ibid.* p. 8.
19. *Ibid.* p. 8.
20. *Ibid.* p. 9.
21. *Ibid.* p. 11.

– Sources for Chapters Twenty to Twenty-Five –

Chapter 20 is taken from Across the Frontiers: Ireland in the 1990s, *edited by Richard Kearney (Wolfhound Press 1988).*

Chapter 21 is taken from The Crane Bag, *edited by Richard Kearney and M.P. Hederman, 6, 1 (1982).*

Chapter 22 is taken from The Crane Bag, *edited by Richard Kearney and M.P. Hederman, 7, 2 (1983).*

Chapter 23 is taken from The Crane Bag, *edited by Richard Kearney and M.P. Hederman, 6, 2 (1982).*

Chapter 24 is taken from The Crane Bag, *edited by Richard Kearney and M.P. Hederman, 9, 1 (1985).* Both quotations are from Alasdair MacIntyre, *After Virtue: A Study in Moral Theory* (Gerald Duckworth & Co. 1981), p. 206.

Chapter 25 is an interview that was originally conducted in Paris in 1982, not long before the death of Georges Dumézil. An edited version was first published in the author's Debates in Continental Philosophy: Conversations with Contemporary Thinkers *(Fordham University Press 2004).*

– Chapter Twenty-Six –
Philosophy at the Limits of Reason Alone

This interview was originally conducted in the University of Leuven, Belgium, in 2005 by the editors of the Leuven University Newsletter and revised and expanded in 2006.

1. See the chapter 'Should We Renounce Hegel?' in Paul Ricoeur, *Time and Narrative*, vol. 3 (University of Chicago Press 1984).
2. R. Kearney, *The God Who May Be* (Indiana University Press 2001), p. 19.
3. J. Greisch, 'The "Maker Mind" and its shade: Richard Kearney's hermeneutics of the possible god', *Research in Phenomenology*, 34 (2004), pp. 246–54.

– Chapter Twenty-Seven –
Conclusion: Myth and the Critique of Ideology

This is a revised and updated version of the original introduction to the author's Transitions: Narratives in Modern Irish Culture *(Wolfhound Press/St Martins Press 1988).*

1. See in particular the structuralist and post-structuralist philosophies of Michel Foucault, Jacques Lacan and Jacques Derrida. For a detailed critique of this tendency see J. L. Ferry and A. Renault, *La Pensée 68: Essai sur l'anti-humanisme contemporain* (Gallimard 1985). See Derrida's defence against such charges in my *Dialogues with Contemporary Continental Thinkers* (Manchester University Press 1984), pp. 123–6.
2. Karl Marx, *The Eighteenth Brumaire of Louis Bonaparte* (1852; Unwin Brothers 1926), pp. 24–6.
3. Roland Barthes, *Mythologies* (Paladin 1973), pp. 157–8.
4. Liam de Paor, *The Peoples of Ireland* (Rainbow Press 1986).
5. See Terry Eagleton, 'Capitalism, modernism and postmodernism', *New Left Review*, no. 152 (1985), p. 64; and also *Walter Benjamin or Towards a Revolutionary Criticism* (Verso Editions and New Left Books 1981).
6. Herbert Marcuse, *Eros and Civilisation* (Beacon Press 1955), p. 19; and also Barry Katz, *Herbert Marcuse and the Art of Liberation: An Intellectual Biography* (Verso Editions and New Left Books 1982), pp. 102, 153.
7. Herbert Marcuse, *The Aesthetic Dimension* (Beacon Press 1978), p. 73.
8. Seán MacBride quoted in *The Cork Examiner* (27 July 1985).
9. Frederic Jameson, *The Political Unconscious: Narrative as a Socially Symbolic Act* (Methuen 1981), p. 298.
10. Basil Chubb, *The Government and Politics of Ireland* (Longman 1982), p. 21.
11. Dick Walsh 'Come on the intellectuals' in *The Irish Times* (20 June 1985).
12. See Walter Benjamin, 'Theses on the history of philosophy' in *Illuminations* (1968; Fontana 1992), p. 57. Paul Ricoeur's definition of a literary tradition in *Time and Narrative* as an interplay of innovation and sedimentation is also most instructive here. The term tradition, suggests Ricoeur, should be understood not as the 'inert transmission of some dead deposit of material but as the living transmission of an innovation always capable of being reactivated by a return to the most creative moments of poetic activity'. Tradition must thus be seen as a sedimented history of innovations. But by the same token, innovation remains relative to sedimentation in the sense that it remains a form of behaviour governed by rules. 'The labour of imagination', as Ricoeur notes, 'is not born from nothing. It is bound in one way or another to the tradition's paradigms. But the range of solutions is vast. It is deployed between the two poles of servile application and calculated deviation, passing through every degree of "rule-governed deformation" the possibility of deviation is inscribed in the relation between sedimented paradigms and actual works. Short of the

extreme case of schism, it is just the opposite of servile application. Rule-governed deformation constitutes the axis around which the various changes of paradigm through application are arranged. It is this variety of application that confers a history on the productive
imagination and that, in counterpoint to sedimentation, makes every narrative tradition
possible' (*Time and Narrative,* vol. 1 [University of Chicago Press 1984], pp. 68–70).

13. Alasdair MacIntyre, *After Virtue: A Study in Moral Theory* (Duckworth Press 1981), p. 206.

14. Seamus Deane, 'Heroic styles: The tradition of an idea', *Field Day,* 4 (1984), p. 18.

15. See Paul Ricoeur, *The Conflict of Interpretations* (Northwestern University Press 1974); *An
Essay on Interpretation* (Yale University Press 1970), and 'The critique of religion' in C.
Regan and D. Stewart (eds), *The Philosophy of Paul Ricoeur: An Anthology of his Work,*
(Boston 1978), p. 215. See also my essay 'Religion and ideology: Ricoeur's hermeneutic
conflict', *Irish Philosophical Journal,* vol. 2, no. 1 (1985), pp. 37–52.

16. Karl Marx and Fredrich Engels, *On Religion* (Foreign Languages Publishing House/
Lawrence and Wishart 1957), p. 50.

17. Barthes, *Mythologies,* pp. 109–59. The negative hermeneutics of myth was by no means
confined to the atheistic masters of suspicion. Many religious thinkers in the twentieth
century also endorsed the demythologizing project. Indeed the very term 'demythologization' was frequently identified with the theological writings of Rudolph Bultmann.
Bultmann held that Christianity must be emancipated from 'mythic' accretions whereby
Christ became idolized as the sacrificial Kyrios of a saviour cult – a cult modelled on the
pagan heroes of Hellenic or Gnostic mystery-rites. (Rudolf Bultmann, *Theology of the
New Testament,* vol. 1 [S.C.M. Cantebury Press 1974; this translation originally published
1952], pp. 295 ff. And also Rudolf Bultmann and Karl Jaspers, *Myth and Christianity: An
Inquiry into the Possibility of Religion without Myth* [Noonday Press 1958], pp. 15 ff.) Bultmann's demythologizing is levelled against the mystification of authentic Christian spirituality. His critique casts a suspecting glance at all efforts to reduce the genuine scandal
of the Cross and Resurrection to an ideological system wherein the newness of the
Christian message is ignored or betrayed. Bultmann systematically exposes the manner in
which the Living Word of the Gospels often degenerated into cultic myths, e.g. the
attempt to express the eschatological promise of the Kingdom as a cosmological myth of
heaven and hell; or the attempt to reduce the historical working of the Spirit through
the Church to a myth of triumphalistic power. To 'demythologize' Christianity is, for
Bultmann, to dissolve these false scandals so as to let the true scandal of the word made
flesh speak to us anew.

   In recent years this work of theistic demythologization has been effectively developed
by the French thinker, René Girard. Girard holds that the most radical aim of the Judaeo-
Christian Revelation is to expose and overcome the mythic foundation of pagan religions in the ritual sacrifice of an innocent scapegoat. Imaginatively projecting the case
of all disharmony and evil onto some innocent victim, a society contrives to hide from
itself the real cause of its *internal* crisis. True Christianity rejects the cultic mythologizing
of the scapegoat, deployed by societies as an ideological means of securing consensus.
Only by demythologizing this ideological lie of sacrificial victimage, that is, by revealing
the true innocence of the scapegoat Christ, can Christianity serve as a genuinely anti-
mythic and anti-sacrificial religion. (René Girard, *Le Bouc Emissaire* [Grasset 1982], in
particular the chapter 'Qu'est-ce qu'un mythe?', pp. 36–7. See also my 'René Girard et
le mythe comme bouc émissaire' in *Violence et Verité: Colloque de Cérisy autour de René
Girard* [Grasset 1985], pp. 35–49.)

18. On this distinction between utopia and ideology see Karl Mannheim, *Ideology and Utopia:
An Introduction to the Sociology of Knowledge* (Routledge and Kegan Paul 1936); Frederic
Jameson, 'The dialectic of utopia and ideology' in Jameson, *Political Unconscious;* and Paul
Ricoeur, 'Science and ideology' in J.B. Thompson (ed.), *Hermeneutics and the Human
Sciences* (Cambridge University Press 1981), pp. 222–46. See also note 26 below.

19. Paul Ricoeur, 'Myth as the bearer of possible worlds', *The Crane Bag,* vol. 2, nos 1 and 2
(1978); reprinted in my *Dialogues with Contemporary Continental Thinkers,* p. 44.

20. On these distinctions between the 'justificatory/explanatory' and 'exploratory/symbolic' functions of myth, and the critical procedures of *demythologization* and *demythization*, see Paul Ricoeur, *The Symbolism of Evil* (Harper and Row 1967), and 'The language of faith', *Union Sem. Quart. Review*, 28 (1973). See also T. Van Leeuwen's lucid commentary in *The Surplus of Meaning: Ontology and Eschatology in the Philosophy of Paul Ricoeur* (Rodopi 1981), pp. 146 ff. Karl Jaspers also has some interesting remarks on this subject in his essay, 'Myth and religion' in his *Myth and Christianity*. For example: 'Mythical thinking is not a thing of the past, but characterises man in any epoch ... The myth is a carrier of meanings which can be expressed only in the language of myth. The mythical figures are symbols which, by their very nature, are untranslatable into other languages ... They are interpreted only by new myths, by being transformed. Myths interpret each other ... Only he has the right to demythologise, who resolutely retains the reality contained in the cipher language of the myth ... We should seek not to destroy, but to restore the language of myth' (pp. 15–7).

21. Ricoeur, *Symbolism of Evil*, p. 5: 'Demythologisation works on the level of the false rationality of myth in its explanatory pretension.'

22. Ricoeur, 'Myth as the bearer', p. 39.

23. Ricoeur, 'Myth as the bearer', pp. 39–40. See also Mircea Eliade, *Myths, Rites, Symbols: A Mircea Eliade Reader*, vol. 1 (Harper 1975), and in particular the sections entitled, 'The corruption of myths' (pp. 109–22) and 'The fallacy of demystification' (pp. 120–3).

24. On this dialectic between ideology and utopia see my 'Religion and ideology', pp. 48–50; also the section on '*mythe et logos*' in my *Poétique du Possible* (Beauchesne 1984), pp. 190–8; and my interview with Ricoeur entitled 'The creativity of language' in my *Dialogues with Contemporary Continental Thinkers*, pp. 29–30. Here Ricoeur suggests the possibility of a complementary dialectic between the retrospective horizon of ideology and the prospective horizon of utopia.

25. Ricoeur, 'Science and ideology', p. 243.

26. *Ibid.* p. 245; see also Ricoeur's study of the Habermas/Gadamer debate on this question in 'Hermeneutics and the critique of ideology' in Thompson (ed.), *Hermeneutics*, pp. 63–100. See my application of the *mythos/logos* dialectic to Irish culture in 'Myth and motherland', *Field Day*, 5 (1984).

27. Tom Nairn, *The Break-up of Britain* (New Left Books 1977), p. 298.

28. Hence the limitations of the 'traditional Marxian negative hermeneutic for which the national question is a mere ideological epiphenomenon of the economic'. Jameson, *Political Unconscious*, p. 298.

29. See John Hume's opening address where he declared that the Forum was not a 'nationalist revival mission' and that one of the reasons for the failure to resolve the national problem up to this point may have been due to an inability to place the creation of a New Ireland 'above some of our most cherished assumptions'. *Proceedings of the New Ireland Forum*, vol. 1 (Dublin Castle 1984).

30. Ricoeur, *Symbolism of Evil*, p. 168.

31. See the analysis of Joyce in my 'Myth and motherland', and in my 'Mythos and Kritik' in *Das Keltisches Bewusstsein* (Dianos-Trikont 1985).

32. Mircea Eliade, *Myths, Dreams and Mysteries* (Fontana 1968), p. 23: 'Myth is thought to express the absolute truth because it narrates a sacred history; that is a transhuman revelation which took place in the holy time of the beginning ... Myth becomes exemplary and consequently *repeatable* ... By *imitating* the exemplary acts of mythic deities and heroes man detaches himself from profane time and magically re-enters the Great Time, the Sacred Time'. (See chapter 3 of this book, 'Myth and Martyrdom'.)

33. Ricoeur, 'Science and ideology', p. 225.

34. *Ibid.* p. 229.

35. *Ibid.* p. 227.

36. *Ibid.* p. 227.

37. See chapter 5, 'Faith and Fatherland', in this book and also my 'Myth and motherland'.

38. Jürgen Habermas, *Legitimation Crisis* (Beacon Press 1973).

CIRCULATING STOCK WEXFORD PUBLIC LIBRARIES		
BLOCK LOAN		
BUNCLODY		
ENNISCORTHY		
GOREY		
MOBILE NORTH		
MOBILE SOUTH		
NEW ROSS		
WEXFORD		